THE ANALYSIS OF COMPETITION POLICY AND SECTORAL REGULATION

World Scientific–Now Publishers Series in Business

ISSN: 2251-3442

Vol. 1 Games and Dynamic Games
by Alain Haurie, Jacek B. Krawczyk and Georges Zaccour

Vol. 2 Dodd–Frank Wall Street Reform and Consumer Protection Act: Purpose, Critique, Implementation Status and Policy Issues
edited by Douglas D. Evanoff and William W. Moeller

Vol. 3 The History of Marketing Science
edited by Russell S. Winer and Scott A. Neslin

Vol. 4 The Analysis of Competition Policy and Sectoral Regulation
edited by Martin Peitz and Yossi Spiegel

World Scientific – Now Publishers Series in Business: **Vol. 4**

THE ANALYSIS OF COMPETITION POLICY AND SECTORAL REGULATION

Editors

Martin Peitz
University of Mannheim, Germany & CERRE

Yossi Spiegel
Tel Aviv University, Israel & CEPR & ZEW

now

World Scientific

Published by

World Scientific Publishing Co. Pte. Ltd.
5 Toh Tuck Link, Singapore 596224
USA office: 27 Warren Street, Suite 401-402, Hackensack, NJ 07601
UK office: 57 Shelton Street, Covent Garden, London WC2H 9HE

and

now publishers Inc.
PO Box 1024
Hanover, MA 02339
USA

Library of Congress Cataloging-in-Publication Data
The analysis of competition policy and sectoral regulation / [edited] by Martin Peitz (Univ of Manheim, Germany; MaCCI, & CERRE) and Yossi Spiegel (Tel Aviv Univ, Israel; CEPR & ZEW).
pages cm. -- (World Scientific-now publishers series in business, ISSN 2251-3442 ; v. 4)
Conference proceedings.
"This volume contains a selection of papers that were presented at the CRESSE Conferences held in Chania, Crete, from July 6th to 8th, 2012, and in Corfu from July 5th to 7th, 2013."
Includes bibliographical references and index.
ISBN 978-9814616355 (alk. paper)
1. Competition--Congresses. 2. Competition, Unfair--Congresses. 3. Commercial law--Congresses. I. Peitz, Martin, editor of compilation. II. Spiegel, Yossi, editor of compilation.
HF1414.A6235 2014
338.6'048--dc23
2014014496

British Library Cataloguing-in-Publication Data
A catalogue record for this book is available from the British Library.

In-house Editors: Sandhya Venkatesh/Chitralekha Elumalai

Typeset by Stallion Press
Email: enquiries@stallionpress.com

Printed in Singapore

Contents

About the Editors **ix**

About the Contributors **xi**

Introduction **xv**
Martin Peitz and Yossi Spiegel

Part I: Competition **1**

Chapter 1 Market Consolidation and Pricing Developments in Grocery Retailing: A Case Study 3
Ratula Chakraborty, Paul W. Dobson, Jonathan S. Seaton and Michael Waterson

Chapter 2 The Price Effects of Mergers in Airline Networks 31
Kai Hüschelrath and Kathrin Müller

Chapter 3 Pattern Asymmetry in the Pass-Through of Input Price Shocks in the Road Fuels Sector: New Evidence on the United Kingdom 59
Enrico Pesaresi, Conor Flanagan and Boryana Miteva

Chapter 4 Better Product at Same Cost: Leader Innovation vs. Generic Product Improvement 93
David J. Balan and George Deltas

Chapter 5 Industry Structure and Pricing Over the Business Cycle 115
Yossi Spiegel and Konrad Stahl

Chapter 6 Price Competition between Platforms: The Case of eBay vs. Yahoo! Auctions 141
Stefan Behringer

Part II: Anticompetitive Practices **173**

Chapter 7 Cartel Sales Dynamics when Monitoring for Compliance is More Frequent than Punishment for Non-Compliance 175
Joseph E. Harrington, Jr. and Juan-Pablo Montero

Chapter 8 Exploitation and Induced Tacit Collusion: A Classroom Experiment of Corporate Leniency Programs 193
Jeroen Hinloopen and Adriaan R. Soetevent

Chapter 9 Quantity Discounts and Market Power: The Michelin Case Revisited 213
Liliane Giardino-Karlinger

Chapter 10 Technology Transfer, Contracting, and Product Market Competition 231
Frago Kourandi, Sabina Sachtachtinskagia and Nikolaos Vettas

Part III: Competition Policy and Regulation **277**

Chapter 11 How Can Competition Policy and Competition-Policy Economics Contribute to Solving the Healthcare Crisis? 279
Michael L. Katz

Chapter 12 Regulation Mismatch in Tackling CO_2 Emissions 339
Claude Crampes

Chapter 13 Public Policies in Investment-Intensive Industries 365
Giovanni Immordino and Michele Polo

Chapter 14 The Role of Legal Principles in the Economic Analysis of Competition Policy 389
Harold Houba, Evgenia Motchenkova and Quan Wen

Chapter 15 Deterrence in Competition Law 423
Paolo Buccirossi, Lorenzo Ciari, Tomaso Duso, Giancarlo Spagnolo and Cristiana Vitale

Chapter 16 The Risks and Tricks in Public–Private Partnerships 455
Elisabetta Iossa, Giancarlo Spagnolo and Mercedes Vellez

Index **491**

About the Editors

Martin Peitz is a Professor of Economics at the University of Mannheim (since 2007), a Director of the Mannheim Centre for Competition and Innovation — MaCCI (since 2009), an Academic Director of the Centre on Regulation in Europe, CERRE (since 2012), and a member of the economic advisory group on competition policy (EAGCP) at the European Commission (since 2013).

Martin Peitz is Editor of *Review of Network Economics*, Co-Editor of *International Journal of Industrial Organization*, Associate Editor of *Journal of Industrial Economics*, and *Information Economics and Policy*, and member of the editorial boards of *Telecommunications Policy* and *Journal of Media Economics*. He is Research Fellow of CEPR, CESifo and ENCORE, CRESSE Associate, and ZEW Research Associate. He has widely published in leading economics journals. He is author of the books *Industrial Organization: Markets and Strategies* (with Paul Belleflamme) and *Regulation and Entry into Telecommunications Markets* (with Paul de Bijl), both published by Cambridge University Press, and editor of the *Oxford Handbook of the Digital Economy* (with Joel Waldfogel), published by Oxford University Press. His research covers various topics in industrial organization, competition policy, regulation, and microeconomics.

Yossi Spiegel is a Full Professor at the Recanati School of Business of Tel Aviv University and a Research Fellow at the CEPR and ZEW. His fields of research include Industrial Organization, Economics of Regulation and Antitrust, and Corporate Finance. He holds a PhD in Economics from Northwestern University (1991), MA in Economics from Tel Aviv University (1987), and BA in Economics and Accounting from Tel Aviv University (1985). Before joining Tel Aviv University, he was a member of technical staff at the Economics Research Group at Bell Communication Research for three years. He is a Co-editor of the *International Journal of Industrial Organization*, *Journal of Economics and Management Strategy*, and *Foundations and Trends*. For complete CV, see http://www.tau.ac.il/~spiegel.

About the Contributors

David J. Balan
Bureau of Economics, Federal Trade Commission
dbalan@ftc.gov

Stefan Behringer
Universität Duisburg-Essen
stefan.behringer@uni-due.de
www.stefanbehringer.com

Paolo Buccirossi
Laboratorio di economia, antitrust e regolamentazione
paolo.buccirossi@learlab.com

Ratula Chakraborty
University of East Anglia
r.chakraborty@uea.ac.uk

Lorenzo Ciari
European Bank for Reconstruction and Development
ciaril@ebrd.com
lorenzociari@hotmail.com

Claude Crampes
Toulouse School of Economics
Claude.Crampes@tse-fr.eu

George Deltas
University of Illinois at Urbana-Champaign
deltas@illinois.edu

Paul W. Dobson
University of East Anglia
p.dobson@uea.ac.uk

Tomaso Duso
–DIW and DICE
TDuso@diw.de

Conor Flanagan
Competition and Markets Authority
conor.flanagan@cma.gsi.gov.uk

Liliane Giardino-Karlinger
Università LUISS Guido Carli
lilianegk@gmail.com

Joseph E. Harrington, Jr.
The Wharton School of the University of Pennsylvania
harrij@wharton.upenn.edu

Jeroen Hinloopen
University of Amsterdam
J.Hinloopen@uva.nl

Harold Houba
VU University
hhouba@feweb.vu.nl

Kai Hüschelrath
ZEW, MaCCI, and University of Mannheim
hueschelrath@zew.de

Giovanni Immordino
University of Salerno
giimmo@tin.it

Elisabetta Iossa
University of Rome Tor Vergata, CEPR and IEFE-Bocconi
Elisabetta.Iossa@uniroma2.it

Michael L. Katz
University of California
katz@haas.berkeley.edu

Frago Kourandi
Athens University of Economics and Business
kourandi@aueb.gr

Boryana Miteva
Expedia Affiliate Network
bmiteva@expedia.com

Juan-Pablo Montero
Pontificia Universidad Católica de Chile
jmontero@uc.cl

Evgenia Motchenkova
VU University
emotchenkova@feweb.vu.nl

Kathrin Müller
ZEW and MaCCI
kathrin.mueller@zew.de

Enrico Pesaresi
European Commission, Directorate General for Competition
enrico.pesaresi@ec.europa.eu

Michele Polo
Bocconi University and IEFE
michele.polo@unibocconi.it

Sabina Sachtachtinskagia
Athens University of Economics and Business
sabina@aueb.gr

Jonathan S. Seaton
Loughborough University
j.s.seaton@Lboro.ac.uk

Giancarlo Spagnolo
University of Rome Tor Vergata, SITE-Stockholm, and CEPR
Giancarlo.Spagnolo@uniroma2.it
Giancarlo.Spagnolo@hhs.se

Yossi Spiegel
Tel Aviv University, CEPR, and ZEW
spiegel@post.tau.ac.il

Konrad Stahl
Universität Mannheim, CEPR, CESifo, and ZEW
kos@econ.uni-mannheim.de

Adriaan Soetevent
University of Groningen
A.R.Soetevent@rug.nl

Mercedes Vellez
University of Rome Tor Vergata and CEDES
mervellez@yahoo.com.ar

Nikolaos Vettas
Athens University of Economics and Business and CEPR
nvettas@aueb.gr

Cristiana Vitale
Organisation for Economic Cooperation and Development (Paris)
Cristiana.VITALE@oecd.org

Michael Waterson
University of Warwick
michael.waterson@warwick.ac.uk

Quan Wen
University of Washington
wenq2@u.washington.edu

Introduction

The Competition and Regulation European Summer School and Conference (*CRESSE*) is an informal network of academics and professionals with an interest in Competition Policy and Sectoral Regulation. It was initiated by Yannis Katsoulacos (Athens University of Economics and Business) in 2005. The annual conference organized by CRESSE has since grown to become an important event in the competition and regulation conferences calendar. The objective is to provide a forum in which the latest research in the areas of competition and regulation is presented and discussed. Presentations in the three-day annual conference include several invited papers and a selection of papers that were submitted in response to a call for papers in major IO journals and the Conference web site (www.cresse.info). The annual CRESSE Conference is organized in early July in Greece; the institution responsible for the organization is the Athens University of Economics and Business.

CRESSE also organizes an annual Summer School in which Visiting Faculty from a number of European and U.S. Universities provide high-quality training to practitioners of competition policy and sectoral regulation that wish to be acquainted with the most recent economic and legal developments. It is also active in disseminating research in the areas of competition policy and regulation and in contributing through the organization of special policy sessions and roundtables that deliver public debates on topical policy issues.

This volume contains some of the papers that were presented at the 2012 *CRESSE* Conferences which was held in Chania, Crete, on July 6–8, 2012, and the 2013 *CRESSE* Conferences which was held in Corfu on

July 5–7, 2013. We are grateful to several colleagues who were generous to help us evaluating the papers for the volume and provided authors with constructive comments and suggestions.

We have grouped the chapters in three parts. Part I contains chapters that examine various aspects of competition. The first three chapters are empirical contributions. Of these, the first two consider price effects of mergers in grocery retailing (Chakraborty *et al.*) and in airlines (Hüschelrath and Müller), while the third (Pesaresi *et al.*) focuses on cost pass-through in the road fuel sector. The other three chapters in Part I of the book are theoretical contributions and they address the effect of innovation on sales and consumer surplus (Balan and Deltas), the effect of demand fluctuations on prices, price-cost margin entry, and capacity utilization (Spiegel and Stahl), and the effect of endogenous seller charges on platform competition (Behringer).

Part II contains chapters on anticompetitive practices. The first two address horizontal practices: cartels (Harrington and Montero) and tacit collusion (Hinloopen and Soetevent). The remaining two chapters address vertical exclusionary practices: Quantity and loyalty discounts (Giardino-Karlinger) and technology transfers (Kourandi *et al.*).

Finally, Part III of the book contains chapters on competition policy and on regulation. The two first chapters elaborate on two key policy issues, health care (Katz) and regulations of CO_2 emissions (Crampes). Both chapters look at these public policy issues from an industrial organization perspective. The other four chapters in Part III of the book study a number of general policy issues, including public policies in innovative industries (Immordino and Polo), the role of legal principle in competition economics (Houba *et al.*), deterrence in competition law (Buccirossi *et al.*), and various problems in the design of public–private partnership contracts (Iossa *et al.*)

The chapters in this volume are at the frontier of empirical or theoretical research on competition issues and they either contain original research, or put recent research into perspective. Each chapter is preceded by a short abstract.

Martin Peitz
Yossi Spiegel
December 2013

Part I

Competition

Chapter 1

Market Consolidation and Pricing Developments in Grocery Retailing: A Case Study*

Ratula Chakraborty

University of East Anglia
r.chakraborty@uea.ac.uk

Paul W. Dobson

University of East Anglia
p.dobson@uea.ac.uk

Jonathan S. Seaton

Loughborough University
j.s.seaton@Lboro.ac.uk

Michael Waterson

University of Warwick
michael.waterson@warwick.ac.uk

Abstract

When large retailers merge, there is a concern that a sudden and marked increase in concentration will alter the intensity and nature of price competition to the detriment of consumers. This chapter considers just such a situation in regard to UK grocery retailing, which has witnessed steadily increasing concentration over recent years, advanced by a series of mergers. Specifically, we examine

*This work was supported by the Economic and Social Research Council (grant number RES-062-23-1962). We are extremely grateful to Arvind Yadav and Andrew Farrell for their research assistance in helping to collect and organize the data used in this study. Helpful comments on aspects of this research were received at the CRESSE meeting 2012 and from our editor, Martin Peitz. Michael Waterson is a member of the UK Competition Commission but was not involved in any of the grocery market inquiries and has not had access to any materials from them not in the public domain.

the nature of price competition amongst the major "one-stop-shop" retail chains before, during, and after the Safeway/Morrison merger in March 2004. We find the merger offered consumers an immediate windfall benefit — with average prices falling straight after the merger — and more intriguingly appears to have led to (or at least is associated with) a marked change in the character of price competition in the market.

Keywords: Price competition, concentration, pricing strategies, grocery retailing.

JEL Classification Codes: L40, L81, L11.

1. Introduction

Prices in the UK grocery sector fell in real terms by 7.3% in the early 2000s (Office of Fair Trading, 2006). Yet, over the same period, concentration increased sharply, with the top four UK supermarket retailers increasing their joint share from approximately 60% to 75%. Doubtless, costs might have been lowered through scale efficiencies, improved organization, and the exercise of buyer power. Even so, the falling prices may be symptomatic of changes taking place in regard to how retailers compete, and in particular, the pricing strategies that they employ, and not merely to do with passing on cost savings. To analyze this, we investigate pricing strategies with particular reference to a large merger. At issue is whether a change in market structure can fundamentally change market behavior in an unanticipated, but in this case apparently beneficial, manner with implications for evaluating future scenarios of how market outcomes might evolve post-merger.

This chapter explores this issue using a balanced panel sample from a novel dataset that covers prices for a wide range of grocery and household products across all four major supermarket chains jointly accounting for over 90% of the UK one-stop shopping grocery retail market (defined in the UK as grocery sales from stores greater than 1,400 sq. m). The dataset used is based on weekly-updated price data on individual items covering the period from November 2003 to November 2006, during which time, there was significant change in the structure of the market, the completion of the *Safeway/Morrison* (hereafter, S/M) merger in March 2004, consolidating the position of the fourth player. Otherwise, this time period is characterized by the macroeconomically benign environment of growth and mild inflation now called the Great Moderation. For the period investigated, we find a strong incidence of net price reductions. The evidence suggests that the primary driver of falling prices during this period has been higher priced firms cutting prices (rather than lower priced firms cutting prices further) as they shifted from traditional high-low ("HiLo") promotional-based pricing toward value-oriented every-day low pricing ("EDLP"), whilst retaining promotional elements — a hybrid strategy that all four major players appear to have adopted to a greater or lesser extent by the end of the period studied.[1]

For this market, a move toward price convergence is associated with a change in the character of price competition triggered by increased concentration and an intensifying battle for market share. Yet, the real price reductions overall mask a more complex picture of price changes, with many falls at the same time as substantial increases in prices on other products.

Viewed in policy terms, this era may have an important bearing on how competition authorities should view retail mergers, with the need to distinguish those likely to promote a shift toward more intense, rather than less intense, competition to the benefit of consumers. The UK competition authorities were faced with four possible merger scenarios, out of which they chose one (with relatively minor restrictions regarding the small number of areas where the merging parties overlapped significantly). The short-term indications are that they got this right, in the sense that the other possible mergers would have led to a more asymmetric concentrated structure and an outside firm is likely to have found greater difficulty in delivering cost reductions.

There remains a lingering concern that as the post-merger market settles, and positions stabilize, then competitive intensity may wane, leading to the prospect of future price rises. Yet, at least for the period studied here, examined purely in terms of the impact on consumer welfare through

---

[1]Bolton and Shankar (2003) provide empirical support for the view that retailers' pricing policies operate along a spectrum of positions (rather than simple "either–or" choices) in respect of the average price levels used, the frequency of price changes, and the nature of retail promotions. Moreover, as shown by Ellickson and Misra (2008) in the context of U.S. supermarkets, retailers may tailor their pricing strategy choices (e.g., EDLP, HiLo, or a hybrid position) at store level, according to prevailing local market conditions and the nature of local competition. This position is noticeably different to that applying in the UK where grocery retailers generally commit to a pricing strategy that applies across their entire store chain or at least to different store-size categories and linked to their retail brand and store fascia (e.g., Competition Commission, 2000).

effects on prices, our analysis provides support for the arguments made by the UK competition authorities in allowing the S/M merger (rather than the other contemplated mergers) in an already quite concentrated market. Our sample suggests that consumers saw an immediate windfall benefit from the merger — with price cuts across a wide range of products following completion of the merger; although, we establish close correlation in timing, this is clearly not the same as establishing causation.[2]

Beyond the rapid post-merger drop in prices, we also find evidence that the nature of price changes and competitor responses changed more generally over the period. In particular, leader–follower patterns and response timings appear to have shifted as the price gap narrowed across the main retailers. Indeed, there is evidence of asymmetric leader–follower positions, with one retailer tending to lead on price rises while another retailer tends to lead on price falls. We also find that, while an increasing number of products were identically priced across all the main retailers, even where price gaps remained, they were often as small as a single penny across the four retailers. A significant proportion of the price changes, particularly decreases, were a single penny, indicating a willingness to pass on lower costs and/or seeking to gain or maintain the lowest price position (and thus enhance their reputation with consumers) — and suggesting low menu costs.

The chapter is organized as follows. In Section 2, we briefly review developments in the UK grocery sector, examining changes in market concentration and the nature of the leading players in the "one-stop shopping" market. In Section 3, we discuss the source and nature of the pricing data used. In Section 4, we assess the four main retailers' price change decisions in terms of patterns over time (particularly in view of the S/M merger, examining average prices, direction and magnitude of price changes, and the extent of price alignment across the retailers), patterns

[2]A quite different structural approach to the analysis of this merger is carried out by Skrianka (2012). He focuses on the geographic distribution of demand using TNS Worldpanel consumer micro-data. Given the structural nature of the model, he is able (subject to his maintained assumptions) to recover estimates of consumer welfare, as well as profits. His paper suggests that the S/M merger had little impact, but that a merger of Safeway with Tesco would have had a greater negative impact on consumers. His model relies on recovering marginal costs and also is comparative static in nature, so he is not able, for example, to investigate leader–follower behavior and the like.

across product types, and evidence of leader–follower behavior. Section 5 concludes the chapter.

2. UK Grocery Retailing and One-Stop Shopping

Grocery retailing is significantly the largest retail sector in the UK. Total sales through UK grocery outlets were around £120 billion (approximately $200 billion) in 2005 (Office of Fair Trading, 2006). Of this total, around £95 billion comprised grocery sales, with the remainder made up of sales of non-grocery items. Groceries account for nearly half of all UK retail sales, and around 13% of all household spending (IGD, 2005). Four retailers — Tesco, Sainsbury, Asda (owned by Wal-Mart), and Morrison/Safeway — dominate the national market, accounting for around 75% of grocery retail sales (covering food and drink, cleaning products, toiletries, and household goods), and indeed 30% of all retail sales in the UK.[3]

These four supermarket retailers have primarily positioned themselves as "one-stop shops", operating with very wide product ranges in large format stores. They jointly account for over 90% of grocery sales for stores with sales areas exceeding 1,400 sq. m (approximately 15,000 sq. ft) — the critical size above which the UK competition authorities view as distinguishing one-stop grocery shops, serving a separate economic market for primary shopping needs (where consumers could buy all their grocery needs in a single store, perhaps with a single weekly shopping trip), from smaller stores catering more for secondary (e.g., "top-up" and "convenience") grocery shopping needs.[4]

With such high concentration and concerns about the exercise of market power, the UK authorities have investigated the sector several times in recent years. The Competition Commission's market investigation completed in

[3]For further details, see IGD (2005) and Mintel (2005). Tesco alone is estimated to take more than one-eighth of UK consumer retail expenditure.

[4]More formally, the Competition Commission (2000, Paragraph 2.26) defined "one-stop shopping" as "the shop for the bulk of a household's weekly grocery needs, carried out in a single trip and under one roof". This is distinguished by the Competition Commission from other forms of shopping, characterized as "secondary shopping", which typically involve the greater use of other types of grocery stores, a different product mix and a lower average basket spend.

Table 1. Market Characteristics in UK Grocery Retailing, 1998–1999

Main UK grocery retailers	General character and pricing policy	Total grocery stores	National market shares		
			All grocery stores (%)	Grocery stores >1,400 sq. m (%)	Grocery stores >2,300 sq. m (%)
One-stop shops					
Tesco	Value-led HiLo	642	23.0	28.5	29.5
Sainsbury	HiLo	424	18.7	24.8	27.5
Asda	EDLP	227	12.2	16.8	20.8
Safeway	HiLo	498	11.5	13.8	11.0
Morrison	EDLP + deals	95	3.9	5.4	6.6
Other chains					
Somerfield/ Kwik Save	HiLo Soft Discount	1,442	9.8	3.1	0.8
M&S	Premium	294	4.9	2.2	2.0
Waitrose	Premium	119	3.0	2.5	0.4
Aldi	Hard Discount	219	1.4	0.0	0.0
Lidl	Hard Discount	173	0.9	0.0	0.0
Netto	Hard Discount	120	0.7	0.0	0.0
Budgens	HiLo	177	0.7	0.0	0.0
Iceland	Specialized/deals	770	3.0	0.0	0.0
Booth	Premium	24	0.2	0.1	0.0
Co-operatives	HiLo	1,920	6.4	2.8	1.5

Source: Dobson and Waterson (2008) adapted from Competition Commission (2000; Tables 5.2 and 5.6, Appendices 5.2 and 7.1).

2000 provided a very detailed analysis of the structure of the relevant markets and the behavior and performance of the main supermarkets groups. Table 1 shows some of the key market characteristics identified at that time, with just five players dominating the one-stop shopping market as served by larger grocery stores.

In March 2004, the "Big 5" became the "Big 4" with the merger of Safeway and Morrison. This followed an investigation by the Competition Commission in 2003 into contemplated mergers with Safeway as considered by all four of the other top 5 one-stop shopping retailers. However, prospective mergers with Tesco, Sainsbury, and Asda/Wal-Mart were all blocked on grounds that competition would likely be significantly reduced

Table 2. Retailer Market Shares for Stores Greater than 1,400 sq. m in Great Britain, 1998–2003

	01/1998	01/1999	01/2000	01/2001	01/2002	01/2003	1998/2003 gain/loss
Tesco	28.5	28.8	29.5	29.9	30.8	31.3	2.8
Sainsbury	26.5	26.0	25.1	23.6	22.4	21.9	−4.6
Asda	17.1	17.6	18.7	19.8	20.4	21.5	4.4
Safeway	12.6	12.9	12.2	13.0	12.7	12.0	−0.6
Morrison	5.4	5.7	6.4	7.1	7.5	7.6	2.2
Others	9.9	9.0	8.1	6.6	6.2	5.7	−4.2

Source: Dobson (2005) adapted from Competition Commission (2003; Tables 3.2 and 5.17) (based on TNS till roll data).

(as identified by the Commission's consideration of potential unilateral and coordinated effects arising from such mergers). Morrison was allowed to proceed subject to a number of store divestments. Table 2 shows the trends in market shares identified in the Competition Commission's inquiry, revealing strong growth in the positions of Tesco, Asda, and Morrison, relative decline in the position of Sainsbury and some decline in Safeway and other retailers in the one-stop shopping market.

Nevertheless, continued concern about the market power held by the main players and increasing levels of concentration, as well as the move by some of the key players (notably Tesco and Sainsbury) to enter the convenience store sector, led to a further full sector inquiry in 2008. This latest inquiry focused on relations in the supply chain (with concerns about the buyer power of the major retailers), possible anticompetitive practices in retail markets (with concerns about below cost selling and targeted pricing), and entry barriers (notably, the role and implications of current planning restrictions in the UK and high levels of local concentration).

In the period after the 2000 Competition Commission market investigation, it was noticeable that the positions of the leading firms changed somewhat, especially with regard to their pricing policy. In particular, "HiLo" promotional pricing was largely abandoned, with Safeway's extreme HiLo pricing being replaced by Morrison's more consistent value-oriented pricing policy, and a move by Sainsbury toward a similar value-oriented position, operating with broadly low everyday prices with some promotional deals. This is also the position essentially adopted by Tesco and even Asda modified its EDLP approach to encompass promotional deals. Thus, the previously more polarized positions gave way to a more common value-led approach shared by all leading players, if to slightly different degrees and with different emphases.[5] The common emphasis became building chains with consistent national appeal through the adoption of national pricing and marketing policies, rather than tailoring offers to local markets (as may be more common in other countries and other retail sectors). For example, local price flexing (that is adjusting prices according to local competitive conditions) largely gave way to a situation where all four major players adopted national prices in the UK one-stop shopping market (i.e., for large sized stores) — a market feature that will prove particularly useful in the context of our price comparison analysis over what has what has turned out to be a very important period in the development of this sector.

3. The Data

Our price data are drawn from a price comparison service provided by tesco.com (at www.tesco.com/pricecheck) — the UK's leading Internet retail operation and run by the UK's leading retailer, Tesco plc. Starting from late 2003, this website provided price comparisons, updated weekly, on initially about 4,000 items, growing to over 10,000 individual items, across the leading four supermarket retailers in the UK — Tesco, Sainsbury, Asda, and Safeway (replaced later with Morrison).[6] The reported prices, stated by Tesco as being independently collected, are based on the most common (i.e., mode) value for one to three similarly sized superstores (i.e., excluding

[5]For details on the points of difference in the nature of the pricing policies used by the key players, see Verdict Research (2005), also Competition Commission (2003, 2008) on pricing policies more generally.

[6]The Pricecheck service was used by Tesco as a marketing ploy to allow it to demonstrate how many lower prices it had compared to rivals in its advertising claims. Of course, it is possible that the presence of the website itself led to behavioral changes. Certainly, we see some price alignment taking place between Tesco and Asda in the early weeks (Seaton and Waterson, 2013). The Tesco Pricecheck service ended in late 2008 with a move to a different marketing ploy and advertising campaign, Tesco Baskets, showing comparisons across baskets of products, rather than individual items.

smaller store formats operated by these retailers, such as Tesco Metro and Sainsbury's Local) around Great Britain for each of these four retail chains and the prices relate to single items/packages (i.e., they do not cover multi-buy offers such as "buy one, get one free", "three for the price of two", etc.).[7]

Crucially (and very different from countries such as the U.S. and France, where retailer chains invariably price locally), these retailers have adopted uniform national pricing policies. Specifically, in keeping with their publicly stated commitments, the "Big 4" retailers, i.e., Tesco, Sainsbury, Asda, and Morrison, each use a national pricing policy at superstore level with no local price deviations in this market (Competition Commission, 2003). Accordingly, the reported prices would normally be expected to apply across every superstore operated by that retailer for the whole of Britain.[8] Hence, this price comparison service should provide reliable coverage for individual item prices for the supermarkets that account for over 90% of the one-stop shopping grocery market expected to operate in Britain.

Our data covers a complete three-year period. Data collection began with the published comparisons for November 10, 2003, on the basis of prices ordered by "aisle" within the store. All available price comparisons made in respect of "aisles" were then subsequently collected from the Tesco

[7]In operating the Pricecheck service, Tesco stated that they tried to ensure that the prices displayed on the website were fair, representative, and accurate. Tesco argued there was no bias in the choice of products for comparison with equivalent products always compared (e.g., Tesco's "Value" brand was always compared with the other supermarkets' own budget brands). More broadly, it was claimed that a like-for-like basis was consistently used for comparisons. If the price collector did not obtain a comparable size for a product, then the nearest size was taken and the price converted pro-rata. If there was no size that would fairly compare with the Tesco product, then it was not included. If a product was found to be sold out in a store, then the price recorded on the shelf was used. If a product had a price mark that was different from the shelf price, then whichever was the lower price was taken.

[8]It is this feature of national pricing policies that makes this particular price comparison service and more recently developed ones, like mysupermarket.co.uk, extremely useful and amenable in allowing analysis of prices in the present UK context. Clearly, such a service would be less useful in other countries (e.g., the U.S.) where local pricing in the retail grocery sector predominates (e.g., Montgomery (1997), Chintagunta *et al.* (2003), and Ellickson and Misra (2008)).

Pricecheck website for each week in which the data were updated through to November 13, 2006. While prices were updated for most weeks, there were a number of early weeks in which prices were not updated on the website. For the 158 weeks covered in this period, we were able to collect data for 129 weeks (i.e., 29 missing weeks).[9]

In any given week, only around a third of the items had comparisons across all four retailers. Also, the goods on which all four comparisons were made changed over time, and even from week to week.[10] In addition, there were changes in the composition of products covered, as well as individual product introductions and deletions over time. The net result is that we were left with 539 items on which we had prices at all four retailers for every week in which data were collected to allow us to construct a balanced panel over this period of three years. These items cover products in 9 of the 12 broad categories ("aisles") identified on the website, with a mix of branded and own-label goods, a range of different package sizes, and broad spread of prices, thus providing a wide but not full representation of products stocked.[11] Table 3 provides some summary details.

[9]Prices were updated weekly up to mid-December 2003 but then were updated more erratically (sometimes only twice a month) through to July 2004, after which they were updated more consistently on a weekly basis through to December 2004, but then again erratically (though often fortnightly) through to July 2005, after which the prices were mostly updated weekly. The most noticeable and consistent gap in the series relates to the two weeks covering each Christmas and New Year (which could be an indication that store prices were themselves not changed significantly over this interval — as found by other studies, e.g., Müller *et al.* (2006)).

[10]Absences on the website were shown as "not found" ("N/F"), indicating that the product (or its like-for-like equivalent) could not be found in the retailer (which may have been because it was not stocked, but could also have been due to the researchers not having sufficient time to locate and record the price — hence accounting for the fluctuation in weekly recorded prices and why coverage varies across categories and across retailers). Four-way comparisons ranged from as high as 40% of the items covered in some weeks to as low as 25% in other weeks, though commonly around 30–35% of items covered.

[11]In particular, we note that there is an absence of "fruit and vegetable" and "meat, fish, and poultry" prices as these only became available from mid-2004 onwards. Also, there were no recorded prices in the "newsagent" aisle (e.g., cigarettes) during this period. In addition, there were certain "shelves" within "aisles" where either recorded prices commenced at a later date or were never covered (e.g., "sweet morning goods" in the bakery aisle and "bags of sweets" in the grocery aisle, amongst several others).

Table 3. Sample Characteristics

Aisle	Number of items	Own-label (%)	Minimum price (£)	Maximum price (£)	Mean price (£)	Median price (£)	Mode price (£)
Bakery	11	64	0.19	2.39	0.81	0.73	1.04
Grocery	289	28	0.15	5.86	0.99	0.84	0.64
Frozen foods	10	10	0.46	5.69	1.79	1.48	1.79
General goods	51	24	0.33	6.71	1.68	1.39	1.28
Deli and dairy	40	28	0.19	16.90	1.35	0.98	0.38
Health and beauty	37	14	0.29	9.25	1.86	1.67	1.68
Off-license	41	7	1.22	26.65	8.47	7.12	1.54
Pet foods	20	10	0.24	4.99	1.34	0.98	0.47
Beverages	40	18	0.13	6.58	2.01	1.93	2.98
Full Sample	**539**	**24**	**0.13**	**26.65**	**1.81**	**1.05**	**0.98**

4. Pricing Developments

We examine in some depth across various dimensions the pricing developments in the British grocery market as the S/M merger was taking place.

The data consists of prices, p_{fiw}, charged by firm $f = 1, \ldots, 4$ (*Tesco, Sainsbury, Safeway/Morrison, and Asda*) for item $i = 1, 2, \ldots, 539$ for weeks $w = 1, 2, \ldots, 158$ (running from November 10, 2003 ($w = 1$) to November 13, 2006 ($w = 158$)). As 29 of the 158 time periods are missing, it proves convenient to redefine our observations to replace w with t covering observations $t = 1, \ldots, 129$ — see Table A1 in the Appendix for details. With 129 weekly observations on 539 goods, we have 69,531 price observations for each retailer, 278,124 observations overall. The number of "valid" price change Δp_{fiw} observations is reduced measurably by missing observations; this can of course be addressed by both careful estimation and appropriate interpolation procedures.

A further complicating feature of the sample relates to the merger of Safeway and Morrison, formally completed on March 8, 2004 but with Safeway store conversions, into the Morrison format, taking place over subsequent months. Pricecheck recorded Safeway prices until mid-August 2004, after which it replaced Safeway with Morrison. Accordingly, our data can be split into three key sub-periods: "pre-merger" (from November 10, 2003 to February 23, 2004, i.e., $w = 1$–16, $t = 1$–11), "post-merger with

Safeway data" (from March 15, 2004 to August 16, 2004, i.e., $w = 19$–41, $t = 12$–24); and "post-merger with Morrison data" (from August 23, 2004 to November 13, 2006, i.e., $w = 42$–158, $t = 25$–129).

4.1. *Firm-level average prices*

To provide a broad indication of how prices developed over the observed time period, Figure 1 shows the indexed (unweighted) firm-level mean average prices for the sample of items. The market exhibits sharply declining prices in S/M[12] (labeled simply Morrison in the figure, for brevity) and more modestly declining prices in Sainsbury, after which the trend is more flat except in pre-Christmas periods where prices dip and then rise again each post-New Year. The latter feature appears to be driven by heavy discounting of particular relatively more expensive products in the sample, notably alcoholic beverages.

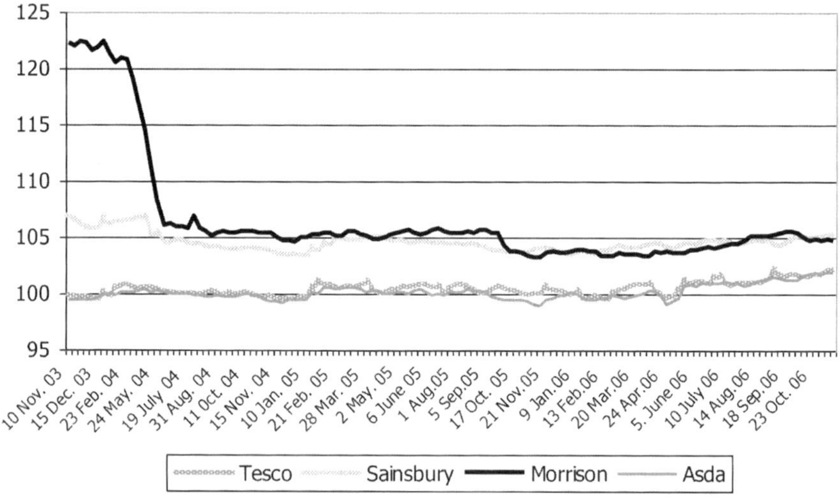

Figure 1. Mean prices over time (unweighted mean with Tesco first week as base = 100).

[12]This is consistent with casual speculation at the time that Safeway faced a relatively high cost base.

4.2. *Direction of price changes*

Tesco, the market leader and the retailer that changed its prices most, made 4,492 price changes, representing just over 5% of the data or equivalent to about eight price changes for each item over the entire period (i.e., a change approximately every 16 weeks). Asda, in line with its declared EDLP approach, changed its prices the least often, with 2,858 price changes, about five changes per item over the three years.

Despite the appearance from Figure 1 of the trends in average prices for the retailers being broadly flat, with the notable exception of Safeway/Morrison, there were in fact substantially more price falls than price rises over the period, as shown in Figure 2. The falls tend to be small in size and the rises larger. Interestingly, this finding is the reverse of U.S. evidence, e.g., Levy *et al.* (2004) who found for a U.S. grocery chain that price rises outnumbered price falls but with rises typically being small compared to price falls, perhaps indicative of a different competitive dynamic at play than in the U.S. (Levy *et al.*, 2004; Hosken *et al.*, 2000).[13]

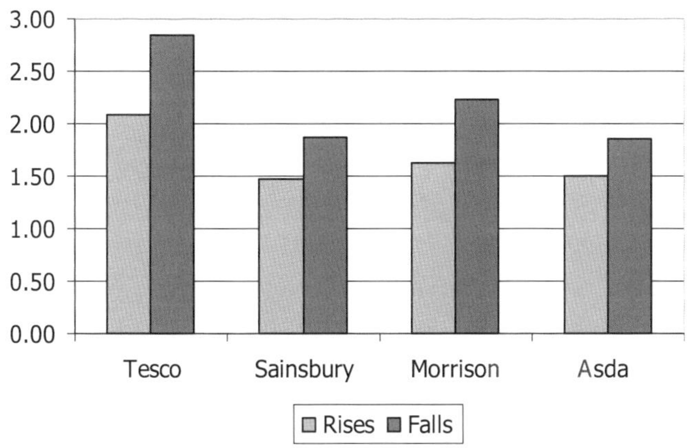

Figure 2. Percentage of price changes by each retailer (average percentage of falls/rises per week).

[13]Note there is little evidence of price stickiness in our data. Nakamura (2008), with a different U.S. supermarket sample, also finds scant evidence of price stickiness.

4.3. *Magnitude of price changes*

Examining the monetary amounts involved in the price changes reveals that, in a large proportion of cases, price changes involved just a few pence. Indeed, a change of just one penny was the most common price change. Figures 3a and 3b respectively show the cumulative frequencies for price falls and price rises (1p–50p) for each retailer.

Investigating further whether the patterns were different for price rises than price falls, and whether these altered over the three sub-periods associated with the S/M merger, Table 4 details the extent of price changes in percentage terms. The upper panel shows the price increases in the ranges up to 10% for all four retailers through each of three sub-periods. It can be observed that such price increases account for less than a sixth of all increases made by Safeway in sub-period one, whereas they account for around a half by the other three retailers, but the pattern is more similar for all four retailers in the two subsequent sub-periods. The lower panel shows the position regarding price falls. Here again we find that Safeway has a relatively small number of low price falls (see Figure 3a). Its price cuts tend to be larger, especially in sub-periods one and two but in sub-period three

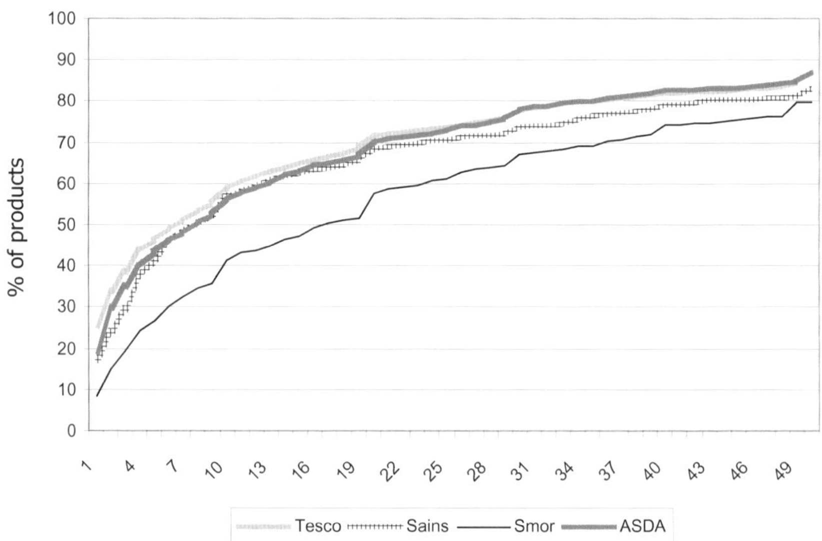

Figure 3a. Cumulative frequency: price falls (1p–50p).

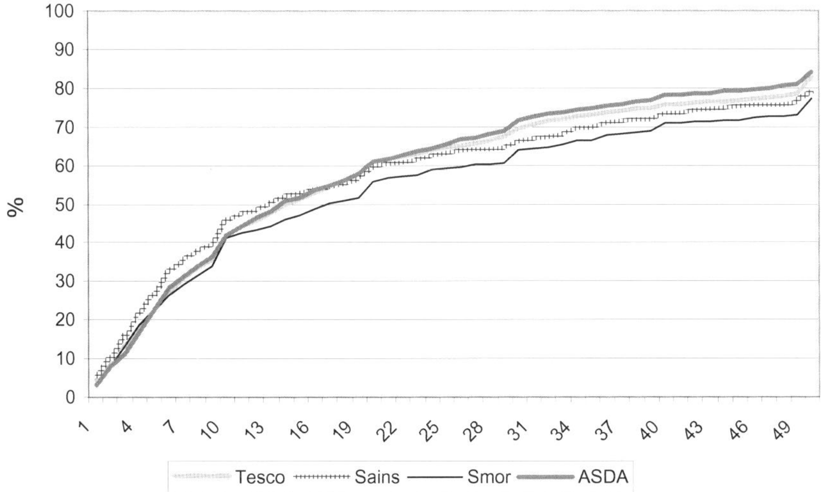

Figure 3b. Cumulative frequency: price rises (1p–50p).

Table 4. Extent of Price Change (Percentage) over Different Sub-Periods

Sub-period	Percent range	Tesco	Sainsbury's	Safeway/ Morrison	Asda
	Price rises (in pence)				
One	0–1	2.4	0.8	0	1.3
	0–10	47.2	50.4	16.6	50.7
Two	0–1	0.6	1.1	1.1	3.5
	0–10	48.9	45.2	45.1	65.2
Three	0–1	2.2	1.7	1.6	1.2
	0–10	41.5	48.2	47.2	42.2
	Price falls (in pence)				
One	0–1	13.6	1.5	0.5	11.6
	0–10	71.7	45.3	15.7	86.0
Two	0–1	8.5	7.2	0.2	10.6
	0–10	54.4	66.7	22.1	68.2
Three	0–1	13.5	5.7	4.6	10.6
	0–10	61.2	59.2	53.6	56.5

these become roughly the same as the other three retailers. In contrast, the Tesco and Asda price falls are relatively small, particularly in sub-period one. Sainsbury generally adopted an intermediate position but with high proportion of price falls in period two, most of which were small

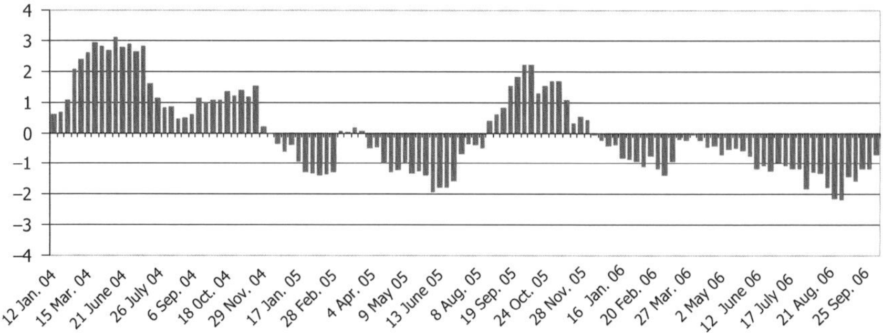

Figure 4a. Net price falls of 10p or more.

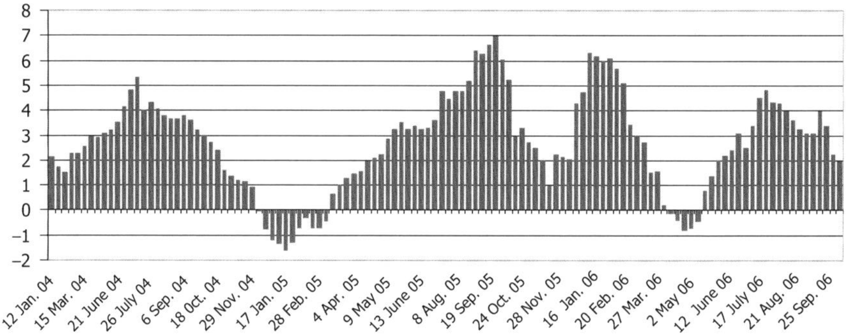

Figure 4b. Net price falls of 9p or less.

Note: Averaged (falls minus rises) over retailer per week for 539 products.

but serving to bring its prices closer into line with Tesco and Asda, as well as Safeway following a wave of cutting prices after the Morrison takeover.

At the market level, it is not uncommon simultaneously to observe net price falls in regard to small price changes but net price rises with larger price changes. This is shown in Figures 4a and 4b, where particularly toward the end of the period, there were many small price falls but these were largely offset by fewer but larger price rises. Indeed, only near the start of the period, when Safeway stores were experiencing price cuts after being acquired by Morrison, do we observe significant net falls in both large and small amounts.

4.4. *Price alignment*

The price data indicates that the S/M merger in 2004 had a profound effect in terms of the alignment of prices in the market. As discussed in Section 2, where formerly there was a marked difference in the pricing policies employed by each of the leading retailers, ranging from extreme HiLo pricing to pure EDLP, positions considerably narrowed such that all four main players subsequently adopted to a greater or lesser degree a similar hybrid strategy, EDLP-based but combined with limited intense promotional pricing. Consistent with this development, Figure 5 reveals a very significant narrowing in the gap in prices over the period studied. At our starting point, prior to the S/M merger, there was significant price dispersion with almost no products identically priced by all four players and with the spread of prices less than 10p for only around 15% of items. However, subsequent to the merger, prices dramatically converged. By the end of our sample period, a third of the items were identically priced across retailers, over half exhibited a price gap of 3p or less, and 70% a spread of 10p or less. As a measure of the spread of prices and a further indication of the extent of price convergence, we find the average coefficient of variation declined by three-quarters. While product characteristics appear relevant in explaining the extent of price alignment, the merger appears to have

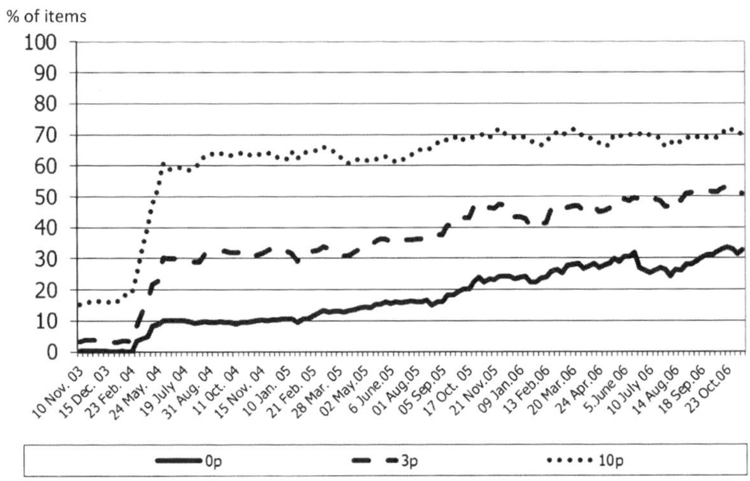

Figure 5. Price gap (in pence) across all four retailers on all items.

played a critical role, leading immediately to lower prices in Safeway (on being acquired by Morrison), and a subsequent response by Sainsbury also lowering prices, drawing both retailers much closer to the prices offered by Tesco and Asda, a trend which continued over time. Accordingly, we find that prices not only drew closer, but generally converged toward a lower level.

4.5. *Patterns across product types*

Differences in the volatility of prices by aisles are shown in Figure 6. Alcohol items in particular appear subject to more frequent price changes, with a tendency for many of these items to have short-term discounts before reverting back to higher prices (particularly around each Christmas/New Year period).[14] Examining more detailed data, it is evident that there is a greater propensity for leading branded goods, especially in relation to alcohol and beverages, household and pet food goods, to have more volatile prices, characteristic of short-term promotional activity on such

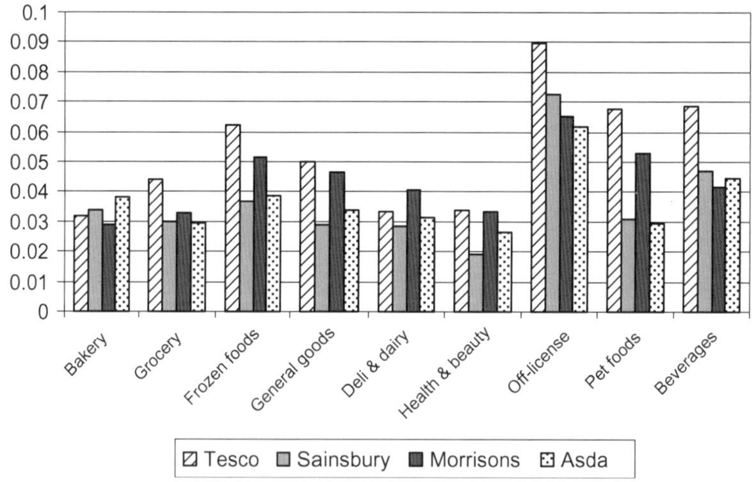

Figure 6. Probability of price change by Aisles.

[14]This is consistent with recent empirical work showing that prices can fall on products in periods of high demand — see McDonald (2000), Chevalier *et al.* (2003), and Nevo and Hatzitaskos (2005).

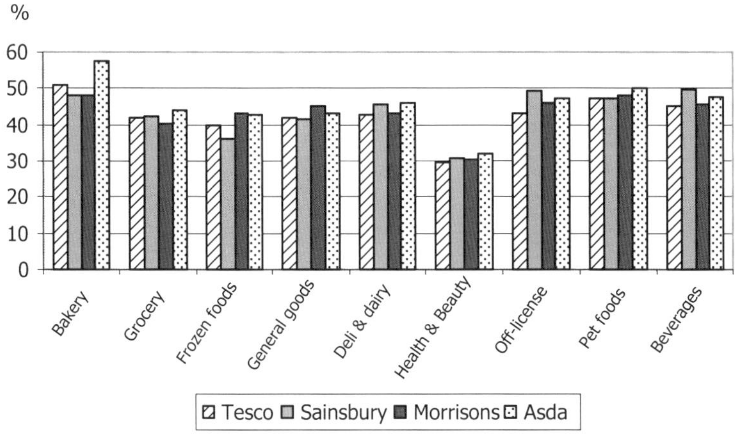

Figure 7. Percentage of price changes that are rises by Aisle.

items (e.g., Hosken and Reiffen, 2004). In addition, though, the extent of changing prices for such products varies from retailer to retailer. Tesco and Sainsbury appear to change prices more frequently on these products (perhaps indicative of their greater use of short-term promotional discount pricing by these two retailers).

As evident from Figure 7, only one category — health and beauty — stands out for having considerably more price falls than price rises. Even so, net price falls over the period characterized almost all categories.

4.6. *Leader–follower behavior*

We next consider the individual price changes made by each retailer to see whether there are any discernible patterns of competitive interaction in terms of the timing of price changes with respect to rivals' behavior.[15] For each price change made by a retailer on a particular item, we consider price changes around this event made by the other retailers on this same item. Specifically, for a $2n + 1$ week window around each retailer's price change, we record whether any other retailer raises or lowers their price

[15]A more extensive investigation of price leadership as between Tesco and Asda over an extended period is reported in Seaton and Waterson (2013). Though the methodology differs significantly, and the timeframe is somewhat different, the results are broadly in line with those reported here.

for that product in the same week (w), the preceding n weeks ($w-1, w-2, \ldots, w-n$) and the following n weeks ($w+1, w+2, \ldots, w+n$). A high count of price changes before the retailer moves indicates that the retailer is a *price follower*, a clump of high counts following w suggests that the retailer is a *price leader*, while a peak around w indicates that the retailers move together (changing prices in the same week). In order to avoid the problem of missing observations, we calculate our results using the maximal window possible up to $n = 3$.

To simplify exposition, we compute a statistic to examine the symmetry of competitor price change, in the same direction, around the firm's price change event at w,

$$\mathrm{LF}(n)\% = 100 \times \left\{ \frac{\begin{array}{l}[\text{Sum of counts } (w+1, \ldots, w+n) \\ \qquad - \text{Sum of counts } (w-1, \ldots, w-n)]\end{array}}{\begin{array}{l}[\text{Total counts at} \\ \qquad (w-n, \ldots, w-1, w+1, \ldots, w+n)]\end{array}} \right\}.$$

This statistic compares the symmetry of price changes on each side of the one firm's price changes at time w. A value of plus one (100%) indicates every other firm that has reacted, did so after this leader firm (f) — whereas minus one (-100%) means all react before, and this firm is a follower. A value close to zero implies price changes were mostly in the same week, or that the distribution is uniform. The results of our analysis are presented in Table 5, where we disaggregate the data, by price type (rise or fall) and sample period (all weeks, pre-merger, S/M merger, post-merger Morrison). We use a chi-squared test to assess the whether the distribution is significantly different from a symmetric one at the 5% level (indicated by *).

Taking first the whole sample period, there is evidence that in terms of price leadership both Tesco and Asda play a strong role. However, their roles appear asymmetric. Asda often leads on price reductions while Tesco often leads price increases. Furthermore, follower behavior appears to be strongly associated with Asda in regard to following the price rises made by others. In contrast, it is Sainsbury and Morrison that both appear to be followers in response to price changes; Sainsbury's having by far the stronger reaction.

The dynamics become particularly interesting when the sample is split into the three sub-periods discussed above in relation to the S/M merger.

Table 5. Price Change Event Window (±3 Weeks)

	Period	Falls chi sq	Falls LF%	Falls indicate	Chi sq	Rises LF%	Rises indicate
Tesco	All	0.82	2.34	Leader	302.76*	50.21	Leader
Sainsbury	All	34.37*	−20.13	Follower	20.40*	−15.34	Follower
Morrison	All	1.75	−5.15	Follower	1.38	−4.17	Follower
Asda	All	33.78*	17.41	Leader	153.28*	−39.92	Follower
Tesco	1	2.17	−21.74	Follower	3.77	53.85	Leader
Sainsbury	1	0.29	−14.29	Follower	2.00	−50.00	Follower
Morrison	1	1.00	−20.00	Follower	0.89	−22.22	Follower
Asda	1	0.33	16.67	Leader	7.36*	−81.82	Follower
Tesco	2	0.86	−17.24	Follower	0.39	13.04	Leader
Sainsbury	2	0.00	0.00	/	0.14	14.29	Leader
Morrison	2	1.92	38.46	Leader	1.29	42.86	Leader
Asda	2	30.77*	76.92	Leader	2.57	−42.86	Follower
Tesco	3	1.76	3.52	Leader	301.84*	50.90	Leader
Sainsbury	3	36.81*	−20.80	Follower	19.81*	−15.26	Follower
Morrison	3	1.86	−5.47	Follower	1.34	−4.18	Follower
Asda	3	22.00*	14.48	Leader	145.32*	−39.38	Follower

*Significantly different from symmetric at the 5% level.

Again from Table 5, in sub-period 1 (i.e., prior to S/M merger), Tesco and Asda appear to set the price change agenda but with largely asymmetric positions — Tesco leading price rises, Asda leading price falls. Meanwhile, Sainsbury and Safeway generally act as price followers: the former consistently in regard to price rises, the latter in regard to price falls. As sample sizes diminish though, so does the statistical power of our tests, and only one relationship is found significant here (Asda as price follower for rises).

In sub-period 2, similarly we only have one significant result — this time for Asda as a leader in price falls. Safeway (after its takeover by Morrison) is largely lowering prices on its own, and while Sainsbury leads on some price increases, it is predominantly Asda that leads on both reductions and Tesco on increases. However, in sub-period 3, Tesco is again a price leader in raising prices, while Asda is a leader in lowering prices (if not to the same degree as in the previous two periods) and also a follower in raising prices. Both Sainsbury and Morrison appear as followers in both price rises and price falls.

In terms of net positions, for the pre-merger sub-period, Tesco and Asda appear to balance each other with asymmetric leadership positions, respectively in price increases and price reductions. Post-merger, Tesco appears to have a greater impact on price increases, with the other three players and especially Asda following Tesco, while Asda's role as setting lower prices for others to follow seems somewhat reduced in the final sub-period.

Accordingly, we find evidence of leader–follower behavior but that the patterns have changed somewhat over time, partly in the aftermath of the S/M merger where just one retailer — the market leader, Tesco — increasingly tended to act as price leader in price rises, perhaps reflecting its growing domination of the sector (possessing double the market share of its nearest rivals) and the reduced influence of the other players to lead price changes.

5. Conclusion

As a tight oligopoly, with four retailers controlling 90% of the national market, the UK's "one-stop-shopping" retail grocery market has witnessed considerable consolidation in recent years, driven by organic growth of the leading players and a major merger (S/M) in 2004.

Given this context, this chapter has sought to draw on a novel data source to examine the nature and extent of price competition in this market, examining the character of price changes and competitor responses amongst the four leading UK supermarket chains over a three-year period. We provide summary data analysis on three specific aspects: (i) the nature and pattern of price changes and whether changes in market structure have altered price change behavior, (ii) the extent of price dispersion and whether price gaps are widening or narrowing; and (iii) any evidence of price leadership behavior.

Despite increased concentration in an already concentrated market, price competition appears to have remained intense, with each major retailer competing to increase its level of sales and improve its market share. We find that Safeway/Morrison prices fell post-merger (as promised), offering consumers an immediate windfall benefit. This is consistent with the view that Safeway was a high-cost firm with the merger achieving lower costs across the merged group; a straightforward Bertrand–Nash model would predict this outcome, provided the cost falls are large enough relative to the impact of concentration on margins. Associated with this, we find that price differences across the Big 4 narrowed considerably over time, as prices set by Morrison and indeed Sainsbury moved closer to those of Tesco and Asda. Much less easily explained by such oligopoly models are various other phenomena. Whilst the number of price falls exceeded price rises by around a third, most falls tended to be small, with the net result that average prices were almost exactly the same at the end of the three-year period as they were at the start (suggesting significant real price deflation over the period). Yet, we observed changed pricing behavior of all four players over different sub-periods relating to the S/M merger. There is also some indication of asymmetric leadership roles — Tesco leading price increases, Asda leading price falls. Of course, there are likely to have been other drivers of these phenomena, apart from the merger.

This case study shows how the nature of competition can change quite markedly and yet subtly in the wake of market consolidation. Such a prospect makes predicting the outcomes from proposed mergers and other concentrations difficult for competition authorities, given the limited concordance with oligopoly theory. The usual assumption in merger analysis is that in the absence of significant cost savings being generated and (at least partly) passed on to consumers then concentration-increasing mergers may well be anticompetitive based on the assumption that competitive interaction will continue in a predictable manner from past behavior. The analysis here demonstrates that the whole nature of competitive interaction can change if price strategies change. For the UK authorities simultaneously investigating four different contemplated mergers between Safeway and other leading industry players all having a concentrating effect on the market, they appear to have made the right decision in allowing the acquisition by Morrison given the subsequent evolution of market prices, at least in the time period considered here. At the time of the investigation, Morrison promised to make immediate and significant price cuts in Safeway stores and they duly delivered these, but it was the subsequent scramble for market share that appears to have led to the other pricing changes identified in this study emerging, with the apparent change in the whole dynamic of competitive interaction in this industry. Such consequences need very detailed and careful consideration.

Appendix

Table A1. Observation Dates

Week no. (w)	Obs (t)	Day	Month	Year	Week no. (w)	Obs (t)	Day	Month	Year
1	1	10	November	2003	91	66	1	August	2005
2	2	17	November	2003	92	67	8	August	2005
3	3	24	November	2003	93	68	15	August	2005
4	4	1	December	2003	94	69	22	August	2005
5	5	8	December	2003	95	70	29	August	2005
6	6	15	December	2003	96	71	5	September	2005
10	7	12	January	2004	98	72	19	September	2005
12	8	26	January	2004	99	73	26	September	2005
14	9	9	February	2004	100	74	3	October	2005
15	10	16	February	2004	101	75	10	October	2005
16	11	23	February	2004	102	76	17	October	2005
19	12	15	March	2004	103	77	24	October	2005
22	13	5	April	2004	104	78	1	November	2005
25	14	26	April	2004	105	79	7	November	2005
27	15	10	May	2004	106	80	14	November	2005
29	16	24	May	2004	107	81	21	November	2005
33	17	21	June	2004	108	82	28	November	2005
34	18	28	June	2004	109	83	5	December	2005
35	19	5	July	2004	110	84	12	December	2005
36	20	12	July	2004	113	85	3	January	2006
37	21	19	July	2004	114	86	9	January	2006
38	22	26	July	2004	115	87	16	January	2006
39	23	2	August	2004	116	88	23	January	2006
41	24	16	August	2004	117	89	30	January	2006
42	25	23	August	2004	118	90	6	February	2006
43	26	31	August	2004	119	91	13	February	2006
44	27	6	September	2004	120	92	20	February	2006
46	28	20	September	2004	121	93	27	February	2006
47	29	27	September	2004	122	94	6	March	2006
48	30	4	October	2004	123	95	13	March	2006
49	31	11	October	2004	124	96	20	March	2006
50	32	18	October	2004	125	97	27	March	2006
51	33	25	October	2004	126	98	3	April	2006
52	34	1	November	2004	127	99	10	April	2006
53	35	8	November	2004	128	100	18	April	2006
54	36	15	November	2004	129	101	24	April	2006
56	37	29	November	2004	130	102	2	May	2006
57	38	6	December	2004	131	103	8	May	2006
58	39	13	December	2004	133	104	22	May	2006

(Continued)

Table A1. (*Continued*)

Week no. (w)	Obs (t)	Day	Month	Year	Week no. (w)	Obs (t)	Day	Month	Year
61	40	3	January	2005	134	105	30	May	2006
62	41	10	January	2005	135	106	5	June	2006
63	42	17	January	2005	136	107	12	June	2006
64	43	24	January	2005	137	108	19	June	2006
66	44	7	February	2005	138	109	26	June	2006
67	45	14	February	2005	139	110	3	July	2006
68	46	21	February	2005	140	111	10	July	2006
69	47	28	February	2005	141	112	17	July	2006
70	48	7	March	2005	142	113	24	July	2006
71	49	14	March	2005	143	114	1	August	2006
72	50	21	March	2005	144	115	7	August	2006
73	51	28	March	2005	145	116	14	August	2006
74	52	4	April	2005	146	117	21	August	2006
75	53	11	April	2005	147	118	29	August	2006
76	54	18	April	2005	148	119	4	September	2006
77	55	25	April	2005	149	120	11	September	2006
78	56	2	May	2005	150	121	18	September	2006
79	57	9	May	2005	151	122	25	September	2006
80	58	16	May	2005	152	123	2	October	2006
81	59	23	May	2005	153	124	9	October	2006
82	60	30	May	2005	154	125	16	October	2006
83	61	6	June	2005	155	126	23	October	2006
84	62	13	June	2005	156	127	30	October	2006
85	63	20	June	2005	157	128	6	November	2006
89	64	18	July	2005	158	129	13	November	2006
90	65	25	July	2005	/	/	/	/	/

References

Bolton, R. N. and V. Shankar (2003). "An Empirically Derived Taxonomy of Retailer Pricing and Promotion Strategies," *Journal of Retailing*, 79(4), pp. 213–224.

Chevalier, J. A., A. K. Kashyap, and P. E. Rossi (2003). "Why Don't Prices Rise During Periods of Peak Demand? Evidence from Scanner Data," *American Economic Review*, 93(1), pp. 15–37.

Chintagunta, P., J.-P. Dube, and V. Singh (2003). "Balancing Profitability and Customer Welfare in a Supermarket Chain," *Quantitative Marketing and Economics*, 1(1), pp. 111–147.

Competition Commission (2000). *Supermarkets: A Report on the Supply of Groceries from Multiple Stores in the United Kingdom*, Cm 4842, TSO. London.

Competition Commission (2003). *Safeway plc and Asda Group Limited (Owned by Wal-Mart Stores Inc); Wm Morrison Supermarkets PLC; J Sainsbury plc; and Tesco plc: A Report on the Mergers in Contemplation*, Cm 5950, TSO, London.

Competition Commission (2008). *The Supply of Groceries in the UK: Market Investigation*, Competition Commission, London, 30 April.

Dobson, P. W. (2005). "Exploiting Buyer Power: Lessons from the British Grocery Trade," *Antitrust Law Journal*, 72(2), pp. 529–562.

Dobson, P. W. and M. Waterson (2008). "Chain Store Competition: Customized vs. Uniform Pricing," *Warwick Economic Research Papers* No. 840.

Ellickson, P. B. and S. Misra (2008). "Supermarket Pricing Strategies," *Marketing Science*, 27(5), pp. 811–828.

Hosken, D., D. Matsa, and D. Reiffen (2000). "How do Retailers Adjust Prices? Evidence from Store-Level Data," *Working Paper* No. 230, Bureau of Economics, Federal Trade Commission.

Hosken, D. and D. Reiffen (2001). "Pricing Behavior of Multi-Product Retailers," *Working Paper* No. 225 *(revised)*, Bureau of Economics, Federal Trade Commission.

Hosken, D. and D. Reiffen (2004). "Patterns of Retail Price Variation," *RAND Journal of Economics*, 35(1), pp. 128–146.

IGD (2005). *Grocery Retailing 2005*. Institute of Grocery Distribution, UK.

Levy, D., H. Chen, S. Ray, and M. Bergen (2004). "Asymmetric Price Adjustment in the Small: An Implication of Rational Inattention," *Discussion Paper 04-23*, Tjalling C. Koopmans Research Institute, Universiteit Utrecht.

McDonald, J. M. (2000). "Demand, Information and Competition: Why Do Food Prices Fall at Seasonal Demand Peaks?" *Journal of Industrial Economics*, 48(1), pp. 27–45.

Mintel (2005). *Food Retailing — UK — November 2005*. Mintel Group, UK.

Montgomery, A. L. (1997). "Creating Micro-Marketing Pricing Strategies Using Supermarket Scanner Data," *Marketing Science*, 16(4), pp. 315–337.

Müller, G., M. Bergen, S. Dutta and D. Levy (2006). "Private Label Price Rigidity During Holiday Periods," *Applied Economics Letters*, 13, pp. 57–62.

Nakamura, E. (2008). "Pass-Through in Retail and Wholesale." *American Economic Review*, 98(2), pp. 230–237.

Nevo, A. and K. Hatzitaskos (2005). "Why Does the Average Price of Tuna Fall During Lent," *Working Paper*.

Office of Fair Trading (2006). "The Grocery Market," *OFT Paper* No. 845, May, HMSO.

Seaton, J. S. and M. Waterson (2013). "Identifying and Characterising Price Leadership in British Supermarkets," *International Journal of Industrial Organization*, 31(5), pp. 392–403.

Skrianka, B. S. (2012). "The Geography of Grocery Demand in the UK: An Evaluation of the 2003 Morrisons- Safeway Merger," Mimeo, University of Chicago, Harris School of Public Policy.

Verdict Research (2005). *Grocery Retailers 2006*, Verdict Research, UK.

Chapter 2

The Price Effects of Mergers in Airline Networks*

Kai Hüschelrath

ZEW, MaCCI, and University of Mannheim
hueschelrath@zew.de

Kathrin Müller

ZEW and MaCCI
kathrin.mueller@zew.de

Abstract

We study the price effects of mergers in airline networks. Guided by a review of the existing theoretical and empirical literature, we develop two classifications of routes possibly affected by an airline merger. Subsequently, we apply a difference-in-differences approach to exemplarily investigate the price effects of the America West Airlines — US Airways merger completed in 2005. We find that although average prices increased substantially on routes in which both airlines competed either on a non-stop or one-stop basis prior to the merger, substantial average price reductions observed for routes without any pre-merger overlap suggest that the merger led to a net increase in consumer welfare.

Keywords: Airline industry, merger, market power, consumer welfare, price effects.

JEL Classification Codes: L40, L93.

*Parts of this article make use of earlier research of both authors published in Hüschelrath and Müller (2013a, 2014). This is especially the case for the empirical analysis presented in Section 4. We are thankful to Martin Peitz and Yossi Spiegel for their comments on earlier versions of the paper. The usual disclaimer applies.

1. Introduction

The study of the price effects of horizontal mergers has captivated generations of researchers. A substantial part of this extraordinary appeal might originate from the general dichotomy such mergers are exposed to: increases in market power — which (in the short run) go hand in hand with consumer welfare-reducing price increases — and countervailing factors such as the realization of efficiencies or the inducement of market entry by competitors — which might (in the medium and long run) translate into consumer welfare-increasing price decreases post-merger. From an antitrust policy perspective, the key challenge of horizontal merger investigations consequently lies in an appropriate assessment and weighting of these potential anti- and procompetitive effects to arrive at a robust conclusion whether the proposed transaction should be blocked, approved, or approved subject to the fulfillment of specific remedies (which aim at healing identified competition concerns).

In the aftermath of decisions on proposed merger transactions by competition authorities, the question is often raised whether the respective decisions were correct. For example, if prices are found to increase after the respective merger is cleared (with or without remedies), one possible explanation could be an erroneous analysis and decision of the case by the responsible competition authority (leading to a significant increase in market power of the merged entity that allowed the observed price increases). The value of conducting such *ex-post* merger reviews, however, goes beyond the mere identification of problematic decisions but especially provides a fruitful basis to learn from weaknesses in past case assessment thereby improving future merger decisions.

For several reasons, the U.S. airline industry provides an ideal environment for an empirical *ex-post* investigation of the price effects of industry consolidation through merger. First, since its deregulation in 1978, the industry experienced many merger and acquisitions thereby providing a large selection of possible cases to investigate. Second, larger airlines offer their service in a large number of route markets thereby providing a good basis for an empirical analysis of the respective economic effects. Last but not least, unlike in many other markets and industries, detailed price and quantity data on a route basis is available (for the United States) providing the possibility to conduct sophisticated *ex-post* merger reviews.

Against this background, we study the price effects of mergers in airline networks. Guided by a review of the existing theoretical and empirical literature, we develop two classifications of routes possibly affected by an airline merger. Subsequently, we apply a difference-in-differences (D-i-D) approach to exemplarily investigate the price effects of the America West Airlines–US Airways merger completed in 2005. We find that although average prices increased substantially on routes in which both airlines competed either on a non-stop or one-stop basis prior to the merger, substantial average price reductions observed for routes without any pre-merger overlap suggest that the merger led to a net increase in consumer welfare.

The chapter is structured as follows. Section 2 provides an overview of the key contributions from both theory and empirics with respect to the consumer welfare effects of mergers in airline networks. Subsequently, Section 3 focuses on the development of two separate classifications of routes possibly affected by a merger of two airlines with a largely complementary network. We will differentiate between overlapping and switching routes (classification 1) and non-stop and one-stop overlaps (classification 2). In Section 4, we apply the second route classification to a real airline merger. Specifically, we concentrate on the merger between America West Airlines and US Airways completed in 2005 and study the price effects of the merger by applying a D-i-D approach. In contrast to Hüschelrath and Müller (2014) who concentrate on a route-carrier level estimation approach, we apply a route-level estimation approach to isolate the effects of the merger on average prices. Section 5 concludes the chapter with a review of its main insights and a discussion of possible avenues for future research.

2. Review of Existing Research

Any study focusing on the price effects of (horizontal) mergers can build on a significant amount of existing research. In this section, we provide an overview of the key contributions from both theory (Section 2.1) and empirics (Section 2.2). As several general surveys on the consumer welfare effects of mergers in general and the price effects of mergers in particular are available,[1] we restrict our review of the existing literature to horizontal mergers in airline networks.

2.1. *Theoretical research*

A hub-and-spoke (HS) network is defined as a route system in which many "spoke" locations are connected to one or a small number of "hubs" which serve the function of bundling incoming and outgoing transactions. Such bundling is typically not only associated with improvements in productive efficiency through economies of traffic density (and scope) but also reaches a better spatial coverage of the respective service (see generally, e.g., Brueckner *et al.* (1992), Brueckner and Spiller (1994), or Caves *et al.* (1984)). Although HS networks by construction lead to substantial concentration and therefore potential bottleneck and market power concerns at the respective hub locations, they are considered as an efficient way to organize traffic flows.

The general characteristics of airline HS networks have been studied quite extensively from a theoretical perspective. Guided by the well-known cost- and demand-related characteristics of such networks, the majority of papers assume an airline network of a monopoly airline and investigate, e.g., under which conditions a monopolist airline has incentives to switch from a point-to-point network to a HS network, how such an airline would allocate costs and set prices across routes, or whether a monopolist airline has possibilities to strategically impede competition by excessively increasing its hub presence (see, e.g., Bittlingmayer (1990), Brueckner and Zhang (2001), or Hendricks *et al.* (1995)).

[1] From a theoretical perspective, Werden and Froeb (2008) as well as Kaplow and Shapiro (2007) and Whinston (2007) provide surveys. Following Pautler (2003), existing empirical research can be subdivided further into multi-industry studies, industry studies, and case studies of specific mergers in specific industries. Concentrating on the later type of studies, Kaplan (2000) and Weinberg (2008) provide selective overviews of such case studies for a diverse set of industries including banking, hospitals, microfilms, telecommunications, computers, railroads, cement, and tires.

The welfare effects of competition and mergers in airline HS networks are only investigated by a small number of papers (see especially Brueckner and Spiller (1991), Oum *et al.* (1995), and Aguirregabiria and Ho (2010)). In their seminal paper, Brueckner and Spiller (1991) differentiate between competition in three different HS route structures — interhub competition, direct competition, and leg competition[2] — and investigate the implications for competition and mergers on traffic and fares. The authors find that competition is not necessarily beneficial in HS networks as soon as both the effects on hub-to-hub and hub-to-spoke routes are taken into account (see also Bittlingmayer (1990)). As an increase in competition is likely to reduce traffic for the incumbent airline(s) on that route, cost complementarities and economies of traffic density are reduced possibly causing increases in marginal costs (and therefore prices) on complementary — seemingly unaffected — routes of the network. Whether the benefits of additional competition overtop these cost increases depend on the (demand and cost) characteristics of the respective routes/network. As a consequence, mergers in HS networks cannot be considered as generally consumer welfare reducing as the costs of a reduction in competition might be overtopped by additional efficiencies created by the larger network operated by the merged entity.

Although any investigation of the consumer welfare effects of a merger has to consider market price as a key variable, it is equally undisputed that additional service-related variables might also influence consumer welfare. For example, Bailey and Liu (1995) study the effects of airline consolidation on price *and* service (measured by scope of operations or network density). They assume that consumers prefer larger airline networks as they basically allow them to reach a higher number of destinations with a higher level of convenience in a shorter amount of time. In a two-stage model with free entry, they show that the service-enhancing effects of further consolidation may indeed outweigh the price-increasing effects of a reduction in the

[2] *Interhub competition* refers to a route network in which cities A and B cannot be reached by a non-stop flight but only by one-stop connections via hub 1 or hub 2. *Direct competition* refers to a route network in which cities A and B can be reached either by a non-stop flight or an one-stop connection via hub 1. *Leg competition* refers to direct competition on a spoke route, e.g., the non-stop route from city A to hub 1.

number of effective competitors. In another contribution, Richard (2003) concentrates on flight frequency as a service-related driver of consumer welfare. Based on a model of firms' decisions which endogenizes flight frequency, the results of various simulation exercises suggest that although a merger typically causes decreases in passenger volume and consumer surplus, some markets show net welfare gains as soon as merger-induced changes in flight frequency are included into the welfare assessment.

2.2. *Empirical research*

Existing empirical research on the price effects of US airline mergers largely refers to the late 1980s. Two U.S. airline mergers — both completed in 1986 — experienced a particularly detailed *ex-post* investigation of their consumer welfare effects: Northwest Airlines–Republic Airlines (NW-RC) and Trans World Airlines–Ozark Airlines (TW-OZ). Both mergers involved a shared major hub airport and therefore led to substantial increases in market power post-merger. In a first influential paper, Werden *et al.* (1991) investigate the price and output effects of the two mergers *at their respective hub airports* and find yield increases of about 5.6% and service decreases (measured in number of departures) of about 17.9% for the NW-RC merger. Yield increases (1.5%) and service decreases (13.0%) were somewhat smaller for the TW-OZ merger. Borenstein (1990) analyzes the effects of the same two mergers at their hub airports and finds evidence for price increases for the NW-RC merger of about 9.5% in total (with about 6.7% price increases if other airlines remain as route competitors and about 22.5% if the merger led to a monopoly route). For the TW-OZ merger, however, his analysis resulted in largely insignificant results with the exception of a significant price decrease of about 12.3% on monopoly routes which were operated by TW or OZ before the merger.[3] Borenstein's analysis therefore provides evidence that airline mergers can have an either increasing or decreasing impact on average prices "... not just on routes that both airlines

[3] It is important to note here that the observed price decrease is rather unexpected and might be explained by a general period of low demand at TWA's St. Louis hub. For the NW-RC merger, Borenstein (1990) finds significant price increases of about 6% for NW or RC routes in which (a) competitor(s) remain(s) after the merger and price increases of about 12% for NW or RC routes which became a monopoly post-merger.

had served prior to the merger, but also on routes where only one of the two merger partners competed with another airline or operated without active competition" (Borenstein, 1990, p. 404).

Borenstein's key result of merger effects on routes in which only one of the merging carriers was active pre-merger is also found in studies of Kwoka and Shumilkina (2010) and Kim and Singal (1993). While Kwoka and Shumilkina (2010) also analyze a single merger (US Air and Piedmont in 1987) and find that prices rise by 5 to 6% on routes which were only served by one of the merging carriers and the other was a potential entrant, Kim and Singal (1993) analyze the effects of 14 U.S. airline mergers between 1985 and 1988 and find that relative fares on the merging firms' routes rose by about 9.4%. Significant price increases were particularly found on routes in which the merging parties did not compete (directly) prior to the merger. They explain this observation by an increase in multi-market contact (MMC) triggered by the merger. Furthermore, the authors identified a substantial difference in the behavior of "mergers including a failing firm" and "mergers without a failing firm". Fares of failing airlines were found to be much lower on average before the merger, providing an explanation for the substantially larger price increases after the merger compared to cases of mergers between "healthy" firms.

Partly due to the substantial reduction in merger activity in the 1990s and 2000s, existing research on the competitive effects of more recent U.S. airline mergers is very limited. From an *ex-post* perspective, Bilotkach (2011) investigates the America West–US Airways merger with a particular focus on its implications for MMC. He finds that the merger changed the way that the airlines take into account the extent of MMC when making strategic choices as to frequency of service. Furthermore, most recently, Luo (2014) estimates the price effects of the Delta Air Lines–Northwest Airlines merger while controlling for, e.g., changes in legacy carrier and low cost carrier competition. Her results suggest that the merger only generated a small fare increase, basically because competition among legacy carriers generally has a weak effect on fares compared to low cost carrier competition. From an *ex-ante* perspective, constant rumors of possible mega-mergers led to several policy studies on the possible effects of such mergers (see, e.g., U.S. General Accounting Office, 2001, U.S. Government Accountability Office, 2010). However, academic contributions are restricted to a paper by Benkard *et al.* (2010) in which the authors simulate the dynamic effects of three proposed horizontal U.S. airline mergers. Using data for 2003–2008, they find that a merger between two major hub carriers leads to increased entry by both other hub carriers and low cost carriers thereby offsetting some of the initial concentrating effects of the merger.[4]

3. Development of Two Classifications to Study the Price Effects of Mergers in Airline Networks

Although the preceding section revealed significant existing research on the question after the price effects of mergers in airline networks, the large majority of these papers refer to U.S. airline mergers completed in the 1980s. On the one hand, this period was characterized by substantial industry consolidation leading to a large number of mergers as possible study objects. On the other hand, the U.S. Department of Justice (DOJ) followed a *laissez-faire* approach to antitrust policy at that time — strongly influenced by the theory of contestable markets by Baumol *et al.* (1982) — and leading to the approval of basically all merger proposals independent of their potential for anticompetitive effects. This general policy led to the approval of airline mergers which had a substantial non-stop route overlap due to the sharing of a common hub.

More recently, however, antitrust authorities tend to take account of the anticompetitive potential of airline mergers with a significant degree of non-stop route overlap. For example, the European Commission (EC) recently prohibited two mergers which both involved shared hubs: Dublin in case of the Ryanair–Aer Lingus merger proposal (Case No. COMP/M.4439,

[4]Complementary to a few theoretical studies focusing on service-related effects of airline mergers, several papers provide empirical evidence for the relevance of such factors. For example, Mazzeo (2003) investigates the relationship between high market concentration and airline service. However, his analysis concentrates on on-time performance only and finds that flight delays are more common and longer on routes operated by a single airline and on routes through airports where the carrier has a large market share. Most recently, Israel *et al.* (2011) study the consumer welfare effects of a greater connectivity and more convenient schedules in an empirical framework and conclude that a full assessment of the welfare effects of mergers demands an inclusion of quality effects, i.e., quality-adjusted post-merger fares have to be compared to the pre-merger fares.

decided in 2007) and Athens in case of the Olympic Air–Aegean Airlines merger proposal (Case No. COMP/M.5830, decided in 2011). In both cases, the EC concluded that (route) competition would be harmed substantially by the mergers and therefore prohibited the transactions.

In the United States, several merger proposals were abandoned after the DOJ signaled competition concerns. For example, in 2001, United Airlines and US Air ended their merger plans after the DOJ announced its intent to block the transaction (see, e.g., U.S. General Accounting Office, 2001 for an analysis of the expected competitive effects of the proposed merger). Three years earlier, in 1998, a proposal of Northwest Airlines to acquire Continental Airlines received similar signals from the DOJ and was subsequently abandoned.

Due to the tougher enforcement of antitrust rules in recent years, approved airline mergers are characterized by largely complementary networks. Although the empirical results of earlier studies remain relevant, the new merger characteristic raises the demand for route classifications that explicitly takes the complementarities of the merging network into account. In the following two sub-sections, we therefore develop two alternative classifications of routes that might be affected by a merger between two airlines with largely complementary networks. While Section 3.1 introduces a classification that differentiates between overlapping and switching routes in direct route markets, the subsequent Section 3.2 provides an extension by also considering one-stop connections as a possible (lower quality) substitute for direct flights.

3.1. *Classification 1: Overlapping and switching routes*

Guided by the theoretical contributions of Bittlingmayer (1990) and Brueckner and Spiller (1991), the first classification is based on a simple differentiation between overlapping routes and switching routes. This differentiation is illustrated in Figure 1.

The two hubs H_1 and H_2 of airlines 1 and 2 are connected by services of both carriers (route H_1H_2) while the respective spokes are only served by the respective hub airline, i.e., routes AH_1, BH_1, and CH_1 by airline 1 and H_2D, H_2E, and H_2F by airline 2. In order to derive hypotheses on the effects of mergers on competition, we introduce a separation of possibly affected

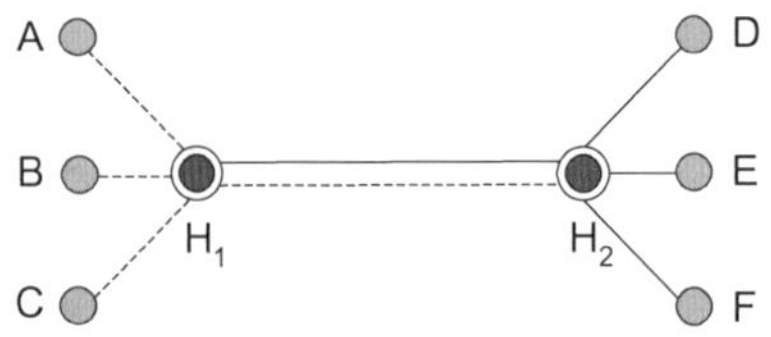

Figure 1. A simple non-stop route network with two airlines.
Source: Hüschelrath and Müller (2013a).

routes. So-called *overlapping routes* are characterized by the presence of both merging carriers before the merger, i.e., they are direct competitors in the respective non-stop markets (route H_1H_2 in Figure 1).[5] In contrast, we introduce a second category of routes for which possible merger effects cannot be ruled out: the so-called *switching routes*. Switching routes are operated by one merger partner *ex-ante* but are taken over by the other merger partner as a consequence of the merger (routes AH_1, BH_1, and CH_1 in Figure 1 if airline 2 acquires airline 1).

3.1.1. Overlapping routes

Focusing on *overlapping routes* first, in the short run, the capacity of one of the merging carriers is unlikely to be removed entirely from the market. However, mergers might lead to an increase in market power thereby incentivizing the merged entity to reduce quantity and increase price. In the medium and long run, the potential effects are again less clear. On the one hand, capacity expansions of existing competitors or entry by potential competitors might constrain the market power of the merged parties. On the other hand, barriers to entry such as hub dominance might reduce the threat of entry substantially thereby allowing the merged parties to permanently increase prices. Comparing liquidation-related exits and merger-related exits, it can be expected that capacity increases through entry are more likely after liquidations given the substantial loss of capacity due to the exit of one carrier. Merger-related exits, however, are more likely to put the merging parties in a stronger position on the respective overlapping

[5]Although Figure 1 only shows one overlapping route (H_1H_2), overlaps in real airline networks are not restricted to hub-to-hub operations but can also be observed in other constellations such as route CH_2 or route AD.

routes suggesting a dissuading effect on the entry incentives of potential competitors.

3.1.2. Switching routes

Turning from overlapping routes to *switching routes*, an initial assessment of this route type might suggest that competitive effects are rather unlikely, especially because the number of competitors on these routes is unaffected by the merger. However, a closer look reveals that the merger-induced change in the operator might trigger price changes. Generally, referring to the theory of HS networks, a merger might have a significant impact of the overall number of passengers traveling on the respective routes. *Ceteris paribus*, an increase (decrease) in the number of passengers is associated with decreases (increases) in marginal costs due to cost complementarities and economies of traffic density and would consequently suggest a downward (upward) trend in price. Furthermore, post-merger (network) reorganization (possibly including hub closures, etc.) might affect route-related costs, demand and average prices as well as the quality of the merged product (e.g., in terms of number of cities served, number of departures, or number of available seats). Additionally, the merger inevitably reduces the overall number of carriers in the industry thereby increasing the probability of MMC among the remaining airlines (possibly triggering tacitly collusive market outcomes and therefore increasing prices). Last but not least, potential competition might be eliminated by the merger possibly making it easier for the remaining carriers to increase price.

3.2. *Classification 2: Non-stop overlap and one-stop overlap*

Although classification 1 does allow a first assessment of the price effects of a merger, it leaves out an important possible driver of competition in HS networks, namely the existence of one-stop connections as (lower quality) substitute for direct connections. In order to study these effects in more detail, we draw on the simple route network shown in Figure 2.

We assume that two airlines provide services in the above network. Airline 1 operates hub A while airline 2 operates hub B (black dots with white circle). Airline 1 offers direct flights to cities B, C, D, and E (dashed lines), while airline 2 provides direct services to cities A, C, D, and F (solid

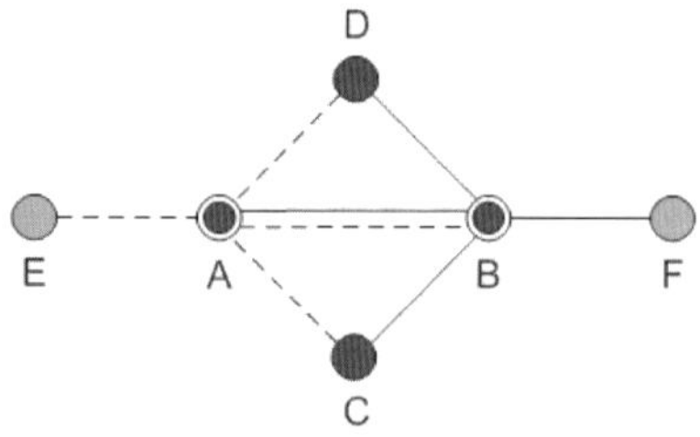

Figure 2. A simple non-stop/one-stop route network with two airlines.
Source: Hüschelrath and Müller (2014).

lines). As a consequence, both airlines are present at the respective airports in cities A, B, C, and D (black dots), while airlines 1 and 2 has an exclusive position at airport E and F respectively (gray dots). Based on this simple airline network, we define the following types of routes possibly affected by the merger.

3.2.1. Routes with non-stop overlap

This route type is characterized by direct competition of both merging airlines in a particular non-stop airport-pair. In this route category, a merger by definition leads to an increase in market concentration and is susceptible of increasing market power of the merging airlines. As a consequence, this route type typically is the major focus of antitrust investigations. In the simple airline network defined in Figure 2, airlines 1 and 2 only compete directly on the AB airport-pair.

3.2.2. Routes with one-stop overlap

This route type is characterized by the presence of indirect competition of one of the merging airlines in a particular airport-pair: while one carrier offers a direct connection, the other carrier operates a one-stop connection between origin and destination airports. Although one-stop connections must be considered as a lower-quality product compared to a direct flight (e.g., due to longer travel times and the need to change airplanes *en-route*), such imperfect substitutes can still act as effective competitive constraint particularly in medium and long-haul markets. A merger reduces or even eliminates this low-quality competition through one-stop connections and might consequently harm consumers through higher prices post-merger.

In the simple airline network above, airline 1 faces one-stop competition on routes AC and AD, as consumers can also travel with airline 2 from A to C via B and from A to D via B. Vice versa, airline 2 might be constrained in its price-setting behavior on routes BC and BD due to one-stop connections by airline 1 (B to C via A and B to D via A).

3.2.3. Routes with no overlap

This route type is characterized by the absence of non-stop or one-stop overlaps, i.e., no direct or indirect competition exists between the merging airlines. In the simple airline network above, this is the case for route AE for airline 1 and route BF for airline 2. Although at first glance, one might think that these routes are unaffected by the merger, our discussion of the "switching routes" category as part of classification 1 above has identified several reasons for price changes in the aftermath of a merger such as changes in the cost and demand structure (of particular routes or even particular routes types) due to network reorganizations, an increased probability of MMC, or the elimination of potential competition.

Based on this classification of routes possibly affected by the merger,[6] an empirical implementation has to differentiate between five different route types: non-stop overlaps between airlines 1 and 2, one-stop competition by airline 1 (airline 2) on a particular non-stop route from airline 2 (airline 1), and routes with no overlap operated by airlines 1 and 2. While we expect average price increases on non-stop and one-stop overlap routes after the merger, our theoretical reasoning and review of existing empirical research suggests that it is not possible to identify a clear direction of possible price effects of the merger on routes with no overlap.

Although the remainder of this chapter will concentrate on an application of the derived classification to a particular merger, i.e., will conduct an *ex-post* merger review, the proposed classification can be of great use in *ex-ante* assessments of proposed mergers as well (basically because

[6]It is important to note that an application of our route classification does not lead to a full coverage of all airline routes in a certain unit of observation (e.g., a country). Depending on the size and characteristics of the merger under investigation, a substantial fraction of routes is unlikely to be (directly) affected by the merger and would therefore not be captured by our classification (which was predominantly designed to conduct *ex-post* merger reviews).

it provides guidance on which route types to include in the antitrust assessment).

4. Application of a Route Classification to the America West–US Airways Merger

Given the development of two classifications for an assessment of the price effects of mergers in airline networks in the preceding section, this section applies the second "richer"[7] classification (based on non-stop and one-stop overlaps) to the merger between America West and US Airways ("HP–U.S. merger") completed in 2005 (third quarter).[8] Although the last decade has seen a couple of mergers between U.S. airlines, several arguments suggest focusing on the HP–U.S. transaction. First, the merger took place at a time without severe external or internal shocks such as terrorist attacks, economic recession, or other larger airline mergers. Second, the networks of both carriers were truly complementary showing only four non-stop route overlaps at the time of the merger. Third, the hubs of both airlines were located quite distant from each other with Phoenix and Las Vegas in case of America West Airlines and Charlotte, Philadelphia, and Pittsburgh in case of US Airways. This characteristic, *ceteris paribus*, makes one-stop connections a closer substitute to non-stop connections than in cases of closely located hubs.[9]

The remainder of the section is structured as follows. Section 4.1 describes the construction of the dataset, while Section 4.2 specifies our empirical approach and presents our results. Section 4.3 finally provides an interpretation of our empirical results.

---

[7]The key advantage of the second classification lies in the consideration of one-stop competition; it is therefore more likely to provide a full picture of the effects of the merger on market price than the first classification.

[8]Applications of the first classification can be found in Hüschelrath and Müller (2013a) to a selection of U.S. airline mergers and in Hüschelrath and Müller (2012) to the specific case of the Delta Air Lines–Northwest Airlines merger completed in 2009. In both papers, a before-and-after approach is applied to study the price effects of the merger(s).

[9]Although it might not be acceptable for most passengers to travel from New York via Boston to Philadelphia, it might be considered as a close substitute to go from New York to Phoenix on either a direct flight or a connecting flight via, e.g., Salt Lake City or Denver.

4.1. *Construction of the dataset*

Our dataset was constructed by collecting and merging data from several sources. We use airline traffic data for the years from 2003 (fourth quarter) to 2007 (third quarter) from the U.S. DOT T-100 Domestic Segment database. This data contains monthly domestic non-stop segment data reported by U.S. air carriers when both origin and destination airports are located within the boundaries of the United States and its territories. We use T-100's information on origin, destination, non-stop distance, available capacity, number of departures, and number of passengers to construct a quarterly panel dataset of non-directional non-stop route airport-pair markets. In addition, we use fare data from the U.S. DOT DB1B Market Origin and Destination Survey to enrich the constructed panel dataset with quarterly route-level fare data. In calculating average non-stop fares, zero fares and abnormally high fares were excluded from the dataset. We only use average fares which are based on at least 10 observations and 1,000 quarterly passengers. We also used DB1B data to identify one-stop overlap routes.[10] We further add demographic information on the population and the number of establishments of the respective Metropolitan Statistical Areas (MSA) from the U.S. Bureau of Labor Statistics.

4.2. *Empirical approach and results*

The implementation of our empirical approach is guided by the second route classification derived above and studies the average price effects of the merger between America West and US Airways for the five different route categories. Table 1 initially characterizes the different route types included in our estimations.

As shown in Table 1, the HP–U.S. merger in sum (directly) affected 239 airport-pairs. Referring to our route classification, we have only four airport-pairs in the "non-stop overlap" category, compared to $7 + 24 = 31$ in the "one-stop overlap" category and $147 + 57 = 204$ routes showing

[10]We started with the identification of all non-stop routes of either U.S. or HP and used DB1B information to identify all stop-over connections available from the respective airports. As a consequence, our subset of routes excludes all markets in which non-stop services of at least one of the merging parties were unavailable.

Table 1. Characteristics of Routes Included in the Estimations

	Number of routes	Number of direct competitors	Distance	Quarterly passengers
Comparator routes	1,364	1.4	798.8	72,864
1. Direct competition	4	2.1	1993.8	131,633
2. US route (no HP comp.)	147	1.6	636.6	103,668
3. US route (HP one-stop comp.)	7	1.7	2231.3	97,951
4. HP route (no U.S. comp.)	57	2.4	897.4	232,978
5. HP route (U.S. one-stop comp.)	24	2.1	2013.5	111,513
Total/Average (unweighted)	*239*	*1.98*	*1554.5*	*135,549*

Sources: U.S. DOT, T-100 Domestic Segment Data, Airline Origin and Destination Survey (DB1B), authors' calculations.

"no overlap". As further revealed by Table 1, HP routes have a higher number of direct competitors in the respective airport pairs suggesting — *ceteris paribus* — more intensive competition. Additionally, data on the average distances show that — due to the locations of the hubs of the merging parties — non-stop and one-stop competition largely take place in long distance markets, while the no overlap routes are (on average) substantially shorter and basically aim at distributing traffic from the respective hubs to airports in the Western parts of the U.S. in case of America West and in the Eastern parts of the U.S. in case of US Airways. Last but not least, the figures for the average number of passengers per quarter reveal that America West routes are denser for both routes with one-stop competition and routes with no competition (between the merging parties).

In order to isolate the price effect of the merger on the five route types, we apply a D-i-D approach. Generally, a D-i-D approach analyzes the change in price for a market category affected by the merger over time (the so-called "treatment group") and compares this change against the change in price for a market category unaffected by the merger over the same time period (the so-called "control group"). A crucial aspect of the D-i-D approach therefore lies in the choice of a suitable control group.

In our case, we started with the entire set of routes (between the fourth quarter of 2003 and the third quarter of 2007) of the 18 largest U.S.

domestic carriers.[11] We continued by excluding any route with fewer than 10 observations and 1,000 quarterly passengers. Subsequently, we dropped all routes in which either U.S. or HP was active. We ended up with a sample of 1,364 routes as our control group. Table A1 in the Appendix presents the descriptive statistics for the comparator routes. Comparing these descriptive statistics with the summary statistics provided in Table A2 in the Appendix reveals that both sets of routes actually have very similar characteristics. Although individual route entry and competition is likely to differ quite substantially, on average, there is no indication that the characteristics of both sets of routes differ substantially from each other. This has partly to do with the construction of the dataset as we focused on major carriers only (who are likely to have similar key characteristics such as a HS network structure, etc.).

Turning to our estimation results, we apply the D-i-D approach to route level data, i.e., we observe one average price per quarter for every affected route and the comparator routes defined above two years before and two years after the completion merger. We use the exit of the HP routes in the T-100 dataset as the quarter in which the merger was completed (fourth quarter of 2005).[12] Regression results with *ln*(*avg. yield*) as dependent variable and several independent variables (characterized further below) are shown in Table 2 while the summary statistics are reported in Table A2 in the Appendix.

As shown in Table 2, across all route types, two years after its completion, the merger led to about 9.9% higher prices than observed on the comparator routes over the same time frame. This is a surprising first result given the largely complementary route network of both carriers. Turning from this general analysis across all affected routes to the application of our route classification reveals that the merger led to significant price increases in four out of five route types. Two years after the completion of the merger, average prices on routes with non-stop overlap were about

---

[11]The 18 largest airlines are AA, AS, B6, CO, DH, DL, F9, FL, G4, HA, NK, NW, SY, TZ, UA, VX, WN, YX_1.

[12]This approach is in accordance with other sources such as "Airlines for America". See http://www.airlines.org/Pages/US-Airline-Mergers-and-Acquisitions.aspx, last accessed on November 18, 2013).

Table 2. Fixed-Effects Regressions of Merger's Price Effects (Route Level)

Variable	ln(avg. yield) coeff.		(s.e.)
Post merger	0.099***		(0.006)
1. Post # direct comp.	0.105***		(0.027)
2. Post # US route (no HP comp.)	−0.115***		(0.016)
3. Post # US route (HP one-stop comp.)	0.063*		(0.033)
4. Post # HP route (no U.S. comp.)	0.028**		(0.014)
5. Post # HP route (U.S. one-stop comp.)	0.071***		(0.016)
# Airlines w/o merger parties	−0.024***		(0.009)
# LCCs	−0.173***		(0.021)
ln(avg. plane size)	−0.043**		(0.021)
Airport size (max)	0.042**		(0.018)
HHI of airport with larger size	0.039		(0.077)
Airport size (max) # HHI of larger airport	−0.128***		(0.023)
Airport size (min)	0.044*		(0.026)
HHI of airport with smaller size	0.032		(0.056)
Airport size (min) # HHI of smaller airport	−0.109***		(0.042)
ln(population) (mean)	0.212		(0.165)
ln(# establ.) (mean)	0.485***		(0.116)
Constant	−5.177**		(2.230)
Observations		25,648	
Routes		1,603	
R^2 (within/between/overall)	0.111	0.058	0.052

Notes: Significance levels $^{***}p < 0.01$, $^{**}p < 0.05$, $^{*}p < 0.1$, cluster-robust standard errors in parentheses. Hausman test prefers the fixed-effects over the random-effects model. Yearly and quarterly dummies included (and highly significant) but not reported.
Sources: U.S. DOT, T-100 Domestic Segment Data, Airline Origin and Destination Survey (DB1B), U.S. Census and U.S. Bureau of Labor Statistics, authors' calculations.

10.5% higher than on comparator routes ("*post # direct comp.*" in Table 2). On routes in which the merger eliminated one-stop competition by U.S. or HP, prices increase by about 6.3% or about 7.1% respectively, supporting the expected significant but reduced competitive pressure created by these imperfect substitutes. For the group of routes with no non-stop or one-stop overlap, results diverge substantially. While we find a substantial and highly significant decrease in price of on average about 11.5% on US routes, the corresponding value for the HP routes shows a moderate increase of about 2.8%.

The control variables largely show the expected behavior. The number of competitors (*# airlines w/o merger parties*) as well as the number of low cost carriers on a particular route (*# LCCs*) have negative effects on average market price. However, the effect of the presence of a low cost carrier is by far larger than the presence of other carriers. This finding is supported by prior studies on the effects of entry (see Brueckner *et al.* (2013) and Hüschelrath and Müller (2013b)). Furthermore, average prices decrease with an increase in plane size (*ln*(*avg. plane size*)) due to the well-known cost advantages of operating larger airplanes. Turning from route-related to airport-related control variables, we also control for the influence of airport size as measured by the mean of the two endpoint airports' passenger share (*airport size* (*max*)). As revealed by Table 2, average prices increase slightly with the overall size of the airport. Interestingly, if not airport size but airport concentration (measured by the Herfindahl–Hirschman Index (HHI)) is the control variable of interest, the results reported in Table 2 show that average prices are reduced with a larger concentration at the larger and the smaller airport used for the operation of a certain route connection. Furthermore, two demographic variables on the MSA level enter the analyses which aim to capture demand effects. The population (*ln*(*population force*) (*mean*)) shall capture potential total demand. The number of establishments (i.e., firms; *ln*(*# establ.*) (*mean*)) is included to capture the demand of less price-sensitive business people. As revealed by Table 2, only the number of establishments is found to have a large and positive effect on average yield.

4.3. *Interpretation of estimation results*

Recapitulating the key results of our estimations, we basically find that especially passengers traveling on routes which were only operated by US Airways pre-merger (and did not face HP one-stop competition) benefitted substantially from the merger (in the form of an average price reduction of 11.5%) while passengers in all other route categories had to cope with price increases between 2.8 and 10.5% post-merger.

Does this finding support the conclusion that the merger was anti-competitive? Although a sophisticated econometrics-based answer to this question is beyond the scope of this chapter, our estimation results, together

Table 3. Characteristics of Affected Routes and Estimated Price Changes

	# of routes	Estimated price change	Average number of passengers	Average number of passengers	Total passenger share
	#	%	quarter	two years	%
1. Direct comp.	4	10.5	131,633	4,212,256	2
2. US route (no HP comp.)	147	−11.5	103,668	121,913,568	47
3. US route (HP one-stop comp.)	7	6.3	97,951	5,485,256	2
4. HP route (no U.S. comp.)	57	2.8	232,978	106,237,968	41
5. HP route (U.S. one-stop comp.)	24	7.1	111,513	21,410,496	8

Source: Own calculations based on results reported in Tables 1 and 2.

with several route characteristics reported in Table 1, allow some back-of-the-envelope calculation suggesting that, overall, consumers benefitted substantially from the merger. The analysis which supports this conclusion is shown in Table 3.

As shown in Table 3, our estimations reveal substantial price increases of 10.5% on routes with non-stop competition, 6.3% on US routes with HP one-stop competition and 7.1% on HP routes which had U.S. one-stop competition pre-merger. However, it is important to point to the fact that only about 12% (2% + 2% + 8%) of the overall number of passengers (in the two-year period following the merger) traveled in these markets. For the majority of passengers, the merger either led to substantial price reductions of on average 11.5% (47%) or a rather small price increase of 2.8% (41%). In absolute terms, while about 31.1 million passengers faced substantially higher prices post-merger, about 106.2 million passengers experienced only small increases in average fares and about 121.9 million enjoyed significant fare reductions. Although admittedly a rough estimate, the derived figures suggest that the merger between US Airways and America West Airlines led to substantial increases in consumer welfare.

Despite this presumably positive net effect of the HP–U.S. merger on consumer welfare, it is important to note that this merger was highly complementary with only four non-stop overlaps and 31 one-stop overlaps. However, as soon as the degree of overlap becomes larger, our empirical results derived above would suggest that competition concerns might become more serious. For example, the merger between Delta Air Lines and Northwest Airlines (completed in 2009) showed 58 non-stop route overlaps; *ceteris paribus*, such a transaction would demand a much more detailed assessment whether the expected price increases on the overlapping parts of the network are still overcompensated by price reduction in markets without a non-stop or one-stop overlap.

On a more general level, the results reported in Table 3 suggest the importance of a disaggregated approach in an *ex-post* analysis of the consumer welfare effects of airline mergers. According to our estimation results for all affected routes reported in Table 2, the merger caused an average fare increase of 9.9%. The implementation of our detailed route classification derived in Section 3, however, revealed that these results are largely driven by two relatively small groups of passengers who were actually harmed by the merger, while the large majority of passengers remain either nearly unaffected or profit substantially from the transaction.

5. Summary and Conclusion

The US airline industry has recently experienced a substantial consolidation trend. In the last 10 years, five large mergers[13] raise concerns about the (consumer) welfare consequences of these consolidations. Against this background, we develop two classifications of routes possibly affected by an airline merger. Subsequently, we apply a D-i-D approach to investigate the price effects of the America West Airlines–US Airways merger completed in 2005. Our estimation results show that, across all route types, two years after its completion, the merger led to 9.9% higher prices than observed on the comparator routes over the same time frame. However, introducing our "non-stop/one-stop" classification of routes revealed substantial variation in the merger-induced price effects. While average prices on routes with non-stop overlap were 10.5% higher than on comparator routes, routes on which the merger eliminated one-stop competition by the U.S. showed prices increase of 7.1% suggesting that this "imperfect substitute" constrained HP significantly in its price-setting behavior. A comparable result of a price increase of about 6.3% is found for routes on which the merger eliminated one-stop competition by HP. For the "no overlap" route category, however,

[13]The large mergers were American Airlines–Trans World Airlines (2001), America West–US Airways (2005), Delta Air Lines–Northwest Airlines (2009), United Airlines–Continental Airlines (2010) and Southwest Airlines–AirTran Airways (2011).

results diverge. While we find a substantial and highly significant price decrease of on average 11.5% on US routes, the corresponding value for the HP routes shows a moderate price increase of on average 2.8%.

With respect to the overall consumer welfare effects of the merger, our estimation results suggest that the merger might have been anticompetitive as it led to either smaller or larger price increases in four route categories and to price decreases in only one category. However, taking the number of passengers traveling in the respective categories into account reveal that only about 12% of the overall number of passengers in the two-year period following the merger traveled in markets which experienced a substantial price increase post-merger. For the majority of passengers, the merger either led to substantial price reductions (47%) or had a rather small positive effect (of below 3%) on average prices (41%).

Although we propose and apply a full-fledged framework to investigate the consumer welfare effects of airline mergers, several potential extensions of our approach can be identified. First, as our study concentrates on the average price effects of the merger, future studies might investigate its impact on price dispersion (taking better account for the fact that airlines typically apply sophisticated price differentiation strategies). Second, as we restrict our empirical analysis of the merger to price effects, future studies might profit from the inclusion of other potential determinants of consumer welfare such as service quality. Third, our empirical analysis concentrates on airport-pairs. Although this (rather defensive) assumption is made by many airline-related papers, it would be interesting to investigate whether our results hold for city-pair markets.[14] Fourth, our general classification of routes suggests an application to other airline mergers. Given the partly substantial differences with respect to both general size and network characteristics of mergers such as Delta Air Lines–Northwest Airlines (2009) or United Airlines–Continental Airlines (2010), important additional insights on the effects of competition and mergers in airline networks might be gained.

---

[14]As none of the five cities with hub presences of the merging parties — Phoenix, Las Vegas for America West and Charlotte, Philadelphia, and Pittsburgh for US Airways — has a larger (alternative) primary or secondary airport, the changes in results triggered from a switch to city-pair markets can be expected to be rather limited for the merger case at hand.

Appendix

Table A1. Summary Statistics — Comparator Routes

	Pre-merger period		Post-merger period		Overall	
	Mean	(s.d.)	Mean	(s.d.)	Mean	(s.d.)
ln (yield)	3.010	(0.702)	3.036	(0.699)	3.023	(0.701)
yield (market fare per passenger mile)	26.304	(21.363)	26.941	(21.837)	26.622	(21.603)
Δ airlines w/o merger parties	−0.001	(0.232)	0.003	(0.217)	0.001	(0.224)
# airlines w/o merger parties	1.363	(0.614)	1.360	(0.639)	1.362	(0.627)
Comparison routes	1.000	(0.000)	1.000	(0.000)	1.000	(0.000)
1. Post # direct comp.	0.000	(0.000)	0.000	(0.000)	0.000	(0.000)
2. Post # US route (no HP comp.)	0.000	(0.000)	0.000	(0.000)	0.000	(0.000)
3. Post # US route (HP one-stop comp.)	0.000	(0.000)	0.000	(0.000)	0.000	(0.000)
4. Post # HP route (no U.S. comp.)	0.000	(0.000)	0.000	(0.000)	0.000	(0.000)
5. Post # HP route (U.S. one-stop comp.)	0.000	(0.000)	0.000	(0.000)	0.000	(0.000)
# LCCs	0.288	(0.463)	0.319	(0.496)	0.303	(0.480)
ln(avg. plane size)	4.520	(0.548)	4.503	(0.542)	4.511	(0.545)
Avg. Plane size	104.981	(49.674)	103.121	(49.216)	104.051	(49.453)
Airport size (max)	2.438	(1.468)	2.406	(1.417)	2.422	(1.443)
HHI of airport with larger size	0.433	(0.199)	0.448	(0.209)	0.440	(0.204)
Airport size (min)	0.562	(0.605)	0.559	(0.605)	0.560	(0.605)
HHI of airport with smaller size	0.351	(0.210)	0.350	(0.209)	0.351	(0.209)
ln(population) (mean)	14.824	(0.832)	14.849	(0.827)	14.836	(0.830)
Population (mean)	3,672,870	(2,924,154)	3,745,043	(2,932,688)	3,708,957	(2,928,579)
ln(# establ.) (mean)	11.233	(0.851)	11.278	(0.851)	11.255	(0.851)
# establ. (mean)	104,436	(89,637)	109,187	(93,522)	106,812	(91,629)

Notes: Yield (market fare per passenger mile) measured in 1995 $ cents; means calculated over all observations 8 quarters before, 8 quarter after the merger and over the whole 16 quarters.

Sources: U.S. DOT, T-100 Domestic Segment Data, Airline Origin and Destination Survey (DB1B), U.S. Census and U.S. Bureau of Labor Statistics, authors' calculations.

Table A2. Summary Statistics

	Pre-merger period		Post-merger period		Overall	
	Mean	(s.d.)	Mean	(s.d.)	Mean	(s.d.)
ln (yield)	2.996	(0.722)	3.014	(0.705)	3.005	(0.714)
Yield	26.376	(22.469)	26.505	(21.910)	26.441	(22.191)
Δ airlines w/o merger parties	0.000	(0.238)	0.003	(0.212)	0.002	(0.225)
Comparison routes	0.851	(0.356)	0.851	(0.356)	0.851	(0.356)
1. Post # direct comp.	0.002	(0.050)	0.002	(0.050)	0.002	(0.050)
2. Post # US route (no HP comp.)	0.092	(0.289)	0.092	(0.289)	0.092	(0.289)
3. Post # US route (HP one-stop comp.)	0.004	(0.066)	0.004	(0.066)	0.004	(0.066)
4. Post # HP route (no U.S. comp.)	0.036	(0.185)	0.036	(0.185)	0.036	(0.185)
5. Post # HP route (U.S. one-stop comp.)	0.015	(0.121)	0.015	(0.121)	0.015	(0.121)
# Airlines w/o merger parties	1.289	(0.682)	1.292	(0.694)	1.291	(0.688)
# LCCs	0.300	(0.475)	0.339	(0.513)	0.319	(0.495)
ln(avg. plane size)	4.555	(0.529)	4.536	(0.523)	4.546	(0.526)
Avg. plane size	107.594	(48.050)	105.484	(47.695)	106.539	(47.883)
Airport size (max)	2.453	(1.403)	2.438	(1.354)	2.446	(1.379)
HHI of airport with larger size	0.428	(0.205)	0.441	(0.210)	0.434	(0.208)
Airport size (min)	0.645	(0.664)	0.643	(0.672)	0.644	(0.668)
HHI of airport with smaller size	0.346	(0.206)	0.342	(0.203)	0.344	(0.205)
ln(population) (mean)	14.844	(0.802)	14.871	(0.796)	14.858	(0.799)
Population (mean)	3,685,147	(2,861,681)	3,760,907	(2,869,394)	3,723,027	(2,865,735)
ln(# establ.) (mean)	11.254	(0.822)	11.302	(0.820)	11.278	(0.822)
# establ. (mean)	104,720	(87,773)	109,651	(91,541)	107,186	(89,709)
Observations	10,912		10,912		21,824	

Notes: Yield (market fare per passenger mile) measured in 1995 $ cents; means calculated over all observations 8 quarters before, 8 quarter after the merger and over the whole 16 quarters.

Sources: U.S. DOT, T-100 Domestic Segment Data, Airline Origin and Destination Survey (DB1B), U.S. Census and U.S. Bureau of Labor Statistics, authors' calculations.

References

Aguirregabiria, V. and C.-Y. Ho (2010). "A Dynamic Game of Airline Network Competition: Hub-and-Spoke Networks and Entry Deterrence," *International Journal of Industrial Organization*, 28, pp. 377–382.

Bailey, E. and D. Liu (1995). "Airline Consolidation and Consumer Welfare," *Eastern Economic Journal*, 21, pp. 463–476.

Baumol, W., J. Panzar and R. Willig (1982). *Contestable Markets and the Theory of Industry Structure*, Harcourt Brace Jovanovich, San Diego.

Benkard, L., A. Bodoh-Creed and J. Lazarev (2010). "Simulating the Dynamic Effects of Horizontal Mergers: US Airlines," *Working Paper*, Stanford University, Palo Alto.

Bilotkach, V. (2011). "Multimarket Contact and Intensity of Competition: Evidence from an Airline Merger," *Review of Industrial Organization*, 38, pp. 95–115.

Bittlingmayer, G. (1990). "Efficiency and Entry in a Simple Airline Network," *International Journal of Industrial Organization*, 8, pp. 245–257.

Borenstein, S. (1990). "Airline Mergers, Airport Dominance, and Market Power," *American Economic Review-Papers and Proceedings*, 80, pp. 400–404.

Brueckner, J. and P. Spiller (1994). "Economies of Traffic Density in the Deregulated Airline Industry," *Journal of Law and Economics*, 37, pp. 379–415.

Brueckner, J. and P. Spiller (1991). "Competition and Mergers in Airline Networks," *International Journal of Industrial Organization*, 9, pp. 323–342.

Brueckner, J. and Y. Zhang (2001). "A Model of Scheduling in Airline Networks: How a Hub-and-Spoke System Affects Flight Frequency, Fares and Welfare," *Journal of Transport Economics and Policy*, 35, pp. 195–222.

Brueckner, J., D. Lee and E. Singer (2013). "Airline Competition and Domestic US Airfares: A Comprehensive Reappraisal," *Economics of Transportation*, 2, pp. 1–17.

Brueckner, J., N. Dyer and P. Spiller (1992). "Fare Determination in Airline Hub-and-Spoke Networks," *RAND Journal of Economics*, 23, pp. 309–333.

Caves, D., L. Christensen and M. Tretheway (1984). "Economies of Density Versus Economies of Scale: Why Trunk and Local Service Airline Costs Differ," *RAND Journal of Economics*, 15, pp. 471–489.

Hendricks, K., M. Piccione and G. Tan (1995). "The Economics of Hubs: The Case of Monopoly," *Review of Economic Studies*, 62, pp. 83–99.

Hüschelrath, K. and K. Müller (2014). "Airline Networks, Mergers, and Consumer Welfare," *Journal of Transport Economics and Policy*, 48(3), pp. 385–407.

Hüschelrath, K. and K. Müller (2013a). "The Competitive Effects of Firm Exit: Evidence from the US Airline Industry," *Economics of Transportation* 2(2–3), pp. 72–85.

Hüschelrath, K. and K. Müller (2013b). "Patterns and Effects of Entry in US Airline Markets," *Journal of Industry, Competition and Trade*, 13(2), pp. 221–253.

Hüschelrath, K. and K. Müller (2012). "Market Power, Efficiencies, and Entry — Evidence from an Airline Merger," *ZEW Discussion Paper* No. 12-070, Mannheim, forthcoming *Managerial and Decision Economics*.

Israel, M., B. Keating, D. Rubinfeld and R. Willig (2011). "Airline Network Effects & Consumer Welfare: A Preliminary Overview of Methodology and Findings," *Working Paper*, Compass Lexecon, Washington DC.

Kaplan, S. (2000). *Mergers and Productivity*, The University of Chicago Press, Chicago.

Kaplow, L. and C. Shapiro (2007). Antitrust, in M. Polinsky and S. Shavell (Eds.), *Handbook of Law and Economics*, Volume 2, North Holland Publishing, Amsterdam, pp. 1073–1225.

Kim, E. and V. Singal (1993). "Mergers and Market Power: Evidence from the Airline Industry," *American Economic Review*, 83, pp. 549–569.

Kwoka, J. and E. Shumilkina (2010). "The Price Effect of Eliminating Potential Competition: Evidence from an Airline Merger," *Journal of Industrial Economics*, 58, pp. 767–793.

Luo, D. (2014). "The Price Effects of the Delta/Northwest Airline Merger," *Review of Industrial Organization*, 44, pp. 27–48.

Mazzeo, M. (2003). "Competition and Service Quality in the US Airline Industry," *Review of Industrial Organization*, 22, pp. 275–296.

Oum, T., A. Zhang and Y. Zhang (1995). "Airline Network Rivalry," *Canadian Journal of Economics*, 28, pp. 836–857.

Pautler, P. (2003). "Evidence on Mergers and Acquisitions," *Antitrust Bulletin*, 48, pp. 119–221.

Richard, O. (2003). "Flight Frequency and Mergers in Airline Markets," *International Journal of Industrial Organization*, 21, pp. 907–922.

U.S. General Accounting Office (2001). "*Airline Competition — Issues Raised by Consolidation Proposals, GAO-01-370T*," Washington DC. Available at http://www.gao.gov/products/GAO-01-370.

U.S. Government Accountability Office (2010). "*Airline Mergers — Issues Raised by the Proposed Merger of United and Continental Airlines, GAO-10-778T*," Washington DC. Available at http://www.gao.gov/assets/130/124805.html.

Weinberg, M. (2008). "The Price Effects of Horizontal Mergers," *Journal of Competition Law and Economics*, 4, pp. 433–447.

Werden, G. and L. Froeb (2008). Unilateral competitive effects of horizontal mergers, in P. Buccirossi (Ed.), *Handbook of Antitrust Economics*, The MIT Press, Cambridge, pp. 43–103.

Werden, G. and L. Froeb (1998). "The Entry-Inducing Effects of Horizontal Mergers: An Exploratory Analysis," *Journal of Industrial Economics*, 46, pp. 525–543.

Werden, G., A. Joskow and R. Johnson (1991). "The Effects of Mergers on Price and Output: Two Case Studies from the Airline Industry," *Managerial and Decision Economics*, 12, pp. 341–352.

Whinston, M. (2007). Antitrust policy toward horizontal mergers, in M. Armstrong and R. Porter (Eds.), *Handbook of Industrial Organization*, Volume 3, North Holland Publishing, Amsterdam, pp. 2369–2440.

Chapter 3

Pattern Asymmetry in the Pass-Through of Input Price Shocks in the Road Fuels Sector: New Evidence on the United Kingdom*

Enrico Pesaresi

European Commission, Directorate General for Competition
enrico.pesaresi@ec.europa.eu

Conor Flanagan

Competition and Markets Authority
conor.flanagan@cma.gsi.gov.uk

Boryana Miteva

Expedia Affiliate Network
bmiteva@expedia.com

Abstract

It is widely believed that fuel prices tend to rise swiftly when oil prices increase, but take longer to fall after oil prices decrease. This "rockets and feathers" pattern could be due to tacit collusion at some level of the supply chain. We test the "rockets and feathers" hypothesis for the UK market, at the national level and for a set of local markets. Specifically, we estimate an error-correction model and test for the symmetry in the speed of adjustment of fuels prices to fluctuations in the

*The authors would like to thank Steve Brown, Stephen Davies, Kirsten Edwards-Warren, Amelia Fletcher, Claire Hart, Liz Hurley, Nenad Njegovan, Maureen Paul, Alan Reilly, Jon Riley, Apurva Shah, Chris Walters, Panagiotis Fotis, Yossi Spiegel and the participants in the CRESSE 2013 conference for their valuable comments and suggestions. A particular thank to Ilaria Fanton and Gary Mills for their outstanding support. The authors were all economists at the Office of Fair Trading (OFT) at the time when the first draft of this chapter was prepared. The views expressed in this chapter are the authors' own and cannot be regarded as stating an official position of the OFT, the Competition and Markets Authority, the European Commission or Expedia.com Ltd.

input prices. In contrast with previous empirical literature on the UK, we reject the existence asymmetric pass-through, as positive shocks are not transmitted along the supply chain at a higher speed than negative ones. Some evidence of asymmetry is found at the retail level in a few local markets, though this evidence is not clear-cut.

Keywords: Asymmetric pass-through of cost shocks, road fuels, retail, wholesale.

JEL Classification Codes: D43, L13, L71, L81.

1. Introduction

In September 2012, the OFT launched a Call for Information (CfI) to investigate various alleged irregularities in the markets for diesel and petrol in the United Kingdom. Among other claims, that include excessive prices in local areas and inability to compete of independent dealers, one of the main issues of concern brought to the attention of the OFT is the fact that changes in the price of petrol and diesel might not reflect the underlying variations in the crude oil price. In particular, prices for petrol and diesel would adjust to cost shocks in an asymmetric way: pump prices would tend to rise swiftly to a rise in the input price, while the same price would take longer time to decrease following a fall in crude oil prices. This pattern often referred to as "rockets and feathers" is periodically held by consumers and by the media as an undisputable proof that oil companies' misbehave at the expense of consumers. While it would be imprudent for the OFT to embrace this view without careful assessment, it is clear from the literature that "rockets and feathers" could indicate the presence of market malfunctioning, possibly related to supra-competitive market power at some level in the supply chain.

This issue of asymmetric cost pass-through has attracted significant attention by the economic literature, and, in recent years, also by competition authorities. The empirical literature has tested for the presence of "rocket and feather" pricing in different markets, concluding in favor of asymmetric adjustment in a remarkably high number of cases.[1] As one would expect that cost shocks are transmitted swiftly and symmetrically in well-functioning markets, it is not surprising that the traditional economic

[1] See Deltas (2008) for an overview of the empirical literature.

explanation for the stickiness of downward adjustment would link it to instances of tacit collusion. In this framework, first proposed by Green and Porter (1984), past output price would act as focal points when input price decreases, leading to the "feathering" down of prices.

Other models have been proposed to explain the reasons for such a phenomenon to occur. These alternative explanations consider "rockets and feathers" as consistent with effective competition, and in some cases, as a natural manifestation of the competitive process. Following Borenstein and Shephard (2002), some authors link asymmetric transmission of input price shocks to the relatively higher rigidity of the supply chain to expansions — as expected in the case of a cost decrease — as compared to the contraction that happens when input prices rise. Others, like Tappata (2009) and Lewis (2011) consider that asymmetric pass-through may be due to consumer behavior: different search intensity from consumers for different price levels may drive the asymmetry. According to Noel (2009), the asymmetric fluctuations of prices could be considered as a distinctive feature of competition in certain markets. In this case, the reduction in price toward the marginal cost level can be followed by a quick price adjustment once the margin gets close to zero, as first described in Maskin and Tirole (1988).

The empirical analysis presented in this chapter was conducted as part of the CfI on the road fuel sector conducted by the OFT. This type of enquiry is periodically conducted by the OFT to gain a better understanding of specific markets, in terms of their functioning and the level of competition involved. This is a screening exercise through which the OFT comes to an informed view on the *prima facie* competition concerns raised by a sector that would warrant further inquiry.[2] With an exploratory intent consistent with the purposes of the inquiry, we have tested for the existence of "rocket and feather" pricing to provide an updated and state-of-the-art empirical analysis of the issue more than 20 years since the last time this was done

[2] If the presence of competition concerns or other market malfunctioning is found, a more in-depth Market Study is normally conducted to investigate those specific issues. This could lead to a referral to the Competition Commission under the Enterprise Act 2002. Evidence gathered through Market Studies and CfIs could also lead to competition enforcement actions. For an overview of the markets' work of the OFT, see "Market Studies — Guidance on the OFT approach", 2010. Available at http://www.oft.gov.uk/shared_oft/business_leaflets/enterprise_act/oft519.pdf.

by Manning (1991).[3] As the analysis was carried out also as a reaction to the claims of consumers associations, the finding that oil price increases and decreases are pass-through at the same speed, if confirmed by the data, would allow the OFT to safely dismiss the claim of "rocket and feather" pricing raised by drivers and consumers' associations. If, on the other hand, asymmetric pass-through was found, then additional analysis — likely involving the opening of full-fletched Market Study — would be required to identify its main drivers and its relation with the competitive process in each market.

Following the framework first proposed in Borenstein *et al.* (1997), and the recent application made in Chesnes (2012), we have estimated an error-correction model to test for the symmetry in the transmission of input cost shocks for road fuels. Using the two-steps procedure first proposed by Engle and Granger (1987), our method allows for the inclusion of the long-run relationship between input and output price series directly into the specification. We have estimated our model for diesel and petrol and for two distinct segments of the supply chain: the upstream segment, crude oil price to ex-refinery price, and the downstream segment of the market, ex-refinery to retail.

We have carried out our analysis on weekly data for crude oil, ex-refinery, and retail petrol and diesel from 2000 to 2012 for the United Kingdom. We have used the Brent Oil price and the Platts petrol prices as proxies for the crude and ex-refinery prices respectively; for the retail level, we have used data provided by the Department of Energy and Climate Change (DECC). In addition, we have used our model to estimate the speed of transmission of the ex-refinery price to the retail price observed in 18 local areas across the UK; for this purpose, we have used weekly data on pump prices between November 2011 and October 2012 provided by Experian Ltd.

We find that shocks in the price of crude oil, either positive or negative, are transmitted to a large extent to the price of refined products within the first two weeks since the shock occurred. The pass-through is slower

[3]The UK refining and fuel retailing have undergone substantial changing since then: the reduction of the refining capacities, the higher reliance on imports of refined products and, at the retail level, the successful entry of supermarkets have contributed to change the structure of the industry.

between ex-refinery and retail prices, where it takes up to five weeks to pass-through to the retail price most of the average price variation. We also find that shocks are passed through symmetrically at both levels; "rocket and feather" pricing is therefore rejected. We did not find compelling evidence of "rocket and feather" pricing in our analysis on the 18 local areas; results for some areas reported some level of asymmetry, especially in the case of petrol, yet this evidence is not clear-cut.

This chapter is organized as follows. Section 2 provides a review of the empirical literature on the subject. Section 3 describes the empirical strategy. Section 4 provides a description of the data used for the analysis. Section 5 illustrates the main findings.

2. Previous Work on "Rockets and Feathers"

The analysis of cost pass-through in petrol markets has received significant attention in the academic literature. The empirical literature has particularly focused on the identification of asymmetric cost pass-through at the different levels of the supply chain. Along with empirical analysis, researchers have also proposed different economic explanations of the asymmetry.

The earliest empirical researches on asymmetric cost pass-through on the fuel market date back to the works of Bacon (1990) and Manning (1991). Using data from the UK retail gasoline market, they were the first to document the asymmetric price responses of firms to cost increases and decreases. Following Bacon's paper, the literature labeled "rockets and feathers" the phenomenon by which prices shoot up, like rockets, as a response to increases in costs and then slowly adjust downward, like feathers, following a decrease in costs. Bacon and Manning both found asymmetry in the pricing response to shocks, using different methods.

Bacon (1990) uses data on ex-refinery and retail diesel and petrol for the UK from 1982 to 1990. He introduces a model where both a linear and a quadratic adjustment term are included in the regression. He finds a significant result on the coefficient for the quadratic term, suggesting the presence of asymmetric adjustment. Mean and standard deviations for the first two lags are also presented, reporting different results for positive and negative cost shocks.

Manning (1991) estimates an error-correction model on data on retail petrol and crude oil monthly prices in the UK over the period 1973–1988.

An error-correction model allows disentangling the long-run relationship between oil price and retail prices and the short-run adjustment to their equilibrium relationship. This methodology, first proposed by Engle and Granger (1987), relies on a first-stage regression of the output price on the input price and a constant. If the series are cointegrated, then the residuals from this regression can be directly introduced in a second regression, where positive and negative short-run input shocks are separately introduced in the specification. The author finds some evidence of asymmetry in short-run speed of adjustment to positive and negative input shocks.

The paper by Borenstein *et al.* (1997) serves as a benchmark for recent academic work in this field. Examining prices for a set of cities in the United States, they use an error-correction model similar to Manning (1991) and find evidence for asymmetric responses of retail petrol prices to crude oil price changes. They also suggest several possible explanations for this finding, including potential short-run retailer market power and inventory asymmetries. They analyze the entire distribution chain using weekly and semi-monthly over six years for several U.S. cities.

A common feature of the early literature on the topic is the fact that evidence of asymmetric pass-through is generally associated with instances of temporary collusion or short-run market power. More recent papers suggest alternative explanations for the asymmetry in the response to cost shocks observed in the data. Tappata (2009) and Lewis (2011) suggest that different levels of search intensity on the consumers' side might explain the "rockets and feathers" phenomenon. According to this explanation, consumers have some expectation of what petrol prices should be — possibly based on recent purchases, price displays, or media reports — and they have a general sense that petrol prices are either rising or falling. If consumers see a price higher than expected, they are more likely to search for a better price than if the observed price is lower than expected. Thus, during periods of rising prices, search intensity is higher than during periods of falling prices. Conversely, when costs are falling, retail stations need only to reduce their prices enough to discourage search so they can maintain higher margins while customers' expectations adjust to the new equilibrium price level.

Radchenko and Shapiro (2011) suggest that the reasons for asymmetries have to be found in the extent to which changes in the gasoline inventory level can be anticipated by suppliers. This explanation, introduced in Borenstein *et al.* (1997) and presented more formally in Borenstein and Shepard (2002), relates the asymmetry to the short-term cost of adjusting inventories and supply following an input price decrease. The existence of such cost would create a lag in the reaction of price to input price decreases that would not be present in the case of input price increases.

While the majority of the empirical works in the area finds evidence of "rocket and feather" pricing, some papers dismiss the existence of asymmetries in the transfer of cost shocks to downstream prices. Bachmeier and Griffin (2003) apply a variant of the method proposed by Borenstein *et al.* (1997) and estimate the error-correction model using the two-steps' procedure as proposed by Engle and Granger (1987). They find no evidence of asymmetric pass-through, either using weekly or daily data.

Another interesting application of the Borenstein *et al.* (1997) model is the one put forward by Deltas (2008) where he stresses the importance of local market conditions and price-cost margins in the asymmetry. By adapting the model of Borenstein *et al.* (1997) to a panel data set including multiple U.S. states, Deltas points out that low margin states adjust more rapidly to an increase in costs than high margin ones, while the converse happens in case of a decrease in costs. These findings allow Deltas to highlight the relationship between market power and price adjustments.

In recent years, the issue of asymmetric pass-through of input cost shocks has also been investigated empirically by national competition authorities. The analysis was primarily motivated by the presumption that "rocket and feather" pricing could be associated to anticompetitive behavior at the different levels of the supply chain. The Bundeskartellamt published the final report of their Fuel Sector Inquiry in May 2011. The Sector Inquiry was conducted following numerous complains about malfunctioning in the German markets for road fuels. "Rocket and feather" pricing was found to be present at retail level using weekly level. The Bundeskartellamt's conclusion stress out that this could be consistent with anticompetitive conduct, though it would not represent sufficient proof for it.

Recently, the Comisión Nacional de la Competencia has also looked at the issue. They use weekly import and retail prices over the period 2005–2011 for the Spanish market to estimate an error-correction model. They find that on average it would take 10 weeks to pass 95% of the input price change into the retail price; this pass-through is found to take place asymmetrically, as input price increases are passed through quicker than decreases. The results, read in conjunction with the other features of the Spanish market for road fuels, are interpreted as evidence of limited competition. This is mainly due to the presence of entry barriers in the different parts of the supply chain.

A very recent piece of research is Chesnes (2012), where asymmetry in pass-through is tested applying an error-correction model to a data set containing rack and retail daily prices for 27 metropolitan areas in the U.S. over the period 1999–2009. He estimates the model at the different levels of the supply chain using both daily and weekly data and finds a significant asymmetry in the pass-through of cost shocks at the retail level, though different in magnitude across the different cities.

3. Methodology

In the design of our empirical model, we followed the recent work of Chesnes (2012) since it is similar to ours in terms of aim of the analysis and of data used. Our methodology is also similar to the work done by the Comisión Nacional de la Competencia.

We estimate an error-correction model of pass-through for the two levels of the supply chain for which data is available, i.e., crude oil to ex-refinery and ex-refinery to retail, for both diesel and petrol. For simplicity, we present the model for the pass-through of wholesale shocks to retail price.

$$\begin{aligned}\Delta\text{Retail}_t = & \sum_{i=1}^{k} \beta_i^+ \Delta\text{Retail}_{t-i}^+ + \sum_{i=1}^{k} \beta_i^- \Delta\text{Retail}_{t-i}^- \\ & + \sum_{i=0}^{k} \gamma_i^+ \Delta\text{ex-refinery}_{t-i}^+ + \sum_{i=0}^{k} \gamma_i^- \Delta\text{ex-refinery}_{t-i}^- \\ & + \delta^+ z_{t-1}^+ + \delta^- z_{t-1}^- + \varepsilon_t, \qquad (1)\end{aligned}$$

where:

- ΔRetail_t is the weekly change in the retail price of either diesel or petrol at time t.

- $\sum_{i=1}^{k} \beta_i^{+} \Delta\text{Retail}_{t-i}^{+}$ is the sum of lagged positive changes in the retail price.
- $\sum_{i=1}^{k} \beta_i^{-} \Delta\text{Retail}_{t-i}^{-}$ is the sum of lagged negative changes in the retail price.
- $\sum_{i=0}^{k} \gamma_i^{+} \Delta\text{ex-refinery}_{t-i}^{+}$ is the sum of the current and lagged positive changes in the ex-refinery price.
- $\sum_{i=0}^{k} \gamma_i^{-} \Delta\text{ex-refinery}_{t-i}^{-}$ is the sum of the current and lagged negative changes in the ex-refinery price.
- $\delta^{+} z_{t-1}^{+}$ and $\delta^{-} z_{t-1}^{-}$ are positive and negative error-correction terms (see below).
- ε_t is the residual variation in prices that is not explained by the model.

In the equation, the change in the retail price for diesel and petrol is regressed on a set of its own lagged differences, on current and lagged differences in the input price and on an error-correction term. Each variable is included in the specification separately for positive and negative variations. This allows distinguishing upward and downward movements in the underlying price series.

The inclusion of the error-correction term z_{t-1} allows for the integration of the long-run relationship between ex-refinery and retail price in our model. Following Engle and Granger (1987), we obtain the error-correction term taking the lagged one period residuals of the regression of the retail price on a constant and the input price, as in the following expression

$$z_t = \text{Retail}_t - \theta_1 - \theta_2 \text{Wholesale}_t. \quad (2)$$

If the ex-refinery and retail price series are found to be cointegrated, then regressing the level of the retail price on the level of the wholesale price and a constant provides a consistent estimate of the long-run relationship between ex-refinery and retail prices, given by θ_1 and θ_2. The residuals z_t are stationary and they can be inserted directly into the main regression as shown in equation (1). This is the error-correction term of our model; the coefficient δ can be interpreted as a measure of how quickly prices revert to their long-term equilibrium relationship. As in the case of short-term pass-through, the specification allows for the estimation of this relationship separately for positive and negative values of z_{t-1}.

After the equation in (1) is estimated, symmetry of pass-through can be tested applying an F-test to the following equalities:

$$\gamma_i^+ = \gamma_i^- \text{ for some } i \tag{3}$$

$$|\delta^+| = |\delta^-|. \tag{4}$$

If either of the equalities in (3) and (4) is rejected, then some type of asymmetry is present in the data.[4]

Equations (3) and (4) present two different formulations of the pattern asymmetry, i.e., asymmetry in the speed at which cost shocks are passed through to downstream prices. Equation (3) tests for the symmetry in the short-term pass-through, while equation (4) represents the long-term speed of adjustment to the equilibrium gross margin.

Evidence of "rockets and feathers" would be found in (3) if $\gamma_i^+ > \gamma_i^-$ in the short-term relationship. If this is the case, positive cost shocks are passed on through retail prices faster than negative ones.

With respect to the long-term relationship, evidence of "rockets and feathers" would be found if $|\delta^+| < |\delta^-|$, that is, if reversion to the long-term level in price takes longer when retail prices are above their long-term level, and are therefore adjusting downward, as compared to the case where they are below it, and are "rocketing" up to get back to their equilibrium level.

4. Data

The aggregate UK-level data set contains ex-refinery and retail weekly prices over the period 2000 to 2012. The ex-refinery price is based on data obtained from Bloomberg Finance LP that report the Brent Oil price and

[4] It could be possible to test also for the symmetry in the *amount* of pass-through. This would imply testing if

$$\sum_{i=0}^{k} \gamma_i^+ = \sum_{i=0}^{k} \gamma_i^-.$$

If the equality does not hold, then the two price series would drift apart overtime. This would result in the long run to firm obtaining either zero or infinite margin, which would be highly unrealistic. Using an error-correction model, we assume that price series would always revert to their long-run equilibrium relationship. This implies that all short-run cost shocks are completely passed through over a sufficiently long time horizon; it does not exclude the possibility that the extent of pass-through could be different from the long-term one in different periods.

the Platts quoted price for each day over the period, averaged at the weekly level. The retail prices for diesel and petrol are computed by DECC on the basis of a survey of six companies, four oil major retailers and two supermarkets, run every week.[5]

For the local analysis, 18 local areas were selected on the basis of a data set obtained from Experian Ltd. containing information the universe of the UK forecourts. For each of these areas, forecourt-level daily prices for diesel and petrol over the period from November 1, 2011 to October 31, 2012 were obtained from Experian. This data set has been complemented with daily Platts prices for UK Diesel, UK Petrol and Dated Brent over the same period, obtained directly from Platts.[6]

The quoted price for diesel and petrol was used for the ex-refinery/wholesale price for both the aggregate and the local-level analysis. This could generally be considered as a good proxy for the actual wholesale price, as the daily quoted diesel and petrol prices are used in the industry as a benchmark for negotiations.[7]

Local areas for analysis were defined as the areas included in the 10 and 20 minutes driving radius from a randomly selected central forecourt for urban and rural areas respectively. The size of local areas was primarily chosen in order to capture the market structure in the area.[8]

5. Analysis and Results

In implementing the model described in Section 3, we proceed as follows:

- We first analyze the behavior of the time-series of the three variables of interest (Brent oil price, wholesale and retail petrol, and diesel prices),

---

[5]For a detailed description of all the data used in the empirical analysis run by the OFT, see OFT (2013), "UK petrol and Diesel Sector — Call for Information", Annex C.

[6]Platts, a division of The McGraw-Hill Companies, Inc., © 2011, 2012.

[7]Retailers normally buy fuel from wholesalers or directly from UK refiners at a price anchored to a reported benchmark, generally by Platts, which is computed on a daily basis from information on bilateral trades of the products taking place in the previous day. A certain mark-up is added to the Platts quotation in each transaction, usually in the range of a few percentage points. This takes into account the size of the shipment, insurance, transport costs, and possible ancillary services.

[8]This approach does not constitute an attempt to reach a firm conclusion about the geographic boundaries of local markets. A more in-depth, case-by-case analysis would in fact be required to define the market for each specific area.

in order to test whether they are integrated of the same order, as it would be necessary for our model. We first test for the presence of a unit root in each of them.[9] Once non-stationarity of all the series in levels is established by the tests,[10] we compute the first differences for each series and confirm their stationarity through the same tests, concluding that all the series are integrated of order one.

- Following Engle and Granger (1987), we proceed with estimating equation (2) for each pair of series using Ordinary Least Squares (OLS). If oil price, ex-refinery, and retail prices are cointegrated, then θ_2 should be a consistent estimate of the relationship between each of the series. As this is the case for all the price series,[11] we take the residuals from this regression and include them, lagged one week, directly into the final model as the error-correction term. The error-correction term is introduced separately for positive and negative variations as shown in equation (1).
- Lagged variables up to 30 lags for the daily analysis and 5 lags for the weekly analysis are then constructed for first difference series of input and output prices. In equation (1), we include separate variables for positive and negative variations of these lags.
- The model presented in equation (1) is then estimated.
- In Chesnes (2012), a preferred model in terms of number of lags for each input/output price pair was chosen using the Bayesian Information Criterion (BIC). In our analysis, a selection exclusively based on BIC could give as result models with very limited number of lags. In the

[9]Augmented Dickey Fuller test (ADF), its Generalized Least Squares version (GLS ADF) and the Phillips–Perron test were conducted for each series, testing in each case with and without the inclusion of a trend.

[10]The ADF test reported that the series are trend-stationary, while the Phillips–Perron test did not reject presence of a unit root. If the series were consistently found trend-stationary, this would have in theory required the inclusion of a constant term in equation (1). We tried this alternative specification and the reported coefficient is not statistically different from zero. For this reason, we followed Chesnes (2012) and present results for the estimation without the constant term.

[11]The estimated value for θ_2 can be interpreted as the extent to which simultaneous movements in the upstream price are transmitted to the downstream price. In the case of the upper portion of the supply chain, crude oil price to refined product quoted price, the estimates are 0.99 and 1.12 for petrol and diesel respectively. Regarding the transmission of ex-refinery prices to pump prices, the estimate is 1.06 for petrol and 1.03 for diesel. All coefficients are significant at the 1% level.

analysis presented below, we proceeded by selecting the best model according to the BIC and to the adjusted R-squared, and compared them with a default model including five lags.[12] The results are in almost all the cases very similar. For the national analysis, we present the analysis based on five lags, while for the local areas analysis, we used the number of lags maximizing the adjusted *R*-squared.

- Finally, an F-test is conducted for each pair of lags, the positive and negative one, to test for the parameters' equality. If their equality is not rejected by the test, then the hypothesis of the existence of "rocket and feather" pricing is rejected by the data.

5.1. *National level results*

Figures 1 and 2 show the Brent crude oil price, the ex-refinery price, and the retail price for diesel and petrol.

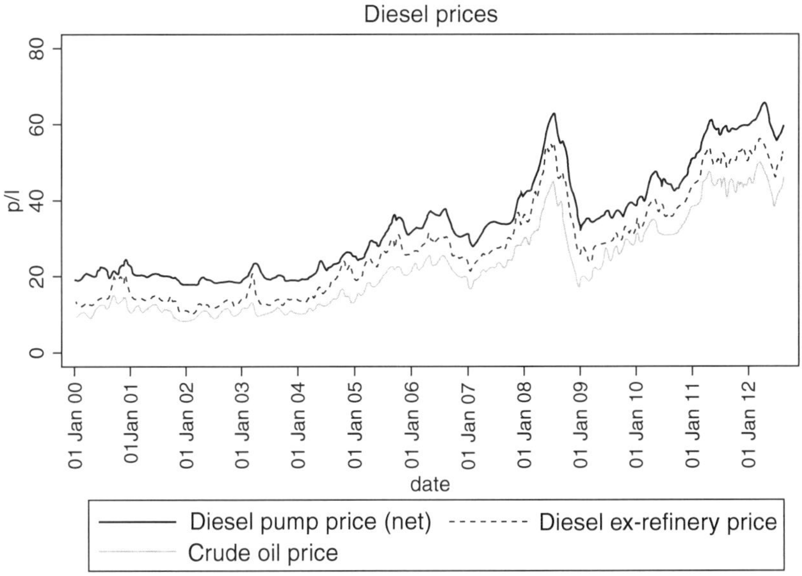

Figure 1. Crude oil, ex-refinery diesel, and diesel net price, 2000 to 2012.
Source: OFT analysis of data from Bloomberg Finance LP and DECC.

[12]We included up to 30 in the case of local-level analysis at the daily level.

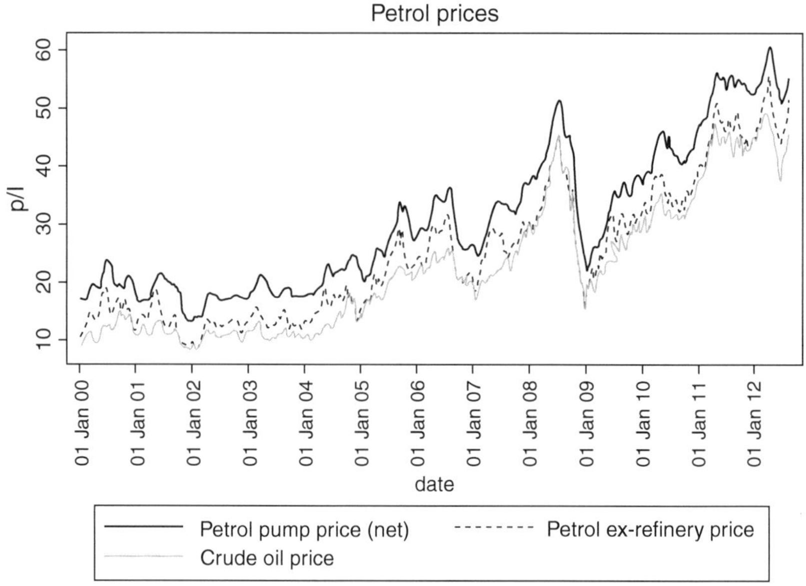

Figure 2. Crude oil, ex-refinery petrol, and petrol net prices, 2000 to 2012.
Source: OFT analysis of data from Bloomberg Finance LP and DECC.

The estimation of specification (1) has been carried out for both levels of the supply chain. For the upstream level, we have estimated the model using the crude oil price as input price and the ex-refinery price for diesel and petrol as output price. For the downstream level, average retail net diesel and petrol price have been regressed on ex-refinery diesel and petrol prices.

Tables 1 and 2 present the results of our upstream analysis, i.e., assessing whether "rockets and feathers" occur when crude oil cost shocks are passed through to refined diesel prices. Tables 3 and 4 present the results of our analysis downstream for diesel and petrol respectively.

In each table, the first column indicates the coefficient and the lag; the second and third columns report the estimated coefficient for a positive variation in the variable and its standard error; the fourth and fifth columns report the estimated coefficient for a negative variation and its standard error; the last two columns report the results of the F-test for the equality of the two coefficients and the associated p-value. For each pair of prices,

Table 1. Results for Crude Oil to Refined Diesel

Coeff.	*coeff.*$^+$	St. error	*coeff.*$^-$	St. error	$F(coeff.^+ = coeff.^-)$	p-value
γ_0	0.742***	0.064	0.852***	0.099	0.66	0.416
γ_1	0.305***	0.107	0.154**	0.063	1.15	0.284
γ_2	−0.015	0.065	−0.030	0.076	0.02	0.888
γ_3	0.045	0.082	0.017	0.089	0.04	0.841
γ_4	−0.080	0.071	−0.029	0.100	0.13	0.721
γ_5	−0.020	0.111	−0.048	0.092	0.03	0.852
δ	−0.076**	0.035	−0.066	0.042	0.02	0.885

Note: *, **, *** means the results are statistically significant at the 90%, 95%, and 99% level of confidence, respectively.

Table 2. Results for Crude Oil to Refined Petrol

Coeff.	*coeff.*$^+$	St. error	*coeff.*$^-$	St. error	$F(coeff.^+ = coeff.^-)$	p-value
γ_0	0.677***	0.060	0.764***	0.070	0.66	0.415
γ_1	0.183**	0.089	0.202**	0.091	0.02	0.896
γ_2	0.041	0.095	0.055	0.087	0.01	0.917
γ_3	−0.061	0.085	−0.063	0.081	0.00	0.990
γ_4	−0.059	0.075	−0.029	0.085	0.06	0.809
γ_5	0.102	0.079	−0.036	0.082	1.04	0.309
δ	−0.092**	0.037	−0.132***	0.039	0.51	0.474

Note: *, **, *** means the results are statistically significant at the 90%, 95%, and 99% level of confidence, respectively.

Table 3. Results for Refined Diesel to Retail Diesel

Coeff.	*coeff.*$^+$	St. error	*coeff.*$^-$	St. error	$F(coeff.^+ = coeff.^-)$	p-value
γ_0	0.175***	0.034	0.208***	0.040	0.27	0.606
γ_1	0.136***	0.038	0.152***	0.055	0.04	0.835
γ_2	0.047	0.036	0.048	0.037	0.00	0.975
γ_3	0.049*	0.026	0.065**	0.033	0.15	0.697
γ_4	0.011	0.027	0.045	0.033	0.52	0.472
γ_5	0.070**	0.032	−0.005	0.033	1.98	0.160
δ	−0.045**	0.020	−0.045**	0.021	0.00	0.992

Note: *, **, *** means the results are statistically significant at the 90%, 95%, and 99% level of confidence, respectively.

Table 4. Results for Refined Petrol to Retail Petrol

Coeff.	*coeff.*$^+$	St. error	*coeff.*$^-$	St. error	$F(coeff.^+ = coeff.^-)$	p-value
γ_0	0.173***	0.044	0.124**	0.061	0.35	0.552
γ_1	0.110**	0.045	0.118***	0.040	0.02	0.890
γ_2	0.128***	0.033	0.114**	0.047	0.07	0.795
γ_3	0.029	0.031	0.084**	0.040	0.90	0.342
γ_4	0.009	0.031	0.039	0.047	0.23	0.629
γ_5	0.036	0.030	0.051	0.035	0.07	0.787
δ	−0.061**	0.025	−0.084***	0.022	0.38	0.538

Note: *, **, *** means the results are statistically significant at the 90%, 95%, and 99% level of confidence, respectively.

we report results from a regression using five lags, and we present results for each of the lags. The last line in the table reports the estimates for the error-correction term.

The results in the first row show contemporaneous pass-through. The coefficients are 0.742 and 0.852 for positive and negative shocks respectively, both highly statistically significant. This means that when the price of crude oil increases, the majority of the price change is passed on in the same time period to the refined diesel price, regardless of the direction of the shock. The fact that the coefficient for negative input price movements is slightly higher than the one for positive ones suggests that, as far as contemporaneous pass-through is concerned, negative shocks in crude oil price are passed on slightly quicker than positive ones to the price of refined diesel.

Once the difference between the coefficients is tested formally, the F-test does not reject the null hypothesis of parameter equality, implying equal speed of adjustment.

The second row in the table shows the results for one lag and can roughly be interpreted as the amount of input price shock that is passed through after one week. The results are 0.305 for positive shocks and 0.154 for negative shocks; the former estimate is significant at the 99% level of confidence, while the latter is significant at the 95% level of confidence. This implies that, in the week after a cost shock takes place, around 30% of positive shocks is passed through, as compared to 15% for negative shocks.[13] The tests of the equality of the positive and negative coefficients for each lag and their *p*-values are presented in the last two columns. Again in this case, the test does not reject the null hypothesis that the coefficients are equal. Each of the estimates of the coefficients on the positive and negative crude oil movements for the second through fifth lag is small and not statistically significant. This indicates that the shocks in the oil price, either negative or positive, are transmitted to refined product within the first two weeks. Furthermore, each of the tests for the equality of the positive and negative coefficients does not reject the null hypothesis that the coefficients are equal.

The estimate on the positive error-correction term is presented in the last row of the table and it is similar to that for the negative error-correction term, but only the former is significant. The test for the equality of the two coefficients does not reject, again, the null hypothesis that the coefficients are equal.

Table 2 reports the results of the same analysis for petrol.

Looking at results for contemporaneous pass-through (lag 0), the cost pass-through rate is around 70%, and slightly higher for negative cost changes compared to positive cost changes. For the first lag, the coefficient for negative shocks is again slightly higher than for positive ones. For each of the two lags, the F-tests do not reject the equality of the coefficients for positive and negative shocks. As in the case of diesel, results for higher lags are not statistically significant. This suggests that a large proportion of the transmission takes place within the first two weeks.

The estimates on the error-correction terms show a higher coefficient for negative adjustments than for positive ones, and both are statistically significant. The test for the equality of the two coefficients does not reject the null hypothesis and we conclude that, also in this case, the coefficients are not significantly different from each other.

Tables 3 and 4 present the results for the downstream markets of diesel and petrol respectively.

[13]The estimated coefficient provides only an indication for such measure. In order to have a precise measure, also the effect of the lags in the dependent variable and the error-correction term has to be taken into account and an impulse response function has to be computed.

In the case of the downstream segment for diesel, the results suggest that around 20% of input price shocks are transmitted during the first week, and an additional 14–15% during the second one. The estimates of the coefficients for the second through fifth lag are small and most are not statistically significant. For each lag, the F-test does not reject the null hypothesis of no difference in the extent of pass-through of positive and negative shocks.

The estimate on the positive error-correction term is the same (to three significant digits) as that for the negative error-correction term, and both are statistically significant.

In the case of petrol, the coefficient for positive shocks is higher for contemporaneous shocks, slightly lower for one-week lagged shocks and higher again for two-weeks lagged shocks than the respective coefficients for negative shocks. The coefficients on lags three through five are small and most are not statistically significant. For each lag, the test does not reject the equality between the two coefficients.

The results presented so far show a different pattern of pass-through for the upstream level as compared to the downstream level. In the case of the upstream level, most of the variations, either positive or negative, seem to be transmitted within the first week. In the case of pass-through of ex-refinery prices variation to the final retail price, transmission seems to take longer. More importantly, the aggregate UK-level analysis seems to reject the existence of asymmetric pass-through in the case of both diesel and petrol and for both levels of the supply chain.[14]

In order to give a more precise measure of the speed of adjustment and fully assess the extent of asymmetry, long-term and short-term pass-through relationships have to be combined by deriving a full impulse response function. The impulse response function shows the response over time of the product prices to a temporary shock in the input price. This is obtained

[14]As an additional test, the same analysis was conducted for crude oil and retail diesel and petrol prices. Even in this case, the model rejects the existence of rocket and feathers pricing. As this analysis encompasses the whole supply chain, we consider this latter test as less informative than the ones presented.

by predicting the adjustment of ex-refinery prices to hypothetical positive and negative 10 pence per liter shocks in the crude oil price.[15]

Impulse response functions for diesel and petrol and for the upstream and downstream segments are presented in Figures 3–6. The graphs present on the horizontal axis the number of weeks since the shock occurred. The vertical axis shows the pence per liter that are transmitted for each week since the shock occurred, up to the fifth week.

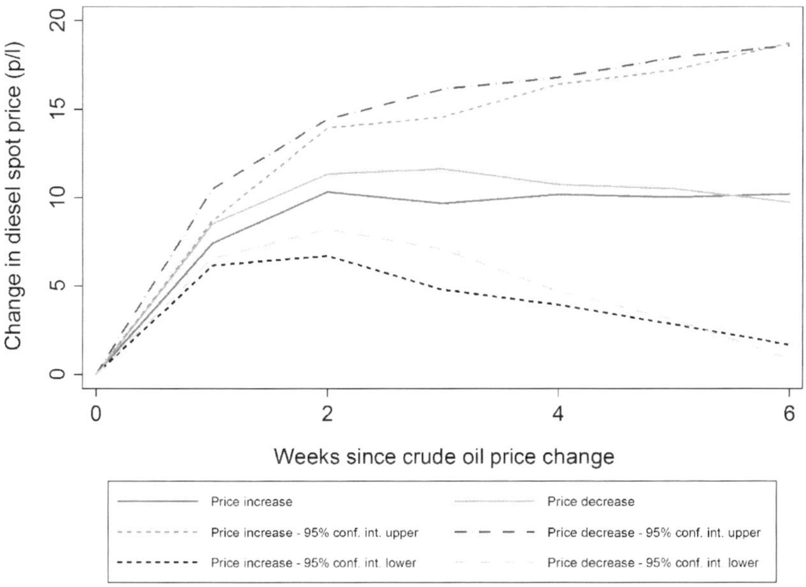

Figure 3. Impulse response function — crude oil prices to ex-refinery diesel prices.
Source: OFT analysis of data from Bloomberg Finance LP and DECC.

[15]The curve was constructed by applying the estimate results to a representative 10 pence price shock applied at the average level of the downstream price. For both positive and negative shocks, the predicted product price change was computed from the estimates of the relevant lag, the previous lags, and error-correction term. The curves take therefore into account both the long- and short-term relationship between each pair of prices, and give an accurate account of the difference in the transmission. In the graphs, the horizontal axis is set to zero for the long-term equilibrium. So, for the sake of interpretation, the shock is considered to take place at week one.

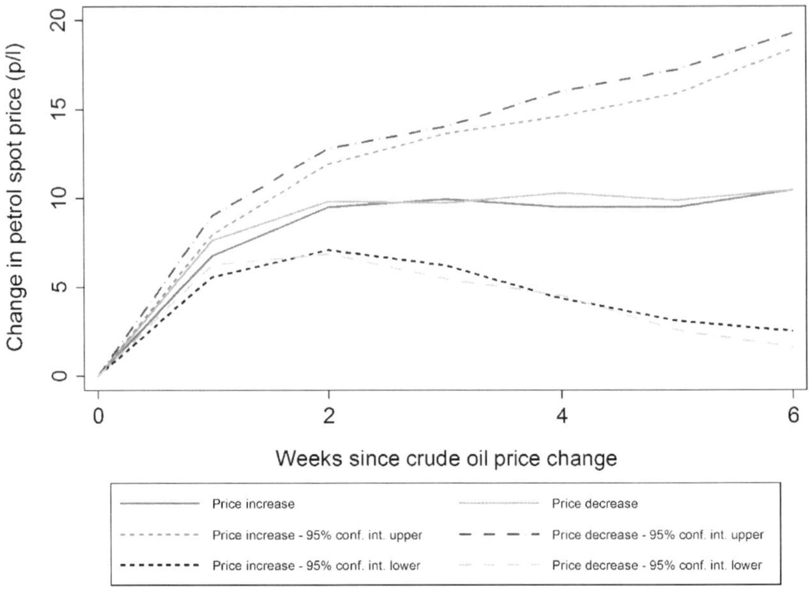

Figure 4. Impulse response function — crude oil prices to ex-refinery petrol prices. *Source*: OFT analysis of data from Bloomberg Finance LP and DECC.

In the case of the upstream market for diesel, around 70–80% of the average price shock, whether positive or negative, is transmitted within the first week. At the second week, the shock seems fully passed through to ex-refinery price.[16] This pass-through happens at a slightly higher rate in the case of a negative shock and convergence is found at week 5. The size of the confidence intervals clearly indicates that the difference is not statistically significant.

The entire shock is transmitted to the price of refined petrol within the first two weeks. Even in this case, a representative negative shock seems to be transmitted in a slightly quicker way than a positive one during the first

[16]The fact that the fitted lines, in particular the one for a price decrease, exceed the value of 10 on the y-axis for a few weeks is consistent with our results for the short term amount of pass-through, obtained from estimating equation (2). Results for pass-through from crude oil to ex-refinery diesel report a coefficient higher than 1, suggesting that on average more than 100% of the original price increase is pass-through to diesel price in the period under analysis.

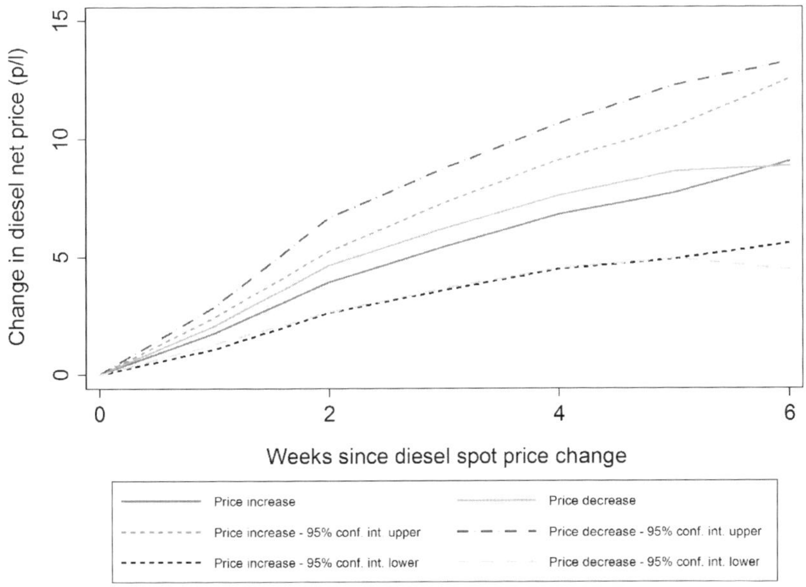

Figure 5. Impulse response function — ex-refinery diesel prices to diesel retail prices. *Source*: OFT analysis of data from Bloomberg Finance LP and DECC.

week, though this difference is not statistically significant at any point in time.

Figures 5 and 6 report the impulse response functions for the downstream portion of the market for diesel and petrol respectively.

For both diesel and petrol, the pass-through at the retail level seems to take place over a longer time horizon than for the upstream portion of the market. In both cases, around 90% of the original shock is passed through five weeks after the shock occurred.

In the case of diesel, the amount of price decreases passed through in each week observed is slightly higher than for price increases. The opposite seems to take place for petrol. In both cases, the difference is very small and not surprisingly the equality in the coefficients is not rejected for any lag, as shown in the last two columns of Tables 3 and 4.

Following the framework proposed by Chesnes (2012), our work rejects the presence of "rocket and feather" pricing at the aggregate UK level for petrol and diesel and for both levels of the supply chain. Our findings differ

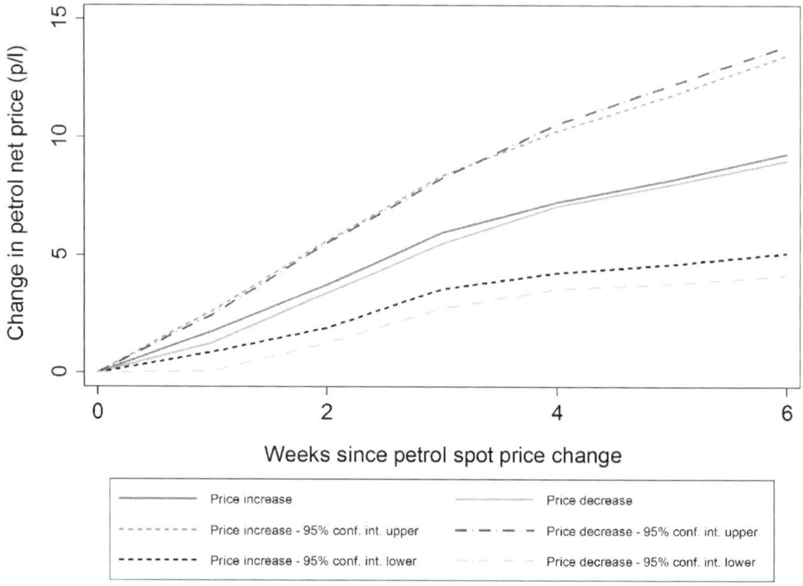

Figure 6. Impulse response function — ex-refinery petrol prices to petrol retail prices. *Source*: OFT analysis of data from Bloomberg Finance LP and DECC.

from previous empirical literature on the UK, as in the works by Bacon (1990) and Manning (1991). These authors, using data on the UK market for the 1970s and 1980s, found that asymmetric pass-through did indeed exist, though the difference found is generally small and short-lived. Bacon (1990) analyzed input price transmission introducing a quadratic and a linear term to account for the two types of cost shocks. Manning (1991) estimated an error-correction model for the pass-through of crude oil to retail fuels, in a way similar to ours.[17] We consider the latter as a more suitable approach, as it takes jointly into account both the short and long-term effects of cost shocks. Both the authors also estimate their models for the whole supply chain, from ex-refinery to retail prices; as explained above, this approach may bear the risk of aggregating multiple effects, precluding the identification of the source of the asymmetry. Given that the size of

[17] Manning (1991) used for his analysis data at the monthly level.

the asymmetry found is small, also a composition effect of multiple small asymmetries for different supply level, not significant if taken in isolation, could not be excluded.

More in general, we note that the two empirical studies used data from a period, the 1970s and the 1980s, where the oil industry and the UK market for fuels were substantially different from the period 2000–2012, which is the focus of our study. The developments in the oil industry in the last 20 years, the increase in the price of crude oil and the change in the macroeconomic conditions are likely to have had an impact also on the UK market. At the same time, technological change, higher fuel efficiency, and changes in consumer preferences have modified the demand for diesel and petrol. All this taken together makes plausible that the UK may have developed feature that would make those results not applicable to the current economic context. Finally, if one had to consider — as we do — absence of "rockets and feathers" as an indication of generally competitive markets, the characteristics of the current UK market may give confidence to our results. The higher reliance of the UK wholesale markets on imports from overseas, imposing price competition in the upstream segment, and the entry of supermarkets as fuel retailers are factors that are likely to benefit consumers, in spite of the constant rise in the price of raw petrol. This is consistent with swift and symmetric transmission time for cost increases and decreases.

5.2. *Local-level analysis*

The analysis at the retail level was performed at the UK aggregate level and also replicated, using a different and more granular data set, for a set of local markets in the UK. The areas were chosen in order to include a representative selection of the different types of local markets, e.g., rural area, urban, commercial, etc. — as well as of the different regions in the UK.[18] As competition in the retail segment is considered to take place primarily at the local level, the UK-wide analysis may not capture the

[18]For the selection of the local areas, 18 combinations of region and type of areas were selected to represent the proportion of each type of areas in each region. For each combination, a fuel station was randomly selected on a data set containing the universe of the fuel stations in the UK. This station was then used as the centroid for the computation of the 10 and 20 minutes isochrones for urban areas and rural areas respectively.

local competition dynamics that affects the transmission of input prices. Therefore, the application of the analysis to a selection of local markets could shed light on the links between market structure and possible evidence of asymmetric pass-through.[19] The local areas included in our analysis are listed in Table 5.

A weighted average price measure for each day in the period from November 1, 2011 to October 31, 2012 was computed for both diesel and petrol.[20] This price index for each area was then averaged at the weekly

Table 5. Local Areas

Area code	Location type	County	Region
1	Urban transient	Greater London	London
2	Residential	East Sussex	South East
3	Residential	Somerset	South West
4	Rural	Hampshire	South East
5	Rural	Powys	Wales
6	Residential	Gwent	Wales
7	Urban transient	Tyne and Wear	North
8	Residential	West Yorkshire	Yorkshire and Humber
9	Urban transient	County Antrim	Northern Ireland
10	Industry/office	Staffordshire	West Midlands
11	Industry/office	Lancashire	North West
12	Urban transient	Hertfordshire	South East
13	Residential	Nottinghamshire	East Midlands
14	Residential	Suffolk	East Anglia
15	Rural	Gloucestershire	South West
16	Rural	Lanarkshire	Scotland
17	Urban transient	County Sntrim	Northern Ireland
18	Residential	Ross-shire	Scotland

[19] In the context of the CfI, the OFT also conducted a price concentration analysis aimed at identifying the determinants of price differences across areas. See OFT (2013), "UK Petrol and Diesel Sector — Call for Information", Annex D. On the relationship between local market conditions and "rockets and feathers", see Deltas (2008).

[20] In order to avoid the risk of composition effects, i.e., changes in the average value that are due to a different number of forecourts observed in the two subsequent days, only those forecourts for which we had good quality data were included in the analysis. Specifically, for each local area, forecourts were ranked on the basis of the total daily price data points observed over the period. Only those forecourts that provided the best coverage in terms of availability of prices were used to compute the daily averages.

level.[21] As input prices, we have used the quoted Platts price for diesel and petrol on the same week.

Descriptive statistics confirmed that the areas have different average price levels and different price evolution overtime. The retail price series showed also a significant level of inertia in many cases, with fuel stations reporting the same price for several days in a row, and even weeks in certain instances.

In testing for the asymmetry for each local area, we proceeded in the same way as for the national-level analysis. The analysis at the daily level proved to be largely inconclusive, insofar as the large majority of lags were reporting insignificant results even in the symmetric model. This finding is nevertheless informative, as it suggests that daily level may be too granular to detect any observable pattern, and cost pass-through is better observed over the larger time span provided by the weekly analysis. Also, the fact that many fuel stations do not adapt prices more frequently that at the weekly level indicates contemporaneous Platts price does not feed into the daily pricing decision, but rather prices are mostly influenced by the actual price paid for the fuel when contracts are signed.

Tables 6 and 7 summarize the results for diesel and petrol. The number of lags to include for each local area was selected by running the standard, symmetric model for each area with zero through five lags, in turn, and selecting the number of lags that maximizes the adjusted R-squared.[22]

The local-level analysis results share some similarities with the national-level analysis, though in many areas positive and negative coefficients are not significant for each individual lag. For each area, significant results are generally found for lags within the first two or three weeks.[23] By and large, the F-test rejects the difference in adjustment for positive and negative shocks.

[21]The data also reported many missing values, especially for days of the week close to the weekend. To overcome this shortcoming, an alternative weekly price was computed using the days of the week with the highest number of observations (Tuesday and Wednesday). The Platts price for the same day was used as input price.

[22]The final results are not sensitive to the alternative of using five lags for all the areas, as done for the national-level analysis.

[23]Area 16 was not included in the weekly analysis due to missing data.

Table 6. Results for Local Areas' Analysis — Weekly Data — Diesel

Area code	Lag (1)	Γ (2)	p-value (3)	γ^+ (4)	p-value (5)	γ^- (6)	p-value (7)	F-stat $(\gamma^+ = \gamma^-)$ (8)	p-value (9)
1	0	0.14**	0.02	−0.08	0.52	0.39***	0.00	4.56	0.04
1	1	0.12	0.10	−0.09	0.50	0.34*	0.06	2.62	0.12
1	2	0.12	0.13	0.01	0.91	0.42**	0.03	2.36	0.14
1	3	0.01	0.92	0.06	0.64	−0.06	0.73	0.21	0.65
1	4	0.10	0.19	0.01	0.96	0.12	0.56	0.16	0.69
1	5	0.08	0.24	0.09	0.44	0.21	0.25	0.23	0.64
2	0	0.11	0.12	−0.08	0.57	0.34**	0.05	2.42	0.13
2	1	0.28***	0.01	0.11	0.51	0.60***	0.00	3.07	0.09
2	2	0.22**	0.02	0.05	0.77	0.41**	0.03	1.83	0.19
2	3	0.16*	0.07	0.17	0.34	0.14	0.48	0.01	0.91
2	4	0.04	0.62	0.03	0.84	0.01	0.97	0.01	0.93
3	0	0.11*	0.08	0.07	0.53	0.17	0.21	0.18	0.68
3	1	0.18**	0.03	−0.01	0.94	0.39**	0.01	2.90	0.10
3	2	0.00	0.96	0.05	0.75	0.06	0.70	0.00	0.95
3	3	−0.08	0.31	0.16	0.26	−0.24	0.13	2.69	0.11
4	0	0.11***	0.00	0.03	0.73	0.21***	0.01	2.17	0.15
4	1	0.16***	0.00	0.04	0.62	0.28***	0.00	3.27	0.08
4	2	0.10**	0.03	0.10	0.20	0.13	0.11	0.08	0.78
5	0	0.20***	0.00	0.03	0.85	0.34**	0.02	2.06	0.17
5	1	0.22*	0.07	0.19	0.25	0.32	0.11	0.28	0.60
5	2	0.12	0.34	0.28*	0.09	0.06	0.74	0.90	0.35
5	3	0.14	0.13	0.14	0.40	−0.05	0.77	0.56	0.46
5	4	0.14	0.11	0.06	0.72	−0.05	0.79	0.16	0.69
5	5	0.14*	0.07	0.08	0.63	0.11	0.49	0.01	0.91
6	0	0.14***	0.00	−0.02	0.84	0.32***	0.00	4.53	0.04
6	1	0.14**	0.01	−0.04	0.67	0.36***	0.00	5.22	0.03
6	2	0.01	0.87	−0.08	0.46	0.16	0.13	1.89	0.18
7	0	0.15**	0.02	0.14	0.38	0.23	0.11	0.14	0.71
7	1	0.16*	0.10	0.08	0.62	0.14	0.50	0.05	0.83
7	2	0.18**	0.05	0.03	0.82	0.30*	0.10	1.11	0.31
7	3	0.09	0.28	0.07	0.65	0.19	0.25	0.21	0.65
7	4	0.04	0.65	−0.08	0.56	0.08	0.67	0.39	0.54
7	5	0.14*	0.06	0.13	0.40	0.16	0.38	0.01	0.90
8	0	0.15***	0.01	−0.02	0.86	0.39***	0.00	4.91	0.03
8	1	0.16**	0.03	−0.08	0.54	0.35***	0.00	4.75	0.04
8	2	0.10	0.15	−0.08	0.56	0.26**	0.02	3.01	0.09
9	0	−0.01	0.93	−0.02	0.85	0.07	0.58	0.19	0.67
9	1	0.15**	0.04	0.04	0.78	0.30**	0.04	1.28	0.27
9	2	0.18**	0.01	0.03	0.84	0.40***	0.00	2.96	0.09

(Continued)

Table 6. (*Continued*)

Area code	Lag (1)	Γ (2)	p-value (3)	γ^+ (4)	p-value (5)	γ^- (6)	p-value (7)	F-stat ($\gamma^+ = \gamma^-$) (8)	p-value (9)
10	0	0.15**	0.02	0.22*	0.08	0.12	0.37	0.21	0.65
10	1	0.16*	0.06	−0.13	0.33	0.44***	0.00	7.13	0.01
10	2	0.04	0.65	−0.06	0.64	0.23	0.16	1.42	0.24
10	3	0.16**	0.05	0.25*	0.06	0.08	0.63	0.53	0.47
11	0	0.16***	0.00	0.07	0.39	0.28***	0.00	1.98	0.17
11	1	0.15***	0.01	−0.07	0.49	0.36***	0.00	8.09	0.01
12	0	0.10**	0.01	0.06	0.41	0.15*	0.06	0.42	0.52
12	1	0.13***	0.01	0.00	0.99	0.26***	0.00	3.75	0.06
13	0	0.15**	0.02	0.06	0.69	0.32**	0.04	1.02	0.32
13	1	0.14	0.12	−0.09	0.62	0.27	0.20	1.42	0.25
13	2	0.09	0.28	0.04	0.80	0.06	0.75	0.01	0.92
13	3	0.11	0.16	0.07	0.62	0.21	0.26	0.25	0.62
13	4	0.13*	0.08	0.20	0.18	0.25	0.21	0.05	0.83
13	5	0.10	0.17	0.26	0.12	−0.04	0.82	1.21	0.28
14	0	0.17***	0.00	0.13	0.26	0.30**	0.03	0.70	0.41
14	1	0.24***	0.00	0.03	0.81	0.37***	0.01	2.41	0.13
14	2	0.08	0.32	−0.04	0.76	0.25*	0.07	1.80	0.19
14	3	0.13*	0.06	0.05	0.71	0.27**	0.05	0.94	0.34
15	0	0.07	0.44	−0.21	0.29	0.33	0.15	2.18	0.15
15	1	0.34**	0.01	0.65**	0.03	−0.06	0.78	3.07	0.09
15	2	0.32***	0.01	0.21	0.43	0.13	0.55	0.04	0.85
15	3	0.19*	0.08	0.23	0.40	0.04	0.84	0.20	0.66
15	4	0.14	0.17	0.13	0.60	0.01	0.96	0.10	0.76
17	0	0.06	0.18	0.03	0.75	0.14	0.26	0.30	0.59
17	1	0.20***	0.00	0.04	0.74	0.36**	0.01	2.53	0.12
17	2	0.09	0.14	−0.02	0.83	0.24*	0.07	1.85	0.19
17	3	0.04	0.50	0.09	0.44	−0.03	0.83	0.36	0.55
17	4	0.09	0.13	0.08	0.44	0.01	0.94	0.15	0.70
18	0	0.18**	0.01	0.08	0.62	0.27	0.16	0.41	0.53
18	1	0.15	0.10	0.01	0.95	0.44*	0.07	1.62	0.21
18	2	−0.01	0.95	0.09	0.64	0.19	0.40	0.09	0.77
18	3	−0.02	0.79	−0.14	0.46	0.29	0.18	1.68	0.21
18	4	0.10	0.20	−0.06	0.76	0.32*	0.09	1.66	0.21

Note: *, **, *** means the results are statistically significant at the 90%, 95%, and 99% level of confidence, respectively.

Table 7. Results for Local Areas' Analysis — Weekly Data — Petrol

Area code	Lag (1)	Γ (2)	p-value (3)	γ^+ (4)	p-value (5)	γ^- (6)	p-value (7)	F-stat ($\gamma^+ = \gamma^-$) (8)	p-value (9)
1	0	0.02	0.69	−0.04	0.67	0.12	0.24	1.08	0.31
1	1	0.10*	0.06	0.12	0.32	0.03	0.75	0.26	0.62
1	2	0.10*	0.09	0.32**	0.01	−0.08	0.52	4.56	0.04
1	3	0.09	0.11	0.27**	0.05	−0.03	0.79	2.47	0.13
1	4	0.16***	0.00	0.15	0.29	0.26**	0.02	0.29	0.60
1	5	0.08	0.15	0.19	0.13	0.03	0.81	0.52	0.48
2	0	0.08*	0.06	0.14	0.22	0.09	0.38	0.07	0.79
2	1	0.29***	0.00	0.38**	0.01	0.23*	0.08	0.46	0.51
2	2	0.29***	0.00	0.29**	0.05	0.40**	0.01	0.26	0.62
2	3	0.20***	0.01	0.22	0.15	0.24*	0.07	0.01	0.90
2	4	0.13*	0.07	0.01	0.94	0.20	0.13	0.79	0.38
3	0	−0.03	0.55	0.06	0.63	0.03	0.82	0.02	0.88
3	1	0.20***	0.00	0.43***	0.00	−0.03	0.83	4.25	0.05
3	2	0.11	0.17	0.34**	0.04	0.03	0.83	1.54	0.23
3	3	0.14*	0.06	−0.03	0.86	0.23*	0.07	1.10	0.30
3	4	0.16**	0.04	0.17	0.28	0.12	0.34	0.03	0.85
4	0	0.06	0.14	0.14	0.11	0.10	0.31	0.10	0.76
4	1	0.16***	0.01	0.27**	0.04	0.21**	0.03	0.15	0.70
4	2	0.14**	0.05	0.50***	0.00	0.05	0.71	7.65	0.01
4	3	0.04	0.61	0.41**	0.04	−0.16	0.13	8.53	0.01
4	4	0.06	0.32	0.13	0.46	0.08	0.41	0.05	0.82
4	5	0.00	0.94	0.05	0.74	−0.04	0.72	0.18	0.68
5	0	0.04	0.68	0.40**	0.04	0.02	0.91	1.76	0.19
5	1	0.18	0.21	0.84***	0.00	−0.37	0.10	11.68	0.00
5	2	0.05	0.74	−0.08	0.78	0.13	0.60	0.22	0.64
5	3	0.21	0.13	−0.08	0.77	0.29	0.23	0.74	0.40
6	0	0.10**	0.04	0.24*	0.05	0.09	0.41	0.64	0.43
6	1	0.14*	0.06	0.22	0.13	0.15	0.22	0.11	0.75
6	2	0.25***	0.00	0.45***	0.01	0.10	0.57	2.03	0.17
6	3	0.18**	0.04	0.45**	0.02	−0.09	0.55	5.51	0.03
6	4	0.21**	0.01	0.25	0.17	0.24*	0.07	0.00	0.99
6	5	0.10	0.13	0.27	0.10	−0.01	0.94	1.40	0.25
7	0	0.06	0.11	0.16*	0.07	0.07	0.28	0.44	0.51
7	1	0.25***	0.00	0.45***	0.00	0.09	0.31	5.81	0.02
7	2	0.24***	0.00	0.40***	0.00	0.09	0.39	3.29	0.08
7	3	0.27***	0.00	0.24**	0.02	0.29***	0.01	0.07	0.80
8	0	0.09**	0.02	0.11	0.25	0.12	0.21	0.00	0.97
8	1	0.11*	0.08	0.08	0.50	0.16	0.17	0.15	0.70

(*Continued*)

Table 7. (*Continued*)

Area code	Lag (1)	Γ (2)	*p*-value (3)	γ^+ (4)	*p*-value (5)	γ^- (6)	*p*-value (7)	F-stat ($\gamma^+ = \gamma^-$) (8)	*p*-value (9)
8	2	0.20***	0.00	0.40***	0.01	0.01	0.93	3.17	0.09
8	3	0.11	0.11	0.30*	0.07	−0.09	0.54	2.57	0.12
8	4	0.10	0.13	0.20	0.19	0.16	0.21	0.04	0.84
8	5	0.06	0.28	0.23	0.13	−0.09	0.47	2.12	0.16
9	0	0.01	0.84	−0.12	0.30	0.18*	0.07	3.01	0.09
9	1	0.04	0.57	0.21*	0.09	−0.14	0.24	3.35	0.08
9	2	0.19***	0.01	0.18	0.22	0.23	0.12	0.04	0.85
9	3	0.16**	0.03	0.00	0.99	0.33**	0.02	1.78	0.19
9	4	0.07	0.31	0.02	0.86	0.09	0.50	0.08	0.77
10	0	0.03	0.46	0.10	0.45	0.08	0.49	0.01	0.93
10	1	0.17**	0.02	0.26	0.10	0.11	0.43	0.33	0.57
10	2	0.23***	0.00	0.45**	0.01	0.15	0.37	1.25	0.27
10	3	0.17**	0.04	0.26	0.17	0.16	0.28	0.14	0.71
10	4	0.08	0.30	0.14	0.45	0.09	0.56	0.04	0.85
11	0	0.01	0.84	0.10	0.19	0.14	0.11	0.09	0.76
11	1	0.19***	0.00	0.26***	0.01	0.06	0.59	1.76	0.20
11	2	0.19***	0.00	0.51***	0.00	0.10	0.35	4.54	0.04
11	3	0.17***	0.01	0.20	0.19	0.19**	0.04	0.00	0.96
11	4	0.13**	0.04	0.20	0.14	0.06	0.57	0.62	0.44
12	0	0.03	0.46	0.07	0.47	0.03	0.75	0.09	0.76
12	1	0.10*	0.06	0.16	0.14	0.06	0.59	0.33	0.57
12	2	0.06	0.23	0.06	0.57	0.08	0.49	0.01	0.93
12	3	0.04	0.41	−0.01	0.92	0.11	0.31	0.44	0.51
13	0	0.07*	0.07	0.17*	0.08	0.09	0.43	0.24	0.63
13	1	0.17***	0.01	0.34***	0.01	0.07	0.49	2.24	0.15
13	2	0.20***	0.00	0.37**	0.02	0.13	0.32	1.03	0.32
13	3	0.21***	0.00	0.25	0.14	0.22	0.10	0.02	0.88
13	4	0.15**	0.03	0.26	0.14	0.17	0.20	0.14	0.72
13	5	0.12**	0.04	0.28*	0.05	0.03	0.81	1.26	0.27
14	0	0.07	0.45	0.19	0.46	−0.14	0.55	0.66	0.42
14	1	0.15	0.26	0.15	0.59	0.21	0.43	0.02	0.88
14	2	0.26**	0.05	−0.02	0.96	0.70*	0.06	1.49	0.24
14	3	0.29**	0.03	0.24	0.47	0.31	0.35	0.01	0.92
14	4	0.21	0.13	0.23	0.50	0.24	0.43	0.00	0.99
14	5	0.00	0.99	0.05	0.85	0.24	0.46	0.12	0.73
15	0	0.07	0.22	−0.07	0.57	0.21**	0.03	2.30	0.14
15	1	0.27***	0.00	0.59***	0.00	0.07	0.57	5.83	0.02
15	2	0.13	0.11	0.26*	0.08	0.11	0.45	0.43	0.52

(*Continued*)

Table 7. (*Continued*)

Area code	Lag (1)	Γ (2)	p-value (3)	γ^+ (4)	p-value (5)	γ^- (6)	p-value (7)	F-stat $(\gamma^+ = \gamma^-)$ (8)	p-value (9)
17	0	0.10**	0.03	0.09	0.52	0.15	0.20	0.08	0.78
17	1	0.04	0.59	0.17	0.31	−0.02	0.90	0.53	0.47
17	2	0.14*	0.06	0.26*	0.10	0.03	0.87	0.61	0.44
17	3	0.07	0.37	0.09	0.54	0.12	0.45	0.01	0.91
17	4	0.05	0.48	0.17	0.29	−0.01	0.93	0.48	0.50
18	0	0.16**	0.03	0.36**	0.03	0.13	0.35	0.81	0.38
18	1	−0.02	0.84	0.45**	0.03	−0.36**	0.04	8.17	0.01
18	2	0.24**	0.04	0.33	0.15	0.21	0.38	0.10	0.75
18	3	0.14	0.19	0.18	0.40	0.11	0.59	0.05	0.83
18	4	0.09	0.40	0.23	0.28	0.03	0.90	0.34	0.56

Note: *, **, *** means the results are statistically significant at the 90%, 95%, and 99% level of confidence, respectively.

The results for diesel seem to point in a few instances in the direction of asymmetric transmission. This is for instance the case for Area 2 (East Sussex). In this case, results from column (2) suggest that lags 1 and 2 are those in which most of the pass-through takes place. In both cases, a clear asymmetric pattern is found, with quicker adjustment for negative shocks. Similar instances are found in areas 4, 9, and 12 (Hampshire, County Antrim, and Hertfordshire), none of which are consistent with "rocket and feather" pricing, but rather with the opposite, i.e., quicker transmission of price decreases.

In the case of petrol, the symmetric model tends to perform relatively well in almost all the areas. Results suggest that a significant proportion of ex-refinery price shocks are generally passed through within the first 2–3 weeks.

Columns (4)–(7) present our results for the asymmetric model. For most of the areas, we do not find significant results for γ^+ and γ^- for the same lag. Asymmetry consistent with "rocket and feather" pricing is found in some areas, but the evidence is not clear-cut. The F-test reported in columns (8) and (9) only rejects symmetry at the 10% level for two consecutive lags in two of the areas (area 4, Hampshire, and area 7, Tyne and Wear).[24]

We have further looked at the areas that reported possible asymmetric pass-through to see if this could be associated with certain area characteristics, such as type of location, population density, level of concentration or presence of supermarkets. We have not found a clear association between our result and any specific area characteristic.[25]

Despite the F-test does not reject equality in the large majority of cases, the pattern of significance of lags' coefficient may suggest that some asymmetry could be found if one had to apply a less stringent test or to expand the time series at our disposal. Even aware of this possibility, we have considered the results as sufficient indication for absence of asymmetric pass-through not to warrant further analysis at the local level. This is consistent with the exploratory nature of our local analysis, where a very small selection of local areas was picked for the analysis.[26]

6. Conclusion

This chapter presents the empirical work undertaken in the context of the CfI on the market for road fuels. It analyses whether cost shocks are passed through in an asymmetric way along the supply chain for road fuels. This represents, to our knowledge, the first comprehensive empirical investigation on the existence of asymmetric pass-through of input price in the road fuel industry in the UK market since the work of Manning (1991). Following Chesnes (2012), we have estimated an error-correction model for petrol and diesel and for the two levels of supply chain, ex-refinery and retail, on weekly price series of crude oil, ex-refinery and retail diesel

[24]While this is also the case for area 9 (County Antrim), the results show asymmetry consistent with "rocket and feather" pricing only for one lag, i.e., lag 1. The asymmetry is in the opposite direction for lag 0. As such, the evidence in this area is not clear-cut.

[25]The price concentration analysis run by the OFT in parallel to this analysis indicated that concentration level and absence of supermarkets are associated with less intense competition at the local level. For this reason, these features were considered as possible causes of asymmetric pass-through.

[26]A more detailed local-level analysis, possibly entailing the selection of a richer sample of areas and a thorough market definition exercise for each of them, was beyond the scope of the OFT's CfI.

and petrol prices for the period 2000–2012 at the national level. In order to investigate the link between asymmetric reaction to cost shocks and local market characteristics, we have replicated the analysis for the retail segment on a data set containing daily and weekly prices for the time period from November 1, 2011 through October 31, 2012 for 18 areas in the UK.

We find that shocks in the price of crude oil are transmitted to a large extent to the price of refined products within the first two weeks since the shock occurred. The pass-through is slower between ex-refinery and retail prices, where it takes up to five weeks to pass-through to the retail price most of the average price variation. We reject the presence of asymmetric pass-through, i.e., "rocket and feather" pricing, for both levels of the supply chain for road fuels over the period 2000–2012. Our analysis on the 18 local areas selected broadly confirms that pass-through from ex-refinery to retail level happens within the first three to four weeks. We did not find compelling evidence of "rocket and feather" pricing neither in diesel nor in petrol; results for some areas reported some level of asymmetry, especially in the case of petrol, yet this evidence is not clear-cut. We did not consider this evidence to be sufficiently clear to warrant additional in-depth analysis by the OFT.

Overall, the empirical analysis described in this chapter suggests that, on the basis of the data available, "rocket and feather" pricing is not a distinctive feature of the UK markets for road fuels. This finding constitutes an important update to the previous empirical evidence that did find evidence of "rocket and feather" pricing. In addition, it provided a valuable indication to the OFT's CfI, which concluded that the markets for road fuels were overall working well for consumers, and no further sector-wide investigation was required.

References

Bachmeier, L. J. and J. M. Griffin (2003). "New Evidence on Asymmetric Gasoline Price Responses," *Review of Economics and Statistics*, 85(3), pp. 772–776.

Bacon, R. (1990). *Rockets and Feathers: The Asymmetric Speed of Adjustment of UK Retail Gasoline Prices to Cost Changes*, EE10, Oxford Institute for Energy Studies, Oxford, United Kingdom.

Borenstein, S., S. C. Cameron and R. Gilbert (1997). "Do Gasoline Prices Respond Asymmetrically to Crude Oil Price Changes?" *Quarterly Journal of Economics*, 112(1), pp. 305–339.

Borenstein, S. and A. Shepard (2002). "Sticky Prices, Inventories, and Market Power in Wholesale Gasoline Markets," *RAND Journal of Economics*, 33, pp. 116–139.

Bundeskartellamt (2011). Fuel Sector Inquiry, Final Report, May.

Chesnes, M. (2012). "Asymmetric Pass-Through in U.S. Gasoline Prices," *U.S. Federal Trade Commission Bureau of Economics Working Paper* No. 302.

Comisión Nacional de la Competencia (2012). "Report Monitoring the Automotive Fuel Distribution Market in Spain," June.

Deltas, G. (2008). "Retail Gasoline Price Dynamics and Local Market Power," *Journal of Industrial Economics*, 56(3), pp. 613–628.

Engle, R. F. and C. W. J. Granger (1987). "Co-Integration and Error Correction: Representation, Estimation, and Testing," *Econometrica*, 55(2), pp. 251–276.

Green, E. and R. Porter (1984). "Non-Cooperative Collusion under Imperfect Price Information," *Econometrica*, LII, pp. 87–100.

Lewis, M. S. (2011). "Asymmetric Price Adjustment and Consumer Search: An Examination of the Retail Gasoline Market," *Journal of Economics and Management Strategy*, 20(2), pp. 409–449.

Manning, D. N. (1991). "Petrol Prices, Oil Price Rises and Oil Price Falls: Some Evidence for the UK since 1972," *Applied Economics*, 23, pp. 1535–1541.

Maskin, E. and J. Tirole (1988). "A Theory of Dynamic Oligopoly II: Price Competition, Kinked Demand Curves and Edgeworth Cycles," *Econometrica*, 56, pp. 571–599.

Noel, M. D. (2009). "Do Gasoline Prices Respond Asymmetrically to Cost Shocks? The Effect of Edgeworth Cycles," *RAND Journal of Economics*, 40(3), pp. 582–595.

Radchenko, S. and D. Shapiro (2011). "Anticipated and Unanticipated Effects of Crude Oil Prices and Gasoline Inventory Changes on Gasoline Prices," *Energy Economics*, 33, pp. 758–769.

Tappata, M. (2009). "Rockets and Feathers: Understanding Asymmetric Pricing," *RAND Journal of Economics*, 40(4), pp. 673–687.

Chapter 4

Better Product at Same Cost: Leader Innovation vs. Generic Product Improvement*

David J. Balan

Bureau of Economics, Federal Trade Commission
dbalan@ftc.gov

George Deltas

University of Illinois at Urbana-Champaign
deltas@illinois.edu

Abstract

We develop a parametric model in which a high-quality dominant firm faces a low-quality competitive fringe. We show that in this model, an increase in the dominant firm's product quality increases total welfare and consumer surplus. An increase in fringe firm quality has an ambiguous effect on total welfare, but always increases consumer surplus. Moreover, an increase in fringe quality always leads to a bigger increase in consumer surplus than does an increase in dominant firm quality, but the analogous comparison for total welfare is ambiguous. Finally, we show that an increase in dominant firm quality always increases total welfare by more than it increases consumer surplus, whereas for an increase in fringe firm quality, the opposite is true. The first of these findings relies on our parametric assumptions, but the others appear not to. We discuss the relevance of these results to public policy.

Keywords: Product innovation, dominant firm, competitive fringe, vertical differentiation.

JEL Classification Codes: L15, L13, J60, O31.

---

*We would like to thank Maria Luisa Mancusi, Tom Ross, David Ulph, Tommaso Valletti, and seminar participants at the U. of Pireus and at CRESSE 2013 (Corfu) for helpful comments and discussion. Ania Jaroszewicz provided expert research assistance. The views expressed in this chapter are those of the authors and do not necessarily reflect those of the Federal Trade Commission.

1. Introduction

A product innovation can make it possible to produce a higher-quality version of an existing product, sometimes at the old production cost. All else equal, such an improvement tends to increase welfare, at least net of any R&D costs incurred. But if the higher-quality product is introduced into a market characterized by distortions due to market power, then the welfare effect will also depend on whether it makes those distortions bigger or smaller. In this chapter, we consider a market structure that does contain such a distortion, namely that of a high-quality dominant firm competing with a low-quality competitive fringe. Within this framework, we derive the total welfare and consumer surplus effects of a quality increase in the dominant firm's product and in the fringe's product, and we also derive several results on how these welfare effects compare with each other. Our results have a direct bearing on the question of what kind of innovation is more valuable, a pushing out of the quality frontier (i.e., an increase in the quality of the dominant firm's product, also referred to as the "branded" product), or catchup innovation by the fringe (i.e., an increase in the quality of the "generic" product). Most analyses of innovation focus on the former, but we show that, somewhat surprisingly, the latter can be more valuable. A major theme of our results is that the comparison of the two types of quality increase depends on the welfare standard adopted, i.e., innovation has redistributive effects, and the nature of the redistribution depends on which product's quality is improved.

Our framework can be applied to a number of settings, such as in consumer electronics, where there is often a clear quality leader (e.g., the iPad), competing with a number of sellers of lower-quality products that compete mainly on price (e.g., other tablet computers). Another such setting is the competition between branded drugs under patent protection and older generic drugs that are less effective but also much cheaper. Yet another might be CT scans vs. MRI scans. For some purposes, these two technologies are substitutes for each other, meaning that either could potentially be appropriate for a particular diagnostic purpose (see Borgen *et al.*, 2006 for an example). A major disadvantage of CT scans is that they expose the patient to radiation, while MRI scans do not. In the framework of our model, an improvement to CT technology, for example a reduction in patient radiation exposure, could be thought of as a quality improvement of a trailing product relative to a frontier product. Notice that in the last two examples, the trailing technology is not simply a lower-quality version of the frontier technology, but is technologically distinct. Our model applies to these cases as well; all that is required is that the trailing product be a lower-quality substitute in demand.

Our findings have implications for public policy. Given that governments have finite resources with which to encourage innovation, there exists a trade-off between encouraging innovation of new or frontier products and encouraging improvements in existing generic technologies that may be less advanced. For example, support for basic science and university research can help foster frontier innovations, but is unlikely to lead to improvements in well-established technologies. Support for corporate R&D, whether direct or through tax incentives, can lead to improvement in either type of product. In contrast, a broader tax incentive, such as accelerated depreciation of all investments including product redesign, will likely have a relatively larger effect at the trailing edge. As a specific example, the U.S. government faces such a trade-off with respect to investments in improving healthcare. The Agency for Healthcare Research and Quality (AHRQ) conducts and funds a variety of research activities to develop new methods of measuring and improving the quality of patient medical care; these activities improve the "frontier" of care. At the same time, the U.S. government also funds and operates, through the Centers for Medicare and Medicaid Services (CMS), the Electronic Health Record (EHR) Incentive Programs for Medicare and Medicaid, which establish incentives for providers who participate in those programs to adopt existing EHR technologies; these activities improve quality of care by bringing providers closer to the existing frontier. Our results are also relevant to public policies that do not involve expenditures or taxation, such as those related to intellectual property (IP) protection. For example, a stricter IP policy, such as stronger patents, might provide stronger incentives for investment in frontier innovation, but at the expense of technology diffusion or imitation, resulting in higher quality at the frontier and lower quality inside it. Our model speaks to the welfare implications of such quality differences.

We use a standard model of vertical differentiation, and also adopt the common parametric assumption that the distribution of consumer willingness-to-pay for quality is distributed uniformly. This assumption yields linear demand structures and closed form expressions for our comparative statics results. Though these results, being derived from a parametric model, may not always generalize, they do yield a number of insights. In our parametric model, an increase in the quality of the dominant firm's product leads to an increase in total welfare. The basic analytics behind this result are as follows. A quality increase of the dominant firm's product provides infra-marginal consumers of that product with higher quality at the same social cost of production, which tends to increase total welfare. In the special case where quality changes have no effect on who buys which product (which in our model occurs when the two marginal costs are equal), the analysis described above is complete. But if the two costs are not equal, then changes in quality cause some customers to switch products. When consumers switch from the generic (fringe) product to the branded (dominant firm's) product, they consume a product of higher value. This product is also more expensive to produce, but the net effect of the switches on total welfare is positive. When consumers switch from the branded product to the generic, these effects are reversed and the net effect of the switches is negative; however, the aggregate effect is positive in this case as well.

In contrast, an increase in the quality of the fringe firms' product has an ambiguous effect on total welfare. As in the case of the dominant firm, a quality increase to the fringe firms' product benefits infra-marginal fringe firm consumers. But all else equal, consumers who buy the fringe firms' product value quality by less than do those who buy the dominant firm's product, so the welfare benefit per infra-marginal consumer is smaller. The total effect across all infra-marginal consumers is also smaller than for an increase in the dominant firm's quality, unless the number of infra-marginal consumers of the fringe firms' product is sufficiently greater than the number of infra-marginal consumers of the dominant firm's product. The effects due to switches are exactly the same as what they are in the case of the dominant firm. There is an additional positive effect of an increase in fringe firm quality that is not present for an increase in dominant firm quality, because an increase in fringe product quality causes some consumers to buy from the fringe instead of not buying at all. The aggregate effect is ambiguous, as stated at the outset. Consumer surplus is increasing in the quality of either product. The analysis is similar to that for total welfare, except that the effects of quality changes on dominant firm profits are given zero weight.

Regarding the comparison between the effects of an increase in dominant firm quality vs. fringe firm quality, we show that under a consumer surplus standard, the latter is unambiguously more valuable than the former. This is because higher fringe firm quality increases the value of the fringe firms' product without increasing its price, and it also, by narrowing the quality gap, reduces the dominant firm's price and profits, leading to a transfer from the dominant firm to consumers. This reduction in profits also has the effect of making consumer surplus more responsive than total welfare to an increase in fringe product quality. In contrast, under a total welfare standard, it is possible that welfare increases by more from an increase in dominant firm quality than from an increase in fringe firm quality. Relatedly, total welfare is more responsive than consumer surplus to an increase in dominant firm quality.

The model in this chapter is based on the framework in Balan and Deltas (2013). However, the questions addressed in that paper are quite different from those addressed here; that paper deals with the quantity and welfare effects of changes in the dominant firm's quality, and touches only tangentially on the effects of changes in fringe firm quality. However, one result from that paper plays a significant role in the results derived in this one. Specifically, that paper shows that the effect of an increase in the dominant firm's quality on its equilibrium quantity depends on how its marginal cost compares to the (common) marginal cost of the fringe firms. Higher quality has no effect on the dominant firm's quantity when the two costs are equal, increases quantity when the dominant firm's costs are higher, and *decreases* quantity when they are lower. In this chapter, we derive closely related results on the effect of fringe product quality on the quantity of either product, as a function of relative marginal costs.

As far as we are aware, there are no other papers that explicitly compare the welfare effects of changes in product quality at the frontier vs. inside the frontier, and certainly not in the case of a dominant firm facing a competitive fringe. But there is a substantial theoretical literature on issues related to ones discussed in this chapter, particularly regarding the effect of market structure on incentives to invest in R&D. We make no attempt to summarize this broad literature, but we mention here a few tangentially relevant papers. Early contributions by Benoit (1985) and Pepall and Richards (1994) analyze the effect of imitation costs on a firm's incentive to invest in developing new products. Greenstein and Ramey (1998) use a vertical differentiation framework similar to ours to analyze the effect of market structure for an existing product on the incentive to invest in developing a new product. Chen and Schwartz (2013) use a similar model to compare the innovation incentives of a monopolist facing no competition with those of a firm that is one of many producers of an older product, which may remain available post-innovation. Finally, Matsushima and Liu (2012) use a model with two dominant firms facing a competitive fringe, and analyze the effect of changes in the fringe firms' cost or quality on R&D investment levels.

2. The Model and Market Equilibrium

Our basic framework follows Balan and Deltas (2013). This framework modifies the standard vertical differentiation duopoly model of Mussa and Rosen (1978) by assuming that a high quality dominant firm competes against a low quality competitive fringe.[1] There is a unit mass of consumers, who differ in their marginal willingness-to-pay for quality. The indirect utility of consumer i for product j is given by

$$U_{ij} = \theta_i s_j, \tag{1}$$

where θ_i is the marginal willingness of consumer i to pay for a unit increase in quality, and s_j is the quality of product j. The parameter θ_i is distributed uniformly on the [0, 1] interval. Fixing the upper and lower bounds of the distribution does not result in any loss of generality, given that the units of

[1] See Beath and Katsoulacos (1991) for a detailed discussion of the foundations of the vertical differentiation literature.

product quality can be arbitrarily rescaled. The value of θ_i can depend on the consumer's intrinsic preferences and also on his or her income.[2] The dominant firm's quality and price are denoted by s_D and P_D, respectively. Those of the fringe are denoted by s_F and P_F.[3] We will sometimes refer to the dominant firm's product as the "branded product," since often (as in pharmaceuticals) it will be a branded product. The fringe's product will sometimes be referred to as the "generic product," since brand is of no importance given that the product is sold by many firms. We assume that $s_D > s_F$ but make no assumptions about the relative values of marginal costs; the dominant firm's marginal cost, c_D, can be greater than, equal to, or less than the (common) fringe firm marginal cost, c_F. That is, the dominant firm's higher quality need not come exclusively from using more expensive inputs, but instead may come from superior technology or some other advantage over the fringe firms.[4] The dominant firm chooses its price to maximize its profits, given its marginal cost. The price of the competitive fringe is equal to c_F. Consumers choose the product that maximizes their utility, net of the product price. Consumers have the option of making no purchase and earning a utility of zero.

In what follows, we assume that both the dominant firm and the competitive fringe have positive market shares in equilibrium and that some consumers choose to purchase neither version of the product. This assumption is equivalent to the set of inequalities given below (Assumption 1), to which we will refer on a number of occasions.

Assumption 1. $1 > \frac{1}{2} + \frac{1}{2}\frac{c_D - c_F}{s_D - s_F} > \frac{c_F}{s_F} > 0.$

We now proceed to the derivation of market shares. The critical value θ_D such that a consumer is indifferent between purchasing from the dominant

[2]The early literature (Gabszewicz and Thisse, 1979; Gabszewics *et al.*, 1986) emphasized differences in income, but the source of the variation in θ is not important for this chapter. See also Shaked and Sutton (1983).

[3]The modeling environment is somewhat simplified relative to that in Balan and Deltas (2013), but with limited loss of generality. The simplifications result in more transparent analytics and closed form solutions. There is also a minor change in notation.

[4]There are alternative ways to define a firm as dominant, for example, based on equilibrium market shares or based on the ratio of quality over production cost. Our definition is the easiest one to use.

firm and purchasing from the fringe is

$$\theta_D s_F - P_F = \theta_D s_D - P_D \Rightarrow \quad (\text{using } P_F = c_F)$$
$$\theta_D = \frac{P_D - c_F}{s_D - s_F}. \tag{2}$$

Every consumer with $\theta_i > \theta_D$ will purchase from the dominant firm. Thus, the demand function of the dominant firm is equal to $Q_D = 1 - \frac{P_D - c_F}{s_D - s_F}$, and the dominant firm chooses P_D to maximize $\pi_D = (P_D - c_D)\left(1 - \frac{P_D - c_F}{s_D - s_F}\right)$, yielding an optimal price of

$$P_D^* = \frac{s_D - s_F + c_D + c_F}{2}. \tag{3}$$

Substituting into the demand function, we obtain the equilibrium sales volume of the dominant firm

$$Q_D^* = \frac{1}{2} - \frac{1}{2}\frac{c_D - c_F}{s_D - s_F}. \tag{4}$$

Substituting P_D^* into (2), we get $\theta_D^* = \frac{1}{2} + \frac{1}{2}\frac{c_D - c_F}{s_D - s_F}$, which Assumption 1 ensures is below 1 (the upper bound of the support of θ). We now turn to comparative statics on the dominant firm's equilibrium price and quantity in (3) and (4). The dominant firm's price is increasing in the quality difference between the branded and the generic product, and also increasing in the production cost of either product. The comparative statics of the dominant firm's sales volume are more interesting. Though sales volume goes up with c_F and down with c_D, as expected, a change in s_D or in s_F has an effect of indeterminate sign. When the dominant firm's cost exceeds that of the fringe, then the expected sign prevails; Q_D^* goes up with s_D and down with s_F. But when the dominant firm's cost is lower than that of the fringe, then its optimal output *decreases* with its own quality and *increases* with the quality of the fringe. When the marginal costs of the firms are equal to each other, the dominant firm's sales volume is independent of either firm's quality.

This surprising result is explained in detail and in a more general framework in Balan and Deltas (2013). The basic intuition is that higher quality of the dominant firm's product causes an outward pivot, rather than a parallel shift, of its residual demand curve. This pivoting of demand causes the marginal revenue curve to rotate clockwise about a point whose height is equal to the fringe firms' (common) marginal cost. When the dominant firm's marginal cost is higher than that of the fringe, the intersection point of its marginal cost and marginal revenue curves moves to the right, and output increases. Similarly, when the dominant firm's marginal cost is lower than that of the fringe, the intersection point moves to the left and quantity falls. When the two marginal costs are equal, the intersection point does not change, and so quantity does not change either.[5]

As for the fringe, perfect competition drives its price to its marginal cost. Thus, the willingness-to-pay for quality, θ_F, of the consumer who is indifferent between purchasing from the fringe and not purchasing at all satisfies

$$\theta_F s_F - P_F = 0 \Rightarrow \quad (\text{using } P_F = c_F)$$
$$\theta_F^* = \frac{c_F}{s_F}. \tag{5}$$

Every consumer with a value of θ_i in the interval $\left[\theta_F^*, \theta_D^*\right]$ purchases from the fringe. Note that Assumption 1 ensures that this interval has positive length. Given that θ_i has a standard uniform distribution, the sales volume of the fringe is given by $Q_F = \frac{P_D - c_F}{s_D - s_F} - \frac{c_F}{s_F}$. Substituting in P_D^* and simplifying we obtain

$$Q_F^* = \frac{1}{2} + \frac{1}{2}\frac{c_D - c_F}{s_D - s_F} - \frac{c_F}{s_F}. \tag{6}$$

It can be easily seen from equation (6) that an increase in the marginal cost of the fringe decreases its sales volume, while an increase in the marginal cost of the dominant firm increases the fringe's sales volume. The comparative statics effect of a change in s_D on Q_F^* is exactly the reverse of its effect on the dominant firm's quantity, since every sale lost by the dominant firm is gained by the fringe (and vice-versa). The effect of a change in s_F is slightly more complicated because a second margin is present, namely the margin between buying from the fringe and not buying at all. On this second margin,

[5] In models with horizontal product differentiation and consumers who value quality equally, an increase in a firm's product quality leads to an increase in that firm's equilibrium sales regardless of relative costs. See, for example, Deltas *et al.* (2013).

an increase in s_F unambiguously increases sales, as some consumers who initially did not buy either product will purchase from the fringe at the higher quality. The net effect can be negative, meaning that an increase in the quality of the fringe firms' product can result in a decrease in its sales, as we show next. The derivative of the generic product sales volume with respect to s_F is

$$\frac{\partial Q_F^*}{\partial s_F} = \frac{1}{2}\frac{c_D - c_F}{(s_D - s_F)^2} + \frac{c_F}{s_F^2}. \tag{7}$$

This is negative if

$$\frac{c_F}{s_F^2} < -\frac{1}{2}\frac{c_D - c_F}{(s_D - s_F)^2} \Rightarrow$$

$$c_F < \frac{s_F^2}{2}\frac{c_F - c_D}{(s_D - s_F)^2}. \tag{8}$$

Notice that the order of marginal costs in the numerator on the right-hand side has been flipped in the last step. This condition could be satisfied if $c_F = \epsilon$, where ϵ is a small positive number that exceeds c_D. Indeed, there are parameter values that can satisfy condition (8) and also Assumption 1.[6] We summarize the above discussion on equilibrium sales volumes in Proposition 1.

Proposition 1 *The dominant firm's sales volume is increasing in s_D and decreasing in s_F if $c_D > c_F$, decreasing in s_D and increasing in s_F if $c_D < c_F$, and invariant to either quality if $c_D = c_F$. These results are reversed for the comparative statics of the fringe's sales volume with respect to s_D. The sales volume of the fringe decreases in s_F only if c_D and c_F are sufficiently small and $c_F > c_D$.*

An examination of this proposition shows that neither the dominant firm's nor the fringe's sales volume is guaranteed to increase in its own quality. However, if an increase in the fringe's quality reduces its sales volume, then it must be the case that an increase in the dominant firm's quality decreases its sales volume as well, but the reverse does not

[6] For example, when $c_F = \frac{1}{50}$, $c_D = \frac{1}{100}$, $s_F = \frac{4}{5}$, and $s_D = 1$, both Assumption 1 and inequality (8) are satisfied. Moreover, $Q_D = \frac{21}{40}$, $Q_F = \frac{9}{20}$, and $P_D = \frac{23}{200}$.

necessarily hold. We next turn to the welfare effects of changes in the dominant firm or fringe firm quality.

3. Consumer Surplus and Total Welfare

In this section, we evaluate the total welfare, W, and consumer surplus, CS, and we derive their comparative statics with respect to the quality of the two products. Suppressing the stars in the critical values of θ, total welfare is given by

$$\begin{aligned} W &= \int_{\theta_D}^{1} \theta s_D - c_D \, d\theta + \int_{\theta_F}^{\theta_D} \theta s_F - c_F \, d\theta \\ &= \left(\frac{1}{2} s_D \theta^2 - c_D \theta\right)\Bigg|_{\theta=\theta_D}^{\theta=1} + \left(\frac{1}{2} s_F \theta^2 - c_F \theta\right)\Bigg|_{\theta=\theta_F}^{\theta=\theta_D} \\ &= \frac{s_D}{2} - c_D - \left(\frac{s_D}{2}\theta_D^2 - c_D\theta_D\right) + \frac{s_F}{2}\theta_D^2 - c_F\theta_D - \left(\frac{s_F}{2}\theta_F^2 - c_F\theta_F\right) \\ &= \frac{s_D}{2} - \frac{s_D}{2}\theta_D^2 + \frac{s_F}{2}\theta_D^2 - \frac{s_F}{2}\theta_F^2 - c_D(1-\theta_D) - c_F(\theta_D - \theta_F) \\ &= \frac{s_D}{2} - \frac{s_D - s_F}{2}(1 - Q_D)^2 - \frac{s_F}{2}(1 - Q_F - Q_D)^2 - c_D Q_D - c_F Q_F, \end{aligned} \tag{9}$$

where the last line replaces θ_D and θ_F with the corresponding functions of Q_D and Q_F. Substituting in the equilibrium values of Q_F^* and Q_D^* and simplifying we get

$$W = \frac{1}{8}\left(3s_D + s_F - 6c_D - 2c_F + \frac{3(c_D - c_F)^2}{s_D - s_F} + \frac{4c_F^2}{s_F}\right). \tag{10}$$

Consumer surplus is given by

$$\begin{aligned} CS &= \int_{\theta_D}^{1} \theta s_D - P_D \, d\theta + \int_{\theta_F}^{\theta_D} \theta s_F - P_F \, d\theta \\ &= \left(\frac{1}{2} s_D \theta^2 - P_D \theta\right)\Bigg|_{\theta=\theta_D}^{\theta=1} + \left(\frac{1}{2} s_F \theta^2 - P_F \theta\right)\Bigg|_{\theta=\theta_F}^{\theta=\theta_D} \\ &= \frac{s_D}{2} - P_D - \left(\frac{s_D}{2}\theta_D^2 - P_D\theta_D\right) + \frac{s_F}{2}\theta_D^2 - P_F\theta_D - \left(\frac{s_F}{2}\theta_F^2 - P_F\theta_F\right) \end{aligned}$$

$$
\begin{aligned}
&= \frac{s_D}{2} - \frac{s_D}{2}\theta_D^2 + \frac{s_F}{2}\theta_D^2 - \frac{s_F}{2}\theta_F^2 - P_D(1-\theta_D) - P_F(\theta_D - \theta_F) \\
&= \frac{s_D}{2} - \frac{s_D - s_F}{2}(1-Q_D)^2 - \frac{s_F}{2}(1 - Q_F - Q_D)^2 \\
&\quad - P_D Q_D - P_F Q_F, \qquad (11)
\end{aligned}
$$

where, as above, the last line replaces θ_D and θ_F with the corresponding functions of Q_D and Q_F. Substituting in the equilibrium values of Q_F^* and Q_D^* and simplifying we get

$$
CS = \frac{1}{8}\left(s_D + 3s_F - 2c_D - 6c_F + \frac{(c_D - c_F)^2}{s_D - s_F} + \frac{4c_F^2}{s_F}\right). \qquad (12)
$$

We now derive the comparative statics of total welfare and consumer surplus with respect to changes in product quality.[7] We do not consider simultaneous changes in production costs and product quality because the partial effect of increases in marginal costs are known. We start with the comparative statics of total welfare with respect to the quality of the branded good, whose derivation is immediate. They are stated in Proposition 2.

Proposition 2 *When consumer willingness-to-pay for quality, θ, is distributed $U[0, 1]$, an increase in s_D increases welfare. In particular,*

$$
\frac{\partial W}{\partial s_D} = \frac{1}{8}\left(3 - \frac{3(c_D - c_F)^2}{(s_D - s_F)^2}\right). \qquad (13)
$$

This is positive if $\frac{c_D - c_F}{s_D - s_F} < 1$, which is directly implied by Assumption 1.

We now examine more closely the expression in Proposition 2, starting with the case where $c_D = c_F$. Recall that when the dominant and the fringe firms have the same marginal cost, a change in s_D does not change the dominant firm's output. It is easy to see that in this case, the effect of an increase in the dominant firm's quality must increase total welfare; the number of consumers who buy the dominant firm's product does not change,

[7] Strictly speaking, the comparative statics approach implies that quality changes are "exogenous," for example, being different realizations of a stochastic process, such as an R&D project with an uncertain outcome. However, even if quality changes are the result of deterministic profit-maximizing firm decisions, the effect of quality changes on W and CS would still be as derived here.

and they enjoy a higher-quality product with no change in production costs. When $c_D \neq c_F$, an increase in s_D affects the dominant firm's quantity, which introduces an additional welfare effect. As in the $c_D = c_F$ case, infra-marginal consumers enjoy higher quality at the same production cost, which tends to increase welfare. When $c_D > c_F$, an increase in s_D also causes some consumers to switch from the fringe to the dominant firm. These consumers get a higher-quality product but at a higher production cost. Since $\theta_D(s_D - s_F) = P_D - c_F > c_D - c_F$ (see equation 2), the net contribution of these switches to welfare is positive, and thus the aggregate effect is also positive. When $c_D < c_F$, higher s_D causes some consumers to switch from the dominant firm to the fringe, getting a lower-quality product but at a lower production cost. Under Assumption 1, the net contribution of these switches to welfare is negative, but not by enough to reverse the sign of the derivative when θ is distributed uniformly (as assumed here).[8]

Also note that marginal costs enter in (13) only though the absolute value of their difference, which has a negative sign. When c_D is much greater than c_F, there are very few consumers of the dominant firm's product, so the welfare gain from an increase in s_D is small. When c_D is much smaller than c_F, an increase in s_D causes many consumers to switch from the dominant firm to the fringe, which also causes the welfare gain to be small.

We next derive the comparative statics of welfare with respect to the generic product, which are reported in Proposition 3.

Proposition 3 *When consumer willingness-to-pay for quality, θ, is distributed $U[0, 1]$, an increase in s_F is not guaranteed to increase welfare. In particular,*

$$\frac{\partial W}{\partial s_F} = \frac{1}{8}\left(1 + \frac{3(c_D - c_F)^2}{(s_D - s_F)^2} - \frac{4c_F^2}{s_F^2}\right), \tag{14}$$

which under Assumption 1 is positive when $c_D \leq c_F$, but is of ambiguous sign when $c_D > c_F$.

Proof. Notice that c_D enters only in the second term inside the bracket of Equation (14), and that this non-negative term is minimized (and becomes

---

[8]As discussed in Balan and Deltas (2013), this result is not guaranteed to hold for non-uniformly distributed θ.

zero) when setting $c_D = c_F$. Therefore, a starting point is to consider this case. Notice that under the condition $c_D = c_F$, Assumption 1 becomes $\frac{c_F}{s_F} < \frac{1}{2} \Rightarrow \frac{4c_F^2}{s_F^2} < 1$. This demonstrates that $\frac{\partial W}{\partial s_F} > 0$ when $c_D = c_F$. This might appear to guarantee that the derivative is also positive when $c_D \neq c_F$, since the derivative is increasing in the absolute value of the difference between the two marginal costs. However, this is not the case. Recall that under Assumption 1, $\frac{c_F}{s_F} < \frac{1}{2} + \frac{1}{2}\frac{c_D - c_F}{s_D - s_F}$, the right-hand side of which is increasing in $c_D - c_F$. Therefore, when $c_D > c_F$, $\frac{c_F}{s_F}$ can take on larger values. Since an increase in this term reduces $\frac{\partial W}{\partial s_F}$, sufficiently high values of $\frac{c_F}{s_F}$ can make the derivative turn negative. This is demonstrated in Figure 1 which plots $\frac{\partial W}{\partial s_F}$ as a function of c_F for specific values of the remaining parameters (in particular, $c_D = \frac{9}{32}$, $s_D = 1$, and $s_F = \frac{1}{4}$).[9]

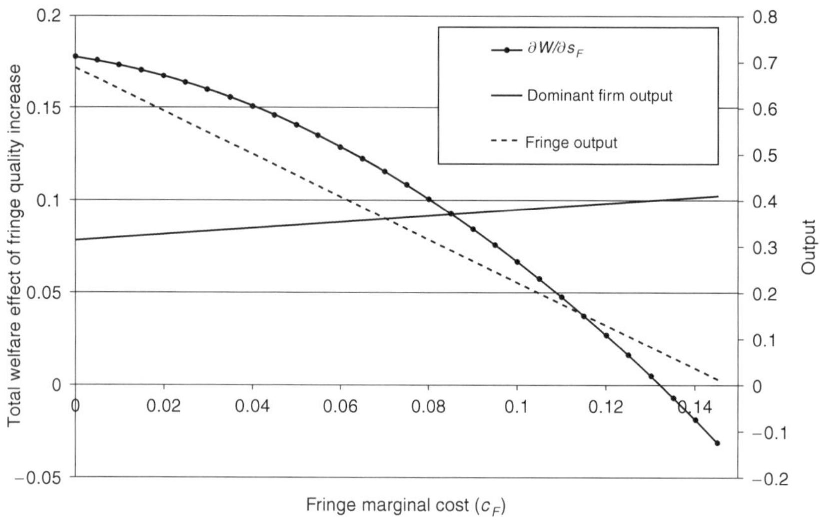

Figure 1. Total welfare effect of fringe quality increase (left axis) and associated firm outputs (right axis) as a function of fringe marginal cost, c_F, with $c_D = \frac{9}{32}$, $s_D = 1$, and $s_F = \frac{1}{4}$.

[9]Figure 1 also plots the equilibrium quantities for the dominant firm and the fringe, showing that both are indeed positive throughout the plotted range. Note that an increase in s_F decreases total welfare when the market share of the fringe is very small. In this case, the negative effect on welfare from consumers switching from the dominant firm to the fringe outweighs the positive effect on welfare from the increased utility of the continuing consumers of the fringe (in Figure 1 $c_D > c_F$, so a narrowing of the quality gap leads to consumer switching from the dominant firm to the fringe).

For values of c_F that are sufficiently high, but are still low enough for the fringe market share to be positive, total welfare decreases with s_F. By contrast, when $c_D < c_F$, the constraint in Assumption 1 becomes more binding, and thus $\frac{\partial W}{\partial s_F}$ is guaranteed to be positive. □

We now turn to the intuition behind Proposition 3. As above, we begin with the case where $c_D = c_F$. Once again, an increase in s_F does not cause any consumers to switch from the dominant firm to the fringe, or vice-versa; the welfare change attributed to the continuing consumers of the fringe product from an increase in s_F is positive. An increase in s_F does cause some consumers to switch from not buying at all to buying from the fringe, which by revealed preference also increases welfare. When $c_D \neq c_F$, these effects are still present (and still tend to increase welfare), but now there is also an effect due to switching from the dominant firm to the fringe, or vice-versa. This latter effect is exactly the same as in the comparative statics on s_D described above, but in the opposite direction, which is why the right-hand side of expressions (13) and (14) have a common term, but with opposite signs. As the proof of Proposition 3 demonstrates, it is possible that the net welfare effect can be negative.

We now show that not only is the effect of an increase in s_F on welfare of ambiguous sign, but so is the difference between $\frac{\partial W}{\partial s_D}$ and $\frac{\partial W}{\partial s_F}$, even under the assumption of uniformly distributed θ. This fact, which is relevant for the appropriate targeting of potentially scarce public resources to encourage R&D, is stated in Corollary 1.

Corollary 1 *The difference between* $\frac{\partial W}{\partial s_D}$ *and* $\frac{\partial W}{\partial s_F}$ *can be written as*

$$\frac{\partial W}{\partial s_D} - \frac{\partial W}{\partial s_F} = \frac{1}{8}\left(2 - \frac{6(c_D - c_F)^2}{(s_D - s_F)^2} + \frac{4c_F^2}{s_F^2}\right). \tag{15}$$

This is positive when c_D *is not too different from* c_F*, but is of ambiguous sign otherwise.*

As can be seen in (4) and (6) above, when $c_D = c_F$, then $Q_D^* = \frac{1}{2}$, and when (in the limit) $c_F \approx 0$, then $Q_F^* \approx \frac{1}{2}$ as well. In this special case, an increase in s_D or in s_F each affect half of all consumers. However, the consumers who buy from the dominant firm have higher values of θ (they value the quality increase more), so the difference between the two derivatives is positive. Under an alternative assumption regarding the distribution of θ, this effect can be reversed only if the initial number of fringe firm customers is sufficiently greater than dominant firm customers, or if the distribution of θ above the median has a sufficiently short-tail.

Higher values of c_F lead more consumers to not buy the product at all, and therefore to more consumers who do not benefit from an improvement in fringe quality. This tends to increase the difference between the two derivatives. The difference between the derivatives is decreasing in the absolute value of the cost difference, $|c_D - c_F|$. When this difference is large enough, it is possible that $\frac{\partial W}{\partial s_D} - \frac{\partial W}{\partial s_F} < 0$, i.e., that welfare is more responsive to an increase in the quality of the generic product than to an increase in the quality of the branded product. This is illustrated in Figure 2, which plots $\frac{\partial W}{\partial s_D} - \frac{\partial W}{\partial s_F}$ as a function of c_F for specific values of the remaining parameters (in particular, for $c_D = \frac{155}{256}$, $s_D = 1$, and $s_F = \frac{1}{16}$). For low values of c_F, when the difference $c_D - c_F$ is large, the difference in the derivatives is negative (an increase in s_F has a bigger effect on welfare than an increase in s_D), while the converse is true for high values of c_F. Figure 2 also plots the equilibrium quantities for the dominant firm and the

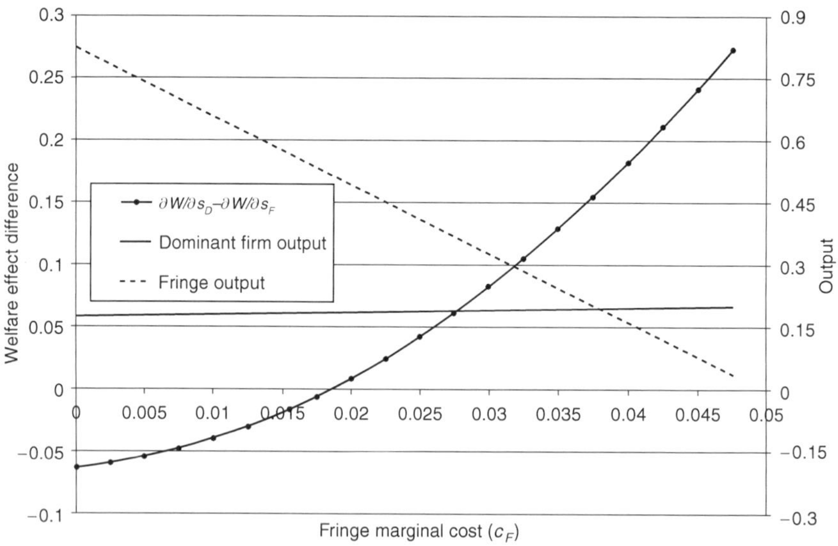

Figure 2. Difference in total welfare effects of dominant firm vs. fringe firm quality increases (left axis) and associated firm outputs (right axis) as a function of fringe marginal cost, c_F, with $c_D = \frac{155}{256}$, $s_D = 1$, and $s_F = \frac{1}{16}$.

fringe, showing that they are indeed positive throughout the plotted range. Note that when total welfare is more responsive to fringe quality than to dominant firm quality, the market share of the fringe greatly exceeds that of the dominant firm, which is consistent with the intuition conveyed earlier in this section.

We now turn our attention to the comparative statics on consumer surplus, which are derived in Proposition 4.

Proposition 4 *When consumer willingness-to-pay for quality, θ, is distributed $U[0, 1]$, an increase in either s_D or s_F increases consumer surplus. In particular,*

$$\frac{\partial CS}{\partial s_D} = \frac{1}{8}\left(1 - \frac{(c_D - c_F)^2}{(s_D - s_F)^2}\right), \tag{16}$$

and

$$\frac{\partial CS}{\partial s_F} = \frac{1}{8}\left(3 + \frac{(c_D - c_F)^2}{(s_D - s_F)^2} - \frac{4c_F^2}{s_F^2}\right) \tag{17}$$

which are both positive under Assumption 1.

Proof. The derivative of *CS* with respect to s_D can easily be shown to be positive following the first inequality of Assumption 1, which implies that $\frac{c_D - c_F}{s_D - s_F} < 1$. Now consider the derivative of *CS* with respect to s_F. From the second inequality of Assumption 1, we have $1 + \frac{c_D - c_F}{s_D - s_F} > \frac{2c_F}{s_F}$. Given that both sides are positive, squaring yields $1 + \frac{(c_D - c_F)^2}{(s_D - s_F)^2} + 2\frac{c_D - c_F}{s_D - s_F} > \frac{4c_F^2}{s_F^2}$. Since from Assumption 1 we know that $\frac{c_D - c_F}{s_D - s_F} < 1$, replacing $\frac{c_D - c_F}{s_D - s_F}$ by 1 in the previous inequality implies that $1 + \frac{(c_D - c_F)^2}{(s_D - s_F)^2} + 2 > \frac{4c_F^2}{s_F^2}$ which finally implies that the bracketed expression in equation (17) is positive. □

Proposition 4 states that consumer surplus is unambiguously increasing in s_D. We should note that this result does not necessary hold for a general distribution of θ, as was discussed in Balan and Deltas (2013). Proposition 4 also states that consumer surplus is unambiguously increasing in s_F. This is in contrast to Proposition 3, which showed that $\frac{\partial W}{\partial s_F}$ is of ambiguous sign. The reason is that part of the effect of higher s_F is to lower dominant firm price and profit, which tends to decrease welfare but increase consumer surplus.

Though, as Proposition 4 states, consumer surplus increases in both s_D and s_F, one can show that it is more responsive to changes in s_F. This is important from a policy standpoint if the government has limited resources to spend on encouraging R&D. Comparing expressions (16) and (17), it is easy to see that when $c_D = c_F$ and $c_F = 0$, the increase in consumer surplus is larger when s_F goes up than when s_D goes up ($\frac{3}{8}$ instead of $\frac{1}{8}$). Corollary 2, the proof of which parallels arguments in the proof of Proposition 4, shows that this ranking holds more generally.

Corollary 2 *The difference between* $\frac{\partial CS}{\partial s_D}$ *and* $\frac{\partial CS}{\partial s_F}$ *is given by*

$$\frac{\partial CS}{\partial s_D} - \frac{\partial CS}{\partial s_F} = \frac{1}{8}\left(-2 - \frac{2(c_D - c_F)^2}{(s_D - s_F)^2} + \frac{4c_F^2}{s_F^2}\right) < 0. \tag{18}$$

This expression is always negative, i.e., consumers always benefit from an improvement in the fringe firm's quality by more than from an increase in the dominant firm's quality. One reason for this is that an increase in s_F benefits not only the consumers of the generic product, but also the consumers of the branded product by forcing the dominant firm to reduce prices. That is, an increase in s_F also has a redistributive effect by shifting surplus from the dominant firm to its consumers.[10]

We conclude this section with a discussion of the distribution of gains from innovation, i.e., we pose the question of who benefits from innovation: the consumers or the firms? Let us first examine the expression (16) and compare it with that in Proposition 2. It is easy to see that when $c_D = c_F$, consumer surplus is less responsive than total welfare to an increase in s_D ($\frac{1}{8}$ instead of $\frac{3}{8}$), because some of the welfare increase is captured by the dominant firm in the form of higher prices. It is possible to show that $\frac{\partial W}{\partial s_D} > \frac{\partial CS}{\partial s_D}$ even when the costs are different, and for the same reason. In other words, an innovation by the dominant firm benefits society by more than it benefits consumers, since only part of the welfare gain is reflected in consumer surplus and the rest contributes to increased profits. Let us now

[10]It is also easily shown that $\frac{\partial CS}{\partial s_D} - \frac{\partial CS}{\partial s_F} < \frac{\partial W}{\partial s_D} - \frac{\partial W}{\partial s_F}$, i.e., the difference in the responsiveness of total welfare to changes in s_D and s_F always exceeds that of consumer surplus.

examine the expression (14) and compare it with (17). It is easy to see that when $c_D = c_F$, consumer surplus is more responsive than total welfare to an increase in s_F. In fact, $\frac{\partial W}{\partial s_F} < \frac{\partial CS}{\partial s_F}$ even when the costs are different, and for the same reasons as those described in the discussion following the proof of Proposition 4. Intuitively, an increase in fringe quality does not increase fringe profits, since fringe firms are perfectly competitive with constant marginal cost. The increase in fringe quality always reduces the profits of the dominant firm, by making the generic product a closer substitute to the branded product. Thus, aggregate profits go down, which directly implies that consumer surplus goes up by more than total welfare.

4. Concluding Remarks

In this chapter, we examine the effects of increases in product quality on total welfare and on consumer surplus. We show that these effects differ depending on whether the quality increase is to the product of a dominant branded firm at the technological frontier, or to the products of generic fringe firms inside the frontier. We show that these effects are not always positive, and that the welfare and consumer surplus effects of a quality improvement to the branded product vs. the generic products cannot always be unambiguously ranked.

Our framework abstracts from the incentives of firms to undertake costly investments in increasing the quality of their products, and also from the fact that the cost of a given quality increase is likely different for branded firms than for generic firms. Our results, then, are best viewed as comparative statics on the continuation payoffs of a given quality increase abstracting from any up-front costs. Endogenizing R&D for the fringe would require a somewhat different cost structure than the one used in this chapter, so that fringe firms earn some quasi-rents, or alternatively an assumption that firms compete in quantities rather than in prices.[11] Either assumption would increase the complexity of the modeling. Moreover, our results should not be taken to the limit: even under the conditions where marginal improvements to fringe product quality are more valuable than are marginal improvements to branded product quality, eventually significant

[11]See Motta (1993) for some related discussion.

increases in total welfare and consumer surplus cannot be achieved with improvements in fringe firm quality but rather require improvements at the technological frontier.

The results of this chapter can be thought of as illustrations of more general principles. When a technological improvement interacts with market imperfections and reduces them, the benefits are not limited to the benefits of a better product, but also include the benefits of a more competitive market structure. Similarly, if the technological improvement aggravates market imperfections, then the net benefit will be smaller and possibly negative.

References

Balan, D. and G. Deltas (2013). "Better Product at Same Cost, Lower Sales and Lower Welfare," *International Journal of Industrial Organization*, 31, pp. 322–330.

Beath, J. and Y. Katsoulacos (1991). *The Economic Theory of Product Differentiation*, Cambridge University Press, Cambridge, UK.

Benoit, J-P. (1985). "Innovation and Imitation in a Duopoly," *Review of Economic Studies*, 52, pp. 99–106.

Borgen, L., H. Ostensen, E. Stranden, H. M. Olerud and T. E. Gudmundsen (2006). "Shift in Imaging Modalities of the Spine through 25 Years and its Impact on Patient Ionizing Radiation Doses," *European Journal of Radiology*, 60, pp. 115–119.

Chen, Y. and M. Schwartz (2013). "Product Innovation Incentives: Monopoly vs. Competition," *Journal of Economics and Management Strategy*, 22, pp. 513–528.

Deltas, G., D. Harrington and M. Khanna (2013). "Oligopolies with (Somewhat) Environmentally Conscious Consumers: Market Equilibrium and Regulatory Intervention," *Journal of Economics and Management Strategy*, 22(3), Fall, pp. 640–667.

Gabszewicz, J. J., A. Shaked and J. Sutton (1986). "Segmenting the Market: The Monopolist's Optimal Product Mix," *Journal of Economic Theory*, 39, pp. 273–289.

Gabszewicz, J. J. and J.-F. Thisse (1979). "Price Competition, Quality and Income Disparities," *Journal of Economic Theory*, 20, pp. 340–359.

Greenstein S. and G. Ramey (1998). "Market Structure, Innovation and Vertical Product Differentiation," *International Journal of Industrial Organization*, 16, pp. 285–311.

Matsushima, N. and R.-J. Liu (2012). "Quality Improvement to Meet Competitive Fringe," *Osaka University Institute of Social and Economic Research Discussion Paper* No. 854.

Motta, M. (1993). "Endogenous Quality Choice: Price vs. Quantity Competition," *Journal of Industrial Economics*, 41, pp. 113–131.

Mussa M. and S. Rosen (1978). "Monopoly and Product Quality," *Journal of Economic Theory*, 18, pp. 301–317.

Pepall, L. M. and D. J. Richards (1994). "Innovation, Imitation, and Social Welfare," *Southern Journal of Economics*, 60, pp. 673–684.

Shaked, A. and J. Sutton (1983). "Natural Oligopolies," *Econometrica*, 51, pp. 1469–1483.

Chapter 5

Industry Structure and Pricing Over the Business Cycle

Yossi Spiegel
Tel Aviv University, CEPR, and ZEW
spiegel@post.tau.ac.il

Konrad Stahl
Universität Mannheim, CEPR, CESifo, and ZEW
kos@econ.uni-mannheim.de

Abstract

We consider the interaction between an incumbent firm and a potential entrant, and examine how this interaction is affected by demand fluctuations. Our model gives rise to procyclical entry, prices, and price-cost margins, although the average price in the market can be countercyclical if the entrant is a first mover, and capacity utilization can be either pro- or countercyclical if the incumbent is a first mover. Moreover, our results show that entry deterrence by the incumbent firm can either amplify or dampen the effect of demand fluctuations on prices, price-cost margins, and capacity utilization.

Keywords: Price competition, business cycle, entry, entry deterrence.

JEL Classification Codes: D43, L41.

1. Introduction

The pricing behavior of firms over the business cycle has been the subject of an ongoing debate among economists. In particular, there is a debate on whether price-cost margins and profitability are pro- or countercyclical. One reason why economists pay attention to the pro- or countercyclicality of price-cost margins and profitability is because they can either amplify or dampen the effects of other business cycle shocks. For instance, high price-cost margins in recessions keep prices from falling and hence may slow down the recovery process. Likewise, low price-cost margins in booms keep prices low and hence boost demand and may extend the boom. Moreover, understanding how market structure and prices respond to external shocks is one of the core issues in Industrial Organization.

There is an extensive empirical literature on the cyclical behavior of prices and price-cost margins. The evidence in this literature is mixed. Domowitz *et al.* (1986a, b, 1987, 1988) find that price-cost margins in U.S. manufacturing industries are procyclical in concentrated industries, but tend to be countercyclical in relatively unconcentrated industries. Price-cost margins are especially procyclical in intermediate goods industries, in non-durable goods industries, in capital-intensive industries, and in low price-cost margin industries. Haskel *et al.* (1995) obtain similar results for UK manufacturing industries.

Other authors, however, find strong evidence for countercyclical price-cost margins, including Bils (1987) and Rotemberg and Woodford (1991) for U.S. data, Portier (1995) for French data, and Oliveira Martins *et al.* (1996) for 14 OECD countries.[1] More recently, Nekarda and Ramey (2013) have revisited the methodology used by, among others, Bils (1987) and Rotemberg and Woodford (1999). Using updated empirical methods and updated U.S. data, they show that prices over marginal costs are procyclical, conditional on technology shocks, and either procyclical or acyclical, conditional on demand shocks. These results hold both when they use quarterly aggregate data on the U.S. private economy, as well as when they use annual four-digit manufacturing data.

A possible reason why the empirical evidence is inconclusive is that entry and exit, and therefore the structure of the industry, are also affected by business cycles. This suggests that in order to fully understand how prices and price-cost margins vary over the business cycle, one needs to study the joint determination of industry structure and pricing. In this chapter, we develop a simple theoretical model intended to examine the nexus between prices and entry in response to demand shocks. To this end, we consider two

[1]Oliveira Martins *et al.* (1996) find that price-cost margins are especially countercyclical in concentrated industries. They attribute this finding to "increased competition during economic booms" which is "likely to be more apparent for the industries characterized by the dominance of large firms with market power."

firms which produce a homogenous product and compete by setting prices. The two firms face a step demand function; the quantity demanded and the willingness of consumers to pay are both larger in booms than in recessions. The two firms differ in two respects. First, firm 1 is an incumbent, while firm 2 is a potential entrant and needs to incur an avoidable fixed cost in order to enter the market. Second, firm 1 has a larger capacity than firm 2. We consider both the timing where firm 1 is a first mover, as well as the opposite timing where firm 2 is a first mover.[2]

In spite of its simplicity, our model yields predictions on the cyclical behavior of prices, price-cost margins, output levels, profitability, entry, and capacity utilization. In particular, we find that entry, prices, and price-cost margins are all procyclical, regardless of which firm is a first mover. By contrast, the average price in the market can be countercyclical if firm 2 is a first mover and firm 1's capacity utilization can be either pro- or countercyclical when firm 1 is a first mover. Moreover, our analysis shows that prices, price-cost margins, and capacity utilization can be more or less volatile than the demand function. This implies that entry deterrence by the incumbent firm can either amplify or dampen the effect of demand fluctuations on these variables.

The theoretical literature on the cyclicality of prices and price-cost margins can be roughly divided into four classes of models. First, price-cost margins will be cyclical if either prices or marginal costs are rigid. For instance, if prices are sticky while marginal costs vary procyclically, then price-cost margins are countercyclical. This explanation, however, also implies that profits should be countercyclical, which is at odds with empirical evidence (see e.g., Rotemberg and Woodford (1999)). By contrast, if marginal costs are rigid while prices are procyclical, then price-cost margins will also tend to be procyclical.[3]

Second, several authors argue that price-cost margins are countercyclical because the elasticity of demand is higher in booms than in recessions; the inverse elasticity rule then implies that price-cost margins should be

[2]When the two firms move simultaneously, our model is essentially a Bertrand duopoly with capacity constraints and hence it does not admit an equilibrium in pure strategies. We do not study the resulting mixed strategy equilibrium in this chapter.

[3]For instance, Domowitz *et al.* (1986b) argue that, due to a large degree of unionization in concentrated industries, real wages, which are a main contributor to costs, tend to be rigid.

lower in booms. Warner and Barsky (1995) argue that demand is more elastic in booms because each consumer wishes to buy more units in high demand states (e.g., holidays and weekends) and hence price reductions in these states generate more sales. In Bils (1989) and in Klemperer (1995), a firm faces a mix of repeat and new customers. The latter have a lower willingness-to-pay.[4] In booms, there are more new customers who respond to low prices, so demand is more elastic than in recessions. Edmond and Veldkamp (2009) argue that demand is more elastic in booms because consumers' income, and hence buyers' willingness-to-pay, are less dispersed than in recessions. As a result, price reductions in booms attract more consumers. In all of these models, however, strategic interaction among firms, which is the main driving force in our model, does not play a role.

Third, some authors like Gottfries (1991) and Chevalier and Scharfstein (1996) develop models in which price-cost margins can be countercyclical due to capital market imperfections. Firms face a trade-off between raising prices and boosting their short-run profits, and keeping prices low in order to build long-run market share. In Gottfries (1991), cash flows during recessions are low relative to liabilities, so firms give more weight to their short-run goals and set high prices. By contrast, in booms, firms can meet their financial obligations, and hence they give more weight to long-term goals which justify low prices. In Chevalier and Scharfstein (1996), firms favor short-term goals during recessions because their low cash flow during recessions mean that they face a risk of bankruptcy; this creates a debt overhang problem, which makes firms more short-term oriented. They provide empirical support for their model using data from the U.S. supermarket industry.

Our model belongs to the fourth class of models, in which the cyclicality of price-cost margins is due to strategic interaction among firms. Green and Porter (1984) consider an infinitely-repeated oligopoly model in which firms are subject to unobserved demand shocks. When sales are low, firms

[4]In Bils (1989), the good is an experience good. New customers have a lower willingness-to-pay because they are still unsure about the good's quality. In Klemperer (1995), the lower willingness-to-pay is due to the fact that new customers need to pay a switching cost when they adopt the firm's product for the first time.

are unsure whether this is due to low demand or to a deviation by a rival firm from a collusive arrangement. To sustain collusion, firms start periodic price wars when demand is low and hence the equilibrium features high collusive prices in booms and low competitive prices in recessions.

By contrast, Rotemberg and Saloner (1986) consider an infinitely-repeated oligopoly model with publicly observable *i.i.d.* demand shocks. During booms, when demand is high, firms are more tempted to deviate from collusion and steal market share. Hence, the collusive price must adjust downward to eliminate the incentive of firms to deviate.[5] Haltiwanger and Harrington (1991) consider a model with deterministic demand fluctuations. They define booms as periods in which demand is increasing and recessions as periods in which demand is decreasing. Since the future gain from collusion is lower when demand is decreasing, collusive prices must decrease to eliminate the incentive of firms to deviate. Hence, for the same level of demand, the collusive price is lower during periods of falling demand than during periods of rising demand.[6] Bagwell and Staiger (1997) consider a model in which demand follows a Markovian structure and identify booms with periods of fast-growing demand and recessions with periods of slow-growing demand. They show that collusive prices move procyclically when demand growth rates are positively correlated over time and countercyclically when they are negatively correlated over time.[7]

---

[5]Staiger and Wolak (1992) consider a related model in which firms must determine their capacities at the start of each period before demand shocks are realized. They show that collusion tends to break down in periods of low demand when firms have excess capacity. Ellison (1994) assesses the applicability of the Green and Porter (1984) and Rotemberg and Saloner (1986) models, using data from the "Joint Executive Committee" railroad cartel from the late 19th century. His estimates provide some support for the predictions of the Green and Porter model.

[6]Fabra (2006) shows that this prediction can be overturned if firms' capacities are sufficiently small. Rosenbaum and Sukharomana (2001) use data from the U.S. Portland cement industry and find support for Haltiwanger and Harrington's predictions that for a given level of demand, the price in the rising part of the cycle is above the price in the falling part of the cycle and that profits reach a peak before market demand.

[7]Galeotti and Schiantarelli (1998) examine data on 19 U.S. industrial sectors over the period 1949–1987 and show that price-cost margins are negatively related to the current state of demand and positively related to expected future demand. This evidence is consistent with Haltiwanger and Harrington (1991) and Bagwell and Staiger (1997).

In these models, demand fluctuations affect the ability of firms to collude. In our model by contrast, demand fluctuations affect the incentive of an incumbent firm to either accommodate or deter an entrant. Hence, our model yields results not only on the cyclicality of prices, but also on the cyclicality of entry and capacity utilization.[8] These results are essentially robust to whether the incumbent or the entrant are first movers. In addition, when the entrant is the first mover, our model also gives rise to price dispersion and shows that it can be either larger or smaller in booms than in recessions.

The rest of this chapter is organized as follows. In Section 2, we describe the model. In Section 3, we characterize the equilibrium under the assumption that firm 1 is a first mover and in Section 4, we consider the opposite situation in which firm 2 is a first mover. Concluding remarks are in Section 5.

2. The Model

Two price-setting firms produce a homogeneous product and face a step demand function that depends on the state of the economy, which is either a boom (state b), or a recession (state r). In booms, consumers wish to buy Q^b units and their willingness-to-pay per unit is α^b, while in recessions, they wish to buy Q^r units and their willingness-to-pay per unit is α^r, where $Q^b > Q^r$ and $\alpha^b > \alpha^r$. That is, consumers wish to buy more and are willing to pay more in booms than in recessions. Albeit simple, this demand specification allows us to conduct separately two interesting comparisons: one is between the variation in consumers' willingness-to-pay

[8]Portier (1995) also studies the joint determination of entry and prices in the context of a simple quantity competition model with an incumbent firm, who acts as a Stackelberg leader, and a potential entrant. In the equilibrium of his model, the number of firms is procyclical and the price (there are no marginal costs in his model so the price is also the markup) is countercyclical. Another paper which considers a non-collusive model of competition under demand fluctuations (but with a fixed number of firms) is Wilson and Reynolds (2005). Their model predicts that during a demand expansion, firms charge the short-run competitive price, but in a recession, they set prices above the competitive price. Thus, price markups over the competitive price are countercyclical in their model. Consistent with this prediction, they find evidence from U.S. manufacturing industries that price changes have higher variance in recessions than in booms.

and equilibrium prices, and the other between the variation in quantities demanded and capacity utilization.

The two firms differ both in terms of their fixed costs and capacities. Firm 1 is an incumbent that has no fixed cost and has a capacity normalized to 1. Firm 2 is a potential entrant that needs to spend a cost F in order to enter the market with exogenous capacity k, where

$$k < Q^r < 1 < Q^b < 1 + k. \tag{1}$$

This assumption implies that firm 2 cannot serve the entire market even in recessions, firm 1 can serve the entire market in recessions but not in booms, and together, the two firms can always serve the entire demand.

Both firms produce at constant marginal cost c. Hence, the average cost of firm 2 when operating at full capacity k, is $AC \equiv c + \frac{F}{k}$. To ensure that firm 2's entry is never blockaded, we assume that $AC < \alpha^r$. In addition, to restrict the number of different cases we would need to consider, we assume that

$$F > \left(Q^b - 1\right)\left(\alpha^b - c\right). \tag{2}$$

This assumption rules out the possibility that in booms, firm 2 will enter the market by charging a price of α^b, above firm 1's price, and will serve the residual demand, $Q^b - 1$, left after firm 1 sells up to its capacity. In other words, this assumption means that in order to enter the market profitably, firm 2 must undercut firm 1's price (though as we shall see below, this is possible only when firm 1's price is sufficiently high).[9]

In what follows, we will characterize the equilibrium under two alternative scenarios: (i) firm 1 sets its price before firm 2 decides whether or not to enter, and if so, at which price; and (ii) firm 2 decides whether or not to enter and at which price before firm 1 sets its own price. In both cases, the two firms know the state of the economy before they make their choices.

[9]We should emphasize that assumption (2) is made only for convenience. In a more general setting, firm 2 should be allowed to enter at a higher price if consumers' willingness-to-pay and/or quantity demanded are sufficiently high.

Before proceeding, it is worth noting that although we consider a single period model, our results can also be interpreted as the Markov perfect equilibrium of an infinite period model in which demand is *i.i.d.* across periods and firm 2 needs to incur an avoidable fixed cost whenever it chooses to operate in the market. We leave the more interesting case, where firm 2 needs to incur a fixed cost only when it (re)enters the market after being out (but not if it already operates in the market), for future research. This case is substantially harder because then firm 1 may wish to drive firm 2 out of the market in order to make it costly for firm 2 to reenter, while firm 2 may wish to stay in the market even when it is currently losing money in order to save on the cost of reentering the market later on.

3. Firm 1 is the First Mover

Let p_1^i be the price that firm 1 sets in state $i = r, b$, before firm 2 decides whether or not to enter the market. Since the products are homogeneous, it is clear that if firm 2 decides to enter, it will set its price, p_2^i, just below p_1^i, and will sell up to its capacity k. Firm 1 will then serve the residual demand, $Q^i - k$, at a price p_1^i. If p_1^i is sufficiently low, then firm 2 decides not to enter because undercutting p_1^i entails a loss. Although firm 2 could still enter in booms by charging a price above p_1^b and then serve the residual demand not served by firm 1, $Q^b - 1$, its resulting profit would be negative since (2) implies that $(Q^b - 1)(p_2^b - c) - F \leq (Q^b - 1)(\alpha^b - c) - F < 0$.[10] Hence, under (2), firm 2 will never enter the market by setting a price above p_1. If firm 2 decides to stay out, then firm 1 either serves the entire demand in recessions by selling Q^r, or sells up to its capacity, 1, in booms. Consequently, the profits of the two firms in state $i = b, r$ are given by

$$\pi_1^i = \begin{cases} \min\left\{Q^i, 1\right\}\left(p_1^i - c\right) & \text{if firm 2 stays out,} \\ \left(Q^i - k\right)\left(p_1^i - c\right) & \text{if firm 2 enters,} \end{cases} \tag{3}$$

and

$$\pi_2^i = \begin{cases} 0 & \text{if firm 2 stays out,} \\ k\left(p_1^i - AC\right) & \text{if firm 2 enters.} \end{cases} \tag{4}$$

[10]In recessions, $Q^r < 1$, so firm 1 serves the entire market if $p_1^r < p_2^r$.

Firm 1 as the first mover has two options that dominate all others: (i) accommodate firm 2 by setting the maximal price $p_1^i = \alpha^i$; or (ii) deter firm 2's entry by setting a limit price just below firm 2's average cost AC, which is a feasible pricing strategy as $AC < \alpha^r$. Under option (i), firm 2 will undercut α^i slightly and will sell up to its capacity k. Firm 1 in turn will serve the residual demand $Q^i - k$. The resulting profits of firms 1 and 2 are $(Q^i - k)(\alpha^i - c)$ and $k(\alpha^i - AC)$, respectively. Under option (ii), firm 2 cannot profitably undercut firm 1, so firm 1 will serve the entire market in a recession and will sell up to its capacity in booms (the demand in booms exceeds firm 1's capacity since $Q^b > 1$). The resulting profit of firm 1 is then $Q^r(AC - c)$ in recessions and $AC - c$ in booms. Firm 2 in turn faces no residual demand in recessions, and due to (2), it cannot make a positive profit in booms by serving the residual demand, $Q^b - 1$. Hence, firm 2 will stay out of the market whenever $p_1^i = AC$.

To determine firm 1's equilibrium choice, note that since it can always ensure itself a profit of $(Q^i - k)(\alpha^i - c)$ by serving the residual demand at α^i, firm 1 will never set a limit price p_1^i such that

$$\min\left\{Q^i, 1\right\}\left(p_1^i - c\right) \leq \left(Q^i - k\right)\left(\alpha^i - c\right).$$

Hence, the lowest limit prices that firm 1 will ever charge in booms and in recessions, respectively, are

$$J^b \equiv c + \left(Q^b - k\right)\left(\alpha^b - c\right), \qquad J^r \equiv c + \left(1 - \frac{k}{Q^r}\right)\left(\alpha^r - c\right). \quad (5)$$

Notice that $J^b > J^r$ since

$$\left(Q^b - k\right)\left(\alpha^b - c\right) > \left(1 - k\right)\left(\alpha^r - c\right) > \left(1 - \frac{k}{Q^r}\right)\left(\alpha^r - c\right), \quad (6)$$

where the first inequality follows because $Q^b > 1$ and $\alpha^b > \alpha^r$ and the second inequality follows because $Q^r < 1$. Recalling that in order to deter entry, firm 1 needs to set a price of AC both in booms and in recessions, we have the following result:

Proposition 1 *Suppose that firm 1 is the first mover. Then the subgame perfect equilibrium is as follows:*

(i) *If $AC < J^r$, then firm 1 accommodates firm 2 both in booms and in recessions and both firms charge α^i in state $i = b, r$. Firm 1 sells $Q^i - k$ and firm 2 sells k.*
(ii) *If $J^r < AC < J^b$, then firm 1 accommodates firm 2 in booms by charging α^b, but deters firm 2's entry in recessions by charging a limit price $p_1^r = AC$. When firm 2 enters in booms, it also charges α^b and the resulting quantities sold by firms 1 and 2 are $Q^b - k$ and k, respectively. In recessions, firm 2 stays out of the market and firm 1 sells Q^r.*
(iii) *If $AC > J^b$, then firm 1 deters firm 2's entry both in booms and in recessions by charging a limit price $p_1^r = p_1^b = AC$. Firm 1 sells 1 in booms and Q^r in recessions.*

Intuitively, to deter firm 2's entry, firm 1 needs to set a limit price equal to firm 2's average cost. Firm 1, however, is willing to cut its price only to J^b in booms and to J^r in recessions in order to deter entry. Equation (6) shows that $J^b > J^r$, implying that firm 1 is more eager to deter entry in recessions. The reason is that firm 1's profit from accommodation is lower in recessions than in booms because firm 1's quantity, as well as its price, are procyclical ($Q^b - k$ and and α^b in booms vs. $Q^r - k$ and α^r in recessions). Although firm 1's quantity under deterrence is also lower in recessions than in booms (1 in booms and Q^r in recessions), the effect of booms on firm 1's profits under accommodation is larger, so firm 1 is more willing to accommodate entry in booms, and by implication, it is more eager to deter entry in recessions.

Proposition 1 is illustrated in Figure 1 (prices in recessions are in solid lines and prices under booms in broken lines). When $AC < J^r$, firm 2 enters the market both in booms and in recessions and both firms charge the monopoly prices α^b in booms and α^r in recessions. When $J^r < AC < J^b$, firm 2 enters only in booms and if it does, both firms charge the monopoly price α^b. In recessions, firm 1 deters entry by charging a limit price AC. When $AC > J^b$, firm 1 charges a limit price of AC both in booms and in recessions and firm 2 stays out of the market. An interesting implication of the fact that the price is α^b or α^r when firm 2 is accommodated, but only

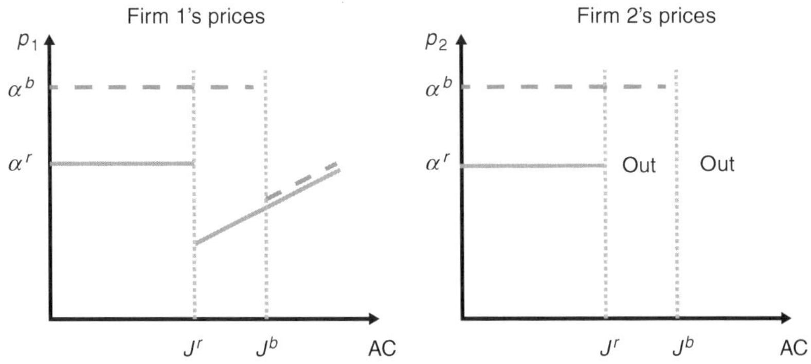

Figure 1. The equilibrium prices when firm 1 is a leader.

AC when firm 2 is deterred, is that we get an inverse relationship between prices and concentration: duopoly is associated with relatively high prices, whereas (contested) monopoly is associated with relatively low prices.[11]

As Figure 1 shows, the interesting case arises when $J^r < AC < J^b$ because then entry occurs in booms, but not in recessions. Consequently, the resulting market structure is state-dependent: duopoly with high monopoly prices during booms, and contested monopoly with a low predatory price in recessions.

Proposition 1 yields the following predictions:

Procyclical prices: Prices are higher in booms than in recessions. The only exception arises when $AC > J^b$, in which case, firm 1's price is equal to AC both in booms and in recessions. The question, however, is whether the equilibrium price variations merely reflect the change in consumers' willingness-to-pay. It turns out that the strategic interaction between the two firms, and the potentially different industry structure in booms and recessions, has interesting effects on the volatility of equilibrium prices, relative to that of consumers' willingness-to-pay.

We will measure the volatility of equilibrium prices and consumers' willingness-to-pay in terms of their respective coefficients of variation, defined as the standard deviation divided by the mean. To compute the

[11] Our assumption that consumers have identical willingness-to-pay implies that high prices in our model do not entail a deadweight loss. But since firm 2 needs to incur an entry cost, total welfare is higher under (contested) monopoly than under duopoly. Moreover, consumer surplus is higher under monopoly due to the threat of firm 2's entry into the market.

coefficients of variation, let β denote the probability of a boom and $1 - \beta$ the probability of a recession. Then, the expected willingness of consumers to pay, W, is

$$E(W) = \beta\alpha^b + (1 - \beta)\alpha^r,$$

and its variance over the business cycle is

$$\begin{aligned} Var(W) &= \beta\big(\alpha^b - E(W)\big)^2 + (1 - \beta)\big(\alpha^r - E(W)\big)^2 \\ &= \beta(1 - \beta)\big(\alpha^b - \alpha^r\big)^2. \end{aligned}$$

Now the coefficient of variation of W is

$$CV(W) = \frac{\sqrt{Var(W)}}{E(W)} = \frac{\sqrt{\beta(1 - \beta)}\big(\alpha^b - \alpha^r\big)}{E(W)}.$$

We now compare $CV(W)$ with the coefficient of variation, $CV(p)$, of equilibrium prices. The expected value and variance of the equilibrium prices are given by

$$E(p) = \begin{cases} \beta\alpha^b + (1 - \beta)\alpha^r & AC \leq J^r, \\ \beta\alpha^b + (1 - \beta)AC & J^r < AC \leq J^b, \\ AC & AC > J^b, \end{cases}$$

and

$$Var(p) = \begin{cases} \beta(1 - \beta)\big(\alpha^b - \alpha^r\big)^2 & AC \leq J^r, \\ \beta(1 - \beta)\big(\alpha^b - AC\big)^2 & J^r < AC \leq J^b, \\ 0 & AC > J^b. \end{cases}$$

Hence, the coefficient of variation of the equilibrium price is

$$CV(p) = \begin{cases} \dfrac{\sqrt{\beta(1 - \beta)}\big(\alpha^b - \alpha^r\big)}{\beta\alpha^b + (1 - \beta)\alpha^r} & AC \leq J^r, \\ \dfrac{\sqrt{\beta(1 - \beta)}\big(\alpha^b - AC\big)}{\beta\alpha^b + (1 - \beta)AC} & J^r < AC \leq J^b, \\ 0 & AC > J^b. \end{cases}$$

It is easy to check that $CV(W) = CV(p)$ if $AC \leq J^r$, $CV(W) < CV(p)$ if $J^r < AC \leq J^b$, and $CV(W) > CV(p)$ if $AC > J^b$.

We summarize the results as follows:

Proposition 2 *The strategic interaction between the two firms has the following implications for equilibrium price volatility:*

(i) *If* $AC \leq J^r$, *equilibrium prices exhibit the same volatility as consumers' willingness-to-pay.*
(ii) *If* $J^r < AC < J^b$, *equilibrium prices are more volatile than consumers' willingness-to-pay.*
(iii) *If* $AC > J^b$, *equilibrium prices are less volatile than consumers' willingness-to-pay.*

Hence, the volatility of consumers' willingness-to-pay and equilibrium prices are identical only when $AC \leq J^r$, in which case firm 2 is accommodated in both booms and recessions. Whenever $J^r < AC < J^b$, however, the equilibrium prices are more volatile than is the consumers' willingness-to-pay. That is, the equilibrium price volatility is amplified by firm 1's strategic decision to deter entry in recessions, because while the equilibrium price is equal to the willingness-to-pay, α^b in booms, it is lower than that in recessions, as $AC < \alpha^r$. Finally, if $AC > J^b$, the volatility of equilibrium prices is zero, and thus obviously smaller than that of consumers' willingness-to-pay.

No price dispersion: Whenever firm 2 enters the market, the two firms charge the same price so there is no price dispersion within the same period. As we shall see in Section 4, this is no longer true when firm 2 is a first mover.

Procyclical price-cost margins: We measure price-cost margins by the Lerner index. When firm 2 is accommodated, the Lerner index of both firms is $\frac{\alpha^i - c}{\alpha^i}$. When firm 1 deters firm 2's entry by setting a price AC, the Lerner index of firm 1 is $\frac{AC-c}{AC} < \frac{\alpha^i - c}{\alpha^i}$. Hence, the industry Lerner index in state i is given by

$$L^i = \begin{cases} \dfrac{\alpha^i - c}{\alpha^i} & AC \leq J^i, \\ \dfrac{AC - c}{AC} & AC > J^i. \end{cases}$$

Since $J^b > J^r$, it follows that $L^b \geq L^r$, with strict inequality whenever $J^r < AC \leq J^b$ (i.e., when the market is a duopoly in booms and a contested monopoly in recessions). As mentioned in the Introduction, the empirical evidence on the cyclicality of price-cost margins is mixed. It should be noted that our results are driven by the fact that firm 1 finds it more profitable to charge a low limit price and deter firm 2's entry during recessions. But since we only consider two firms, our predictions apply only to concentrated markets in which entry deterrence is a relevant possibility.

Procyclical entry: To derive predictions about entry, let us assume that AC is drawn from some distribution function $G(AC)$ on the interval $[0, \alpha^r]$, and is observed by both firms before any decisions are taken. Then, Proposition 1 implies that in equilibrium, the probability of entry is $G(J^b)$ in booms, and $G(J^r)$ in recessions, where $G(J^b) > G(J^r)$. This prediction is consistent with Portier (1995) who shows that the number of firms in France is positively correlated with the French GDP during the period 1977–1989. Likewise, Campbell (1998) finds significant positive correlation between the entry rates in the U.S. manufacturing sector and the U.S. GDP during the 1972–1988 period, and Lee and Mukoyama (2013) find that entry rates of U.S. manufacturing plants during the 1972–1997 period are on average significantly higher in booms than in recessions.

Procyclical profits and profit margins: When $AC \leq J^r$, firm 1's profit in state i is $(Q^i - k)(\alpha^i - c)$. Since $Q^b > Q^r$ and $\alpha^b > \alpha^r$, firm 1's profit is procyclical. Likewise, when $AC > J^b$, firm 1's profit in state i is $Q^i(AC - c)$, so again it is procyclical. When $J^r < AC \leq J^b$, firm 1's profit in booms, $(Q^b - k)(\alpha^b - c)$, is also higher than firm 1's profit is recessions, $Q^r(AC - c)$, since

$$\left(Q^b - k\right)\left(\alpha^b - c\right) \geq Q^r\left(Q^b - k\right)\left(\alpha^b - c\right) = Q^r\left(J^b - c\right) \geq Q^r\left(AC - c\right),$$

where the first inequality arises since $Q^r \leq 1$, the equality follows from the definition of J^b, and the last inequality arises since $AC \leq J^b$. Hence, firm 1's profit is also procyclical in this range. As for firm 2, its profit when $AC \leq J^r$ is $k(\alpha^i - AC)$ which is procyclical since $\alpha^b > \alpha^r$. When $J^r < AC \leq J^b$, firm 2 operates in the market and makes a positive profit only in booms; hence, its profit is also procyclical in this range. When

$AC > J^b$, firm 2 is out of the market in both states. The procyclicality of profits is well-documented empirically (see e.g., Rotemberg and Woodford (1999)).

Our model also yields predictions regarding profit margins, i.e., profits divided by quantities. The profit margin of firm 1 is $\alpha^i - c$ when $AC \le J^r$, $\alpha^b - c$ in booms and $AC - c$ in recessions when $J^r < AC \le J^b$, and $AC - c$ in both booms and recessions when $AC > J^b$. Firm 2's profit margin is $\alpha^i - AC$ when $AC \le J^r$, $\alpha^b - AC$ in booms and 0 in recessions when $J^r < AC \le J^b$, and 0 when $AC > J^b$. Hence, our model predicts that profit margins should be (weakly) procyclical. This result is consistent with Machin and Van Reenen (1993) who study a panel of 709 large UK firms over the 1970s and 1980s and find that firm-level profit margins are strongly procyclical.

Pro- or countercyclical capacity utilization by firm 1: Clearly, if the industry structure (and capacities) would stay unchanged over the business cycle, then capacity utilization would vary procyclically, as firms produce more in booms than in recessions. The question is what happens when the endogenous determination of industry structure is explicitly taken into account. In what follows, we study the cyclical behavior of firm 1 which operates in our model for all parameter values.

To address this question, recall that firm 1's capacity is 1, so firm 1's capacity utilization is equal to firm 1's output. In booms, firm 1 produces $Q^b - k$ if $AC < J^b$ and 1 if $AC > J^b$, so its expected output, and hence its expected capacity utilization, is

$$CU_1^b = (Q^b - k)G(J^b) + 1 - G(J^b).$$

In recessions, firm 1 produces $Q^r - k$ if $AC < J^r$ and Q^r if $AC > J^r$, so its expected capacity utilization is

$$CU_1^r = (Q^r - k)G(J^r) + Q^r(1 - G(J^r)).$$

Since $Q^b - k > Q^r - k$ and $J^b > J^r$, then $(Q^b - k)G(J^b) > (Q^r - k)G(J^r)$. At the same time, if Q^r is sufficiently close to 1, then it is also possible that $1 - G(J^b) < Q^r(1 - G(J^r))$, so the relationship between CU_1^b and CU_1^r is in general ambiguous.

It is interesting to note that the capacity utilization of firm 1 in state i declines with J^i, which in turn varies with α^i. Intuitively, the larger α^i is, the more tempting it is for firm 1 to accommodate firm 2, in which case, firm 1's capacity utilization is lower than in the case where it deters entry.

As in the case of equilibrium prices, the question now is whether the cyclical behavior of capacity utilization merely reflects the volatility of quantities demanded, or whether it is also affected by the strategic interaction between the two firms. To address this question, note that the expected quantity demanded is

$$E(Q) = \beta Q^b + (1-\beta)Q^r,$$

and its variance over the business cycle is

$$\begin{aligned} Var(Q) &= \beta\left(Q^b - E(Q)\right)^2 + (1-\beta)\left(Q^r - E(Q)\right)^2 \\ &= \beta(1-\beta)\left(Q^b - Q^r\right)^2. \end{aligned}$$

Hence, the coefficient of variation of demand is

$$CV(Q) = \frac{\sqrt{Var(Q)}}{E(Q)} = \frac{\sqrt{\beta(1-\beta)}\left(Q^b - Q^r\right)}{E(Q)}.$$

We now compare $CV(Q)$ with the coefficient of variation of the capacity utilization of firm 1. Recalling that firm 1's capacity utilization is equal to firm 1's output, and noting from Proposition 1 that firm 1's output is $Q^b - k$ if $AC < J^b$ and 1 if $AC > J^b$ in booms and $Q^r - k$ if $AC < J^r$ and Q^r if $AC > J^r$ in recessions, the expected value and variance of firm 1's capacity utilization are given by

$$E\left(CU_1\right) = \begin{cases} \beta\left(Q^b - k\right) + (1-\beta)\left(Q^r - k\right) = E(Q) - k & AC \leq J^r, \\ \beta\left(Q^b - k\right) + (1-\beta)Q^r = E(Q) - \beta k & J^r < AC \leq J^b, \\ \beta + (1-\beta)Q^r = E(Q) - \beta\left(Q^b - 1\right) & AC > J^b, \end{cases}$$

and

$$Var\left(CU_1\right) = \begin{cases} \beta(1-\beta)\left(Q^b - Q^r\right)^2 & AC \leq J^r, \\ \beta(1-\beta)\left(Q^b - Q^r - k\right)^2 & J^r < AC \leq J^b, \\ \beta(1-\beta)\left(1 - Q^r\right)^2 & AC > J^b. \end{cases}$$

Hence, the coefficient of variation of firm 1's capacity utilization is

$$CV\left(CU_1\right) = \begin{cases} \dfrac{\sqrt{\beta(1-\beta)}\left(Q^b - Q^r\right)}{E(Q) - k} & AC \leq J^r, \\ \dfrac{\sqrt{\beta(1-\beta)}\left(Q^b - Q^r - k\right)}{E(Q) - \beta k} & J^r < AC \leq J^b, \\ \dfrac{\sqrt{\beta(1-\beta)}\left(1 - Q^r\right)}{E(Q) - \beta\left(Q^b - 1\right)} & AC > J^b. \end{cases}$$

It is now easy to check that $CV(CU_1) > CV(Q)$ if $AC \leq J^b$, and $CV(CU_1) < CV(Q)$ if $AC > J^b$. We summarize the comparison of $CV(CU_1)$ with $CV(Q)$ in the following result:

Proposition 3 *The strategic interaction between the firms has the following implications for the volatility of equilibrium capacity utilization of firm* 1:

(i) *If* $AC \leq J^b$, *the equilibrium capacity utilization of firm* 1 *is more volatile than the quantity demanded.*
(ii) *If* $AC > J^b$, *the equilibrium capacity utilization of firm* 1 *is less volatile than the quantity demanded.*

Proposition 3 shows that the strategic interaction between the two firms either dampens or amplifies the volatility of capacity utilization of firm 1 which is the incumbent. This result corresponds nicely to Proposition 2: when $AC \leq J^b$, i.e., when firm 2's fixed costs is low relative to demand, firm 1 finds it optimal to accommodate firm 2 at least in booms. The equilibrium prices then are (weakly) more volatile than the willingness of consumers to pay, while firm 1's capacity utilization is (strictly) more volatile than the quantity demanded. In the opposite case, where $AC > J^b$, firm 1 finds it optimal to deter firm 2's entry both in booms and in recessions, and in this case, the equilibrium price and firm 1's capacity utilization are less volatile than the corresponding demand primitives.

4. Firm 2 is the First Mover

We now turn to the alternative scenario in which firm 2 first decides whether or not to enter; and if it does, it sets a price p_2^i in state $i = b, r$. Firm 1 observes firm 2's entry decision and price and then sets p_1^i. This scenario corresponds to the Judo Economics model of Gelman and Salop (1983), in which the entrant moves before the incumbent responds. In recessions, firm 2 sells a positive quantity only if firm 1 does not undercut it. In booms, firm 2 could also serve the residual demand $Q^b - 1$ when firm 1 undercuts it, but by equation (2), its profit would be negative: $(Q^b - 1)(p_2^b - c) - F \leq (Q^b - 1)(\alpha^b - c) - F < 0$. Hence, firm 2 can profitably enter the market only if it sets a sufficiently low "judo" price, which firm 1 does not wish to undercut. From Section 3, it should be clear that the required judo prices are J^r in recessions and J^b in booms. Obviously, firm 2 is willing to set these prices only if they exceed its average cost AC. Hence,

Proposition 4 *Suppose that firm 2 is the first mover. Then the subgame perfect equilibrium is as follows:*

(i) *If $AC < J^r$, then firm 2 enters the market in both states and sets $p_2^b = J^b$ in booms and $p_2^r = J^r$ in recessions. Firm 1 in turn sets $p_1^i = \alpha^i$ and sells $Q^i - k$, while firm 2 sells k.*
(ii) *If $J^r < AC \leq J^b$, then firm 2 enters the market only in booms and sets $p_2^b = J^b$. Firm 1 in turn sets $p_1^b = \alpha^b$. Firm 1 sells $Q^i - k$, and firm 2 sells k. In recessions, firm 2 stays out of the market. Firm 1 sets $p_1^r = \alpha^r$ and sells Q^r.*
(iii) *If $AC > J^b$, then firm 2 cannot profitably enter the market in either state. Firm 1 then sets $p_1^i = \alpha^i$ and sells Q^r in recessions, and 1 in booms.*

Proposition 4 shows that the patterns of entry and output levels are exactly as in Proposition 1. Moreover, Figure 2 shows that as in the case

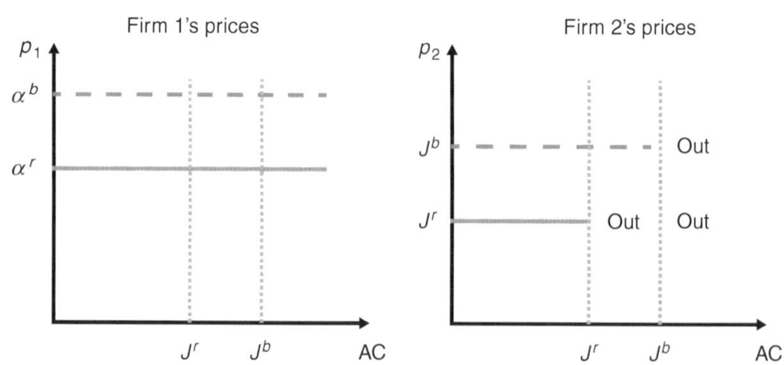

Figure 2. The equilibrium prices when firm 2 is a leader.

where firm 1 is the first mover, the equilibrium prices when firm 2 is a first mover are also procyclical in the sense that they are higher in booms than in recessions (the prices in booms are α^b and J^b and in recessions, they are α^r and J^r). Hence, the predictions on entry, sales, and the procyclicality of prices are robust to the identity of the leading firm.

As for price-cost margins, Proposition 4 implies that the industry Lerner index in state i is given by

$$L^i = \begin{cases} \dfrac{Q^i - k}{Q^i} \times \dfrac{\alpha^i - c}{\alpha^i} + \dfrac{k}{Q^i} \times \dfrac{J^i - c}{J^i} & AC \leq J^i, \\ 1 \times \dfrac{\alpha^i - c}{\alpha^i} & AC > J^i. \end{cases}$$

Since $\alpha^b > \alpha^r$, $J^b > J^r$, and $Q^b > Q^r$, it is clear that $L^b > L^r$ when $AC \leq J^r$ and when $AC > J^b$. If we assume in addition that

$$Q^b - k > \frac{\alpha^r - c}{\alpha^b - c}, \tag{7}$$

then

$$\begin{aligned} J^b \equiv c + \left(Q^b - k\right)\left(\alpha^b - c\right) &= \alpha^r + \left(Q^b - k\right)\left(\alpha^b - c\right) - \left(\alpha^r - c\right) \\ &= \alpha^r + \left(\alpha^b - c\right)\left[Q^b - k - \frac{\alpha^r - c}{\alpha^b - c}\right] \\ &> \alpha^r, \end{aligned}$$

which implies that $\frac{J^b - c}{J^b} > \frac{\alpha^r - c}{\alpha^r}$. This ensures in turn that $L^b > L^r$ when $J^r < AC \leq J^b$. Hence, as in the case where firm 1 is a first mover, here (under the additional constraint (7)), we also get procyclical price-cost margins.[12]

Proposition 4 also implies that the procyclicality of profits is robust to the identity of the first mover. To see why, note that firm 1's profit in state i is $(Q^i - k)(\alpha^i - c)$ when $AC \leq J^r$ and $Q^i(AC - c)$ when $AC > J^b$. Since $Q^b > Q^r$ and $\alpha^b > \alpha^r$, firm 1's profit is procyclical in both cases. When $J^r < AC \leq J^b$, firm 1's profit is $(Q^b - k)(\alpha^b - c)$ in booms and $Q^r(\alpha^r - c)$

[12] It should be noted that combined, (1) and (7) require that $\frac{\alpha^r - k}{\alpha^b - k} < Q^b - k < 1$. That is, the gap between Q^b and k is not too small and not too large.

in recessions. Noting that $Q^r \leq 1$, (7) ensures that firm 1's profit is also procyclical in this case. Firm 2's profit is also procyclical since it is equal to $k(\alpha^i - AC)$ if $AC \leq J^r$, and if $J^r < AC \leq J^b$, firm 2 operates in the market and makes a positive profit only in booms.

Although Propositions 1 and 4 generate similar predictions regarding entry, sales quantities, prices, price-cost margins, and profits, there are at least two important differences between the case where firm 1 is a first mover and the opposite case where firm 2 is a first mover. First, Figures 1 and 2 show that when firm 2 is a first mover, the equilibrium prices are weakly lower for firm 1 and strictly lower for firm 2. The reason is that when firm 2 is a first mover, it must set at low judo prices to induce firm 1 to accommodate it. By contrast, when firm 1 is a first mover, it accommodates entry by setting high monopoly prices. In this sense, we get a more competitive outcome when firm 2 is a first mover than when firm 1 is a first mover.

Second, the low judo price that firm 2 sets when it enters the market gives rise to price dispersion. This is in contrast to Proposition 1 where the two firms set the same price when they are both active in the market. To examine how the extent of price dispersion varies over the business cycle, let us measure price dispersion in state i by the coefficient of variation of prices.[13] To this end, note that the average price in state $i = b, r$ is

$$\hat{p}^i = \frac{Q^i - k}{Q^i}\alpha^i + \frac{k}{Q^i}J^i = \alpha^i - \frac{k(\alpha^i - J^i)}{Q^i},$$

and the variance of price in state $i = b, r$ is

$$Var(p^i) = \frac{Q^i - k}{Q^i}(\alpha^i - \hat{p}^i)^2 + \frac{k}{Q^i}(J^i - \hat{p}^i)^2 = \frac{Q^i - k}{Q^i} \times \frac{k}{Q^i} \times (\alpha^i - J^i)^2,$$

where $\frac{Q^i - k}{Q^i}$ is the market share of firm 1 and $\frac{k}{Q^i}$ the market share of firm 2. Using these expressions, the coefficient of variation of prices in state $i = b, r$ is

$$CV(p^i) = \frac{\sqrt{Var(p^i)}}{\hat{p}^i} = \frac{\sqrt{k(Q^i - k)}(\alpha^i - J^i)}{Q^i\alpha^i - k(\alpha^i - J^i)}.$$

[13]This is a common measure of price dispersion, see e.g., Table 1 in Baye *et al.* (2006).

Noting that $\alpha^b - J^b = (\alpha^b - c)(1 + k - Q^b)$ and $\alpha^r - J^r = (\alpha^r - c)\frac{k}{Q^r}$, and simplifying, yields

$$CV(p^b) = \frac{\sqrt{\frac{Q^b}{k} - 1}}{\frac{Q^b}{k}\frac{1}{1+k\left(1-\frac{Q^b}{k}\right)}\frac{\alpha^b}{\alpha^b - c} - 1}, \qquad CV(p^r) = \frac{\sqrt{\frac{Q^r}{k} - 1}}{\left(\frac{Q^r}{k}\right)^2 \frac{\alpha^r}{\alpha^r - c} - 1}.$$

It turns out that $CV(p^b)$ could be above or below $CV(p^r)$.

An interesting implication of Proposition 4 is that although both firms charge higher prices in booms than in recessions, the average price paid by consumers is not necessarily procyclical. To see this, consider the case where $J^r < AC \leq J^b$, so that firm 2 enters in booms, but stays out in recessions. Then the average price in booms is $\hat{p}^b$. In recessions, firm 2 stays out of the market and firm 1 serves the entire market at a price α^r. If (7) holds, then $J^b > \alpha^r$, which implies in turn that $\hat{p}^b > \alpha^r$; hence, the average price is higher in booms than in recessions. However, if (7) fails, then $\alpha^r > \hat{p}^b$ whenever

$$\alpha^r > \alpha^b - \frac{k\left(\alpha^b - c\right)\left(1 + k - Q^b\right)}{Q^b}. \tag{8}$$

Hence when (8) holds, the average price in booms is lower than in recessions. The reason for this counterintuitive possibility is a composition effect: although firm 1 charges higher prices in booms than in recessions, firm 2 enters the market only during booms, and its price is lower than firm 1's price. When firm 2's price, J^b, is sufficiently below firm 1's price in recessions, α^r, the average price in booms will end up being below the average price in recessions. Notice that this case arises only when α^r is sufficiently close to α^b.

We report these results in the following proposition:

Proposition 5 *When firm 2 is the first mover,*

(i) *there is price dispersion whenever firm 2 enters the market;*
(ii) *the extent of price dispersion is pro- or countercyclical;*
(iii) *the average price during booms is below the average price during recessions if (8) holds.*

Part (i) of Proposition 5 suggests that price dispersion can arise due to the low price that firm 2 sets in order to induce firm 1 to accommodate it. While this result replicates the familiar judo economics result, part (ii) of Proposition 5, which as far as we know is novel, shows that the extent of price dispersion varies over the business cycle and can either be pro- or countercyclical. Evidence for procyclical price dispersion is found in Cornia *et al.* (2012). They examine the prices of domestic, direct, coach-class airline tickets in the U.S. over the period 1993 to 2009 and find that price dispersion is highly procyclical, especially for legacy carriers and especially when concentration is high.

A number of papers have documented that retail prices for many products tend to fall during periods of peak demand (see e.g., Warner and Barsky (1995), MacDonald (2000), and Chevalier *et al.* (2003)). Part (iii) of Proposition 5 suggests that this phenomenon may be due to a composition effect: lower price firms increase their market shares when demand peaks, and this may lead to an overall decrease in average prices. Interestingly, Hatzitaskos and Nevo (2006) use the Chevalier *et al.* (2003) data and find support for the existence of a composition effect.[14]

5. Concluding Remarks

We develop a simple model intended to explore the joint determination of prices, sales, and entry and examine how they vary over the business cycle. Our model is based on the idea that demand fluctuations affect the incentives of an incumbent firm to set low prices to keep a potential entrant out of the market. It predicts that prices, price-cost margins, and entry are all procyclical, but capacity utilization by the incumbent firm can be either pro- or countercyclical when the incumbent is a first mover and price dispersion can also be either pro- or countercyclical when the entrant is a first mover. Our model also shows that entry deterrence by the incumbent firm can either amplify or dampen the effect of demand fluctuations on prices, price-cost margins, and capacity utilization.

[14]For instance, they find that when the demand for tuna peaks during Lent, much of the increase in sales is due to two relatively cheap products, whose market share is tripled despite the fact that their prices do not fall.

As mentioned in Section 1, our paper belongs to the class of models in which the cyclical behavior of prices and price-cost margins (as well as entry and capacity utilization) is due to strategic interactions among firms. Most other papers in this class study the effect of demand fluctuations on the ability of firms to collude. The two most influential papers in this class are Green and Porter (1984) and Rotemberg and Saloner (1986). In Green and Porter (1984), collusion can be sustained in high demand states, but it completely breaks down in low demand states because firms cannot tell if their low sales are due to low demand, or due to a deviation from the collusive agreement by a rival. Hence, like in our model, their model predicts procyclical prices and price-cost margins. By contrast, Rotemberg and Saloner (1986) predict countercyclical price-cost margins, which is the opposite of what our model predicts. In both models, symmetric firms are assumed to operate at unlimited capacity. At least, the Rotemberg and Saloner result is clearly driven by this assumption. Also, unlike our paper, neither paper allows for entry and exit and hence these papers do not generate predictions regarding the joint determination of prices, price-cost margins, and entry.

Finally, the firms in our model have asymmetric capacities. Compte *et al.* (2002) show that asymmetric capacities hinder the ability of firms to collude if the aggregate capacity of all active firms is small relative to market size, but may facilitate collusion otherwise. To the extent that the market expands in booms and contracts in recessions, their results suggest that collusion should be harder to sustain in booms than in recessions. Contrary to our results, this would generate countercyclical price-cost margins.

References

Bagwell, K. and R. Staiger (1997). "Collusion Over the Business Cycle," *RAND Journal of Economics*, 28(1), pp. 82–106.

Baye, M., J. Morgan and P. Scholten (2006). Information, Search, and Price Dispersion, in T. Hendershott (Ed.), *Handbook in Economics and Information Systems*, Volume 1, Chapter 6, Elsevier, Amsterdam.

Bils, M. (1987). "The Cyclical Behavior of Marginal Cost and Price," *The American Economic Review*, 77(5), pp. 838–855.

Bils, M. (1989), "Pricing in a Customer Market," *The Quarterly Journal of Economics*, 104(4), pp. 699–718.

Campbell, J. (1998), "Entry, Exit, Embodied Technology, and Business Cycles," *Review of Economic Dynamics*, 1(2), pp. 371–408.

Chevalier, J., A. Kashyap and P. Rossi (2003). "Why Don't Prices Rise During Periods of Peak Demand? Evidence from Scanner Data," *The American Economic Review*, 93(1), pp. 15–37.

Chevalier, J. and D. Scharfstein (1996). "Capital-Market Imperfections and Countercyclical Markups: Theory and Evidence," *The American Economic Review*, 86(4), pp. 703–725.

Cornia, N., K. Gerardi and A.-H. Shapiro (2012). "Price Dispersion over the Business Cycle: Evidence from the Airline Industry," *Journal of Industrial Economics*, 60(3), pp. 347–373.

Compte, O., F. Jenny and P. Rey (2002). "Capacity Constraints, Merger, and Collusion," *European Economic Review*, 45, pp. 1–29

Domowitz, I., G. Hubbard and B. Petersen (1986a). "Business Cycles and the Relationship between Concentration and Price-Cost Margins," *RAND Journal of Economics*, 17(1), pp. 1–17.

Domowitz, I., G. Hubbard and B. Petersen (1986b). "The Intertemporal Stability of the Concentration-Margins Relationship," *Journal of Industrial Economics*, 35(4), pp. 13–34.

Domowitz, I., G. Hubbard and B. Petersen (1987). "Oligopoly Supergames: Some Empirical Evidence on Prices and Margins," *Journal of Industrial Economics*, 35(4), pp. 379–398.

Domowitz, I., G. Hubbard and B. Petersen (1988). "Market Structure and Cyclical Fluctuations in Manufacturing," *The Review of Economics and Statistics*, 70(1), pp. 55–66.

Edmond, C. and L. Veldkamp (2009). "Income Dispersion and Counter-Cyclical Markups," *Journal of Monetary Economics*, 56, pp. 791–804.

Ellison, G. (1994). "Theories of Cartel Stability and the Joint Executive Committee," *RAND Journal of Economics*, 25(1), pp. 37–57.

Fabra, N. (2006). "Collusion with Capacity Constraints Over the Business Cycle," *International Journal of Industrial Organization*, 24(1), pp. 69–81.

Galeotti, M. and F. Schiantarelli (1998). "The Cyclicality of Markups in a Model with Adjustment Costs: Econometric Evidence for US Industry," *Oxford Bulletin of Economics and Statistics*, 60, pp. 121–142.

Gelman, J. R. and S. C. Salop (1983). "Judo Economics: Capacity Limitation and Coupon Competition," *Bell Journal of Economics*, 14(2), pp. 315–325.

Gottfries, N. (1991). "Customer Markets, Credit Market Imperfections and Real Price Rigidity," *Economica*, 58, pp. 317–323.

Green, E. and R. Porter (1984). "Noncooperative Collusion Under Imperfect Price Information," *Econometrica*, 52(1), pp. 87–100.

Haltiwanger, J. and J. Harrington (1991). "The Impact of Cyclical Demand Movements on Collusive Behavior," *RAND Journal of Economics*, 22(1), pp. 89–106.

Haskel, J., C. Martin and I. Small (1995). "Prices, Margial Cost and the Business Cycle," *Oxford Bulletin of Economics and Statistics*, 57(1), pp. 25–41.

Hatzitaskos, K. and A. Nevo (2006). "*Why Does the Average Price Paid Fall During High Demand Periods*?" Mimeo, Northwestern University.

Klemperer, P. (1995). "Competition when Consumers have Switching Costs: An Overview with Applications to Industrial Organization, Macroeconomics, and International Trade," *The Review of Economic Studies*, 62(4), pp. 515–539.

Lee Y. and T. Mukoyama (2013). "*Entry, Exit, and Plant-level Dynamics over the Business Cycle*," Mimeo.

MacDonald, J. (2000). "Demand, Information and Competition: Why Do Food Prices Fall at Seasonal Demand Peaks?" *Journal of Industrial Economics*, 48(1), pp. 27–45.

Machin, S. and J. Van Reenen (1993). "Profit Margins and the Business Cycle: Evidence from UK Manufacturing Firms," *Journal of Industrial Economics*, 41(1), pp. 29–50.

Nekarda, C. and V. Ramey (2013). "The Cyclical Behavior of the Price-Cost Markup," Mimeo, *NBER Working Paper* No. 19099, see http://www.nber.org/papers/w19099.

Oliveira Martins J., S. Scarpetta and D. Pilat (1996). "Mark-Up Pricing, Market Structure, and the Business Cycle," *OECD Economic Studies*, 27, pp. 71–105.

Portier, F. (1995). "Business Formation and Cyclical Markups in the French Business Cycle," *Annals of Economics and Statistics*, 37/38, pp. 411–440.

Rotemberg, J. and G. Saloner (1986). "A Supergame-Theoretic Model of Price Wars During Booms," *American Economic Review*, 76(3), pp. 390–407.

Rotemberg, J. and M. Woodford (1991). "Markups and the Business Cycle," *NBER Macroeconomics Annual 1991*, 6, pp. 63–140.

Rotemberg, J. and M. Woodford (1999). The Cyclical Behavior of Prices and Costs, in J. B. Taylor and M. Woodford (Eds.), *Handbook of Macroeconomics*, Edition 1, Volume 1, Chapter 16, Elsevier, pp. 1051–1135.

Rosenbaum, D. and S. Sukharomana (2001). "Oligopolistic Pricing Over the Deterministic Market Demand Cycle: Some Evidence from the US Portland Cement Industry," *International Journal of Industrial Organization*, 19(6), pp. 863–884.

Staiger, R. and F. Wolak (1992). "Collusive Pricing with Capacity Constraints in the Presence of Demand Uncertainty," *RAND Journal of Economics*, 23(2), pp. 203–220.

Warner, E. and R. Barsky (1995). "The Timing and Magnitude of Retail Store Markdowns: Evidence from Weekends and Holidays," *Quarterly Journal of Economics*, 110(2), pp. 321–352.

Wilson, B. and S. Reynolds (2005). "Market Power and Price Movements over the Business Cycle," *Journal of Industrial Economics*, 53(2), pp. 145–174.

Chapter 6

Price Competition between Platforms: The Case of eBay vs. Yahoo! Auctions*

Stefan Behringer

Universität Duisburg-Essen
stefan.behringer@uni-due.de
www.stefanbehringer.com

Abstract

We investigate the equilibrium market structure on competing online auction sites such as those of eBay or Yahoo! Building on the model of Ellison *et al.* (2004), we take full account of the complexity of network effects on such platforms. We extend the model by looking at the implication of exogenous and endogenous buyer and seller charges making use of contingent tariffs. This extension brings in line the theory with the empirical findings of Brown and Morgan (2009) that eBay sellers enjoy higher prices and more favorable buyer–seller ratios than Yahoo! sellers. We also investigate welfare effects and look at the viability of duopoly with size differentials, at large markets, and at implications for policy.

Keywords: Platform competition, two-sided markets, auctions, equilibrium coexistence, eBay.

JEL Classification Codes: L11, L13, D43, D44.

1. Introduction

Virtual market platforms such as auctions often reveal very different price strategies despite the fact that such intermediaries offer homogenous

*I am grateful for comments by Matthias Blonski, Federico Boffa, Björn Brand, Thomas Gall, Germain Gaudin, Dominik Grafenhofer, Michael Katz, Lucia Visconti Parisio, Martin Peitz, Yossi Spiegel, Alex White, Julian Wright, and Pai-Ling Yin as well as participants of the "Two-sided Markets" Seminar at Universität Frankfurt, INTERTIC 2010 Milan, the 10th ICT conference at ZEW, CRESSE 2012, RSA Matera 2012, Oligo2013 Budapest, and the SEARLE Conference on Internet Search and Innovation 2013. Financial support of the PREMIUM project of the BMBF is gratefully acknowledged.

products. Competition between eBay and Yahoo! auctions are a case in point with Yahoo! auctions having substantially lower fees and commissions than eBay both in the U.S. and in Japan. Despite these similarities, markets were eventually dominated by eBay in the U.S. and by Yahoo! auctions in Japan (see Yin, 2004).

One explanation for this observation is the presence of network externalities. Intermediation between heterogenous agents such as bargaining buyers and sellers generates direct externalities (from agents of their own type) and indirect network externalities (from agents of the other type). This complex interaction of network externalities often remains unmodeled; an exception being the work "Competing Auctions" of Ellison, Fudenberg, and Möbius (EFM, 2004).[1] The analysis in EFM shows that stable equilibria in such duopoly markets exist and that they may be asymmetric.

EFM provide a simple model of static network competition between two competing auctions, i.e., *two-sided markets* involving buyers and sellers of a homogenous good. The network externalities on such auction markets are diametrically opposed, i.e., a buyer benefits if there are fewer other buyers in his/her auction (negative own-side effects or congestion externalities) and if there are more sellers (positive cross-side effects or indirect network effects). Inversely, a seller benefits from having more buyers and fewer sellers in his/her auction platform. The magnitudes of these effects can be calculated and compared as auctions are well-understood bargaining processes in the economics literature.

EFM have pointed out that when aggregating and netting these network effects, a "scale effect" dominates, i.e., the fact that larger auctions are more efficient than smaller ones implies that losses from own-side effects are more than outweighed by gains from cross-side effects. Still there is a countervailing "market impact effect", i.e., the fact that a single buyer or seller when switching auction platforms will have an impact on the outcome of the auctions by changing the buyer–seller ratio and thus the expected auction price for the good. In conjuction, these two effects allow for the co-existence of small and large auction platforms in equilibrium, i.e., a situation where neither buyers nor sellers on any of the two auctions prefers to switch platforms or abstain from the auction.

---

[1]Another exception is Nocke *et al.* (2007).

In their Section 7, EFM also look at the consequences of the two auction sites choosing an endogenous *common charge* that is assumed not to violate participation constraints and upset equilibrium allocations. This choice of modeling is partly motivated by the 1975 price-fixing allegations for Sotheby's and Christie's and partly because more general pricing strategies would lead to additional (ad-hoc) assumptions about selection rules in order to tackle the resulting *equilibrium multiplicity*. Whence the consequences of *asymmetry* for optimal platform pricing (that is generically observed in practice absent price-fixing arrangements) were not pursued.[2]

The aim of this chapter is to explain why undifferentiated platforms may charge *different* charges in equilibrium and potentially earn positive profits and what comparative statics these charges will have. We first identify conditions for an equilibrium in the agents' (buyers and sellers) allocation between the two platforms, for *exogenous* entry fees. Intuitively, if platform 2, for example, charges buyers a higher entry fee than platform 1, then the equilibrium allocation should involve a higher ratio of buyers–sellers in platform 1 than in platform 2. This is because platform 1 should become less attractive to buyers (to compensate for its lower entry fee) by including more buyers and less sellers than in platform 2. Similar logic applies for sellers.

The implications of the EFM framework for online trading platform competition between the most important players in the online auction platform markets *eBay* and *Yahoo! auctions* have been investigated in Brown and Morgan (2009).[3] In their extension of the EFM model, they also look at exogenous vertical platform differentiation (as in Shaked and Sutton (1982)) that could result from differing fixed entry fees.

One of their findings (see Proposition 4 in their paper) is that given eBay is the dominant platform and provides an exogenous vertical differentiation advantage to sellers, firstly, more buyers are attracted to a given Yahoo! auction than an eBay auction, and secondly, prices for the traded goods are higher on Yahoo! auctions than on eBay. The authors note that

---

[2]The objective to also investigate asymmetric price with elastic demands on competing two-sided platforms (albeit not in an auction setting) can be traced back to the foundational work of Rochet and Tirole (2003).

[3]Alternative applications include the competition of exchanges, see Cantillon and Yin (2011).

both predictions are *exactly contradicted* by their evidence from field experiments. As an alternative, they offer a dynamic disequilibrium model with boundedly rational players that will eventually lead to "tipping".

In this chapter, we are offering a more parsimonious extension of EFM that is in accordance with equilibrium coexistence taking differences in seller charges into account. This extension is empirically warranted as eBay has almost always been the more expensive platform for sellers in practice, charging listing fees *and* commissions. However, treating pricing/vertical differentiation as exogenous is clearly not fully satisfactory in the context of competing platforms either.

We therefore move on to investigate the effects of *endogenous* seller charges (e.g., entry fees) on the equilibrium market structure. These equilibria may be asymmetric in the proportion of buyers and sellers that join each platform, and in the sellers' access fees. We are able to show that introducing seller charges and thus vertical differentiation is sufficient to reconcile the empirical findings in Brown and Morgan (2009) with their use of the EFM model independently whether such differentiation is the result of an endogenous competitive outcome or an exogenous advantage. It is thus robust and supported by the empirical findings.

In analogy with the common agency literature, it seems straightforward that platforms as principals should be able to make their actions (the payments required from agents) *contingent* on the choice of the agent, i.e., the observable allocation decision of buyers and sellers. This is strongly related to the idea of *insulating fees* on two-sided platforms (put forward in Weyl (2010) for monopoly and White and Weyl (2012) for competition) where platform pricing may be made conditional on this eventual allocation mitigating the coordination problems.

A major advantage of such contingent tariffs over the employment of equilibrium refinements is that they are flexible enough to accommodate the potentially *asymmetric* market shares of buyers and sellers on each platform and endogenously reflect these asymmetries. While we are aware of the fact that such tariffs are only sufficient to bring about the observed changes in charges as eBay gains market dominance in many empirical markets (see Yin, 2004), we think that the investigation of price menus is warranted in its own right and may open new perspectives for platform operators. For example, it would be technically feasible for eBay to make seller charges contingent on the number of competing products and/or the number of buyers who decide to monitor a given auction on their watchlist.

From a policy perspective, a satisfactory analysis of *asymmetric* competition in such two-sided markets is clearly of vital importance as it reflects the most pressing cases of policy concern. The fact that effective competition and antitrust policy in standard markets generically do not carry over to two-sided markets with strong indirect network effects is well established (see e.g., Wright, 2004) and hence satisfactory and robust theoretical models have an impact on regulation policy.

The economic literature on two-sided markets in particular on platform competition has been blossoming recently. Auctions sites as special kinds of platforms with a clear and well-understood game structure are thus amenable to this analysis. Based on the pioneering work of Caillaud and Jullien (2003) and Armstrong (2006), one focus has been to try to deal with the inherent *multiplicity of equilibria*. These may arise for example from coordination failures, congestion externalities as in EFM, the possibility of multi-homing, i.e., joining multiple platforms, and/or simple price setting processes where, even in monopoly, equilibrium prices need not be unique despite the fact that equilibrium allocations of agents are (and indeed would determine unique equilibrium prices).

In order to tackle the issue, early research has resorted to *belief restrictions* such as "bad-expectation beliefs" (originating in Caillaud and Jullien (2003), and refined in Armstrong and Wright (2007)) such that agents are assumed to join one particular platform unless it is a dominant strategy for them not to do so. The consequences of such "responsive" as compared to "passive" expectations and hybrid forms of monopoly and duopoly pricing have been investigated recently in Hagiu and Halaburda (2013).

Viewing the problem of platform competition as a (multi) principal-agent problem (albeit with important externalities) with platforms trying to induce players to take certain actions using take-it-or-leave-it offers, the issue has parallels with the common agency literature originating in Bernheim and Whinston (1986). In an incomplete information setting, Halaburda and Yehezkel (2013) are employing these parallels using a *sequential* game under "*ex-post* asymmetric information", i.e., the same informational structure as EFM. Argenziano (2008) and Jullien and Pavan (2012) are investigating these issues within a global-game framework.

A paper that is close to our motivation to explain the coexistence of asymmetric outcomes in two-sided markets is Ambrus and Argenziano (2009). While their paper also starts with heterogenous consumers, the informational structure differs strongly as agents know their types when choosing the platform already. Also due to their assumption that agents are atomistic, the reasons for finding equilibrium coexistence are fundamentally different.

2. The Model

We model the duopolistic platform competition departing from a simple two-stage game presented in EFM (2004).

The timing of the game is as follows: In the first stage, B risk-neutral buyers ($B \in \mathcal{N}_0$) with unit demand and S risk-neutral sellers ($S \in \mathcal{N}_0$) with a single unit of the good to sell and no reservation value simultaneously decide whether to attend platform 1 or platform 2. In the second stage, buyers learn their valuations that are uniformly i.i.d. distributed on the unit interval and the object is auctioned off. We model this bargaining as a uniform price (multiobject if $S > 1$) auction on each platform. By the revenue equivalence theorem, this choice of the bargaining process is quite general. Each buyer only demands one homogeneous good. In order to guarantee strictly positive prices, we make the "non-triviality assumption" that

$$B > S + 1, \tag{1}$$

for both being positive integers. Sellers have their expected utility given by the expected price on their chosen platform. A buyer's utility on a platform with B buyers and S sellers is given by his/her expected net utility conditional on winning the good i.e.,

$$u_B = E\left\{v - v^{S+1,B} \middle| v \geq v^{S,B}\right\} \Pr\left\{v \geq v^{S,B}\right\}, \tag{2}$$

where $v^{k,n}$ gives the k highest order statistic of a draw of n values and thus in this auction format, the uniform price is simply the $S + 1$ highest of the buyers valuations $v^{S+1,B}$ (i.e., the highest losing bid). This is the typical mathematical convention as long as we deal with a discrete model.

Larger markets are more efficient than smaller ones as they come closer to the *ex-post* efficient outcome to allocate a good to a buyer if and only if his/her valuation is high. The *ex-post* efficient outcome implies that the buyers with the S highest values obtain the good, so that the expectation of the maximum total *ex-ante* surplus (welfare) is

$$B\Pr\left\{v \geq v^{S,B}\right\}E\left\{v \middle| v \geq v^{S,B}\right\} = SE\left\{v \middle| v \geq v^{S,B}\right\}$$
$$= SE\left\{v \middle| v > v^{S+1,B}\right\} = S\int_0^1 \left(\int_x^1 vf(v|v > x)dv\right) f^{S+1,B}(x)dx, \tag{3}$$

where $f^{S+1,B}$ is the density function of $v^{S+1,B}$, the $S+1$ highest order statistic of a draw of B values under the uniform distribution.

Lemma 1 (EFM) *Under the uniform distribution, total welfare on one platform can be written as the sum of buyer and seller utilities*

$$w(B,S) = S\left(1 - \frac{1}{2}\frac{1+S}{B+1}\right) = S\left(\frac{B-S}{B+1}\right) + B\left(\frac{S(1+S)}{2B(B+1)}\right).$$

Proof. See EFM (2004). □

The result is intuitive: The total value of a sale is the expected value of v *given* $v > p$, where p is the equilibrium price of the product within the platform. Under the uniform distribution, this is $1 - \frac{1}{2}\frac{1+S}{B+1} = p + \frac{1-p}{2}$. Clearly, the second term is the value for one buyer with the remaining p (as calculated above) going to the seller. To obtain total welfare, we multiply with the number of sales.

Note that

$$\frac{\partial w(1, \frac{S}{B} = \bar{x} < 1)}{\partial B} = \frac{1}{2}\bar{x}\frac{(2-\bar{x})(B+2)B+1}{(B+1)^2} > 0, \tag{4}$$

showing that for constant shares of sellers to buyers, larger markets are more efficient than smaller ones. The efficiency deficit makes it more difficult for small markets to survive but the sequential structure of the game allows for equilibria with two active platforms whenever the impact of switching of buyer and/or seller on his/her expected surplus more than outweighs the efficiency advantage.

The game is solved by backward induction and the solution concept is Subgame Perfect Nash equilibrium (SPNE). The transaction of the good in stage two yields *ex-ante* utility in stage one for a seller of

$$u_S(B, S) = p = \frac{B - S}{B + 1}, \tag{5}$$

and for a potential buyer of

$$u_B(B, S) = \frac{1 - p}{2}\frac{S}{B} = \frac{S(1 + S)}{2B(1 + B)}. \tag{6}$$

Note that holding S/B (the relative advantages of buyers and sellers) constant, sellers prefer larger, *more liquid* markets (where the expected equilibrium price is higher) and buyers prefer small, less efficient markets as

$$\frac{\partial u_S(1, \frac{S}{B} = \bar{x} < 1)}{\partial B} = \frac{\partial p(1, \frac{S}{B} = \bar{x} < 1)}{\partial B} > 0, \tag{7}$$

and

$$\frac{\partial u_B(1, \frac{S}{B} = \bar{x} < 1)}{\partial B} < 0. \tag{8}$$

Extending the setting of EFM, we assume that platforms can charge buyers and/or sellers some fee for participating but do not allow for price-discrimination, i.e., all buyers and sellers are assumed to face the same fee. Remember that consumers choose homogenous platforms *ex-ante*, i.e., before knowing their types. This *ex-ante* homogeneity of agents makes price discrimination using a "divide and conquer" type strategy by (heterogenous) platforms targeting specific subsets of heterogenous consumers (with possibly negative prices) as in Jullien (2011) a less obvious possibility and, on the other hand, voids the need for sophisticated belief refinements to counter the resulting multiplicity of equilibria.

As buyers and sellers simultaneously decide which platform to join in stage one, we can set up the relevant constraints that determine the set of *all* possible SPNE of the game subject to the qualification that the integer constraint holds. Otherwise, we will speak of a *quasi-equilibrium*.

This restriction is investigated in detail in Anderson *et al.* (2010). The constraints to keep buyers in place in stage one given buyer charge difference $p_{2B} - p_{1B} \equiv \Delta_B \geq 0$ are

$$u_B(B_1, S_1) \geq u_B(B_2 + 1, S_2) - \Delta_B, \tag{B1}$$

and

$$u_B(B_2, S_2) - \Delta_B \geq u_B(B_1 + 1, S_1). \tag{B2}$$

In words: A buyer on platform 1 needs to have an expected utility from the auction stage correcting for charges paid to the platform owner such that a change to the other platform and the implied effect on the equilibrium outcome of the auction there deters him from doing so.

To keep sellers in place in stage one given seller charge difference $\Delta_S \geq 0$, we need

$$u_S(B_1, S_1) \geq u_S(B_2, S_2 + 1) - \Delta_S, \tag{S1}$$

and

$$u_S(B_2, S_2) - \Delta_S \geq u_B(B_1, S_1 + 1), \tag{S2}$$

to hold. The motivation for the constraints is analogous. Clearly, these constraints matter only for interior equilibria.

2.1. *Exogenous buyer charges*

We now look explicitly at the form of the constraints and thus at the set of possible SPNE with some exogenous charge differences $\Delta_B > 0$ to (winning) buyers in auction two. Note that this does not imply that charges are made only by one of the platforms but only that it is the difference between such charges that influence location incentives.

Denoting s as the *share* of sellers on platform 1 and β as the *share* of buyers at platform 1, the buyer constraint (B1) becomes

$$\frac{sS(1+sS)}{2\beta B(1+\beta B)} \geq \frac{(1-s)S(1+(1-s)S)}{2((1-\beta)B+1)(1+(1-\beta)B+1)} - \Delta_B,$$

and (B2) is

$$\frac{(1-s)S(1+(1-s)S)}{2(1-\beta)B(1+(1-\beta)B)} - \Delta_B \geq \frac{sS(1+sS)}{2(\beta B+1)(1+\beta B+1)}.$$

A numerical example (with $B = 10$, $S = 5$) illustrates how the buyer constraints change. The two buyer constraints with $\Delta_B = 0$ (*solid lines*) and $\Delta_B = 0.3$ (*dashed lines*) are:

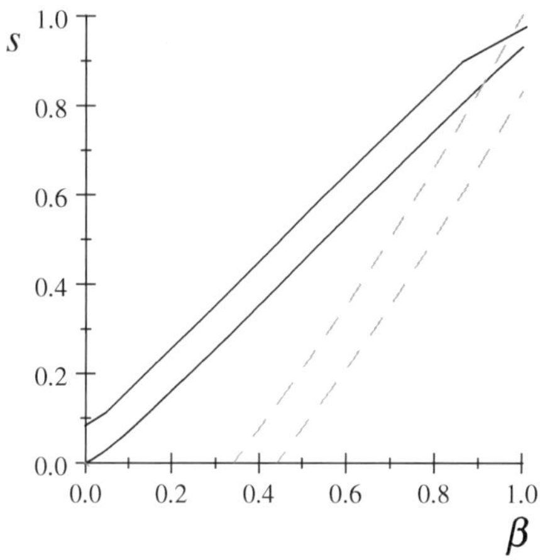

where the share of sellers on platform 1 (s) is on the ordinate and the share of buyers on platform 1 (β) is on the abscissa.

The interpretation of this finding is as follows: The lower *solid line* is the (B1) constraint gives the condition that buyers stay on platform 1 if the fraction of sellers s is large enough or, alternatively if β is low enough. The higher *solid line* is the (B2) constraint gives the condition under which buyers stay on platform 2, i.e., if s is small (and thus $(1-s)$ the fraction of seller on his/her own platform is large enough). Between the two curves is the candidate set of SPNE (we still need to check if the seller constraints hold).

Now with a charge of $\Delta_B > 0$ to buyers on platform 2 both the (B1) and the (B2) constraint shift downwards to the *dashed lines*, i.e., the set of SPNE allows for equilibria with a lower share of sellers on platform 1 for a given share of buyers. The (B2) constraint also shifts downwards. i.e., buyers move from platform 2 at higher levels of s already (and thus for a lower fraction of seller $(1 - s)$ on his/her own platform) than before given the new charge.

2.2. *Exogenous seller charges*

We now introduce an exogenous charge difference Δ_S for sellers of platform 2. Seller constraints are

$$\frac{\beta B - sS}{\beta B + 1} \geq \frac{(1-\beta)B - ((1-s)S + 1)}{(1-\beta)B + 1} - \Delta_S, \tag{S1}$$

and

$$\frac{(1-\beta)B - (1-s)S}{(1-\beta)B + 1} - \Delta_S \geq \frac{\beta B - (sS + 1)}{\beta B + 1}. \tag{S2}$$

With $\Delta_S = 0$ (*solid lines*) and $\Delta_S = 0.3$ (*dashed lines*), we find the picture with the seller constraints becomes:

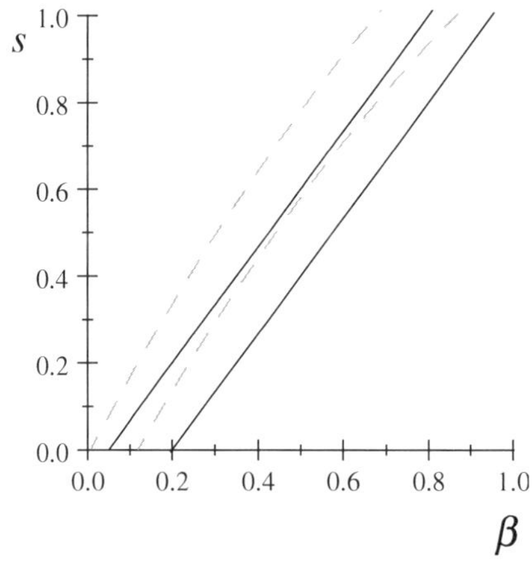

The interpretation of this finding is as follows: For the upper *solid line* is the linear (S1) constraint, a seller stays on platform 1 if s is not too high for a given share of β, otherwise he will go to platform 2. For the lower *solid line*, the linear (S2) constraint, a seller stays at platform 2 if s is high (i.e., his/her own seller share $1 - s$ is low), otherwise he will go to platform 1. Between the two curves is the candidate set of SPNE (we need to check if the buyer constraint holds simultaneously).

Now that there is a charge of $\Delta_S > 0$ to the sellers on platform 2, the (S1) constraint is no longer linear and shifts upwards to the upper *dashed line*: Sellers stay on platform 1 even if s is much higher than before for given β. Similarly, the (S2) constraint is no longer linear and also shifts upwards to the lower *dashed line*: Sellers will move from platform 2 even if s is much higher (hence their own seller share $1 - s$ much lower) than before.

The numerical example with $\Delta_S = 0.3$ (*dashed lines*) and the original buyer constraints for $\Delta_B = 0$ (*solid lines*) yields both seller and buyer constraints as:

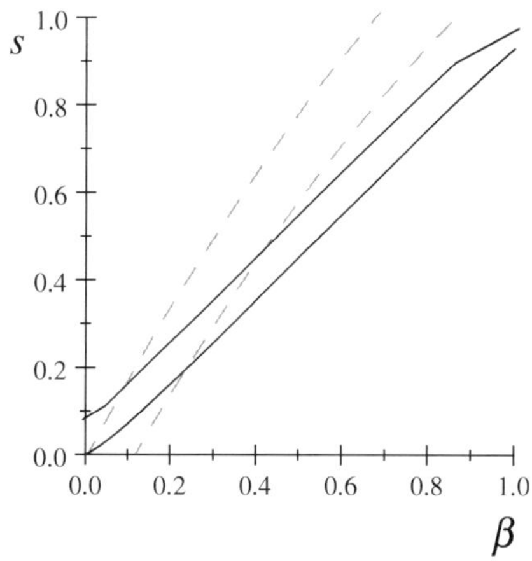

Only $\beta = 0.2, s = 0.2$ is a viable equilibrium here and the previous candidate $\beta = 0.4, s = 0.4$ is no longer viable.

The result reveals that charging sellers on platform 2 allows for higher s tolerance for given β on platform 1. Also, equally sized platforms are no longer viable. As sellers like larger, more liquid platforms where the uncertainty about the resulting final price is lower, we find that a positive and exogenous relative seller charge difference of platform 2 can only be an equilibrium if platform 2 also has the larger share of sellers.

3. Endogenous Seller Price Competition

We next look at duopoly competition where platforms may charge sellers for using the platform only. We focus on seller charges mostly because of the major application of this chapter, i.e., the competition between eBay and Yahoo! auctions where eBay explicitly forbids seller-fee-shifting. The assumption also holds for many other examples of platform competition and hence we consider it the more interesting variant. Again, we abstract from the possibility of price-discrimination.[4]

In order to investigate the issue, we extend setup and timing of the game: In the *first stage*, platforms $j = 1, 2$ simultaneously choose seller charges that may be *contingent* on realized allocations of buyers and sellers, i.e., a *function* that specifies charges as a function of buyer and seller allocations, $p^{S,j}, p^{S,-j}: (\beta, B, s, S) \to \mathbb{R}^+$.

In the *second stage*, buyers and sellers simultaneously decide which platform to join, learn their valuations that are uniformly distributed on the unit interval and the object is auctioned off. Payoffs to buyers, sellers, and platforms are realized (this was described as a separate stage above but can be collapsed into a single stage as we have shown for the EFM model above).

We make use of a very weak equilibrium refinement for the second stage: Instead of implementing belief/expectation restrictions or a new solution concept we define:

Definition 1 *An "efficient equilibrium" for the EFM model is the welfare maximizing equilibrium taken from the set of stable candidate equilibria.*

It is then possible to show that the efficient equilibrium will be *unique*. Intuitively as can be seen from the example above, the buyer switching constraints absent any buyer charges are "tight" around the diagonal, 45° line, i.e., there is no room for additional candidate equilibria neither above or below, nor to the right or to the left of the diagonal:

---

[4]Note that with endogenous "insulating fees" for which we allow here, it could be a profitable strategy to target initial sellers with a fee for a small number of buyers that is small (or even negative) but is then increasing (and positive) for a higher number of buyers. This would convince all sellers to join which in turn implies that all buyers will, in line with the idea of a "divide and conquer" strategy. This strategy also seems empirically plausible (e.g., *early adopters* with technical products) but again we abstract from such price discrimination due to a lack of buyer heterogeneity and because we believe that such sophisticated temporal strategies should most profitably be investigated in a truly dynamic framework (see Cabral, 2012).

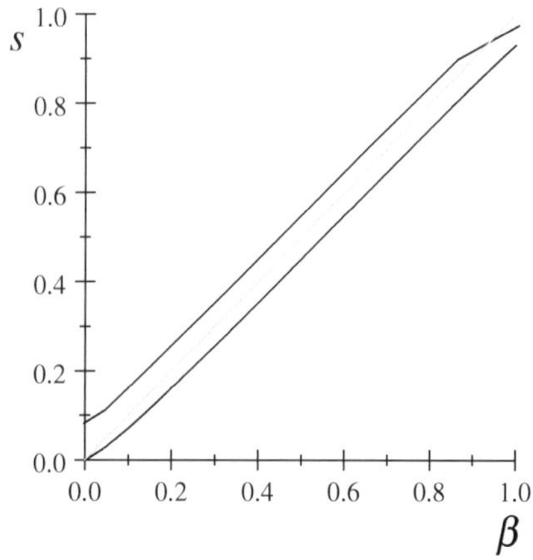

The buyer switching constraint thus forces all candidate equilibria to be *on* the diagonal. Now from what EFM call the "scale effect", we know that independently of the interplay of the four network effects (direct, indirect on both platforms), the aggregate effect is such that welfare is always maximized at the corner i.e., for a monopoly situation and that this monotony implies a unique efficient candidate equilibrium.[5] It is again obvious from this finding that any relevant policy implication from this model needs to take into account charges and thus the distributive issues that would result from a monopoly situation.

In order to discuss price formation in the above platform game, we now introduce platforms' *pricing strategies* to the first stage of the model that have the spirit of the *insulating fees* used in Weyl (2010) and White and Weyl (2012) (i.e., a mapping or menu from buyer and seller allocations into charges) to select their "*target allocations*" which mitigates the coordination problems. Lee (2013) also investigates contingent transfers in a one-sided setting. In the continuation equilibrium, the buyers and sellers then choose the platforms contingent on these price mappings. Platform profits are simply

$$\Pi_j = S_j p^{S,j} \quad \text{for } j = 1, 2, \tag{9}$$

where the charge $p^{\cdot}$ can be interpreted as a markup net of seller unit costs.

[5]For more details, see Behringer (2012).

Definition 2 *A "seller pricing strategy" is a map that specifies the charge to sellers as a function of the buyer and seller platform choices:*

$$p^{S,1}(B_1, B_2, S_1, S_2) \quad and \quad p^{S,2}(B_2, B_1, S_2, S_1),$$

or

$$\Delta^S(\beta, B, s, S).$$

This allows charges to be used as a non-cooperative tool to induce coordination on a desired outcome. The solution concept for the first stage is then *pure strategy Nash equilibrium* so that

$$p^{S,j*} = p^{S,j}(B_j^*, B_{-j}^*, S_j^*, S_{-j}^*) \quad \text{for } j = 1, 2 \text{ when } -j = 2, 1,$$

denotes the SPNE of the two-stage game where platforms maximize profits holding the other platforms price map constant and anticipate correctly that buyers and sellers will play the unique *efficient* equilibrium in stage two.

In most analyses of platform competition, it is assumed that *participation constraints* of the buyers are always met. For example, in a Hotelling model where the fixed benefit always outweighs possibly high charges by platforms. An explicit treatment of participation constraints often obscures results substantially (e.g., Lee, 2013, fn.11) or renders solutions implausible. On the contrary, we are able to investigate participation constraints and profit conditions (feasibility) in detail below.

Furthermore, demand also should depend on charges: If platform j charges a high enough seller charge, then it should lose all its sellers. In order to meet these intuitive requirements, we will assume the following assumption:

Assumption 1(A1). Agents do react to price changes of platforms in a way that their incentive (switching) constraints remain binding. Hence, a bounded and non-trivial demand elasticity can be calculated.

Proposition 1 *The equilibrium seller charge difference (of the price maps) resulting under competition and A1 are given by*

$$\Delta^{S*R} = -3\frac{B_1 - B_2 - S_1 + S_2 + B_1 S_2 - B_2 S_1}{(B_2 + 1)(B_1 + 1)},$$

if charges are rigid (R) and by

$$\Delta^{S*F} = -3\frac{2B_1 - B_2 - S_1 + S_2 + B_1S_2 - B_2S_1 + 1}{(B_2+1)(B_1+1)},$$

if charges are fully flexible (F).

Proof. See Appendix. □

The equilibrium target charges have the expected comparative statics as:

$$\frac{\partial p^{S_1,1*}}{\partial S_1} = -\frac{1}{B_1+1} < 0, \quad \frac{\partial p^{S_1,1*}}{\partial B_1} = \frac{S_1+2}{(B_1+1)^2} > 0$$

$$\frac{\partial p^{S_1,1*}}{\partial S_2} = \frac{2}{B_2+1} > 0, \quad \frac{\partial p^{S_1,1*}}{\partial B_2} = -\frac{2S_2+1}{(B_2+1)^2} < 0.$$

The comparative statics with flexible charges are identical except

$$\frac{\partial p^{S_1,1*}}{\partial B_2} = -\frac{2S_2+3}{(B_2+1)^2} < 0,$$

which differs in magnitude but not in sign. We focus on the rigid charge case in what follows.

3.1. *Participation constraints*

Note that (27) as calculated in the appendix can be written as

$$p^{S_1,1*} = \frac{(2\beta B+2)(1-s)S - ((1-\beta)B+1)sS + (\beta B - 2(1-\beta)B - 1)}{((1-\beta)B+1)(\beta B+1)}. \tag{10}$$

The participation constraints of a *seller on platform 1* is thus

$$U^{S1} = \frac{B_1 - S_1}{B_1+1} - p^{S_1,1*} = \frac{2B_2 - 2S_2 + B_1B_2 - 2B_1S_2 + 1}{(B_2+1)(B_1+1)} \geq 0, \tag{11}$$

which does not depend on S_1 anymore. The comparative statics reveal:

$$\frac{\partial U^{S1}}{\partial S_2} = -\frac{2}{B_2+1} < 0, \qquad \frac{\partial U^{S1}}{\partial B_1} = -\frac{1}{(B_1+1)^2} < 0,$$
$$\frac{\partial U^{S1}}{\partial B_2} = \frac{2S_2+1}{(B_2+1)^2} > 0,$$

so that taking price competition into account, the seller utility now decreases in the number of sellers on the other platform, decreases in the number of buyers on its own, but increases in the number of buyers on the other platform.

Expressing the constraint in terms of shares we find,

$$\frac{\partial U^{S1}}{\partial S} = -\frac{2(1-s)}{B-B\beta+1} < 0, \qquad \frac{\partial U^{S1}}{\partial s} = \frac{2S}{B-B\beta+1} > 0,$$

which clearly follows from the fact that U^{S1} does not depend on S_1 anymore. The remaining statistics are

$$\frac{\partial U^{S1}}{\partial B} = \frac{\begin{array}{c}(\beta(1-\beta)(2\beta+2S\beta(1-s)-1))B^2 + (4S\beta(1-\beta)(1-s))B \\ +2S(1-\beta)(1-s)+(1-2\beta)\end{array}}{(B(1-\beta)+1)^2(B\beta+1)^2},$$

and

$$\frac{\partial U^{S1}}{\partial \beta} = B\frac{\begin{array}{c}(2\beta(1-\beta-S\beta(1-s))-1)B^2 + (4S\beta(s-1)-2)B \\ +2(S(s-1)-1)\end{array}}{(B(1-\beta)+1)^2(B\beta+1)^2},$$

which are increasing and decreasing in large markets respectively.

If we introduce the seller participation constraint (11) into the example above ($B = 10$, $S = 5$), we get the following picture with new switching constraints for endogenous charges (*solid line*) and the participation constraint for sellers on platform 1 (*dashed line*):

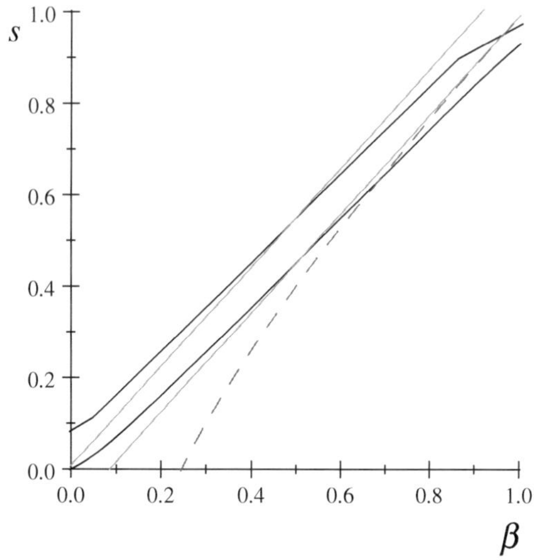

The example motivates the more general proof.

Lemma 2 *The participation constraint for sellers will be satisfied in any candidate equilibrium.*

Proof. See Appendix. □

3.2. *Platform profits*

Profits for platform 1 are given by

$$\Pi^1 = p^{sS,1} sS = \frac{\begin{bmatrix}(2\beta B + 2)(1-s)S - ((1-\beta)B + 1)sS \\ +(\beta B - 2(1-\beta)B - 1)\end{bmatrix}}{((1-\beta)B+1)(\beta B+1)} sS,$$

which is non-negative and thus feasible if the allocation in interior and platform equilibrium charges are non-negative. As seller charges on platform 1 (10) are decreasing in s, non-negative profits imply

$$s \leq \frac{2S - 2B + 3B\beta + 2BS\beta - 1}{3S + BS + BS\beta}. \tag{12}$$

For the example above ($B = 10$, $S = 5$), we find the zero-profit line (*dashed line*) as:

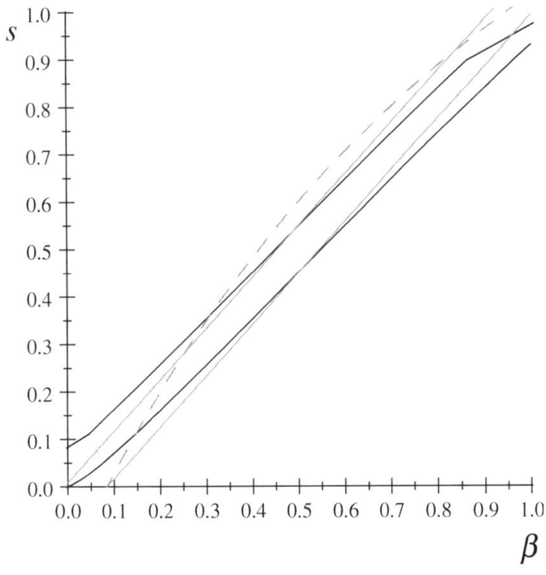

Note that despite the fact that with endogenous charges, from the consumer perspective all equilibria along the diagonal are now feasible, a non-negative-profit constraint on firms implies that extreme outcomes are still not possible and cannot be in the set of targeted allocations. The example generalizes to showing that extreme outcomes will be feasible:

Lemma 3 *The participation constraint for platforms cannot be satisfied for extreme candidate equilibria.*

Proof. Extreme candidate equilibria have $\beta, s \to 0$ (or $\beta, s \to 1$) respectively. We can solve the non-negative profit constraint (12) for β

at equality as

$$\beta = \frac{1}{3B + 2BS}(2B - 2S + 1) > 0,$$

i.e., strictly positive by non-triviality. Hence, extreme candidate equilibria cannot satisfy the feasibility constraints for duopoly. □

The above analysis finds that equilibria of this game may have non-Bertrand outcomes (despite homogeneity of the technology of the platforms and the product of the transaction) where pricing differences between the two platforms can prevail in subgame perfect equilibrium.

Making use of insulating fees and focusing on efficient equilibria allows to tackle the inherent multiplicity of equilibria in this two-sided market setting. As in Section 7 EFM, we focus on endogenous seller charges only but contrary to their analysis, we are able to investigate *asymmetric* insulating seller fees and are able to explicitly analyze asymmetric equilibrium outcomes. We also check for participation constraints and profit conditions without making additional assumptions about selection rules or employ belief restrictions.

4. Implications for Brown and Morgan (2009)

For very large platforms, it is quite intuitive that we cannot observe any charge differentials as the friction of the EFM model and hence the "market impact" effect vanishes. This finding is shared with Proposition 3 in Brown and Morgan (2009) who show that with exogenous vertical differentiation (i.e., a charge difference $\Delta_S > 0$ in our case) equilibrium coexistence in very large markets is impossible.

As the paper by Brown and Morgan is motivated by a detailed empirical and theoretical investigation of the competition between eBay and Yahoo! auctions, we phrase the following findings in this duopoly setting in order to make our findings more easily commensurable. A version of their Proposition 4 holds that in addition:

Proposition 2 *In any quasi-equilibrium in which the sites coexist and eBay (here* 1*) enjoys an* exogenous *vertical differentiation advantage for sellers (here $\Delta_S > 0$) and a more than 50% market share, relatively more sellers* *are attracted to a given eBay auction than an Yahoo! auction for sufficiently many buyers.*

Proof. The seller constraint (S2) from (S2) can be transformed into

$$s_{S2} \geq \frac{1}{S(B+2)}(S - 2B + \Delta_S + B\Delta_S - 1) + B\beta\frac{S + B\Delta_S - B\Delta_S\beta + 3}{S(B+2)}. \tag{13}$$

Also given participation constraints hold the maximal advantage for sellers is bounded by

$$\Delta_S < \max_{\beta,s}\left\{\frac{(1-\beta)B - (1-s)S}{(1-\beta)B + 1}\right\}. \tag{14}$$

Now we show that if $\Delta_S > 0$ and $\beta > 1/2$, then $s > \beta$ for sufficiently many buyers.

Note that s_{S2} is strictly concave in β given that $\Delta_S > 0$. The difference between s_{S2} and the 45° line (where $\beta = s$) is

$$d \equiv s_{S2} - \beta = \frac{1}{S(B+2)}(S - 2B + \Delta + B\Delta - 1) + \beta\frac{3B - 2S + B^2\Delta - B^2\Delta\beta}{S(B+2)}, \tag{15}$$

and still strictly concave in β. Thus, the difference d attains a maximum at

$$\beta_{\max} = \frac{3B - 2S + B^2\Delta_S}{2B^2\Delta_S} > 0, \tag{16}$$

at $\beta = 0$, the difference is

$$d = \frac{1}{S(B+2)}(S - 2B + \Delta + B\Delta - 1),$$

which is strictly negative given (14). As derivatives are smooth, there exists a unique intermediate value of β such that $d = 0$. This value can be found as

$$\beta_k = \frac{S - B(2 - \Delta_S) + \Delta_S - 1}{2S - B(B\Delta_S + 3)}. \tag{17}$$

Note that

$$\frac{\partial \beta_k}{\partial \Delta_S} = -\frac{(3B - 2S + B(B+2)(2B - S))}{(\Delta B^2 + 3B - 2S)^2}, \tag{18}$$

which given non-triviality $B > S + 1$ is negative. Hence, the difference is falling in Δ_S. Then there is a critical level of seller advantage such that the critical level of the intersection of s_{s2} and the 45° line is exactly at $\beta = 1/2$. This level is

$$\Delta_k = \frac{B + 2}{2B + B^2 + 2}, \tag{19}$$

and is *falling* in B. With sufficiently many buyers for any $\Delta_S > \Delta_k (\rightarrow 0)$, we have given $\beta > 1/2$ that $s > \beta$, i.e., the seller switching constraint (S2) can only be satisfied strictly above the 45° line. Thus, platform 1 faces $s > \beta$ and so a seller–buyer ratio of

$$\frac{sS}{\beta B} > \frac{S}{B}, \tag{20}$$

and by adding up

$$\frac{(1 - s)S}{(1 - \beta)B} < \frac{S}{B} < \frac{sS}{\beta B}. \tag{21}$$

□

The original Proposition 4 in Brown and Morgan holds that with an *exogenous* vertical differentiation advantage for sellers and a more than 50% market share, relatively more buyers are attracted to a Yahoo! than an eBay auction (platform 1) which contradicts their data. Once charges are endogenized using Proposition 6, we note that the theoretical implication is *exactly reversed* as sellers on eBay will actually face relatively more favorable buyer seller ratios as they will have to pay the higher seller charge and thus face an endogenous vertical differentiation disadvantage (i.e., $\Delta_S < 0$).

It turns out that endogenizing charges to sellers is also sufficient to reverse the result in Brown and Morgan (2009) about the relative *transaction prices* on both platforms and hence bring the model in line with their data in this respect too. We can show that:

Proposition 3 *In any quasi-equilibrium in which the sites coexist and eBay (here* 1*) enjoys an* endogenous *vertical differentiation* disadvantage for sellers *(here $\Delta^{S*F} < 0$) and a more than 50% market share, for sufficiently many buyers, the transaction price on eBay is higher than that on Yahoo! auctions.*

Proof. See Appendix. □

Hence, we find that with endogenous seller charges the transaction prices on eBay will be larger than those of Yahoo! auctions, in line with the data findings in Brown and Morgan (2009).

Alternatively, we can also use an exogenous vertical differentiation advantage for *buyers* to similarly show that:

Proposition 4 *In any quasi-equilibrium in which the sites coexist and eBay (here* 1*) enjoys an* exogenous *vertical differentiation* advantage for buyers *(here $\Delta_B > 0$) and a more than 50% market share, relatively more buyers are attracted to a given eBay auction than an Yahoo! auction for sufficiently many buyers and the transaction price on eBay is higher than on Yahoo! auctions.*

Proof. See Appendix. □

We have thus shown two alternatives by which the empirical results reported in Brown and Morgan (2009) can be brought in line with the theory. The first implies that the liquidity effects of a large market will dominate the effect of the endogenous seller charges on large platforms leading to a higher expected transaction price to the detriment of its buyers. Alternatively, one may argue that if eBay has an exogenous vertical differentiation advantage for buyers in addition to being the dominant platform in a liquid market, this is also sufficient to explain the more favorable buyers–seller ratio for its buyers and for it to have larger transaction prices than at Yahoo! auctions.

Note that endogenous seller charges satisfy

$$\lim_{B\to\infty}(\Delta^{S*F}) = \lim_{B\to\infty}(3\frac{(B-S)(1-2\beta)}{(B\beta+1)(B(1-\beta)+1)}) = 0. \qquad (22)$$

The intuition for this limit result is straightforward: The possibility that the switching of either buyer or seller has a tangible impact on expectations decreases as the number of buyers and sellers increases so that in the limit as markets get very large, all friction disappears from the model and we get a Bertrand type outcome with regard to the charge differences and proportional equilibria. This proposition can be easily extended to an unspecified distribution of valuations and is thus robust.

We also have a result for welfare on large platforms: As total welfare of a platform goes out of bounds, if the platform gets very large, we look at total welfare per buyer and seller respectively

$$\frac{w(B,S)}{B} = u_B(B,S) + \bar{x}u_S(B,S) = \bar{x}\left(1-\frac{\bar{x}}{2}\right), \qquad (23)$$

and

$$\frac{w(B,S)}{S} = \frac{1}{\bar{x}}u_B(B,S) + u_S(B,S) = 1-\frac{\bar{x}}{2}, \qquad (24)$$

where $\bar{x}$ is the limit of the total seller to buyer ratio. By the non-triviality assumption, the per capita welfare contribution of a buyer is thus always lower than that of a seller.

5. Conclusion

Often buyers cannot be charged for participating on a platform as for example on eBay where seller-fee-shifting is not allowed. Alternatively, the final transactions may not be observable as on used-car platforms. In these cases, the strictness of the buyer switching constraints implies that independently of whether or not there are charges to the sellers, the equilibrium market structure of the platform duopoly will imply proportional equilibria. This strongly restricts the set of equilibria of the game in EFM.

The original Proposition 4 in the paper by Brown and Morgan (2009) exactly contradicts their data which finds that: "eBay sellers enjoy higher prices and more favorable buyer–seller ratios than do Yahoo! sellers." Endogenizing the platform's pricing decision for sellers using the motivation for an "insulating equilibrium", we are able to show that theory and practice actually reveal an endogenous vertical disadvantage for sellers on eBay being the dominant platform. This observation exactly reverses their theoretical findings bringing them in line with the data from their field experiments.

A similar finding pertains with respect to the predicted relative transaction prices on both platforms. Once charges to sellers are endogenized, being the dominant platform implies that transaction prices will indeed be larger on eBay, the more liquid platform, again as observed in their field experiments. An alternative theoretical derivation of these results can be observed for an exogenous vertical differentiation advantage for buyers on eBay.

In conclusion, we have been able to explain why undifferentiated platforms may charge different prices in equilibrium. Our extension of the EFM model taking into account optimal platform pricing behavior results in a unique equilibrium target allocation and, as its mirror image, a set of participation-contingent equilibrium seller charges that fits the empirical results of Brown and Morgan (2009) for competition in the online auction market between eBay and Yahoo! auctions.

6. Appendix

Proof of Proposition 1: The game is solved using backward induction. W.l.o.g. we will focus on platform 1 with profits $\Pi_1 = S_1 p^{S_1,1}$. Using A, we can assume that (S1) is strictly binding thus

$$\frac{\beta B - sS}{\beta B + 1} - p^{S_1,1} \geq \frac{(1-\beta)B - ((1-s)S + 1)}{(1-\beta)B + 1} - p^{S_2+1,2}, \tag{25}$$

can be written as

$$p^{S_1,1} = p^{S_2+1,2} + \frac{B_1 - S_1}{B_1 + 1} + \frac{S_2 - B_2 + 1}{B_2 + 1}. \tag{26}$$

We investigate two cases:

(a) Prices are *rigid* (R) so that platforms cannot change their prices quickly and hence

$$p^{S_2+1,2} = p^{S_2,2}.$$

Substituting into the profit condition, the concave program for the optimal target allocation is

$$\max_{S_1} \Pi_1 = S_1 \left(p^{S_2+1,2} + \frac{B_1 - S_1}{B_1 + 1} + \frac{S_2 - B_2 + 1}{B_2 + 1} - c^{S,1} \right),$$

with the necessary and sufficient first-order conditions yielding best responses

$$S_1^{BR} = \frac{1}{2}(B_1 + 1)\, p^{S_2+1,2} + \frac{1}{2}\frac{2B_1 - B_2 + S_2 + B_1 S_2 + 1}{B_2 + 1},$$

and by symmetry

$$S_2^{BR} = \frac{1}{2}(B_2 + 1)\, p^{S_1,1} + \frac{1}{2}\frac{2B_2 - B_1 + S_1 + B_2 S_1 + 1}{B_1 + 1}.$$

Solving simultaneously the equilibrium target allocation then has

$$S_1^{*} = \frac{1}{3}(B_1 + 1)\left(p^{S_1,1} + 2p^{S_2+1,2} + \frac{3}{B_2 + 1} \right),$$

and

$$S_2^{*} = \frac{1}{3}(B_2 + 1)\left(p^{S_2+1,2} + 2p^{S_1,1} + \frac{3}{B_1 + 1} \right).$$

These can be implemented with *conditional* equilibrium charges

$$p^{S_1,1*} = \frac{(2B_1 + 2)S_2 - (B_2 + 1)S_1 + (B_1 - 2B_2 - 1)}{(B_2 + 1)(B_1 + 1)}, \tag{27}$$

and

$$p^{S_2+1,2*} = \frac{(2B_2 + 2)S_1 - (B_1 + 1)S_2 + (B_2 - 2B_1 - 1)}{(B_1 + 1)(B_2 + 1)}, \tag{28}$$

yielding

$$\Delta^{S*FP} = p^{S_2+1,2*} - p^{S_1,1*} = -3\frac{B_1 - B_2 - S_1 + S_2 + B_1S_2 - B_2S_1}{(B_2+1)(B_1+1)},$$

with rigid prices, as given above.

(b) If prices are *flexible* (F), we have the Nash targets still as

$$S_1^* = \frac{1}{3}(B_1+1)\left(p^{S_1,1} + 2p^{S_2+1,2} + \frac{3}{B_2+1}\right),$$

and again by symmetry

$$S_2^* = \frac{1}{3}(B_2+1)\left(p^{S_2+1,2} + 2p^{S_1,1} + \frac{3}{B_1+1}\right).$$

These can be implemented by

$$p^{S_1,1} = -2p^{S_2+1,2} + \frac{3B_2S_1 + 3S_1 - 3B_1 - 3}{B_1 + B_2 + B_1B_2 + 1},$$

but now prices adjust so that

$$p^{S_2+1,2} = -2p^{S_1,1} + \frac{3B_1(S_2+1) + 3(S_2+1) - 3B_2 - 3}{B_1 + B_2 + B_1B_2 + 1},$$

and equilibrium charges are

$$p^{S_1,1*} = \frac{3B_1 - 2B_2 - S_1 + 2S_2 + 2B_1S_2 - B_2S_1 + 1}{B_1 + B_2 + B_1B_2 + 1},$$

and

$$p^{S_2+1,2*} = -\frac{3B_1 - B_2 - 2S_1 + S_2 + B_1S_2 - 2B_2S_1 + 2}{B_1 + B_2 + B_1B_2 + 1},$$

which are no longer symmetric. The charge differencc for flexible prices is then

$$\Delta^{S*F} = -3\frac{2B_1 - B_2 - S_1 + S_2 + B_1S_2 - B_2S_1 + 1}{(B_2+1)(B_1+1)},$$

as given above. □

Proof of Lemma 2: We show that the participation constraint will remain outside the S2 switching constraint in general. Note that (11) can be written as

$$\frac{2(1-\beta)B - 2(1-s)S + \beta B(1-\beta)B - 2\beta B(1-s)S + 1}{((1-\beta)B+1)(\beta B+1)} \geq 0,$$

which can be solved as

$$s \geq \frac{1}{2S + 2BS\beta}(-2B + 2S + B^2\beta^2 + 2B\beta - B^2\beta + 2BS\beta - 1).$$

The RHS is an increasing and strictly concave function in β as

$$\frac{\partial RHS}{\partial \beta} = \frac{1}{2}\frac{B}{S(B\beta+1)^2}(B^2\beta^2 + 2B\beta + B + 3) > 0,$$

and

$$\frac{\partial^2 RHS}{\partial \beta^2} = -\frac{B^2\,(B+2)}{S\,(B\beta+1)^3} < 0.$$

It thus takes its maximum value at $\beta = 1$ where the constraint becomes

$$s_{PC} \geq \frac{1}{2S + 2BS}(2S + 2BS - 1).$$

The S2 constraint is from above

$$\frac{(1-\beta)B - (1-s)S}{(1-\beta)B+1} - \Delta_S \geq \frac{\beta B - (sS+1)}{\beta B + 1}, \tag{29}$$

where, if we replace the equilibrium rigid prices from above and solve for the binding s, we find:

$$s = \frac{1}{4S + 2BS}(2S - B + 3B\beta + 2BS\beta + 1),$$

which is linearly increasing in β. Again, the RHS takes a maximum at $\beta = 1$ for which the condition becomes

$$s_{S2} = \frac{1}{4S + 2BS}(2B + 2S + 2BS + 1).$$

Now if we take the vertical difference to the S1 constraint (29), we find:

$$s_{S2} - s_{PC} = \frac{1}{2}\frac{4B - 2S - 2BS + 2B^2 + 3}{S(B+2)(B+1)},$$

the sign of which depends on the numerator only. It is increasing in B and decreasing in S. As non-triviality equation (1) implies $B > S$ then at most $S = B$ and the numerator becomes $2B+3 > 0$ so the term is always positive. Due to symmetry, the result is sufficient for the participation condition to hold in any equilibrium. □

Proof of Proposition 3: The transaction price difference is

$$\begin{aligned} p_y - p_e &= \frac{(1-\beta)B - (1-s)S}{(1-\beta)B+1} - \frac{\beta B - sS}{\beta B + 1} \\ &= \frac{B - S - 2B\beta + 2Ss - BS\beta + BSs}{(B(1-\beta)+1)(B\beta+1)}, \end{aligned} \tag{30}$$

which has the same sign as

$$\begin{aligned} \sigma &\equiv B - S - 2B\beta + 2Ss - BS\beta + BSs \\ &= B - S + Ss(B+2) - B\beta(2+S), \end{aligned} \tag{31}$$

which is increasing in s. The (S2) constraint gives

$$\begin{aligned} s_{S2} \geq{}& \frac{1}{S(B+2)}(S - 2B + \Delta_S + B\Delta_S - 1) \\ &+ B\beta\frac{S + B\Delta_S - B\Delta_S\beta + 3}{S(B+2)}. \end{aligned} \tag{32}$$

With endogenous and rigid prices, the seller charge differential is

$$\Delta_S^* = 3\frac{(B-S)(1-2\beta)}{(B\beta+1)(B(1-\beta)+1)} < 0, \tag{33}$$

and with many buyers $\Delta_S^* \to 0$. Hence, what remains is the condition

$$s_{S2} \geq \frac{1}{S(B+2)}(S - 2B - 1) + B\beta\frac{S+3}{S(B+2)}. \tag{34}$$

Substituting in the above yields

$$\sigma = -B(1-\beta) - 1 < 0, \tag{35}$$

so this is not sufficient for σ to be positive, we need a higher s. Still we know from the existence of the "scale effect" that the buyer switching constraints are forcing equilibria to be *proportional* so that $\beta = s$ has to hold. The transaction price differential then reduces to

$$p_y - p_e = (B - S)\frac{1 - 2\beta}{(B(1-\beta)+1)(B\beta+1)}, \tag{36}$$

and as $B > S + 1$ and $\beta > 1/2$, we find that this difference is indeed negative. □

Proof of Proposition 4: The transaction price difference is

$$\begin{aligned} p_y - p_e &= \frac{(1-\beta)B - (1-s)S}{(1-\beta)B+1} - \frac{\beta B - sS}{\beta B + 1} \\ &= \frac{B - S - 2B\beta + 2Ss - BS\beta + BSs}{(B(1-\beta)+1)(B\beta+1)}, \end{aligned} \tag{37}$$

which has the same sign as

$$\begin{aligned} \sigma &\equiv B - S - 2B\beta + 2Ss - BS\beta + BSs \\ &= B - S + Ss(B+2) - B\beta(2+S), \end{aligned} \tag{38}$$

which is decreasing in β.

Assuming an exogenous vertical buyer advantage for eBay (1), the (B2) constraint implies

$$\frac{(1-s)S(1+(1-s)S)}{2(1-\beta)B(1+(1-\beta)B)} - \Delta_B \geq \frac{sS(1+sS)}{2(\beta B+1)(1+\beta B+1)}, \tag{39}$$

solving for β implicitly yields

$$2\beta_{B2} \geq 2 + \frac{1}{B} - \frac{\sqrt{\begin{array}{l} B^2\big(2(1+\beta B)(2+\beta B)\Delta_B + sS + sS^2\big) \\ \quad \times \big(2(1+\beta B)(2+\beta B)\big(\Delta_B + 2S(1-s) \\ \quad \times (S(1-s)+1)\big) + sS + sS^2\big) \end{array}}}{B^2\big(2(1+\beta B)(2+\beta B)\Delta_B + sS + sS^2\big)}. \tag{40}$$

With sufficiently many buyers $2\beta_{B2} \to 2$ so that $\beta > s$. Also

$$\sigma \equiv B - S + Ss(B+2) - B(2+S) = 2Ss - S - BS - B + BSs. \tag{41}$$

The maximum this can take (at $s = 1$) is

$$\sigma = 2S - S - BS - B + BS = -(B - S), \tag{42}$$

which by non-triviality $B > S + 1$ is *always* negative. □

References

Ambrus, A. and R. Argenziano (2009). "Asymmetric Networks in Two-Sided Markets," *American Economic Journal: Microeconomics*, 1(1), pp. 17–52.

Anderson, R. M., G. Ellison and D. Fudenberg (2010). "Location Choice in Two-Sided Markets with Indivisible Agents," *Games and Economic Behaviour*, 69, pp. 2–23.

Argenziano, R. (2008). "Differentiated Networks: Equilibrium and Efficiency," *RAND Journal of Economics*, 39(3), pp. 747–769.

Armstrong, M. (2006). "Competition in Two-Sided Markets," *RAND Journal of Economics*, 37, pp. 668–691.

Armstrong, M. and J. Wright (2007). "Two-Sided Markets, Competitive Bottlenecks and Exclusive Contracts," *Economic Theory*, 32, pp. 353–380.

Behringer, S. (2012). "Equilibrium Market and Pricing Structures in Virtual Platform Duopoly: Coexistence on Competing Auction Sites revisited," Mimeo.

Bernheim, B. D. and M. D. Whinston (1986). "Menu Auctions, Resource Allocation, and Economic Influence," *Quarterly Journal of Economics*, 51(1), pp. 1–32.

Brown, J. and J. Morgan (2009). "How much is a Dollar Worth? Tipping versus Equilibrium Coexistence on Competing Online Auction Sites," *The Journal of Political Economy*, 117(4), pp. 668–700.

Cabral, L. (2012). "Oligopoly Dynamics," *International Journal of Industrial Organization*, 30, pp. 278–282.

Caillaud, B. and B. Jullien (2003). "Chicken & Egg: Competition Among Intermediation Service Providers," *RAND Journal of Economics*, 34(2), pp. 309–328.

Cantillon, E. and P.-L. Yin (2011). "Competition between Exchanges: A Research Agenda," *International Journal of Industrial Organization*, 29, pp. 329–336.

Ellison, G., D. Fudenberg and M. Möbius (EFM) (2004). "Competing Auctions," *The Journal of the European Economic Association*, 2(1), pp. 30–66.

Halaburda, H. and Y. Yehezkel (2013). "Platform Competition under Asymmetric Information," *American Economic Journal: Microeconomics*, 5, pp. 22–68.

Hagiu, A. and H. Halaburda (2013). "Expectations and Two-Sided Platform Profits," *Working Paper* 12-045, *Harvard Business School*.

Jullien, B. (2011). "Competition in Multi-Sided Markets: Divide and Conquer," *American Economic Journal: Microeconomics*, 3(4), pp. 186–220.

Jullien, B. and A. Pavan (2012). "Platform Competition under Dispersed Information," Mimeo, *Discussion Paper* No. 1568, Kellogg School of Management.

Lee, R. S. (2013). "Competing Platforms," *Journal of Economics and Management Strategy*, forthcoming.

Nocke, V., M. Peitz and K. Stahl (2007). "Platform Ownership," *Journal of the European Economic Association*, 5(6), pp. 1130–1160.

Rochet, J.-C. and J. Tirole (2003). "Platform Competition in Two-Sided Markets," *Journal of the European Economic Association*, 1(4), pp. 990–1029.

Shaked, A. and J. Sutton (1982). "Relaxing Price Competition Through Product Differentiation," *Review of Economic Studies*, 49(1), pp. 3–13.

Weyl, E. G. (2010). "A Price Theory of Multi-Sided Platforms," *American Economic Review*, 100, pp. 1642–1672.

White A. and E. G. Weyl (2012). "Insulated Platform Competition," *NET Institute Working Paper* 10–17.

Wright, J. (2004). "One-Sided Logic in Two-Sided Markets," *Review of Network Economics*, 3, pp. 42–63.

Yin, P.-L. (2004). "Online Auction Markets," *Harvard Business School Case Study*, 9-705-411, August 23, 2004. Available at http://hbr.org/product/online-auction-markets/an/705411-PDF-ENG.

Part II

Anticompetitive Practices

Chapter 7

Cartel Sales Dynamics when Monitoring for Compliance is More Frequent than Punishment for Non-Compliance*

Joseph E. Harrington, Jr.
The Wharton School of the University of Pennsylvania
harrij@wharton.upenn.edu

Juan-Pablo Montero
Pontificia Universidad Católica de Chile
jmontero@uc.cl

Abstract

This study investigates when a cartel that uses a sales quota allocation scheme monitors more frequently than it enforces; for example, monitoring of sales is done on a weekly basis but firms are only required to comply with sales quotas on a quarterly basis. In a simple three-period quantity game with i.i.d cost and demand shocks, we show that the volatility of a cartel member's sales follows a U-shape within the compliance horizon. In comparison, sales volatility is constant over time under competition. This result offers a simple empirical test for distinguishing collusion from competition using sales data.

Keywords: Cartels, collusion, competition policy.

JEL Classification Codes: L13, L41.

1. Introduction

Many cartels, especially those in intermediate goods markets, do not just coordinate on prices but also on an allocation of the market (Harrington,

*The first author acknowledges the financial support of the National Science Foundation (SES-1148129) and the second the support of ISCI (Milenio P05-004F & Basal FBO-16). Both authors thank Martin Peitz for his constructive comments.

2006). One method of market allocation is sales quotas which can take the form of an absolute quantity or a market share. An interesting feature of these quota-allocation schemes is that the timing of monitoring and enforcement are not necessarily the same. Members of the lysine cartel, for example, coordinated on sales quotas to be enforced on a quarterly basis although they reported their sales on a monthly basis. As explained in Harrington and Skrzypacz (2011), one of the member companies of the lysine cartel — Ajinomoto — was assigned the task of preparing monthly "scorecards" for the cartel. Each member company telephoned or mailed their *monthly* sales volumes to an executive of Ajinomoto, who then prepared a spreadsheet that was distributed at the *quarterly* meetings of the cartel. And to enforce compliance, the cartel utilized a "guaranteed buy-ins" scheme: if during the quarter, a company sold more than its quota, it had to buy output from producers that were below quota.

The citric acid cartel, which also operated during the 1990s, is another example. In that cartel, monitoring of sales was done on a monthly frequency but enforcement occurred only annually. Members coordinated on a sales quota scheme in terms of market shares. On a monthly basis, each company reported its sales to an executive of Hoffmann LaRoche. The data were then assembled and reported back to the members by telephone. Enforcement was through a "buy-back system" whereby a company that exceeded its assigned quota in any one year was obliged to purchase product from the companies with sales below their quota in the following year.

It could be argued that a similar phenomenon may apply in an on-going antitrust case in which three chicken producers have been accused of having coordinated on sales quotas in Chile's wholesale chicken market. The defense argues that these were not quota allocations but rather sales projections provided by the trade association. (Without taking a position here on what they were, for our current purposes, we will refer to them as quota allocations.) The companies were accused of restricting competition by allocating weekly sales quotas of total kilos of chicken in its different forms (legs, breast, and whole chicken). This claim was examined in Montero *et al.* (2013) from which we provide Figure 1 which compares companies' actual weekly sales with their weekly "quota allocations" for 2007 (figures for other years are quite similar). It is evident from Figure 1 that the companies systematically and significantly deviated from their

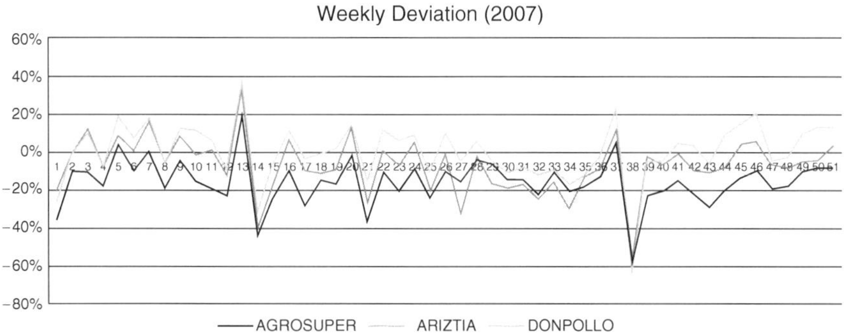

Figure 1. Weekly "deviations" of chicken producers.

Source: Reproduced from Figure 3.3 of Montero *et al.* (2013).

allocations, both individually and as a group. It is common to find weeks in which their sales were 10 or 20% above their "quotas" or 10 or 20% below, and this weekly "deviation" pattern is not unique to the largest company but applies to all three firms.

From our knowledge of the operation of past cartels, however, one cannot rule out the existence of a collusive sales quota agreement because there is a systematic and significant discrepancy between actual weekly sales and purported weekly sales quotas. It is possible that the compliance horizon is not weekly but of some longer length of time. In fact, in its accusation and without being explicit about it, the National Prosecuting Authority (Fiscalia Nacional Económica, FNE) appears open to the idea that the compliance horizon may have not been the week but rather the calendar year based on its extensive discussion of how the companies followed rather closely sales suggestions at the annual level (FNE, 2011, pp. 8–12). Figure 2 shows that "deviations" at the annual level were indeed far smaller, which may lead one to reasonably argue that the compliance horizon with the agreement was not the week but the calendar year; that is, the arrangement was for firms to meet their sales quotas at the annual level with monitoring done at the weekly level in order to provide information to assist in making that happen. Of course, an alternative hypothesis is that the lower deviation from sales projection at the annual level is the product of the law of large numbers and not of collusion. If observed weekly sales equal weekly sales projections plus i.i.d noise, then the variance of annual sales will necessarily

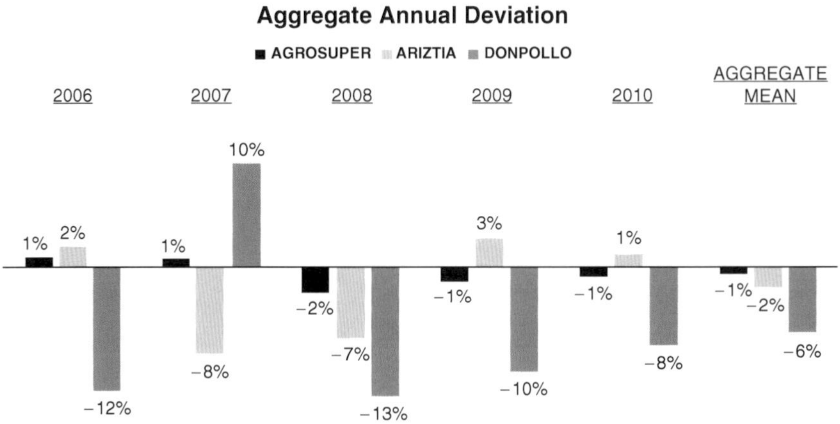

Figure 2. Annual "deviations" of chicken producers.

Source: Reproduced from Figure 3.4 of Montero *et al.* (2013).

be less than the variance of weekly sales. Thus, competition could well produce this pattern. It is then important to develop other tests that could distinguish collusion from competition in the intertemporal pattern of sales, which is the contribution of this chapter.

In this chapter, we exploit the different timing between monitoring and compliance for the purpose of deriving behavior that would allow one to empirically distinguish collusion from competition. This investigation is conducted for a simple linear quantity game with i.i.d cost and demand shocks. We find that early in the compliance horizon (which, as described above, is conjectured to be annual for the purported chicken processing cartel), the sales of a cartel member are more sensitive to contemporaneous shocks than are later sales to contemporaneous shocks. The logic is that a cartel member will take greater advantage of favorable shocks (that is, low cost or high demand) early in the compliance horizon by producing above average, as it knows there will be ample time to offset the over-production with under-production in the remainder of the year and still hit the cumulative quota target established by the cartel. Based on this "adjustment-to-shocks" effect, the prediction is derived that, under collusion, the sensitivity of contemporaneous sales to contemporaneous shocks should decline over the compliance horizon. In comparison, in our stationary environment, the sensitivity of sales to shocks is stationary over time under competition.

There is a second effect which we refer to as the "propagation-of-shocks" effect. As firms move through the compliance horizon, a cartel member's residual or available quota (that is, the quota less sales already realized) is more volatile as the result of previous shocks which adds to the volatility of sales. As the "adjustment-to-shocks" and "propagation-of-shocks" effects operate in different directions, we find that the volatility of sales of a cartel member follows a U-shape as opposed to the constant pattern under competition. That the volatility of sales under collusion follows a distinct path from that under competition could prove useful as a test for the presence of a cartel that engages in sales quotas.

The remainder of the chapter is organized as follows. The model is presented in Section 2 and firms' equilibrium strategies are derived in Section 3. In Section 4, we derive the equilibrium implications for the intertemporal pattern in the variance of sales and how it can allow us to distinguish collusive from competitive behavior. We conclude in Section 5.

2. Model

The model is designed to explore the implications for sales dynamics of a cartel that implements sales quotas with a multi-period compliance horizon. The compliance horizon is three periods in length which is sufficient to draw out the main insight. In this simple model, we do not consider the collusive strategies deployed in the infinite horizon setting but rather presume that it involves sales quotas and just assume that firms are constrained to satisfying the sales quota by the end of the compliance horizon.[1] The environment is enriched, however, by allowing for cost and demand shocks. After presenting the model, we then solve for equilibrium strategies for firms over the compliance horizon. In the following section, we explore the implications of equilibrium behavior for the cartel sales path.

Consider an industry with two firms, i and j, and a collusive agreement in which each firm is allocated a total output quota of $\rho^i = \rho^j = \rho$ every

[1] As described and analyzed in Harrington and Skrzypacz (2007, 2011), some cartels imposed a penalty to exceeding the sales quota which is continuous in the discrepancy between sales and the quota. Thus, firms could violate the quota without dire consequences. In the future, it is our intention to explore the questions of this chapter with such a specification but for this chapter we implicitly assume that the consequences of violating the sales quota are sufficiently severe that firms ensure that the quota is satisfied.

three periods. This is the same as to say that firms receive a quota of $\rho/3$ per period but compliance is only enforced at the end of the third period. A firm is free to allocate its sales any way it wants over the three periods as long as, at the end of period 3, its cumulative sales do not exceed ρ. We assume that the firms compete in the market by simultaneously choosing output q_t^i and q_t^j in each period, $t = 1, 2, 3$. Sales are publicly observed. There is no discounting over the three periods (which is unimportant for our results).

Firms face cost and demand shocks. Each firm has constant marginal cost where the realized cost is i.i.d across firms and time. Let $f : [\underline{c}, \overline{c}] \to [0, \infty)$ be the continuous density function on cost, and $\gamma \equiv \int_{\underline{c}}^{\overline{c}} sf(s)ds$ and $\sigma_c^2 \equiv \int_{\underline{c}}^{\overline{c}} (s-\gamma)^2 f(s)ds$ denote the mean and variance of cost, respectively. At the beginning of each period t and before choosing its quantity q_t^i, firm i learns its current period cost, c_t^i, but does not observe the other firm's cost. As is standard in the Cournot model, the market clears according to the linear inverse demand function $P(Q_t) = a_t - bQ_t$, where $Q_t = q_t^i + q_t^j$ is total output, and a_t is a demand shock that is i.i.d over time. Let $g : [\underline{a}, \bar{a}] \to (\overline{c}, \infty)$ be its continuous density function, and $\alpha \equiv \int_{\underline{a}}^{\bar{a}} sg(s)ds$ and $\sigma_a^2 \equiv \int_{\underline{a}}^{\bar{a}} (s-\alpha)^2 g(s)ds$ denote the associated mean and variance, respectively. Firms observe a_t before setting quantities for the period.

It is evident that in the absence of shocks (that is, $a_t = a$ and $c_t^i = c$ for sure and for all t), it would be impossible for the analyst to separate competitive (Cournot) behavior from collusive behavior by just looking at the evolution of sales. With either form of conduct, production is constant over time. Our focus is on how cost and demand shocks can allow us to separate collusive from competitive behavior using sales data.

3. Equilibrium Behavior

To facilitate the exposition, we consider first the case of cost shocks and then add demand shocks.

3.1. *Case of cost shocks*

Assume for now that inverse demand is deterministic: $P(Q) = a - bQ$. Denote by $\phi_1 : [\underline{c}, \overline{c}] \to [0, \infty)$ a firm's period 1 (symmetric) equilibrium strategy — which prescribes a quantity given its period 1 cost — and by $\phi_2 : [\underline{c}, \overline{c}] \times [0, \rho]^2 \to [0, \infty)$, a firm's period 2 (symmetric) equilibrium strategy — which prescribes a quantity given its period 2 cost and the available quotas of both firms from period 1.[2] Setting ρ sufficiently small for the problem to be non-trivial (that is, it is a binding constraint for colluding firms), a firm's period 3 strategy is simply to produce an amount equal to its available quota: $q_3^i = \rho - q_2^i - q_1^i$. To find equilibrium strategies ϕ_1 and ϕ_2, we proceed by backward induction.

Suppose we are in period 2 and the available quotas at the beginning of the period are $\rho_2^i \equiv \rho - q_1^i$ and $\rho_2^j \equiv \rho - q_1^j$. Note that the available quotas are observed by both firms at the beginning of each period which is the result of their quantities being observed. Firm i's expected total payoff as of period 2 (given its period 2 cost) is:

$$\begin{aligned}\int_{\underline{c}}^{\overline{c}} \int_{\underline{c}}^{\overline{c}} &[(a - bq_2^i - b\phi_2(c_2^j, \rho_2^j, \rho_2^i) - c_2^i)q_2^i \\ &+ (a - b(\rho_2^i - q_2^i) - b(\rho_2^j - \phi_2(c_2^j, \rho_2^j, \rho_2^i)) - c_3^i)(\rho_2^i - q_2^i)] \\ &\times f(c_2^j) f(c_3^i) dc_2^j dc_3^i. \qquad (1)\end{aligned}$$

Note that the expectation is taken with respect to the other firm's period 2 cost and a firm's own period 3 cost (The other firm's period 3 cost does not matter given the assumption that firm i will produce $\rho_2^i - q_2^i$ in period 3.). Note also that the equilibrium strategy for the other firm, $\phi_2(c_2^j, \rho_2^j, \rho_2^i)$, depends not only on the firm's own cost but may also depend on the available quotas of both firms.

Recalling that γ is the expected cost, (1) is equivalent to

$$\begin{aligned}\int_{\underline{c}}^{\overline{c}} &[(a - bq_2^i - b\phi_2(c_2^j, \rho_2^j, \rho_2^i) - c_2^i)q_2^i \\ &+ (a - b(\rho_2^i - q_2^i) - b(\rho_2^j - \phi_2(c_2^j, \rho_2^j, \rho_2^i)) \\ &- \gamma)(\rho_2^i - q_2^i)] f(c_2^j) dc_2^j.\end{aligned}$$

[2]Conditioning on the available quotas is equivalent to conditioning on the period 1 quantities. In principle, the period 2 strategy could also condition on a firm's period 1 cost, but that will not be the case in equilibrium.

Take the first-order condition (FOC), and solve for optimal q_2^i which is $\phi_2(c_2^i, \rho_2^i, \rho_2^j)$:

$$\phi_2(c_2^i, \rho_2^i, \rho_2^j) = \left(\frac{1}{4b}\right)\left[2b\rho_2^i + b\rho_2^j - 2bE\left[\phi_2(c_2^j, \rho_2^j, \rho_2^i)\right] + \gamma - c_2^i\right], \tag{2}$$

where

$$E[\phi_2(c_2^j, \rho_2^j, \rho_2^i)] = \int_{\underline{c}}^{\overline{c}} \phi_2(c_2^j, \rho_2^j, \rho_2^i) f(c_2^j) dc_2^j.$$

Taking the expectation of (2) and using the fact that c_2^i and c_2^j are independent:

$$E[\phi_2(c_2^i, \cdot)] = \int_{\underline{c}}^{\overline{c}} \left(\frac{1}{4b}\right)\left[2b\rho_2^i + b\rho_2^j - 2bE[\phi_2(c_2^j, \cdot)] + \gamma - c_2^i\right] \times f(c_2^i)dc_2^i$$

$$E[\phi_2(c_2^i, \cdot)] = \left(\frac{1}{4b}\right)\left[2b\rho_2^i + b\rho_2^j - 2bE[\phi_2(c_2^j, \cdot)] + \gamma - \gamma\right]$$

$$E[\phi_2(c_2^i, \cdot)] = \left(\frac{1}{4b}\right)\left[2b\rho_2^i + b\rho_2^j - 2bE[\phi_2(c_2^j, \cdot)]\right]. \tag{3}$$

Similarly, we have

$$E[\phi_2(c_2^j, \cdot)] = \left(\frac{1}{4b}\right)\left[2b\rho_2^j + b\rho_2^i - 2bE[\phi_2(c_2^i, \cdot)]\right].$$

We have two equations, (2) and (3), and two unknowns. Solving, we obtain

$$E[\phi_2(c_2^i, \cdot)] = \frac{\rho_2^i}{2}, \quad E[\phi_2(c_2^j, \cdot)] = \frac{\rho_2^j}{2},$$

and using these values in (2) leads to

$$\phi_2(c_2^i, \rho_2^i, \rho_2^j) = \frac{\rho_2^i}{2} + \frac{\gamma - c_2^i}{4b}. \tag{4}$$

On average, a firm produces half of its available quota in period 2, leaving the other half for period 3. When its period 2 cost is favorable (in the sense that it is below the mean value for cost), then it produces above the level of $\rho_2^i/2$ in order to take advantage of the low cost realization. If instead the cost realization is unfavorable, then it produces below $\rho_2^i/2$ in order to save more quota for period 3 when, on average, the cost realization will be better than that for period 2.[3]

Recall that (4) was derived under the conjecture that a firm would want to produce at its remaining quota $\rho_2^i - q_2^i$ in period 3. We then need to verify that is indeed optimal for a firm given its period 2 equilibrium quantity and do so for all cost realizations in periods 2 and 3 and for all available period 2 quotas. For that, we just need to check what happens when firms' available quotas are at their maximum values in period 3, which occurs, in equilibrium, when both firms had the highest cost of $\overline{c}$ in periods 1 and 2. In that case, the myopic (unconstrained) best reply in period 3 exceeds the available quota if and only if:

$$\frac{a-\overline{c}}{2b} - \left(\frac{1}{2}\right)\left[\rho - \phi_1(\overline{c}) - \phi_2(\overline{c}, \rho - \phi_1(\overline{c}))\right]$$
$$> \rho - \phi_1(\overline{c}) - \phi_2(\overline{c}, \rho - \phi_1(\overline{c})). \tag{5}$$

We cannot proceed any further with the verification of this conjecture without first deriving the period 1 equilibrium strategy ϕ_1, which we do next.

Given ρ_2^i and ρ_2^j, deriving period 1 equilibrium strategies requires that we first compute firms' payoffs in period 2 onwards as a function of the unused allocations coming out of period 1. Denote these payoffs by $V_2^i(\rho_2^i, \rho_2^j)$ and $V_2^j(\rho_2^i, \rho_2^j)$. Thus, firm i's expected payoff in period 2 (given the available quotas) is:

$$\begin{aligned}
&E\left[V_2^i(\rho_2^i, \rho_2^j)\right] \\
&= \int_{\underline{c}}^{\overline{c}} \int_{\underline{c}}^{\overline{c}} \left[\left(a - b\phi_2(c_2^i, \cdot) - b\phi_2(c_2^j, \cdot) - c_2^i\right)\phi_2(c_2^i, \cdot)\right. \\
&\qquad + \left(a - b\left(\rho_2^i - \phi_2(c_2^i, \cdot)\right) - b\left(\rho_2^j - \phi_2(c_2^j, \cdot)\right) - \gamma\right) \\
&\qquad \times \left.\left(\rho_2^i - \phi_2(c_2^i, \cdot)\right)\right] f(c_2^i) f(c_2^j) dc_2^i dc_2^j.
\end{aligned}$$

[3]Note that the equilibrium strategy (4) is independent of the rival's available quota which is probably due to the linearity of the problem (that is, linear demand and cost functions), and thus need not hold more generally.

It takes a bit of algebra to show that

$$\frac{d}{d\rho_2^i}E\left[V_2^i(\rho_2^i,\rho_2^j)\right]=\int_{\underline{c}}^{\overline{c}}\int_{\underline{c}}^{\overline{c}}\left[a-\frac{1}{2}\gamma-\frac{1}{12}c_2^j-\frac{5}{12}c_2^i-\frac{1}{2}b\rho_2^j-b\rho_2^i\right]$$
$$\times f(c_2^i)f(c_2^j)dc_2^i dc_2^j$$
$$=a-\frac{1}{2}bE\left[\rho_2^j\right]-b\rho_2^i-\gamma.$$

Now, firm i's expected total payoff as of period 1 (given its period 1 cost) is:

$$\int_{\underline{c}}^{\overline{c}}\left[(a-bq_1^i-b\phi_1(c_1^j)-c_1^i)q_1^i\right]f(c_1^j)dc_1^j+E\left[V_2^i(\rho_2^i,\rho_2^j)\right],$$

where recall $\rho_2^i\equiv\rho-q_1^i$ and $\rho_2^j\equiv\rho-q_1^j$. Firm i's problem is to choose q_1^i, given the cost realization c_1^i. The FOC for this problem is

$$a-2bq_1^i-bE\left[\phi_1(c_1^j)\right]-c_1^i=a-\frac{1}{2}b(\rho-E\left[\phi_1(c_1^j)\right])-b(\rho-q_1^i)-\gamma,$$

which, after rearranging, leads to the optimal period 1 quantity $\phi_1(c_1^i)$:

$$\phi_1(c_1^i)=\frac{1}{6b}(3b\rho-3bE\left[\phi_1(c_1^j)\right]+2\gamma-2c_1^i).$$

Proceeding as we did in solving for the period 2 equilibrium strategy, we have

$$E\left[\phi_1(c_1^i)\right]=\frac{1}{6b}(3b\rho-3bE\left[\phi_1(c_1^j)\right]),$$

and, using the symmetry of the problem, we get

$$E\left[\phi_1(c_1^i)\right]=E\left[\phi_1(c_1^j)\right]=E[\phi_1(c_1)]=\frac{\rho}{3}.$$

Therefore,

$$\phi_1(c_1^i)=\frac{\rho}{3}+\frac{\gamma-c_1^i}{3b}. \quad (6)$$

Similar to the period 2 case, a firm produces above (below) the per period quota of $\rho/3$ when its cost realization is below (above) average.

In comparing the period 1 and period 2 equilibrium strategies in (4) and (6), respectively, we find that the period 1 quantity is more sensitive to the period 1 shock than the period 2 quantity is to the period 2 shock, which in turn is more sensitive than the period 3 quantity to the period 3 shock (which, by the assumption that the quotas are binding with probability one, is not sensitive at all to period 3 cost):

$$\frac{\partial \phi_1}{\partial c_1^i} = -\frac{1}{3b} < -\frac{1}{4b} = \frac{\partial \phi_2}{\partial c_2^i} < 0 = \frac{\partial \phi_3}{\partial c_3^i}.$$

Property 1: A firm's quantity is more sensitive to the contemporaneous cost shock when it is earlier in the compliance horizon.

A firm's quota for the compliance horizon is a scarce resource and when it produces above its quota in a given period, there is less quota available for later production. Given that cost is stochastic, a firm wants to save up its quota so that it can produce more when its cost is low. If a firm produces more in period 2 in order to take advantage of low period 2 cost, there is necessarily less output that can be produced in period 3 which means a firm could not take advantage of a low period 3 cost realization. In comparison, in period 1, a firm does not have to be as frugal when it comes to using up its quota because there are two periods with which to adjust its quantity in order to comply with the quota. Thus, even if firm 1 produces at a high level in period 1 because of a low period 1 cost, it will still be in a position to produce at a high level in period 2 if there is a low period 2 cost. In sum, early in the compliance horizon, quantities are more sensitive to cost shocks as a firm can depart from "average quantity" knowing it will have more periods to adjust its quantity and still hit the cumulative quantity target. As a firm gets near the end of the compliance horizon, its quantity becomes less sensitive to contemporaneous cost shocks and more sensitive to the available quota as it has a shorter time to manage its quantities in order to ensurc that its sales do not exceed its sales quota.

Notice, however, that equilibrium quantities are more sensitive to cost shocks in period 1 than in period 2 does not necessarily imply that the sales path of a cartel firm is more volatile at the beginning of the compliance window than at the end. There is a second force that operates in the opposite direction: the quantity in period 2 is not only subject to period 2 cost shocks but also to period 1 cost shocks which operate indirectly through the available quota (i.e., ρ_2^i). In the next section, we study how the combination of these two forces determines the evolution of sales volatility.

Before closing the section, we return to the verification we initiated in equation (5), which can be rewritten as

$$\frac{a-\bar{c}}{2b} > \left(\frac{3}{2}\right)(\rho - \phi_1(\bar{c}) - \phi_2(\bar{c}, \rho - \phi_1(\bar{c})))$$

$$\frac{a-\bar{c}}{3b} > \left[\rho - \left(\frac{\rho}{3} + \frac{\gamma - \bar{c}}{3b}\right) - \left(\frac{\rho}{3} + \frac{\gamma - \bar{c}}{12b}\right)\right]$$

$$\frac{a-\bar{c}}{3b} > \frac{\rho}{3} + \frac{5(\bar{c}-\gamma)}{12b} \Rightarrow \frac{a-\bar{c}}{3b} - \frac{\rho}{3} > \frac{5(\bar{c}-\gamma)}{12b}. \tag{7}$$

Recall that we want to ensure that firm i finds it optimal to produce in period 3 so that its sales quota is binding; that is, it produces $\rho_2^i - q_2^i$ for any cost realizations for both firms in periods 1 and 2 and for any cost realization for this firm in period 3. Let us assume the per period collusive allocation $\rho/3$ is less than the average static Nash equilibrium quantity,

$$\frac{a-\gamma}{3b} > \frac{\rho}{3},$$

so that, on average, the sales quota is less than the competitive supply. In that case, (7) holds as $\bar{c} \to \gamma$. Hence, if the support on cost is not too large, then (7) holds, and the equilibrium strategies found above, (4) and (6), are valid for any cost realizations in $[\underline{c}, \bar{c}]$.

3.2. *Case of cost and demand shocks*

It is straightforward to add i.i.d demand shocks to the model.[4] As before, equilibrium strategies are found by backward induction. Suppose we are in period 2 and $\rho_2^i \equiv \rho - q_1^i$ and $\rho_2^j \equiv \rho - q_1^j$. Then a firm's payoff as of

[4]Given that demand shocks are market-wide, we also expect the same implications to emerge from a common cost shock to firms as would occur, for example, from a common change in an input price.

period 2 is

$$\int_{\underline{a}}^{\bar{a}}\int_{\underline{c}}^{\overline{c}}\int_{\underline{c}}^{\overline{c}} \left[\left(a_2 - bq_2^i - b\phi_2\left(c_2^j, a_2, \cdot\right) - c_2^i\right)q_2^i \right.$$
$$+ \left(a_3 - b\left(\rho_2^i - q_2^i\right) - b\left(\rho_2^j - \phi_2\left(c_2^j, a_3, \cdot\right)\right) - c_3^i\right)\left(\rho_2^i - q_2^i\right)\Big]$$
$$\times f\left(c_2^j\right) f\left(c_3^i\right) g\left(a_3\right) dc_2^j dc_3^i da_3.$$

Proceeding as before to derive the optimal q_2^i, we obtain the equilibrium strategy

$$\phi_2\left(c_2^i, a_2, \rho_2^i, \rho_2^j\right) = \frac{\rho_2^i}{2} + \frac{a_2 - \alpha}{6b} + \frac{\gamma - c_2^i}{4b}, \tag{8}$$

where recall $\alpha = \int_{\underline{a}}^{\bar{a}} sg(s)ds$.

We next turn to period 1 quantities given the derived equilibrium quantity rules for period 2. Firm i's expected total payoff as of period 1 (given period 1 demand and cost) is:

$$\int_{\underline{c}}^{\overline{c}} \left[\left(a_1 - bq_1^i - b\phi_1\left(c_1^j, a_1, \cdot\right) - c_1^i\right)q_1^i\right] f\left(c_1^j\right) dc_1^j + E\left[V_2^i\left(\rho_2^i, \rho_2^j\right)\right],$$

where $E\left[V_2^i\left(\rho_2^i, \rho_2^j\right)\right]$ is the expected equilibrium payoff in the continuation game with available quotas ρ_2^i and ρ_2^j and it is equal to

$$\int .. \int \left[\left(a_2 - b\phi_2^i - b\phi_2^j - c_2^i\right)\phi_2^i + \left(a_3 - b\left(\rho_2^i - \phi_2^i\right)\right.\right.$$
$$\left.\left. - b\left(\rho_2^j - \phi_2^j\right) - \gamma\right)\left(\rho_2^i - \phi_2^i\right)\right]$$
$$\times f\left(c_2^i\right) f\left(c_2^j\right) g(a_3) g(a_2) dc_2^i dc_2^j da_3 da_2,$$

where $\phi_2^i \equiv \phi_2\left(c_2^i, a_2, \rho_2^i, \rho_2^j\right)$.

Proceeding as in Section 3, it is not difficult to show that the period 1 equilibrium strategy is

$$\phi_1\left(c_1^i, a_1\right) = \frac{\rho}{3} + \frac{2(a_1 - \alpha)}{9b} + \frac{\gamma - c_1^i}{3b}. \tag{9}$$

Since $2/9 > 1/6$, we find a similar relationship to that in Section 3.1 in that period 1 quantities are more sensitive to period 1 demand shocks than period 2 quantities are to period 2 demand shocks, which in turn are more sensitive than period 3 quantities to period 3 demand shocks. In fact, the equilibrium strategy for any period $t = 1, 2, 3$ can be written more generally as

$$\phi_t\left(c_t^i, a_t, \rho_t^i\right) = \frac{\rho_t^i}{T - t + 1} + k_t\left(\frac{2}{9b}(a_t - \alpha) + \frac{1}{3b}\left(\gamma - c_t^i\right)\right), \quad (10)$$

where $T = 3$ is the number of periods within the compliance window, $k_1 = 1$, $k_2 = 3/4$, and $k_3 = 0$. Note how the "adjustment" coefficients k_t's go down overtime. Furthermore, from looking at the regularity in (10), it should be possible to find the equilibrium strategies for any T recursively (something we do not do here).

Property 2: A firm's quantity is more sensitive to the contemporaneous demand shock when it is earlier in the compliance horizon.

4. Volatility of Sales

The volatility of period 1 sales depends only on the volatility of period 1 shocks. From the equilibrium strategy (9), we obtain that the variance of period 1 sales is

$$\text{Var}\left[q_1^i\right] = \frac{1}{9b^2}\left(\frac{4}{9}\sigma_a^2 + \sigma_c^2\right), \quad (11)$$

where σ_a^2 and σ_c^2 are the variances of demand and cost shocks, respectively. Furthermore, given perfect compliance with the cartel agreement (that is, $q_3^i = \rho - q_1^i - q_2^i$), it is evident that period 3 sales are more volatile than sales in any previous period. In fact, the unconditional variance of period 3 sales is simply

$$\text{Var}\left[q_3^i\right] = \text{Var}\left[q_1^i\right] + \text{Var}\left[q_2^i\right].$$

Much less evident is how the volatility of period 2 sales compares to the volatility of period 1 sales because of the operation of the two effects identified earlier. Equilibrium strategies show that firms adjust less to contemporaneous shocks as we move toward the end of the compliance window — this is the adjustment-to-shocks effect — but at the same time, these later sales are not only subject to contemporaneous shocks but also to previous shocks through changes in the available quota left to cover future sales — this is the propagation-of-shocks effect. Using the equilibrium strategy (8) and the fact that $\rho_2^i = \rho - \phi_1(c_1^i, a_1)$ along the equilibrium path, the unconditional variance of period 2 sales is

$$\mathrm{Var}[q_2^i] = \frac{1}{4}\mathrm{Var}[q_1^i] + \frac{1}{16b^2}\left(\frac{4}{9}\sigma_a^2 + \sigma_c^2\right).$$

Using (11), we have

$$\mathrm{Var}[q_2^i] = \frac{13}{16}\mathrm{Var}[q_1^i].$$

In sum,

$$\left(\frac{13}{16}\mathrm{Var}[q_1^i] =\right)\mathrm{Var}[q_2^i] < \mathrm{Var}[q_1^i] < \mathrm{Var}[q_3^i]\left(= \frac{29}{16}\mathrm{Var}[q_1^i]\right).$$

There is then the implication that period 2 sales are less volatile than both period 1 and period 3 sales. This lower volatility is the result of the adjustment-to-shocks effect dominating the propagation-of-shocks effect. Thus, early in the horizon, one would expect a high adjustment effect to dominate a low propagation effect in that sales would be mostly sensitive to contemporaneous cost shocks. As the firm moves forward, its sales become less sensitive to contemporaneous cost shocks and more sensitive to previous shocks as reflected in the remaining quota. In the intermediate time period, a lower adjustment effect dominates a higher propagation effect which results in overall less volatility. When the firm gets near the end of the compliance horizon, there is virtually no room for adjustment to contemporaneous shocks; its sales are nevertheless highly volatile because of the propagation effect. This implies that the volatility of sales of a cartel member follows a U-shape as opposed to the volatility of a firm's sales in the absence of collusion which exhibit a stable path.

Property 3: Sales volatility is minimized in the middle of the compliance horizon.

That the volatility of sales under collusion follows a distinct path from that under competition is a useful finding that has a simple intuition and a clean prediction that one can take to sales data. For example, if a fraction of firms of an industry are suspected of forming a cartel one can use this theory to test for differences between the volatility of sales of those firms suspected of being part of the cartel and those that are not. Provided that one can get access to monthly series of sales data of both cartel and non-cartel firms, the citric acid cartel is a potentially good example to run such a test as it comprised the five largest producers which together controlled about 60% of global production and 67% of production in the European Union (Harrington, 2006).

In applying our theory to less than all inclusive cartels, however, it is important to keep in mind that the volatility of sales of a non-cartel firm is also affected by the way cartel firms price their products and adjust their quantities to shocks.[5] This interaction makes for an interesting extension to our theory, but one that should not undermine the main result that collusive and competitive behavior can be distinguished by looking at the volatility of sales. Take for example, a positive demand shock early on the compliance horizon. Cartel members would increase their production to take advantage of the favorable shock while non-cartel firms would not react as much to the positive shock because of the strategic substitutability of quantities. This would make cartel sales look even more volatile relative to those of non-cartel firms. This is just one example illustrating why our theory should still apply in the case of a "partial" cartel, but obviously a more formal extension is required before any conclusions are drawn.

In the case of an all-inclusive cartel, which probably better applies to the case of the allegedly chicken cartel mentioned in Section 1 and which controlled about 90% of domestic production (Montero *et al.*, 2013), the test may require a time series of sales data long enough to cover periods where the cartel was not in operation. This data may correspond to the period before the cartel was formed or after the accusation was initiated (though provided the cartel would no longer be able to maintain cooperation). In the absence of such "counterfactual" sales data, one can still run the test if shocks are expected to follow a pattern that can be explained by other observables (e.g., prices of relevant inputs and prices of other meat products).

[5] In a model in which monitoring and enforcement follow the same timing, Montero and Guzman (2010) study how a cartel that faces a fringe of competitive suppliers adjust its overall quota to changes in demand.

5. Conclusions

In a simple model, we have explored collusive behavior in the context of a sales quota scheme when monitoring occurs at a higher frequency than is enforcement imposed for non-compliance. There are two main contributions. The first contribution is identifying two dynamic forces at work with regards to a firm's quantity. The adjustment-to-shocks effect is that a cartel member's quantity is less responsive to contemporaneous cost and demand shocks as we move toward the end of the compliance (or enforcement) horizon. Early on in the compliance horizon, a firm takes greater advantage of low cost shocks by producing at a higher rate, knowing that it has more periods to adjust its sales in order to ensure compliance by the end of the compliance horizon. The propagation-of-shocks effect is that, as a cartel member moves toward the end of the compliance horizon, its available quota is more volatile as it is the cumulative product of more cost and demand shocks. While the adjustment-to-shocks effect results in greater sales volatility *earlier* in the compliance horizon, the propagation-of-shocks effect results in greater sales volatility *later* in the compliance horizon. The second contribution is showing that, when both of these effects are taken account of, sales volatility is initially decreasing as a cartel member moves through the compliance horizon and is then increasing so that sales volatility is minimized at an intermediate stage of the compliance horizon. This finding provides a test for a cartel with a sales quota scheme since, under competition, sales volatility is stationary and thus does not exhibit this intertemporal pattern.

Under standard models of competition, if cost and demand are stationary stochastic processes, then firms' quantities are stationary stochastic processes, too. However, when firms collude using sales quotas and the timing of monitoring and compliance do not coincide, then firms' quantities are no longer stationary. The distribution on firms' quantities will depend on where they are in the compliance window. It was this non-stationarity property that was exploited in deriving the collusive markers for distinguishing collusion from competition. While our analysis assumed i.i.d processes for cost and demand shocks, the general approach can be used to derive collusive markers as long as the cost and demand processes are stationary. Thus, the analysis could be extended in a straightforward way to allow cost and demand shocks to be serially correlated.

The model used for this analysis assumes a three-period compliance horizon and that firms produce subject to the constraint of satisfying the three-period sales quota. While useful for gaining some initial insight into how a sales quota scheme with an enforcement horizon exceeding the monitoring horizon impacts sales dynamics, a proper approach would set the problem up in an infinite horizon setting, endogenize the penalty from exceeding the sales quota (rather than presuming it is so severe that a firm would never exceed it), and derive equilibrium behavior given that penalty function. Of particular interest is to use that structure to solve for the optimal frequency of monitoring and enforcement. Understanding how market conditions — such as the number of firms and cost and demand volatility — impact the length of the enforcement horizon could deliver additional properties on collusive behavior and thus allow for a richer set of tests for assessing whether a cartel is present in a market.

References

Fiscalía Nacional Económica (FNE, 2011). Requerimiento contra Agrosuper Agrícola S.A. y otros (FNE's complaint against Agrosuper and others), Santiago (the document can be accessed from Chile's Competition Tribunal website: www.tdlc.cl).

Harrington, J. E. (2006), "How Do Cartels Operate?" *Foundations and Trends in Microeconomics*, 2(1), pp. 1–108.

Harrington, J. E. and A. Skrzypacz (2007). "Collusion under Monitoring of Sales," *RAND Journal of Economics*, 38(2), pp. 314–331.

Harrington, J. E. and A. Skrzypacz (2011). "Private Monitoring and Communication in Cartels: Explaining Recent Collusive Practices," *American Economic Review*, 101(6), pp. 2425–2449.

Montero, J.-P. and J. I. Guzman (2010). "Output-Expanding Collusion in the Presence of a Competitive Fringe," *Journal of Industrial Economics*, 58(1), pp. 106–126.

Montero, J.-P., J. E. Harrington and F. Gallego (2013). "A Competition Analysis of Chile's Wholesale Chicken Market" (the document can be accessed from Chile's Competition Tribunal website: www.tdlc.cl).

Chapter 8

Exploitation and Induced Tacit Collusion: A Classroom Experiment of Corporate Leniency Programs*

Jeroen Hinloopen
University of Amsterdam
J.Hinloopen@uva.nl

Adriaan R. Soetevent
University of Groningen
A.R.Soetevent@rug.nl

Abstract

Recent laboratory experiments support the popular view that the introduction of corporate leniency programs has significantly decreased cartel activity. We develop a classroom experiment that captures key features of leniency programs. Our treatments include an exploitable and a non-exploitable leniency program to highlight possible adverse effects of leniency programs that are too generous. We also examine to what extent a non-exploitable leniency program triggers tacit collusion. The experimental results show that if the efforts of the antitrust authority and the leniency program are directed exclusively to the most straightforward collusive scheme, subjects manage to switch to a more intricate form of coordination. This shift from overt collusion to tacit collusion can serve as the basis for a classroom discussion about the effectiveness of actual leniency programs.

Keywords: Classroom experiment, collusion, tacit collusion, corporate leniency program.

JEL Classification Codes: C72, C92, L41.

*Thanks are due to Aufa Doarest and Jona Linde for their assistance during the experiment. We further thank Sander Onderstal and seminar participants at the European Commission (DG Competition) for helpful comments. The involvement of the Editor, Yossie Spiegel, greatly improved the exposition of our ideas. Soetevent's research is supported by the Netherlands Organisation for Scientific Research under grant 451-07-010.

1. Introduction

To better enforce the ban on collusion, the United States introduced in 1978 a corporate leniency program.[1] This policy initiative was followed by the European Commission in 1996 (Hinloopen, 2003). According to these programs, antitrust authorities can offer fine reductions to cartel members that report their cartel and provide legal proof toward conviction of the cartel. Meanwhile, leniency programs are part of antitrust law in all modern economies (OECD, 2002).[2]

In recent years, a number of high-profile cartel cases have illustrated the success of leniency programs, including the citric acid, lysine, and vitamin cartels (Connor, 2001; see also Harrington, 2006). Policy makers are apt to stress the success of leniency programs in diminishing cartel activity.[3] As Scott Hammond, the former Director of the Criminal Enforcement Antitrust Division of the U.S. Department of Justice, remarks: "Leniency is the single greatest investigative tool available to antitrust investigators. It destabilizes cartels by increasing the risk and fear of detection. It breaks up cartels by causing members to compete again, only this time the competition is a footrace to the government's door. [...] The stakes are so high that the competitors can no longer afford to trust each other. Panic ensues, and it is a race for leniency" (Hammond, 2003, p. 14).[4]

[1]Estimates of the probability that in a given year a cartel is detected (in absence of a leniency program) vary between 13 and 17% (Bryant and Eckard, 1991; Combe *et al.*, 2008).

[2]The fine reductions depend on several factors, including the extent to which the self-reporting firm cooperates with the antitrust authorities, whether or not it has been convicted in the past for participating in a cartel, and if it is the cartel's ring leader. Leniency programs differ across jurisdictions (Roux and von Ungern-Sternberg, 2007; Spagnolo, 2008). Choi and Gerlach (2012) show that cartel members can exploit these differences in that it may help cartel members to coordinate on reduced self-reporting.

[3]The American Central Intelligence Agency freely disseminates a video with excerpts from cartel meetings that were obtained with the help of the whistle blower in the infamous lysine cartel, Marc Whitacre. The popular narrative of the rise and fall of the lysine cartel by Kurt Eichenwald (Eichenwald, 2000) was the basis of a Holywood feature film, starring Matt Damon as Marc Whitacre.

[4]The success of leniency programs is also hailed by Neelie Kroes at the time she was EU Commissioner for competition: "The leniency program is proving to be an efficient tool to detect and punish cartels" (*New York Times*, 2005).

The theoretical support for the effectiveness of leniency programs is mixed however. Carefully designed leniency programs can destabilize existing cartels and may deter future cartel formation (Spagnolo, 2004). But leniency programs could also induce firms to collude tacitly. To illustrate this possibility, consider the empirical study of Goeree and Helland (2010). In 1993, the U.S. changed its corporate leniency program and made it easier and more attractive to apply for leniency. Goeree and Helland (2010) use this policy change to examine if research joint ventures (RJVs) serve as a collusive device. They find that the policy change significantly reduces the probability that a firm joins an RJV.[5] One interpretation of this finding is that the policy change makes it more likely that firms will apply for leniency suggesting that the leniency program before the policy change encouraged firms to collude tacitly under the wings of an RJV.

Badly designed leniency programs may even stimulate collusion. Indeed, leniency programs that offer fine reductions that are too generous can be exploited. Applying for leniency is then part of the collusive agreement: cartel members take turn in applying for leniency, and cartels do not break down upon reporting. The leniency program then triggers collusion if this type of collusion yields higher expected profits than either colluding and not reporting or not colluding at all, while colluding without leniency applications is not incentive compatible (Motta and Polo, 2003).[6] A generous *ad hoc* leniency program in The Netherlands targeted at a specific, widely-defined industry ("construction") might have been exploited. In 2001, an anonymous whistle blower came forward with evidence of about 3,000 rigged bids during the period 1986–1998. When the Dutch competition authority subsequently initiated a rather generous leniency program, granting amnesty to anyone who pleaded guilty of bid rigging and other types of price fixing agreements, 486 companies from different industries applied for leniency. This massive reporting of illegal

[5]Because the policy change should not have an effect on firms' incentives to join an RJV unless it has some collusive purpose, Goeree and Helland (2010, p. 7) conclude that "Our results are consistent with RJVs serving (at least in part) a collusive function."

[6]An optimal leniency program would maximize the likelihood that a cartel is reported while not becoming exploitable. According to such a program, fine reductions should be offered to the first applicant only but it should not be restricted to first-time offenders (Chen and Rey, 2009).

firm conduct did not, however, resort in significant price reductions in the Dutch construction industry (Van Bergeijk, 2007). This suggests that applying for leniency was a profitable means to escape fine payments while it did not affect subsequent firm conduct.

In this chapter, we present a classroom experiment that captures key features of a leniency program. We consider both an exploitable and a non-exploitable leniency program, and we examine to what extent leniency programs induce tacit collusion. The results of the experiment can be used to start a classroom discussion about the acclaimed success of leniency programs.[7]

The effectiveness of various leniency programs has been examined in a number of recent experimental studies. The strand of papers that is closest to our classroom experiment starts with Apesteguia *et al.* (2007). They consider a one-shot homogeneous goods Bertrand game with three players. Explicit cartel formation is possible before the pricing stage, and cartels can be reported after all prices are posted. Offering cartel members a fine reduction in return for reporting the cartel reduces the average price to levels observed in treatments where the possibility to form a cartel is blocked. The setting of Apesteguia *et al.* (2007) is extended in three directions by Hinloopen and Soetevent (2008): cartels can be detected and punished in the absence of reporting, fine reductions depend on the order of leniency application, and subjects interact repeatedly. The leniency program of Hinloopen and Soetevent (2008) is also effective: it destabilizes cartels, it reduces the probability that a cartel is re-established, and it reduces average price. Yet another innovation is introduced by Bigoni *et al.* (2012). They introduce the possibility for subjects to report cartels also before the pricing stage. These secret reports allow the authors to distinguish between two motives for leniency applications: to punish defecting cartel members and to escape possible fine payments. In this setting, leniency programs also deter cartel formation and significantly reduce cartel recidivism.[8]

---

[7]Field studies shed light on the working of real-life cartels but overlook by definition cartels that have not been detected (although Miller (2009) and Brenner (2009) conduct empirical tests that permit inference for the entire population).

[8]Another strand of the literature considers the effects of leniency programs in auctions (Hamaguchi *et al.*, 2007; Hinloopen and Onderstal, 2013).

The experiments reported in the literature have focused exclusively on non-exploitable leniency programs. The designs rule out situations where regularly applying for leniency can be part of a profitable collusive arrangement. The objective of our classroom experiment is not only to illustrate the working of a leniency program, but also to examine if an exploitable leniency program will be exploited. In addition, our design illustrates the workings of different leniency programs in a setting where it is less difficult for cartel members to collude tacitly.

We conducted a pen-and-paper experiment that is an extension of the classroom experiment of Holt and Capra (2000). Subjects repeatedly interact with the same person. In each round, participants have to play either a red (R) or a black (B) card. Only if both players play a red card, they collude overtly.[9] There are four different treatments. In the first, labeled BENCHMARK, there is no penalty for playing (R, R). This is different in ANTITRUST where a cartel detection probability of 40% is introduced. The concomitant fine equals what subjects earn when playing (R, R). The first leniency program is EXPLOITABLE. Upon self-reporting, subjects receive full amnesty if they are the only one to report the cartel. A 90% fine reduction is given when both subjects self-report. In NON-EXPLOITABLE, the latter is reduced to 50% while full amnesty is given to a single self-reporting subject.

The results of the classroom experiment conducted in a first-year PhD course clearly illustrates the undesirable effects of introducing leniency programs that are too generous: a significant fraction of all subjects was able to exploit the program if it is exploitable. Another observation that could steer a classroom discussion is that in case of the non-exploitable leniency program, a substantial number of subject pairs succeeded in switching to a more intricate form of collusion whereby subjects took turn in capturing the entire market. Because this behavior does not qualify as collusion in the experiment, it successfully avoids the probability of having to pay a fine.

In what follows, we first present the theoretical framework that corresponds to our classroom experiment. Section 3 presents the experimental procedures. We have conducted the experiment in a first-year economics PhD course, the results of which are discussed in Section 4. Section 5 concludes.

[9]Collusion is synonymous for overt collusion. Tacit collusion is always explicitly identified.

2. The Game

The experiment is a card game that builds on the classroom experiment of Holt and Capra (2000). In this game, each subject is given two playing cards, a red (R) card and a black (B) card, and an identification number. Each round subjects are asked "to play" one card, which means holding it to one's chest with the back side up. In this way, it is clear that a card is played but not which color. Next, the identification numbers are called in pairs according to a pre-determined pairing scheme. Subjects have to show the color of their card whenever their identity number is called. The experimenter then calls out the colors of the two cards and the choices are recorded. Subjects that have been asked to reveal their card put down their card, record their private earnings in their income table, and wait for the round to end. All treatments involve repeated play. To implement a common discount factor, while at the same time secure enough observations, we followed Dal Bó (2005) in that after each round a 10-sided die was thrown to determine if subject pairs would be re-matched. We implemented a 20% re-matching probability.

How much subjects earn depends on their own card choice and that of the subjects with whom they are matched. Table 1 shows the per-period earnings in our BENCHMARK treatment, which correspond to a classic prisoner's dilemma. When played only once, playing B is for both players the dominant strategy and (B, B) is the unique Nash equilibrium. At the same time, each player would receive a higher payoff when (R, R) is played.[10]

Table 1. The One-Shot Prisoner's Dilemma that is Repeated in BENCHMARK

		Column player	
		R	B
Row player	R	(10, 10)	(20, 0)
	B	(0, 20)	(4, 4)

[10]The game can be interpreted as a repeated Bertrand pricing game with homogeneous goods and constant marginal costs. Suppose there is a market with two firms who each have constant marginal cost of 5 and where in each period market demand equals $D(p) = 14 - p$. Demand is rationed in that the firm charging the lowest price captures the entire market while

Playing the game repeatedly allows for equilibrium outcomes that are no equilibrium in the one-shot game. The obvious alternative to the single-stage Nash equilibrium is playing (R, R) in each period. A trigger strategy whereby each player plays R in each round conditional on the other player having done the same, and otherwise B as of the next period for ever after (Friedman, 1971), could sustain (R, R) as an equilibrium. The individual net present value (NPV) of adherence to this strategy is $V^C = 10/(1-0.8) = 50$, where superscript C stands for "Collusion".[11] Assuming both players to adhere to the trigger strategy, the NPV of playing B rather than R is $V^D = 20 + 0.2 \times 4/(1-0.8) = 36$, which shows that playing (R, R) repeatedly is incentive compatible in BENCHMARK.

Playing (R, R) in each period is not the only possible strategy profile to avoid playing (B, B) in every period. Another, somewhat more complicated scheme is that players alternate between playing R and B. Subjects receive full undercutting profits of 20 in periods in which they play B and 0 in all other periods. This strategy profile is based on players returning favors. Of course, the NPV of this scheme in a given period is the lowest for the player whose turn it is to play R, and equals $V^{TC} = 0.8 \times 20/(1-0.8^2) = 44.4$, where TC stands for "Tacit Collusion" as there is no penalty when alternating between (R, B) and (B, R).[12] Note that this type of collusion is also incentive compatible in BENCHMARK, and that it yields the highest possible payoff and is the least difficult to implement amongst all possible forms of tacit collusion that are aimed at avoiding playing (B, B) in every

the market is split evenly in case both firms charge the same price. There are no capacity constraints and firms can only charge integer prices. Both firms setting a price of 6 is a Nash equilibrium of the one-shot game with each firm receiving a payoff of 4 (both firms setting a price equal to 5 is another Nash equilibrium, but in that case payoffs are 0). This corresponds to the situation where both players play B. Joint profits are maximized when the market price is 10 (or 9), in which case, total demand is 4 and the individual firm's profit equals 10. This situation corresponds to both players playing R. Undercutting is mimicked if one player chooses B while the other plays R. Playing B then corresponds to a price of 9 while R reflects a price of 10, yielding as payoffs 20 and 0, respectively. In sum, (R, R) corresponds to (10, 10), (B, B) is equivalent to (6, 6) and (B, R) mimics (9, 10).

[11] Strictly speaking, some form of binding communication is required for (R, R) to qualify as collusion in a legal sense.

[12] The player whose turn it is to play B earns 20 and has no incentive to deviate by playing R. Her NPV equals $20 + 0.8 \times 44.4 = 55.6$.

period. At the same time, because $V^C > V^{TC}$ in BENCHMARK, in this treatment, we expect to observe more collusion than tacit collusion.

In ANTITRUST, the 10-sided die was also thrown in case of (R, R). If either of four numbers (0, 3, 6, and 9) came up, both players earned 0 rather than 10. This mimics the efforts of competition authorities to detect cartels and to fine cartel members accordingly absent a leniency program. Colluding is then no longer incentive compatible because the expected value of collusion reduces to $V^C = 0.6 \times 10/(1 - 0.8) = 30$ while the expected value of cartel defection is not affected by possible cartel detection.[13] The value of colluding tacitly is also not affected by possible fine payments. In ANTITRUST, we thus expect to observe tacit collusion only.

In both leniency treatments, playing (R, R) implied that both players had to put down their card face down, and then play either card again. If a second (R, R) appeared, the die was thrown and the same rule applied as with (R, R) in ANTITRUST. This situation corresponds to collusion while not applying for leniency. Alternatively, B was played in the second stage, which mimicked an individual leniency application. The number of points then earned depends on the leniency program in place and whether the other subject also applied for leniency, see Table 2.

With a leniency program in place, applying for leniency can be part of the collusive agreement. In NON-EXPLOITABLE, the expected value of

Table 2. Payoffs in the Reporting Phase in the Leniency Treatments Following (R, R) in the Pricing Phase

		EXPLOITABLE			NON-EXPLOITABLE	
		Column player			Column player	
		R	B		R	B
Row player	R	(10, 10)*	(0, 9)	R	(10, 10)*	(0, 9)
	B	(9, 0)	(8, 8)	B	(9, 0)	(4, 4)

*In case of (R, R), a 10-sided die was thrown to determine if a fine of size 10 had to be paid.

[13]We assume that cartel detection does not affect subject's propensity to play (R, R) in future rounds.

playing (R, R) followed by (B, B) is $V_L^C = 4/(1 - 0.8) = 20$ while in EXPLOITABLE, it equals $V_L^C = 8/(1 - 0.8) = 40$. If applying for leniency is not part of the collusive agreement, the expected value of collusion is no different than in ANTITRUST: $V^C = 0.6 \times 10/(1 - 0.8) = 30$. The value of defection (at the pricing stage) is also not affected by the leniency program: $V^D = 20 + 0.2 \times 4/(1 - 0.8) = 36$.[14] The leniency program in EXPLOITABLE can thus be expected to induce collusion: absent the leniency program collusion is not incentive compatible while it is incentive compatible if subjects continuously apply for leniency. Still, also in EXPLOITABLE does tacit collusion come with the highest expected profits. But because of the more intricate type of coordination tacit collusion requires, one could expect to observe tacit collusion more often in circumstances where any other type of collusion is not incentive compatible, that is, in both ANTITRUST and NON-EXPLOITABLE. Table 3 summarizes the value of the different strategies across the four treatments.

3. Experimental Procedures

The experiment was conducted at the Tinbergen Institute in Amsterdam. It began with distributing the instructions for the BENCHMARK treatment. These are in Appendix A. After reading out loud the instructions, subjects could indicate if they had a question by raising their hand. These were then answered in private. Once everyone understood the rules of the game,

Table 3. Values of Different Strategies Across Treatments

	BENCHMARK	ANTITRUST	EXPLOITABLE	NON-EXPLOITABLE
V^C	50	30	30	30
V^{TC}	44.4	44.4	44.4	44.4
V^D	36	36	36	36
V_L^C	—	—	40	20

[14] In both EXPLOITABLE and NON-EXPLOITABLE defecting at the reporting stage in case applying for leniency is no part of the collusive agreement yields $V^D = 9 + 0.2 \times 4/(1 - 0.8) = 25$. Defection at the reporting stage is thus always dominated by defection at the pricing stage.

the experiment started. The experiment lasted in total for 60 minutes and 16 subjects took part. These were first-year economics PhD students. In addition to a show-up fee of €5, the points subjects earned during the experiment were converted to euros whereby 1 point was worth €0.05. Average earnings were €17.90, with a minimum of €15.50 and a maximum of €21.80. Four people administered the experiment. One called out the pairs and the cards being played, another recorded play in an Excel spreadsheet, a third rolled the die after each round to determine whether or not there would be a re-matching of pairs, and, when appropriate, to decide whether or not a fine was to be paid, and the fourth person overlooked the room to spot any irregularity.

Upon arrival in the (large) seminar room, subjects had to sit at designated places according to the seating pattern in Figure 1 with ample space in between subjects. This allows for pairings that made non-verbal communication impossible. Obviously, matching subject 1 with subject 9, subject 2 with subject 10, and so on, qualifies as such a pairing. But other pairings are possible as well. In total, 6 different pairing schemes were used, which are listed in Appendix B. We need for more pairing schemes because we follow Dal Bó (2005) in that the continuation probability specifies the probability of a re-matching of pairs within the same treatment. In this way, enough observations are obtained for each treatment while it preserves the notion of a common discount factor. The treatments lasted 9 (BENCHMARK), 8 (ANTITRUST), 9 (EXPLOITABLE), and 10 (NON-EXPLOITABLE) rounds, for which respectively 2 (#1, #2), 3 (#6, #5, #4), 1 (#3), and 3 (#3, #2, #1) different pairings were used, where the numbers in brackets refer to the matching scheme numbers in Appendix B. This yielded in total 36 (BENCHMARK), 32 (ANTITRUST), 36 (EXPLOITABLE), and 40 (NON-EXPLOITABLE) observations. All subjects participated in all treatments, whereby the order of treatments being played was as in Table 3.

1	2	3	4
5	6	7	8
9	10	11	12
13	14	15	16

Figure 1. Seating pattern of subjects.

4. Experimental Results

In discussing the experimental results, we first focus on the extent of collusion *per se* across the four different treatments. We then examine to what extent the exploitable leniency program is exploited. And we conclude with analyzing subjects' propensities toward tacit collusion.

We want to stress that the results in this section come from a single classroom experiment. The observations are therefore not of the same quality as those obtained in computerized experiments in properly controlled environments. For instance, all subjects took part in all treatments, which creates an undesirable dependence between treatment results. Indeed, there is ample room for subjects to learn how to coordinate. This caveat notwithstanding, we do think that the results display broad patterns that would also be observed in properly conducted computerized experiments. They could also serve as the starting point for a classroom discussion about the expected effectiveness of actual leniency programs.

4.1. *Collusion*

Figure 2 gives for each treatment the distribution by pairs of cards played at the pricing stage. The figure shows that in BENCHMARK collusion is paramount: over 70% of all decisions is (R, R). The introduction of a

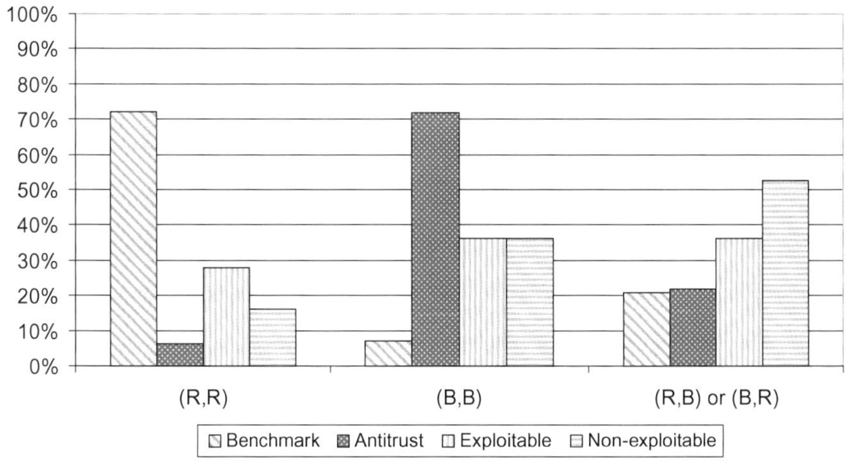

Figure 2. Distribution of card color in the pricing stage at the group level.

detection probability has a strong effect on this behavior. Compared to BENCHMARK, the fraction of pairs playing (R, R) is reduced with 90%, a finding that corroborates previous experimental results (see Hinloopen and Soetevent (2008) and Bigoni *et al.* (2012)). As conjectured, introduction of an exploitable leniency program increases the number of pairs playing the collusive strategy (R, R). At the same time, the fraction of pairs that collude in NON-EXPLOITABLE is substantially below that in EXPLOITABLE. Yet, the fraction of 16% of all pairs that collude in NON-EXPLOITABLE is above the comparable fraction in ANTITRUST. If anything, these results show that introducing a detection probability and/or some leniency program significantly affects subjects' propensity to collude.

4.2. *Exploitability*

Figure 2 does not tell whether pairs who play (R, R) in the pricing stage in one of the leniency treatments really exploit the leniency program by subsequently filing for leniency, that is, play B in the reporting stage. Figure 3 shows the distribution of the cards played in the reporting stage in both EXPLOITABLE and NON-EXPLOITABLE. The figure clearly illustrates that the exploitable leniency program is indeed exploited: more than 70% of subjects in pairs that play (R, R) at the pricing stage decide to apply for leniency. Under the less generous leniency program in NON-EXPLOITABLE, this percentage drops to about 10%. That is, the exploitable leniency

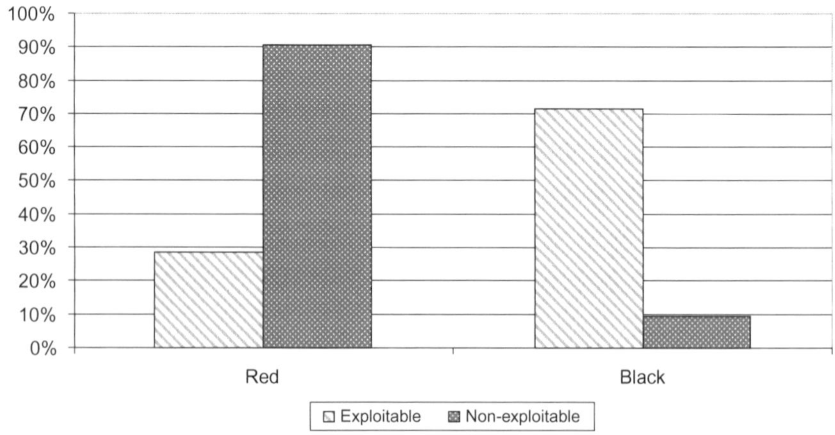

Figure 3. Distribution of the card color in the reporting stage at subject level.

program is indeed exploited; implementation of the exploitable leniency program triggers significantly more collusion.

4.3. *Induced tacit collusion*

On basis of the evidence above, it is tempting to conclude that non-exploitable leniency programs are a great way to reduce collusion. Care is needed however, because so far, we have considered overt collusion only: both subjects playing R in the pricing stage. But not observing (R, R) does not necessarily imply that all subjects play black cards, the socially preferred outcome.

Figure 4 plots the average earnings of subjects for each treatment.[15] As expected, average net earnings in BENCHMARK are close to 10 ($p = 0.490$) because almost none of the pairs plays (B, B) and the other combinations (R, R), (B, R), and (R, B) all imply average net earnings of 10 per subject.[16]

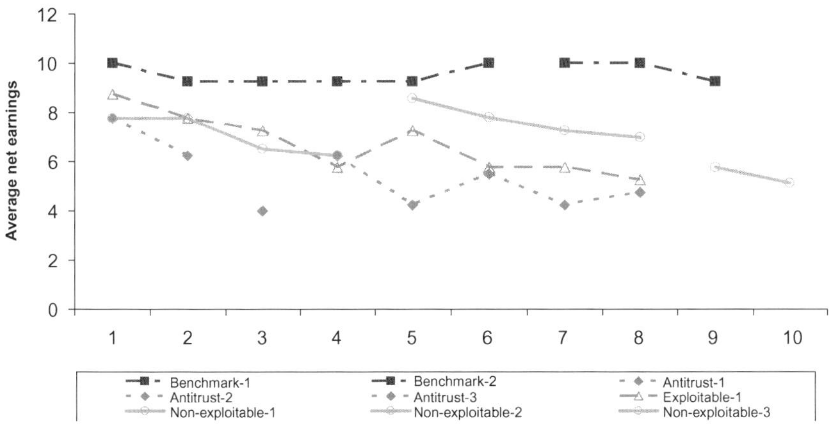

Figure 4. Average net earnings of subjects per treatment.

[15]The lines are disconnected at points where a re-matching of subjects occurs. In some instances such a re-start creates a substantial shift in play, as in NON-EXPLOITABLE. But there appears to be no systematic shift in play after any re-start.

[16]The p-values in this section are calculated on the basis of Wilcoxon signed rank tests. The test compares two treatments using the paired difference of subjects' average net earnings in the two treatments as observations (16 in total for each test). An objection to using this test is that subjects play in pairs such that there is dependence between subjects' average earnings. For this reason, one should interpret the reported p-values with care.

Likewise, earnings in ANTITRUST are significantly lower ($p < 0.001$) because of the detection probability. Theory predicts that in EXPLOITABLE, subjects *en masse* exploit the leniency program and earn 8 units on average. Figure 4 however shows that realized earnings are significantly lower ($p = 0.008$) and are comparable to earnings in ANTITRUST in later periods ($p = 0.109$). Most striking however is that in NON-EXPLOITABLE, subjects' average net earnings are not below those in EXPLOITABLE ($p = 0.535$) while they exceed those in ANTITRUST ($p = 0.052$). Further, as Figure 2 illustrates, increased collusion cannot be the reason for the difference in earnings between EXPLOITABLE and NON-EXPLOITABLE. Increased popularity of colluding tacitly might offer an alternative explanation.

To investigate this, we first have to specify how we identify tacit collusion. Recall that the idea behind the tacitly collusive scheme is that subjects alternate between playing R and B in the pricing stage, whereby the subject who plays B receives the full collusive profits of 20 in that period and is expected to return the favor in the next period by playing R. Therefore, we calculate for each subject the correlation between the color of the cards played in subsequent periods in the pricing stage conditional on subjects not being re-matched between the two periods of investigation. For a subject that alternates continuously between R and B, the correlation score is -1. In principle, we end up with 16 individual correlation scores for each treatment, but for subjects who play the same color in each period of a treatment, the correlation score cannot be calculated.[17] The average scores per treatment for the remaining subjects are given in Figure 5. The figure shows a sharp drop in average correlation scores in NON-EXPLOITABLE, which suggests an increased popularity of tacit collusion. However, to conclude that the non-exploitable leniency program triggers tacit collusion, we have to examine further what drives playing B in the pricing stage across treatments.

Figure 6 displays per period the average earnings of subjects playing a black card in BENCHMARK and ANTITRUST. The few subjects that play

[17] Recall that the correlation score equals $cov(color_t, color_{t+1})/\sqrt{var(color_t)var(color_{t+1})}$ and that $var(color_t) = 0$ if the same card is played in each period. In BENCHMARK, ANTITRUST, EXPLOITABLE, and NON-EXPLOITABLE, the fraction of subjects who never change card color in the pricing stage is 44%, 56%, 50%, and 13%, respectively.

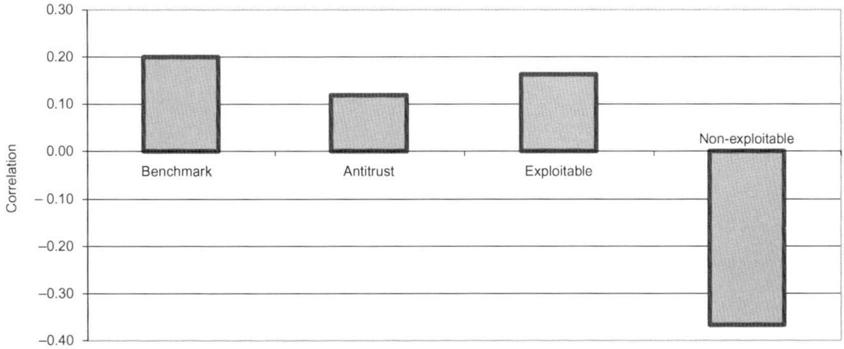

Figure 5. Correlation over time of card color played in pricing stage at the subject level.

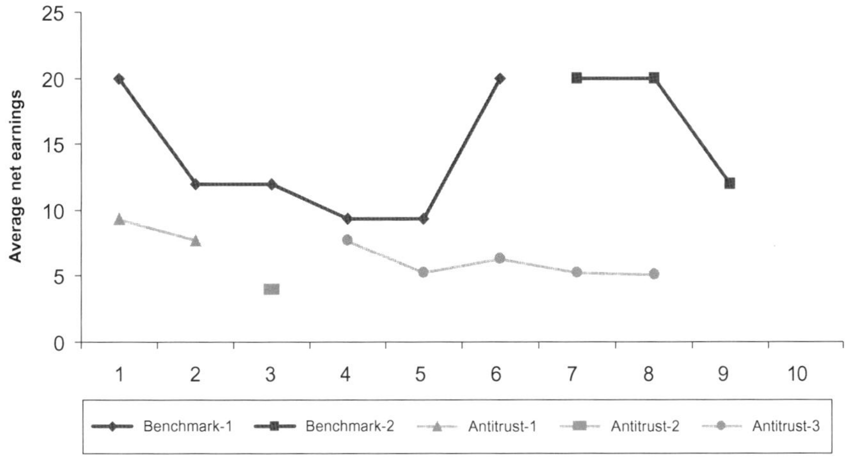

Figure 6. Average net earnings for subjects who play B: BENCHMARK vs. ANTITRUST.

B in BENCHMARK cheat in most cases and earn defection profits of 20. In ANTITRUST, playing B is most often part of the one-shot Nash equilibrium (B, B), and for this reason, subjects that play black earn on average only slightly more than 4 units. That is, there is no clear evidence that in ANTITRUST playing B is part of a scheme to collude tacitly, whereby subjects take turn in playing R and B.

Turning now to the leniency treatments, we have to contrast the two motivations for playing B: to cheat on a collusive agreement or to play it as part of a tacitly collusive scheme. The difference between the two

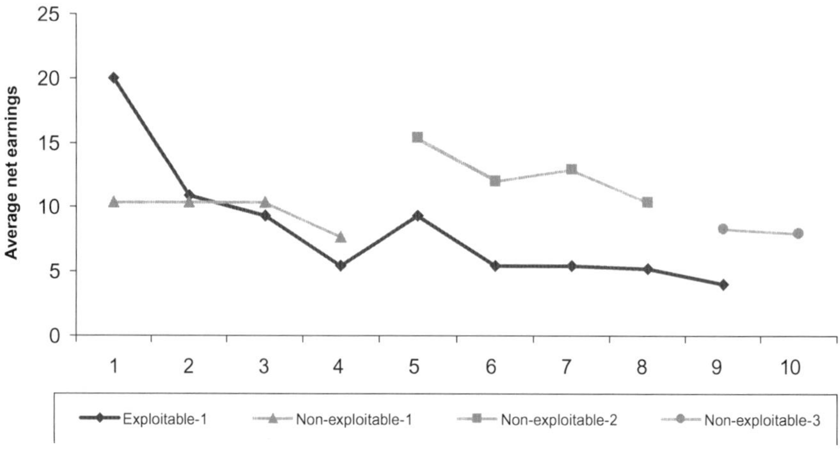

Figure 7. Average net earnings for subjects who play B in the pricing stage: EXPLOITABLE vs. NON-EXPLOITABLE.

explanations for observing B in the pricing stage is that we expect the payoff of cheating to die out in time. Figure 7 indicates that subjects playing B in NON-EXPLOITABLE indeed achieve average earnings in the range of 10 to 15 units. Over time, these earnings somewhat decrease but stay well above the levels observed in ANTITRUST and EXPLOITABLE. This suggest that playing B in the pricing stage in NON-EXPLOITABLE is part of a tacitly collusive scheme whereby subjects take turn in playing R and B, and that this type of play is triggered by the implementation of the non-exploitable leniency program.

5. Conclusions

Leniency programs are part of competition policy in most modern economies. Policy makers are apt to declare the success of these programs in reducing cartel activity, typically referring to the sharp increase in the number of cartels that are revealed since the introduction of these programs. In this chapter, we have focused on two potential drawbacks of leniency programs: the possibility that a leniency program is exploited and the possibility that a leniency program triggers tacit collusion.

Our classroom experiment illustrates that these concerns could be more than mere theoretical artifacts. A leniency program that by design is exploitable, is in fact exploited. And a non-exploitable leniency program appears to trigger tacit collusion. In both cases, the leniency program does more harm than good. Of course, the results presented here come from a single classroom experiment and should be treated with care. Indeed, the main objective of this chapter is to provide a pedagogical device that allows for an illustration of the possible drawbacks of corporate leniency programs.

Appendix A: Instructions

Setup

We are going to play a card game in which every person in the room will be matched with another person in the room. The game consists of several rounds and in each round, you will face the same opponent.

I will give each of you two playing cards, a red card (Hearts or Diamonds) and a black card (Clubs or Spades). The number or faces on the cards will not matter, just the color. You will be asked to play one of these cards by holding them to your chest (so we can see that you have made your decision, but not what that decision is). Your earnings are determined by the card that you play and by the card played by the person matched with you.

Points

If you each play your black card, you will each earn 4 points. If you each play your red card, you will each earn 10 points. If you play your red card and the other person plays her black card, then you earn no points and the other person earns 20 points (and vice versa).

Game Play

After you choose which cards to play, hold them to your chest. I then call out the identification numbers in pairs, and you can cach reveal the cards that you played. Record your earnings in the table on the other side of this form. After I have called out all identification numbers, a 10-sided die will be thrown. In case the numbers 0 or 5 occur, the next round starts with a new matching of pairs. In all other cases, the existing matching applies for the next round.

Earnings

The points that you earn during the experiment will be converted to euros at a rate of 1 point being €0.05. Payment will be done in the next recitation class.

Any questions? If not then I ask you to play your first card.

Appendix B: Matching Schemes

Matching scheme 1		**Matching scheme 2**		**Matching scheme 3**	
1	9	1	10	1	11
2	10	2	11	2	12
3	11	3	12	3	9
4	12	4	9	4	10
5	13	5	14	5	15
6	14	6	15	6	16
7	15	7	16	7	13
8	16	8	13	8	14
Matching scheme 4		**Matching scheme 5**		**Matching scheme 6**	
1	12	1	15	1	7
2	9	2	16	2	15
3	10	3	13	3	14
4	11	4	14	4	6
5	16	5	11	5	12
6	13	6	12	8	9
7	14	7	9	10	16
8	15	8	10	11	13

References

Apesteguia, J., M. Dufwenberg and R. Selten (2007). "Blowing the Whistle," *Economic Theory*, 31, pp. 143–166.

Bigoni, M., S.-O. Fridolfsson, C. Le Coq and G. Spagnolo (2012). "Fines, Leniency and Rewards in Antitrust: An Experiment," *RAND Journal of Economics*, 43, pp. 368–390.

Brenner, S. (2009). "An Empirical Study of the European Corporate Leniency Program," *International Journal of Industrial Organization*, 27, pp. 639–645.

Bryant, P. G. and E. W. Eckard (1991). "Price Fixing: The Probability of Getting Caught," *Review of Economics and Statistics*, 73, pp. 531–536.

Chen, Z. and P. Rey (2009). "On the Design of Leniency Programs," *Working Paper*, Toulouse University.

Choi, J. P. and H. Gerlach (2012). "Global Cartels, Leniency Programs and International Antitrust Cooperation," *International Journal of Industrial Organization*, 30, pp. 528–540.

Combe, E., C. Monnier and R. Legal (2008). "Cartels: The Probability of Getting Caught in the European Union," *BEER Working Paper* 12.

Connor, J. M. (2001). *Global Price Fixing: Our Customers are the Enemy*, Kluwer Academic Publishers, Boston.

Dal Bó, P. (2005). "Cooperation under the Shadow of the Future: Experimental Evidence from Infinitely Repeated Games," *American Economic Review*, 95(5), pp. 1591–1604.

Eichenwald, K. (2000). *The Informant*, Broadway Books, New York.

Friedman, J. W. (1971). "A Non-cooperative Equilibrium for Supergames," *Review of Economic Studies*, 38, pp. 1–12.

Goeree, M. S. and E. Helland (2010). "Do Research Joint Ventures Serve a Collusive Function?" Institute for Empirical Research in Economics, University of Zurich, *Working Paper* No. 448.

Hamaguchi, Y., T. Ishikawa, M. Ishimoto, Y. Kimura and T. Tanno (2007). "An Experimental Study of Procurement Auctions with Leniency Programs," *CPRC Discussion Paper.*

Hammond, S. D. (2003). "Beating Cartels at their Own Game — Sharing Information in the Fight Against Cartels," Speech delivered at the Capitol Tokyo Hotel, Tokyo, November 20. Available at www.usdoj.gov/atr/public/speeches/201614.pdf.

Harrington, J. E., Jr. (2006). "How Do Cartels Operate?" *Foundations and Trends in Microeconomics*, 2, pp. 1–105.

Hinloopen, J. (2003). "An Economic Analysis of Leniency Programs in Antitrust Law," *De Economist*, 151, pp. 415–432.

Hinloopen, J. and A. M. Onderstal (2013). "Gong Once, Going Twice, Reported! The Effectiveness of Corporate Leniency Programs in Experimental Auctions," *Tinbergen Institute Discussion Paper* No. 2010-120/1

Hinloopen, J. and A. R. Soetevent (2008). "Laboratory Evidence on the Effectiveness of Corporate Leniency Programs," *RAND Journal of Economics*, 39, pp. 607–616.

Holt, C. A. and M. C. Capra (2000). "Classroom Games: A Prisoner's Dilemma," *Journal of Economic Education*, 31(3), pp. 229–236.

Levenstein, M. C. and V. Y. Suslow (2006). "What Determines Cartel Success?" *Journal of Economic Literature*, 44, pp. 43–95.

Miller, N. H. (2009). "Strategic Leniency and Cartel Enforcement," *American Economic Review*, 99, pp. 750–768.

Motta, M. and M. Polo (2003). "Leniency Programs and Cartel Prosecution," *International Journal of Industrial Organization*, 21, pp. 347–380.

New York Times (2005). "EU to Beef Up its Cartel Busters," March, 11, 2005.

OECD (2002). *Fighting Hard-Core Cartels; Harm, Effective Sanctions and Leniency Programs*, OECD, Paris.

Roux, C. and T. von Ungern-Sternberg (2007). "Leniency Programs in a Multimarket Setting: Amnesty Plus and Penalty Plus," *CESifo Working Paper*, No. 1995.

Spagnolo, G. (2004). "Divide *et impera*: Optimal Leniency Programs," *CEPR Discussion Paper* 4840.

Spagnolo, G. (2008). "Leniency and Whistleblowers in Antitrust," in P. Buccirossi (ed.), *The Handbook of Antitrust Economics*, MIT Press, Cambridge, MA, pp. 259–304.

Van Bergeijk, P. A. G. (2007). "On the Allegedly Invisible Dutch Construction Sector Cartel," *Journal of Competition Law and Economics*, 4, pp. 115–128.

Chapter 9

Quantity Discounts and Market Power: The Michelin Case Revisited*

Liliane Giardino-Karlinger

Università LUISS Guido Carli

lilianegk@gmail.com

Abstract

Quantity discounts of all kinds — be it pure quantity discounts, bundled discounts, or market-share discounts — have raised considerable antitrust concerns. Unlike its U.S. counterpart, the European Commission (EC) has adopted a fairly tough stance on such business practices, to the point of even outlawing standardized pure quantity discounts. In this chapter, we will briefly review the literature on anticompetitive effects of vertical restraints in general, before discussing in more detail the recent contributions on the economics of quantity discounts and market-sharing discounts. We will then explore how fidelity rebates can be used by a dominant supplier to achieve both horizontal and vertical control in an industry where two retailers first contract with the dominant supplier, and then compete for the supplies of a vertically differentiated entrant. Our findings are then applied to the EC's Michelin II decision of 2001, to help us understand the impact it had on the structure of vertical relations and on consumer welfare in the French truck tire market.

Keywords: Sequential contracting, vertical restraints, opportunism, input price discrimination, Stackelberg leader.

JEL Classification Codes: L12, L14, L42.

*This chapter is based on my presentation at the 2012 CRESSE Conference in Chania (Crete). I am indebted to Martin Peitz and Yossi Spiegel for helpful comments on an earlier version of this chapter. Financial support from University of Bologna is gratefully acknowledged. The usual disclaimer applies.

1. Introduction

The potential anticompetitive effects of vertical restraints in general, and fidelity rebates in particular, have been a major concern to antitrust authorities. Fidelity rebates encompass a wide range of business practices, such as pure quantity discounts (which may be all-units discounts or incremental-units discounts), bundled discounts, and market-share discounts. So far, U.S. authorities and courts have refrained from interfering with the use of fidelity rebates, primarily to avoid setting adverse precedents. Instead, the European Commission (EC) has consistently found such rebates to be anticompetitive when employed by a dominant firm. In fact, market-share discounts and discounts based on purchase growth are *per se* illegal. The only admissible type of rebate used to be a standardized quantity discount. However, in its surprising Michelin II decision of 2001,[1] the EC even found such standardized quantity discounts to be unlawful, at least if the reference period exceeds three months.[2]

This chapter will give an overview over the literature on anticompetitive vertical restraints in general, and on some of the more recent contributions on the economics of quantity discounts. We will then come back to the Michelin II case to study the implications of a ban on quantity discounts for the structure of vertical relations in this industry.

2. Vertical Contracts and Market Power

The idea that vertical contracts may be used to maintain monopoly power goes back to Aghion and Bolton (1987). They study a model where a single buyer purchases at most one unit from one of two sellers and there is sequential contracting; under complete information, the buyer and the first seller can extract all the surplus from the second seller by agreeing to an

[1] *Michelin II* Commission decision 2002/405/EC [2002] OJ L 143/1, Case COMP/E-2/36.041, upheld by the Court of First Instance in its 2003 decision, *Manufacture française des pneumatiques Michelin v. Commission* (Michelin II), [2003] ECR II-4071.

[2] "The Court of Justice has ruled against the granting of quantity rebates by an undertaking in a dominant position where the rebates exceed a reasonable period of three months (as is the case here) on the grounds that such a practice is not in line with normal competition based on price" (Recital 216 of Commission decision 2002/405/EC).

exclusive-dealing contract in which the buyer must pay a lump-sum penalty to the first seller if it buys from the second seller.

The penalty, called "liquidating damages", therefore acts as a rent-shifting device: To attract the buyer, the second seller has to make an offer that compensates the buyer for the penalty it will have to pay if it defaults on its exclusive-dealing contract with the first seller. To convince the buyer to switch supplier, the second seller may therefore have to offer up to its entire surplus to the buyer, which is then shared with the first seller through the penalty.

A rational buyer will agree to such a contract because this contract gives the buyer access to the second seller's surplus, which the buyer would not have if it refused to sign the contract. While such an agreement is certainly unfavorable to the second seller, it is not welfare detrimental: Whenever the second seller is more efficient than the first seller, it will be able to serve the buyer, i.e., the exclusive dealing arrangement will not lead to exclusion of a more efficient seller.

The situation is different when the exact efficiency rent generated by the second seller is not known *a priori*: In this case, the first seller and the buyer will fix the penalty at the *expected* level of the second seller's surplus. But then, whenever the second seller's actual surplus is lower than the expected level (though still positive), it cannot offer enough surplus to the buyer to induce the latter to switch supplier: In this case, rather than shifting rent from the second to the first seller, the exclusive dealing contract preserves the first seller's monopoly over the buyer even in the presence of a more efficient competitor.

Aghion and Bolton (1987) were among the first to jolt the general consensus that vertical restraints tend to be welfare-enhancing, and inspired a growing literature on the possible anticompetitive effects of vertical restraints. This research gravitates around three central themes:[3]

Exclusive dealing contracts used by dominant firms to play buyers off against each other: Rasmusen *et al.* (1991), Innes and Sexton (1994), Segal and Whinston (2000), Fumagalli and Motta (2006).

This strand of the literature differs from Aghion and Bolton (1987) insofar as exclusion of an efficient rival can even arise under complete

[3]For an excellent review, see Miklós-Thal *et al.* (2010).

information. In these models, there are multiple buyers (usually two), and for entry to be viable, the entrant must serve both of them. The incumbent supplier can then make a highly competitive (below-cost) offer to one of the buyers to induce this buyer to sign an exclusive dealing contract. As a result, the more efficient new supplier will no longer find it profitable to enter the market as it cannot reach the critical market share. The incumbent supplier can then cover the losses made on the first buyer with the profits made on the second buyer, who will be forced to buy from the incumbent at the monopoly price once the first buyer signed up with the incumbent.

The key concept here is that of "contracting externalities": A buyer who signs an exclusive dealing contract with a supplier will only take into account his own benefits from this contract, but not the possible harm inflicted on other buyers who will not have access to a more efficient second supplier. Exclusive dealing contracts are thus at the heart of a "divide-and-conquer" strategy employed by the incumbent to prevent buyers from coordinating on the more efficient rival supplier.

Vertical restraints and opportunism: Hart and Tirole (1990), O'Brien and Shaffer (1992), McAfee and Schwartz (1994), Rey and Vergé (2004), Rey and Tirole (2007).

Suppose a monopoly seller and a retailer (or franchisee) signed a vertical contract granting the seller a franchise fee equal to the monopoly profits which the franchisee expects to earn on the final consumer market. If there are other potential franchisees available in the market, the monopoly seller then has an incentive to cheat on the first franchisee by signing up a second (third, fourth, ...) franchisee who will compete with the first one on the final market. The first franchisee will then not be able to recover on the retail market the franchise fee it paid to the monopoly seller. A rational franchisee will therefore not be willing to sign such a contract in the first place, thus making it impossible for the monopoly seller to sell its franchise at the monopoly price. Vertical restraints such as exclusive territories then offer guarantees to the franchisee against opportunistic behavior by the monopoly seller, thus allowing the latter to restore its market power.

The role of Retail Price Maintenance (RPM) and slotting allowances in facilitating upstream collusion: Bernheim and Whinston (1985, 1986), Winter (1993), Rey and Vergé (2010), Innes and Hamilton (2006, 2009).

Consider an industry where two competing upstream firms sell their products through the same retailer, i.e., they operate under "common agency". If these firms can use two-part tariffs, they will end up setting their retail prices so as to maximize the retailer's profits, i.e., as though they were fully colluding, because they can extract these profits through the fixed fee. Common agency thus eliminates the incentives to price competitively. This effect is also present when there is more than one retailer, as long as each retailer carries all products (i.e., an industry characterized by "interlocking relationships").

Thus, exclusivity clauses, RPM, and refusal to supply have been at the center of the academic debate on vertical restraints for a long time, and have a status of *per se* illegality under the EU jurisdiction. It was only recently that a much "softer" form of vertical restraints, namely quantity discounts in all their manifestations, have received more scrutiny. There are in fact very few papers which specifically study the effects of quantity discounts in vertical relations. Since these papers are most relevant for our analysis of the Michelin II decision, we shall discuss them here in more detail.

3. Anticompetitive Effects of Market-Share Discounts and Quantity Discounts

The literature on vertical restraints has struggled very hard (and with little success) to deliver clear-cut welfare results, and the recent work on quantity discounts is no exception to this rule. There are a number of papers which find either pro-competitive, or adverse welfare effects, or no welfare effects at all, as we shall see shortly.

Marx and Shaffer (2008) revisit the Aghion and Bolton (1987) framework of one monopoly buyer contracting sequentially with two sellers. However, they allow for more than one unit to be traded, and study the impact of various constraints on the structure of supply contracts (bans on below-cost prices and/or market share contracts) on the degree of rent extraction under complete information. They find that bans on below-cost pricing and on market share contracts lead to imperfect rent extraction, but leave the first seller's (contemporaneous) output decisions unaffected. In other words, there are no welfare losses associated with such pricing strategies, at least in the short run.

However, with more than one buyer, quantity discounts can be used to generate contracting externalities that do have a negative impact on welfare. Karlinger and Motta (2012) consider an incumbent firm and a more efficient entrant who both produce a network good and compete for the orders of several asymmetric buyers. The buyers who buy from the same supplier (i.e., join the same network) exert strong positive externalities on each other, so that the industry gravitates toward monopoly (i.e., competition is of the winner-takes-all type). The socially efficient equilibria are those where the entrant serves all buyers. Karlinger and Motta (2012) show that price discrimination (with quantity discounts being an instance of indirect price discrimination) reduces the set of achievable socially efficient entry equilibria: if the efficiency gap between the two firms is not too large, allowing the incumbent to use discriminatory offers out-of-equilibrium will break equilibria in which the buyers coordinate on the more efficient entrant.

In two recent contributions by Elhauge and Wickelgren (2012a, b), loyalty discounts play a key role in softening competition between two symmetric upstream firms. In their models, buyers may either sign a loyalty discount contract with one of the two suppliers or remain "free" buyers. A buyer who signed the loyalty discount contract always receives the good at a lower price than a "free" buyer who ends up buying from the same supplier as the "loyal" buyers. This arrangement thus reduces sellers' incentives to compete fiercely for the free buyers: Whenever a seller offers a very low price to such a free buyer to attract its orders, the seller has to lower the price on all its "loyal" buyers as well (because the loyal-buyer price is expressed as a percentage of the free-buyer price). Quite like a non-discrimination clause, this clearly reduces the profitability of competitive pricing, thus inflating prices for all buyers, raising seller profits and reducing overall welfare.

The remaining papers discussed here all rely on adverse selection as a key element. Majumdar and Shaffer (2009) consider a dominant supplier selling to a monopoly retailer who also carries a differentiated product supplied by a competitive fringe. The retailer has private information on the state of demand, and so the supplier can offer standard incentive contracts (with the typical downward output level distortion for low-demand realizations) to induce the retailer to reveal the state of demand. These incentive contracts can be made even more effective if they are allowed to include market-share clauses: The dominant supplier will require a very high market share for his own product if the low demand state is realized, so that concealing a high demand state is even less profitable for the retailer than if he were free to choose his level of the competitively supplied product. Consumers are therefore negatively affected by such market-share agreements because they will get to consume inefficiently low levels of both goods in case the low demand state is realized.

Asymmetric information also plays a key role in Herweg and Müller (2013), who study price discrimination by a monopolistic supplier who sells to several downstream firms which are privately informed about their retail costs. In this setup, retailers differ in their *ex-ante* distribution of retail costs, and so the incentive contracts offered by the monopolistic upstream firm will differ across retailers (interpreted as "third-degree discrimination"), with the typical output distortion "at the bottom" being a function of the retailer-specific probability of realizing a low-demand state. Banning price discrimination will then increase welfare whenever it does not lead to a reduction in total output.

Calzolari and Denicolò (2013) study a model where two symmetric firms supply horizontally differentiated products but do not know the buyers' willingness-to-pay for the products. Thus, buyers obtain informational rents even if firms can use non-linear prices. In this context, firms have a unilateral incentive to use exclusive contracts, because they allow for better rent extraction; however, if both firms use exclusive contracts, this actually intensifies competition among the firms, leading to lower prices and higher consumer welfare. If such contracts are allowed, then offering market-share discounts in addition to exclusive dealing will weaken competition, and harm consumers. In the more realistic scenario where exclusive contracts are prohibited, however, the effect of market-share discounts is ambiguous.

4. Horizontal and Vertical Control

In practice, a dominant firm will often want to exert control both vertically and horizontally. The need for vertical control arises whenever retailers compete against each other for the patronage of final consumers. And horizontal control could be necessary when retailers compete for the supplies of a (more or less) differentiated product offered by a rival manufacturer.

In Karlinger (2012), I therefore consider an industry composed of two upstream firms, a dominant supplier producing a high-quality product (good

A), and an entrant producing a low-quality variant of the same product (good B). Consumers are heterogenous in their valuation for quality, which is unobservable to the firms, so that a monopolist would always want to offer both varieties in order to extract rents through quality discrimination.

In a duopoly setting, the notion of quality differentiation allows for broader interpretations: We can think of the incumbent's quality advantage also as a short-cut for inherent asymmetries between incumbent and entrant (such as switching costs, installed base, etc.) which favor the incumbent while allowing for the two manufacturers to coexist, each serving a different consumer segment.

Retailers first contract with the dominant manufacturer, and then turn to the entrant to compete for exclusivity of the entrant's supply of the low-quality product. Sequential contracting arises naturally when there are technology spillovers from incumbent to entrant which are necessary for the latter to be able to produce her variety, and which take time to materialize (Figure 1).[4]

If there was a single retailer who contracts with both suppliers, the incumbent could exploit her first-mover advantage to extract the entrant's profits through the contracts she writes with the retailer (see Aghion and

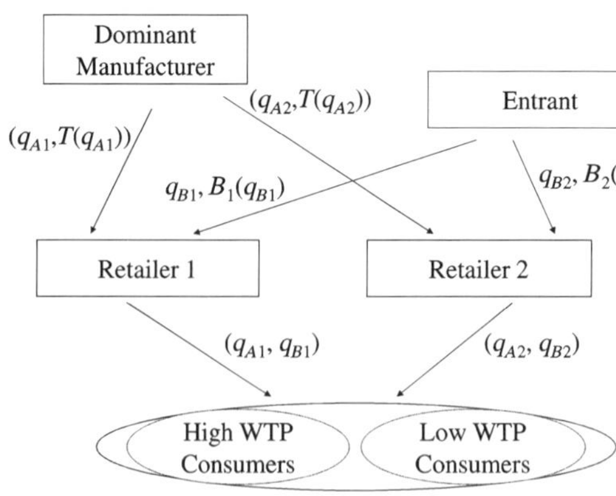

Figure 1. Industry structure under sequential contracting.

[4]Examples include the pharmaceutical industry (brand-name drugs followed by generic equivalents after patent expiry), the food industry (supermarket chains retail both branded products and private labels), and consumer electronics (iPhone vs. low-end smartphones).

Bolton, 1987). In Karlinger (2012), however, retailer competition for the entrant's supplies will bid up their price, thus allowing the entrant to earn a positive rent. The level of this rent will depend on the available level of the high-quality good, and its distribution across retailers, which are determined beforehand in the negotiations between dominant manufacturer and retailers.

More precisely, if marginal cost is zero at all levels, and the dominant firm, I, can use simple forcing contracts, its profits are equal to industry profits minus the profits appropriated by the entrant (firm E) through the franchise fee paid by the retailer who wins the bidding contest for the supply of good B:

$$\Pi_I(q_A, q_B) = q_A p_A(q_A, q_B) + q_B p_B(q_A, q_B) - \Pi_E(q_A, q_B).$$

Firm I has two choices to make: how much to produce of good A, q_A, and how to split this output among the two retailers: $q_A = q_{A1} + q_{A2}$. Since the output level of good B is chosen at a later stage, q_B is also a function of q_A. In particular, the higher q_A, the lower the profit Π_E that can be earned for any given level of q_B, because a higher supply of good A crowds out some of the demand for good B.

Relative to the industry profit-maximizing solution, this induces two distortions in the dominant firm's supply decisions: (i) a tendency to oversupply the high-quality good, and (ii) an incentive to discriminate among the two retailers, in the sense that they will carry different levels of the incumbent's good.

An abundant supply of the high-quality good reduces the profits that can be earned on the entrant's variety, and hence the franchise fee, $\Pi_E(q_A, q_B)$, offered for it by any of the retailers. Thus, the dominant supplier essentially acts as a Stackelberg leader, expanding own market share at the expense of the follower. Note that consumer welfare increases as a result of the incumbent's oversupply: more consumers will enjoy the high-quality good, and more consumers will consume at all, than under the industry profit-maximizing solution.[5]

[5]This result is driven by the assumption that the incumbent's good is of higher quality than the entrant's. If the quality ranking was reversed, or the goods were just horizontally differentiated and the market is fully covered, the normative results in Karlinger (2012) would no longer hold.

The reason why the dominant firm wants to discriminate among *ex-ante* identical retailers is more subtle: If both retailers carried the same amount of the high-quality good (i.e., are identical when turning to the entrant), both retailers will bid the same amount to win the supply of good B, and so the entrant could fully extract all surplus on its variety. But with asymmetric supplies of the incumbent's good, the retailer who carries less of it is also a weaker competitor for the entrant's variety, thus lowering the franchise fee at which the stronger retailer can acquire the entrant's supply in equilibrium.

The franchise fee paid by the winning retailer (call it $R1$) is simply the incremental profit which the losing retailer, $R2$, could have made on good B if he had been given the supply instead.

$$\Pi_E = q_{A2}p_A(q_{A1}, q_{A2}, 0, q_{B2}) + q_{B2}p_B(q_{A1}, q_{A2}, 0, q_{B2}) - q_{A2}p_A(q_{A1}, q_{A2}, q_{B1}, 0).$$

The retailer who holds less of good A, here Retailer 2, is also less profitable in marketing good B, because he internalizes less of the externality of good B on the price of good A than Retailer 1 does. Thus, the dominant supplier has an incentive to deviate from the simple 50:50 split between the two retailers; by allocating less to one retailer than to the other, firm I can soften retailer competition for good B, thus reducing the rent extracted by E.

Discrimination among the retailers has yet another advantage for the incumbent: it also helps her align the retailer's supply level of the rival product with her own preferred level, which differs systematically from that of the retailers: the latter have a tendency to oversupply the low-quality good, because they do not fully internalize the negative externality this has on the profit margins of the high-quality product.

Karlinger (2012) also explores in detail how the policy maker can intervene to modify the distribution of rents across firms, and how this affects consumers.

If the incumbent cannot directly control the levels of both her own and the rival's good, retailer discrimination is beneficial for consumers, as it leads both to an expansion of the overall consumption as well as to a higher average quality of consumption (i.e., a higher proportion of consumers will enjoy the high-quality product).

Allowing the dominant firm to use fidelity rebates (interpreted here as penalties or "taxes" on the sales of the rival good) will however fully restore her market power, and hence harm consumers. As suspected by many antitrust authorities (but not corroborated by the academic literature on the subject), these fidelity rebates have effects very similar to those of exclusive dealing contracts between incumbent and the retailers.

It seems natural to wonder what would be the effects of preventing dominant firms not only from offering fidelity rebates, but also from discriminating in any way among their retailers (a scenario very close to the current legal situation in the European Union). Not surprisingly, banning discrimination will benefit the entrant at the expense of the incumbent. This will benefit consumers indirectly if viability of entry into this market depends on the extra profit made by the entrant in the uniform-contracts scenario.

Whether consumers also benefit directly from this intervention is less clear: While overall consumption expands, output of the high-quality good (and therefore the average quality of consumption) will fall, so that the net effect on consumer surplus can only be evaluated by trading off the losses of high-valuation consumers against the gains for low-valuation consumers.

This framework also allows us to analyze the impact of changes to the market structure such as horizontal and vertical mergers. I argue that a horizontal merger among the retailers will distribute profits away from both incumbent and entrant and toward the (monopolized) retail sector. The latter will in fact find itself in a bilateral monopoly with the incumbent manufacturer, who will therefore be able to implement maximal industry profit.

However, the incumbent can no longer play the two retailers off against each other, so that it will be forced to share profits with the monopoly retailer: absent retailer competition, the outside option of contracting with the entrant alone now yields positive profits for the retailer, who will therefore be willing to accept the incumbent's contract only if compensated for this outside option. While a downstream merger is bound to be detrimental for consumers, I show that it also reduces the dominant manufacturer's profits, who will therefore unambiguously prefer a strong rival manufacturer over a concentrated retailer sector.

A vertical merger between the dominant manufacturer and one of the retailers will similarly lead to an elimination of downstream competition for the low-quality good (i.e., elimination of the entrant's rents). The incumbent will want to channel most or all of her business to this retailer, and use the vertically integrated retailer only as a threat so as to fully extract all rents from the independent retailer.

5. The *Michelin* Case

Let us see what lessons we can draw from the arguments above to better understand the implications of the Commission decision in the Michelin case. The *Michelin II* case concerned the market for replacement truck tires in France, which the Commission identified as independent from the car tire market.[6] The Commission furthermore distinguished between the market for new truck tires, and the market for retreaded tires (where "retreaded" means that the tread of a worn tire casing was renewed). The retreading technology is available both to manufacturers of new tires and to a competitive sector of middle-sized firms specialized in retreading. While retreaded tires are considered inferior substitutes to new ones, they account for almost half of the market for replacement tires.

On the French market for new tires, Michelin had a market share of 55–60% in 1995, and owned 11 out of the 19 tire production plants operating in France at the time.[7] Recent entrants into the French market were Continental and Sumitomo/Dunlop, who each owned two tire plants in France, and Bridgestone/Firestone and Goodyear, with one plant each. Table 1 shows the market shares of Michelin and its main competitors on the European market for 1993 and 1995, as reported in Recital 25 of Commission decision 2002/405/EC.

The table shows that Michelin's position on its home market is much stronger than on the broader European market; while still the market leader, its 30% market share on the European market is a far cry from the 55–60% on the French market. Arguably, the substitutability between Michelin tires

[6]Truck and bus tire prices are more than five times higher than those of car tires, which — according to Michelin representatives — reflects the fact that "the resources employed to design and produce truck and bus tires are radically different from those required to manufacture the other types of tire" (Recital 7 of Commission decision 2002/405/EC).
[7]See also Motta (2009).

Table 1. Market Shares in Europe, All Tires Combined (%)

Manufacturer	1993	1995
Michelin	31.9	31.4
Continental	13.9	17.1
Goodyear	13.1	13.3
Pirelli	9.2	8.6
Bridgestone	9.3	7.7
Sumitomo	9.3	7.7
Others		
Yokohama, Toyo, Vredestein + 16 others	13.3	13.5
Total	**100.0**	**100.0**

Source: The Economist Intelligence Unit. (Study entitled "The World Tyre Industry, a new perspective to 2005; the EIV, 1997).

and the rival brands is much lower on the French market than on the export market.

Unlike car tires, the retailing of truck tires requires technological knowledge and special skills, which explains why 78 to 85% of the truck tire retailing is carried out by specialized distributors. Michelin is vertically integrated into the distribution sector through its retailer "Euromaster", which ran about 330 outlets out of a total of 2,225 specialized sales outlets in France, thus being the single largest chain in the industry at the time. Michelin's competitors were also partially vertically integrated: Sumitomo/Dunlop owned 120 specialized outlets, while Bridgestone/Firestone had 26.

The remaining outlets were run by independent tire retailers, whose vertical contracts with Michelin soon called the EC into action. In its decision, the EC observed that competition between the dealers is very intense and margins are small (Recital 206). Michelin offered its retailers a number of rebate and bonus programs, ranging from standardized quantity rebates applying uniformly to all its retailers, to individualized sales growth bonuses (the so-called "progress bonus"), and to market share rebates rewarding retailers who joined the "club des amis de Michelin". Under the latter scheme, the "club" members (some 375 outlets covering about

20% of the market) would guarantee for a certain “Michelin temperature”, i.e., for certain sales volumes and market shares. In return, Michelin would contribute to investment and training of the retailer’s staff, and also provide financial contributions.

The Commission found these rebate schemes to be fidelity-enhancing and exclusionary, the allegation being that Michelin tried to defend its dominant position on the French tire market by making it impossible for rival manufacturers to access the retail sector.

The French tire industry at the time of the EC decision resembles the model studied in Karlinger (2012). The sequential contracting setting was certainly present there because all tire retailers had signed up with Michelin before the rival manufacturers entered the French market and started to trade with these retailers. While it is certainly true that Michelin’s rivals sold to more than one French tire retailer (so that we cannot speak of exclusive relationships with respect to the national market), it may well be that exclusivity applied to some of the regional or local sub-markets.

In Karlinger (2012), the incumbent manufacturer has no interest in excluding the entrant, and certain aspects of Michelin’s business practices raise doubts about the Commission conviction that the main purpose behind Michelin’s conduct was to exclude the other tire manufacturers. For instance, Michelin did carry the rival brands at its own outlets, i.e., the Euromaster store. This lends support to the idea that Michelin found multi-brand retailing more profitable compared to an own-brand-only policy.

However, it is unlikely that the independent retailers would be as careful in protecting the Michelin tires from oversupply of rival brands as Euromaster, which was directly controlled by Michelin. Therefore, Michelin had to design its vertical contracts with these independent retailers in a way to protect the margins earned on Michelin tires, and also to reduce the rents that the rival manufacturers could extract from the common-agency retailers.

That such rents were actually earned by the other tire manufacturers is quite likely considering their market power in other markets, which sets them apart from the “white-brand” manufacturers and the suppliers of so-called “retreaded” (i.e., recycled) tires who also operate on the French market. The fact that Michelin’s competitors have a high-quality brand image on markets outside of France is not in contrast with the assumptions of our model, which assigns the high-quality good to the incumbent and a low-quality variant to the entrant: The notion of quality in the tire market does not only refer to the technological characteristics of the tire itself, but also to the quality of the retail services, i.e., choosing and fitting the right tires for each client. The EC decision discusses repeatedly how Michelin invested heavily into the quality of the sales services offered by its retailers, and that Michelin's strong position in the French market is at least partly explained by consumers' preferences for these high-quality services.

The fact that Michelin's market share was stable and even slightly decreasing over the 1990s should not be seen as evidence of dwindling market power (as Michelin itself claimed in its appeal against the Commission's decision): as Karlinger (2012) shows, if the incumbent is successful at defending her market power, she will be able contain her output, while a drastically expanding market share of the dominant brand is a symptom of failure to control retailer competition for the rival brands in any other way: Absent any alternatives, an abundant supply of good A is makeshift to reduce the residual demand for good B, and hence the competitive price for the available stocks of good B that the retailers are willing to pay.

Thus, the post-EC-decision market structure is closest to a uniform-contracts scenario. We would therefore expect to see Michelin losing market share and profits, while the rival manufacturers should gain along both lines. Thus, there is no doubt that the decision hurt Michelin and favored its newcomer competitors. The more controversial question is whether the decision benefitted consumers or not.

To assess this question, we have to identify the most likely pre-decision scenario: If we think that the vertical restraints employed by Michelin were sufficient to fully restore its market power, i.e., that the market was at its industry profit-maximizing equilibrium, then the EC decision was unambiguously beneficial, in that it lead to an output expansion for all brands, with lower prices and higher consumption at all quality levels.

If, however, the only effect of the decision was to impose uniform contracts where previously Michelin used discriminatory contracts, it is unclear whether consumers benefitted or not: The decision is most likely to have been beneficial if the perceived quality difference between Michelin's products (and the services provided by its retailers) and the rival tires was not too large, and the expansion of the rival brands' sales was sufficiently strong to compensate for the drop in average quality of consumption.

6. Conclusion

This chapter discusses the most recent contributions on possible anticompetitive effects of quantity discounts and loyalty discounts. It then presents in more detail the central findings of Karlinger (2012), the first model to show how vertical and horizontal control interact with each other when a dominant firm faces constraints on the vertical restraints it can use, and how these constraints affect consumers. Most of the existing literature on vertical restraints studied the two objectives — vertical and horizontal control — in isolation, and therefore identified effects on consumers which differ from the ones I find.

In particular, I highlight the role of fidelity rebates (a form of cross-market controls) in reducing the rent extracted by the competing supplier, and in aligning the retailers' incentives in supplying the competing good with those of the dominant supplier. I argue that the EC's Michelin decision, which outlawed quantity discounts even in their softest form (uniform pure quantity discount), may have reduced Michelin's market power in a welfare enhancing way even if Michelin's main intent was not exclusion: Outlawing quantity discounts may have made it harder for Michelin to exert control over its retailers' contracts with rival tire producers, thus forcing Michelin to expand its output and lower prices to all its retailers.

References

Aghion, P. and P. Bolton (1987). "Contracts as a Barrier to Entry," *American Economic Review*, 77(3), pp. 388–401.

Bernheim, D. and M. Whinston (1985). "Common Marketing Agency as a Device for Facilitating Collusion," *RAND Journal of Economics*, 16, pp. 269–281.

Bernheim, D. and M. Whinston (1986). "Common Agency," *Econometrica*, 54, pp. 923–942.

Calzolari, G. and V. Denicolò (2013). "Competition with Exclusive Contracts and Market-Share Discounts," *American Economic Review*, 103(6), pp. 2384–2411.

Elhauge, E. R. and A. L. Wickelgren (2012a). "Robust Exclusion Through Loyalty Discounts With Buyer Commitment," *Harvard Discussion Paper* No. 722.

Elhauge, E. R. and A. L. Wickelgren (2012b). "Anti-Competitive Market Division Through Loyalty Discounts Without Buyer Commitment," *Harvard Discussion Paper* No. 723.

Fumagalli, C. and M. Motta (2006). "Exclusive Dealing and Entry, when Buyers Compete," *American Economic Review*, 96(3), pp. 785–795.

Hart, O. and J. Tirole (1990). "Vertical Integration And Market Foreclosure," *Brookings Papers on Economic Activity*, 1990, pp. 205–276.

Herweg, F. and D. Müller (2013). "Price Discrimination in Input Markets: Quantity Discounts and Private Information," *The Economic Journal*. doi: 10.1111/ecoj.12061.

Innes, R. and S. F. Hamilton (2006). "Naked Slotting Fees for Vertical Control of Multi-Product Retail Markets," *International Journal of Industrial Organization*, 24(2), pp. 308–318.

Innes, R. and S. F. Hamilton (2009). "Vertical Restraints and Horizontal Control," *RAND Journal of Economics*, 40(1), pp. 120–143.

Innes, R. and R. J. Sexton (1994). "Strategic Buyers and Exclusionary Contracts," *American Economic Review*, 84(3), pp. 566–584.

Karlinger, L. and M. Motta (2012). "Exclusionary Pricing When Scale Matters," *Journal of Industrial Economics*, 60(1), pp. 75–103.

Karlinger, L. (2012). "Discrimination and Fidelity Rebates in a Vertically Differentiated Industry," Mimeo, May 2012.

Majumdar, A. and G. Shaffer (2009). "Market-Share Contracts with Asymmetric Information," *Journal of Economics & Management Strategy*, 18(2), pp. 393–421.

Marx, L. M. and G. Shaffer (2008). "Rent-Shifting, Exclusion, and Market-Share Discounts," *Working Paper*, University of Rochester.

McAfee, P. and M. Schwartz (1994). "Opportunism in Multilateral Contracting: Nondiscrimination, Exclusivity and Uniformity," *American Economic Review*, 84(1), pp. 210–230.

Miklós-Thal, J., P. Rey and T. Vergé (2010). "Vertical Relations," *International Journal of Industrial Organization*, 28(4), pp. 345–349.

Motta, M. (2009). Michelin II: The Treatment of Rebates, in B. Lyons (Ed.), *Cases in European Competition Policy — The Economic Analysis*, Cambridge University Press, Cambridge.

O'Brien, D. P. and G. Shaffer (1992). "Vertical Control with Bilateral Contracts," *RAND Journal of Economics*, 23(3), pp. 299–308.

Rasmusen, E. B., J. Mark Ramseyer and J. S. Wiley (1991). "Naked Exclusion," *American Economic Review*, 81(5), pp. 1137–1145.

Rey, P. and J. Tirole (2007). A Primer on Foreclosure, in M. Armstrong and R. Porter (Eds.), Handbook of Industrial Organization, Vol. III, North Holland, pp. 2145–2220.

Rey, P. and T. Vergé (2004). "Bilateral Control with Vertical Contracts," *RAND Journal of Economics*, 35(4), pp. 728–746.

Rey, P. and T. Vergé (2010). "Resale Price Maintenance And Interlocking Relationships," *Journal of Industrial Economics*, 58(4), pp. 928–961.

Segal, I. R. and M. D. Whinston (2000). "Naked Exclusion: Comment," *American Economic Review*, 90(1), pp. 296–309.

Winter, R. A. (1993). "Vertical Control and Price Versus Nonprice Competition," *Quarterly Journal of Economics*, 108(1), pp. 61–76.

Chapter 10

Technology Transfer, Contracting, and Product Market Competition*

Frago Kourandi

Athens University of Economics and Business
kourandi@aueb.gr

Sabina Sachtachtinskagia

Athens University of Economics and Business
sabina@aueb.gr

Nikolaos Vettas

Athens University of Economics and Business and CEPR
nvettas@aueb.gr

Abstract

We examine aspects of how new technology may be transferred to firms that use it in a final product market. Should technology transfer take place to a single firm or to more than one, and should it happen gradually or at once? How do the incompleteness of contracts and the nature of product market competition affect the transfer of technology? Such issues are central in the challenges that multinationals face when they need to transfer technology to local firms. First, we review the main related ideas in the literature. Second, we set up a simple model of gradual transfer of a cost-reducing innovation by its owner to the product market. We illustrate why, in the absence of vertical integration and complete contracts, technology transfer tends to be slower and at a lower than the optimal level and discuss the crucial role of potential competition in determining the level and allocation of profits between the upstream and the downstream firms.

*This chapter partly draws on a presentation at the 2012 CRESSE conference at Chania. The present research has been partly financed by the EU-ESF and Greek national funds, through the Thalis Research Funding Program of the National Strategic Reference Framework.

Keywords: Technology transfer, incomplete contracts, licensing, hold-up.

JEL Classification Codes: O3, L1, L22, D23.

1. Introduction

Technology is a major driver for profitability — when firms are able to decrease their costs or to improve the quality of their products, not only can they directly increase their demand, but they also gain an advantage relative to their competitors in the market. At the same time, technology is a major contributor to consumers' welfare, again, through the improvement of the quality of products or the decrease in their costs. It is not a surprise, therefore, that many aspects of the issue, how new technology is generated and used, have been studied extensively in the literature. More specifically, these aspects include the development of basic technology, the relation between invention and innovation in the market, process and product innovation, patenting and intellectual property rights (IPR), the structure of licensing contracts, and the relation between product market competition and the diffusion of innovations. In this chapter, we examine some specific issues related to how new technology may be possibly transferred from its current owner to other firms that will use in a final market, highlighting the crucial role or product market competition in such a relation. It has two parts, first, a review of the relevant literature and, second, a description of a simple model and its analysis to capture some novel aspects of the problem.

In the first part of the chapter, the main issues around the problem of technology licensing are discussed, along with presenting the related literature. This discussion covers what we consider as the main aspects of the problem that will be related, directly or indirectly to our subsequent analysis. We focus on the possible exclusivity of the technology transfer, its pace over time, the role of various contracting instruments, the possible lack of contract enforceability, contract incompleteness, and related moral hazard issues. We also discuss some particular issues that arise when technology is transferred in foreign markets, usually by multinational enterprises to local agents. Our discussion is not meant to be a comprehensive review of all the important contributions in the general area of technology transfer and contracting; after all, there are already many books covering the general area. It is necessarily partial and eclectic, focusing on the particular issues that are more important when technology is to be transferred in an environment where contracts are expected to offer only limited protection. We emphasize more recent contributions, also so that we can set the stage for our model in the second part of the chapter.

In the second part of the chapter, we set up and analyze a simple model of technology transfer. Our analysis sheds light to the role that market structure and potential competition among firms play when technology transfer occurs over time from "upstream" to "downstream" firms. In particular, while technology transfer in a static model has been studied in the literature, little attention has been paid to the pace and the amount of technology transfer in a dynamic environment. The objective of our model is to study the strategic timing of the technology transfer when the protection of IPR is not complete. The possibility that a downstream firm may not fully compensate the upstream firm for the benefits that it has received creates serious hold-up issues. We examine whether competition at the downstream level may resolve or diminish such problems. A leading example for our analysis would be a multinational enterprise which enters a local market (say, in a less developed country) and licenses superior technology to one or more local firms, and when the contracts that are signed are not fully enforceable. A number of issues arise. Should technology transfer take place to a single seller or to a larger number of rivals, and should it happen gradually or at once? How does the incompleteness of contracts, the nature of product market competition, and other aspects of the institutional framework affect the transfer of technology?

More specifically, our model studies the dynamics of a cost-reducing technology transfer over two periods. It may make sense that technology is transferred gradually and not at once, since typically both its transfer and its absorption require the use of significant human and other resources, an appropriate adjustment or even redesign of the receiving institution or changes in management practices. To capture such issues, we model the cost of technology transfer within each period as convex. We consider an upstream monopolist who wishes to transfer technology downstream, while at the downstream level there is potential competition. In principle, in this framework, we can have the optimal use of the technology when the seller can become vertically integrated (VI) or when it is possible that complete contracts replicate such vertical integration. Nevertheless, vertical integration or complete contracts are not always feasible or desirable in reality. We find that under vertical separation and when the protection of

IPR is imperfect, in equilibrium, technology transfer occurs to the same downstream firm in both periods. However, the type of the contractual relationship is crucially affected by the presence of competitors. In particular, there is a delay in technology transfer relative to the vertical integration benchmark. The upstream firm tries to limit the downstream firm's bargaining power, in an effort to pay a lower rent or no rent to the downstream firm in the subsequent period. Price competition downstream does not fully eliminate the opportunistic behavior of a downstream firm. We identify and describe scenarios when a downstream firm may capture a positive rent.

The remainder of the chapter is as follows. Section 2 presents an eclectic literature review on technology licensing. Section 3 sets up the basic model and sketches the corresponding game under vertical integration and vertical separation. The equilibrium outcome and its properties are also illustrated via some numerical examples. Section 4 concludes and discusses some possible future research.

2. Literature Review

The licensing of technology by an innovator to other firms that operate in the final product market provides a way to diffuse technology for compensation. The world market for licensing of technology is of considerable size. For example, the total receipts of U.S. firms from cross-border royalties and licensing fees for industrial processes and products, taking into account only non-affiliated buyers, amount to $47.5 billions for 2012.[1] In the UK, evidence from a recent SIPU survey, commissioned by the Intellectual Property Office and authored by Arora *et al.* (2013), suggests that the expenditure on technology in-licensing (i.e., licensing and R&D purchase) for 2009–2012 was around £6.9 billion per year, which corresponds to almost 40% of the total business enterprise spending on R&D. The same survey also finds that licensing typically helps to catch-up with innovations rather than to access the very latest technology and that industries where innovation rates are low often rely on licensing. On the contrary, industries where innovation rates tend to be high are less likely to use licensing and

[1] Online data from U.S. Bureau of Economic Analysis: U.S. International Services, Table F: http://www.bea.gov/international/international_services.htm.

more likely to maintain exclusivity by the owner of technology. Another survey by Arora and Gambardella (2010) has identified the factors that limit the growth of the market for technology. These factors include: high transaction costs of licensing and uncertainty about the property rights, as well as about the value of the technology and about the transaction process.

The protection of intellectual property typically gives to the inventor monopoly rights over his invention for a limited period of time. This protection is intended to provide incentives for research and a way to cover the development costs.[2] Although technology patents are generally protected much like all other intellectual products, such as books and works of art, their nature is somewhat different. Knowledge itself is an intangible asset and may be viewed as a public good — once knowledge is produced, it can be shared among multiple users without much additional cost. However, when knowledge is applied to a particular technological innovation, the situation becomes more complex. The transfer of knowledge which is applied to the production of goods is likely to be costly, for example, when some significant training of the firms' personnel is necessary in order for the new technology to become operational. In addition, access to a new technology usually provides some competitive advantage and therefore exclusive ownership of this technology may be highly desirable for a firm (in essence, sharing of the innovation may create negative externalities for a firm that may reduce its profits).

Naturally, there are various types of innovation, each with its own features, including product innovations, that create new products or improve the quality of existing products. Optimal license fees for a new product have been examined by Kamien *et al.* (1988). Rockett (1990) discusses the quality of technology that the innovator chooses to license. Stamatopoulos and Tauman (2008) analyze the licensing of a quality-improving innovation. However, for the purpose of the analysis of technology transfer, most models in the relevant literature focus on cost-reducing innovation. Using Arrow's (1962) definition, such an innovation can be classified as drastic — which gives to the inventor monopolistic price in the product market — or

[2]For an overview of alternatives to patenting (e.g., public sponsorship) and for possible improvements of the patenting system to avoid the deadweight loss associated with monopoly, see a detailed analysis in Scotchmer (2004).

non-drastic. Hence, the effect of innovation on public welfare is not always positive, since it can lead to monopoly.

A thorough survey of the early research on the theory of licensing has been provided by Kamien (1992). Seminal contributions on cost-reducing innovations when property rights are perfect include Katz and Shapiro (1985, 1986) and Kamien and Tauman (1984, 1986) who develop models for the transfer of technology. More recently, Sen and Tauman (2007) consider the optimal licensing schemes for a cost-reducing innovation by both incumbent and potential innovators in a Cournot oligopoly model. They find that for any non-drastic innovation, patents are sold to all firms, and that an outsider has a greater incentive to innovate than an incumbent.

An important question is whether licensing stimulates cost-reducing innovation or not. According to Gallini and Winter (1985), licensing stimulates innovation when the initial costs of competing firms are relatively symmetric, but harms innovation when these costs are asymmetric. They also find that licensing reduces innovation in concentrated industries and encourages innovation in less concentrated industries. There is a large number of alternative formulations and extensions of the generic models of cost-reducing innovations. In this section, we present an eclectic review of some important issues centering around technology transfer. These issues, studied in more or less detail in the extant literature, are the following: the type of technology contracting, specific issues that may arise in foreign markets, the role of competition and market structure, incomplete contracting, and the dynamics of technology transfer. Each of these issues is discussed separately below. Naturally, these issues are not usually independent of each other and, on the contrary, they tend to be interconnected.

2.1. *Technology contracting*

***Ex-post* and *ex-ante* licensing.** Licensing contracts can be signed either *ex-post*, for fully developed technologies or *ex-ante*, for emerging technologies. A study by Siebert and von Graeventiz (2011) examines *ex-ante* licensing agreements and finds that, in the markets studied, they are more common than *ex-post* licensing agreements. The authors provide an empirical analysis with data from the semiconductor industry between

1989 and 1999. Their research is motivated by the fact that although the number of patents has been increasing steadily during this decade (and more than doubled), the number of (*ex-post*) licensing agreements followed an inverse U-shape. This phenomenon is explained by the evolution of *ex-ante* licensing agreements in the early 1990s, when contracts were signed before research was completed. The authors demonstrate that *ex-ante* licensing agreements are effective to prevent patent races. In contrast, *ex-post* licensing agreements help to rectify the situation when the importance of a blocking technology has been underestimated *ex-ante*. We note, however, that the Siebert and von Graeventiz (2011) model appears to apply primarily to a horizontal market structure where manufacturers conduct R&D themselves, and not to a vertically separated industry.

Licensing fees. The two major forms of licensing fees are fixed fees and royalty payments. Under complete information, when licensing to a single downstream firm that is not the licensor's competitor, fixed fees would be preferred, since royalties would tend to distort the marginal cost of production and decrease the total surplus. However, when incomplete information or strategic considerations are important, the choice between fees and royalties becomes less straightforward. While the early theory suggests that the optimal licensing schemes should involve fixed payments,[3] empirical evidence shows that royalties are used quite often, either alone or within a two-part tariff scheme. For example, according to a survey by Rostoker (1984), royalties alone were used in 39% of all the cases studied, and two-part tariffs in 46%. A more recent empirical study by Mendi (2005) that uses Spanish data also notes that royalties are used quite often.

The use of royalties, rather than fixed fees, may be preferred due to contractual incompleteness or informational asymmetries that hinder the use of fixed fees. For example, an upfront payment could not be possible due to imperfect access of the licensee to the financial markets, or when there can be uncertainty about the size of the demand. It seems logical to assume that the longer is the expected contractual relationship, the harder it is to predict possible future demand shocks and to calculate all the risks, and thus the more likely it is that some form of output-based fees will

[3]See e.g., Katz and Shapiro (1986).

be used. Also, under asymmetric information, the use of royalty fees may constitute a signal.[4] Wang (1998) finds another reason for the inventor to prefer royalties, in a model where a non-drastic innovation is licensed to a rival and the product market is a Cournot duopoly with homogenous product. He concludes that the patent-holding firm enjoys a cost advantage in the Cournot game under a royalty licensing scheme, but not under a fixed-fee licensing scheme. Saracho (2002) examines how of strategic delegation and managerial incentives relate to the choice of the licensing fee. Since in the modern corporation, there is a separation of ownership from managerial decisions, the owners can strategically induce the managers to act aggressively, e.g., by paying them on the basis of sales rather than profits, and in that case, the profits from royalties would increase with sales. Muto (1993) examines optimal licensing in a differentiated Bertrand duopoly. He finds that when the cost reduction that the innovation provides is small, the use of royalty fee can be optimal. On the contrary, when the cost reduction is large, a fixed fee is preferred. Bousquet *et al.* (1998) analyze the role that risk aversion plays in licensing. They find that when demand is uncertain, *ad valorem* royalties tend to outperform per unit royalties. The intuition here is that *ad valorem* royalties make the payment dependent on revenues rather than on output, and therefore the risk is shared by the licensor and the licensee. Jensen and Thursby (2001) study the licensing of university inventions and observe that there are inventions where the probability of success is small at the time of licensing, but increases with additional inventor effort. This feature creates a moral hazard problem that can be resolved by writing a contract with output-based payments, such as royalties or equities.

It should be noted that it is not always possible to use royalties, as they can be implemented only when sales are observable. Similarly, when technology transfer includes elements that are difficult to verify or to quantify (such as management techniques) and that are not immediately tied to production, royalties are not quite relevant, and fixed payments could be easier to implement. Related to their regulatory and competition policy implications, the availability of both fixed fees and royalties is important. Fauli-Oller and Sandonis (2003) show that when either instrument is

[4] For a detailed analysis, see "incomplete information and signaling".

unavailable, the possibility of licensing cannot be used as a definitive argument against horizontal mergers. This is because licensing might be unprofitable when the seller is restricted to the use of only one instrument (royalties or fixed fee). In that case, a merger becomes the more reasonable way or in fact the only way to transfer superior technology and may be welfare improving.

A strong substitute for licensing is selling the patented technology. An empirical research by Jeong *et al.* (2013) that uses data from Korean market of technology shows that firms tend to license their patents when uncertainty is low or transaction costs are high, and tend to sell their patents under the opposite conditions.

Resale terms and other special clauses. Apart from the licensing fees, contracts often include other provisions that bring benefits to the licensor. Hence, licensing contracts can have special terms that prohibit the resale of technology, although it is not always easy to confirm in practice whether this obligation is kept or not. Another possible clause in licensing contracts is a resale price maintenance (RPM) arrangement for the final good that is produced with the use of licensed technology. Such a clause specifies a fixed price or a floor/ceiling price (minimum/maximum RPM) for the final good. It is often presumed that RMP has anticompetitive effects, reducing intra-brand competition and, under some conditions, facilitating collusion. Fixed and minimum RPM are illegal in the EU, and have been *per se* illegal in the U.S. until the 2007 Supreme Court decision about Leegin case that has suggested a more compromising approach, based on the economics of each case.

It is also worth mentioning here some special clauses often used in practice: there can be an exclusive dealing clause, which constrains the licensee from dealing with other firms, and a grant-back clause, where the licensee agrees to license back to the original inventor any improvements that will be made to the patent. Joint licensing, agreed strategically by two or more IPR holders, is possible for complementary technologies. However, large collective rights management organizations, such as the ASCAP (American Society of Composers, Authors and Publishers) in the U.S. or ECL (Extended Collective Licensing) in the Nordic countries, tend to replace customized contracts by generic templates.

The role of bargaining power. The leading and well-studied case in the literature is that the innovator is a multinational corporation and the buyer of the technology is a small local firm, picked from a large enough pool of possible competitors each with low bargaining power. However, more generally, it is not always given that the initial distribution of the bargaining power is in favor of the innovator. Especially for licensing within the same country, it may be that the relatively small size of the innovator's firm or its inferior access to financial markets relative, say, to the final goods producers, diminishes its bargaining power. In a sense, the size of the innovator and the distance from the final goods market is also an endogenous variable — the innovator could be instead a joint venture (JV) or a partner of the firm that sells in the final goods market. Moreover, the final goods market structure is endogenous too, depending on the strategic interactions and choices that are made by the upstream and the downstream firms. Therefore, a strong interdependency exists between the market structure at the upstream level (vertically separated/integrated innovators) and at the downstream level (the number of firms in the final goods market). This feature also raises the issue of exclusionary practices and bottlenecks in the vertical chain along which technology is transferred.

The role of bargaining for the licensing of a cost-reducing innovation has been examined by Sempere Monerris and Vannatelbosch (2001). They find that, although from the social point of view, the best option is a fixed licensing fee, from the point of view of the inventor, direct negotiation might be preferred to both an auction and a fixed fee, as it can extract a larger rent from the downstream duopolistic industry. Naghavi and Ottaviano (2008) analyze the impact that the bargaining power has on the choice between producing and outsourcing. They assume that all research is conducted by independent labs and that outsourcing production requires complementary upstream and downstream inventions. They find that the relationship between the incentives to outsource and the bargaining power of the upstream firm has an inverted-U shape. Therefore, innovation is maximized when the supplier's bargaining power does not take extreme values.

2.2. *Foreign markets, technology, and FDI*

Licensing to a foreign firm is a special case of licensing. The peculiarity here is that the upstream firm, the innovator, is typically a large multinational enterprise (MNE) that may enter a market in a less developed country (or, in any event, one with a different and possibly poorer legal system), and can do so via licensing. So, here the study of technology transfer has to be understood in relation to the literature about the various types of foreign direct investment (FDI).

A distinction can be made between vertical and horizontal FDI. The general theory of vertical FDI has been first developed in depth by Helpman (2004). When two countries have different endowments in production factors, such as labor and capital, and the stages of production involve different intensity of these factors, there are incentives for outsourcing. Typically, a developed country, endowed with capital, would conduct R&D and build the machines, while the labor-intensive production would be carried in a less developed country, where the labor is cheaper, so as to exploit the competitive advantage that this country has. Horizontal FDI, in contrast, presupposes that there is demand for the final good in a foreign country. In this case, offshoring of production is a substitute for exporting to satisfy the demand abroad. When the final good is exported, transportation costs, tariffs and taxes must be taken into account. If the corresponding economies of scale are not significant, and the production costs abroad are low enough, it is often more profitable to offshore than to export. Of course, a firm can have both vertical and horizontal motives for offshoring. While horizontal FDI is arguably more common,[5] our main interest here is in vertical FDI, which has similarities to the transfer of technology to a foreign firm. An empirical study of U.S. multinationals by Ramondo *et al.* (2011) suggests that the comparative advantage of MNEs comes primarily from transferring intangible rather than physical inputs along the vertically linked production chain.

The role of FDI in international technology transfer has been studied by several authors. Saggi (2002) emphasizes the role of international knowledge spillovers for growth. More recently, Glass and Saggi (2008) review the relevant literature. Marin *et al.* (2013) find that transfer of an innovative technology to the host country is one of the major factors that lead to the transplantation of the MNE's business model (i.e., decisions about

[5]For a review of vertical vs. horizontal explanation of motives for FDI, see Brakman and Garretsen (2008), Chapter 1, pp. 19–22.

acquisitions, finance, budget, R&D, new strategy, firing of personnel, etc.) to the affiliate.

There are many papers that consider the formation and dissolution of vertical FDI relations, vertical chains, and JVs, without studying the issue of imperfect IPR or the timing of technology transfer issues. The main intuition is that when one firm has superior access to capital and another firm has superior access to the workforce, cooperation between these firms can develop. The model by Chowdhury and Chowdhury (2001) applies this idea to examine JVs life cycles. Their model has two periods and, in each period, firms decide whether to form a JV or to compete in Cournot market. The authors assume that JVs are formed because they create synergies, e.g., the MNE can supply capital more cheaply, while the domestic firm can supply labor more cheaply. JVs are assumed to involve some coordination cost (otherwise they would always be formed). There exists organizational learning which is both-sided and symmetric, so that firms gradually become more efficient in the field where their partner excels, which reduces the value of synergetic cost savings. Depending on the values of parameters, JVs can be formed or not, and can be broken or not. Hence, the market structure with vertical relations is endogenized. We note here, of course, that JVs are only one example and there are many alternative ways to create synergies by developing one or another form of a vertical relation, which are discussed below.

Possible modes of entry into the foreign market (most of which form some sort of vertical relations) include: licensing, establishing a new subsidiary (greenfield investment), acquiring an existing local firm and exporting. Hence, there is a choice of the mode of entrance into a foreign market. Apart from access to low cost labor, an MNE's motives for FDI include, for example, avoiding problems with information exchange, as explored in Ethier (1986), or avoiding transportation costs, as in the study of Helpman *et al.* (2004). Brakman and Garretsen (2008) emphasize that acquisition allows to face low intra-union trade cost when serving a foreign market, and call this the export-platform gain. Also, they note that acquisitions make the market structure more concentrated that greenfield investments, therefore every acquisition increases the incentive for further acquisitions. Of course, developing countries may have legislative restrictions on direct foreign entrance in domestic market, and this factor makes licensing particularly useful to access those markets. Also, it must be taken into account that in developing countries, there is often only imperfect intellectual rights protection and possibly some other forms of market imperfections that do not allow in practice the use of complete contracts.

Horstmann and Markusen (1996) explore a model where different modes of serving the foreign market emerge endogenously. In a multi-period model, an MNE, being uncertain about the characteristics of demand (especially, the size of the foreign market) must decide whether to invest and enter the market directly or to contract with a local agent first. Using an agent, the multinational firm can avoid making costly investments in case the market is not large enough to render them profitable. If the market proves large, the MNE will switch to direct investment in subsequent periods, but if the market proves small, it will stick to contractual relations. The local agent, being better informed about the local market, is able to extract information rents from the multinational firm. It should be noted, however, that competition is not present in this model. It is found that entrance through direct investment will be preferred to contracting when the market is large and variability in profits is small.

There is a more recent literature about the choice between various modes of entry into a foreign market.[6] For example, Rob and Vettas (2003) examine the choice between FDI and exports under the assumption of demand uncertainty and irreversibility of investment. Kotseva and Vettas (2005) study this choice in presence of demand shocks that, while increasing expected profits, impede learning because of persistence of uncertainty. Nocke and Yeaple (2007) develop a general equilibrium model with heterogeneous firms to study alternative modes of foreign market access (FDI vs. acquisition).

Sinha (2010) considers the possibility of the strategic use of licensing prior to the choice of the mode of entrance into a foreign market. In his model, there are two domestic firms that operate in a Cournot market and an MNE that seeks to enter the market. In the first stage, the MNE licenses technology to the downstream firms and chooses the type of licensing contract (royalty, fixed fee or two-part tariff). In the second stage, the MNE enters the foreign market with either exports or FDI (acquiring a subsidiary).

[6]For a comprehensive analysis of the modes of entry, see Feenstra (2010).

The author finds that, for some values of the parameters, choosing royalties rather than fixed fees helps to shift market conditions in favor of the MNE. As a result of this shift, in the second stage, the MNE prefers to enter the foreign market through exports rather than with FDI. This can potentially reduce the welfare of the developing country.

Another important issue here is what effects the mode of entry has on technology transfer. In a model by Mattoo *et al.* (2004), the MNE has a choice between direct entry and acquisition of a domestic firm. The authors consider the incentives for the MNE to transfer technology to the downstream firm in both cases. They find that, although direct entry obviously has a greater effect on enhancing competition than acquisition, neither mode of entry clearly dominates the other in terms of the level of technology transfer. The acquired firm enjoys a larger market share that increases the technology transfer due to scale effects. However, the increased level of competition due to direct entry also benefits technology transfer as a strategy to increase one's market share.

The dynamic impact of acquisitions on R&D is studied by Guadalupe *et al.* (2012), who use a Spanish manufacturing firms' dataset and propose a model of endogenous selection and innovation. Their estimation is that MNEs acquire the most productive domestic firms. These acquired firms, after adopting foreign technology, become even more productive and are likely to innovate.

2.3. *The role of competition and market structure*

Exclusivity and foreclosure. The licensing of technology essentially creates a vertical relation between the innovator who "supplies" the technology and the downstream firm who receives the technology (to use it in the final market). A large strand of the industrial organization literature examines the vertical contractual relations and how the various types of contracts affect the final and the intermediate prices and the competition in both vertical levels.[7] An important part of this literature concerns the exclusivity of relations between the upstream and the downstream firms. For example, Marx and Shaffer (2007) examine the use of upfront payments

[7]For a general review, see Motta (2004).

(such as slotting allowances or listing fees) that are made by an upstream firm to the downstream firms to gain access to their retail distribution network. In their model, two competing downstream firms make a take-it-or-leave-it offer to a single upstream firm. The model predicts that the dominant retailer will use his bargaining power, so as to exclude the rival retailer. Rey and Tirole (2007) focus on vertical market foreclosure, where not all competitors have access to a bottleneck input, while Rey and Vergé (2008) offer a comprehensive overview of several vertical contacting issues.

A contract clause that ties a buyer to a supplier, restricting him from buying from other suppliers, is called "exclusive dealing". Rasmusen *et al.* (1991) and Segal and Whinston (2000) argue that exclusive dealing contracts can be used to deter entry when economies of scale are present. For example, when there are 100 customers, and the minimum efficient scale is $n < 50$, it is enough to lock up $100 - n$ customers to become a monopoly. Therefore, the upstream firm exploits the lack of coordination between multiple buyers with little bargaining power, who are likely to agree to sign exclusive contracts if they expect the other buyers to sign too. One could say that signing an exclusive contract imposes a negative externality on the other buyers. But what happens if the buyers are not the final consumers of the product? Could perhaps downstream competition between the buyers solve the problem of exclusive dealing? Wright (2009), commenting on a model by Fumagalli and Motta (2006) where buyers are homogenous price competitors, shows that despite the downstream competition between buyers, exclusion persists. In this framework, entry can be deterred even when entrants have a relatively large cost advantage or when the economies of scale are small. Simpson and Wickelgren (2007) obtain similar results in a setting when competing downstream firms could breach contracts and pay expectation damages.

Many of the considerations that govern vertical relations, partly also apply to technology licensing as a special case. For example, the (upstream) technology innovator may choose to transfer technology to a specific downstream firm and this may lead to the (downstream) foreclosure of competitors that now have become less efficient. However, there could be a trade-off between creating a downstream monopoly vs. having multiple downstream firms competing for the implementation of the innovation. A firm's willingness to license technology to multiple downstream firms may be affected by a number of factors, such as incomplete information, incomplete IPR protection, product differentiation, capacity constraints, bargaining power, managerial incentives, and the use of strategic intertemporal planning (e.g., to reduce rival's incentive to research or to reduce the future bargaining power of licensees by increasing their number). According to Schmitz (2001), when the value of invention is private information, the monopolistic inventor may have to license in equilibrium to more than one firm, even though he would otherwise have preferred an exclusive contract.

While antitrust law sometimes prohibits exclusive dealing contracts, it is usually more permissive with contracts that grant exclusive rights to a buyer. According to an empirical study by Anand and Khanna (2000), 11% of all licensing contracts grant worldwide exclusivity, 26% grant local exclusivity, and in another 45%, the type of exclusive rights granted cannot be ascertained, while only 18% of all contracts are explicitly non-exclusive.[8] These facts illustrate the extent and importance of foreclosure issues in licensing. The authors also find that about 13% of all licensing contracts are cross-licensing which means that the two parties share their patents or technologies.

Licensing to rivals. Another important issue, closely related to foreclosure, concerns the incentives of a firm to license technology to rivals. The problem is twofold. On the one hand, when the inventor refuses to license to rivals, this may exclude them from the downstream market and thus have anticompetitive effects. On the other hand, when the inventor agrees to license to rivals, this may decrease the rivals' incentives to invent, and thus also have anticompetitive effects.[9] As noted by Gallini (1984), licensing generally decreases incentives to invent around the patent. Thus, rival firms can be encouraged to enter the product market via licensing as a way of deterring them from R&D activity. This helps to reduce inefficient R&D

[8]These percentages vary across industries. Exclusive contracts are somewhat less frequent in industries such as computers and electronics.

[9]However, the increase in downstream competition may offset these effects. For example, Spulber (2012) finds that competing inventors have greater expected returns to invention when the downstream market is competitive, therefore downstream competition increases the incentives to invent.

costs, which is a welfare-improving effect, although potentially efficient innovations are also reduced. In a recent paper by Duchene *et al.* (2012), the strategic use of technology transfer to deter downstream entry is analyzed. The inventor could license technology to another incumbent via a low royalty so as to exclude potential entrants to the market. Hence, a trade-off exists between using a high licensing fee and having a more concentrated market structure. From a different viewpoint, Arora and Fosfuri (2003) find that when the technology holder is not a monopolist in the market of technology or, at least, when he is threatened with competition, his incentives to license the technology to rivals increase. Fauli-Oller and Sandonis (2012) show that in a Bertrand market with differentiated product, licensing to rivals can be used as a collusive device to keep prices high, which could result to a reduction in welfare.

2.4. *The role of incomplete contracts for technology transfer*

Incomplete information and signaling. There can be various reasons why complete contracts are not feasible in practice. Incomplete or asymmetric information plays a major role here. For instance, the innovator or the licensee (or both) may be unable to foresee the full extent of implications that an innovation may have. In fact, it might be an oversimplification to assume that the innovator always has higher information about the value of innovation than the licensee. If the innovator specializes in research rather than in production and sales of the final product, then his knowledge of the market conditions could be limited. In any case, it can be hard to write a perfect contract in advance. The role of asymmetric information concerning the value of innovation has been first analyzed by Gallini and Wright (1990), where an inventor signals his innovation type by choosing an output-based payment, such as a royalty rather than a fixed fee. Beggs (1992) also shows how the presence of asymmetric information about the value of the patent may provide an explanation for the existence of royalties. According to his analysis, the use of royalties constitutes a signal that increases the likelihood of the patent being allocated to the right firm. Hernandez-Murillo and Llobet (2006) characterize the optimal contracts in a framework with differentiated products and private information about the value of the new technology, and analyze the use of licensing for softening competition.

Moldavanu and Sela (2003) show, in an auction setting, how incomplete information about production costs creates inefficiencies when a cost-reducing innovation is licensed to Bertrand competitors. In addition, an asymmetry in information can be used strategically to facilitate collusion. Das Varma (2003) explores bidding for a process innovation in a first-price, sealed bid auction under alternative modes of competition. In his model, bids are used to signal the value of the innovation. He finds that an efficient equilibrium exists under Cournot competition, but not under Bertrand competition at the downstream level (unless the number of firms is very large). Under Cournot competition, bidders have the incentive to overstate the value that the innovation has for them to induce the competitors to reduce their output and, thus, the highest bidder indeed wins the auction. On the contrary, under Bertrand competition, bidders have the incentive to understate the value that the innovation has for them to induce the competitors to raise their price and this tends to create a distributive inefficiency in first-bid auctions.

Spillovers and imitation. In addition to the ones discussed above, a reason that contracts can be incomplete is because of imperfect IPR protection that leads to spillovers or imitation. Technological spillovers from FDI to local firms through worker's mobility arise in Fosfuri *et al.* (2001). The MNE may pay a wage premium to prevent local firms from hiring its workers and thus gaining access to their knowledge in Glass and Saggi (2002a). The impact of the host country policies on the technology transfer when there is the fear of spillovers is analyzed by Mőller and Schnitzer (2006). Additionally, Glass and Saggi (2002b) develop a product life-cycle model with endogenous innovation, imitation and FDI. Technology that is licensed and used to produce goods, tends to diffuse to other firms in the downstream market, for example via worker mobility. While the licensed technology could often be patent-protected, this is not always the case, as sometimes firms prefer not to disclose their current innovations by going through the patent system, so as not to incentivize the rivals to invent around the patent. In addition, even a patent-protected technology can be imitated in practice. Such diffusion and imitation are sometimes considered beneficial for public welfare. Generally, in such cases the innovator is not fully compensated and this constitutes a case of imperfect intellectual rights protection.

The strategic interaction of the innovator with the potential licensees under imperfect IPR protection can be rather complex. A model by Jehiel *et al.* (1996) illustrates this point and, as the authors note, it could be applied to the study of the sale of a patent to downstream competitors. The model explains how outside options of agents become endogenous in the problem, when an agent's decision whether to acquire the good or not generates an externality (e.g., spillovers). The example they use for illustrating their insights is the sale of nuclear weapons. The central idea is that a buyer's behavior must take into account the effect of his decisions on the subsequent game. The authors find that, paradoxically, surplus can be extracted also from agents who do not obtain the auctioned object, and that the seller may be better off when he is paid from all potential buyers for not selling the good.

Does insufficient IPR protection hurt innovation and decrease social welfare? Generally, and in the short run, strong protection of IPR is expected to encourage innovation, at least in the "developed" countries, while imperfect protection is expected to discourage innovation. Yet, this relation may not be so straightforward when strategic interactions are added in the analysis. Market structure issues must be then taken into account. O'Donoghue and Zweimuller (2004) suggest, for example, that if the incumbent firm is threatened by entry, IPR protection allows fewer ideas to be patented and therefore hurts competition and slows innovation in the long run. Another argument, expressed e.g., by Helpman (1993), is that strong IPR protection reduces imitation, while imitation could play an important role in technological growth. Akiyama and Furukawa (2009) replicate this result in the classical North–South setting, which takes into account international markets. They find that the relation between IPR protection and innovation follows an inverted "U", in other words, relatively moderate patent protection helps innovation, while relatively strict patent protection hurts innovation. Aoki and Tauman (2001) find that when innovation is relatively significant, more licenses will be sold in the presence of spillovers. Pack and Saggi (2001) find that the double marginalization problem in a vertical chain is reduced when technology is transferred via international outsourcing, and its diffusion leads to entry in the domestic country market.

Spillovers and imitation do not always have an adverse effect on the inventor's profits. The idea of open source technology is gaining ground during the last few years. Sharing technology (which is not necessarily of state-of-the-art quality, since proprietary and open source technologies can coexist without competing directly) can have beneficial effects on the inventor's reputation, create positive network effects, and help to dominate the market (a particularly effective strategy if switching costs are present). The signaling effect of technology sharing when information is asymmetric is emphasized in Jansen (2009). Also, two or more competitors can decide to share their information. Their willingness to share depends primarily on the quality of information and on the intensity of competition. Cho and Jun (2013) examine a model where two firms have private information. They show that when the information that the firms have is independent, i.e., uncorrelated, sharing information tends to be beneficial to the firms. The opposite happens if the information that firms have is correlated, and in that case, sharing is less likely to take place.

From a regulator's point of view, when considering IPR protection and spillovers, the goal is to find the optimal balance between giving long-run incentives to innovate and maximizing short-run social welfare by encouraging competition. Still, the IPR law needs to be general rather than taking into account the peculiarities and the market structure of every industry. Therefore, it seems unavoidable in practice that the law gives the same protection to an innovation that creates monopoly (and, thus, implies some deadweight loss) and to an innovation that does not create monopoly and only improves production efficiency. However, what can and must be considered when granting IPR protection, is how broad is the field that protection will cover, and what types of bottlenecks are created. For example, the famous "1-click" patent (the technique of allowing customers to make online purchases with a single click), owned by Amazon.com, is considered by some a classic example of an overly broad patent. Also, a patent can lead to additional innovations. Therefore, another key choice that a regulator has to make is whether to grant IPR for improvements over the original patent, if they are made by the licensee. For example, the Plant Variety Protection Act of 1970 (in the U.S.) states that the use of a protected variety for further plant breeding or research does not constitute an infringement.

The choice of length of patent protection is also a difficult problem. Greater length of patent is usually believed to provide more protection to innovator and thus greater length for his monopoly, but this may be not always so. For example, Galini (1992) finds that when imitation is possible but costly, a long length of patents stimulates imitation. The cost to obtain a pattern must also be taken into account, along with the cost to enforce the patent. In the U.S., the application fee for a patent is under $1,000, but writing a patent properly usually costs $5,000–10,000 and often much more in attorney fees. Enforcing a patent is much more costly, since it has to be done in a court of law. Scotchmer (2004) presents evidence that the litigation cost is on average more than $0.5 million in the U.S., which is far more than the value of most patents.[10] She notes that, although litigations in the EU are generally less costly, they might have to be repeated in different countries.

Hold-up and moral hazard. Apart from spillovers and imitation, the licensing of technology under imperfect IPR protection can lead to a hold-up problem under conditions of moral hazard. This problem can be very significant in a setting where a party in a developed country licenses technology to another party in a developing country. Since the transfer of technology constitutes a relationship-specific ("idiosyncratic") investment, the licensee may break the contractual relationship without fully compensating the upstream firm for the benefits that it has received. This incentive constitutes the basis of the hold-up problem. The issue here is the shift of bargaining power, followed by renegotiation of the contract. Overall, the possibility of renegotiation of the licensing contract is important for two reasons. The first reason is the resolution of various asymmetries and market imperfections that happens naturally as time progresses. For example, the value of innovation becomes evident or the demand for the product becomes known gradually. Either the buyer or the seller (or both) may have an incentive to renegotiate the contract to take the new information into account. The second reason is that the distribution of the bargaining power may shift after the technology transfer begins, either because of the sunk costs for firm-specific investments or because of the changes in the final goods market structure that the innovation has provoked. Even when renegotiation option is formally absent, if IPR are not protected

[10] See Chapter 7, "Litigation and Enforcement".

perfectly, e.g., due to insufficient legal framework, then moral hazard (hold-up) problems may arise. This problem is quite common in the developing countries that are recipients of technological transfers. Lafontaine and Slade (2007) review the empirical evidence for the formation of vertical chains and their evidence supports that moral hazard is an important reason to avoid outsourcing.

There are many ways that a licensee may exploit insufficient IPR protection and appropriate part of the profits associated with technology production. An influential paper by Ethier and Markusen (1996) could serve as a good introduction to the problem. This chapter explores a model with two countries, where each is endowed with labor, but only the source country is endowed with capital. The innovation race in the source country produces a new product with a two-period life cycle. The MNE that developed this product must choose between costly exporting, licensing, and acquiring a subsidiary in the host country. Ownership advantage is tied to knowledge-based capital, and there is a risk of technology diffusion, since intellectual rights in the host country are not protected, in other words, anyone involved in producing the good in the first period can produce it in the second. There are many firms in the host country, but the authors assume that the source firm cannot establish a new license in the second period unless this was foreseen (i.e., licensing to another firm is not a possible response to an unanticipated, out-of-equilibrium move of a host firm). For different cost and technology parameters, alternative modes of serving the foreign market emerge endogenously. Often, an MNE finds the moral hazard problem so severe that it prefers to dissipate some rents through costly exporting rather than to share the rents with a subsidiary or licensee in order to induce them not to defect. The analysis also shows that similarities in relative factor endowments of countries are likely to promote direct investment.

In a subsequent paper, Markusen (2001) presents a model where the moral hazard problem is double-sided and finds that contract enforceability constraints on an MNE would allow it to credibly offer a lower licensing fee. However, it is quite usual in the literature to assume that an MNE has a good reputation and credibility that guarantees its contracts, thus, making any potential hold-up problem one-sided rather than two-sided.

Choi (2001) develops a model where technology transfer is susceptible to the moral hazard problem because of incomplete contracts. He assumes that there are costly inputs that are necessary for the efficient transmission of knowledge, which cannot be contracted directly, either because they are not easily observable or because they are not verifiable by a third party. This creates a moral hazard problem, which may be resolved if the contract includes royalties which depend on the verifiable production quantity, or simply by FDI instead of licensing.

2.5. *Dynamics of technology transfer*

For a number of reasons, related to both technology and strategy, technology transfer usually does not happen at once, but is spread over a longer time. Technological reasons for such a delay could be, for example, the increasing cost of a speedy technology transfer (technically, a quadratic cost function for transferring technology within each period could be regarded as a standard assumption in this strand of literature), or the increasing cost of technology absorption, due to lack of qualified personnel. The strategic reasons for delay in technology transfer usually have to do with the incomplete contracts that were analyzed in Section 2.4. Also, as already discussed in Section 2.3, licensing choices can sometimes be used as a strategic instrument to shape the market structure.[11] For these reasons, a study of multi-period strategy of technology transfer is essential. While many papers belong to the general field of licensing with incomplete contracts, only very few study the strategic timing, i.e., the pace of technology transfer. We provide a brief survey of this strand of the literature and pose some questions that arise.

Incomplete information and dynamics. A recent paper by Allain *et al.* (2011) finds that asymmetric information about the value of invention may lead to deviations from the socially optimal timing of technology transfer, depending on the bargaining power of the innovator. It sets up a two-period model with one innovator and many producers. In either period, the innovator bargains sequentially with the producers, so that an

[11] It is worth noting that MNEs can provide to their affiliates access to foreign markets for exports, as observed, for example, by Hanson *et al.* (2005). This can be part of an MNE's strategy to make technology more valuable in the future, by increasing the demand for the final product.

exclusive licensing can be signed. In the first period, there is asymmetric information, since only the innovator is informed about the value of his invention, while in the second period, this uncertainty is resolved. The development of the product from the first to the second period is costly for the innovator, but costless for the producer, thus, it is socially optimal that the innovation is transferred to one of the producers in the first period. However, asymmetric information may lead to deviations from the socially optimal timing. In particular, the more producers there are, the greater is the bargaining power of the innovator, and the greater is the price he can ask for the invention in the second period, which gives him an incentive to delay the licensing until he can prove the value of invention. In this way, the innovator gets a larger slice of a smaller pie. However, there is also a countervailing effect. If there is a large number of producers that intensify competition and decrease the profits derived from the innovation in the second period, this leads the innovator to earlier signing, in order to save on the cost of developing the invention. However, the more competitors there are downstream, the larger is the share of the pie for the inventor, but the smaller is this pie. For non-concentrated markets, the second effect dominates. So, mergers downstream might make technology transfer take place faster, as they increase the potential profit downstream. The higher the asymmetry of information, the greater is any impact that the number of competitors has on the delay of technology transfer.

Spillovers and imitation and dynamics. Another strategic reason for the innovator to delay transfer of technology to a downstream firm is to avoid imitation by other downstream firms, as technology is being diffused. Lin and Saggi (1999) propose a dynamic model where technology transfer generates cost-lowering spillovers for the competitor. They find that imitation risks may intensify competition. Henry and Ponce (2011) study the dynamic pricing of knowledge by examining the incentives to imitate rather than to innovate. They find that, when imitation is legal but costly, the inventor may prefer to offer contracts that allow the resale of knowledge and that the profit of the inventor increases with the number of potential imitators. The intuition here is that, if knowledge trading is possible, imitators prefer to strategically delay their entry awaiting for the price of knowledge to fall. Thus, the original inventor enjoys monopolistic profits for a random period of time, before the first contract is sold. In another recent paper, Henry and Ruiz-Aliseda (2012) note that many inventions are not protected by patents. Instead, the innovators can partially control the speed and the scope of imitation, by making their technologies harder to reverse-engineer. The dynamics of investment in protective measures vs. investment in imitation can explain the high rents that some firms enjoy when they choose secrecy over patenting.

Hold-up and dynamics. Transferring much technology at once could lead to a hold-up problem, by enabling the licensee to operate alone, breaking the contract with the upstream firm. This ability would give to the licensee additional bargaining power, which may enable him to get a larger share in the vertical chain's profits. Therefore, the innovation may have incentives to diminish the pace of technology transfer.[12]

Long *et al.* (2009) study a dynamic vertical model, where the downstream firm can quit without penalties, and find that the pace of technology transfer in this case departs from the optimal. They examine the relationship between a JV, consisting of a technologically advanced MNE and a local firm that operates in a developing country. The MNE owns the technology that is necessary to produce the good and that reduces its production cost. This technology can be transferred over time to a local firm, and the transfer has an increasing absorption cost. The local firm is drawn from an infinitely large pool of firms that all have the necessary qualifications to sell in the local market. The MNE protects its reputation and can commit credibly to certain actions, but a local firm's contracts cannot be enforced, which means that the local firm may break away at any point and produce the good by itself. If a breakup happens, the authors assume that the MNE leaves the host country. Also, it is assumed that there are financial market imperfections

[12]Schnitzer (1999) analyzes how an investor can use his control rights to protect his investment if he faces a hold-up problem. While his paper does not actually examine the pace of technology transfer, it studies how a multinational investor can be protected from a hold-up. In the model, once the investment is sunk, the government of the host country may partly expropriate it, e.g., by changing the tax policy. The investor can react and "punish" the government by exercising his control rights to shift production to other country. As a result, there may be underinvestment if the outside option of the investor is too weak, and overinvestment if it is too strong.

that make the MNE unable to collect a proper compensation from the local firm as soon as it receives any technology transfer, since this would imply negative cash-flows for the local firm. In order to prevent an early breakup, the MNE designs a scheme of technology transfer (both in terms of pace and aggregate amount), as well as a flow of side payments to the local firm. Note that the agent's value is changing over time, as he accumulates more and more capital. The optimal speed of technology transfer is examined. Since the technology transfer pace serves as a tool to counter the breakaway incentives, it deviates from the first best, i.e., both the rate and the amount of technology transfer are reduced, and the joint surplus is not maximized.

The role of competition and market structure and dynamics. There seems to be a major gap in the literature concerning the relation between the pace of technology transfer and the market structure. First, it could be possible that intensive downstream competition would help to resolve the problems that are created by incomplete contracts. Second, the pace of technology transfer could be used dynamically by the innovator in order to endogenize the market structure. It could be used to foreclose entrance, to exclude a rival, to facilitate collusion and to reduce the bargaining power of either current or potential licensees. There are models, discussed in our Section 2.3, that deal with some of these issues, but they are not dynamic with respect to the speed of technology transfer. Another question that remains largely unanswered by the current literature is whether the transfer of technology and know-how promotes vertical integration or vertical separation.[13]

[13]An empirical research by Bloom *et al.* (2013) using a dataset of American and European firms makes a distinction between information acquisition costs and communication costs. Empirical results imply that a fall in information acquisition costs has the effect of making the employees more autonomous. This could also be true for the firms that acquire access to MNE's superior knowledge via licensing or some other form of affiliation. As their costs of information acquisition fall, they might gain incentives to operate autonomously, being vertically separate and taking their own managerial decisions. On the other hand, a fall in communication costs tends to reduce the autonomy of employees, since it becomes easier to take and implement centralized decisions. Indeed, the gradual development of cooperation between MNE and its affiliates tends to lower their communication costs, and this may give incentives for vertical integration.

The model that we set up and study in Section 3 is compatible with the FDI setting and focuses on two key dynamic issues presented above: the imperfect IPR protection that may lead to hold-up and the role of competition and market structure. The model of hold-up that was developed by Long *et al.* (2009) avoids examining the impact of the pace of transfer on market structure, by assuming that after suffering a hold-up the inventor cannot reenter the market. In contrast, we explore this possibility. Some important questions that involve strategic decision making are the following: Will the licensees be able to extract rents due to the threat of moral hazard, if the upstream firm has the means to endogenize the market structure by controlling the pace of technology transfer? How do the speed and the total level of technology transfer under imperfect property rights compare to the socially optimal level? One could expect them to be reduced, but this is not necessarily so, since competition between the downstream producers for the license contract might be able to resolve the moral hazard problem, in line with what Felli and Roberts (2000) have suggested. More generally, how is the hold-up problem affected by the mode of competition downstream? How do the types of contractual relations in the vertical chain relate to the pace of technology transfer, especially if we compare vertical integration vs. decentralized production? We try to explore these issues in a simple model of technology transfer in Section 3.

3. A Simple Model of Technology Transfer

In this section, we set up a simple model of technology transfer. The model abstracts away from incomplete information considerations and explores a scenario where, if there would be no other restrictions, it is efficient that technology is transferred gradually. We explore how the presence of potential competition in the downstream market and alternative assumptions about the contracts that can be used affect the level and speed of technology transfer and the allocation of profits across the parties involved.

Suppose that there is one upstream firm (U) and a large pool of downstream firms (D, D', ...). The downstream firms have legal permission to operate in the final products market and produce homogeneous goods. Initially, they all produce at the same marginal production cost c (the technology of production is linear). Firm U owns an advanced technology that reduces the production cost of the downstream firms when this technology is transferred to them. This cost reduction is cumulative, as the technology transfer of the previous period continues to contribute to the cost reduction in the future. We examine a two-period model ($t = 1, 2$) where the discount factor between periods is denoted by $\delta \in [0, 1]$. We could denote the production cost of a downstream firm by $c_1 = c - h_1$ in the first period and by $c_2 = c_1 - h_2$ in the second period, where c_t is the marginal cost in period t and h_t is the technology transferred to this firm in period t.

Transferring technology is costly, as for example in the case where training costs are necessary to adopt the new technology. As technology transfer increases, the adoption cost increases in an increasing rate. Formally, this is reflected by a quadratic function $C(h_t) = \frac{\tau h_t^2}{2}$, $\tau \geq 0$. This cost is paid by firm U each time that it transfers technology to a downstream firm. We consider a linear demand function $Q_t = a - p_t$, where the highest value a of the buyers surpasses the initial production cost c. Competition in the final goods market takes place *à la* Bertrand. Finally, U charges fixed fees, a lump-sum transfer F_t, to the downstream firms when transferring technology h_t. Further, we assume that there are cash constraints, therefore, the fixed fee F_1 may not be drawn from the expected downstream profits in the subsequent period.

Consider first the benchmark case where U is VI with D and no fees have to be paid when technology is transferred within the VI chain. The joint profits of the VI chain in period t are given by

$$\Pi_t^{\mathrm{VI}} = (p_t - c_t)Q_t - \frac{\tau h_t^2}{2}.$$

The timing of the game is as follows. In the first period, U chooses the level of technology transfer h_1 and subsequently the downstream firms compete in the final market by setting the final price p_1. In the second period, U chooses the level of technology transfer h_2 that is will possibly make and then the final price p_2 is set by the downstream firms.

Turning next to vertical separation, the profit function of the upstream firm in period t is

$$\Pi_t^U = \begin{cases} F_t - \dfrac{\tau h_t^2}{2} & \textit{if } h_t \text{ is transferred} \\ 0 & \text{otherwise,} \end{cases}$$

while the profit function of the downstream firm is

$$\Pi_t^D = \begin{cases} (p_t - c_t)\, Q_t - F_t & \textit{if } h_t \text{ is transferred} \\ (p_t - c_{t-1})\, Q_t & \text{otherwise.} \end{cases}$$

The game is as follows.

1.1 First period. Firm U makes a take-it-or-leave-it offer available to any of the downstream firms, consisting of the level of technology transfer h_1 and the compensation fee F_1. Since there is a large pool of identical downstream firms and there are cash constraints, U chooses randomly to supply, say to some downstream firm D. Thus, D produces with a reduced cost in the first period.[14]

1.2 First period. The downstream firms compete *à la* Bertrand and the final price p_1 is set. D pays the agreed compensation fee F_1 to U.

2.1 Second period. U makes a take-it-or-leave-it offer (h_2, F_2) to firm D (specifying the transfer of some additional technology for an additional fee) and D decides whether to stop dealing with U or not, i.e., to reject or accept the offer. If D rejects the offer, no further technology is transferred to D. U then may make a take-it-or-leave-it offer (h_2', F_2') to another downstream firm, say D'.

2.2 Second period. The downstream firms compete *à la* Bertrand by setting the product price p_2 and the agreed compensation fee is paid to U.

3.1. *Analysis*

We now sketch how the model can be analyzed under the two basic alternative assumptions and present some numerical examples. Next we compare the VI to the vertically separated case numerically and comment on the findings. Each case is solved by backwards induction.

Vertical Integration. Under this vertical structure, the VI firms (U and D), maximize their joint profits.[15] We solve the game backwards

[14] Note that U transfers technology to only one firm each period. Downstream firms compete *à la* Bertrand and the more cost-efficient firm obtains the whole demand each period.

[15] Consider the case where an MNE firm U operates its own subsidiary in the foreign local market or that U signs a long-run contract with a single downstream firm for dealing with it both periods.

starting from the second period. Given that in the first period, U has transferred technology h_1 to its downstream partner D, U would never transfer technology to another downstream firm in the second period since downstream firms compete in final prices and the firm with the lower cost always obtains the whole demand. Therefore, in the second period, the downstream firm D is the most cost-efficient firm with production cost $c_2 = c - h_1 - h_2$ and the final price is set at the initial level of the production cost c (the price is set at the limit below the initial production cost and the VI chain obtains the whole demand).[16] The VI chain chooses the level of technology transfer h_2 to maximize its joint profit. Note also that special care should be taken for the possible corner cases which play an important role in this model.[17] Finally, all other downstream firms get zero demand and obtain zero profits.

In the first period, D faces the lowest cost ($c_1 = c - h_1$) compared to all other downstream firms and, thus, the final price is set at cost c. Then, given the continuation of the game, the VI chain chooses the level of technology transfer h_1 to maximize the present value of the joint profits $PV^{\text{VI}} = \Pi_1^{\text{VI}} + \delta\Pi_2^{\text{VI}}$. From the first-order conditions and again taking care about the corner cases, we can obtain the optimal level of h_1. All other downstream firms obtain zero profits. Figure 1 illustrates the equilibrium outcome by using a numerical example.

We see that when the cost parameter τ is low enough, meaning that the technology transfer is not very costly, the upstream firm transfers technology $h_1 = c$, thus, the marginal production cost is zero already from the first period ($c_1 = 0$). When, for example, the training costs necessary to adopt a new cost-reducing technology are low enough, firm D tends to adopt this technology at once to enjoy full cost reduction from the first period. For intermediate values of τ, the marginal production cost is reduced

[16]This holds when the monopoly price is higher than the cost of the competitors c. If, instead, the technology transfer is so high that the monopoly price is lower than the cost of the competitors c, then profits are maximized at the monopoly price. For simplicity, we can assume that the demand parameter a is sufficiently high to make sure that the monopoly price is always higher than the initial production cost c.

[17]The production costs cannot be negative. Whenever, the interior solution for h_t derived by the first-order conditions does not meet the constraint $c_t \geq 0$, due to the concavity of the profit function, the equilibrium level of h_t is set at the maximum possible level; here this level is $h_2 = c - h_1$.

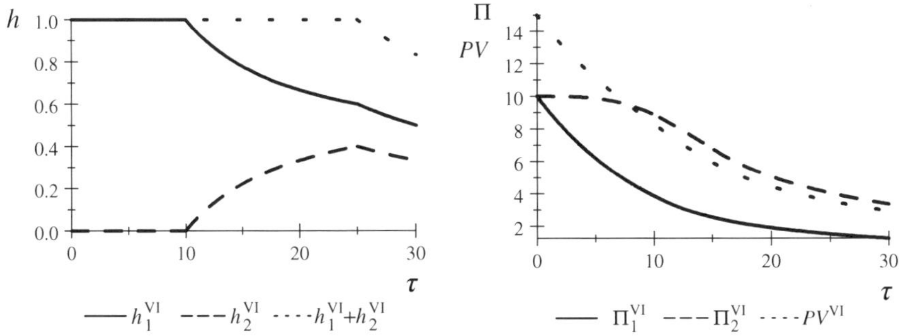

Figure 1. Equilibrium technology transfer and profits for every τ and $a = 11$, $c = 1$, $\delta = 0.5$.

to zero only in the second period ($c_2 = 0$ or $h_1 + h_2 = c$). But when τ is high enough, the marginal cost never reaches the zero level, since technology transfer is too costly ($c_2 > 0$ or $h_1 + h_2 < c$). Also the profits are decreasing in τ.

Vertical Separation. We now sketch how the vertical separation case can be analyzed. Under this structure, firm U charges a fixed fee F_t when it transfers technology h_t to a downstream firm. We look for a subgame perfect equilibrium.

Stage 2.2 Final prices in the second period. In this stage, the downstream firms compete by setting the final price p_2. This decision depends on the second period's production costs and, thus, on the technology already transferred. Downstream competition drives the final price to the second lowest marginal cost. Three alternative cases can be distinguished, depending on whether technology in the second period is transferred to the same downstream firm D (which has dealt with U also in the first period), to another downstream firm D' or to none at all.

First, suppose that firm D has accepted the offer (h_2, F_2) made by U at Stage 2.1. Thus, D has a production cost equal to $c_2 = c - h_1 - h_2$ and all other downstream firms face the initial cost c. Under Bertrand competition, the price p_2 is set at level c. Note that D pays the fee F_2 to firm U, while all other downstream firms obtain zero demand and profits.

Suppose now that firm D has rejected the offer (h_2, F_2) made by U, thus, it enjoys no additional cost reduction in the second period. Nevertheless, U

transfers technology h'_2 to another downstream firm D' that has not dealt with before. In such a case, we would have two downstream firms with reduced production cost; D with cost $c - h_1$ and D' with cost $c - h'_2$. Importantly, a necessary condition for firm D' to become the more cost-efficient firm and to have positive demand is that h'_2 is greater than h_1. Under this constraint and due to Bertrand competition, the final price is set at $c - h_1$. D' obtains the whole demand and pays a fee F'_2 to firm U, while firm D and all other downstream firms get zero profits.

Finally, suppose that U transfers no technology in the second period. D produces without a further cost reduction, but still is the most cost-efficient firm with cost equal to $c - h_1$. All other firms face the initial production cost c, thus, price p_2 is set again at the initial cost c. Firm D obtains the whole demand with all other downstream profits being zero.

Stage 2.1 Contract terms in the second period. In this stage, U sets the contract terms, that is, the level of technology transfer and the payment for this technology transfer. There are four alternative cases, depending on whether U makes an offer to D, such that D is still supplied with technology in the second period or not and depending on whether D extracts a rent, i.e., obtains positive profits or not. We discuss the four cases in turn below.

First, suppose that firm D accepts the take-it-or-leave-it offer (h_2, F_2) made by U and extracts no rent. This holds when D's profits are not lower than the profits obtained by rejecting the offer and producing without any further cost reduction in period 2.[18] In addition, here, firm U could potentially serve another downstream firm D', thus, if D would have rejected the offer, it would have obtained zero profits (D's outside option is zero, so it extracts no rent). Therefore, D would accept any offer that gives non-negative profits. A necessary condition for this case to hold is that U's profits are non-negative if it would transfer technology h'_2 to D' $\left(\Pi_2^U\left(h'_2, F'_2\right) \geq 0\right)$. Since U has all the bargaining power, it offers a fixed fee F_2 to extract D's profits. After deriving F_2 by using the constraint $\Pi_2^D = 0$, firm U derives the optimum h_2 by maximizing its own profit. It remains

[18]We can assume that if a downstream firm is indifferent between dealing with firm U and stopping this cooperation, it continues this cooperation.

to calculate the values of h_1 where $\Pi_2^U(h_2', F_2') \geq 0$, after deriving the optimum h_2' and F_2' below. We need to find the maximum value of h_1 which would allow U to give no rent at firm D in equilibrium. When h_1 is low enough, the second period's cost asymmetries, between D and the other downstream firms, are not high enough and it is easy for U to serve another firm D'.

Suppose now that firm D accepts the take-it-or-leave-it offer (h_2, F_2) made by U and extracts a positive rent. This holds when D does not obtain lower profits than the profits obtained by rejecting the offer. Here, firm U could *not* potentially serve another firm D', that is, we have $\Pi_2^U(h_2', F_2') < 0$. If D had rejected the offer, it would have obtained positive profits equal to $h_1(a-c)$, as calculated at Stage 2.2 (its outside option). Thus, F_2 is designed by U to leave a positive rent equal to $\Pi_2^D = h_1(a-c)$ for firm D. Given F_2, U also determines the optimum h_2 by maximizing its profits. It still remains to calculate the values of h_1 where $\Pi_2^U(h_2', F_2') < 0$.

Alternatively, firm D can reject the offer (h_2, F_2) and U can make a new offer (h_2', F_2') to firm D'. Firm D' accepts the offer when it obtains non-negative profits, since D' has not dealt with U before. This case holds when U's profits by dealing with firm D' are non-negative. Firm U extracts all profits by D' through the fixed fee F_2' and sets h_2' to maximize its profits. After deriving the optimum h_2', we calculate the equilibrium profits $\Pi_2^U(h_2', F_2')$ as a function of h_1. Of course, we need $h_2' > h_1$, otherwise D' would obtain zero demand and $\Pi_2^U(h_2', F_2') \geq 0$, otherwise U would not supply D'. Equation $\Pi_2^U(h_2', F_2') = 0$ determines the "rent bound" for h_1. If the transfer h_1 is lower than this bound, U can supply firm D' in the second period and can obtain positive profits, while D obtains zero profits. U has supplied D with a relatively low h_1 at the first period, thus, cost asymmetries are not high in the second period and it is not too costly for U to transfer sufficient technology to D'. Therefore, for these values of h_1, firm D would not extract a positive rent if it has accepted the offer by U.

Finally, suppose that firm D rejects U's offer and U cannot make a new offer (h_2', F_2') to another downstream firm D'. This case corresponds to values of h_1 that make $\Pi_2^U(h_2', F_2')$ negative, i.e., for h_1 higher than the "rent bound". Firm U does not operate in the second period and firm D enjoys positive profits equal to $h_1(a-c)$.

In summary, the first and third case presented above hold for low levels of h_1 $\left(\text{i.e., } \Pi_2^U\left(h_2', F_2'\right) \geq 0\right)$, while the second and fourth for high levels of h_1 $\left(\text{i.e., } \Pi_2^U\left(h_2', F_2'\right) < 0\right)$. However, the equilibrium in Stage 2.1 remains to be derived given all potential values of h_1. Is it more profitable for firm U to make an offer to D, such that D does not stop dealing with it (by, possibly, giving a positive rent to D) or to make an offer to another downstream firm D'? After comparing U's profits across these alternative cases, we find that firm U always prefers in the second period to supply technology to downstream firm D, the one that it has already dealt with in the first period of the game. Intuitively, firm U has already invested in firm D at the first period of the game and stays with the same firm at the second period as well, even if it has to leave a positive rent to it.

Stage 1.2 Final prices in the first period. Given that U has transferred technology h_1 only to firm D, the downstream firms compete *à la* Bertrand and the final price p_1 is set at the level of the initial cost c. Firm D obtains the entire demand and all other downstream firms have zero demand and profits.

Stage 1.1 Contract terms in the first period. In this stage, firm U offers a contract (h_1, F_1) to the downstream firms. All downstream firms have initially the same cost and would accept an offer that yields non-negative profits. Since all downstream firms are identical, firm U chooses randomly to transfer technology h_1 to some firm D, while it cannot supply additional technology to another downstream firm, as firms compete in prices and only one firm may get positive profits in Stage 1.2. Moreover, U has all the bargaining power and extracts all profits by D via the fee F_1. U's decision about the level of technology transfer h_1, affects both its current and its future profits. In particular, firm U determines h_1 by maximizing the present value of its profits $PV^{\text{VS}} = \Pi_1^U + \delta \Pi_2^U$, where, as already discussed, Π_2^U takes different values, depending on whether D is able to extract rent or not. To derive the equilibrium of the entire game, we should then compare the present value of U's profits, with and without rent extraction by D in the second period of the game.

If U transfers, in equilibrium, a relatively low h_1 to D, the cost asymmetry that it creates, between D and the other downstream firms, is relatively low and U extracts the whole profits in the second period of the game, i.e., there is no rent extracted by D. Nevertheless, the investment itself in cost reduction is low, which leads to lower profits in both periods. Therefore, there are two effects when reducing the technology transfer in the first period: one which tends to reduce the rent extracted by D and one that increases the production cost in both periods. The opposite reasoning holds for relatively high levels of h_1. The equilibrium outcome depends on the range of the parameter values.

Figure 2 presents some numerical examples of the equilibrium outcome.

Note that, in the examples presented in Figure 2, rent is extracted by firm D only in the case where $\delta = 0.1$ and τ is relatively high (and in this case, the dashed line is above the solid line). In the other two cases shown in Figure 2, firm D cannot extract a rent by U. In general, under vertical separation, the upstream firm U tends to give a rent to the downstream firm D for relatively low values of the discount factor δ and for relatively high values of the technology cost parameter τ. When future payoffs are not viewed as very important ($\delta \to 0$), U transfers a high level of h_1 to D

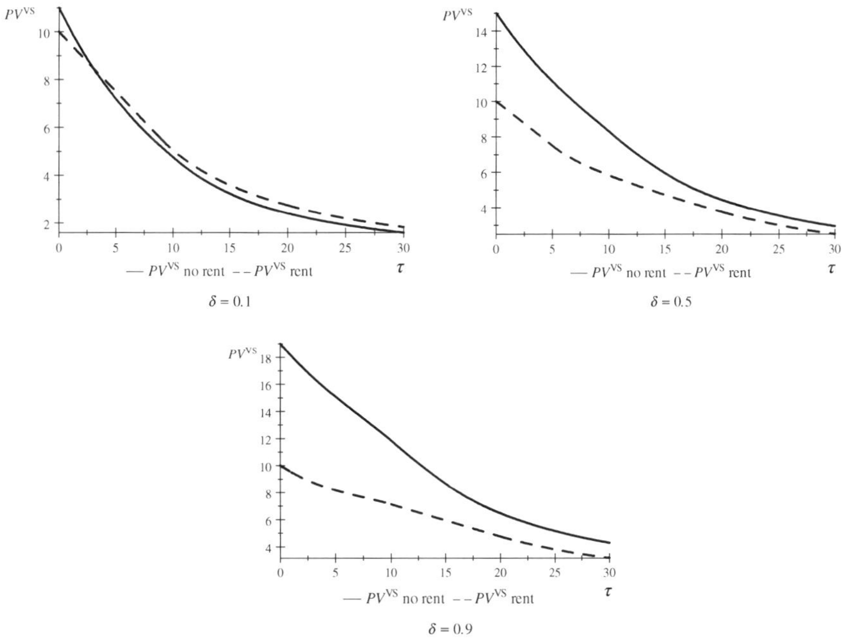

Figure 2. PV^{VS} for every τ and $a = 11$, $c = 1$, $\delta = \{0.1, 0.5, 0.9\}$.

in the first period to enjoy lower marginal cost in this period and this leads to rent extraction by D in the second period. Moreover, for a given level of δ, U tends to give rent to D when the cost parameter τ is high enough. When τ is low, U could easily transfer a high level of technology to another downstream firm D' in the second period if the initial downstream firm D stops dealing with it. Thus, for low τ, rent cannot be extracted by D in equilibrium.

Figure 3 presents the equilibrium level of technology transfer under vertical separation for the same parameter values as in Figure 2.

Note that when $\delta = 0.1$, there is a discontinuity at the level of technology transfer as the equilibrium switches from the "no rent" scenario to the "rent" scenario, as already discussed. Finally, as τ increases and

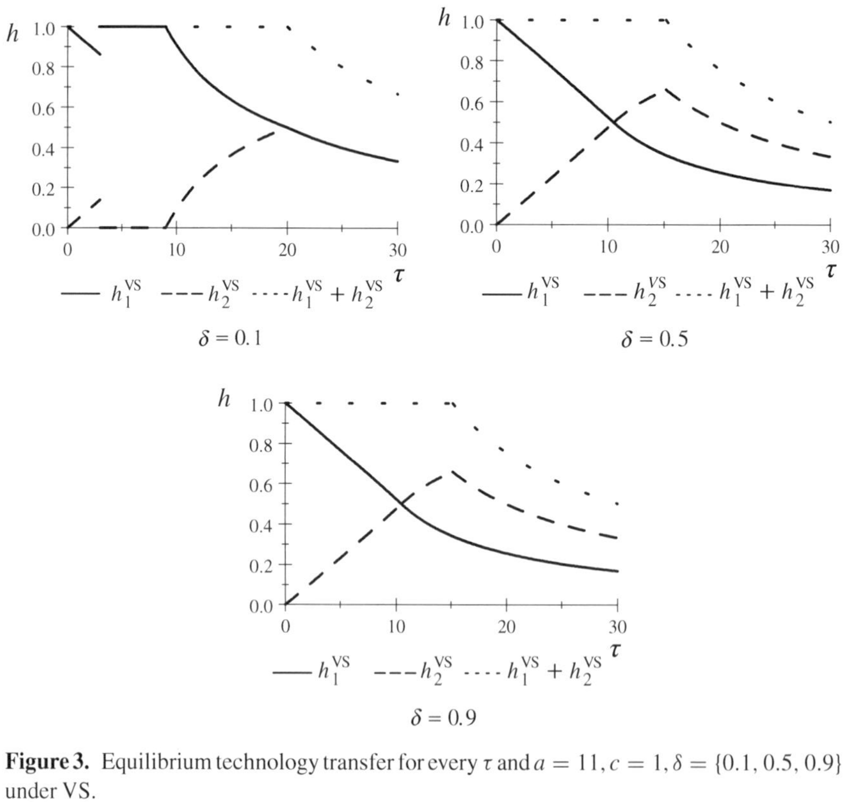

Figure 3. Equilibrium technology transfer for every τ and $a = 11, c = 1, \delta = \{0.1, 0.5, 0.9\}$ under VS.

technology transfer becomes more costly, the total level of technology transfer $h_1^{\text{VS}} + h_2^{\text{VS}}$ does not reach the initial production cost c ($c_2 > 0$).

3.2. *Vertical integration vs. vertical separation*

It is important now to contrast the vertical separation scenario to the vertical integration benchmark. We do this by using a numerical example.

In Figure 4, we observe that h_1^{VI} is higher than h_1^{VS} and decreasing in τ. When firm U is VI with firm D, there is no threat that firm D will stop dealing with firm U in the second period of the game. Rent is never given within the vertical integrated chain and the incentives of U to reduce the technology transfer in the first period are diminished. In contrast, under VS, firm U tends to reduce h_1, compared to the VI case, in an effort to lower the rent paid to firm D in the second period. If h_1 is low enough, the rent paid reduces to zero. Thus, the level of h_1 is used by U as an instrument to reduce D's future bargaining power. On the one hand, U decreases or avoids the

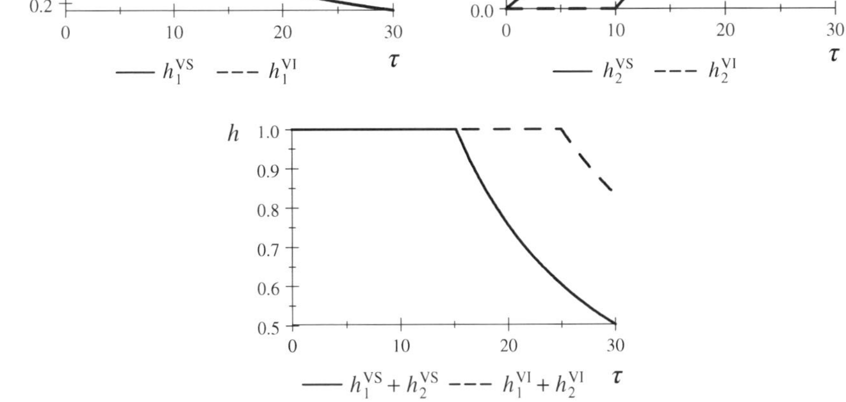

Figure 4. Equilibrium technology transfer under VS and VI for every τ and $a = 11$, $c = 1$, $\delta = 0.5$.

future rent paid, but, on the other hand, sacrifices some short-run profits due to a smaller cost reduction, i.e., U gets a larger share of a smaller pie.

In addition, the total level of technology transfer in both periods under VS is never higher compared to the VI case $\left(h_1^{\mathrm{VI}} + h_2^{\mathrm{VI}} \geq h_1^{\mathrm{VS}} + h_2^{\mathrm{VS}}\right)$. When τ is sufficiently low, we obtain $h_1^{\mathrm{VI}} + h_2^{\mathrm{VI}} = h_1^{\mathrm{VS}} + h_2^{\mathrm{VS}} = c$ and, since $h_1^{\mathrm{VI}} \geq h_1^{\mathrm{VS}}$, we conclude that the technology transfer is shifted toward the second period under VS; there is delay in the technology transfer under VS. When τ is sufficiently high, we obtain $c > h_1^{\mathrm{VI}} + h_2^{\mathrm{VI}} > h_1^{\mathrm{VS}} + h_2^{\mathrm{VS}}$, thus, the reduction in h_1^{VS} is not compensated by an increase of h_2^{VS} and hold-up issues arise.

To sum up, we observe that the possibility that the downstream firm may not fully compensate the upstream firm for the benefits that it has received, creates hold-up issues. Our model, although simple, allows for a number of different strategies and illustrates that studying gradual technology transfer along with potential competition is a rich area. We find that in equilibrium, transfer occurs to the same downstream firm in both periods; however, the contractual relationship is crucially affected by the presence of competitors. In particular, the equilibrium level of technology transfer under vertical separation is *never higher* than the equilibrium level of technology transfer under vertical integration and the technology transfer is *shifted toward the second period* under vertical separation. Price competition downstream does not fully eliminate the opportunistic behavior created by the imperfect IPR.

4. Conclusion and Future Research

Following a review of the relevant literature, we have presented a simple model of gradual technology transfer. In particular, we have studied the strategic timing and pace of cost-reducing technology transfer by an upstream monopolist to a downstream market. Key ingredients in the analysis are the presence of potential competition downstream and that the protection of IPR is imperfect. If the transfer could happen under the protection of vertical integration or complete contracts that would be fully supported by the courts, then it would be gradual. Its optimal pace would reflect a trade-off between the costs and the benefits of transferring technology in each period. But when such protection is rarely present, we show that, in equilibrium, transfer occurs to the same downstream firm in both periods; however, the type of the contractual relationship is crucially affected by the presence of competitors. In particular, there is a delay in technology transfer, relative to the vertical integration benchmark. The upstream firm tries to limit the downstream firm's bargaining power, in an effort to pay a lower rent or no rent to this firm in the subsequent period. Price competition downstream does not fully eliminate the opportunistic behavior created by the IPR.

Our model is simple, but many different possibilities arise within this framework. In addition to solving analytically and characterizing the multiple cases in the analysis, considering a number of extensions of our simple model will offer additional and significant insights into the problem. An interesting extension would be the introduction of uncertain production costs across periods. In such a case, it may no longer be clear that the upstream firm would want to contract with the same firm each period. Then, a potential long-run contract where the upstream firm deals with the same downstream firm in each period may not be an equilibrium outcome. Another interesting extension would be when the downstream firms may be *ex-ante* different with respect to their initial costs. While the one that has the lowest cost is the most attractive target for transferring technology, the cost asymmetry would imply a modified allocation of profits. Finally, it would be useful to examine alternative and richer forms of competition downstream, since Bertrand competition with homogeneous goods has the special feature that in a given period only a single firm could produce, the one with the lowest cost.

References

Akiyama, T. and Y. Furukawa (2009). "Intellectual Property Rights and Appropriability of Innovation," *Economic Letters*, 103, pp. 138–141.

Allain, M.-L., E. Henry and M. Kyle (2011). "Inefficiencies in Technology Transfer: Theory and Empirics," *CEPR Discussion Paper* No. 8206.

Anand, B. and T. Khanna (2000). "The Structure of Licensing Contracts," *Journal of Industrial Economics*, 48(1), pp. 103–135.

Aoki, R. and Y. Tauman (2001). "Patent Licensing with Spillovers," *Economic Letters*, 73, pp. 125–130.

Arora, A. and A. Gambardella (2010). "Ideas for Rent: An Overview of Markets for Technology," *Industrial and Corporate Change*, 19(3), pp. 775–803.

Arora, A. and A. Fosfuri (2003). "Licensing the Market for Technology," *Journal of Economic Behavior & Organisation*, 52, pp. 277–295.

Arora, A., S. Athreye and C. Huang (2013). "Innovation, Patenting and Licensing in the UK: Evidence from the SIPU survey." Available at http://www.brunel.ac.uk/_ _data/assets/pdf_file/0005/328145/Report__draft_01092013.pdf.

Arrow, K. (1962). Economic Welfare and the Allocation of Resources for Inventions, in R. Nelson (Ed.), *The Rate and Direction of Inventive Activity*, Princeton University Press, Princeton.

Brakman, S. and H. Garretsen (2008). Foreign Direct Investment and the Multinational Enterprice: An Introduction, in S. Brakman and H. Garretsen (Eds.), *Foreign Direct Investment and the Multinational Enterprise*, Chapter 1, MIT Press, Cambridge, MA.

Beggs, A. (1992). "The Licensing of Patterns under Asymmetric Information," *International Journal of Industrial Organization*, 10, pp. 171–191.

Bloom, N., L. Garicano, R. Sadun and J. Van Reenen (2013). "The Distinct Effects of Information Technology and Communication Technology on Firm Organisation," *CEPR Discussion Paper* No. 9762.

Bousquet, A., H. Cremer, M. Ivaldi and M. Wolkowicz (1998). "Risk Sharing in Licensing," *International Journal of Industrial Organization*, 16, pp. 535–554.

Cho, M. and B. Jun (2013). "Information Sharing with Competition," *Economic Letters*, 119, pp. 81–84.

Choi, J. P. (2001). "Technology Transfer with Moral Hazard," *International Journal of Industrial Organization*, 19, pp. 249–266.

Chowdhury, I. and P. Chowdhury (2001). "A Theory of Joint Venture Life-Cycles," *International Journal of Industrial Organization*, 19, pp. 319–343.

Duchene, A., D. Sen and K. Serfes (2012). "Technology Transfer and Entry Deterrence." Available at SSRN: http://dx.doi.org/10.2139/ssrn.1952764.

Das Varma, G. (2003). "Bidding for a Process Innovation under Alternative Modes of Competition," *International Journal of Industrial Organization*, 21, pp. 15–37.

Ethier, W. (1986). "The Multinational Firm," *The Quarterly Journal of Economics*, 101(4), pp. 805–834.

Ethier, W. and J. Markusen (1996). "Multinational Firms, Technology Diffusion and Trade," *Journal of International Economics*, 41, pp. 1–28.

Fauli-Oller, R. and J. Sandonis (2003). "To Merge or to License. Implications for Competition Policy," *International Journal of Industrial Organization*, 21, pp. 655–672.

Feenstra, R. (2010). *Offshoring in the Global Economy: Microeconomic Structure and Macroeconomic Implications*, MIT Press, Cambridge, MA.

Fauli-Oller, R. and J. Sandonis (2012). "Welfare Reducing Licensing," *Games and Economic Behavior*, 76(2), pp. 515–518.

Felli, L. and K. Roberts (2000). Competition and Hold-Ups, in T. Atkinson, H. Glennester and N. Stern (Eds.), *Putting Economics to Work: Volume in Honour of Michio Morishima*, Chapter 4, London School of Economics and Political Science, London.

Fosfuri, A., M. Motta and T. Ronde (2001). "Foreign Direct Investment and Spillover through Workers' Mobility," *Journal of International Economics*, 53(1), pp. 205–222.

Fumagalli, C. and M. Motta (2006). "Exclusive Dealing and Entry, When Buyers Compete," *American Economic Review*, 96(3), pp. 785–795.

Gallini, N. (1992). "Patent Policy and Costly Imitation," *RAND Journal of Economics*, 23(1), pp. 52–63.

Gallini, N. (1984). "Deterrence by Market Sharing. A Strategic Incentive for Licensing," *American Economic Review*, 74(5), pp. 931–941.

Gallini, N. and R. Winter (1985). "Licensing in the Theory on Innovation," *RAND Journal of Economics*, 16(2), pp. 237–252.

Gallini, N. and B. Wright (1990). "Technology Transfer under Asymmetric Information," *RAND Journal of Economics*, 21(1), pp. 147–160.

Glass, A. J. and K. Saggi (2002a). "Multinational Firms and Technology Transfer," *Scandinavian Journal of Economics*, 104(4), pp. 495–513.

Glass, A. J. and K. Saggi (2002b). "Intellectual Property Rights and Foreign Direct Investment," *Journal of International Economics*, 56, pp. 387–410.

Glass, A. J. and K. Saggi (2008). The Role of Foreign Direct Investment in International Technology, in A. Dutt and J. Ros (Eds.), *International Handbook of Development Economics*, Edward Elgar, Cheltenham, UK.

Guadalupe, M., O. Kuzmina and C. Thomas (2012). "Innovation and Foreign Ownership," *American Economic Review*, 102(7), pp. 3594–3627.

Hanson, G., R. Mataloni and M. Slaughter (2005). "Vertical Production Networks in Multinational Firms," *Review of Economics and Statistics*, 87(4), pp. 664–678.

Helpman, E. (1993). "Innovation, Imitation and Intellectual Property Rights," *Econometrica*, 61, pp. 1247–1280.

Helpman, E. (2004). "A Simple Theory of International Trade with Multinational Corporations," *Journal of Political Economy*, 92, pp. 451–471.

Helpman, E., M. Melitz and S. Yeaple (2004). "Export versus FDI," *American Economic Review*, 94(1), pp. 300–316.

Henry, E. and F. Ruiz-Aliseda (2012). "Innovation Beyond Patents: Technological Complexity as a Protection Against Imitation," *CEPR Discussion Paper* No. 8870.

Henry, E. and C. Ponce (2011). "Waiting to Imitate: On the Dynamic Pricing of Knowledge," *Journal of Political Economy*, 119(5), pp. 959–981.

Hernandez-Murillo, R. and G. Llobet (2006). "Patent Licensing Revisited: Heterogeneous Firms and Product Differentiation," *International Journal of Industrial Organization*, 24, pp. 149–175.

Horstmann, I. and J. Markusen (1996). "Exploring New Markets: Direct Investment, Contractual Relations and the Multinational Enterprise," *International Economic Review*, 37, pp. 1–19.

Jansen, J. (2009). "Share to Scare. Technology Sharing in the Absence of Intellectual Property Rights," *Working Paper Series of the Max Planck Institute for Research on Collective Goods* 2009/36.

Jensen, R. and M. Thursby (2001). "Proofs and Prototypes for Sale. The Licensing of University Inventions," *American Economic Review*, 91(1), pp. 240–259.

Jehiel, P., B. Moldovanu and E. Stacchetti (1996). "How (not) to Sell Nuclear Weapons," *American Economic Review*, 86(4), pp. 814–829.

Jeong, S., S. Lee and L. Kim (2013). "Licensing Versus Selling in Transactions for Exploiting Patented Technological Knowledge Assets in the Markets for Technology," *Journal of Technology Transfer*, 38(3), pp. 251–272.

Kamien, M., Y. Tauman and I. Zang (1988). "Optimal License Fees for a New Product," *Mathematical Social Sciences*, 16, pp. 77–106.

Kamien, M. (1992). Patent Licensing, in R. J. Aumann and S. Hart (Eds.), *Handbook of Game Theory with Economic Applications*, Chapter 11, North-Holland, Amsterdam.

Kamien, M. and Y. Tauman (1984). "The Private Value of a Patent: A Game Theoretic Analysis," *Journal of Economics* (Supplement), 4, pp. 93–118.

Kamien, M. and Y. Tauman (1986). "Fees Versus Royalties and the Private Value of a Patent," *Quarterly Journal of Economics*, 101, pp. 471–491.

Katz, M. and C. Shapiro (1985). "On the Licensing of Innovations," *RAND Journal of Economics*, 16(4), pp. 504–520.

Katz, M. and C. Shapiro (1986). "How to License Intangible Property," *Quarterly Journal of Economics*, 101(3), pp. 567–589.

Kotseva, R. and N. Vettas (2005). "Foreign Direct Investment and Exports Dynamics with Demand Learning," *CEPR Discussion Paper* No. 5262.

Lafontaine, F. and M. Slade (2007). "Vertical Integration and Firm Boundaries: The Evidence," *Journal of Economic Literature*, 45(3), pp. 629–685.

Lin, P. and K. Saggi (1999). "Incentives for Foreign Direct Investment Under Imitation," *Canadian Journal of Economics*, 32, pp. 1275–1298.

Long, N. V., A. Soubeyran and R. Soubeyran (2009). "Joint Venture Breakup and the Exploration-Exploitation Trade-off," *REPEC Working Paper*.

Markusen, J. (2001). "Contracts, Intellectual Property Rights, and Multinational Investment in Developing Countries," *Journal of International Economics*, 53, pp. 189–204.

Marin, D., L. Rousova and T. Verdier (2013). "Do Multinationals Transplant their Business Model?" *CEPR Discussion Paper* No. 9500

Marx, L. and G. Shaffer (2007). "Upfront Payments and Exclusion in Downstream Markets," *RAND Journal of Economics*, 38(3), pp. 823–843.

Mattoo, A., M. Olarreaga and K. Saggi (2004). "Mode of Foreign Entry, Technology Transfer and FDI Policy," *Journal of Development Economics*, 75, pp. 95–111.

Mendi (2005). "The Structure of Payments in Technology Transfer Contracts: Evidence from Spain," *Journal of Economics & Management Strategy*, 14(2), pp. 403–429.

Motta, M. (2004). Vertical Restraints and Vertical Mergers, in *Competition Policy: Theory and Practice*, Chapter 6, Cambridge University Press, Cambridge, UK.

Moldovanu, B. and A. Sela (2003). "Patent Licensing to Bertrand Competitors," *International Journal of Industrial Organisation*, 21, pp. 1–13.

Mőller, T. and M. Schnitzer (2006). "Technology Transfer and Spillovers in International Joint Ventures," *Journal of International Economics*, 68, pp. 456–468.

Muto, S. (1993). "On Licensing Policies in Bertrand Competition," *Games and Economic Behavior*, 5, pp. 257–267.

Naghavi, A. and G. Ottaviano (2008). Outsourcing, Contracts, and Innovative Networks, in S. Brakman and H. Garretsen (Eds.), *Foreign Direct Investment and the Multinational Enterprise*, Chapter 4, MIT Press, Cambridge, MA.

Nocke V. and Yeaple S. (2007). "Cross-Border Mergers and Acquisitions vs. Greenfield Foreign Direct Investment: The Role of Firm Heterogeneity," *Journal of International Economics*, 72, pp. 336–365.

O'Donoghue, T. and J. Zweimuller (2004). "Patents in a Model of Endogenous Growth," *Journal of Economic Growth*, 9, pp. 81–123.

Pack, H. and K. Saggi (2001). "Vertical Technology Transfer via International Outsourcing," *Journal of Development Economics*, 65, pp. 389–415.

Ramondo, N., V. Rappoport and K. Ruhl (2011). "Horizontal vs. Vertical FDI: Revisiting Evidence from U.S. Multinationals," Mimeo, Columbia Business School.

Rasmusen, E., J. M. Rasmusen and J. Wiley (1991). "Naked Exclusion," *American Economic Review*, 81(5), pp. 1137–1145.

Rey, P. and J. Tirole (2007). A Primer on Foreclosure, in M. Armstrong and R. Porter (Eds.), *Handbook of Industrial Organization III*, North Holland, Amsterdam, The Netherlands.

Rey, P. and T. Vergé (2008). The Economics of Vertical Restraints, in P. Buccirossi (Ed.), *Handbook of Antitrust Economics*, Chapter 9, MIT Press, Cambridge, MA.

Rostoker, M. (1984). "A Survey of Corporate Licensing," *IDEA*, 24, pp. 59–92.

Rob, R. and N. Vettas (2003). "Foreign Direct Investment and Exports with Growing Demand," *Review of Economic Studies*, 70, pp. 629–648.

Rockett, K. (1990). "The Quality of Licensed Technology," *International Journal of Industrial Organization*, 8, pp. 559–574.

Saggi, K. (2002). "Trade, Foreign Direct Investment, and International Technology Transfer: A survey," *World Bank Research Observer*, 17(2), pp. 191–235.

Saracho, A. (2002) "Patent Licensing Under Strategic Delegation," *Journal of Economics and Management Strategy*, 11(2), pp. 225–251.

Schmitz, P. (2002). "On Monopolistic Licensing Strategies Under Asymmetric Information," *Journal of Economic Theory*, 106(1), pp. 177–189.

Schnitzer, M. (1999). "Expropriation and Control Rights: A Dynamic Model of Foreign Direct Investment," *International Journal of Industrial Organization*, 17, pp. 1113–1137.

Scotchmer, S. (2004). *Innovation and Incentives*, MIT Press, Cambridge, MA.

Sempere Monerris, J. and V. Vannatelbosch (2001). "The Relevance of Bargaining for the Licensing of a Cost-Reducing Innovation," *Bulletin of Economic Research*, 53(2), pp. 101–115.

Segal, I. and M. Whinston (2000). "Naked Exclusion: Comment," *American Economic Review*, 90(1), pp. 296–309.

Sen, D. and Y. Tauman (2007). "General Licensing Schemes for a Cost-Reducing Innovation," *Games and Economic Behavior*, 59, pp. 163–186.

Simpson, J. and A. Wickelgren (2007). "Naked Exclusion, Efficient Breach, and Downstream Competition," *American Economic Review*, 97(4), pp. 1305–1320.

Siebert, R. and G. von Graevenitz (2011). "Are Licensing Agreements Appropriate Instruments to Cut through the Patent Thicket?" *Working Paper*.

Sinha, U. (2010). "Strategic Licensing, Exports, FDI, and Host Country Welfare," *Oxford Economic Papers*, 62, pp. 114–131.

Spulber, D. (2012). "Competitive Investors and the Incentive to Invent," *Industrial and Corporate Change*, 22(1), pp. 33–73.

Stamatopoulos, G. and Y. Tauman (2008). "Licensing of a Quality-Improving Innovation," *Mathematical Social Sciences*, 56, pp. 410–438.

Wang, X. H. (1998). "Fee Versus Royalty Licensing in a Cournot Duopoly Model," *Economic Letters*, 60, pp. 55–62.

Wright, J. (2009). "Exclusive Dealing and Entry, When Buyers Compete: Comment," *American Economic Review*, 99(3), pp. 1070–1081.

Part III

Competition Policy and Regulation

Chapter 11

How Can Competition Policy and Competition-Policy Economics Contribute to Solving the Healthcare Crisis?*

Michael L. Katz

University of California

katz@haas.berkeley.edu

Abstract

Public policy makers around the world are concerned with the cost and quality of healthcare. I argue that competition-policy economics can make valuable contributions to solving the healthcare crisis by addressing four fundamental questions:

(i) Why don't insurance companies offer policies that generate greater consumer incentives to seek low-cost providers and generate increased price competition?
(ii) How can consumers be provided with information that will induce stronger quality competition?
(iii) What organizational structures promote the most efficient coordination among complementary care providers and between insurers and care providers?
(iv) How do structure and conduct in markets for healthcare insurance and healthcare services affect the incentives to create and adopt new healthcare goods and services?

Preliminary lines of research to address these questions are identified and discussed.

Keywords: Competition policy, health insurance, health care, quality competition.

JEL Classification Codes: I1 (I11, I13, and I18), K2, L4.

---

*The author is grateful to Yossi Spiegel and participants in the 2013 CRESSE Conference and the 6th Annual Searle Antitrust Conference for useful comments and suggestions.

1. Introduction

There is widespread agreement that increasing public and private expenditures on healthcare threaten to overburden both household and governmental budgets. In the United States, combined public and private expenditures on healthcare rose from 5.2% of GDP in 1960 to 17.9% in 2011.[1] As illustrated by Figure 1, the percentage of GDP devoted to expenditures on health has risen in many countries, albeit not as dramatically as in the

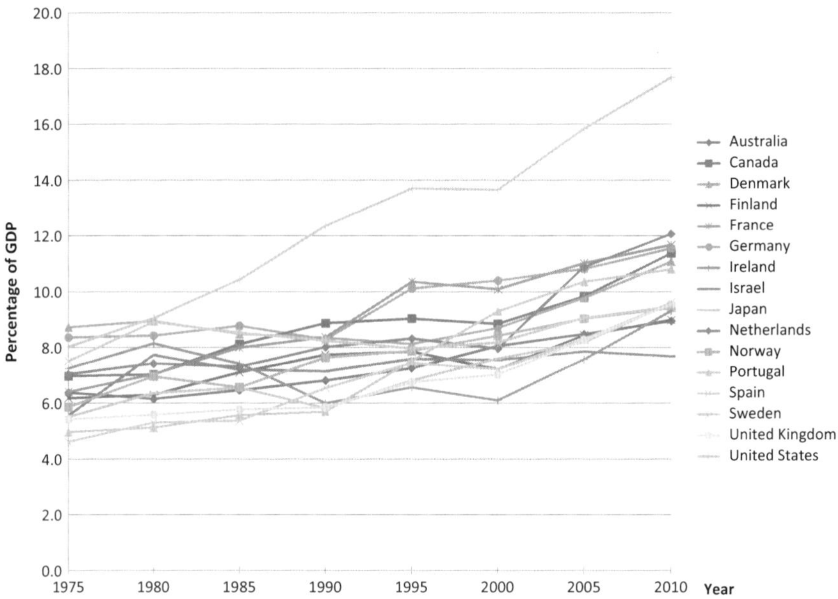

Figure 1. Total expenditures on health as a percentage of GDP in selected countries.
Source: OECD, "OECD Health Data 2013 — Frequently Requested Data." Available at http://www.oecd.org/health/health-systems/oecdhealthdata2013-frequentlyrequesteddata.htm (site visited December 26, 2013).

[1]Centers for Medicare and Medicaid Services (2013) "Table 1. National Health Expenditures; Aggregate and Per Capita Amounts, Annual Percent Change and Percent Distribution: Selected Calendar Years 1960–2011." Available at http://www.cms.gov/Research-Statistics-Data-and-Systems/Statistics-Trends-and-Reports/NationalHealthExpendData/Downloads/tables.pdf (site visited December 9, 2013).

United States. The OECD (2013) predicts that, unless cost-containment policies are enacted, increases in public expenditures for many countries will increasingly strain public budgets. And particularly in the United States, healthcare expenditures place large financial burdens on many households. To make matters worse, there is a widespread perception that the quality of healthcare in many advanced economies is lower than it should be given the levels of expenditures. For example, based on two large studies, the Committee on Quality of Health Care in America (2000, p. 1) estimated that at least 22,000, and possibly more than 49,000, deaths a year in the United States were due to preventable medical errors, such as medication errors caused by illegible handwriting.[2] There are widespread failures to apply best practice and evidence-based medicine[3] and, as discussed below, a lack of coordination among healthcare providers is common in many countries.[4]

Private and public entities in countries around the world are seeking ways to lower the costs and raise the quality of healthcare services. Policy makers in several countries, including England, France, Italy, the Netherlands, Sweden, and the United States, are attempting to use competitive market forces to achieve these objectives.[5] These attempts prompt the questions: What role does competition policy have to play in helping to solve the healthcare crisis, and what role do industrial organization economists have to play in informing competition policy with respect to the healthcare sector?

---

[2]More recently, Levinson (2010, Executive Summary) estimated that 1.5% of hospitalized Medicare beneficiaries (180,000 patients annually) experienced an event that contributed to their deaths and another 25.5% experienced events during their hospital stays the resulted in permanent or temporary harm. Physicians determined that 44% of all events were preventable.

[3]See, for example, U.S. Department of Health and Human Services (2012).

[4]In their survey of adults with complex care needs in 11 nations, Schoen *et al.* (2011, p. 2437) "found that in all of them, care is often poorly coordinated."

[5]Beckert *et al.* (2012, p. 400). This is so even in the case of national health services, where policy makers have tried to create competition among care providers within the national health system. See, for example, Cooper *et al.* (2011) and Gaynor *et al.* (2012). For a multi-country history of public–policy attitudes toward competition in healthcare, see Toth (2010).

I will argue that competition policy has a large and potentially very beneficial role to play. However, I will also argue that, to date, economists and competition-policy enforcers have tended to focus on areas that, while important, are not the ones in which the potential contributions of competition policy are the greatest. Specifically, in Section 2, I survey the drivers of increasing expenditures, which are shown to be the product of both rising quantities and rising prices. Economists have devoted considerable attention analyzing the competitive effects of horizontal mergers among hospitals and the possible exclusionary effects of various vertical arrangements.[6] I argue that competition policy must look elsewhere to understand — and significantly slow — the increasing prices of healthcare products and services. In Section 3, I summarize key characteristics of healthcare markets (most notably, uncertainty and asymmetric information) that tend to weaken or distort competition to the detriment of both static and dynamic efficiency.

In Sections 4–7, I consider ways in which competition policy can address these market failures. I do so by considering four dimensions of competition policy other than the scrutiny of horizontal mergers to prevent harm to static price competition. I argue that competition-policy economics can make significant contributions to slowing the excessive growth of healthcare expenditures and improving healthcare quality by: (1) understanding why, to date, insurance policies tend to have consumers pay prices that are too *low* at the relevant margin and fail to induce consumers to shop for low-cost providers; (2) guiding the design of public policies that strengthen competition by providing information to consumers regarding the prices and quality levels of products and services offered by insurance companies and healthcare providers; (3) understanding when vertical restraints and vertical integration promote greater coordination of care delivery and increased adherence to medical best practices; and (4) analyzing whether various public policies applied to healthcare markets (e.g., regulation of the scope of provider networks offered by healthcare insurance companies) promote or harm competition. The chapter closes with a brief conclusion.

---

[6]See, for example, Gaynor and Vogt's (2000) survey.

I should disclose at the outset that I do not offer a comprehensive review of healthcare competition policy — my goal is to stimulate new work, not to catalog the field. In each section below, I review some of the relevant literature and identify some of the open issues I believe may be fruitful areas for further research.

2. Rising Healthcare Expenditures: What is the Problem?

As noted above, the rapid increase in healthcare expenditures over the last several decades is widely perceived to be a very significant problem or even crisis.[7] It is not a foregone conclusion that rising expenditures should be seen as a problem. After all, it is also the case that expenditures on smart phones in many countries rose dramatically over the last decade. Yet, this increase has not triggered concern about a "smart-phone crisis." One difference is that the amounts of money involved are much lower for smart phones than healthcare. There is also a more profound difference. Smart-phone expenditures have risen because new, improved products have been brought to market that consumers find to be very valuable. The increased expenditures are a sign that markets are working well. In contrast, there is a widespread perception that much of the additional expenditures on healthcare do not represent commensurate additional value.[8] In order to understand why there is a problem — and what, if anything competition policy can contribute to addressing it — we need to understand why healthcare expenditures are rising.

As a matter of arithmetic, healthcare expenditures equal the quantity consumed times the price. As shown in Table 1, both prices and quantities

[7]Although the growth in U.S. healthcare expenditures slowed dramatically in recent years (see, for example, Martin *et al.* (2012) and Table 1), it remains to be seen whether this was largely due to the Great Recession and whether the growth rates will rise again as the economy continues to recover.

[8]There can also be problems even when increased healthcare expenditures do represent increased value. I suspect most citizens feel that they are more entitled to government-subsidized healthcare than to subsidized smart-phone service, which can create strong political pressures and budgetary problems even when the additional services are of high value to patients. Moreover, care-improving innovations might lower consumer well-being to the extent that the resulting therapies are unaffordable and available to many people and, consequently, create a sense of regret or resentment.

Table 1. Changes in U.S. National Health Expenditures

Year	2004	2005	2006	2007	2008	2009	2010	2011
Growth in nominal health expenditures from prior year (%)	7.1	6.8	6.5	6.2	4.7	3.9	3.9	3.9
Growth in real expenditures from prior year (%)	3.5	3.2	3.2	2.8	2.6	1.5	1.2	1.5
Growth in prices from prior year (%)	3.4	3.4	3.2	3.3	2.1	2.4	2.7	2.4

Source: Centers for Medicare and Medicaid Services, Office of the Actuary, National Health Statistics Group. Table 2, National Health Expenditures; Nominal Dollars, Real Dollars, Price Indexes, and Annual Percent Change: Selected Calendar Years 1980–2011. Available at http://www.cms.gov/Research-Statistics-Data-and-Systems/Statistics-Trends-and-Reports/NationalHealthExpendData/Downloads/tables.pdf (site visited December 26, 2013).

have risen, with higher prices contributing more to the growth in healthcare expenditures than have increased care-consumption levels, at least in the United States.[9]

2.1. *Rising quantities*

There are several possible explanations for rising consumption levels, and for the fact that the United States spends much more per capita on healthcare than do other countries. One factor is income. Richer populations consume greater amounts of healthcare services, and differences in income over time and across countries explain at some — but far from all — of the observed variation. For example, Farrell *et al.* (2008, p. 10) estimated that, in 2006, "the United States spent nearly $650 billion more on healthcare than peer OECD countries, even adjusting for wealth."[10] Aging

[9] In a more detailed decomposition, Farrell *et al.* (2008, p. 16) estimated that U.S. same-day hospital care expenditures increased 2.1 percentage points between 2003 and 2006 due to "volume" growth and 7.0 percentage points due to shifts toward a mix of more-expensive procedures and increases in the prices for given procedures.

[10] For a contrasting view, see Hall and Jones (2007), who conclude that, due to rising incomes, the optimal level of healthcare spending in the United States as a share of GDP may be over 30% by 2050.

populations are another possible driver of healthcare expenditures but directly account for only a small portion of the increase in the consumption of healthcare.[11] And, although, one might suspect that Americans spend more on healthcare because they lead unhealthy lifestyles and consequently have a greater demand for healthcare, Farrell *et al.* (2008, p. 11) found that Americans were not more disease prone than citizens in peer OECD countries.[12]

Just as with smart phones, technological progress plays a major role in the increasing consumption of healthcare services. Indeed, Dranove and Garthwhite (2013) have asserted that "There is a broad consensus . . . that technological change is the most important long-run driver of cost and quality."[13] There are many new medical products that may generate large patient benefits but that are extremely costly. For example, in recent years, there have been pharmaceutical breakthroughs leading to drugs that allow patients with certain cancers (e.g., chronic myeloid leukemia) to live near-normal life spans as long as they continue to receive the recommended treatments, which can cost well over $100,000 annually.[14] Consequently, the increased consumption of innovative therapies can have significant effects on expenditures. Moreover, not only are there greater expenditures on the new treatments that result from innovation, but overall healthcare expenditures increase to the extent that patients live longer than they would have absent the innovation *and* require expensive care during some or all of their extended life spans.

In summary, differences in population characteristics cannot explain much of the variation in consumption levels across countries or over time, and while innovation is thought to play an important role in consumption increases over time, it cannot explain cross-country differences in adoption patterns.

[11]For a survey of the effects of aging on healthcare expenditures, see Breyer *et al.* (2010).

[12]Although a greater proportion of Americans are obese than are the citizens of many OECD countries, the rate of obesity has grown more slowly in the U.S., and there are both a lower prevalence of smoking and faster rate of decline. See, also, Muennig and Glied (2010).

[13]For an early expression of this view, see Newhouse (1992).

[14]Experts in Chronic Myeloid Leukemia (2013).

2.2. *Rising prices*

Next, consider prices. When a new treatment is both much more efficacious and much more costly than the treatments for which is a substitute, there are difficult issues in constructing a meaningful price index.[15] However, it is clear that even the prices of existing healthcare services (e.g., hospital care) have been rising faster than overall inflation.

Consideration of prices brings us squarely into the domain of competition policy. Economists and competition policy authorities have focused considerable attention on the pricing behavior of care providers, insurance companies, pharmaceutical companies, and medical device makers. In the research literature, there has been an especially pronounced emphasis on the effects of hospital concentration on pricing.[16] There have also been studies of the price effects of insurer mergers,[17] and American politicians appear to be particularly fond of attacking insurance companies and blaming price increases on high industry profits resulting from a lack of competition.[18] However, there are several reasons to believe that competition-policy enforcement with respect to care-provider and insurance-provider horizontal concentration does *not* address the key sources of the healthcare crisis, in general, and rising prices, in particular.

First, the amounts of money involved are not big enough. In the 1990s, the United States went through a wave of over 900 hospital mergers and acquisitions, and several empirical studies have found that increased concentration leads to higher prices in specific markets.[19] However, Capps

---

[15]More generally, decompositions into price and quantity effects should be taken only as broad indicators of trends. The problem of constructing quantity and price indexes is an extremely difficult one because there are thousands of components of healthcare services and the consumption mix changes over time as the result of technological progress and demand shifts.

[16]In Gaynor and Vogt's (2000) survey of healthcare competition-policy economics, hospital mergers receive by far the most attention of any topic.

[17]See Dafny *et al.* (2012) for a recent analysis.

[18]See, for example, the press release by then-Speaker of the U.S. House of Representatives, Nancy Pelosi, "Pelosi: 'The Days of Allowing Insurance Companies to Place Profits Over Public Health Must End'," February 19, 2010. Available at http://pelosi.house.gov/news/press-releases/pelosi-the-days-of-allowing-insurance-companies-to-place-profits-over-public (site visited December 9, 2013).

[19]Vogt (2009). See, also, Vogt and Town (2006) and the papers cited therein.

(2009) has estimated that increased concentration has led to an increase in overall health expenditures of between only 0.4 and 0.5% and, hence, cannot explain why healthcare expenditures have risen so dramatically over the past several decades.[20] Similarly, the strength of insurance company competition is unlikely to be an important driver of increasing healthcare costs, at least on *traditional* antitrust grounds, because insurance industry profit margins are not large relative to overall price increases.[21] U.S. data show that, in 2011, the Net Cost of Health Insurance accounted for just over 6% of Health Consumption Expenditures and the increase in the Net Cost between 2010 and 2012 accounted for a similar percentage of the increase in Health Consumption Expenditures over that period.[22] And for both 2007–2008 and 2008–2009, consumption expenditures rose while administrative and net insurance costs fell.[23] In short, the price effects of mergers among hospitals and among insurance companies represent two (admittedly big) drops in a huge bucket of overall healthcare expenditures. The potential

[20]Even if hospital mergers had increased hospital prices in all geographic markets by 20% and led to no reduction in quantities (assumptions that almost certainly overstate mergers' effects on expenditures), the change would account for approximately two years of increases in total U.S. healthcare expenditures. In other words, the share of expenditure increases potentially explained by hospital mergers is far less than the share of the healthcare competition-policy literature devoted to hospital mergers. (Calculations based on Centers for Medicare and Medicaid Services (2013) "Table 1. National Health Expenditures; Aggregate and Per Capita Amounts, Annual Percent Change and Percent Distribution: Selected Calendar Years 1960–2011" and "Table 7. Hospital Care Expenditures; Levels, Annual Percent Change and Percent Distribution, by Source of Funds: Selected Calendar Years 1970–2011." Available at http://www.cms.gov/Research-Statistics-Data-and-Systems/Statistics-Trends-and-Reports/NationalHealthExpendData/Downloads/tables.pdf (site visited December 9, 2013).)

[21]The U.S. Government Accountability Office (2011a, Table 1) found that, in 2009, the mean value of (premiums — medical care claims)/premiums in the large-group insurance market was 11.2%, while the corresponding figures for the individual market and small-group market were 15.3% and 16.9%, respectively. Because these margins account for neither corporate administration and marketing costs, nor expenses for activities to improve care quality, they are upper bounds on insurance companies' profit margins.

[22]Centers for Medicare and Medicaid Services (2013) "Table 2. National Health Expenditures; Aggregate and Per Capita Amounts, Annual Percent Change and Percent Distribution: Selected Calendar Years 1960–2011." Available at http://www.cms.gov/Research-Statistics-Data-and-Systems/Statistics-Trends-and-Reports/NationalHealthExpendData/Downloads/tables.pdf (site visited December 9, 2013).

[23]*Id.*

price effects of horizontal mergers among either hospitals or insurers clearly merit economists' and policy enforcers' attention, but merger policy is not going to solve the healthcare crisis.

A second problem with the view that high levels of concentration and a resulting lack of price competition are important drivers of the healthcare crisis is that it does not explain why prices keep rising for years and even decades, and do so even in markets where mergers are not occurring. In many concentrated industries, such as wireless telecommunications and microprocessor manufacturing, quality-adjusted prices *fall* over time.

A third reason to believe that solving the healthcare crisis is about more than preventing increases in horizontal concentration is that factors other than supply-side concentration clearly are major drivers of market prices. For instance, proprietary drugs are produced and sold by the same companies around the world and, despite the similarities on the supply side, drug prices are on average 50% higher in the United States than in other OECD countries for equivalent molecules.[24]

In addition to failing to account for the observed magnitude and pattern of price increases, concentration and changes in concentration do not explain either why quantities keep rising or why the quality of healthcare delivery is low due to failure to implement best practices or coordinate care among providers.[25] If all that were happening was that firms were increasingly exercising market power by raising prices, then *ceterus paribus* one would expect to see consumption levels falling. And with respect to quality, there is no general theorem stating that a firm with market power will choose quality that is inefficiently low.[26]

[24]Farrell *et al.* (2008, p. 19). The price differences can be very large in both absolute and relative terms. For example, a one-year dose of Imatinib or Nilotinib costs over $100,000 per year in the United States, which has been estimated to be approximately twice as high as in Germany and roughly three times as high as in the United Kingdom even though the set of suppliers and competing drugs are the same. (Experts in Chronic Myeloid Leukemia (2013).)

[25]Similar critiques regarding both rising consumption levels and pricing dynamics can be applied to other antitrust policies that have received considerable attention from economists, such as pay-for-delay deals among branded and generic pharmaceutical manufacturers.

[26]See Spence (1975). For a survey on quality competition with fixed prices, see Katz (2013).

If concentration in hospital and healthcare insurance markets cannot explain the continuing increases in prices, the increasing quantities of care consumed, or the low quality of care, what can?[27] As noted above, innovation helps explain this pattern, but as I will now argue, does so only incompletely. First and fundamentally, innovation is endogenous, so one needs to understand the underlying drivers of innovation in order to fully understand the problem and identify potential solutions. Second, although innovation leading to new or improved products and services can explain a pattern of increasing consumption levels, it does not explain the phenomenon of paying higher prices for new therapies and procedures that may offer little incremental benefit relative to existing alternatives. For example, in a competitive market with well-informed buyers, a new product typically can succeed only if it is sold at quality-adjusted prices that are lower (or at least no higher) than those of incumbent products. Lastly, innovation does not offer an obvious explanation of the failures to implement even long-standing best practices or to engage in coordination among care providers treating a common patient.

In order to understand the pattern of innovation and the lack of market forces promoting high quality, it is necessary to take into account several important features of the healthcare sector that distinguish it from other markets and have significant effects on the nature of competition. These features are the subject of the next section.

3. What Makes Healthcare Competition Special?

To understand where competition policy might usefully intervene, it is important to understand how competition operates in healthcare markets. Markets for healthcare and healthcare insurance have several features that distinguish them from many other markets.

---

[27]The so-called service-sector disease might appear to be an explanation for the continuing increase in prices. However, there are many potential innovations using information technology and pharmaceuticals that could reduce labor costs. Hence, this explanation can be considered to be part of a broader analysis of innovation below.

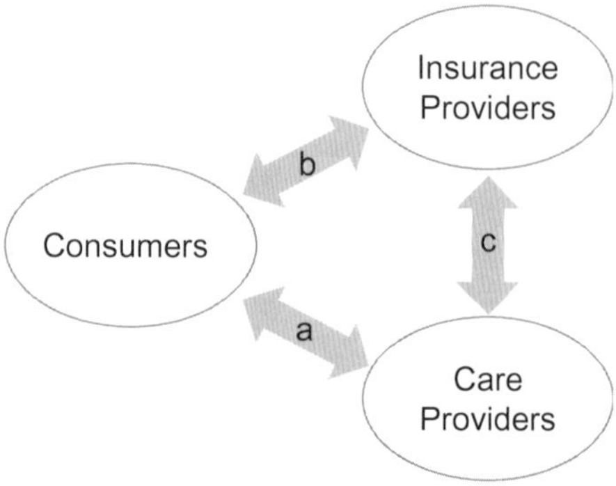

Figure 2. The nexus of competition.

3.1. *Uncertainty and asymmetric information*

In his pathbreaking article, Arrow (1963, p. 941) identified pervasive uncertainty as the critical feature of healthcare markets. In today's terminology, one would elaborate and say that pervasive uncertainty and asymmetric information together are the critical features. Uncertainty with respect to future health states creates a demand for insurance, but, by itself, uncertainty about health states and the efficacy of healthcare is not an obstacle to well-functioning, competitive healthcare insurance and healthcare delivery markets. It is the combination of uncertainty and asymmetric information that can lead to market failures.

Figure 2 illustrates three important areas in which competition potentially occurs in the provision of healthcare services and insurance: (a) care providers compete with one another to attract both insured and uninsured patients; (b) insurance plans compete to attract policyholders; and (c) care providers compete to be included in insurance plans' provider networks.[28] Asymmetric information can attenuate and distort competition in each area.

Consider the competition among care providers to attract patients and how it is affected by asymmetric information. Quality in healthcare markets

[28]As discussed below, U.S. employers often select the insurance plans offered to their employees. In addition, patients often rely on physicians for referrals to other care providers. Hence, there is competition to attract the patronage of employers and referring physicians. For the sake of brevity, I will focus on the types of competition illustrated in the figure.

is complex, multidimensional, and can be difficult to observe. Unlike many products, the quality of healthcare can be difficult for consumers to assess both before and *after* consumption. This is so because the vast majority of consumers have little knowledge of appropriate treatment, and health outcomes can: have large stochastic components; be very dependent on specific, unobservable patient conditions; and be very poor even for patients who received the best available care. If households cannot observe quality, then they cannot reward high-quality providers by patronizing them to a greater extent than low-quality providers, and competition will generate little incentive to provide costly quality.[29] The presence of poorly informed consumers even raises the possibility that competition will degrade quality. In recent years, there has been an increasing recognition by healthcare experts that the overconsumption of care can worsen health outcomes because many treatments run the risks of harmful side effects or errors.[30] However, a poorly informed patient may judge a higher quantity of care (e.g., invasive testing or surgery) to be evidence of a higher quality of care even when it is, in fact, the opposite. Competition to attract such consumers could make the problem of excessive — and, thus, low-quality — care worse.

Poor information regarding quality can also affect price competition. In theory, poor quality information could strengthen price competition by reducing the degree of perceived product differentiation.[31] However, the lack of quality information could also weaken price competition, either because consumers perceive there to be greater differentiation than there truly is or because — in the absence of such information — price may serve as a signal of quality. When the latter occurs, the provider-specific

---

[29]Brekke *et al.* (2012) show that a similar attenuation of incentives may arise if consumers learn about a provider's quality only slowly over time.

[30]In addition, Berwick and Hackbarth (2012) estimate that, in 2011 alone, U.S. patients received between 158 and 389 billion dollars in "care that, according to sound science and the patients' own preferences, cannot possibly help them".

[31]Whenever discussing the effects of strengthening competition in a static, one-shot sense, it should be noted that the effects on competition in a repeated game could be the opposite due to what Shapiro (1989) has labeled the "topsy-turvy" principle: higher cross-elasticities can make threats of future punishment more effective and thus better support collusive outcomes.

price elasticity of demand is lower because its perceived quality falls as a provider lowers its price.

Quality and price competition can interact in other ways. Price competition can undermine the use of supplier reputations as a means of generating incentives to supply high quality. In market in which consumers (imperfectly) learn care quality after consuming it, care providers may develop reputations that affect consumers' future choices. The prospect of profitable future sales resulting from a good reputation can motivate a care provider to offer high quality today even though consumers cannot determine quality before making purchase decisions. As discussed by Kranton (2003), if price competition reduces expected future margins, then it can also reduce the incentive to invest in building a good reputation by providing high quality today.

Healthcare consumers are often very poorly informed about price, as well as quality. Consumers' lack of price information arises both because care providers (particularly U.S. hospitals) do not make it available in a convenient form (if at all) prior to treatment, and because prices can depend on the particulars of a consumer's insurance policy and (due to deductibles and variable coinsurance rates) the total amount of health care a policyholder consumes in a given period.

Competition to attract patients is also distorted by the fact that, in addition to being poorly informed about prices and qualities, consumers typically are heavily insured.[32] A highly insured patient has an economic incentive to focus on quality without regard for the cost, and patients may also consume excessive quantities of healthcare services.[33] These distortions, too, are the result of a lack of information: A moral hazard problem exists because an insurer has a limited ability to observe the care that a given policyholder should receive and, thus, it is difficult for the insurer to control care-provider and policyholder behavior.

[32]Even in the United States, the majority of patients are covered by either public or private insurance.

[33]Although it does not prove the point, data cited by Victor Fuchs (2012) show the out-of-pocket percentage of healthcare expenses fell in half between 1950 and 1980 and half again between 1980 and 2009, while over the same time periods, annual, per-capita expenditures measured in 2009 dollars rose from 407 to 2,050, to 6,807.

Consider next the competition among insurance companies to attract policyholders. There can be informational asymmetries between consumers and insurers running in both directions that lead to competitive problems. In one direction, consumers may be poorly informed about the financial terms of alternative insurance policies, in addition to having poor information about both the quality of the care providers in the insurance plans' networks and the effects of insurance companies' policies on the quality of care provided to policyholders. This lack of information can attenuate and distort competition among insurance companies. In the other direction, policyholders can be better informed about their prospective healthcare consumption than are insurers.[34] This asymmetry can lead to adverse selection problems and even the breakdown of insurance markets.[35]

In part to offset possible moral hazard in fully insured consumers' choices of care providers, healthcare insurance companies often create financial incentives for patients to utilize specific care providers, such as those physicians and hospitals within a plan's provider network. A care provider's volume of business can be strongly influenced by its inclusion in — or exclusion from — a particular health plan's network. Hence, as illustrated by arrow C in Figure 2, a third form of competition arises to the extent that insurers engage in *selective* contracting: Care providers compete on the basis of price and quality to be included in the insurers' provider networks. Although they are better-informed and more sophisticated buyers than are households, insurers also suffer from difficulties observing quality, which can weaken or distort competition.

In summary, various forms of asymmetric information potentially lead to severe distortions in all three areas of competition identified in Figure 2. In order to accurately predict the welfare effects of firms' actions, competition policy must take these effects into account. Moreover, competition policy should recognize that asymmetric information in one of the three areas can affect competition in another. For example, differences

[34] Or insurers may have information about consumers that the insurers are not allowed to use in setting their prices. The Patient Protection and Affordable Care Act, Pub. L. No. 111–148, 124 *Stat.* 119 (hereinafter, the Affordable Care Act) contains provisions having this effect.
[35] Classic papers by Akerlof (1970) and Rothschild and Stiglitz (1976) demonstrate this point theoretically, and Cutler and Reber (1998) describe an adverse selection "death spiral" that led to the elimination of an insurance plan offered by Harvard University.

among insurance plans' care-provider networks can be an important determinant of consumers' choices among insurance plans (arrow B in Figure 2), which creates insurers' derived demand for healthcare providers (arrow C). Hence, if consumers cannot perceive quality differences among care providers, insurers may not perceive the providers to be differentiated either.

Competition policy should also recognize that the potential problems induced by uncertainty and asymmetric information are not limited to static distortions. For most industries, competition policy presumes that more innovation is better. Although innovation may lead to increased expenditures on new and improved goods and services, it typically is associated with lower quality-adjusted prices and higher levels of consumer welfare.[36] Stated another way, because their choice sets are enlarged, one typically expects consumers to benefit from new-product development.

Once one accounts for the way in which healthcare consumption decisions are made, however, it becomes evident that healthcare innovation may harm, as well as benefit, consumers. One reason is that new technologies may create new opportunities to provide unnecessary care that financially benefits care providers but not patients. Technology adoption may also be non-optimal because of behavioral biases that arise even when providers are not intentionally distorting care provision to increase their profits. One bias may be toward new therapies, with the result that physicians recommend courses of treatment that are much more expensive than existing alternatives yet have few, if any, incremental benefits relative to those alternatives. The case of the drug Zaltrap provides a striking indication of the problem. In 2012, a group of physicians publicly announced that they would not prescribe the drug, which cost more than twice as much what it was intended to replace while offering virtually no incremental benefits.[37] Remarkably, a pledge not to adopt an extremely costly therapy with no

[36]An important exception is that suppliers with market power may be able to use new products to sort consumers and engage in second-degree price discrimination.

[37]Bach, P. B., L. B. Saltz, and R. E. Wittes (2012). "In Cancer Cost Matters," *The New York Times*, October 14. Available at http://www.nytimes.com/2012/10/15/opinion/a-hospital-says-no-to-an-11000-a-month-cancer-drug.html?_r=0 (site visited December 24, 2013).

incremental benefits was considered remarkable and even attracted media attention.[38]

The problem is not innovation *per se*. Innovation by pharmaceutical companies, medical device manufacturers, and information technology providers has the potential to generate large benefits in the form of higher-quality and/or less-costly care. Rather, the problem is the severe distortions in adoption decisions, which in turn lead to distorted research and development investment incentives, particularly a bias toward new therapies with little regard to cost and a bias against innovation aimed at reducing costs. These fundamental distortions in innovation incentives arise from the behavior of physicians and consumers, and the structure of insurance contracts, all of which are driven by pervasive uncertainty and asymmetric information.[39]

Given innovation's substantial contribution to increasing healthcare expenditures and its potentially large effects on consumer welfare, it is important to ask how competition policy can help promote efficient innovation. It certainly is not evident that less concentration of pharmaceutical companies, care providers, or insurance companies will lead to better-aligned innovation incentives. A much more promising tack is to give consumers the information and incentives to undertake informed searches to find high-quality, low-cost care, which will create a derived demand for innovation supporting such care.

3.2. *Other factors*

Pervasive uncertainty and asymmetric information are not the only features of the healthcare sector that raise interesting issues for competition analysis. As noted above, care providers may compete to be included in the provider

[38]For example, S. S. Hall (2013). "The Cost of Living," *The New York Times*, October 20. Available at http://nymag.com/news/features/cancer-drugs-2013-10/ (site visited December 24, 2013).

[39]This is not to say that device manufacturers and pharmaceutical companies do not contribute to the problem through their choices of pricing strategies and actions such as gaming the intellectual property protection laws to limit competition (e.g., pay-for-delay deals).

networks or *portfolios* that insurers offer to potential policyholders.[40] Portfolio competition can give rise to several novel effects. For example, "competing" products may be complements or substitutes for one another depending on the specifics of the market under consideration.[41] The reason can be seen by decomposing the demand for a care provider's services into two components: (1) the overall sales of the portfolio to which it belongs, and (2) its share of that total. When various providers are substitutes from the perspective of a specific patient, a decrease in the price of one provider leads its share of the portfolio total to rise and those of other providers to fall. However, the price decrease also raises the overall sales of the portfolio because it is more attractive relative to other portfolios. When the share shifts are sufficiently small relative to the overall-sales effect, other providers in the portfolio gain sales from the fall in price — the care providers' services are complements.[42] Whether products are substitutes or complements can have powerful implications for competition policy. By the logic of Cournot (1838), oligopolists offering complementary products set their prices above the joint profit-maximizing levels that would be set by multi-facility monopoly.

The heavy involvement of governments and private employers is another interesting characteristic of the healthcare sector. One form of government involvement is the tax treatment of healthcare insurance and healthcare purchases, which can have significant impacts on the demand for healthcare insurance and healthcare. Governments also act as insurers and

[40]As observed by Bardey and Rochet (2010), insurance companies function in this regard as platforms in a two-sided market.

[41]Katz (2011a) models this feature in the context of hospital competition, while Rey and Tirole (2013) discuss the adoption of a technology coupled with the choice of products within that technological class. Similar issues also arise with portfolios of programming offered by cable television and direct-to-the-home satellite broadcasting companies.

[42]For this effect to rise, it must be that agents who are attracted to buy more insurance because the price of provider i has fallen also have some demand for the services of provider j. This case naturally arises when providers are complements from the perspective of any individual patient. But it can also arise when the two providers are substitutes from the perspective of any given patient. One way this can happen is that the buyer is actually an employer with a collection of employees with heterogeneous preferences. Similar effects could arise at the household level or even for an individual who has uncertain demand for care providers and is willing to pay an insurer for the option to be treated by different care providers.

care providers, and thus can affect competition directly. Lastly, governments extensively regulate insurance and care markets.

As will be discussed below, some regulation conflicts with competition. In some cases, this conflict is not intended while in others it is. Competition is not always viewed favorably by public policy makers. In the late 1990s, there was a backlash in several countries, including Germany and the United Kingdom, that earlier had introduced greater competition into their health systems in attempts to reduce costs.[43] Over the past decade, there has been a renewed emphasis on competition in several of these countries,[44] but even today, many public policies attempt to manage the competitive outcome (e.g., by limiting the degree of risk-adjustment that can be reflected in insurance prices).

Turning to employers, the majority of Americans under age 65 with health insurance obtain it through an employer-based program.[45] All else equal, an employer selecting an insurance plan to offer its employees seeks one that offers a range of care providers that can efficiently satisfy diverse employee preferences. Katz (2011a) showed that, because it aggregates employee demands, an employer may view two care providers as close substitutes even though individual employees consider them highly differentiated. This effect potentially strengthens care-provider competition to be included in insurers' provider networks.

Another unusual characteristic of U.S. markets for healthcare services is the extensive presence of both for-profit and not-for-profit providers. For example, 58% of U.S. community hospitals are non-government, not-for-profit, 21% are for-profit, and 21% are state and local government.[46] Managers of a not-for-profit care provider might be modeled as maximizing their utility subject to a constraint that profits not fall below a certain level (e.g., zero).[47] Both care quality and management perquisites are possible arguments of managers' utility functions. Despite different possible

[43]Toth (2010).
[44]*Id.*
[45]DeNavas-Walt *et al.* (2013, p. 24).
[46]American Hospital Association (2013). "Fast Facts on US Hospitals." Available at http://www.aha.org/research/rc/stat-studies/fast-facts.shtml (site visited December 29, 2013).
[47]See, e.g., Newhouse (1970) and Pauly (1987).

objective functions, empirical studies generally have found relatively little difference in the behavior of for-profit and not-for-profit hospitals with respect to either pricing[48] or the quality of care.[49]

The biggest competition-policy implication of the empirical literature is that not-for-profit providers should not be exempt from scrutiny; there is little or no support for the claim that the management of a not-for-profit provider would choose to "spend" increased revenues from the loss of price competition on quality improvements or charity care. However, despite the similarity of conduct, the interaction of for-profit and not-for-profit care providers and insurance companies remains an interesting issue of competition policy.[50] One question to address is whether some combination of favorable tax treatment, charitable donations, and a lack of a market for corporate control allows not-for-profit care providers or insurance companies to behave less efficiently in certain dimensions. For example, a not-for-profit insurance company might face less pressure to implement efficient insurance policies.

A final important market characteristic is that the efficient provision of healthcare services is a team sport. For severely ill patients, a large number of providers (e.g., different physician specialists, nurses, medical technicians, and facilities operators) working together typically is needed to produce favorable health outcomes. Even for less severely ill patients, cooperation between a general practitioner and a smaller set of specialists may be necessary. Actions taken by one care provider can affect the efficacy and cost of actions taken by other providers. There are potential market failures because cooperation is beneficial but individually costly, and the

[48] See, for example, Capps (2003), Connor *et al.* (1998, p. 173); Keeler *et al.* (1999, p. 80); Town and Vistnes (2001, pp. 749–750); Capps *et al.* (2003, p. 753); and Melnick and Keeler (2007, pp. 408–409).

[49] See Keeler *et al.* (1992, p. 1712).

There is also little evidence of differences in the costs of providing a given level of care (Sloan 2000, p. 1156), the adoption of technology (*id.* p. 1161), or the provision of charity care (Vogt, 2002; Sloan, 2000, p. 1160).

[50] For a recent analysis of quality competition under administered prices between a for-profit provider and one that does not purely maximize profits, see Herr (2011). For a theoretical analysis of mergers between non-profit enterprises, see Prüfer (2011).

degree to which a care provider undertakes cooperative activities may be difficult to observe or verify.

3.3. *Implications for competition policy*

In the remainder of this essay, I discuss ways in which competition policy — and economic research regarding competition policy — might contribute to improving the performance of healthcare and healthcare insurance markets. I focus on addressing four striking features of behavior in markets for healthcare and healthcare insurance:

(1) The first is how little effort consumers make to seek lower-cost care. The lack of consumer concern about prices is generally a rational response to current insurance contracts, which tend create little incentive to shop among care providers based on price. Hence, a central question for competition policy is the following: Why aren't insurance contracts structured to create greater incentives for consumers to seek low-cost care providers, and to what extent are there obstacles to more-efficient contracting that competition policy can address?

(2) The second striking feature is how little effort consumers apparently make in seeking higher-quality healthcare. Several studies have found that consumers make relatively little use of quality data that are available to them.[51] Given the importance of healthcare quality to consumers' welfare, and given that highly insured consumers bear little, if any, cost of receiving more-expensive care, one might have expected consumers to devote substantial effort to obtaining the highest quality care available. An important question for competition policy is thus: What can be done to strengthen competition by providing consumers

[51] For example, in their literature survey, Schauffler and Modavsky (2001, p. 83) concluded that "the evidence suggests that most consumers do not use report cards to choose health plans, hospitals, or doctors, and most employers do not use them to choose the health plans they offer to their employees." Kolstad and Chernew (2009) summarize the literature as finding that consumers often are unaware of — or are confused by — care-provider report cards, but that the release of these report cards has statistically significant, if small, effects on choices. Kolstad and Chernew also summarize the literature as generally finding that the release of insurance-plan report cards has a positive and significant effect on the market shares of higher-quality plans although only a small fraction of consumers actually change their plan choices following the release of report cards. See, also, Dranove and Jin (2010).

with information regarding quality that they will use to make informed choices?

(3) The third striking feature is the widespread lack of coordination among care providers in many countries.[52] To a large extent, the lack of coordination is the result of both: (a) the lack of consumer shopping for high-quality care, and (b) the nature of the contracts between insurance companies and care providers — in the United States today, each care provider typically is paid separately without regard for either the overall health of the patient or the effects one care provider's actions have on the costs incurred by other providers. Hence, here, too, it would be valuable to understand why insurance contracts are not more efficiently structured. The lack of coordination also raises questions of whether certain forms of organization and contracting (e.g., vertical integration and extensive vertical restraints) would be beneficial even if aspects of such organization and contracting risked diminishing competition. The Committee on Quality of Health Care in America (2000, p. 3) concluded that "The decentralized and fragmented nature of the [U.S.] healthcare delivery system . . . contributes to unsafe conditions for patients, and serves as an impediment to efforts to improve safety."

(4) The final feature is the distorted nature of innovation and the possibility that innovation lowers consumer welfare. As I have described above, this problem largely derives from the first two features, as well as agency problems between insurance companies and care providers.

These features all suggest that it would be valuable for competition policy to improve consumer search with respect to price and quality. One way to motivate consumers to search over prices is to implement insurance contracts that result in consumers' paying *higher* prices, but at the right margins. It is also important that consumers be aware of the prices and qualities of the options available to them, which raises the possibility of improvements through better education and the provision

[52] See, Blendon *et al.* (2003), Commonwealth Fund (2012), and Schoen *et al.* (2011). In addition to having adverse consequences for patients' health outcomes and experiences, Berwick and Hackbarth (2012) estimated that care coordination failures resulted in between $25 billion and $45 billion in wasteful spending in the U.S. in 2011, which was equal to approximately 1 to 2% of U.S. healthcare expenditures.

of information. The striking lack of care-provider coordination can be addressed by implementing contracts between insurers and care providers that explicitly or implicitly reward coordination and, possibly, by allowing care providers to organize themselves in new ways. These policies are the subject of the next three sections.

4. Promoting Higher Prices at the Correct Margins

As discussed above, because they often bear little or none of the cost of using more-expensive care providers, consumers have at best weak incentives to shop for and patronize low-cost providers. To a certain degree, moral hazard is endemic to the provision of insurance in the presence of asymmetric information. Moreover, the optimal design of insurance contracts is a difficult and complex problem. Although the fundamental aim of insurance is to equalize the marginal utility of income across different states of the world (in this case, underlying health states), problems of asymmetric information make it necessary to consider patient and care-provider incentives with respect to the mix of services a policyholder consumes. There can be complex trade-offs. Arrow (1963) showed that a deductible (i.e., no insurance payment is made to the policyholder for healthcare expenditures below a threshold level) coupled with full insurance above the deductible is optimal when the loading (i.e., the amount by which the price of insurance exceeds the expected value of the insurance payout) is proportional to the expected payout and there is no moral hazard. Other authors have extended Arrow's result regarding deductibles to other forms of loading and to non-expected utility maximization, and as Drèze and Shokkaert (2013, p. 148) explain, its "robustness . . . reflects its simple logic: since it is better to insure expenditures when disposable income is low rather than high, insurance funds should always be spent on the highest expenditures."

Yet, depending on its level, a deductible can effectively result in a higher coinsurance rate (i.e., a higher percentage of healthcare costs borne by the policyholder rather than insurer) for inframarginal payments than marginal ones, which tends to worsen problems of moral hazard relative to, for instance, a constant coinsurance rate. For example, high-deductible policies (which are a popular proposal for insurance reform) do not address the problem of moral hazard for expenditures that exceed the deductibles.

Drèze and Shokkaert (2013) allow for moral hazard with respect to the quantity of healthcare consumed and show that a deductible remains optimal but is coupled with a positive coinsurance rate even for high levels of healthcare expenditures.[53]

It is very difficult to characterize the optimal insurance contract in the presence of administrative costs, patient and care-provider moral hazard with respect to multidimensional actions, and other forms of policyholder conduct discussed below.[54] Nevertheless, insurance contracts appear to be non-optimal in certain respects. Specifically, although it is difficult to reduce moral hazard with respect to the quantity of care consumed without reducing the benefits of insurance, it is notable that 39% of workers with private health insurance in the United States in 2013 had *no* coinsurance for hospital admissions.[55] One might argue that moral-hazard concerns are minimal for healthcare expenditures triggered by serious medical conditions, for which treatment is "essential." Such a view, however, implicitly assumes that there is a single course of treatment offered at a single price. In fact, there typically are options, and the prices of those options can vary widely. Even for essential treatments, there can be significant concern regarding moral hazard with respect to price search (what one might call "shopping moral hazard").

Perhaps more strikingly, little use is made of a policy that explicitly target consumers' choices among alternative providers providing the same treatment at different costs and which could provide consumers with incentives to shop for lower prices while at the same time enjoying the benefits of insurance.[56] Under *reference pricing*, an insurance plan

---

[53]Somewhat confusingly, Drèze and Shokkaert refer to the combination of a deductible and coinsurance rates as a system of "implicit deductibles."

[54]In addition to the issues discussed in the text, there is a need to account for moral hazard with respect to preventative care, where consumers may under-invest to the extent that costs of ill health are heavily insured. Similarly, it can make sense to have lower coinsurance rates for certain types of chronic and acute care. For a survey of the optimal design of healthcare insurance, see Cutler and Zeckhauser (2000).

[55]Kaiser Family Foundation (2013, p. 100). Almost half of workers with private health insurance had no coinsurance as recently as 2010.

[56]Prior to implementation of the Affordable Care Act, there was another way in which some insurance policies were structured that was almost surely inefficient: they had lifetime payment caps, which provided poor coverage for truly catastrophic events. Potential

"establishes a standard price for a drug, procedure, service or bundle of services, and generally requires that health plan members pay any allowed charges beyond this amount."[57] A reference-price policy can be viewed as collecting a coinsurance payment on the *difference* between the actual cost of care and the benchmark price.[58]

The poor design of current insurance contracts with respect to shopping moral hazard search raises a central question for competition policy: Why don't insurance companies offer contracts that promote greater price search, such as those containing reference-price clauses or positive coinsurance rates? The failure of offer such contract terms is particularly puzzling given that their use could be expected to give rise to beneficial selection effects, as well as reducing shopping moral hazard. There are several potential answers to consider.

One candidate answer is that an insurance plan's payment of different insurance benefits to policyholders depending on whether they use in-network or out-of-network care providers might serve as a substitute; the idea being that in-network care providers would be of low cost to the insurance company as well as its policyholders. However, health plans' networks are often quite broad (for example, including all or nearly all hospitals in the relevant geographic area), and it is common for there to exist vary large price differentials (from the insurers' perspective) among care providers within a given plan's network.

Another candidate answer is that insurance contracts have been distorted by the large subsidies resulting from the U.S. tax code, the biggest component of which is that employers can purchase health insurance for their employees without the cost of the insurance being taxed as employee income.[59] This subsidy increases the equilibrium consumption of insurance and creates incentives to design insurance policies that serve as a

---

explanations are that consumers underestimate the probabilities of very large health expenditures or are poorly informed about the terms of the policies they purchase.

[57]Catalyst for Payment Reform, "From Reference Pricing to Value Pricing," Action Brief, p. 1.

[58]Although the industry definition just quoted implicitly limits this coinsurance rate to being either 0 or 100%, in principle it could take other values.

[59]For a comprehensive, if somewhat dated, survey of the literature on taxation and healthcare insurance, see Pauly (1986).

tax-advantaged means for employers to pay their employees. Employer-provided dental insurance that principally covers regularly scheduled examinations and preventative care is a good example: These expenditures are highly predictable, and the primary role of this "insurance" is to avoid income taxation. Similarly, tax subsidies could be expected to lead to smaller deductibles in employer-sponsored plans than otherwise. But it is far from evident that tax subsidies should distort insurance in ways that suppress price competition among care providers. One would expect to see policies designed to transfer income efficiently (as in the case of dental insurance payments for scheduled care) rather than inducing distortions that reduce the collective welfare of insurance companies, employers, and employees. For example, one might expect policies to have low deductibles (in order to transfer income) and relatively high coinsurance rates (to mitigate policyholder moral hazard).

A more plausible reason insurance companies (and employers) do not do more to steer consumers to lower-cost care providers is that such efforts might backfire due to consumers' use of price as a signal of quality.[60] Specifically, consumers might think that an insurer was trying to steer them to low-quality providers that are low cost from the insurer's perspective. Providing consumers information about care-provider quality is a way to address this issue, and it is discussed in Section 5 below.

Another possible reason insurance contracts have the form they do is that, due to a lack of sufficient competitive pressures in healthcare insurance markets, an insurer may be able to prosper while behaving inefficiently. To put it colloquially, an insurance company may be fat and lazy because of a lack of effective governance coupled with either substantial market power, reduced financial pressures due to a not-for-profit status, or because none of its competitors behaves efficiently either and entry by efficient competitors is difficult. To the extent that a lack of competitive pressures allows inefficient behavior, this effect could be a mechanism through which insurance company concentration harms consumers. Note, however, that the source of consumer harm would *not* be the traditional competition-policy concern of increased insurance company margins induced by a loss of competition. Rather, the absence of competition among insurance

[60]Insurance-company executives presented this view to me in personal interviews.

companies allows them to offer inefficient policies that weaken competition among healthcare providers, which results in higher healthcare prices and, ultimately, higher insurance prices. If the necessary data were available, it could be very interesting to explore whether this effect is strong in practice.

It also would be worth exploring whether care-provider market power is a factor driving the lack of insurance terms that promote care-provider price competition. Does a care provider with substantial market power have the incentive and ability to exercise that power, in part, by negotiating agreements with insurers that block them from steering policyholders to other care providers through policies such as making the policyholders pay more if they utilize that care provider than others in the insurance plan's network?

To begin to answer this last question, consider an insurance company bargaining with a hospital over the price that the insurance company will pay when its customers utilize that hospital. Superficially, it might appear that the hospital could not gain from demanding a no-steering provision because the insurer would demand price concessions as compensation. However, this intuition fails to capture some of the complexities of bargaining. To see how, consider bargaining over price with and without a no-steering provision. All else equal, absent a no-steering agreement, the insurer could be expected to make increasingly strong efforts to steer its policyholders away from the hospital as the price paid by the insurer rose. This effect would reduce the benefits to the hospital of obtaining a higher price through bargaining and would lead to a lower equilibrium price than otherwise.

In contrast, with steering restraints in effect, the insurer is confronted with an all-or-nothing choice of whether to include the hospital in its provider network. In this situation, in which a higher price charged to the insurance company does not lead to higher prices or other forms of disincentives imposed on consumers, the hospital unambiguously gains from higher prices as long as the insurance company does not choose to drop the hospital entirely. Hence, in some circumstances, the existence of anti-steering provisions can affect the degree to which the hospital can exercise its market power to obtain higher prices.[61]

[61]This discussion implicitly assumes that there are bargaining frictions (e.g., asymmetric information) that prevent the parties from negotiating their way to an outcome that

Formal modeling and empirical studies could shed light on several interesting questions. How extensive is the use of no-steering clauses in contracts between insurance issuers and care providers? What forms do these clauses take? Do they tend to be used more where care providers have greater market power? Does more intense competition among insurers make it more difficult for them to implement steering policies in the face of care-provider opposition? Are there potential efficiency benefits of no-steering clauses (e.g., to support relationship-specific investment)?

Thus far, the discussion has focused on possible explanations for why insurance policies are not structured to do more to induce price sensitivity among policyholders. Now, consider conduct that actively undermines insurance policy terms intended to induce price sensitivity: subsidies and supplemental insurance covering coinsurance and copayment expenditures. These subsidies are offered by high-cost care providers precisely to offset the incentives created by insurance contracts to steer consumers away from high-cost treatments. For example, a pharmaceutical company may offer a payment card that reimburses a patient for the higher out-of-pocket costs associated with consuming the card-issuer's drug instead of a cheaper alternative. The care provider offering the subsidy benefits from the resulting increase in the sales of its good or service. It could be interesting to explore an equilibrium model of provider and insurance company behavior that captures the interactions among insurance-policy terms, the price of the medical product or service, and the use of copayment and coinsurance subsidies. What are the net efficiency and welfare effects of these subsidies? Do these subsidies represent competitive price reductions, a form of price discrimination (to the extent that distribution of the cards is targeted at only some purchasers), or conduct that undermines incentives to engage in price competition? If the latter, should competition policy prohibit or limit various forms of coinsurance and copayment subsidies?

In contrast to the providers of typical copayment subsidies, the providers of supplemental insurance do not benefit from increased utilization of care services. Indeed, greater utilization typically will trigger greater costs for the supplemental insurance provider. Nevertheless, supplemental

maximizes their joint profits, say through optimal two-part tariffs. There are, of course, considerable bargaining frictions in practice.

insurance can be expected to lead to excessive insurance because the costs of the moral hazard induced by low coinsurance rates are borne, in part, by another insurer. For example, Medicare supplemental insurance offered by private companies increases the payments made by Medicare. Again, an equilibrium model would be helpful and might raise questions regarding whether competition policy authorities should limit certain forms of supplemental insurance that undermine care-provider price competition or, at least, look favorably on efforts by primary insurers to limit their policyholders' purchase of certain forms of supplemental insurance.

Changing the degree to which consumers bear the costs of their medical care might also affect the degree to which they engage in quality search. It could be interesting to consider a model in which price serves as a noisy signal of quality (say because some patients are informed and there is some exogenous heterogeneity in care-provider quality). If the rate of coinsurance rises, consumers may have incentives to make greater use of other sources of quality information in order to identify low-price, high-quality providers. The result could be more intense price and quality competition.

I close this section by noting two other points to keep in mind in designing policies to promote higher consumer prices at the correct margins. One is the presence of what Baicker *et al.* (2012) call *behavioral hazard* (i.e., actions that are the result of mistakes or behavioral biases), which can lead to underuse as well as overuse of care. Beeuwkes Buntin *et al.* (2011) found that consumers with high-deductible insurance policies consumed less preventive care (e.g., childhood vaccinations and various types of cancer screening) than people with low-deductible policies even though the high deductible did not apply to preventative care.[62] Similarly, Lowsky *et al.* (2102) report that, while cost sharing induced policyholders to consume less healthcare, they reduced consumption of "highly beneficial" and "less beneficial" care equally. The possibility of biases and mistakes suggests that insurance plans either need to be structured to account for these effects or education efforts should be undertaken to improve consumer decision

[62] That said, one needs to be careful about interpretation of results with respect to preventative care and the effects of deductibles. Screening and true preventative care are two different things. There may be no point in getting screened for cancer if you cannot afford the treatment that would be recommended conditional on finding a problem.

making. It is also important to understand the implications of these biases and mistakes for competition.

The second point to keep in mind is the effect of pricing on care providers' incentives. Increasing the amounts paid by consumers at the margin need not correspond to increasing the amounts paid to care providers at the margin. Indeed, there are reasons to believe that at least some payments to care providers today are already too high at the margin. For example, Hsu *et al.* (2013) found that hospitals in their study profited from central-line associated bloodstream infections. Even if these hospitals do not attempt to profit from inducing ill health, they clearly lack financial incentives to prevent such infections. More generally, it is desirable for consumers to face higher prices at the margin and providers to receive lower prices when treating patients for conditions triggered by the provider.

5. Information Policy as Competition Policy

The presence of poorly informed consumers opens the possibility that public policy could improve market outcomes by improving consumers' access to — and use of — information about the prices and quality levels of both insurance plans and care providers.[63]

5.1. *Information regarding healthcare providers*

Consider a policy that provides consumers improved information about care-provider quality with the intention of strengthening competition to induce providers to offer higher-quality care. Economic theory identifies several complications that make designing an effective information policy difficult.

First, the incentives created by the availability of additional information are mediated through consumer behavior. To see why this fact matters, consider a standard agency problem, such as would arise if a payor acted as a principal contracting with a care provider as its agent, and the principal

[63]Information disclosure may be voluntary or mandatory. See Dranove and Jin (2010) for a comprehensive review of the literature. Although I will not discuss it in this essay, public policy could also prohibit provision of services receiving ratings below some threshold.

made the payment to its agent conditional on the principal's information regarding provider quality. The principal would seek an optimal reward function, $r^*(\cdot)$, relating the payment received by provider i to the verifiable signal of provider i's quality, s_i, observed by the payor. In a standard agency problem, the principal benefits from information that is better in the Blackwell, sense.[64] In the present situation, the signal is provided to consumers who then choose among care providers that are compensated by the payor. Given signal s_i, consumers take equilibrium actions $x(s_i)$ that determine the provider's revenue, $R(x)$. In many instances, the choice of $R(\cdot)$ will have been made without regard to consumers' information sets or behavior. And even if $R(\cdot)$ were chosen optimally, it may be impossible to find a revenue function such that $R(x(s_i)) \equiv r^*(s_i)$. As discussed above, consumer choice, here $x(\cdot)$, is distorted by the presence of insurance and, even after the provision of various signals, consumers will be imperfectly informed.

In the light of the theory of the second best, it is not surprising that the literature has found that statistical improvements in information can worsen market performance. For example, Gravelle and Sivey (2010) showed that having noisier signals can serve as a form of informational handicapping that allows low-quality care providers to continue to compete with high-quality providers to attract patients and, thus, can create incentives for providers to increase their quality levels above what would be chosen in the absence of competition. And Katz (2013) showed that it can sometimes be optimal to provide signals that aggregate ratings across different dimensions of care (e.g., a hospital's performance with respect to cardiology and oncology) in order to leverage competition for one type of patient (e.g., those needing cardiac care) to improve the quality of another area (e.g., oncology) even though such aggregation may dilute incentives in other instances.[65]

---

[64] See Holmstrom (1979) and Grossman and Hart (1983).

[65] Ma and Mak (forthcoming) show that reporting only aggregate quality indexes can improve welfare in the case of a multiproduct monopolist by blocking the firm from engaging in second-degree price discrimination that it would undertake if disaggregated quality information were provided to consumers.

Another way in which improved information may create perverse incentives arises from forces identified in the literature on multi-task agency (e.g., Holmstrom and Milgrom (1991)) and the fundamental insight that "you get what you pay for." Consumers respond only to the information available to them, so care providers are rewarded for raising quality along the dimensions that are measured and reported, and providers are not rewarded for offering high quality along unreported dimensions. Lu (2012) found that the introduction of report cards under the Nursing Home Quality Initiative led measures of quality along publicly reported dimensions to improve, but measures of quality along unreported dimensions to worsen. Whether consciously or not, nursing homes "gamed" the system.

Gaming is a factor that should be taken into account in designing information policies generally. Another example of gaming is that care providers may influence reported quality signals through patient selection. This mechanism arises because patients differ in the severity of their conditions, which affects the distribution of outcomes. Care providers can take advantage of private information regarding a patient's condition to optimize their case mix against any risk-adjustment system used to create a quality signal.[66] Dranove *et al.* (2003) found evidence that such selection occurs in practice.

The design of policies regarding quality information should also account for effects on the degree of price competition. To the extent that other sources of information diminish the importance of price as a signal of quality, price competition will be more intense because a lower price will less strongly lead consumers to believe the product is of lower quality. In addition, Board (2009) showed that increased consumer information can strengthen price competition when the information reveals that competing care providers are more similar than consumers had believed. However, the opposite is also possible: Information provision could reveal quality

[66]Gaming the risk-adjustment system need not be the only force giving rise to distortions in patient selection. As sketched in Katz (2013), one might consider an analysis that builds on Holmstrom's (1999) career-concerns model of a manager's choice of investment project, in which project (patient) selection is distorted because certain types of projects reveal more about the manager's ability than do others. It would appear that this distortion could arise even if the case mix were publicly reported and the risk-adjustment rating system perfect.

differences that weaken price competition in comparison with consumers' naïve (and incorrect) beliefs that the providers are undifferentiated.

There have been many efforts to create care-provider report cards and other measures of care-provider quality.[67] It is my understanding that these efforts seldom take into account the considerations identified above. Developing useful principles to guide the design of performance measures in ways that do account for these factors is thus a potentially valuable area for research. Relevant questions and potential research topics include the following:

- Are there practical ways to determine if informational handicapping and/or information aggregation would be beneficial in a given situation?
- The multi-task agency perspective suggests that, to the extent that only a limited number of measures are reported, it is best if quality along those dimensions is complementary to quality along unreported dimensions, so that higher reported quality induces higher unreported quality. It is also best to avoid negative spillovers with other activities, as could arise either due to the opportunity cost of resources (e.g., physician or management time) or because of direct conflicts (e.g., avoiding blood clotting may promote bleeding). It would be useful to develop a taxonomy of factors that give rise to complementarities or negative spillovers. Another topic, which also touches on issues of organizational design, is to extend to healthcare settings the literature relating optimal job design to the set of available performance measures.[68]

---

[67] For example, the governments of both the United Kingdom and United States maintain such sites (e.g., http://www.nhs.uk/Service-Search/Hospital/LocationSearch/7/Hospitals and http://www.medicare.gov/hospitalcompare/About/WhatIs/What-Is-HOS.aspx, both sites visited January 13, 2013. Leading examples of private organizations include: a non-profit, organization that provides consumer ratings generally (Consumer Reports, http://www.consumerreports.org/cro/magazine/2012/08/how-safe-is-your-hospital/index.htm); a for-profit magazine (*U.S. News and World Report*, http://health.usnews.com/best-hospitals); a non-profit group aimed at representing employer interests (The Leapfrog Group, http://www.leapfroggroup.org/); and a for-profit firm that provides services to hospitals (HealthGrades, http://www.healthgrades.com/). All sites visited January 13, 2013.

[68] Holmstrom and Milgrom (1991) is a seminal contribution to the economics literature.

- Information policies should account for the well-documented heterogeneity in how consumers make use of available information.[69] Providing improved information could lead sophisticated consumers to be more sensitive to differences in providers' qualities, which could generate a positive externality for unsophisticated consumers if care providers improve their quality to attract sophisticated consumers.[70] One issue to explore is whether an increase in the precision of the information available to sophisticated consumers could lead some providers to give up trying to attract those consumers and, instead, offer low-quality services to unsophisticated consumers.

- Quality measures should not be subject to gaming through selection effects. Gaming can be prevented either by having a measure that cannot be influenced by selection or by having the system contain a means of detecting and/or correcting for selection. Chen (2011) has modeled an example of the latter mechanism in which taking on a high volume of patients (i.e., not engaging in selection) can serve as a signal of quality when publicly reported. It would be useful to extend Chen's model of exogenous provider qualities to the case of endogenous qualities.

Next, consider information regarding prices. Healthcare policy discussions have had several recent calls for greater price transparency in the sense that consumers know what prices they will pay if they are treated at a given provider.[71] The U.S. Government Accountability Office found that it typically is very difficult for consumers to estimate what their out-of-pocket costs of care will be.[72] In part, this is because the quantities are difficult to predict. But consumers also typically do not know the prices charged by care providers. And, in many instances, the net prices patients pay are dependent on insurance policy characteristics (e.g., the size of the

---

[69]See Faber *et al.* (2009), Kolstad and Chernew (2009), and references cited therein.

[70]In Brekke *et al.*'s (2007) model, an increase in the percentage of patients who receive advice regarding hospital choice from general practitioners (and thus become informed consumers) exerts a positive influence on hospitals' equilibrium quality levels.

[71]See, for example, Catalyst for Payment Reform, "Price Transparency: An Essential Building Block for a High-Value, Sustainable Health Care System," Action Brief.

[72]U.S. Government Accountability Office (2011b).

in-network benefit and the deductible). There are several ongoing efforts to increase transparency.[73]

These efforts face many challenges. One is the nature of hospital pricing, which can involve charging for thousands of goods and services separately. Given uncertainty about the quantities that will be consumed upon admission, it can be extremely difficult for a consumer to make meaningful comparisons between two hospitals' price vectors. This problem suggests that there is value in constructing standardized price indexes, but any such index will be imperfect and might be subject to gaming. An alternative approach would be to force hospitals and associated care providers to quote prices for bundles of services (e.g., an all-in charge for a hip replacement). It could be interesting to model the competitive effects of bundling in this context.

An important competition-policy issue is whether making information available to consumers will enable a hospital or insurance company to infer what payment rates have been negotiated by other hospitals and insurers. If so, this information provision raises potential competitive concerns because suppliers who interact repeatedly and have information about one another's prices may be able to use punishment strategies to sustain some degree of collusion. It would be useful to extend the existing literature, which examines the effects of the information structure on collusion when suppliers sell to passive buyers, to settings more closely resembling the active bargaining between insurers and care providers.[74]

Such an extension would be useful because additional considerations come into play when there are strategic players on both the demand and supply sides of the market — buyers might make use of the price information as well. Seeing the price a hospital charges insurer *A* might allow insurer *B* to make inferences about the hospital's payoffs in bargaining with *B*. For instance, observing low prices charged to insurer *A* might lead insurer *B* to infer that the hospital has a weak disagreement point in bargaining with *B* because disagreement would shift share to *A*. Or insurer *B* might infer that the hospital has low marginal costs. However, the knowledge that

[73]See U.S. Government Accountability Office (2011b, pp. 2–3).

[74]Green and Porter (1984) was an important early contribution to this literature. For a recent contribution, see Miller (2012).

its pricing to insurer A will have these effects on the resulting bargain with insurer B will give the hospital incentive to charge higher prices to insurer A than if the information remained secret.[75] An equilibrium model is needed.

Sinaiko and Rosenthal (2011) present an argument suggesting another potential unintended consequence of price transparency: When consumers take price as a signal of quality and consumers care more about quality than price, making comparative price information available to consumers may lead low-price care providers to raise their charges in order to signal higher quality.[76] Sinaiko and Rosenthal do not offer an equilibrium model of pricing, so it is not apparent under what conditions the net effect of increased transparency would be to raise prices. Such a model would be useful.

5.2. *Information regarding insurance policies*

Empirical studies have consistently found that consumers are poorly informed about the prices and financial benefits associated with different insurance policies and tend to make poor choices among plans.[77] This fact suggests that competition potentially could be strengthened by providing consumers additional information about insurance plans and educating them with regard to how to use it. The information could cover plan pricing, the nature of financial benefits provided by different plans, and the qualities of provider networks associated with different plans. Indeed, there are several insurer report cards available, the most well-known in the United States being the National Committee for Quality Assurance's detailed Healthcare Effectiveness Data and Information Set (HEDIS) measures and *U.S. News & World Report*'s five-star rating system

[75]Cutler and Dafny (2011) make a similar intuitive argument and assert that price transparency will give rise to effects akin to those of most-favored nation clauses.

[76]This possibility reinforces the value of having consumers bear some of the costs of choosing high-price care providers and of having consumers have access to good information about quality in a form that they find useful.

[77]See Ho *et al.* (2013) and references therein for a studies examining consumer choice among Part D Medicare plans in the United States.

based on information collected from insurers by the Centers for Medicare and Medicaid Services.[78]

Several of the issues with respect to providing information about care providers also arise with respect to information about insurance plans. For example, insurance contracts can be difficult to evaluate and compare because the financial terms are multi-dimensional. Attempts to summarize insurance plans with a simple index may be susceptible to "gaming," whereby suppliers would be induced to offer policies that look good according to the index instead of designing plans that fit well with many consumers' actual patterns of healthcare expenditures.[79] Of course, there may also be gaming to the extent that consumers systematically miscalculate differences among insurance plans in the absence of such standard measures.

The analysis of Katz (2013) regarding the costs and benefits of aggregating information to leverage competitive pressures across different dimensions of care-provider performance could also be applied to insurance plans. That said, there are also important differences between the analyses of insurance markets and healthcare markets. For instance, Glazer and McGuire (2006) find that reporting only aggregate measures of insurance plans' qualities and characteristics can improve market performance for a reason that is specific to the provision of insurance: it can mitigate problems of adverse selection by preventing insurance companies from successfully pursuing multi-dimensional product strategies that induce consumers to sort themselves.

The issue of whether to report information to consumers in aggregate form naturally arises when considering how to report the quality of an insurance plan's provider network. Several performance measures based on the underlying care-providers' qualities (e.g., HEDIS scores) report only a single score for an insurance plan as a whole, rather than providing separate scores for each provider in the plan's network. Presumably, one

[78]Sternberg, S. and C. I. Young, (2012). "How U.S. News Rates Health Insurance Plans," August 7. Available at http://health.usnews.com/health-news/health-insurance/articles/2012/08/07/how-us-news-rates-health-insurance-plans (site visited January 3, 2014).

[79]Another way to address this problem is for regulators to standardize the policies that may be offered. I will return to this issue in the Section 7.

justification for this approach is to reduce the computational burden placed on consumers. However, different consumers will make different use of the various providers in a plan's network and, consequently, an average figure may not provide a good measure of quality from any given consumer's perspective. Moreover, because the intention of report cards such as HEDIS is to induce insurance plans and care providers to improve the quality of care, the incentive effects of aggregation should be taken into account.

Care providers' incentives to improve quality flow from: (a) patients' and insurers' demands for quality, and (b) the fact that, depending on the nature of insurance contracts, higher-quality care can be more profitable because it avoids the need to incur unreimbursed costs triggered by low-quality care.[80] An insurance provider's demand for care-provider quality comes from: (a) consumers' derived demand for quality, and (b) the fact that higher-quality care can be cheaper overall because it avoids unnecessary readmissions and complications such as hospital-acquired infections.[81] Providing consumers information about care-provider quality can affect both their demand for quality and insurers' derived demand.

The choice of level at which to report care-provider quality will influence how a provider's quality influences demand for its output. When reported only at the aggregate, provider-network level, the effects are mediated solely through the demand for the insurance plan overall, and those demand effects are driven by the marginal plan buyer's evaluation of changes in the average provider quality. When qualities are reported at the provider level, there are changes in the demand for the overall plan and share shifts among providers within the plan portfolio. These share shifts are driven by the marginal consumers as determined at the provider level. The latter approach might appear to generate stronger incentives to provide high quality, but the marginal consumers in the two situations may have very different preferences. Moreover, the Spence (1975) distortion (i.e., that the tastes of the marginal consumer might not represent the average

[80]Recall that Hsu *et al.* (2013) found that, under current insurance contracts, hospitals profited from central-line associated bloodstream infections.

[81]As discussed Section 6 below, in addition to using its purchase behavior to create care-provider incentives to offer high-quality services, an insurer may work to improve care quality in more direct ways, such as providing patient advocates and working with providers to implement best practices of care.

valuation of quality) also needs to be taken into account and significantly complicates the welfare analysis. Whether economic theory can provide concrete guidance in this regard is an area to explore.

The use of an average-provider-quality report also can have implications for an insurer's choice of network scope that could be worth modeling. Intuitively, when a report card offers a quality score separately for each care provider in a plan's network, the insurer has incentives to add any care provider whose combination of characteristics makes that provider attractive for some policyholders. In contrast, if only a mean score is reported, then the insurer has incentives to exclude low-quality providers that would pull down the reported average. Reporting only mean scores could thus narrow networks and harm consumers with idiosyncratic (e.g., location-based) preferences for otherwise low-quality providers.

Lastly, Handel (2013) can be interpreted as identifying another potential downside of improving consumer information with respect to insurance plans in a second-best world. Handel estimated a structural model of the health insurance choices made by employees of a large firm and used the model to simulate the effects of policies that induce consumers to make plan choices that are closer to privately optimal. His central finding is that the effect of these private improvements is to worsen adverse selection and reduce overall welfare. As Handel (2013, pp. 2680–2681) notes, his analysis does not account for changes in firm behavior. If the improvements in consumer choices are due to improved consumer information, there may be increases in competition that have offsetting, beneficial effects. Hence, Handel's analysis does not establish that improved information is harmful, but his analysis is yet another reminder of the complications that arise under asymmetric information and of the value of careful economic modeling.

6. Complementarities, Vertical Relations, and Horizontal Structures

As described above, there is a broad sense that healthcare quality is too low given its cost and that a significant cause of this problem is an inefficiently low level of cooperation among care providers. Governmental and private insurers are trying to address the problem of low quality and poor coordination among healthcare providers through a variety of means. One is to compensate care providers on a joint — rather than individual —

basis. Another is to engage in selective contracting and make care providers compete to be included an insurance plan's provider network based on quality, as well as price. Still another approach is for insurance companies directly to influence provider practices by cooperating with care providers. Insurer activities in this regard include offering best-practice information to the care providers and/or monitoring the treatment of particular patients and making specific care recommendations.[82] These insurer initiatives raise a variety of issues for competition policy.

6.1. *Promoting cooperation among complementary care providers*

Realizing organizational structures that promote care-provider coordination and care quality is one of the most important goals that must be achieved to improve the healthcare sector's performance. In the United States, public and private insurers are promoting formation of Accountable Care Organizations (ACOs).[83] Although a consensus definition of an ACO has yet to emerge, a critical element appears to be the joint compensation of multiple healthcare providers treating a given patient, with a linkage between the compensation amount and the associated health or cost outcomes. The need for the jointly compensated providers to allocate payment among themselves can create demand for new forms of care-provider organizations or contractual relationships among providers. Assessing the competitive effects of different forms of provider organization and contracts will be a very important task for competition policy going forward, and I believe the value of additional research in this area will be very high.

Although insurers have shown increasing interest in creating coordination incentives for care providers by making (partially) capitated payments to the collection of care providers treating a given patient for a particular condition, the fact that collaboration is necessary or desirable is *not*, in itself, a reason to reward groups rather than individuals. Absent physician altruism, collaboration ultimately has to be motivated by financial incentives at

[82] Some insurance company report cards (e.g., HEDIS) contain information reflecting how well an insurance company has induced the care providers treating its policyholders to follow best practice and to deliver high-quality care.

[83] See, for example, https://www.cms.gov/Medicare/Medicare-Fee-for-Service-Payment/ACO/index.html?redirect=/ACO/ (site visited April 13, 2014).

the individual level.[84] Consequently, it is not obvious that the distinction between individual and group payments should matter, particularly if side payments among care providers are allowed.

Katz (2014) considers a simple model in which, if two care providers ("specialists") coordinate their efforts, then overall costs treatment are lower and/or the patient health outcome is better. But coordination is costly and cannot be verified by an outsider. As a consequence, there is a problem of motivating the specialists to undertake efficient levels of coordination that cannot be solved simply by writing contracts that reward or require coordination directly. However, because the specialists can observe one another's degree of cooperation, they can implement relational contracts if they interact with each other repeatedly. These relational contracts can support cooperation that could not be supported by formal contracts alone.

Katz (2014) demonstrates that the effectiveness of these relational contracts depends in subtle ways on the nature of the formal financial contracts with insurers (i.e., whether care providers are capitated on an individual or group basis). Moreover, as is typically the case, the relational contracts are more effective when there is more frequent interaction among the specialists. This fact has potentially important implications for competition policy. It suggests that long-term, exclusive relationships among specialists (perhaps effectuated through a merger of complementary physician groups) could be efficiency enhancing because they would increase the frequency with which the specialists have patients in common. Moreover, commitments to long-term relationships might also allow for relational contracts with harsher punishments and, thus, better support cooperation. However, in addition to promoting greater coordination, such relationships could potentially harm competition. For example, if there are very few specialists of a given type, it would appear that exclusive relationships could lead to foreclosure of other specialists and/or a reduction in the number of viable competitors overall.

There are many other questions about the contractual relationships among — and the organization of — complementary care providers. The

---

[84]This is not to say that no physician is altruistic. But there is ample evidence that financial incentives affect the behavior of many physicians. See, for example, Kouri *et al.*'s (2002) survey of the effects of physicians' financial interests on the use of medical imaging.

complementary nature of efforts raises the question of whether integration or an employment relationship could help address problems of poor cooperation.[85] For example, to what extent would organizing physicians as employees of a common company lead them efficiently to engage in greater cooperation? And to what extent could it also facilitate physician collusion against patients and insurers? For instance, there might be conflict-of-interest concerns when a primary care physician (PCP) acts as a gatekeeper to specialist services in which the PCP has a financial interest. Empirical studies offer grounds for concern; research suggests that a primary effect of physician ownership of medical facilities and equipment is higher rates of treatment without concomitant patient benefits.[86] In thinking about these issues, it is notable that the distortions are not primarily driven by traditional concentration concerns. Rather, the issue is the internalization of the profits earned by the care providers and facilities to which referrals have been made, and the distortions arise because care providers possess private information regarding the appropriate course of treatment.

Gaynor (2006) provides a brief survey of the theoretical and empirical literature on the effects of hospital–physician integration. The results of the empirical literature are best described as "mixed." Cuellar and Gertler (2006) found that such integration did not give rise to efficiencies and appeared to generate increased bargaining power resulting in higher prices. However, Ciliberto and Dranove (2006) found that changes in integration were not associated with significant price changes, and Ciliberto (2006) found that integration led to efficiently higher investment. There clearly is room here for additional empirical work on these issues and others, such as whether integration leads to changes in referral and care patterns.

6.2. *Insurer/care-provider vertical relations*

The actions of insurers and care providers affect one another. For example, insurers may invest in improving the quality of care providers' services, and many decisions taken by care providers affect the amounts paid by insurers.

[85]Although this discussion has focused on labor, the ownership of specialized assets might also be a feature to take into account in determining the optimal organization of care providers.

[86]See, for example, Kouri *et al.* (2002).

Because of pervasive asymmetric information, it is impossible to write arm's-length contracts that provide direct incentives to behave in a jointly optimal manner. These incentive problems raise the possibility that other contractual terms (e.g., exclusivity) or care-provider/insurer integration may be efficient.

First, consider insurer investments in provider quality. When an insurer invests in the quality of a care providers' services (e.g., by assisting care providers with implementing best practices), that investment may be subject to free riding to the extent that it improves the care provider's quality with respect to all of its patients, including those who are not policyholders of the insurer making the investment. Moreover, when the investment makes the care provider more attractive to non-investing insurers, the possibility of hold up arises. There are at least two responses to consider. One is to allow a more concentrated insurance industry so that any one firm internalizes a greater percentage of the quality benefits that it creates. Another is to allow care providers and insurers to enter into exclusive dealing contracts or even vertically integrate. Exclusive dealing contracts eliminate free riding and, as shown by Segal and Whinston (2000), can ameliorate hold-up problems. Of course, both increased horizontal concentration and tighter vertical relations raise other competition issues.

Next, consider economies of scale at the level of a relationship between a care provider and insurer. They may arise because of fixed costs associated with investments of the sort just discussed, or a care provider may incur large fixed costs to comply with an insurance company's claims-processing procedures and policies. The existence of such costs limits the efficient number of insurer–provider relationships. There are at least three possible responses to the existence of economies of scale (in addition to ignoring them). One is to allow a more concentrated insurance industry in order to reduce the number of insurers with which a given care provider has to deal while still being able to serve a large share of potential patients. Second, the party bearing the fixed costs may seek some sort of volume commitment from the other party, which could be equivalent to an exclusive contract in some circumstances. Where the fixed costs arise from a care provider's need to adapt to an insurer's procedures and systems, a third approach is to allow insurers to coordinate certain aspects of their behavior when dealing with care providers, such as setting care protocols or requiring use of electronic medical records. This third approach raises many issues already addressed by the literature on standard setting in industries with network effects, such as assessing the costs and benefits of standards competition.[87] All three approaches potentially raise significant competition-policy issues that can fruitfully be modeled.

More generally, the interrelated decision making of insurers and care providers raises the question of whether an efficient response to the pervasive incentive issues may be either to organize the insurance and care-delivery functions within a single, vertically integrated enterprise or to create a virtual enterprise through a series of exclusive contracts that tightly link an insurance company with a fixed set of care providers.[88] Surprisingly, this important area of research is still largely unexplored beyond the general theory of the firm.[89]

Although there are reasons to expect companies that are integrated insurers and care-providers to offer high-quality services, and several such companies in the United States (e.g., Kaiser) have been very successful in their home markets, these companies generally have had limited success expanding into additional markets. Ho (2009) found that entry by integrated providers into new markets was made difficult by: (a) the need for a large number of plan subscribers to support an exclusive network; (b) difficulties in convincing consumers in new markets that the entrant offered high-quality service;[90] and, to a lesser degree (c) higher costs triggered by the need to comply with certificate-of-need regulations, which limit the ability of entrants to construct their own facilities. These considerations suggest that competition policy might promote efficient organization by allowing

[87]For a recent survey, see Farrell and Klemperer (2007).

[88]Captitated payments represent a step in this direction: a capitated care provider bears the financial risk and, thus, takes on the insurance function with the range of conditions covered by the capitated contract.

[89]Gaynor and Haas–Wilson (1999) summarize the sparse literature on the effects of integration or exclusive dealing between insurance companies and care providers.

[90]Supporting for this conclusion is provided in Sorensen's (2006) empirical finding that social learning affects consumers' choices of insurance plans.

vertical mergers or various forms of exclusive contracting to help overcome the first of these three barriers to entry.[91]

6.3. *Modeling the vertical system*

The vertical relationships between unintegrated insurance companies and care providers raise interesting and complex issues for competition policy. Competition-policy enforcers would be in a much better position to assess the competitive effects of various conduct if economists could develop richer models incorporating two major institutional features: (a) the overlapping bargaining between multiple insurance companies and multiple care providers, and (b) portfolio competition.

Consider first the need to understand how care-provider/insurer bargaining works in settings where there is overlapping bargaining by multiple care providers with multiple insurers. Such settings are relevant because an insurer often negotiates multi-year contracts with most of the hospital systems and physician groups in a given geographic area, and any one care provider typically negotiates with multiple insurers.

Does increased competition among insurers lead to higher or lower prices paid to care providers in these settings? And how do any such price changes translate to the prices paid by consumers? There are intuitive arguments running in both directions. One is that increased insurer concentration will lead to the exercise of bargaining power that drives care providers' price down. The other is that greater competition among insurance companies will make each one less able to "afford" to pay higher prices. More precisely, if insurance companies face higher elasticities of demand, then paying higher provider prices may be more costly to them than otherwise.

Although Melnick *et al.* (2010) and Moriya *et al.* (2010) found that increased insurer concentration lowers care-provider prices, Ho and Lee (2013) found heterogeneous effects in their examination of healthcare-provider/insurer bargaining.[92] Specifically, they found that top hospitals

---

[91]Additionally, improving the availability and use of quality information (Section 5) can address the second barrier, and advocating for the relaxation or, at least, judicious application, of certificate-of-need regulations (Section 7) can address the third one.

[92]A similar question has long been addressed in the context of firm-union bargaining over wages. The literature on union bargaining finds ambiguous theoretical and empirical effects,

benefit from insurer competition, while the average price received by hospitals falls. Ho and Lee also found that increased insurer competition creates incentives for hospitals to merge and to invest in making hospital more attractive.

Unfortunately, there is an absence of any generally accepted model of overlapping, pairwise bargaining with multiple potential partners on each side. Although it is a tall order, further development of relevant bargaining theory could help to identify which elements of market structure are key drivers of equilibrium prices. There are also important empirical questions relevant to fitting bargaining models to these markets, including: How quickly do consumers switch insurance companies versus care providers and what are consumers' relative switching costs? Could public policy reduce these switching costs? Would there be unintended consequences of doing so? Such questions are relevant because the answers provide insights into insurers' and care providers' disagreement points.

Another area of potential interest is the exercise of monopsony power by very large purchasers (e.g., the U.S. government) of pharmaceuticals and other therapies, particularly newly invented ones. Are the higher prices paid in the United States than in other countries due to political constraints that prevent the Medicare administration from exercising its buyer power, or does the United States plays the role of a *pivotal buyer* (i.e., a buyer who is essential to the seller's decision whether to initiate and maintain production of the good)? Although a common intuition suggests that a pivotal buyer should have more bargaining power because its patronage is critical to the product's success, Raskovich (2003) shows that this intuition is incorrect. The central idea of Raskovich's analysis is that, when a buyer is pivotal, the seller's fixed costs, such as R&D, enter into consideration of the disagreement points. This fact redounds to the disadvantage of the buyer. Intuitively, the buyer has to help the seller cover its fixed costs, and the price is no longer based on incremental cost. Moreover, a large buyer may develop a reputation, which puts pressure on a large buyer not to exploit its

and these effects are sensitive to the particulars of the institutional structure (e.g., whether the union bargains with only one firm or with all of the firms in the industry). See Bastos *et al.* (2010) and the literature cited therein.

bargaining power for a short-term gain at the expense of undermining the future supply of therapies.

It would also be helpful to develop a much better understanding of portfolio competition. For example, the following are several interesting features of portfolio competition, all of which could usefully be explored further. First, as discussed in Section 3.2, two care providers that are substitutes from the perspective of any individual patient may be complements in the context of portfolio competition. Second, as also discussed in Section 3.2, because employers and insurance companies aggregate the preferences of their employees and policyholders, respectively, two care providers that are highly differentiated from the perspective of individual patients may be viewed as close substitutes by employers and insurers. One implication of these first two phenomena is that competition policy enforcers need to think carefully about the implications of individual preferences for the assessment of mergers in markets with portfolio competition.

A third feature of portfolio competition is the possibility of "must-have" providers. It has become fashionable to assert that a supplier thought to possess substantial market power is a "must-have" supplier. It is difficult to know what this term means in the context of final goods unless the product is literally essential to life and lacks any substitutes. The term can be more meaningful in the context of portfolio competition. Specifically, "must have" can be interpreted to mean that a portfolio is not commercially viable if it does not contain the must-have supplier's good or service. Katz (2011b) examined a simple model of two horizontally differentiated hospitals, one of which was a must-have provider in selling its services to insurance plans. The model establishes conditions under which the other hospital is a complement to the must-have hospital, and this complementarity has strong implications for the competitive effects of "exclusionary" behavior by the must-have hospital. The model is, however, only a starting point for the analysis of these issues.

A final interesting feature of portfolio competition is its effects on quality competition. As discussed in Section 5.2 in the context of providing consumers with information regarding the quality of an insurance plan's provider network, there are potentially complex effects when quality competition takes place both among providers competing for share within a portfolio and across portfolios.

7. Competition Advocacy

Another way in which competition-policy economists and enforcers can contribute to solving the healthcare crisis is by preventing public policies that interfere with the workings of competitive markets. For example, there is a long history of questioning entry restrictions such as occupational licensing and certificate of need laws, which explicitly restrict new entry or investment and can distort the choice of organizational form when the regulations are differentially applied.[93]

One of the biggest areas for competition advocacy is with respect to the various ways in which policy makers have attempted to interfere with the bargaining between healthcare insurers and care providers. As discussed in Section 3.1, a care provider's volume of business can be strongly influenced by its inclusion in — or exclusion from — a particular health plan's network. Hence, when health insurance plans engage in selective contracting, care providers compete on the basis of price and quality to be included in the plans' provider networks. Competition to serve insurance providers works only if they can exclude care providers from their networks and/or steer consumers' choices of care providers through financial or other incentives. However, insurers may find themselves under political or regulatory pressure to have networks that include most or all care providers, thus weakening the threat of exclusion as a driver of competition.[94,95]

In theory, regulation requiring an insurance plan to have an extensive provider network might serve as a counter to the lack of informed consumers or to prevent the insurer from using the exclusion of certain care providers as a means of screening out potential policyholders having demand for very

---

[93]Kouri *et al.* (2002), citing Hillman (1991) on the distorted choice of organizational form.

[94]For example, because of its high charges, several insurers did not include Seattle Children's hospital in the provider networks of the plans they offered on the Affordable Care Act's insurance exchange in Washington State (Landa, 2013). Seattle Children's Hospital engaged in litigation and a media campaign to force its inclusion (*Id.*). At present, the state insurance commissioner is seeking additional powers to regulate networks in order to be able to compel such inclusion (Egge, 2013).

[95]Similar effects arise when political or regulatory pressures force insurers to reimburse expenditures on very costly and/or unproven therapies.

expensive care offered only by certain providers.[96] It is not clear whether such regulation could be a rational counter to a lack of competition among insurers. By the logic of Spence (1975), it is possible that even a monopoly insurance plan would create a network with inefficiently many providers, rather than too few. Whether or not there are justifications for this type of regulatory intervention, it is important for competition-policy economists identify the costs that derive from diminished competition.

Competition is similarly weakened by "any-willing-provider" regulation, under which an insurance company must include in its provider network any care provider that is willing to accept the health plan's standard terms. Some states enacted such legislation ostensibly to preserve provider competition and give patients choices.[97] Katz (2011a) examines a model of hospital competition and shows that, in fact, such regulation can undermine competition while having no effect on the set of hospitals included in provider networks. Indeed, in the Katz (2011a) model, it is a weakly dominant strategy for each hospital to quote the monopoly price to insurers. Intuitively, there is no point in initially quoting anything less than the monopoly price because, if a hospital loses the initial bidding, it can always accept the price bid by the other hospital.

Katz (2011a) provides one, simple model of care-provider competition to be included in provider networks. There are many other models to consider. For example, one might consider a model in which the equilibrium provider networks vary as a result of public policy intervention, in which case, the following effects would come into play. If a hospital is in some insurance companies' provider networks but not others, then it has an incentive to improve its quality in order to attract more consumers to the insurance plans in which it participates. On the other hand, when it is in fewer networks, the hospital has a smaller addressable market to attract

[96]Although such screening could be inefficient, it should also be noted that a heavily insured patient may choose among care providers with little regard for cost, and consumer choices thus tend to be biased toward higher-cost providers. An important consequence is that it can be socially optimal to exclude a care provider from an insurance plan's provider network because doing so negates some of the ill effects of the lack of appropriate price signals.

[97]For discussion of any-willing-provider regulation, see Marstellar *et al.* (1997) and Sloan and Hall (2002).

through quality improvements. It could be interesting to explore how these effects balance out.

Public–policy constraints on the terms and prices of privately supplied insurance policies are another regulation to examine. In the United States, for example, the Affordable Care Act (ACA) and state insurance commissioners restrict many of the terms (e.g., whether certain treatments are covered and the size of caps on out-of-pocket policyholder expenditures) that can be offered in insurance policies sold on the ACA insurance exchanges and elsewhere. Some of these restrictions may be motivated by the desire to simplify the choice problem confronting insurance buyers, but there are costs of doing so. Policies that limit choice clearly risk preventing firms from offering efficient policies that some or all of their customers would prefer. The effects of such policies on other elements of competition are less evident, and it could be useful to develop models addressing them. For example, does standardization lead to more intense price competition and/or does it drive insurers to seek other, unregulated dimensions along which to differentiate themselves, perhaps more inefficiently?

Regulation may also restrict insurers' ability to use available information about policyholder characteristics to set personalized prices. Absent transaction costs, insurers in a competitive market would set prices reflecting all information available to them regarding a policyholder's likely future healthcare demand. Regulation that limits this use of information can promote adverse selection and distort consumption decisions made by informed consumers. Handel *et al.* (2013) provide an interesting analysis of this issue in the context of the certain regulations contained in the ACA, but there clearly is room for more work in this area. For example, Handel *et al.* examine reactive equilibria among homogeneous insurers. The price differentials observed among insurers successfully offering competing policies on ACA's insurance exchanges suggest that consumers perceive insurers to be differentiated. And reactive equilibrium may not be the appropriate concept for ACA insurance exchanges, where rates are simultaneously set and then locked in for one year. Exploring mixed strategy Nash equilibria along the lines of Luz (2013) could be useful.

Lastly, governments often act as both suppliers and buyers of healthcare insurance and healthcare services. There are many different ways that governmental agencies can influence competition in these roles. For example, governmental insurers and care providers can act as competitive benchmarks for private firms. If politics are not an insurmountable obstacle, government agencies can also foster competition in their roles as major buyers, for example by using competitive auctions and selective contracting in procurement. Competition policy should encourage governmental agencies to act in ways that promote competition, especially with an eye to toward promoting efficient innovation. Economists can contribute to these efforts by analyzing alternative market institutions.

8. Conclusion

Competition policy has a lot to contribute to solving the healthcare crisis. Traditional competition policy, such as the review of horizontal mergers among insurers or care providers, has a valuable role to play. But one should not overestimate that role. The exercise of market power by care providers explains only on a small portion of the change in healthcare expenditures and does not explain why prices and quantities continue to rise. This not to say that the performance of healthcare providers and insurance companies has been good or that the exercise of market power is not detrimental to welfare. But it does suggest that policy makers and researchers should also look elsewhere if competition policy is to make large contributions to solving the problem.

The following four central questions provide a starting point:

- *How can consumers be provided with quality information that will induce stronger quality competition?* Consumers do not act in a manner that promotes price and quality competition. In the case of price search, this is largely a rational response to non-optimal insurance contracts. It is harder to understand the source of the problem with respect to quality search and why consumers do not make greater use of available quality information. That said, there are many ways in which information provision could be improved, and economists can play a valuable role in identifying the competitive effects of different information policies.
- *Why don't insurance companies offer policies that generate greater consumer incentives to seek low-cost providers and generate increased*

price competition? For instance, has a lack of competition among insurers led to X-inefficiency in the form of non-optimal insurance contracts that lead to inefficiently low quality, inefficiently high prices, and distorted innovation incentives for healthcare goods and services? Or has care providers' market power allowed them to prevent insurance companies from undertaking efforts to steer patients away from high-cost providers?

- *What organizational structures will promote the most efficient coordination among complementary care providers and between insurers and care providers?* Organizational innovation may be a critical response to the pervasive incentive problems created by asymmetric information. An understanding of the competitive effects and efficiencies associated with different organizational and industry structures is thus a critical foundation for sound competition policy.
- *How do structure and conduct in markets for healthcare insurance and healthcare services affect the incentives to create and adopt new healthcare goods and services?* In the long run, the pattern of technological progress and technology adoption is a critical driver of healthcare expenditures and the quality of care. Improving innovation and adoption incentives is thus critical to solving the healthcare crisis.

Competition-policy economists can plan an invaluable role in helping to answer these questions and the many others that follow from them.

References

Akerlof, G. A. (1970). "The Market for 'Lemons': Quality Uncertainty and the Market Mechanism," *Quarterly Journal of Economics*, 84(3), pp. 488–500.

Arrow, K. J. (1963). "Uncertainty and the Welfare Economics of Medical Care," *American Economic Review*, 53(5), pp. 941–971.

Baicker, K., S. Mullainathan and J. Schwartzstein (2012). "Behavioral Hazard in Health Insurance," *NBER Working Paper* No. 18468.

Bardey, D. and J.-C. Rochet (2010). "Competition Among Health Plans: A Two-Sided Market Approach," *Journal of Economics & Management Strategy*, 19(2), pp. 435–451.

Bastos, P., U. Kreickemeier and P. W. Wright (2010). "Open-Shop Unions and Product Market Competition," *Canadian Journal of Economics*, 43(2), pp. 640–662.

Beckert, W., M. Christensen and K. Collyer (2012). "Choice of NHS-funded Hospital Services in England," *Economic Journal*, 122(560), pp. 400–417.

Beeuwkes Buntin, M., A. M. Haviland, R. McDevitt and N. Sood (2011). "Healthcare Spending and Preventive Care in High-Deductible and Consumer-Directed Health Plans," *American Journal of Managed Care*, 17(3), pp. 222–230.

Berwick, D. M. and A. D. Hackbarth (2012). "Eliminating Waste in US Health Care," *Journal of the American Medical Association*, 307(14), pp. 1513–1516.

Blendon, R. J., C. Schoen, C. DesRoches, R. Osborn and K. Zappert (2003). "Common Concerns Amid Diverse Systems: Health Care Experiences in Five Countries," *Health Affairs*, 22(3), pp. 106–121.

Board, O. (2009). "Competition and Disclosure," *Journal of Industrial Economics*, 57(1), pp. 197–213.

Brekke, K. R., R. Nuscheler and O. R. Straume (2007). "Gatekeeping in Health Care," *Journal of Health Economics*, 26(1), pp. 149–170.

Brekke, K. R., R. Cellini, L. Siciliani and O. R. Straume (2012). "Competition in Regulated Markets with Sluggish Beliefs about Quality," *Journal of Economics & Management Strategy*, 21(1), pp. 131–178.

Breyer, F., J. Costa-font and S. Felder (2010). "Ageing, Health, and Health Care," *Oxford Review of Economic Policy*, 26(4), pp. 674–690.

Capps, C. S. (2003). "For-Profit and Non-Profit Pricing: The Empirical Evidence," FTC/DOJ Hearing on Health Care and Competition Law and Policy (April 10). Available at http://www.ftc.gov/ogc/healthcarehearings/docs/capps0304.pdf (site visited on March 5, 2008).

Capps, C. (2009). "The Approximate Effect of Hospital Consolidation on National Healthcare Expenditures," *Institute of Medicine Workshop Series Presentation*, May 22.

Capps, C., D. Dranove and M. Satterthwaite (2003). "Competition and Market Power in Option Demand Markets," *RAND Journal of Economics*, 34(4), pp. 737–763.

Chen, Y. (2011). "Why are Health Care Report Cards so Bad (Good)?" *Journal of Health Economics*, 30(3), pp. 575–590.

Ciliberto, F. (2006). "Does Organizational Form Affect Investment Decisions?" *Journal of Industrial Economics*, 54(1), pp. 63–93.

Ciliberto, F. and D. Dranove (2006). "The Effect of Physician–Hospital Affiliations on Hospital Prices in California," *Journal of Health Economics*, 25(1), pp. 29–38.

Committee on Quality of Health Care in America, Institute of Medicine (2000). To Err is Human: Building a Safer Health System, in L. T. Kohn, J. M.

Corrigan and M. S. Donaldson (Eds.), Washington, DC, National Academies Press.

Commonwealth Fund (2013). "2012 Commonwealth Fund International Health Policy Survey of Primary Care Physicians." Available at http://www.commonwealthfund.org/Surveys/2012/Nov/2012-International-Survey.aspx (site visited December 24, 2013).

Connor, R. A., R. D. Feldman and B. E. Dowd (1998). "The Effects of Market Concentration From Horizontal Mergers on Hospital Costs and Prices," *International Journal of the Economics of Business*, 5(2), pp. 159–180.

Cooper, Z., S. Gibbons, S. Jones and A. McGuire (2011). "Does Hospital Competition Save Lives? Evidence From The English NHS Patient Choice Reforms," *Economic Journal*, 121(554), pp. F228–F260.

Cournot, A. A. (1838) (1897). *Researches into the Mathematical Principles of the Theory of Wealth* (translated by N. T. Bacon), Macmillan, London.

Cuellar, A. E. and P. Gertler (2006). "Strategic Integration of Hospitals and Physicians," *Journal of Health Economics*, 25(1), pp. 1–28.

Cutler, D. M. and L. Dafny (2011). "Designing Price Transparency Systems for Medical Care Prices," *New England Journal of Medicine*, 364(10), pp. 894–895.

Cutler, D. M. and S. J. Reber (1998). "Paying for Health Insurance: The Tradeoff between Competition and Adverse Selection," *Quarterly Journal of Economics*, 113(2), pp. 433–466.

Cutler, D. M. and R. J. Zeckhauser (2000). "The Anatomy of Health Insurance," in A. J. Cuyler and J. P. Newhouse (Eds.), *Handbook of Health Economics*, Volume 1A, Elsevier B.V., Amsterdam.

Dafny, L., M. Duggan and S. Ramanarayanan (2012). "Paying a Premium on Your Premium? Consolidation in the US Health Insurance Industry," *American Economic Review*, 102(2), pp. 1161–1185.

DeNavas-Walt, C., B. D. Proctor and J. C. Smith (2013). "Income, Poverty, and Health Insurance Coverage in the United States: 2012," U.S. Census Bureau. Available at http://www.census.gov/prod/2013pubs/p60-245.pdf (site visited December 29, 2013).

Dranove, D. D. and C. Garthwaite (2013). "What We Don't Know Can Hurt Us," The Health Care Blog. Available at http://thehealthcareblog.com/blog/2013/12/18/what-we-dont-know-can-hurt-us/#more-68511 (site visited December 24, 2013).

Dranove, D. D. and G. Zhe Jin (2010). "Quality Disclosure and Certification: Theory and Practice," *Journal of Economic Literature*, 48(4), pp. 935–963.

Dranove, D., D. P. Kessler, M. B. McClellan and M. A. Satterthwaite (2003). "Is More Information Better? The Effects of Report Cards on Health Care Providers," *Journal of Political Economy*, 111(3), pp. 555–588.

Drèze, J. and E. Schokkaert (2013). "Arrow's Theorem of the Deductible: Moral Hazard and Stop-Loss in Health Insurance," *Journal of Risk and Uncertainty*, 47(2), pp. 147–163.

Egge, R. (2013). "More insurance plans to cover Seattle Children's Hospital services," HEALTHworks, *KOMOnews.com*, October 25. Available at http://www.komonews.com/news/health/More-insurance-plans-to-cover-Seattle-Childrens-services-229275221.html (site visited January 3, 2014).

Experts in Chronic Myeloid Leukemia (2013). "The price of drugs for Chronic Myeloid Leukemia (CML) is a reflection of the unsustainable prices of cancer drugs: from the perspective of a large group of CML experts," *Blood*, 121(22), pp. 4439–4442.

Faber, M., M. Bosch, H. Wollersheim, S. Leatherman and R. Grol (2009). "Public Reporting in Health Care: How Do Consumers Use Quality-of-Care Information? A Systematic Review," *Medical Care*, 47(1), pp. 1–8.

Farrell, D., E. Jensen, B. Kocher, N. Lovegrove, F. Melhem, L. Medonca and B. Parish (2008). "*Accounting for the Cost of US Health Care: A New Look at Why Americans Spend More*," McKinsey Global Institute, December.

Farrell, J. and P. Klemperer (2007). "Coordination and Lock-In: Competition with Switching Costs and Network Effects," in M. Armstrong and R. Porter (Eds.), *Handbook of Industrial Organization*, Volume 3, Elsevier B.V., Amsterdam.

Fuchs, V. R. (2012). "Major Trends in the US Health Economy Since 1950," *New England Journal of Medicine*, 366, pp. 973–977.

Gaynor, M. (2006). "Is Vertical Integration Anticompetitive? Definitely Maybe (But That's Not Final)," *Journal of Health Economics*, 25(1), pp. 175–180.

Gaynor, M. and D. Haas-Wilson (1999). "Change, Consolidation, and Competition in Health Care Markets," *Journal of Economic Perspectives*, 13(1), pp. 141–164.

Gaynor, M., C. Propper and S. Seiler (2012). "Free to Choose? Reform and Demand Response in the British National Health Service," unpublished manuscript, Carnegie Mellon University.

Gaynor, M. and W. B. Vogt (2000). "Antitrust and Competition in Health Care Markets," in A. J. Cuyler and J. P. Newhouse (Eds.), *Handbook of Health Economics*, Volume 1B, Elsevier B.V., Amsterdam.

Glazer, J. and T. G. McGuire (2006). "Optimal Quality Reporting in Markets for Health Plans," *Journal of Health Economics*, 25(2), pp. 295–310.

Gravelle, H. and P. Sivey (2010). "Imperfect Information in a Quality-Competitive Hospital Market," *Journal of Health Economics*, 29(4), pp. 524–535.

Green, E. J. and R. H. Porter (1984). "Noncooperative Collusion under Imperfect Price Information," *Econometrica*, 52(1), pp. 87–100.

Grossman, S. J. and O. D. Hart (1983). "An Analysis of the Principal–Agent Problem," *Econometrica*, 51(1), pp. 7–45.

Hall, R. E. and C. I. Jones (2007). "The Value of Life and the Rise in Health Spending," *Quarterly Journal of Economics*, 122(1), pp. 39–72.

Handel, B. R. (2013). "Adverse Selection and Inertia in Health Insurance Markets: When Nudging Hurts," *American Economic Review*, 103(7), pp. 2643–2682.

Handel, B., I. Hendel and M. D. Whinston (2013). "Equilibria in Health Exchanges: Adverse Selection vs. Reclassifcation Risk," unpublished manuscript, University of California, Berkeley.

Herr, A. (2011). "Quality and Welfare in a Mixed Duopoly with Regulated Prices: The Case of a Public and a Private Hospital," *German Economic Review*, 12(4), pp. 422–437.

Hillman, B. J. (1991). "George W. Holmes Lecture. Whose turf is Imaging? Independent practice, academics and research," *American Journal of Roentgenology*, 156(3), pp. 443–447.

Ho, K., J. Hogan and F. Scott Morton (2013). "Insurer (In)Efficiency in the Medicare Part D Program," unpublished manuscript, Columbia University.

Ho, K. and R. Lee (2013). "Insurer Competition and Negotiated Hospital Prices," unpublished manuscript, New York University.

Ho, K. (2009). "Barriers to Entry of a Vertically Integrated Health Insurer: An Analysis of Welfare and Entry Costs," *Journal of Economics & Management Strategy*, 18(2), pp. 487–545.

Holmström, B. (1979). "Moral Hazard and Observability," *Bell Journal of Economics*, 10(1), pp. 74–91.

Holmström, B. (1999). "Managerial Incentive Problems: A Dynamic Perspective," *Review of Economic Studies*, 66(1), pp. 169–182.

Holmström, B. and P. Milgrom (1991). "Multitask Principal-Agent Analysis: Incentive Contracts, Asset Ownership, and Job Design," *Journal of Law, Economics and Organization*, 7, pp. 24–52.

Hsu, E., D. Lin, S. J. Evans, K. S. Hamid, K. D. Frick, T. Yang, P. J. Pronovost and J. Pham (2013). "Doing Well by Doing Good: Assessing the Cost Savings of an Intervention to Reduce Central Line-Associated Bloodstream Infections in a Hawaii Hospital," *American Journal of Medical Quality*. Available at http://ajm.sagepub.com/content/early/2013/04/22/1062860613486173.full.pdf+html (site visited December 29, 2013).

Kaiser Family Foundation and Health Research & Educational Trust (2013). "Employer Health Benefits 2013 Annual Survey." Available at http://kff.org/private-insurance/report/2013-employer-health-benefits/ (site visited January 7, 2014).

Katz, M. L. (2011a). "Insurance, Consumer Choice, and the Equilibrium Price and Quality of Hospital Care," *The B.E. Journal of Economic Analysis & Policy*, 11(2), pp. 1–44.

Katz, M. L. (2011b). "Exclusionary Contracting in Healthcare Markets," unpublished manuscript, University of California, Berkeley.

Katz, M. L. (2013). "Provider Competition and Healthcare Quality: More Bang for the Buck?" *International Journal of Industrial Organization*, 31(5), pp. 612–625.

Katz, M. L. (2014). "Will Bundled Payments Improve Healthcare Provider Cooperation and, if so, How?" unpublished manuscript, University of California, Berkeley.

Keeler, E. B., L. V. Rubenstein, K. L. Kahn, D. Draper, E. R. Harrison, M. J. McGinty, W. H. Rogers and R. H. Brook (1992). "Hospital Characteristics and Quality of Care," *Journal of the American Medical Association*, 268(13), pp. 1709–1714.

Keeler, E. B., G. Melnick and J. Zwanziger (1999). "The Changing Effects of Competition on Non-profit and For-profit Hospital Pricing Behavior," *Journal of Health Economics*, 19(1), pp. 69–86.

Kolstad, J. T. and M. E. Chernew (2009). "Quality and Consumer Decision Making in the Market for Health Insurance and Health Care Services," *Medical Care Research and Review*, Supplement to 66(1), pp. 28S–52S.

Kouri, B. E., R. G. Parsons and H. R. Alpert (2002). "Physician Self-Referral for Diagnostic Imaging: Review of the Empiric Literature," *American Journal of Roentgenology*, 179(4), pp. 843–850.

Kranton, R. E. (2003). "Competition and the Incentive to Produce High Quality," *Economica*, 70(279), pp. 385–404.

Landa, A. S. (2013). "Left off Many Networks, Seattle Children's Sues," *The Seattle Times*, October 4, 2013 (page modified October 5, 2013). Available at http://seattletimes.com/html/localnews/2021968776_acachildrenssuitxml.html (site visited January 3, 2014).

Levinson, D. R. (2010). "Adverse Events in Hospitals: National Incidence among Medicare Beneficiaries," United States Department of Health and Human Services Office of Inspector General.

Lowsky, D., R. Chari, P. S. Hussey, A. Mulcahy, M. E. Vaiana and A. L. Kellermann (2012). "Flattening the Trajectory of Health Care Spending: Engage and Empower Consumers," *RAND Health Research Brief*. Available at

http://www.rand.org/pubs/research_briefs/RB9690z3.html (site visited April 13, 2014).
Lu, S. F. (2012). "Multitasking, Information Disclosure, and Product Quality: Evidence from Nursing Homes," *Journal of Economics & Management Strategy*, 21(3), pp. 673–705.
Luz, V. F. (2013). "Characterization and Uniqueness of Equilibrium in Competitive Insurance," unpublished manuscript, Yale University.
Ma, C. A. and H. Y. Mak (2014). "Public Report, Price, and Quality," *Journal of Economics & Management Strategy*, 23(2), pp. 443–464.
Martin, A. B., D. Lassman, B. Washington, A. Catlin and the National Health Expenditures Accounts Team (2012). "Growth In US Health Spending Remained Slow In 2010; Health Share Of Gross Domestic Product Was Unchanged From 2009," *Health Affairs*, 31(1), pp. 208–219.
Marsteller, J. A., R. R. Bovbjerg, L. M. Nichols and D. K. Verrilli (1997). "The Resurgence of Selective Contracting Restrictions," *Journal of Health Politics, Policy, and Law*, 22(5), pp. 1133–1189.
Melnick, G. and E. Keeler (2007). "The Effects of Multi-Hospital Systems on Hospital Prices," *Journal of Health Economics*, 26(2), pp. 400–413.
Melnick, G. A., Y.-C. Shen and V. Y. Wu (2010). "The Increased Concentration of Health Plan Markets Can Benefit Consumers Through Lower Hospital Prices," *Health Affairs*, 30(9), pp. 1728–1733.
Miller, D. A. (2012). "Robust Collusion with Private Information," *Review of Economic Studies*, 79, pp. 778–811.
Moriya, A. S., W. B. Vogt and M. Gaynor (2010). "Hospital Prices and Market Structure in the Hospital and Insurance Industries," *Health Economics, Policy and Law*, 5, pp. 459–479.
Muennig, P. A. and S. A. Glied (2010). "What Changes in Survival Rates Tell Us About US Health Care," *Health Affairs*, 29(11), pp. 1–9.
Newhouse, J. P. (1970). "Toward a Theory of Nonprofit Institutions: An Economic Model of a Hospital," *American Economic Review*, 60(1), pp. 171–185.
Newhouse, J. P. (1992). "Medical Care Costs: How Much Welfare Loss?" *The Journal of Economic Perspectives*, 6(3), pp. 3–21.
OECD (2013). "What Future for Health Spending?" *OECD Economics Department Policy Notes*, 19, pp. 329–414.
Pauly, M. V. (1986). "Taxation, Health Insurance, and Market Failure in the Medical Economy," *Journal of Economic Literature*, 24(2), pp. 629–675.
Pauly, M. V. (1987). "Nonprofit Firms in Medical Markets," *American Economic Review*, 77(2), pp. 257–262.
Prüfer, J. (2011). "Competition and Mergers Among Nonprofits," *Journal of Competition Law & Economics*, 7(1), pp. 69–72.

Raskovich, A. (2003). "Pivotal Buyers and Bargaining Position," *Journal of Industrial Economics*, 51(4), pp. 405–426.

Rey, P. and J. Tirole (2013). "Cooperation vs. Collusion: How Essentiality Shapes Co-opetition," *IDEI Working Paper* No. IDEI-801.

Rothschild, M. and J. Stiglitz (1976). "Equilibrium in Competitive Insurance Markets: An Essay on the Economics of Imperfect Information," *Quarterly Journal of Economics*, 90(4), pp. 629–649.

Schauffler, H. H. and J. K. Mordavsky (2001). "Consumer Reports in Health Care: Do They Make a Difference?" *Annual Review of Public Health*, 22, pp. 69–89.

Schoen, C., R. Osborn, D. Squires, M. Doty, R. Pierson and S. Applebaum (2011). "New 2011 Survey of Patients with Complex Care Needs in Eleven Countries Finds that Care is Often Poorly Coordinated," *Health Affairs*, 30(12), pp. 2437–2448.

Segal, I. R. and M. D. Whinston (2000). "Exclusive Contracts and Protection of Investments," *RAND Journal of Economics*, 31(4), pp. 603–633.

Shapiro, C. (1989). "Theories of Oligopoly Behavior," in R. Schmalensee and R. D. Willig (Eds.), *Handbook of Industrial Organization*, Volume 1, North Holland Publishing, Amsterdam, pp. 329–414.

Sinaiko, A. D. and M. B. Rosenthal (2011). "Increased Price Transparency in Health Care — Challenges and Potential Effects," *New England Journal of Medicine*, 364(10), pp. 891–894.

Sloan, F. A. (2000). "Not-For-Profit Ownership and Hospital Behavior," in A. J. Cuyler and J. P. Newhouse (Eds.), *Handbook of Health Economics*, Volume 1B, Elsevier B.V., Amsterdam.

Sloan, F. A. and M. A. Hall (2002). "Market Failures and the Evolution of State Regulation of Managed Care," *Law & Contemporary Problems*, 65(4), pp. 169–206.

Sorensen, A. T. (2006). "Social Learning and Health Plan Choice," *RAND Journal of Economics*, 37(4), pp. 929–945.

Spence, A. M. (1975). "Monopoly, Quality, and Regulation," *Bell Journal of Economics*, 6(2), pp. 417–429.

Toth, F. (2010). "Healthcare Policies Over the Last 20 Years: Reforms and Counter-reforms," *Health Policy*, 95, pp. 82–89.

Town, R. and G. Vistnes (2001). "Hospital Competition in HMO Networks," *Journal of Health Economics*, 20(5), pp. 733–753.

U.S. Department of Health and Human Services (2012). "National Healthcare Quality Report 2012," *AHRQ Publication* No. 12-0002.

U.S. Government Accountability Office (2011a). "Private Health Insurance: Early Experiences Implementing New Medical Loss Ratio Requirements," GAO-11-711.

U.S. Government Accountability Office (2011b). "Health Care Price Transparency: Meaningful Price Information Is Difficult for Consumers to Obtain Prior to Receiving Care," GAO-11-791.

Vogt, W. B. (2002). "Testimony of William Vogt at the Federal Trade Commission Health Care and Competition Law and Policy Workshop (September 9, 2002)." Available at http://www.ftc.gov/ogc/healthcare/20909trans.pdf (site visited March 5, 2008).

Vogt, W. B. (2009). "Hospital Market Consolidation: Trends and Consequences," *Expert Voices*, National Institute for Health Care Management Foundation.

Vogt, W. B. and R. Town (2006). "How has hospital consolidation affected the price and quality of hospital care?" *Research Synthesis Report* No. 9, Robert Wood Johnson Foundation.

Chapter 12

Regulation Mismatch in Tackling CO_2 Emissions

Claude Crampes*

Toulouse School of Economics
Claude.Crampes@tse-fr.eu

Abstract

By defining three targets as pillars of their environmental policy (20% cleaning, 20% greening, and 20% saving energy by 2020), European authorities are putting out noisy signals on what the actual objective is and how to achieve it. I show that, whereas the community-wide CO_2 market (named Emissions Trading System, ETS) is one of the right answers to fix greenhouse gas emissions, the policy tools implemented by Member States to achieve the greening and saving objectives reduce the efficiency of ETS and push the CO_2 price down. I then analyze the efficiency distortions created by the forced entry of renewable energy sources into the mix of electricity production.

Keywords: Environmental policy, emissions trading system, renewable energy sources, State aid.

JEL Classification Codes: Q38, Q42, Q48, Q58.

1. Introduction

Starting with "Directive 96/92/EC concerning common rules for the internal market in electricity", the European authorities decided that the electricity industry should join telecoms and similar network activities in the competition adventure. Transmission and distribution infrastructure was recognized as a natural monopoly, and therefore excluded from the field. By contrast, production and supply to final customers have progressively

*I thank the participants of the 2013 CRESSE conference for their comments, and Yossi Spiegel for his attentive reading of the first draft. All remaining errors and omissions are my own.

been opened to competitive mechanisms under the scrutiny of national and community competition authorities. Producers and suppliers can now freely enter and exit the market, as cheap and high-quality firms are allowed to supplant badly performing ones.

Incumbents have however fiercely (and successfully) resisted this opening process, often with the help of Member State governments which like the concept of national champions, particularly on the energy battlefield where independence and security of supply are viewed as strategic. There is another reason why the liberalization process is far from successful in the European Union (EU) electricity industry. Global warming has progressively become a central concern in energy policy[1] and the tools forged by the European Community to tackle greenhouse gas (GHG) emissions have been wrongly designed, resulting in State aid becoming the rule rather than the exception. State aid should be granted only under specific circumstances because it distorts competition mechanisms, frequently on purpose. With the surge of environmental concerns, State aid is everywhere in the energy sector. Not only does it distort market mechanisms, it is also inefficiently adapted to the aim it is supposed to pursue. For example, according to Marcantonini and Ellerman (2013, p. 20), in Germany "the CO_2 abatement cost of wind for 2006–2010 is on average €43/tCO_2, higher than the historical EU Emissions Trading System (ETS) carbon price but of the same order of magnitude. On the contrary, the CO_2 abatement cost of solar is very high, the average for 2006–2010 is €537/tCO_2, much above any possible realistic carbon price." (Recall that during the year 2013, the carbon price has fluctuated between €3 and €5/tCO_2.) In this chapter, I identify the mistakes that have led to the current costly framework and propose arguments in favor of dismantling the system of subsidies to renewable energy sources (RES) of electricity.

In Section 2, I explain the discrepancy between what the policy to reduce CO_2 emissions should be and how it is implemented by the European authorities. In particular, I show that the European Trading System, the flagship of the EU environmental policy, is endangered by complementary policies fixing targets for renewables and energy saving. In Section 3, I discuss the distortions created by State aid aimed at promoting renewable

[1] See OECD (2006).

sources of energy in the technology mix, and in Section 4, I present some brief concluding remarks.

2. Inefficient Environmental Regulation

In 2005, following the Kyoto protocol (1997) which had the objective to slow down global warming, the EU launched the ETS, a cap-and-trade mechanism dedicated to limiting GHG emissions.[2] This initiative, justified on economic grounds, was unfortunately complemented later by mandatory targets in terms of RES and consumption reduction that impair the efficiency of ETS and increase the cost of reaching the GHG target.

2.1. *One objective, three directives*

The environmental policy of the EU is currently driven by three directives:

- Directive 2009/29/EC to achieve at least a 20% reduction in GHG by 2020 compared to 1990.
- Directive 2009/28/EC to reach a 20% share of RES in overall EU energy consumption by 2020.[3]
- Directive 2012/27/EU to save 20% of the EU's energy consumption compared to projections for 2020.

Such profusion of regulation raises many questions, in particular: Why do we need three objectives (and directives)? Are these objectives mutually consistent? Are they consistent with EU competition policy, with EU industrial policy, and with EU tax policy?

Let us first look at the problem starting from the following situation focused on the electricity industry:

- the surplus derived from electricity consumption q is $S(q)$, an increasing and concave function;

[2]Directive 2003/87/CE.

[3]The list of RES is fixed: production of energy from wind, solar, aerothermal, geothermal, hydrothermal and ocean energy, hydropower, biomass, landfill gas, sewage treatment plant gas, and biogases.

- two production technologies have been installed: one serves to produce quantity x at marginal cost c_x, the second to produce y at marginal cost c_y, where $c_x < c_y$.

This very simple situation is not uncommon in national electricity industries, with x standing for electricity from coal-fired plants and y for electricity from an additional primary energy, natural gas for example.[4]

Assume that the installed capacity to produce x, labeled K_x, is such that $S'^{-1}(c_x) < K_x$. The optimal dispatch is the triplet (x, y, q) that maximizes the net social surplus, that is

$$\max_{x,y,q} S(q) - c_x x - c_y y \quad \text{s.t. } q \leq x + y,\ x \leq K_x,\ y \leq K_y. \tag{1}$$

The social planner will then choose

$$q^o = x^o = \arg\{S'(x) = c_x\} < K_x, \quad y^o = 0. \tag{2}$$

This allocation can be implemented by a price for electricity $p^o = c_x$.

Assume now that scientists prove that x is emitting pollutants $e(x)$, which is an increasing function. This generates an environmental cost $c(e)$, which is increasing and convex. By contrast, technology y emits few pollutants, normalized to 0. To simplify, also assume that

$$\arg\{c_x + c'(e(x))e'(x) = c_y\} < S'^{-1}(c_y), \tag{3}$$

which means that the marginal cost of y intersects with the marginal social cost of technology x (including the environmental damage) before it intersects with the marginal surplus curve.

Given these new elements, the social planner must solve

$$\max_{x,y,q} S(q) - c_x x - c(e(x)) - c_y y \quad \text{s.t. } q \leq x + y,\ x \leq K_x,\ y \leq K_y. \tag{4}$$

The solution is the environmentally-friendly dispatch

$$x^* = \arg\{c_x + c'(e(x))e'(x) = c_y\},\ q^* = S'^{-1}(c_y),\ y^* = q^* - x^*. \tag{5}$$

[4]See International Energy Agency (2012), "Key World Energy Statistics", p. 24, www.iea.org.

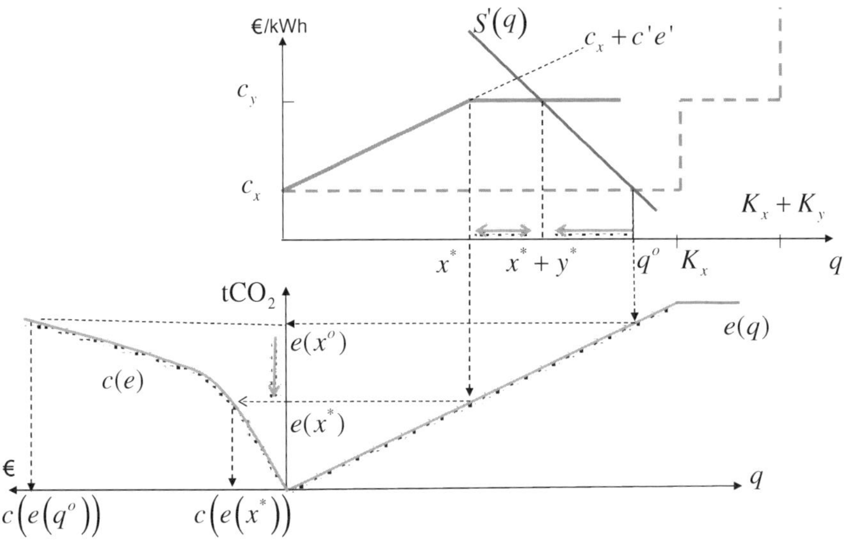

Figure 1. Myopic vs. virtuous dispatch.

The upper panel in Figure 1 shows the marginal cost of electricity (i) with the environmental damage (bold piecewise linear curve) and (ii) without the environmental damage (dotted staircase curve), and the decreasing marginal gross surplus $S^{'}(q)$. The right lower panel shows the polluting emissions; they increase with the production from technology x up to capacity K_x, and then become constant given our hypothesis that y does not emit pollutants. In the left lower panel, we have drawn the environmental cost of pollutants.

As illustrated by arrows in Figure 1, there are three differences between the short-sighted dispatch (2) and the environmentally-friendly dispatch (5):

- the non-polluting technology partially replaces the polluting one: $y^* > y^o = 0,\ x^* < x^o = q^o$,
- polluting emissions are decreased: $e(x^*) < e(x^o)$,
- total consumption is decreased: $q^* = x^* + y^* < q^o$.

Now the question is: how to implement the virtuous dispatch x^*, y^*, q^*?

The economist's answer is very simple: environmental damages are externalities that can be curbed either by a price (Pigou, 1920) or by the allocation of rights to pollute (Coase, 1960). We know since Weitzman (1974) that these two tools are not strictly equivalent,[5] but at least they oblige polluters to internalize the cost of their private decisions.[6] In our illustration, since the marginal environmental damage is $c'(e(x))e'(x) = c_y - c_x$ at the optimum, given the piecewise linear shape of the electricity marginal cost, the tax charged to x's operators should be $t_- < c_y - c_x$ for each kWh below x^* and $t_+ > c_y - c_x$ for each kWh above x^*. The alternative is to give for free or to sell producers the right to emit the quantity $e(x^*)$.

2.2. *The CO_2 market and its toxic companions*

The solution adopted by European authorities to reduce CO_2 emissions is the ETS, launched in 2005. It is a cap-and-trade system where a mandatory target has been imposed on almost 12,000 industrial plants throughout Europe, plus the airlines companies since 2012.[7] They are the obligated parties. For each obligated firm, the adjustment between the individual target and the initial endowment is reached partially, thanks to technical investment to abate polluting emissions, partially through trade. The market part of the mechanism generates a carbon price. *Per se*, it is a good solution:

- it is the market alternative to the Pigovian tax, necessary to fix a negative externality; it is efficient when well designed;
- it sends a scarcity signal to polluters;

---

[5] In our example, they are equivalent because there is no randomness in either preferences or costs. See also Hepburn (2006).

[6] The Polluter Pays Principle (PPP) is established by Article 191 of the "Treaty on the Functioning of the European Union". In fact, a large share of the additional cost is passed through to the consumers who are the ultimate polluters (see Fabra and Reguant, 2013).

[7] In April 2013, the EU decided to temporarily suspend requirements for flights from or to non-European countries. The legislation continues to apply to flights within and between countries in Europe. The International Civil Aviation Organization was expected to reach a global agreement to tackle aviation emissions in line with the EU ETS during its autumn meeting. It reached consensus on October 3, 2013 for a roadmap to create a market-based scheme curbing aviation emissions by 2020, but rejected the EU proposal allowing it to apply its ETS to foreign airlines in the interim.

- it allows firms to adjust the volumes they need;[8]
- it generates public revenues.[9]

With the CO_2 emissions from EU industrial plants under control, one would expect the European authorities to be satisfied. In reality, they are not. First, they are dissatisfied because the quantity controlled is only a small fraction of worldwide emissions, and the EU effort opens the door to free-riding by non-EU countries. The second reason is more surprising. Dissatisfaction comes from the price of the CO_2 ton (formerly in secondary markets, now at the initial auctions). So far, the tCO_2 price has remained rather low, around €3 during the first semester of 2013, well below the penalty for non-compliance (€40/tCO_2 during the first round 2005–2007, €100/tCO_2 during the second 2008–2012, and the third 2013–2020). The authorities have apparently forgotten why ETS was created, and have made fund-raising their main concern because they want to feed high public expenditures and subsidize non-profitable clean energy sources and energy efficiency programs. This is why during spring 2013, the Commission proposed a "backloading" of allowances, which meant postponing a series of carbon permit auctions, in the hope that provisional scarcity would push the price up. The European Parliament rejected the proposal on April 16 but finally accepted it on July 3. Hence, the allocations of some 2014 permits by Member States to their industries will be held back from auction until 2019. This confusion between objectives and tools is counterproductive not only for the control of CO_2 emissions but also for the tax-collecting objective politicians have in mind, as we explain below.

The initial mistake comes from the alignment of the three effects identified in Figure 1. This is an error because with a clear policy to limit GHG emissions, there is no need to subsidize less polluting technologies and to limit consumption: as we have seen, $y^* > y^o$ and $q^* < q^o$ are natural consequences of the carbon policy. Independent quantitative targets for

[8]See OECD (2011).

[9]Since January 2013, we have entered Phase III where all electricity producers must buy the rights to emit CO_2 instead of receiving them for free on a grandfathering basis like in Phases I and II. Overall, 40% of allowances are to be auctioned. On the auctioning rules, see European Commission (2010).

20% energy saving and 20% of renewables in the energy mix are inefficient solutions because

- they are viewed as genuine objectives whereas they do not directly fix an externality;
- they require large amounts of red tape and State aid;
- they increase the cost of reaching the CO_2 target;
- they introduce noise into the CO_2 price and public revenues from allowances auctions.

The latter two points can be explained as follows. Let z_a stand for the direct abatement effort of polluting firms at unit cost w_a (e.g., switching from coal to natural gas, carbon storage), z_b the effort to comply with additional rules at unit cost w_b (i.e., adopt renewable sources or decrease energy consumption), and $g(z_a, z_b)$ the resulting decrease in CO_2 emissions. The optimal combination of efforts is the solution to

$$\min_{z_a, z_b} w_a z_a + w_b z_b \text{ s.t. } g(z_a, z_b) \geq T, \tag{6}$$

where the target is $T = 20\%$ of 1990 emissions. The solution is $z_a^* = z_a(w_a, w_b, T), z_b^* = z_b(w_a, w_b, T)$ defined by $g(z_a, z_b) = T$ and $\frac{\partial g(z_a, z_b)/\partial z_a}{\partial g(z_a, z_b)/\partial z_b} = \frac{w_a}{w_b}$ and the cost of this optimal policy is $C^*(T) = w_a z_a^* + w_b z_b^*$.

As the authorities impose the additional constraint $z_b \geq \underline{z}_b$, we have two possibilities:

(i) either $\underline{z}_b \leq z_b(w_a, w_b, T)$: the new constraint is redundant since it is met by the solution to (6). In that case, all the subsidies allocated to meet the additional constraint are pure windfall gains for beneficiaries;

(ii) or $\underline{z}_b > z_b(w_a, w_b, T)$: the least-cost solution is no longer feasible. The constrained solution is $z_a^o = \arg[g(z_a, \underline{z}_b) = T], z_b^o = \underline{z}_b$. As we can see in Figure 2, there are two important consequences: (a) the solution is more costly than it should be, $w_a z_a^o + w_b z_b^o > C^*(T)$ because of the additional constraint(s) represented by the secondary target(s) and (b) since $z_b^o > z_b^*$, the direct effort to abate CO_2 emissions is reduced: $z_a^o < z_a^*$.

It is important to insist on the second effect ($z_a^o < z_a^*$) because it illustrates how bad policy can impair good economic tools. On the

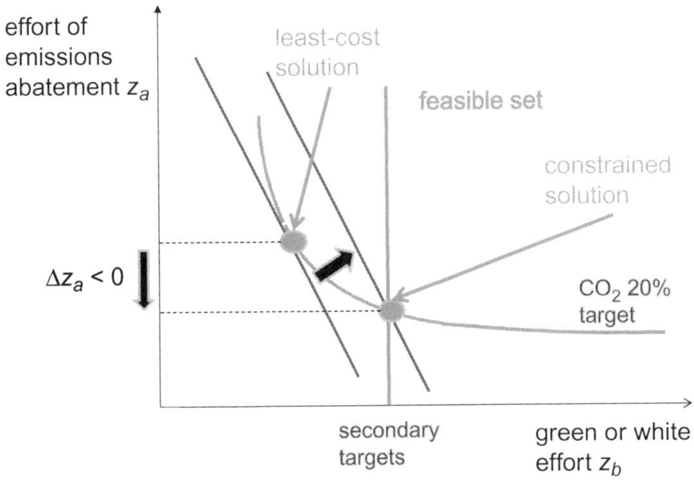

Figure 2. Cost minimization to reach the CO_2 target.

CO_2 market, supply is basically fixed and equal to the European Union Allowances determined for each year of the current phase by the EU authorities.[10] Demand is derived from profit maximization by industrial polluters. As in the case of any input, the demand for allowances decreases in line with the price of allowances and of complementary inputs (for example, coal), and increases with the price of substitutes (for example, abatement technologies) and that of all the output drivers (for example, global activity, electricity price, etc.). Decreasing the need for abatement effort automatically decreases the cost of the related technologies, which depresses the allowance requirement since abatement effort and emission credits are close substitutes. In a price–quantity diagram, it is then easy to understand that because of the secondary targets, the demand for permits is shifted leftwards, resulting in a price decrease.

In a nutshell, the tighter the green constraint (20% of renewables) and the white constraint (20% of energy saving), the lower the price of

[10]There also exist credits from complementary programs: Emissions Reducing Units (from Joint Implementation) and Certified Emission Reduction (from Clean Development Mechanism) that introduce some price-elasticity in supply; see cdm.unfccc.int/about and ji.unfccc.int.

CO_2 on the ETS. This negative side-effect is apparently a bad surprise for governments in needs of tax revenues. The fact that emissions are kept under control has become a secondary concern.

3. The Promotion of Renewables

Regarding direct CO_2 abatement, EU Member States have no choice: ETS is mandatory. By contrast, they remain free to organize as they see fit the path toward 20% renewables and 20% energy saving. This explains the wide variety of regulations and State aid used by various countries to reach the targets.[11] In the EU competition policy toolbox, the control of State aid plays an important role in limiting potential distortions that governments could create when they sustain domestic agents by financial and non-financial means. The principle settled by Article 107 of the Treaty is simple: "State aid is forbidden, except if". Aid in favor of environment protection is one of the categories exempted from notification requirements.[12] In other words, when it comes to the 20-20-20 objective, the principle changes to: "State aid is permitted, except if".

In the following paragraphs, I limit the analysis to the "Green 20" strategy, that is to the promotion of RES. I discuss the current EU environment policy in favor of RES in two steps: (i) RES have several handicaps that impede their efficient entry into the energy mix; and (ii) the various tools used to promote RES, in particular feed-in tariffs (FIT), have severe distortive effects.

3.1. *Efficient energy mix*

3.1.1. Technology choice without RES

The basic model for electricity producers burning coal or natural gas is as follows: to produce quantity q_{ft} at date t, it costs c_f per unit below the equipment capacity K_f. Consequently, the optimal equipment to install and quantities to produce given the increasing and concave surplus functions

[11] See Butler and Neuhoff (2008) and Ragwitz *et al.* (2012).

[12] The others are aid in favor of small enterprises, R&D, employment, and training.

$S_t(.)$ are the solution to

$$\max_{K_f,\{q_{ft}\}} \quad -r_f K_f + \sum_{t=1}^{N_f} \frac{S_t(q_{ft}) - c_f q_{ft}}{(1+\rho)^t} \qquad \text{s.t. } q_{ft} \le K_f \quad \forall t, \tag{7}$$

where N_f is the (exogenously given) life of the equipment, r_f the unit cost of capacity, and ρ the interest rate.

From the first-order conditions, we obtain

$$q^*_{ft} = \begin{cases} \arg\left[S_t^{'}(q_{ft}) = c_f\right] < K_f^* \text{ if } S_t^{'}(K_f^*) < c_f \\ \qquad K_f^* \quad \text{otherwise} \end{cases} \tag{8}$$

$$\text{and } K_f^* = \arg\left[\sum_{t\in N_f^*} \frac{S_t^{'}(K_f) - c_f}{(1+\rho)^t} = r_f\right], \tag{9}$$

where N_f^* is the subset of periods where the equipment is saturated, i.e., $q^*_{ft} = K^*_f$. In addition to the local conditions (8) and (9), we must check whether the overall discounted net surplus is non-negative at the solution:

$$-r_f K_f^* + \sum_{t=1}^{N_f} \frac{S_t(q^*_{ft}) - c_f q^*_{ft}}{(1+\rho)^t} \ge 0. \tag{10}$$

Otherwise, $K_f^* = 0$ and $q^*_{ft} = 0$ at all t.

Under perfect competition, the expected profit of producers is $-r_f K_f + \sum_{t=1}^{N_f} \frac{(p_t^e - c_f) q_{ft}}{(1+\rho)^t}$ where $p_t^e(K_f, c_f) = \max[S_t^{'}(K_f), c_f]$ is the equilibrium electricity spot price at t given K_f.

The non-negativity of discounted cash-flow imposes

$$\sum_{t\in N_f^*} \frac{S_t^{'}(K_f) - c_f}{(1+\rho)^t} \ge r_f. \tag{11}$$

If all firms have the same technology, free entry transforms (11) into an equality by decreasing $p_t^e(K_f, c_f) = S_t^{'}(K_f)$. It determines the equilibrium capacity to install, equal to the optimal one K_f^*. By the free entry process, firms balance their budget at the long-run competitive equilibrium.

If technologies are heterogeneous, there are more than two types of market state to determine the spot price. It remains true that at off-peak periods, the price is equal to the operating cost of the cheapest technology and at peak periods, it is equal to the marginal utility of the whole capacity. In between (low and medium demand), the price is determined by the operating cost of intermediate technologies. The peaking firms (those with a large c_f) are called into operation only for a very small number of peak hours N_f^*. They can therefore survive only if they have a low capital cost r_f and prices $p_t^e = S_t'(\sum_f K_f)$ are sufficiently high during the N_f^* periods.[13] Again, at the long-run competitive equilibrium, all the active firms balance their budget.[14]

3.1.2. Technology choice with RES

How does this mechanism change when electricity from RES is available? Most of the technologies based on RES have two characteristics: (i) they can work only if a non-controllable source of primary energy is available (wind, water along the river, solar energy) and (ii) the operating cost is nil when the source is available. Assume there are two states of nature on the supply side at each period: a state with plenty of primary energy (windy days) with probability ν_t, and a state without any primary energy (days without any wind). The staircase line in Figure 3 is the merit order in windy states of nature when fossil-fuel capacity K_f and RES capacity K_i are available: first, produce at 0 marginal cost up to K_i, then serve additional demand at marginal cost c_f up to $K_i + K_f$. In states of the world without wind, the merit order is just shifted leftwards up to quantity K_i.

Ex-post, if capacity K_i is installed on top of K_f, the market equilibrium price at period t will be as follows:

- with probability ν_t, $p_t^e = 0$ off-peak, $p_t^e = S_t'(K_i)$ at periods of low demand $\widetilde{N}_i^*$, $p_t^e = c_f$ at periods of medium demand N_i^*, and $p_t^e = S_t'(K_i + K_f)$ at peak periods N_{if}^* (see Figure 3);
- with probability $(1 - \nu_t)$, $p_t^e = c_f$ at periods of low demand and $p_t^e = S_t'(K_f)$ at periods of high demand N_f^*.

---

[13] Actually, prices are capped in most wholesale markets: for example €3,000/MWh on EPEXspot. The cap creates a "missing money" problem that some countries solve by capacity payments, capacity obligations, or capacity markets.

[14] The first proof was published in Boîteux (1949).

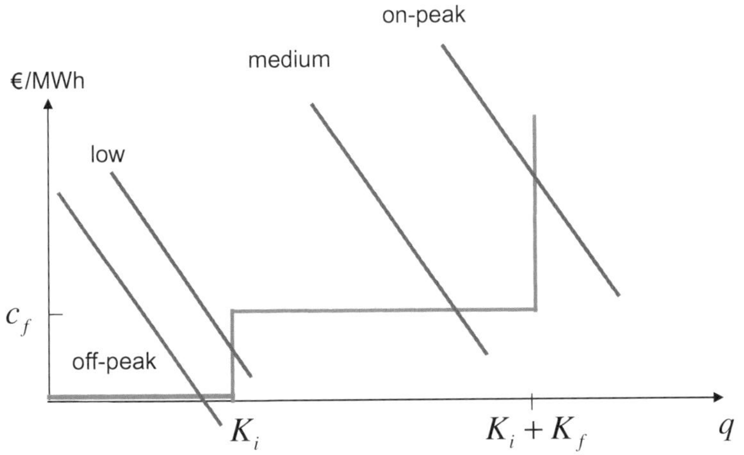

Figure 3. Peak-load pricing with RES and non-RES.

Ex-ante, given the expected electricity market prices and the unit cost r_i of production plants, the entry of RES is profitable if and only if

$$\sum_{t \in \widetilde{N}_i^*} \nu_t \frac{S_t'(K_i)}{(1+\rho)^t} + \sum_{t \in N_i^*} \nu_t \frac{c_f}{(1+\rho)^t} + \sum_{t \in N_{if}^*} \nu_t \frac{S_t'(K_i + K_f)}{(1+\rho)^t} \geq r_i. \qquad (12)$$

Under pure market mechanisms, that is without any public intervention, we see that profitability requires

- a low capital cost r_i, a long life duration N_i, and large probabilities ν_t;
- large operating cost c_f in non-RES;
- small capacities of both types in order to push $S_t'(K_i)$ and $S_t'(K_i+K_f)$ up.

Note that benefits are boosted by positive correlation between RES availability ν_t and marginal willingness-to-pay for electricity, i.e., in regions where ν_t is large at dates t of large $S_t'(.)$. Clearly, windmill producers earn more money if the wind blows in the day rather than at night and solar panel owners would prefer the sun to shine at full capacity at the end of winter working days.[15]

[15]In countries where peak demand is due to air conditioning, photovoltaic (PV) panel production is positively correlated with demand.

As for fossil-fuel plants,

- when a large quantity of RES is available, a positive margin only appears at peak periods N^*_{if}. In states $\widetilde{N}^*_i$ fossil-fuel plants do not produce and $p_t = c_f$ in states N^*_i.
- without RES, margins are positive at peak periods N^*_f.

The profitability of fossil-fuel plants then requires that

$$\sum_{t \in N^*_f} (1 - \nu_t) \frac{S'_t(K_f) - c_f}{(1+\rho)^t} + \sum_{t \in N^*_{if}} \nu_t \frac{S'_t(K_i + K_f) - c_f}{(1+\rho)^t} \geq r_f. \qquad (13)$$

Under free entry, the long-run equilibrium capacities are those determined when (12) and (13) are equalities instead of inequalities. Given the current values of parameters $(c_f, r_f, N_f, r_i, N_i, \rho, \{\nu_t\})$, most renewables-based technologies cannot be profitable when condition (13) is met as an equality.[16] Their cost r_i is still too high, their availability $\{\nu_t\}$ too low, and their life N_i too short as compared to the characteristics of thermal plants (c_f, r_f, N_f). This explains why State aid is necessary for RES to reach profitability. In Section 3.2, we consider alternative policies aimed at making RES profitable, even though we have seen in Section 2 that it should not be an objective *per se*.

3.2. *Certificates, tariffs, taxes, and the like*

Because of high cost, intermittency, and geographical dispersion, RES cannot be developed without government help. The expected "grid parity", that is the possibility for these energies to compete against fossil sources on a level field is a matter of misunderstanding. It may be true that in the future, RES-electricity will have a MWh cost comparable to the cost of fossil-fuel plants. That will however not solve the intermittency feature since $\nu_t < 1$ for most dates t. The guarantee to supply a given quantity at a given date for a given duration will always be out of reach for intermittent sources

[16]Even when cost parameters make RES competitive, long-run equilibrium is feasible only if consumers are reactive to scarcity at production nodes through state-contingent prices. We address this point in Section 3.2.1. For a detailed analysis of the case where there is one single time period, see Ambec and Crampes (2012).

such as wind power and solar energy without additional backup or storage equipment.[17] Consequently, the development of RES-electricity creates a public commitment to constrain the future industry structure. The EU "Green 20" strategy actually authorizes Member States to launch industrial policy in the energy sector.

In this mix of environmental and industrial policy, some Member States use direct subsidies for investment, while others prefer quota obligations, sometimes combined with tradable green certificates. However, the most widely used financial tool across the community is a non-market system: fixed FIT paid to green producers.

In the following paragraphs, I first show how RES are positively impacted by an increase in the operating cost of electricity producers burning fossil fuel. I then compare the effects of the tools currently used to promote RES.

3.2.1. Increasing the carbon cost

As shown in Section 2, the basic tool for environmental regulation should consist in obliging producers who use polluting technologies to internalize their negative externalities. This can be done by a tax equal to the marginal environmental damage, by the obligation to buy the right to emit, or by free allowances up to a given total quantity. The operating cost c_f then becomes $c_f + \Delta$, where Δ stands for the tax, the fee to pay for acquiring rights or the dual value of the quantitative constraint. As inequality (12) shows, by increasing c_f to $c_f + \Delta$, the profitability condition is easier to meet for RES; as (13) shows, it becomes more difficult for non-RES, so that some plants are obliged to stop producing.

More precisely, a drastic CO_2 policy indirectly benefits RES in two ways:

- **Enrichment effect**: when demand is medium ($t \in N_i^*$) and the price is determined by non-RES technologies, RES earn a larger margin $c_f + \Delta - 0$ (if they produce, i.e., with probability ν_t).
- **Replacement effect**: the price at period t is lower when RES are used than when they are not, regardless of whether t is a low or a high demand

[17] On solar energy, see Baker *et al.* (2013); on wind power, Butler and Neuhoff (2008).

period. This means that if fossil-fuel plants were just balancing their budget before the entry of RES, it is no longer the case afterwards. Then, to rebalance inequality (13), type-f firms are obliged to decrease their installed capacity K_f. Prices consequently decrease but remain high at peak periods because of the closure of type-f plants, which is beneficial for RES, in particular if their production is positively correlated with demand.

The replacement effect is a source of potential problems in terms of security of supply. Were RES just cheaper reliable sources of energy, the entry of low-cost technologies pushing expensive ones out of the efficient mix would be good news for consumers.[18] Unfortunately, without smart meters and appliances, electricity consumption is weakly responsive to short-term scarcity signals such as price increases and warning messages sent by the system operator.[19] As a result, at each date t, consumers are not reactive to the state of nature at production plant locations. Assume that Δ is fixed high enough for RES to be profitable. Then $K_i > 0$, but we know that $q_{it} = 0$ with probability $\nu_t > 0$ at period t. Unless we accept black-outs, electricity being non-storable, production at period t must be the same whatever the speed of wind at windfarm sites. For example, at peak periods, we have seen that p_t^e should be equal to $S_t^{'}(K_f)$ with probability $(1 - \nu_t)$ and to $S_t^{'}(K_i + K_f)$ with probability ν_t. Actually, fossil-fuel plants face two *ex-post* obligations: (a) to keep total production independent of the state of nature and (b) to leave priority to RES in the efficient dispatch. Then, if RES are very abundant, fossil-fuel plants must produce $q^i_{ft} = 0$ when RES are available and $q^{\bar{i}}_{ft} = K_i$ when they are not, which requires the installation of $K_f = K_i$.

[18]In Germany, at noon on July 21, 2013, solar production reached the total record of 24 GW, that is more or less the production of 24 nuclear plants. The two main incumbents, RWE and E.ON, are contemplating the closure of some 15 GW of coal and gas-fired plants.

[19]With the exception of big industrial consumers who have contracts at low prices to compensate for curtailment clauses. For smaller customers (small industrial and business clients, households), service providers propose remotely controlled load-shedding (see Crampes and Léautier, 2012).

More generally, denoting by $\overline{p}_t$ the non-state-dependent price at t[20] and by $D_t(\overline{p}_t)$, the corresponding demand, fossil-fuel plants must be ready to produce

$$q_{ft} = \begin{cases} D_t(\overline{p}_t) - K_i & \text{with probability } \nu_t \\ D_t\left(\overline{p}_t\right) & \text{with probability } 1 - \nu_t. \end{cases} \tag{14}$$

Assuming that fossil-fuel firms produce at full capacity at peak periods without RES and that black-outs and brown-outs are not permitted, we have $K_f = D_t(\overline{p}_t)$ or $\overline{p}_t = S_t^{'}(K_f)$ for $t \in N_f^*$. We also have $\overline{p}_t = S_t^{'}(K_f)$ at peak periods with RES $\left(t \in N_{if}^*\right)$ because of the impossibility to have state-contingent prices, but fossil-fuel producers can only sell $D_t(\overline{p}_t) - K_i$. The budget balancing conditions of the two types of producers are then

$$\sum_t \nu_t \frac{\overline{p}_t}{(1+\rho)^t} \geq r_i \tag{15}$$

$$\sum_{t \in N_f^*} (1 - \nu_t) \frac{\overline{p}_t - c_f}{(1+\rho)^t} + \sum_{t \in N_{if}^*} \nu_t \frac{\overline{p}_t - c_f}{(1+\rho)^t} \frac{D_t(\overline{p}_t) - K_i}{K_f} \geq r_f. \tag{16}$$

As shown in Ambec and Crampes (2012), when consumers are not reactive to state-contingent prices, lower energy prices combined with the dramatic fall in non-RES electricity sales due to RES priority results in the impossibility to meet the separate conditions (15) and (16) simultaneously: a zero net present value in (16) gives a strictly positive net profit to RES, and a zero net present value in (15) provokes financial losses of non-RES plants. The intuition is as follows: to satisfy (16), we need $\overline{p}_t \geq c_f$ in all states of nature. The RES producers then earn $\overline{p}_t - 0 \geq c_f > 0$ whenever they are active while at first best where budgets are balanced, the price should be 0 during off-peak periods where RES are available.

To reach a long-run equilibrium, it is necessary to implement structural arrangements (mergers), contractual arrangements (guarantee of supply), or portfolio obligations to balance the producers' budget globally, i.e., to compensate for the financial losses of fossil-fuel plants with the benefits

[20]In real life, because of the absence of smart meters, not only electricity prices cannot depend on the state of nature, but they cannot even depend on date.

of RES. Besides back-up by thermal plants, RES intermittency can also be balanced by demand curtailment, energy storage, and imports.

3.2.2. Technology-pushed vs. demand-pulled entry

The above analysis with or without price-reactive consumers is based on the possibility for RES to be competitive against non-RES, in particular because of a high CO_2 cost. In reality, RES are far from competitive, and EU Member States are obliged to force the entry of technologies based on renewables into the energy mix by violating competition rules.[21] In the following paragraphs, we consider first subsidies to R&D in RES technologies and second subsidies to electricity demand.

Subsidies to R&D. When investors face a technology with

$$\sum_{t=1}^{N_i} \nu_t \frac{p_t q_{it}}{(1+\rho)^t} < r_i K_i, \tag{17}$$

where p_t is exogenous and $q_{it} \leq K_i$, they naturally consider whether the inequality can be reversed by means of R&D investment that could increase N_i and ν_t, and decrease r_i. There are at least two advantages with the R&D solution: (i) decision-makers can choose the best option within their toolbox and (ii) they bear the risk of failure, which is the role of entrepreneurs as they are less risk-averse than the other agents. There are also at least two drawbacks: (i) because of economies of scale and learning by doing, drastic improvement can be out of reach when many agents act separately and (ii) R&D is a source of positive externalities that individual decision-makers cannot easily internalize. Then, since reversing the inequality in (17) is now a community objective for RES, if joint ventures necessitate excessive transaction costs or are impeded under Article 100 of the Treaty, State aid becomes necessary. Given its distortive effects, State aid is limited

[21] "State aid may be justified if the cost of production of renewable energy is higher than the cost of production based on less environmentally-friendly sources and if there is no mandatory community standard concerning the share of energy from renewable sources for individual undertakings. The high cost of production of some types of renewable energy does not allow undertakings to charge competitive prices on the market and thus creates a market-access barrier for renewable energy" (European Commission, 2008, Paragraph 48).

by guidelines issued by EU authorities. In particular *State aid for research, development and innovation in the environmental field is subject to the rules set out in the Community framework for State aid for research and development and innovation. However, the market diffusion stage of eco-innovation (acquisition of an eco-innovation asset) is covered by these Guidelines.*[22] In other words, upstream State aid aimed at reversing (17) for RES must follow the same rules defined in European Commission (2006)[23] as for any innovation in any industry. That is good news for the economist who considers there to be no reason to make the Green 20% strategy a *sui generis* objective. It is bad news for the economist who observes that, given that the Green 20% is now a *sui generis* objective, in the absence of any upstream specific encouragement, Member States will systematically adopt downstream State aid.

Premiums and FIT. Another way to change the sign in (17) is to increase p_t and q_{it}, and decrease ρ.

A reduction in interest rates for loans dedicated to financing green investment is a simple solution, but given the high cost of these technologies, it can be true that they remain unprofitable even when $\rho = 0$. Complementary solutions are then necessary.

The quantity sold can systematically be increased up to the capacity available by means of priority rules: the system operator must accept any injection coming from RES before energy from plants using sources not on the list mentioned by Directive 2009/28/EC.[24] After capacities have been installed, this is not a distortion of competition, given that RES generically have an operating cost close to zero, below the operating cost of thermal plants. Why it then appears as an obligation is unclear: it is actually *ex-post* efficient to include RES first in the merit order when available (see Figure 3). However, this obligation may be a source of inefficiency under specific circumstances: at some hours, nuclear or coal-fueled plants have negative economic costs due to starting, warming, and ramping constraints; therefore, at some hours, they should be ranked before RES that have a zero

---

[22] European Commission (2008), Paragraph 63.

[23] Note that this framework is currently under review.

[24] Except for safety and technical reasons, in particular when lines are congested.

operating cost in the merit order. This is forbidden, given the rule of priority to RES. This can be illustrated as follows:

- there are two types of period: off-peak at night (n), and peak at day (d);
- because of ramping-rate constraints, the unit cost of production at a given hour depends on what the firm was doing during the preceding hour. Specifically, to keep the model simple, the unit cost is $c(0)$ at night and $c(q_n)$ in the day, with $c'(q_n) < 0$.

Then, for the firm that solves

$$\max_{q_n, q_d} S_n(q_n) - c(0)q_n + S_d(q_d) - c(q_n)q_d,$$

the first-order conditions are

$$S_n^{'}(q_n^*) - c(0) - c'(q_n^*)q_d^* = 0 \quad (18)$$

$$S_d^{'}(q_d^*) - c(q_n^*) = 0. \quad (19)$$

During night hours, the economic cost of the thermal producer is $c(0)+c'(q_n^*)q_d^*$. Since it is below $c(0)$, it gives producers the incentive to produce off-peak more than if $c' \equiv 0$. The welfare loss resulting from $S_n^{'}(q_n^*) < c(0)$ is more than compensated at day, thanks to the consecutive decrease from $c(0)$ to $c(q_n^*)$. The point is that if (i) the ramping effect $|c'|$ is strong and (ii) the expected daytime demand q_d^* is high, the accounting cost at night $c(0)$ may be below the opportunity gain $-c'(q_n^*)q_d^*$ so that $c(0) + c'(q_n^*)q_d^* < 0$. This explains why electricity producers are allowed to submit negative bids on wholesale markets.[25] When they do so, they should be ranked first in the merit order since bids from RES should, at the lowest, be equal to 0. Actually, this efficient market mechanism is impaired by wind-mill operators who also submit negative bids. We now explain that it results from the tariff policy in favor of RES.

To change the inequality in (17), many Member States have chosen to pay electricity producers using renewable sources a unit price $\alpha p_t + F_t$,

[25] See for example the auctions organized for France, Germany/Austria and Switzerland on www.epexspot.com/en/market-data/auction/curve/auction-aggregated-curve/ and for the Netherlands and the UK on www.apxgroup.com/market-results/apx-power-nl/aggregated-curves/.

where p_t is the market price, α a coefficient in [0, 1], and $F_t > 0$ a premium raised from other agents of the industry (mainly consumers). In the extreme case where $\alpha = 0$, RES producers are totally disconnected from market signals. France, Germany, Italy, and Spain have hugely subsidized the solar and wind energies by guaranteeing generous selling prices F_t (FIT) for 20 years to the electricity producers equipped with windmills and photovoltaic panels.[26] These programs have been so successful that they have endangered the financial equilibrium of the funding system in the four countries obliging governments to downsize tariffs and redefine conditions for eligibility. Meanwhile, FIT that reward producers using wind resources have also impaired the efficiency of negative bids. If a windmill operator anticipates a reward $\alpha p_t + F_t$ per MWh when producing, any spot price $p_t > \frac{-F_t}{\alpha}$ is still profitable since the operating cost is nil. The operator is then encouraged to bid slightly above $\frac{-F_t}{\alpha}$, which can still be very low,[27] guaranteeing a positive margin on every MWh injected, even though the equilibrium spot price is negative. In Germany, negative equilibrium prices have almost always occurred in early-hour markets of low demand (1:00 am–2:00 am, 2:00 am–3:00 am, etc.) where large quantities of wind energy from the North Sea were available. Whether this can prevent thermal plants from being dispatched at early hours and be operational at low cost when the morning demand is at a peak cannot be taken into consideration by the system operator under the current regulation.

Public authorities often emphasize several side benefits on top of limiting global warming from the promotion of RES. They quote in particular increasing energy security, leading Europe out of the economic crisis and creating new technology jobs.[28] All these side-effects are disputable, in

[26]In other countries, $\alpha = 1$ and F_t is a supplement reward from selling certificates associated with RES production. Certificates are sold to obligated parties (suppliers in Belgium and UK, producers in Italy, grid companies in Germany). The tradable green certificate system looks like the EU ETS except that it is organized on a national basis. It therefore has the same qualities and shortcomings as ETS, in particular the administrative cost of registering and controlling.

[27]However, energy exchanges impose price floors: on Epexspot, bids cannot be below €–3,000/MWh. See www.eex.com/de/document/74115/EEX_MARKET_MONITOR-Q4_2009-english_final.pdf.

[28]In Directive 2009/28/EC Preamble 4 says: "When favouring the development of the market for renewable energy sources, it is necessary to take into account the positive

particular, the possibility to give European industries an advantage in the field of PV panels. By relying on very generous FIT, Member States hoped that consumers would massively buy PV panels so that, thanks to learning-by-doing and economies of scale, the production cost of panels r_i would go down and change the direction of the inequality (17). This did occur, but governments have forgotten that under this subsidization regime (i) consumers, not manufacturers, are the risk-takers: they bear regulatory uncertainty, and they can be stuck for 20 years with obsolete panels, and (ii) consumers behave like any electricity producer, choosing the least-cost equipment, which is eventually imported from Asia. Indeed, high FIT have created a violent shock of demand in the market where parts of green equipment are manufactured. The shock has excluded European champions from the equipment market instead of giving them a boost.[29] The industrial policy slice of the promotion plan is then a total failure.

---

impact on regional and local development opportunities, export prospects, social cohesion and employment opportunities, in particular as concerns SMEs and independent energy producers."

In Preamble 6: "The move towards decentralized energy production has many benefits, including the utilization of local energy sources, increased local security of energy supply, shorter transport distances and reduced energy transmission losses. Such decentralization also fosters community development and cohesion by providing income sources and creating jobs locally."

Similarly, "Renewable energy is crucial to any move towards a low carbon economy. It is also a key component of the EU energy strategy. The European industry leads global renewable energy technology development. It employs 1.5 million people and by 2020 could employ a further 3 million. The promotion of renewable energy also develops a diverse range of mostly indigenous energy resources."

[29]The mechanism behind the expected development of RES through demand subsidies is based on a decrease in production cost thanks to learning-by-doing. Contrary to the logics of subsidies to R&D where an increase in demand is due to lower prices resulting from lower costs, in the FIT system, demand is the driver of the cost decrease. Therefore, with FIT, an increase in demand comes sooner than under the regime of R&D subsidies. This system can have adverse effects for competition as "learning-by-doing involves a form of sunk cost. Production leading to a gain in experience, is the cost which is sunk. Learning therefore manifests itself as an irreversibility in production possibilities" (Dasgupta and Stiglitz, 1988). This implies that under FIT, there is a potential for creating a natural monopoly instead of promoting competition. See also Crampes and Lefouili (2013).

4. Conclusions

Environmental policies commonly used in the EU are an inefficient mix of taxes, markets, subsidies, FIT, and capacity obligations. Their complexity is masking the priority that must be given to the reduction of GHG emissions. Theoretically, several tools are more efficient than only one since they allow fine tuning. Fischer and Neuwell (2008) show that the least-cost tool to reduce polluting emissions is a price or tax or dual value on polluting emissions, not indirect tools.[30] They also insist that "an optimal portfolio of policies achieves emissions reductions at a significantly lower cost than any single policy." This is true if several market failures are identified and if the tools are well chosen and well balanced. In practice, the risks of mistakes, lobbying, and opportunism increase very rapidly with the number of State aids, in particular when each target is sustained by a directive making it mandatory.

My discussion has been based on the drawbacks of the 20% RES objective because the inefficiency of the policy tools aimed at curbing polluting emissions by RES promotion is strong. I have simply mentioned the energy efficiency target because its rationale is very similar.[31] Energy efficiency should be subordinated to the reduction of negative externalities, but it sometimes increase emissions.[32] Also note that energy saving is not the natural outcome of a competition policy that promotes price decreases. Actually, energy retail prices increase whereas wholesale prices decrease because retail prices include the additional costs imposed by the environmental policy. But price increases are much higher than they should be, particularly in Germany, because the authorities have accumulated mistakes in choosing the mix of environmental tools.

[30]In a numerical application to the U.S. electricity sector, they find the following ranking in terms of welfare loss: (1) emissions price, (2) emissions performance standard, (3) fossil power tax, (4) renewables share requirement, (5) renewables subsidy, and (6) R&D subsidy.

[31]See European Council for an Energy Efficient Economy (2012). On demand response, see Torriti *et al.* (2010).

[32]In France for example, one rule to reach the 20% energy saving target requires that new buildings do not consume more than 50 kWh/m^2 of primary energy. This constraint eliminates electric boilers that store hot water at night by consuming electricity from nuclear plants. They are now replaced by gas boilers, which means an increase in the consumption of an energy that emits GHG.

References

Ambec, S. and C. Crampes (2012). "Electricity Provision with Intermittent Sources of Energy," *Resource and Energy Economics*, 34, pp. 319–336.

Baker, E., M. Fowlie, D. Lemoine and S. S. Reynolds (2013). "The Economics of Solar Electricity," *EI@Haas WP*, 240, April.

Boîteux, M. (1949). "La tarification des demandes en pointe: application de la théorie de la vente au coût marginal," Revue générale de l'électricité, août. Translated as "Peak-load pricing" in *Journal of Business* (1960), pp. 157–179. Available at www.trconsultoria.com/up_docs/sug_JTSVINEVRKWXYFMD.pdf.

Butler, L. and K. Neuhoff (2008). "Comparison of Feed in Tariff, Quota and Auction Mechanism to Support Wind Power Development," *Renewable Energy*, 33(8), pp. 1854–1867.

Coase, R. H. (1960). "The Problem of Social Cost," *Journal of Law and Economics*, III, pp. 1–44.

Crampes, C. and T.-O. Léautier (2012). "Distributed Load-Shedding in the Balancing of Electricity Markets," *EUI Working Papers*, RSCAS 2012/40, Loyola de Palacio Programme on Energy Policy.

Crampes, C. and Y. Lefouili (2013). "The Structural Effects of Feed-in Tariffs," IDEI WP.

Dasgupta, P. and J. Stiglitz (1988). "Learning-by-Doing, Market Structure and Industrial and Trade Policies," *Oxford Economic Papers*, New Series, 40(2), June, pp. 246–268.

European Commission (2006). "Community Framework for State Aid for Research and Development and Innovation," *Official Journal of the European Union C*, 323, December 30, 2006.

European Commission (2008). "Community Guidelines on State Aid for Environmental Protection," *Official Journal of the European Union*, (C.82/01).

European Commission (2010). "Commission regulation (EU) No. 1031/2010 of 12 November 2010 on the timing, administration and other aspects of auctioning of greenhouse gas emission allowances pursuant to Directive 2003/87/EC of the European Parliament and of the Council establishing a scheme for greenhouse gas emission allowances trading within the Community."

European Council for an Energy Efficient Economy (2012). "Energy efficiency obligations — the EU experience," ECEEE briefing for DG Energy on EU energy efficiency obligations on energy companies and their importance in meeting climate change and energy security challenges, March.

Fabra, N. and M. Reguant (2013). "Pass-Through of Emissions Costs in Electricity Markets," January, 2013. Available at idei.fr/doc/conf/eem/papers_2013/fabra.pdf.

Fischer, C. and R. G. Neuwel (2008). "Environmental and Technology Policies for Climate Mitigation," *Journal of Environmental Economics and Management*, 55, pp. 142–162.

Hepburn, C. (2006). "Regulation by Prices, Quantities or Both: A Review of Instrument Choices," *Oxford Review of Economic Policy*, 22(2), pp. 226–247.

OECD (2006). "Environmental Regulation and Competition," Competition Committee, November.

OECD (2011). "Emission Permits and Competition," Competition Committee, June.

Marcantonini, C. and A. D. Ellerman (2013). "The Cost of Abating CO_2 Emissions by Renewable Energy Incentives in Germany," WP-2013-005, February, MIT CEEPR.

Pigou, A. C. (1920). "The Economics of Welfare." Available at archive.org/download/economicsofwelfa00pigouoft/economicsofwelfa00pigouoft.pdf.

Ragwitz M., J. Winkler, C. Klessmann, M. Gephart and G. Resch (2012). "Recent Developments of Feed-in Systems in the EU — A Research Paper for the International Feed-In Cooperation," January. Available at www.futurepolicy.org/fileadmin/user_upload/PDF/Feed_in_Tariff/IFIC_feed-in_evaluation_Nov_2.

Torriti, J., M. G. Hassan and M. Leach (2010). "Demand Response Experience in Europe: Policies, Programmes and Implementation," *Energy*, 35(4), pp. 1575–1583, April.

Weitzman, M. (1974). "Prices vs. Quantities," *Review of Economic Studies*, 41(4), pp. 477–491.

Chapter 13

Public Policies in Investment-Intensive Industries*

Giovanni Immordino

University of Salerno
giimmo@tin.it

Michele Polo

Bocconi University and IEFE
michele.polo@unibocconi.it

Abstract

In this chapter, we review some recent work on public intervention in economic environments where firms undertake investments in research or in physical assets, and then select appropriate business practices to extract profits from the outcomes of the investment process. Public policies may take different forms: the release of an authorization; the setting of fines and damages for liability; or the choice of legal standards in antitrust law enforcement. The business practices are privately profitable but may be welfare enhancing or socially harmful. When expectations are optimistic, public policies face a trade-off between *ex-ante* effects on investment, that suggest hands off, and *ex-post* control of practices when harmful, that requires intervention. Our general result suggests that public policies should be softer when innovation is an important source of welfare improvements.

Keywords: Authorization, liability, enforcement, innovation, legal standard.

JEL Classification Codes: D73, K21, K42, L51.

*In developing the research surveyed in this chapter, we received many comments and suggestions. Then, we would like to thank Jacques Cremer, Nuno Garoupa, Louis Kaplow, Yannis Katsoulakos, Dilip Mookherjee, Massimo Motta, Marco Ottaviani, Marco Pagano, Martin Peitz, Patrick Rey, Lars-Hendrik Röller, Maarten Schinkel, Giancarlo Spagnolo, David Ulph, and especially Yossi Spiegel. A preliminary version of the second paper surveyed in this chapter has been presented at CRESSE 2011.

1. Introduction

When private activities may generate negative externalities, it is generally recognized that some form of public intervention may be desirable.[1] The most appropriate policy may be selected within a wide range of different regimes that differ in terms of timing — intervening before or after the relevant activities have been undertaken — and in terms of the tools at the public agent's disposal, from releasing an authorization to levying fines.

So far, the literature has studied this issue looking at environments where technologies were given and public intervention consisted in affecting the behavior of private agents who produced externalities.[2] This chapter, instead, presents a simple framework to survey the effects of different public policies in research-intensive industries. In this setting, the current practices of agents interact with the long-run decision to invest in R&D. We refer to an economic environment where firms first invest in research and then, if research is successful, undertake business practices to exploit the profit potentials of the innovation. Firm's practices, in turn, while privately profitable, may be *ex-ante* welfare enhancing or detrimental. In this framework, a stricter public intervention, reducing the profits *ex-post*, discourages the investment in research although it may better control *ex-post* behavior. There is therefore a potential tension between the *ex-ante* and *ex-post* effects of the policy that works in all the regimes considered.

We mainly draw from our recent work: Immordino *et al.* (2011) focus on the choice between *ex-post* liability and *ex-ante* authorization of innovative products as genetically modified (GM) organisms, or new

[1]This claim is justified as long as the Coase Theorem does not apply, due for instance to transaction costs, difficulties in coordination, imperfect information. We argue that in many instances, some of these elements characterize the economic environments we are interested in.

[2]The literature of Public Economics and Law and Economics has further pointed out that the optimal form of intervention should trade-off the social benefits of the different regimes with their enforcement costs. See, on the public economics side, among others, Krueger (1974); Rose-Ackerman (1978); Banerjee (1997); Acemoglu and Verdier (2000); Glaeser and Shleifer (2003); Immordino and Pagano (2010). Similar arguments can be found in the literature on the optimal design of regulation: see Laffont and Tirole (1993) and Armstrong and Sappington (2007). The law and economics literature, such as Becker (1968), Becker and Stigler (1974) and Polinsky and Shavell (2000), has dealt with similar issues arising from the optimal enforcement of norms.

drugs. They identify when each policy is optimal. In Immordino and Polo (2012), instead, we compare *per se* and discriminating legal standards, within the *ex-post* law enforcement regime, referring to antitrust intervention against abuse of dominance. Hence, the two papers can be read as complementary.

A key feature of our approach is that the effects of the practices, when applied to the new technologies, are unknown at the time the investment is sunk and the policy is set. When the investment decision is taken, therefore, its expected returns depend on the policy implemented in each state of the world, and on the probability of each state. If it is optimal to sustain the investment, then, the policies, including the one applied when the practices are socially detrimental, may be softened.

Uncertainty may be rooted in the very nature of the research activity, so that the features of the innovation are unknown until discovery. For instance, a new GM seed may promise higher yields but may also pose unknown risks to public health, risks that can be properly verified only once the research has been concluded. This setting reminds the class of problems that we address in Immordino *et al.* (2011) and which are reviewed in Section 4.

In other instances, uncertainty may be due to the interaction of the innovation, whose properties may have been controlled and planned by the firm with sufficient confidence, with the economic or social environment at the time the innovation will be introduced. The features of this environment at this later stage, in turn, will depend on the decisions of other agents and cannot be assessed *ex-ante* with certainty. To illustrate, consider the example of a dominant software company that may invest in research to tie a new software application into a new personal computer operating system (OS), a setting that refers to the competition policy issues addressed in Immordino and Polo (2012) and reviewed in Section 5 of this chapter. Beyond the initial intent of the company, the efficiency and foreclosure effects of tying this new software packages will depend, at the time of its commercial introduction, on the alternative packages and applications available from competitors, which may be only imperfectly foreseen at the time of the research investment.

We derive a full range of normative results that depend on the private and social effects of the practices, and on the likelihood that they will cause social harm. Our general result suggests that the more optimistic the expectations of the practices' social effects, the laxer the policy. When comparing *ex-ante* authorization and *ex-post* liability (Section 4), *laissez-faire* initially prevails, for very optimistic expectations, and is then replaced by an *ex-post* liability regime. When damages are capped, because of a limited liability constraint, a (strict) *ex-ante* authorization is finally selected when the probability of social harm is very high. In the analysis of different legal standards (Section 5), *per se* legality initially prevails, then replaced by a discriminating (effect-based) rule, while *per se* illegality is introduced for very pessimistic expectations on the effects of the practice, when fines are capped.

The remainder of this chapter is organized as follows. Section 2 discusses the relevant literature. Section 3 sets up the baseline model. Section 4 compares *ex-ante* regulation to *ex-post* liability. Section 5 compares different legal standards in antitrust. Section 6 concludes.

2. Related Literature

Several strands of the literature are relevant for our work. Starting with the Law and Economics literature, our papers have some common elements with the so-called "activity level" model (see, for instance, Shavell (1980, 2007) and Polinsky and Shavell (2000)). According to this approach, private benefits and social harms depend on two different decisions of private agents: a level of activity (how long the individual drives) and a level of precaution (the speed at which the agent drives). This literature focuses mainly on comparison of different liability rules (strict vs. fault-based). In our model, the innovative effort resembles the activity while the choice of new actions parallels precaution. However, in our setting, the time and information structure are different, since innovative effort is taken before uncertainty is resolved and before actions are chosen, while in the activity level model, activity and precaution are chosen together and uncertainty plays no role.

The analysis performed in Immordino *et al.* (2011) is related to Shavell (1984), who analyzes four determinants of the choice between an authorization and a liability regime, in his context respectively labeled as safety regulation and liability: (i) difference in risk knowledge; (ii) incentive or ability to enforce penalties; (iii) magnitude of administrative costs, and

(iv) magnitude of maximal fines. In our analysis, we hold determinants (i)–(iii) constant across regimes. This is done to focus on the role of innovation in the choice between regimes, eliminating other sources of differential effectiveness between them.

Immordino *et al.* (2011) compare different policy regimes based on *ex-ante* vs. *ex-post* intervention. A model that analyzes similar issues is Schwartzstein and Schleifer (2012), who investigate when and how the optimal policy combines *ex-ante* regulation and *ex-post* litigation in the activity model. They consider a setting where safe and unsafe firms decide whether to produce and may take precautions. Firms face uncertainty as to the liability for damages that will apply to them, due to the assumption that courts can make errors: a judge may mistake a safe firm for an unsafe one, which creates a disincentive effect for safe firms. If the regulator can identify safe firms *ex-ante*, it is optimal for regulation to set these firms free from liability for damages, since the social benefits of their activity exceeds the expected harm from taking too few precautions. This parallels our finding that regulation should be softer when social harm is unlikely. But our analysis differs from Schwartzstein and Schleifer (2012), as we model uncertainty as inherent to the social effects of firms' research activity, rather than as arising from judicial errors. As such, it applies uniformly to any form of policy intervention, and does not *per se* favor any regime over others.

Immordino and Polo (2012) introduce in the analysis the role of judicial errors. Judicial errors and their reduction, i.e., accuracy, are a central concern in law enforcement: they have been analyzed in the standard model of law enforcement proposed by Kaplow (1994), Kaplow and Shavell (1994, 1996), Polinsky and Shavell (2000), and Png (1986) among others, which focuses on the (negative) impact of such errors on marginal deterrence. In this framework, accuracy is always desirable, and it is chosen optimally balancing the marginal benefits and costs. In our framework, errors affect not only *ex-post* (marginal) deterrence, but also *ex-ante* deterrence: type-I errors, inducing over-deterrence, discourage investment, while type-II errors affects positively the research effect due to under-deterrence. The effects of accuracy, therefore, are richer in our setting than in the traditional law enforcement literature.

The impact of antitrust enforcement in innovative industries, at the core of Immordino and Polo (2012), is analyzed also in a paper by

Segal and Whinston (2007). Considering a sequence of innovations, the authors analyze the trade-off between protecting the incumbents, by so doing increasing the rents of the winner and the incentives to invest in innovation, and protecting the innovative entrants, that increases the rate of technical progress. They derive conditions under which the latter effect is the dominant one.

Segal and Whinston (2007) offer interesting results on law enforcement when innovative activity is a crucial component, but they do not consider different legal standards, which instead play a central role in Immordino and Polo (2012). In Katsoulakos and Ulph (2009), a welfare analysis of legal standards is developed, comparing *per se* rules and discriminating (effect-based) rules characterized by a lower probability of errors, in a setting where no innovative investment is required. The authors identify some key elements that can help deciding the more appropriate legal standard and the cases in which type-I or type-II accuracy is more desirable, but do not consider the additional effects arising when decisions on research investment and on the practices interact. The discussion on legal standards has also occupied an important place in the recent debate on the enforcement of competition policy in preventing foreclosure and monopolization, comparing *per se* or form-based rules and discriminating or effect-based rules (see on this point Gual *et al.* (2005); DG Competition (2005, 2008); and Department of Justice (2008)).

Finally, Chang (1995), Green and Scotchmer (1995), and Erkal (2004) consider the interaction of different forms of public intervention, namely antitrust and patent policy, in a setting of sequential innovations. They show that different licensing agreements may have an impact on the incentives to further discover the second innovation as well as on market coordination.

3. A Simple Set Up

Consider a profit-maximizing firm that chooses whether to invest in R&D activity or not. If the firm invests and fails, or if it does not invest at all, it can only implement the status-quo action, $a = 0$, e.g., familiar technologies, and the resulting profit and welfare are normalized to zero. If instead the firm invests and succeeds in its research effort, it discovers how to implement a set of new actions $A = (0; 1]$, with associated profits $\Pi = \pi a$, where $\pi > 0$. In this case, the firm is also assumed to learn the state of nature $s \in \{b; g\}$, where the bad state b occurs with probability β and the good state g occurs with probability $1 - \beta$. In the bad state b, the innovation is socially harmful, and the new actions decrease welfare according to $W_b = -w_b a$, with $w_b > 0$. In the good state g, the innovation raises welfare by $W_g = w_g a$, with $w_g > 0$. That is, in the bad state, private incentives conflict with social welfare since a new action a yields profit but reduces welfare, while in the good state g, new actions raise welfare as well as profits

The resources I that the firm invests in research determine its chances of success: for simplicity, I is assumed to coincide with the success probability, so that $I \in [0, 1]$. The cost of learning is increasing and convex in the firm's investment; for concreteness, we assume it is given by $c(I) = c\frac{I^2}{2}$. After choosing I and learning its outcome, the firm selects the most profitable action a among the feasible actions under the constraints imposed by public policy.

4. *Ex-ante* Authorization vs. *Ex-post* Liability of Innovative Products

We start our comparison of policy regimes by considering a firm that invests in research projects, for instance on GM seeds, potentially able to improve farming, yet exposed to unknown risks to public health; similar issues arise in the nanotechnology industry (Editors, 2010), or in the pharmaceutical and chemical industries (Philipson *et al.*, 2008). To contain the potential hazards posed by innovative activity, public policy may constrain the actions of successful innovators either by subjecting them to an *ex-ante* notification and authorization requirement (*authorization*) or to an *ex-post* liability regime (*liability*), where the firm can be condemned to pay damages. Under the authorization regime, the firm notifies to a public agency (such as the Food and Drugs Administration) the action it plans to undertake based on the results of its research (e.g., the sale of GM seeds), and the agency, after carrying out an investigation on the potential implied harm, decides whether the firm is allowed to go ahead. In contrast, under a liability regime, the firm is free to choose any new action made possible by its research findings (in our example, sell any new GM seed), but may have to pay a fine or damage *ex-post* if this action causes social harm. Public policies must trade off the social gains arising from the firm's innovation (a larger harvest) against their potential social harm (a public health hazard). The key issue to be explored is how this trade-off shapes the optimal design of the policy in each regime, as well as the choice between regimes.

4.1. *Ex-ante authorization*

In the authorization regime, after a firm notifies the action that it wishes to undertake, the authorizing agency investigates whether the notified actions are socially harmful or not, and obtains decisive evidence about their social effects with probability $p \in [0, 1]$, while it finds no evidence in either direction with probability $1-p$. If the evidence is decisive, the authorization is given if and only if the evidence is favorable. If, instead, it is not decisive, the agency can opt for one of two rules: a "lenient authorization" (*LA*) rule, whereby when in doubt the firm is authorized, or a "strict authorization" rule (*SA*), whereby in such circumstances, the authorization is denied. Hence, under the *LA* regime, the firm is authorized as long as no social harm is proved, while under the *SA* rule, new actions are permitted only if proved to be socially beneficial.

If the preliminary review were always to produce decisive evidence ($p = 1$), the two regimes would be equivalent; but if it may fail to yield hard evidence ($p < 1$), the lenient and strict rules differ. *LA* leads to under-enforcement, since with probability $\beta(1-p)$, it gives green light to a harmful action, while *SA* entails over-enforcement, by blocking with probability $(1 - \beta)(1 - p)$ a beneficial action. When the authorization is denied, the firm must take the *status-quo* action $a = 0$.

The timing of the game is as follows. At $t = 0$, the agency chooses between the *LA* and the *SA* rule, committing to the chosen rule for the entire game. At $t = 1$, the firm chooses its innovative activity I and with probability I discovers the new actions A and the state of nature s. At $t = 2$, under the rules *LA* and *SA*, the firm notifies the agency of the new action it wishes to undertake. At $t = 3$, the agency obtains evidence on the social effects of the proposed action with probability p, and decides whether to authorize it or not. At $t = 4$, the firm carries out the authorized action (if any), and the corresponding private and social payoffs are realized.

Since by assumption, the new actions in A are more profitable than the *status-quo* action $a = 0$, if research is successful, the firm always applies to be authorized to carry out the highest (most profitable) new action $a = 1$. If the *LA* rule is in place, the firm anticipates that the agency will always authorize it in the good state (with probability $1 - \beta$) and will authorize it only with probability $1 - p$ in the bad state (with probability β). Hence, under the *LA* rule, the firm will take action $a = 1$ with probability $(1 - \beta) + \beta(1 - p) = 1 - \beta p$. Then, the expected profits at the time the level of investment is chosen are $E(\Pi_{LA}) = I(1 - \beta p)\pi - c\frac{I^2}{2}$.

Under the *SA* rule, instead, the agency will authorize action $a = 1$ only if it uncovers favorable evidence (with probability p), which happens only in the good state (with probability $1 - \beta$). Hence, the action 1 will be authorized with probability $(1-\beta)p$ and the expected profits are $E(\Pi_{SA}) = I(1 - \beta)p\pi - c\frac{I^2}{2}$.

Since the firm is allowed to take the most profitable action more often $(1 - \beta p > (1 - \beta)p)$, the lenient rule, leaving greater expected profits to innovators, is associated with greater investment in innovation than the strict one. Indeed, we have

$$I_{LA} = \frac{(1 - p\beta)\pi}{c} > I_{SA} = \frac{(1 - \beta)p\pi}{c}.$$

Comparing the different authorization rules, Immordino *et al.* (2011) conclude that the *LA* rule, being associated to under-deterrence, boosts innovative investment more than the *SA* rule. When there is a low probability β that the new actions reduce welfare, the former is preferable to the latter.[3] This happens for a larger set of values of the probability β when enforcement becomes more effective (higher p): when the probability of social harm increases, the agency sticks to the lenient rule only if the ability to detect harmful innovations is high enough as to compensate the under-deterrence of this rule.

[3]This result is obtained by comparing the expected welfare under the *LA* rule, $E(W_{LA}) = I_{LA}[(1-\beta)w_g - \beta(1-p)w_b] - c\frac{I_{LA}^2}{2}$, with the one under the *SA* rule, $E(W_{SA}) = I_{SA}(1-\beta)pw_g - c\frac{I_{SA}^2}{2}$, where the profit, maximizing investments have been described above.

4.2. *Ex-post liability*

Having characterized the optimal authorization regime, we now consider the optimal implementation of the liability regime. In this latter case, the successful innovator can implement any action $a \in A$, but anticipates that he may be sanctioned if the action is found to have caused social harm. This occurs when the agency obtains evidence that the chosen action was socially harmful, which happens with probability p as in the authorization regime. Under liability, an action $a \in A$ that causes social harm is punished according to a fine (or damage) schedule $f(a)$ chosen in the interval $[0, F]$ and non-decreasing in social harm:

$$f(a) = \begin{cases} 0 & \text{if } a = 0 \\ \underline{f} \geqslant f & \text{if } 0 < a \leqslant a_f \\ \bar{f} \leqslant F & \text{if } a > \tilde{a}. \end{cases}$$

In the liability regime, the timing of the game is as follows: at $t = 0$, the agency commits to the fine schedule $f(a)$. If the agency sets its fines at zero for any new action $a \in A$, it effectively opts for a *laissez-faire* regime. At $t = 1$, the firm chooses innovative activity I and with probability I discovers the set of new actions A and the state of nature s. At $t = 2$, it decides which action a to take. At $t = 3$, the private and social payoffs are realized. At $t = 4$, the agency investigates the action a, finds decisive evidence about its social effects with probability p and, if it does, levies the fine $f(a)$.

The influence of law enforcement and penalties on firms' behavior is twofold: it affects both the choice of the *action* when the new actions are discovered and are socially harmful, and the *research investment* in the first place, when the firm computes the expected profits from the new actions. The first effect plays *ex-post*, and we can label it as *ex-post deterrence*, that is, the ability of fines to guide private choices among unlawful actions.[4] The second effect, which is absent in standard models, stems from the impact of law enforcement on innovative activity, and therefore on the probability that any new action will be taken. For this reason, we can label this second effect

[4]This effect is known in the Law and Economics literature as marginal deterrence. See Stigler (1970) and Mookherjee and Png (1994).

ex-ante deterrence. The policy will be chosen considering both effects on private choices and ultimately on welfare.

The choice of actions at $t = 2$ depends on the outcome of the firm's innovative activity at $t = 1$ and on the fine schedule $f(a)$ designed by the agency at $t = 0$. When innovative activity is unsuccessful, the firm carries out the *status-quo* action $a = 0$. Instead, when successful, the firm can also take new actions $a \in A$. If these are socially beneficial, no damage can be imposed, so that the firm picks the most profitable action in the good state, i.e., $a_g = 1$. If instead, the new actions $a \in A$ are socially harmful, they might be sanctioned, and the firm chooses the action that maximizes profits net of the expected fine: $\tilde{a}_b = \arg\max_{a \in [0,1]}[\pi a - pf(a)]$. Referring again to our example, if innovative activity is unsuccessful, the firm sells traditional seeds ($a = 0$), while if successful, it markets the most profitable type of seeds if that poses no concern for public health ($a_g = 1$), while it selects a less profitable variety ($\tilde{a}_b$) if it is dangerous, taking into account the corresponding damages it may be called to pay.

At $t = 1$, the firm chooses the innovative activity I so as to maximize its expected profits, anticipating the optimal actions to be taken at $t = 2$. In terms of our example, the biotech firm chooses its investment in R&D, taking into account which GM seeds it will sell if successful. The expected profits of the firm under liability when choosing the level of investment I, given the action, $\tilde{a}_b$, are

$$E(\Pi_L) = I[(1-\beta)\pi + \beta(\pi\tilde{a}_b - pf(\tilde{a}_b))] - c\frac{I^2}{2}.$$

The profit-maximizing investment is therefore:

$$I_L(\tilde{a}_b) = \frac{(1-\beta)\pi + \beta[\pi\tilde{a}_b - p\underline{f}]}{c}.$$

Finally, we can write the expected welfare that the agency maximizes:

$$E(W_L) = I_L(\tilde{a}_b)[(1-\beta)w_g - \beta w_b\tilde{a}_b] - c\frac{I_L^2(\tilde{a}_b)}{2}.$$

The (incentive compatible) action $\tilde{a}_b$ and investment I_L depend on the fine schedule (the parameters $\underline{f}$, $\bar{f}$, and a_f). A convenient way to describe the optimal penalty schedule is to consider its design as equivalent to (indirectly) implementing an action $\hat{a}_b$ in the bad state — and a corresponding investment $I_L(\hat{a}_b)$ — that maximizes expected welfare, among all (profit-maximizing) actions $\tilde{a}_b$ which the firm will want to pick in the bad state.

Two different effects interact in the selection of the optimal action $\hat{a}_b$ in the bad state: *ex-post* deterrence requires to implement a low action to reduce social harm, whereas a higher and more profitable action is desirable to sustain investment, as long as the expected welfare is *ex-ante* positive. Indeed, the first partial derivative of the expected welfare with respect to the action implemented in the bad state, $\tilde{a}_b$ is

$$\frac{\partial E(W_L)}{\partial \tilde{a}_b} = \left[(1-\beta)w_g - \beta w_b \tilde{a}_b - cI_L\right]\frac{\beta\pi}{c} - \beta w_b I_L,$$

where the first term corresponds to the indirect effect through the impact on investment (*ex-ante* deterrence), while the second refers to the direct impact of the action on welfare (*ex-post* deterrence). This latter is always negative, requiring to reduce the action when socially harmful. The sign of the first one depends on the parameters and on the level of the implemented action $\tilde{a}_b$. When innovation has potentially large social benefits ($w_g > w_b + \pi$) and social harm is sufficiently unlikely ($\beta < \frac{w_g - w_b - \pi}{w_g + w_b}$), the first term is positive and large even at $\tilde{a}_b = 1$. In this case, in order to foster investment in innovation, the firm should be allowed to choose the most profitable action even in the (very unlikely) bad state. The liability regime should be suspended, in favor of a *laissez-faire* regime. When β is high ($\beta > \frac{w_g - w_b - \pi}{w_g + w_b}$), instead, the firm must be constrained by setting a fine $\bar{f}$ large enough so as to implement the action $\hat{a}_b(\beta) < 1$ in the bad state.[5] The implemented action $\hat{a}_b(\beta)$ varies continuously from the most profitable one ($a = 1$) to the *status-quo* action ($a = 0$) as the probability of the bad state β, as well as the marginal social loss w_b, increase. The new actions are completely deterred only in the limiting case $\beta = 1$, while for $\beta < 1$, some welfare-decreasing actions $\hat{a}_b(\beta) > 0$ are accepted. This pattern describes the optimal implementation of a liability rule.

[5] In this case, we have an internal solution for $\hat{a}_b < 1$. The first term of the partial derivative is kept positive by reducing $\tilde{a}_b$ when β increases.

4.3. *Optimal policies*

The final step is the selection of the optimal policy through the comparison of the expected welfare associated with each regime. The optimal regime depends on the parameters (w_g, w_b, and π) that describe the private and social effects of the new actions, and on the likelihood of the bad state, β. We describe the optimal policies in terms of the likelihood of social harm, β, and the thresholds that affect the shift in regime in terms of the parameters w_g, w_b, and π. Immordino *et al.* (2011) find that public intervention becomes increasingly stringent as the likelihood of social harm increases: as β goes up, the optimal policy changes from *laissez-faire* to a liability regime, while the authorization regime is always dominated. This is because penalties can be fine-tuned to the likelihood of social harm, whereas authorizations are more rigid, being a "yes-or-no" decision that does not affect at the margin the choice of the action.

When the maximum feasible fine is capped at some upper bound, for instance due to a limited liability constraint on the damages that can be levied, however, the optimal policies become considerably richer. With capped fines, indeed, also the authorization regimes play a role for sufficiently large values of the likelihood of social harm β. More specifically, the constraint on maximum fines hampers the effectiveness of the liability regime for values of β exceeding a certain threshold. For an interval of values above this threshold, the liability and the LA regimes become equivalent, while for even larger values of β, the SA regime dominates both of them. Intuitively, when social harm is very likely and fines are capped at a maximum, the incomplete deterrence of the liability regime becomes too costly for society. At that point, the SA regime dominates, being safer though less sophisticated. Hence, for increasing likelihood of the social harm, β, all the policy regimes are selected, starting from *laissez-faire*, moving to liability, shifting to LA and closing with SA when β is very high.

5. Abuse of Dominance: The Optimal Legal Standards

We now discuss the implementation of competition policies in innovative industries. We maintain a similar set up, with the firm initially investing in research and then undertaking a practice to extract profits from the innovative technology. In this section, however, we explicitly refer to antitrust intervention on unilateral, or monopolization, practices. More precisely, we want to analyze the selection of the optimal legal standards, comparing *per se* rules, where a practice itself may be classified as unlawful, with a discriminating rule, that considers a practice anticompetitive only if its effects reduce welfare. Compared with the previous section, we focus here on *ex-post* intervention.

We argue that the choice of legal standards and the antitrust enforcement against abuse of dominance in investment-intensive industries capture two ingredients that have played a central role in competition policy in the last decade. In recent years, the debate on competition policy has explored in depth the role played by economics in improving the analysis of anticompetitive conducts. The discussion has raised issues concerning the substantial arguments as well as the legal standards that should be adopted in cases involving anticompetitive practices. Following the important reforms on cartel cases (Article 101) and merger control, in 2009, the DG Competition of the European Commission has reshaped the enforcement of Article 82 (now 102) on abuse of dominance, pursuing an approach that rests on a deeper and more intelligent use of the new findings of economic analysis in the enforcement against unilateral practices.[6] The received view from modern Industrial Organization is quite mixed, depending on the specific environments and models. While some economists argue that dominant firms adopt socially harmful practices to maintain their market power, others consider this possibility skeptically, stressing instead the pursuit of superior efficiency as the driving force explaining the emergence of market leaders.[7] Hence, among the Industrial Organization researchers and antitrust practitioners, there is no general consensus that certain business practices always produce desirable or negative welfare effects, while a more articulated view based on the specific conditions seems to prevail.

These developments have suggested a change in the view that legal standards should be selected in antitrust enforcement. A new approach

[6] See Gual *et al.* (2005) and DG Competition (2005, 2008).

[7] See Evans and Padilla (2005) for a brilliant summary of the evolution of economic thinking in antitrust from the traditional view to the Chicago critique to the post-Chicago approaches.

has emerged, labeled "effect-based" as opposed to the traditional form-based approach.[8] The novelty of these proposals refers to identifying anticompetitive practices through a careful analysis of the foreclosure effects of the conducts, beyond their formal description.

The debate on antitrust enforcement against unilateral practices has overlapped with the handling of several landmark cases of abuse of dominance that involved technological market leaders or incumbents in network industries: the U.S. and EC cases against Microsoft, covering a full range of business practices, from bundling to exclusive dealing; the record fine to Intel for loyalty rebates; the recent cases involving Google and Apple. All those cases have posed new and complex issues where business practices and innovative investments are strictly entrenched. Liberalized public utilities in Europe are another arena where incumbents, with a legacy on the monopolistic network infrastructures, have been prosecuted for abuse of dominance. This has happened for the major telecom companies of many European countries, or for the incumbent operators in the electricity and gas markets.[9]

Although the cases mentioned above were specifically addressing the anticompetitive use of certain business practices, in the debate following the decisions, it has been argued that the impact on the incentives to invest in research should be considered. And, similarly, some commentators pointed out that an excessively severe antitrust policy against the established public utility incumbents could reduce their investment incentives in a phase where new important projects should be realized to improve the energy or telecom networks.

How these concerns should be addressed, and what might be the implication for the selection of the appropriate legal standards are still an open issue. In Immordino and Polo (2012), we explore this issue, using

[8]We have several, almost equivalent, definitions in both views. The effect-based approach is often defined as a discriminating rule, since it is contingent on the effects, and closely reminds the rule of reason adopted in the U.S. on certain practices. The form-based is also called *per se* rule, as it considers unlawful a practice *per se*, with no consideration of its effects.

[9]See the cases of margin squeeze that have involved in the last decade Deutche Telecom, British Telecom, France Telecom, Telecom Italia and Telefonica, or the German electricity incumbents and the Italian gas incumbent.

a framework similar to the benchmark model we discussed in the previous section. However, we slightly modify the payoff functions in order to allow for an independent positive effect of the new technologies. This effect works together with the one produced by the business practices chosen to develop and commercialize the innovative products. The private profits are therefore given by $\Pi(a) = \Pi + \pi a$, where Π represents the stand-alone positive effect of the innovation on profits, while the second term captures the extra profits due to the adoption of the practice a. Social effects as well can be described through a (positive) stand-alone effect on welfare, W, and the additional impact of the practice, that may be positive or negative. Therefore, in the good state, total welfare if the innovation is successful is $W_g(a) = W + w_g a$, while the socially harmful case corresponds to $W_b(a) = W - w_b a$.

This framework can be applied, for instance, to the design of a new OS and the related applications, where these latter may be bundled together with the OS. The action a, in this case, may represent the degree of compatibility of the new OS with competitors' applications, a lower compatibility (a higher a) corresponding to larger private benefits for the innovator. Welfare effects of different degrees of compatibility may be negative ($W_b(a)$) if, this way, competitors are foreclosed. But we may also have a case where low compatibility increases welfare ($W_g(a)$), if bundling the OS and applications improves the performance of the software while competitors can still market their packages using alternative OS or middlewares, with no restriction on their ability to compete.

The framework adopted allows to consider not only the optimal legal standards, but also the interaction of competition and patent policy. The effectiveness of this latter, in our framework, can be captured by the level of private benefits Π appropriated by the innovator, for given social value W: when patent protection is effective, Π is close to W, while the innovator hardly receives a return when competitors can easily imitate the new technology and/or the social benefits are transferred to consumers, a case corresponding to a low Π for given W.

Antitrust legal standards, in this setting, differ in the way unlawful practices are defined, in the informational requirements that are needed to implement them, and in the probability of committing judicial errors in their implementation. *Per se* rules establish the legality or unlawfulness with reference to the practice itself, no matter how large is the degree a of its implementation, nor the effects that are produced. *Per se* legality, in this framework, states that the practice is always legal, and cannot be sanctioned, whereas *per se* illegality, that, for instance, considers as unlawful any tying of the OS and apps, gives the enforcer the power to fine the practice at any degree $a > 0$ it is undertaken. Conversely, a discriminating (or effect-based) legal standard considers a practice as unlawful as long as it reduces welfare: compatibility, in this case, can be sanctioned only in case it is a vehicle to foreclosure.

Operationally, *per se* rules require to observe only whether the practice is adopted (if $a > 0$), a much simpler task than assessing the social effects (whether $W(a)$ is larger or lower than W), a process where we assume the enforcer may commit errors.[10] Type-I errors, then, arise when the enforcer mistakenly evaluates the practice as socially damaging while it is welfare enhancing, leading to over-enforcement, whereas type-II errors and under-enforcement occur in the opposite case. We measure how seriously errors affect enforcement by the probability ε^{I} and $\varepsilon^{\mathrm{II}}$ of committing type I or type II errors. Then, enforcement tools in a discriminating regime add to the usual fine schedule $f(a)$ the possibility to costly reduce the probability of errors (accuracy) by collecting additional information. To sum up, we model legal standards according to two dimensions: flexibility and accuracy. In this perspective, discriminating rules are more flexible than *per se*, adapting enforcement to the effects of the practice, but are more prone to errors, requiring more information to be implemented. In this framework, Immordino and Polo (2012) analyze two issues: first, optimal enforcement policies for *per se* and discriminating regimes are characterized; second, the outcomes are compared to select the optimal legal standard.

5.1. *Per se rules*

Per se rules, by their very nature, do not discriminate the practice according to its effects, and therefore cannot induce a different behavior in the bad or the good state. While the firm, under *per se* legality, is never fined, and therefore chooses always action $a = 1$, under *per se* illegality the firm will

[10] More precisely, we assume that the enforcer receives an informative but noisy signal σ that interprets as corresponding to social harm when above a certain threshold x.

select the action that maximizes the net profits, $\tilde{a} = \arg\max_a \Pi + \pi a - f(a)$. The expected profits when the investment is chosen are therefore $E\Pi_{PS} = I(\Pi + \pi\tilde{a} - \underline{f}) - \frac{I^2}{2}$ and the profit-maximizing investment is

$$I_{PS} = \Pi + \pi\tilde{a} - \underline{f}. \tag{1}$$

Finally, expected welfare under *per se* illegality is

$$EW_{PS} = I_{PS}[W + ((1-\beta)w_g - \beta w_b)\tilde{a}] - \frac{(I_{PS})^2}{2}. \tag{2}$$

We show that when the prior β on social harms is sufficiently low, a *per se* legality regime is selected, committing not to intervene in order to boost the innovative investment. For more pessimistic priors, a *per se* illegality regime is introduced, giving the enforcer the power to fine the practice. In this case, by appropriately shaping the fine schedule, the enforcer can implement an action $\hat{a}$, reducing, or even completely deterring, the practice itself. For increasing values of the probability of social harm β, the optimal policy initially still implements the action at the highest level ($\hat{a} = 1$), as in the *per se* legality regime, but reduces the investment through the fine $f(1) > 0$, and then turns to progressively reducing the action $\hat{a}$ until full deterrence is implemented.

5.2. *Discriminating rule*

Turning to the discriminating rule, the enforcer sets the fine schedule conditional on the social effects, and therefore never fines the practice when receiving a good signal, while properly implementing through the fine schedule $f(a)$ the action $\hat{a}_b$ when the signal is bad. Since the signal is noisy, the firm is fined also when the true state is good. The expected profits under the discriminating rule when the investment is chosen are therefore

$$E\Pi_D = I\{\Pi + (1-\beta)[\pi - \varepsilon^{\mathrm{I}}\bar{f}] + \beta[\pi\tilde{a}_b - (1-\varepsilon^{\mathrm{II}})\underline{f}]\} - \frac{I^2}{2}.$$

The optimal investment given the enforcement policy is then:

$$I_D = \Pi + (1-\beta)[\pi - \varepsilon^{\mathrm{I}}\bar{f}] + \beta[\pi\tilde{a}_b - (1-\varepsilon^{\mathrm{II}})\underline{f}].$$

We can notice that type-I errors imply over-deterrence, and, indeed, reduce the investment, while type-II errors have an opposite impact through under-deterrence. The enforcer, then, designs the optimal policy using the fine schedule and the level of accuracy to maximize the expected welfare:

$$EW_D = I_D\left[W + (1-\beta)w_g - \beta w_b \tilde{a}_b - \frac{I_D}{2}\right] - \frac{\gamma}{2}(\overline{\varepsilon} - \varepsilon^{\mathrm{I}})^2 - \frac{\gamma}{2}(\overline{\varepsilon} - \varepsilon^{\mathrm{II}})^2,$$

where the last two terms refer to the cost of reducing type-I and type-II errors by refining accuracy.

The optimal enforcement policy, for increasing values of the probability of social losses β, works as follows: when β is sufficiently low, the most profitable action is implemented even in the bad state ($\hat{a}_b = 1$), setting the fine $\underline{f}$ at the lowest level. Then, as long as the fine $\underline{f}$ may be set to zero, the discriminating rule collapses into a *per se* legality regime for low β. In the potential conflict between *ex-ante* deterrence, that suggests to reduce fines to boost investment when the social loss is unlikely, and *ex-post* deterrence, that instead always requires to fine the practice when socially harmful, the former effect prevails. For higher values of the probability of social harm, instead, the enforcer progressively reduces the action $\hat{a}_b$ in the bad state. In this case, moreover, type-I accuracy is refined, reducing type-I errors and over-deterrence, as a complementary way to sustain the investment while controlling the action $\hat{a}_b$.

5.3. *Optimal legal standards*

These results shed lights also on the optimal legal standards that are selected, according to different values of the likelihood of social harm, β. *Per se* legality prevails for low values of β, as a way to boost investment by committing not to intervene *ex-post* when the practice is harmful. *Per se* rules are then abandoned, in favor of the discriminating rule, when social harm becomes more likely, balancing *ex-ante* and *ex-post* deterrence.

Moreover, the legal standards and associated enforcement policies are adjusted to the effectiveness of patent policy, that we measure through the stand-alone profits of the innovator, Π, for given social welfare W. In Immordino and Polo (2012), we show that *per se* legality is preferred to a discriminating rule for

$$\beta \leq \frac{W - \Pi + w_g - \pi - w_b\frac{\Pi+\pi}{\pi}}{w_g + w_b},$$

and the upper bound moves to the right when Π decreases (for given W). Moreover, we show that the implemented action in the bad state under a discriminating rule, $\hat{a}_b$, increases as well, making the antitrust enforcement less stringent. Both adjustments make the antitrust enforcement laxer, improving the incentives to invest in research whenever the patent policy becomes less effective. Antitrust policy, therefore, acts as a substitute to patent protection in our framework.

When fines are capped, for instance because of limited liability, the optimal enforcement policies are further enriched. Since a higher probability of social harm requires to implement a lower action $\hat{a}_b$ and to increase the fine for $a > \hat{a}_b$, for sufficiently high β, the limited liability constraint becomes binding. The enforcement policy is modified accordingly, choosing a combination of fines, type-I and type-II accuracy that make enforcement more and more costly. When β becomes very high, then, a more rigid but less costly *per se* illegality rule is preferred to save on enforcement costs. Hence, depending on the prior β and the parameters W, Π, w_g, w_b, and π (that enter into the expression of the different thresholds), the full range of legal standards is adopted.

The results in Immordino and Polo (2012) then contribute to the debate on the desirable form of antitrust enforcement of unilateral practices by showing that form-based (*per se*) rules may be desirable in some cases, while effect-based (discriminating) rules may be desirable in others. In particular, when no investment issue is involved, and the only concern of law enforcement is to control the practice (*ex-post* deterrence), then it is shown that the discriminating rule is dominant, even when β is very low, supporting the view of those that claim in favor of a generalized effect-based approach. This result applies to sectors where there is no major issue of research investment interacting with business strategies, as in mature industries where no innovation is expected to replace the current technologies. The desirability of a discriminating over *per se* rules emerges also when the enforcement policy is chosen, or can be redesigned, after the investment is sunk (no commitment case).

Flexible, discriminating rules, however, are not always the dominant legal standard when investment matters and the enforcer can commit to a given legal standard. Indeed, when the practice undertaken on the innovative products is unlikely to harm consumers (low β), a more rigid *per se* legality rule is preferred. This rule ensures no *ex-post* intervention when social harm arises, and thereby it strengthens the *ex-ante* incentive to invest. In this case, the enforcer faces a time inconsistency problem that can be solved through guidelines or precedents, restoring the ability to commit. However when β is large, a discriminating rule dominates the *per se* legality regime, as it preserves the flexibility to implement an enforcement policy when the action is socially harmful. Finally, the discriminating rule displays a second weakness when β is very large, and fines are capped. Then, the only way to control a harmful action is to rely on accuracy.[11] This makes the simpler, but less costly, *per se* prohibition a more appealing regime.[12]

Finally, Immordino and Polo (2012) show that, with minor changes, the same results occur when the firm has to run a preliminary phase of deterministic investments in physical assets, rather than of uncertain investments in research. In this sense, therefore, the prescriptions on the optimal legal standards apply in our framework to a wide range of (research or physical capital) investment-intensive industries, capturing the two classes of technological champions and public utility incumbents that have been at the center of landmark antitrust cases in recent years in Europe.

6. Conclusion

In this chapter, we discussed a research agenda where the agents first have to invest resources in learning — what we call research — and then, if successful, they are able to choose a new action that *ex-post* may be welfare enhancing or reducing. Public policies, determining the instances when the firm is subject to a restrictive policy treatment, affect both the *ex-post* profits from the new actions and the *ex-ante* incentives to invest in research. The

[11]We have seen that type-II accuracy can improve deterrence on actions, while the reduction of type-I error may sustain innovative investments. The possibility of refining type-I or type-II accuracy rests on the following argument. A practice may be welfare enhancing (good state) or detrimental (bad state). Each of the two possibilities can be analyzed within an appropriate model, and their empirical predictions suggest a set of observables. As long as the two sets of predictions are, at least in part, distinct, we can obtain identifying restrictions that allow to validate either of the two explanations. See Polo (2010) for an application to selective price cuts.

[12]The role of commitment and flexibility of a legal system in affecting growth has been recently studied by Anderlini *et al.* (2013).

optimal policy comes out of the interplay between the *ex-ante* effect on investment and the *ex-post* effect on actions, and depends on the priors of the enforcer on the likelihood and magnitude of the positive and negative private and social effects of the new practices.

We compared several policy options: in the first part of the chapter, we analyzed the choice between *ex-ante* authorization and *ex-post* liability of innovative products, as GM seeds, or new drugs. In the second part of the chapter, different legal standards (*per se* vs. discriminating rules) were compared in the enforcement of antitrust intervention against abuse of dominance in investment-intensive industries.

When the social effects of the new practices are likely to be positive, in both cases, the optimal policy prescribes not to intervene, as a way to commit not to penalize the new practices *ex-post* when socially harmful: this result is driven by the goal to sustain the innovative investment. When expectations are more mixed, liability, or a discriminating rule, is selected in the two environments. Finally, for pessimistic expectations, authorization or *per se* illegality is selected.

References

Armstrong, M. and D. E. M. Sappington (2007). Recent Developments in the Theory of Regulation, in M. Armstrong and R. H. Porter (Eds.), *Handbook of Industrial Organization*, Volume 3, North-Holland, Amsterdam.

Acemoglu, D. and T. Verdier (2000). "The Choice Between Market Failures and Corruption," *American Economic Review*, 90(1), pp. 194–211.

Anderlini, L., L. Felli, G. Immordino and A. Riboni (2013). "Legal Institutions, Innovation and Growth," *International Economic Review*, 54, pp. 937–956.

Banerjee, A. V. (1997). "A Theory of Misgovernance," *Quarterly Journal of Economics*, 112(4), pp. 1289–1332.

Becker, G. S. (1968). "Crime and Punishment: An Economic Approach," *Journal of Political Economy*, 76, pp. 169–217.

Becker, G. S. and G. J. Stigler (1974). "Law Enforcement, Malfeasance and Compensation of Enforcers," *The Journal of Legal Studies*, 17(1), pp. 65–81.

Chang, H. F. (1995). "Patent Scope, Antitrust Policy, and Cumulative Innovation," *RAND Journal of Economics*, 26, pp. 34–57.

Department of Justice (2008). "Competition and Monopoly: Single-Firm Conduct under Section 2 of the Sherman Act." Available at http://www.justice.gov/atr/public/reports/236681_chapter1.pdf.

DG Competition (2005). "Discussion Paper on the Application of Article 82 of the Treaty to Exclusionary Abuses." Available at http://ec.europa.eu/competition/antitrust/art82/discpaper2005.pdf.

DG Competition (2008). "Draft Guidance on the Commission's Enforcement Priorities in Applying Article 82 EC Treaty to Abusive Exclusionary Conducts by Dominant Undertakings," *Official Journal of the European Union*, C 45/7, February 24, 2009.

Easterbrook, F. (1984). "The Limits of Antitrust," *Texas Law Review*, 63, pp. 9–14.

Editors (2010). "Big Need for a Little Testing," *Scientific American*, January. Available at http://www.scientificamerican.com/article/big-need-for-a-little-testing/.

Erkal, N. (2004). "The Decision to Patent, Cumulative Innovation, and Optimal Policy," Intellectual Property Research Institute of Australia, wp. 11/03.

Evans, D. and J. Padilla (2005). "Designing Antitrust Rules for Assessing Unilateral Practices: A Neo. Chicago Approach," *The University of Chicago Law Review*, 72, pp. 73–98.

Glaeser, E. L. and A. Shleifer (2003). "The Rise of the Regulatory State," *Journal of Economic Literature*, 41(2), pp. 401–425.

Green, J. and S. Scotchmer (1995). "On the Division of Profit in Sequential Innovation," *RAND Journal of Economics*, 26, pp. 20–33.

Gual, J., M. Hellwig, A. Perrot, M. Polo, P. Rey, K. Schmidt and R. Stenbacka (2005). "An Economic Approach to Article 82," Report for the DG Competition, European Commission, published on *Competition Policy International*, 2, pp. 111–156.

Immordino, G. and M. Pagano (2010). "Legal Standards, Enforcement and Corruption," *Journal of the European Economic Association*, 8, pp. 1104–1132.

Immordino, G., M. Pagano and M. Polo (2011). "Incentives to Innovate and Social Harm: *Laissez-faire*, Authorization or Penalties?" *Journal of Public Economics*, 95, pp. 864–876.

Immordino, G. and M. Polo (2012). "Antitrust in Innovative Industries: The Optimal Legal Standards," *IGIER Working Paper* No. 434.

Kaplow, L. (1994). "The Value of Accuracy in Adjudication: An Economic Analysis," *The Journal of Legal Studies*, 15, pp. 371–385.

Kaplow, L. and S. Shavell (1994). "Accuracy in the Determination of Liability," *Journal of Law and Economics*, 37, pp. 1–15.

Kaplow, L. and S. Shavell (1996). "Accuracy in the Assessment of Damages," *Journal of Law and Economics*, 39, pp. 191–210.

Katsoulakos, Y. and D. Ulph (2009). "On Optimal Legal Standards for Competition Policy: A General Welfare-Based Analysis," *Journal of Industrial Economics*, LVII, pp. 410–437.

Krueger, A. (1974). "The Political Economy of the Rent-Seeking Society," *American Economic Review*, 64(3), pp. 291–303.

Laffont, J.-J. and J. Tirole (1993). *A Theory of Incentives in Procurement and Regulation*, MIT Press, Cambridge, MA.

Mookherjee, D. and I. Png (1994). "Marginal Deterrence in the Enforcement of Law," *Journal of Political Economy*, 102, pp. 1039–1166.

Philipson, T. J., E. C. Sun and D. Goldman (2008). "Is the Food and Drug Administration Safe and Effective?" *Journal of Economic Perspectives*, 22, pp. 85–102.

Png, I. P. L. (1986). "Optimal Subsidies and Damages in the Presence of Judicial Error," *International Review of Law and Economics*, 6, pp. 101–105.

Polo, M. (2010). "Anticompetitive vs Competitive Explanations of Unilateral Pratices: The Identification Problem," *Journal of Competition Law and Economics*, 6, pp. 457–476.

Polinsky, M. A. and S. Shavell, (2000). "The Economic Theory of Public Enforcement of Law," *Journal of Economic Literature*, 38, pp. 45–76.

Posner, R. A. (1992). *The Economic Analysis of Law*, 4th Edition, Little Brown, Boston.

Rose-Ackermann, S. (1978). *Corruption: A Study in Political Economy*, Academic Press, New York, NY.

Schwartzstein, J. and A. Shleifer (2012). "An Activity-Generating Theory of Regulation," *Journal of Law and Economics*, 56, pp. 1–38.

Segal, I. and M. Whinston (2007). "Antitrust in Innovative Industries," *American Economic Review*, 97, pp. 1703–1730.

Shavell, S. (1980). "Strict Liability versus Negligence," *The Journal of Legal Studies*, 9, pp. 1–25.

Shavell, S. (1984). "Liability for Harm versus Regulation of Safety," *The Journal of Legal Studies*, 13, pp. 357–374.

Shavell, S. (1992). "Liability and the Incentive to Obtain Information about Risk," *The Journal of Legal Studies*, 21, pp. 259–270.

Shavell, S. (2007). "Do Excessive Legal Standards Discourage Desirable Activity?" *Economics Letters*, 95, pp. 394–397.

Stigler, G. J. (1970). "The Optimum Enforcement of Laws," *Journal of Political Economy*, 78, pp. 526–536.

Chapter 14

The Role of Legal Principles in the Economic Analysis of Competition Policy*

Harold Houba
VU University
hhouba@feweb.vu.nl

Evgenia Motchenkova
VU University
emotchenkova@feweb.vu.nl

Quan Wen
University of Washington
wenq2@u.washington.edu

Abstract

We study the impact of legal principles on the design and the effectiveness of antitrust fines. Modern antitrust enforcement obeys four basic legal principles: punishments should fit the crime, proportionality, bankruptcy considerations, and minimum fines. We integrate these principles into a Bertrand oligopoly model, where bankruptcy considerations ensure abnormal cartel profits. We discuss the optimal legally-constrained fine schedule that achieves maximal social welfare under these legal principles. This fine schedule induces collusion on a lower price by making it more attractive than collusion on higher prices. This fine structure depends on the characteristics of competition, legal restrictions, and market conditions and can be related to price-cap regulation implemented in several sectors, such as electricity and telecom. We analyze the welfare implications

*We would like to thank Joseph Harrington, Yannis Katsoulacos, Jose Luis Moraga-Gonzalez, Massimo Motta, Michele Polo, Daniel Rubinfeld, Giancarlo Spagnolo, Yossi Spiegel, David Ulph, the anonymous referees and the participants of ALEA (2012), EARIE (2012), CRESSE (2012), and IIOC (2013) conferences for stimulating discussions and valuable comments.

of limited liability restrictions and minimum fines. We conclude that regulations aiming at either reducing legal ceilings or raising minimum fines reduce social welfare and should better be avoided.

Keywords: Antitrust enforcement, Antitrust Law, cartel, oligopoly, repeated game.

JEL Classification Codes: L4, K21, D43, C73.

1. Introduction

The literature on antitrust is rather silent on how to integrate legal principles of antitrust into the economic analysis and how to assess their impact on the design and the effectiveness of competition policy.[1] The principles embedded in the current antitrust sentencing guidelines in both the U.S. and the EU are: punishments should fit the crime, bankruptcy considerations, minimum fines, and proportionality. The punishments-fit-the-crime principle attempts to relate the fine to a rough measure of gravity that is approximated by the cartel's illegal gains in the U.S. and by the cartel overcharge or revenue in the EU. Bankruptcy considerations set restrictive ceilings to the maximum applicable fines. Minimum fines impose a non-negative legal lower bound. The principle of proportionality states that the regulator should not take any action that exceeds the one which is just necessary to achieve the objective.[2] In terms of fine structures, this principle implies that the fine should not be in excess of the lowest fine that suffices to prevent criminal activities.

These legal principles may conflict with the economic principle of efficiency, which makes deterrence less effective. However, we show that, even in the presence of these legal restrictions, it is possible to design antitrust penalties in a way that improves the effectiveness of deterrence compared to standard antitrust policy prescriptions. We also show that the resulting optimal legally-constrained fine schedule depends on the legal restrictions and the characteristics of competition, such as the number of firms and market conditions.

---

[1] Notable exceptions include Buccirossi and Spagnolo (2007) and Cooter and Ulen (2007).
[2] A similar interpretation of this rule can be found in e.g., Burca (1993), Usher (1998), Jacobs (1999), Tridimas (2006), Sullivan and Frase (2008), Fish (2008), or Sauter (2013).

The analysis in this chapter, which applies the more general model developed in Houba *et al.* (2011), focuses on the role of the above listed legal principles in designing optimal antitrust fines, i.e., the fines that minimize cartel harm. In Houba *et al.* (2011), the optimal legally-constrained fine schedule is derived endogenously in an infinitely-repeated oligopoly model with general demand functions and cost functions.[3] In this chapter, we study the special case of the classical Bertrand oligopoly competition with a linear market demand so that we are able to characterize the optimal legally-constrained fine schedule analytically. In this chapter, we also discuss how the presence of a legal ceiling (limited liability constraints) and a minimum fine are likely to affect the optimal fine structure and how optimal fines for corporations should change if bankruptcy considerations are taken into account. We conclude that regulations, which aim at either reducing the legal ceiling or raising the minimum fine, reduce social welfare and should better be avoided. Furthermore, we show that deterrence power can still be improved without increasing the level of fines above the existing (explicit or implicit) legal ceilings. We demonstrate this by constructing the most effective legally-constrained fine schedule that satisfies the four legal principles. This optimal fine schedule induces the lowest profit-maximizing cartel price and, hence, reduces the deadweight loss to its lowest achievable level. This improvement is achieved by making collusion on lower prices more attractive than collusion on higher prices.[4]

Further, in this chapter, we assess the likely effects of cartel enforcement after the implementation of the proposed optimal legally-constrained fine schedule on the resulting cartel overcharges, consumer surplus, and total welfare. In that respect, our analysis is related to the literature that assesses the likely deterrence and welfare effects of antitrust law enforcement policies with numerical simulations, which includes the work by Werden

[3]The main contribution of Houba *et al.* (2011) is to revise previous policy prescriptions for an extension of the model in Buccirossi and Spagnolo (2007) in which the four legal principles are accounted for. In Houba *et al.* (2011), the price is a continuous variable that is set strategically by the cartel to maximize its profit given the antitrust enforcement. Antitrust enforcement is endogenous to maximize social welfare under the four legal principles.

[4]The derived optimal fine schedule and other results can be related to the literature on marginal deterrence by Stigler (1971), Shavell (1992), Wilde (1992), and Mookherjee and Png (1994).

and Simon (1987), Gallo *et al.* (1994), Craycraft *et al.* (1997), Posner (2001), Connor and Lande (2005), Buccirossi and Spagnolo (2007), and Harrington and Chen (2007).

The theoretical model proposed in this chapter allows linking the structure of the fine (the toughness of the penalty regime) to the cartel pricing behavior (the level of cartel overcharge).[5] Moreover, the standard homogeneous product Bertrand oligopoly model with linear demand structure, employed in this chapter, allows comparing the deterrent effects of the three major types of fining structures currently investigated in the literature. These three types include fines based on revenues (see e.g., Bageri *et al.* (2013), Katsoulacos and Ulph (2013), or Souam (2001)), fines based on illegal gains (see e.g., Harrington (2004, 2005) or Houba *et al.* (2010, 2012)), or fixed fines (see e.g., Rey (2003) or Motta and Polo (2003)). We conclude that our optimal legally-constrained fine structure has a stronger deterrent effect compared to fixed fine structures or fines based on revenues or illegal gains. It outperforms all three above-mentioned systems.

It should also be mentioned that the problem we analyze can be viewed as a price-cap implementation problem through antitrust enforcement, rather than through sectorial regulation. Sectorial regulation could impose an *ex-ante* price cap close to the competitive price, such as the price-cap regulation implemented in the electricity and telecom sectors. However, regulating all sectors by price-caps is, probably, not feasible and may be regarded as unwanted. Therefore, governments still rely on *ex-post* antitrust enforcement in the majority of markets.

The rest of this chapter is organized as follows. Section 2 discusses the four legal principles and how we implement these in our analysis. Section 3 outlines the model. The optimal fine schedule is derived in Section 4.1. Further, in Sections 4.2 and 4.3, we provide analyses of the welfare implications of insufficient legal ceiling on fines and analyze the consequences of imposing minimum fines. In Section 4.4, we compare the deterrent effects of four major types of fining structures, which are currently analyzed in the literature on antitrust. Section 5 concludes.

[5] Similar issues have been addressed in Katsoulacos and Ulph (2013).

2. Four Legal Principles

Current legislation in the U.S. and EU restrict fines based on legal principles such as punishments should fit the crime, proportionality, bankruptcy considerations, and minimum fines. In this section, we discuss these four principles and how to incorporate them into economic analysis of antitrust in an oligopoly model of price competition.

Punishments Fit the Crime: Antitrust guidelines in the U.S. and EU are founded on the legal principle that punishment should fit the crime, see DOJ (2010) and EC (2006). In practice, this principle translates into higher fines for more serious offenses. Generally speaking, the gravity of an offence is related to both the harm caused by the offense and the cartel's illegal gains. In the U.S., the gravity is measured by the cartel's illegal gains, while in the EU, it is often approximated by the cartel overcharge or turnover (revenue) involved in the infringement.[6,7] Because both cartel's illegal gains, cartel's overcharge or turnover involved in the infringement are positively related to the cartel price, we model the fine schedule as a non-decreasing function of cartel price. Further, as in Becker (1968) and Posner (1976), our optimal antitrust enforcement consists of a fine schedule and effort level of inspection and prosecution that maximize the social welfare. The principle that punishment should fit the crime is satisfied, since a higher cartel price should cause a higher fine in this setting.

Principle of Proportionality: An important principle of current EU legislation is the principle of proportionality that states that regulators should not take any action that exceeds the one which is just sufficient

[6]The EU 2006 Guidelines revise those adopted in 1998, with a view to increasing the deterrent effect of fines. Council Regulation 1/2003 (as with Council Regulation 17/62 before it) provides that companies may be fined up to 10% of their total annual turnover. Within this limit, the revised Guidelines provide that fines may be based on up to 30% of the company's annual sales to which the infringement relates. In particular, the basic amount of the fine will be related to a proportion of the value of sales, depending on the degree of gravity of the infringement, multiplied by the number of years of infringement.

[7]See also Bageri *et al.* (2013), where fines are based on relevant turnover. However, as relevant turnover is generally increasing in the gravity of the offence or in the size of cartel overcharge, without loss of generality we can assume that the fine schedule can be modeled as non-decreasing function of cartel price (or cartel overcharge).

to achieve the same outcome, see e.g., Burca (1993), Usher (1998), Jacobs (1999), Tridimas (2006), Fish (2008), or Sauter (2013).[8] In the U.S., the application of the principle of proportionality is less transparent. However, concepts of proportionality have long been an instrumental part of the rule of law. These concepts all embody the fundamental value that government and private actions should not be demonstrably excessive relative to their moral and practical justifications (see e.g., Sullivan and Frase (2008)). Interpreting this principle in terms of the antitrust fine structure requires that the fine should not be more than the lowest possible fine that would induce the same market outcome, i.e., the least restrictive means (LRM) test. If fines are considered to be socially costless, there is no reason to adopt this principle. However, excessive fines may amplify the possible negative impact of antitrust enforcement, which can stem from unobservable legal errors. Hence, the legal principle of proportionality requires the adoption of the minimal fine that induces a given social outcome in order to minimize any potential undesirable impact of the antitrust policy.[9]

Bankruptcy Considerations: Both the EU and the U.S. legislation take into account bankruptcy considerations when imposing fines. Normally, this is implemented by imposing (either explicitly or implicitly) ceilings on fines. These ceilings are justified on the ground that legislators do not want to jeopardize the financial stability of the offending firms. Besides employment considerations, high fines that cause bankruptcy are against

[8]In the EU, the principle of proportionality has been developed by the Court of Justice of the European Union and requires that freedom of action should not be limited beyond the degree necessary in the public interest. It appeared for the first time in a judgement of the Court in *Fédéchar* (see Case 8/55, Fédération charbonnière de Belgique v ECSC High Authority, p. 299). Since the Treaty of Amsterdam of 1997, the principle is incorporated in the Treaty of the European Union, see Usher (1998). The principle of proportionality is articulated in Article 5 of the Treaty of the European Union. It states that "Under the principle of proportionality, the content and form of Union action shall not exceed what is necessary to achieve the objectives of the Treaties."

[9]The application of proportionality in the framework of the EU competition law has been discussed in e.g., Sauter (2013). He mentions that Article 7 of the Modernization Regulation includes an explicit proportionality test and directly implies LRM testing. In the recent *Mastercard (2012)* case, the Court further specifies LRM testing of Article 7 decisions (see Case T-111/08, paras 323–324).

the ultimate goal of antitrust law because such high fines would reduce the number of active competitors in the market.

In the EU, fines are limited to up to 10% of overall total annual turnover, see e.g., EC (2006), Bos and Schinkel (2007), or Bageri *et al.* (2013). Total turnover is indirectly related to the illegal gains or price-markups in the markets corrupted by cartel agreements, because it consists of the total sales over all the product markets in which the company operates, while only some of these markets may be involved in the collusive agreement. In the U.S., the final fine for undertakings must not exceed a maximum statutory limit which is the greatest of $100 million or twice the gross pecuniary gains the violators derived from the cartel or twice the gross pecuniary loss caused to the victims (see Bageri *et al.*, 2013). In addition, in many cases in practice, such as the UCAR 1993 case, fines were reduced even below the legal ceiling due to firms' inability to pay.[10] In such a setting, the existence of an implicit legal upper bound on fines, which is determined by the firms' limited liability, can be argued. For modeling purposes, we assume that a combination of formal legal ceilings, specified in the sentencing guidelines, and no-bankruptcy considerations, determined by the firm's limited liability, impose an upper bound on the fine schedule. This upper bound is modeled as an increasing function of an individual firm's illegal profits, plus a constant component that captures the EU rules.[11]

Minimum Fines: According to the current sentencing guidelines in the U.S., the base fine can be zero for some mild offenses, see DOJ (2010). Moreover, rewarding firms that violate antitrust law is not possible according to the current rules both in the U.S. and the EU. This implies that fines must be non-negative. Hence, we model the fine schedule as bounded

[10]The UCAR 1993 case refers to the determination of the fine for the U.S. part of the graphite electrode cartel, UCAR International. According to the U.S. sentencing guidelines, the fine was supposed to be set in the range between $199.64 to $399.28 million. However, the lower fine of $110 million was imposed, because of UCAR's inability to pay. See also Wehmhoerner (2005).

[11]In Houba *et al.* (2011), we show that all the results are robust when the legal upper bound is modeled as an arbitrary non-decreasing function of the cartel price. By doing so, our approach can also accommodate for the three main interpretations of the current guidelines: a constant upper bound, a percentage of annual overall turnover, and bounds related to the cartel's illegal gains.

by a non-negative constant lower bound in order to exclude rewards, which are not allowed in the current U.S. and EU guidelines.

3. The Model

Consider an infinitely-repeated Bertrand oligopoly model with $n \geq 2$ firms which produce a homogenous product at no cost and a linear inverse demand function $Q = 2 - p$.[12] In the symmetric Nash equilibrium of this model, each firm charges a price equal to 0. This outcome is also the competitive outcome. The monopoly price in this model is equal to 1. Hence, when firms collude, they will charge a price between 0 and 1. In every period, the firms decide whether to collude and if so, at what price. If the firms collude at $p \in (0, 1]$, each firm will receive an abnormal per period profit $\pi(p) = \frac{1}{n}p(2 - p)$, which is continuous and strictly increasing in $p \in [0, 1]$.[13]

Firms however face antitrust enforcement: if firms collude, they are detected by the AA with some exogenous probability $\beta \in [0, 1]$ and then they pay a fine $\xi(p)$, which we characterize below. We follow Rey (2003) and assume that only misconduct in the current period is prosecuted. Our objective is to design $\xi(p)$, which satisfies the four legal principles mentioned earlier, in order to induce the lowest collusive price possible. In particular, $\xi(p)$ is continuous, non-decreasing in p, bounded from below by 0 and from above by $\xi^{\max}(p)$, and satisfies proportionality.

We model legal upper bound $\xi^{\max}(p)$ as the lower envelop of the legal ceiling, denoted $\xi_1^{\max}(p)$, and the maximum fine due to no-bankruptcy considerations, denoted $\xi_2^{\max}(p)$. Following the structure of the current EU sentencing guidelines, we assume that the legal ceiling $\xi_1^{\max}(p)$ is determined as a fraction of the undertaking's global turnover.[14] It is

[12] Introduction of positive marginal costs does not change the qualitative aspect of our model and the results.

[13] Since we have normalized this model such that $\pi(p^N) = 0$, we can interpret $\pi(p)$ as abnormal profit.

[14] Recall that in the EU, the maximum amount of the fine imposed shall not exceed the cap of 10% of annual worldwide turnover of the undertaking in the preceding business year (see EC (2006) or Bageri *et al.* (2013)). This translates into a legal upper bound on fines which is given by the sum of the relevant turnover (equal to profit under assumption of zero marginal costs) and turnover in other markets (not corrupted by the cartel agreement) that is independent of the price set by the cartel.

a non-decreasing function of p that has both fixed and proportional components. It is given by $\xi_1^{\max}(p) = t(\pi(p) + T)$, where $t > 0$ denotes the fine multiplier applied to relevant turnover (or illegal profit) and $T \geq 0$ denotes turnover in other markets (not corrupted by the cartel agreement).[15] The maximum fine due to no-bankruptcy considerations we employ takes into account the stream of current and future profits of setting the price p forever. This generates an expected profit of $\pi(p) - \beta\xi(p)$ per period, which is non-negative if $\xi(p)$ is bounded from above by $\xi_2^{\max}(p) = \pi(p)/\beta$.[16] In summary, $\xi^{\max}(p) = \min\left\{\xi_1^{\max}(p), \xi_2^{\max}(p)\right\}$.[17]

$\xi^{\min} \geq 0$ denotes the legal lower bound or minimum fine. We first analyze the case $\xi^{\min} = 0$. In Section 4.3, we extend our analysis to $\xi^{\min} > 0$.

The legal principle of proportionality requires some explanation. A fine schedule that is limited by an insufficient legal upper bound is ineffective to deter some cartel prices and, hence, the cartel will form. Given β and $\xi(p)$, the cartel will choose the *optimal cartel price* that maximizes the present value of its member's profit with discount factor $\delta \in (0, 1)$. The fine schedule $\xi(p)$ satisfies the legal principle of proportionality if there does not exist another fine schedule $\hat{\xi}(p) \leq \xi(p)$ for all $p \in (0, 1]$ (and $<$ for some prices) such that $\hat{\xi}(p)$ induces the same optimal cartel price as $\xi(p)$ does.

If the firms collude at price $p \in (0, 1]$ in any period, the expected profit to every firm is $\pi(p) - \beta\xi(p)$. This process then repeats period after period, and each firm maximizes its discounted continuation payoff with discount factor δ per period. This repeated Bertrand model generally has

---

[15]The proposed structure also incorporates the U.S. system as a special case. Recall, that the U.S. system implies that the final fine for undertakings must not exceed a maximum of \$100 million, twice the gross pecuniary gains or twice the gross pecuniary loss to the victims. So $\xi_1^{\max}(p) = \max\{100 \text{ million}, 2\pi(p), 2\text{Loss}CS(p)\}$. This either translates into constant legal ceiling of \$100 million or into $\xi_1^{\max}(p) = 2\pi(p)$.

[16]Alternatively, we could consider $\xi_2^{\max}(p) = \pi(p)$ neglecting future profits. Our approach is flexible enough to accommodate this.

[17]It is worthwhile to clarify that both upper bounds $\xi_1^{\max}(p)$ and $\xi_2^{\max}(p)$ are motivated by no-bankruptcy considerations. However, the formal legal ceiling, which is a part of the current regulations, may not be feasible sometimes due to firm's inability to pay. The second upper bound is not a part of formal sentencing guidelines, however, it applies whenever firms are unable to pay.

many subgame perfect equilibria (see e.g., Fudenberg and Tirole (1991)). For simplicity, we focus on the class of equilibria that are supported by a simple trigger strategy profile: firms collude at price p in every period, their collusion will be detected with probability β and, if collusion is detected, each firm is fined with $\xi(p)$. However, if any firm deviates in any period by undercutting prices, the firms will repeat the static Nash/competitive equilibrium in all future periods. With such strategies, the present value of a firm's expected profit is simply $v(p, \xi(p)) = (\pi(p) - \beta\xi(p))/(1-\delta)$. In order to support collusion at p under the arbitrary fine schedule $\xi(p)$, no firm should have an incentive to slightly undercut the collusive price p, i.e.,

$$\frac{1}{1-\delta}\left[\frac{1}{n}p\,(2-p) - \beta\xi(p)\right]$$
$$\geq p(2-p) \Leftrightarrow \xi(p) \leq \frac{1-n(1-\delta)}{n\beta}p(2-p), \qquad (1)$$

where the right-hand side of the condition is the profit a firm would receive from undercutting the cartel price. Note that as in Motta and Polo (2003), price-deviating firms will not be prosecuted.[18] Also note that (1) is the general condition for sustainability of any cartel price under any fine schedule.

Given an arbitrary fine schedule $\xi(p)$ that obeys the four legal principles, the set of supportable cartel prices may not be a simple interval. Among all the supportable cartel prices, any cartel price that yields the highest expected profit among all supportable cartel prices is an optimal cartel price:

$$p^C(\xi) = \arg\max_{p\in(0,1]} v(p, \xi(p)) \quad \text{subject to condition (1).} \qquad (2)$$

Observe that a lower cartel price implies a lower deadweight loss, or a higher social welfare. Hence, our objective is to identify which fine schedule induces the lowest equilibrium price in the industry. The design of this fine schedule takes into account the optimal reaction by the cartel to the antitrust enforcement and satisfies the four legal principles.

[18]Alternative assumptions such as the possibility of prosecuting price-deviating firms would only relax the equilibrium condition for collusion to be sustainable. Hence, our results will not qualitatively change if such alternative assumptions were imposed.

Finally, in our analysis, we need a special condition based on (1) that ensures sustainability of monopoly price $p = 1$ under the legal upper bound $\xi(p) = \xi^{\max}(p)$. Note that $\xi^{\max}(p) = \xi_2^{\max}(p)$ for sufficiently low cartel prices and, otherwise, $\xi^{\max}(p) = \xi_1^{\max}(p)$. Also note that the value function $v(p, \xi_2^{\max}(p))$ is constant and that $v(p, \xi_1^{\max}(p))$ is increasing in p on $[0, 1]$. So, the cartel will collude on the monopoly price and $\xi_1^{\max}(p)$ applies at this price, provided this price is sustainable.[19] Then, for $p = 1$ and $\xi(p) = \xi_1^{\max}(p)$ in (1), we obtain the following condition for sustainability of collusion:

$$\delta \geq \frac{n - 1 + \beta t + \beta t n T}{n} > \frac{n-1}{n}. \tag{3}$$

The proof of condition (3) is as follows. After substitution of $\xi(p) = t(\pi(p) + T)$ into (1) and setting $p = 1$, we obtain $t(1/n + T) \leq \frac{1-n(1-\delta)}{n\beta}$. This implies $\delta \geq \frac{n-1+\beta t+\beta t n T}{n} > \frac{n-1}{n}$, which also ensures that the standard textbook condition $\delta > (n-1)/n$ is satisfied. In what follows, we will maintain this assumption.[20]

4. The Role of Legal Principles

In this section, we will first derive a closed-form solution for the optimal legally-constrained fine schedule that satisfies all four legal principles. This fine schedule includes an expression for the minimal cartel price. Next, we investigate the effects of modifying the legal ceiling and the legal lower bound. We conclude this section with demonstrating that the optimal legally-constrained fine schedule is superior to other fine schedules proposed in the literature. Each of these topics will be treated in a separate subsection.

---

[19] In models in which the detection probability also depends upon p, the optimal cartel price may differ from the monopoly price (see e.g., Houba *et al.* (2010 or 2012)).

[20] Note also that Buccirossi and Spagnolo (2007), Bos and Schinkel (2007), and Wils (2007) point out that the current inspection efforts and the existing upper bounds on fines, at least in the EU and several OECD countries, are insufficient to deter all cartels. In a number of related empirical studies, Connor and Lande (2005, 2006, 2008, 2012) also argue that the existing U.S. and EU penalties for cartel violations are too low resulting in high cartel overcharges. This suggests that the existing legal upper bound and levels of detection probability are not high enough to deter cartel formation so that some collusive prices can still be sustained.

4.1. *Optimal legally-constrained fine schedules*

In this section, we will characterize the optimal fine schedule constrained by the four legal principles. We begin by identifying the "maximal cartel profit" that the cartel members can guarantee themselves when facing a fine schedule that satisfies the four legal principles. Next, given the legal lower bound of a fine schedule, we derive the least possible cartel price at which each firm receives the maximal profit identified in step one. Lastly, we provide a unique fine schedule that satisfies all four legal principles and induces the minimal cartel price. This fine schedule is the lowest fine schedule (i.e., satisfies the proportionality principle) that induces the minimal cartel price, thus it is the optimal legally-constrained fine schedule. We conclude with numerical investigation of the tolerated cartel overcharge in order to gain insight into the magnitudes of the theoretical effects.

In the linear Bertrand setting with non-decreasing legal upper bound given by $\xi^{\max}(p)$, **the maximal cartel profit**, $v^* = \max_{p\in(0,1]\text{ s.t. }(1)} v(p, \xi^{\max}(p))$, introduced in Houba *et al.* (2011), is given by[21]

$$v^* = \frac{1 - \beta t(1 + nT)}{n(1 - \delta)}. \tag{4}$$

Hence, v^* can be viewed as the individual cartel member's security level or the lowest maximal profit the cartel can guarantee given the legal upper bound, which is determined by $t(\pi(p) + T)$ for prices close enough to the monopoly price. Figure 1 illustrates the maximal cartel profit v^* and the cartel price $p^* = 1$ supporting it.[22]

[21] By definition of v^*, we maximize $v(p, \xi^{\max}(p))$ subject to sustainability constraint (1). Recall that (1) is satisfied at the monopoly price whenever condition (3) holds. Without loss of generality, we may neglect (1). Also recall that for large prices $p \in [0, 1]$, we have $\xi^{\max}(p) = \xi_1^{\max}(p) = t(\pi(p) + T)$. Then, substitution of $\xi_1^{\max}$ for $\xi^{\max}$ gives $v(p, \xi^{\max}) = \frac{\pi(p)-\beta t\pi(p)-\beta tT}{1-\delta} = \frac{\frac{1}{n}(2-p)p(1-\beta t)-\beta tT}{1-\delta}$. Obviously, this expression is maximized at $p = 1$, which gives $v^* = v(1, \xi^{\max})$ as stated in (4).

[22] Note that the structure of this figure corresponds to the U.S. system with $\xi_1^{\max}(p) = t\pi(p)$ and $\xi_2^{\max}(p) > \xi_1^{\max}(p)$ for all p. Under the EU system, where $\xi_1^{\max}(p) = t(\pi(p) + T)$, with $T > 0$, we will observe a somewhat different shape of the value functions. However, the results will not be qualitatively affected by this variation in the structure of the legal upper bound. Only the ranges of sustainable cartel prices will differ under these alternative legal upper bounds. Note that in Figure 1 all prices $p \in (0, 1]$ are sustainable, since the profit from undercutting $p(2 - p) < v(p, \xi^{\max})$ for all $p \in (0, 1]$.

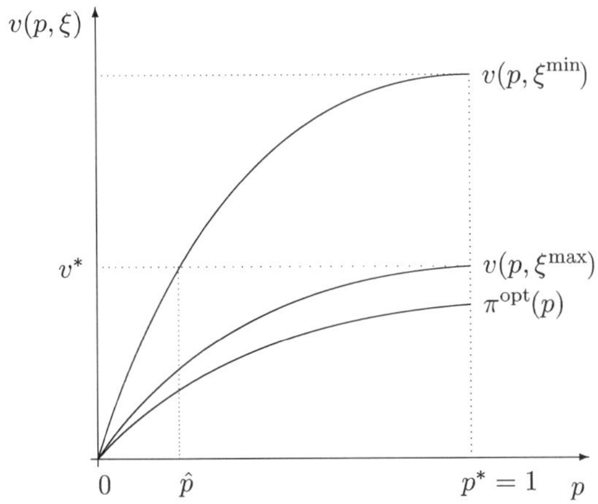

Figure 1. The maximal cartel profit v^*, the minimal cartel price $\hat{p}$, and the profit from undercutting $\pi^{\text{opt}}(p) = p(2-p)$.

Further, in searching for the optimal fine schedule that satisfies the four legal principles to deter cartel activity, the objective of antitrust enforcement should shift to minimize the harm caused by the cartel. This translates into minimization of the profit-maximizing cartel price in order to take into account the cartel's response to the fine schedule set by the AA.

The key idea is to induce the cartel to set a sustainable cartel price $\hat{p} < 1$ that gives it its lowest maximal cartel profit v^* and the cartel will be punished by $\xi^{\min}$ for setting $p \leq \hat{p}$. For that reason, we first define the entire set of sustainable cartel prices when the minimum fine $\xi^{\min}$ is imposed. For the Bertrand oligopoly and $\xi^{\min} = 0$, standard arguments imply

$$\frac{1}{1-\delta}\left[\pi(p) - \beta\xi^{\min}\right] \geq n\pi(p) \Leftrightarrow \delta \geq \frac{n-1}{n}.$$

So, under condition (3), all cartel prices $p \in [0, 1]$ can be sustained under $\xi^{\min} = 0$. Hence, it is without loss of generality to ignore equilibrium condition (1) for the cartel price $\hat{p}$ that we will characterize next.

Expression (5) shows that within the class of fine schedules considered, it is impossible to reduce the cartel price below the minimal cartel price $\hat{p}$. **The minimal cartel price**, $\hat{p}$, is the lowest cartel price that can be supported under optimally set legally-constrained fine schedule and it is given by the solution of the following equation[23]

$$v(\hat{p}, \xi^{\min}) = v^*. \tag{5}$$

Figure 1 illustrates this minimal cartel price $\hat{p}$. The intuition behind this method is based on the "minmax" principle, where we search for the lowest cartel price attainable under minimum fines (or in the absence of enforcement) that would allow cartel to secure the maximal profit v^* attained under the legal upper bound. Given that it is impossible to drive cartel profits below v^* and to prevent cartel formation under the legal upper bound, the objective of antitrust enforcement is not to minimize the cartel profit, but rather to minimize the harm caused by the cartel.

In the setting of the Bertrand oligopoly with linear demand, we can compute the **minimal cartel price**, $\hat{p}$, as the solution of the following equation:[24]

$$\frac{1}{n}\frac{(2-p)p}{1-\delta} = v^* \Leftrightarrow p^2 - 2p + n(1-\delta)v^* = 0, \tag{6}$$

$$\Rightarrow \hat{p} = 1 - \sqrt{1 - n(1-\delta)v^*}.$$

After substitution of (4), we get $\hat{p} = 1 - \sqrt{\beta t(1 + nT)}$.

The next question is whether it is feasible to induce this minimal cartel price with a fine schedule that not only satisfies the upper and lower bounds, but also monotonicity and, more importantly, proportionality. If such a fine schedule exists and indeed induces the minimal cartel price, it is **the optimal legally-constrained fine schedule** under the four restrictions imposed by the legal rules and conventions.

We approach this important issue by first investigating a stepwise fine function that is often discussed in the literature (see e.g., Immordino and Polo (2013)) in which low cartel prices are fined minimally while high prices are fined maximally. There are several reasons to first investigate such stepwise fines. First, we will identify the stepwise fine that (also) implements the minimal cartel price $\hat{p}$. Second, we will demonstrate that

[23]Note that, for general oligopoly models, if $\hat{p}$ cannot be supported as a collusive price under $\xi^{\min}$, then the best the AA can do is to induce the lowest sustainable cartel price when the optimal legally-constrained fine schedule (8) is imposed.

[24]Here we assume that $\xi^{\min} = 0$. In Section 4.3, we will relax this assumption.

this fine function only satisfies three legal principles while it fails proportionality. So, there will be more than one fine schedule that implements the minimal cartel price $\hat{p}$, but only one will satisfy all four legal principles. For stepwise fines, we derive the following result. In the proof, we also establish that (1) holds at $\hat{p}$ under the stepwise fine function.

Proposition 1 *The stepwise fine schedule that satisfies three legal principles (punishments fit the crime, bankruptcy considerations, and minimum fines) and induces the cartel to set* $\hat{p} = 1 - \sqrt{\beta t(1+nT)}$ *is given by*

$$\tilde{\xi}(p) = \begin{cases} 0, & \text{for } 0 \leq p \leq 1 - \sqrt{\beta t(1+nT)}, \\ \xi^{\max}(p), & \text{for } 1 - \sqrt{\beta t(1+nT)} < p \leq 1. \end{cases} \tag{7}$$

Proof. Recall from the proof of condition (3) that, for $p = \hat{p}$ and $\xi(\cdot) = \tilde{\xi}(\cdot)$, $\tilde{\xi}(\hat{p}) = 0$ and, hence, (1) becomes $\frac{1}{1-\delta}\pi(\hat{p}) \geq n\pi(\hat{p})$, which holds for all $\delta \geq \frac{n-1}{n}$. So, all δ that satisfy (3) also satisfy this latter condition. This establishes that (1) holds at $\hat{p}$. Next, for all $p < \hat{p}$, each cartel member gets $v(p, 0) < v^*$. For all $p \in (\hat{p}, 1)$, $v(p, \xi^{\max}(p)) < v^*$, while $v(1, \xi^{\max}(p)) = v^*$. In equilibrium, even though cartel is indifferent between $\hat{p}$ and monopoly price 1, it will choose $\hat{p}$. Because if not, then the cartel would choose the monopoly price and we can extend the zero fine to $\hat{p} + \varepsilon$ for arbitrary small $\varepsilon > 0$ and make $\hat{p} + \varepsilon$ more attractive than the monopoly price, which would break such an equilibrium.

For all cartel prices $p \in [0, 1]$, $\tilde{\xi}(p)$ is equal to either $0 = \xi^{\min}$ or $\xi^{\max}(p)$, hence, it satisfies both legal bounds. $\tilde{\xi}(p)$ also satisfies the punishments-fit-the-crime principle as it implies weakly higher fines for more serious offences. Recall $\xi^{\max}(p)$ is increasing in p on [0, 1].

This completes the proof. □

Figure 2 illustrates the stepwise fine schedule $\tilde{\xi}(p)$ that jumps from 0 to $\xi^{\max}(\cdot)$ at $\hat{p}$. It implements $\hat{p}$ as it makes collusion on any price $p > \hat{p}$ very costly. Since for all cartel prices $p \in [0, 1]$, the fine schedule $\tilde{\xi}(p)$ is equal to either $0 = \xi^{\min}$ or $\xi^{\max}(p)$, it trivially satisfies both legal bounds. It also satisfies the punishments-fit-the-crime principle as it implies weakly higher fines for more serious offences. We note that the principle of proportionality is violated, since imposing the fine $\xi^{\max}(\hat{p})$ in order to block offences just above $\hat{p}$, say $\hat{p} + \varepsilon$, is excessive as the same outcome could also have been achieved with any sufficiently large fine $\hat{\xi}(\hat{p} + \varepsilon) < \xi^{\max}(\hat{p} + \varepsilon)$. So,

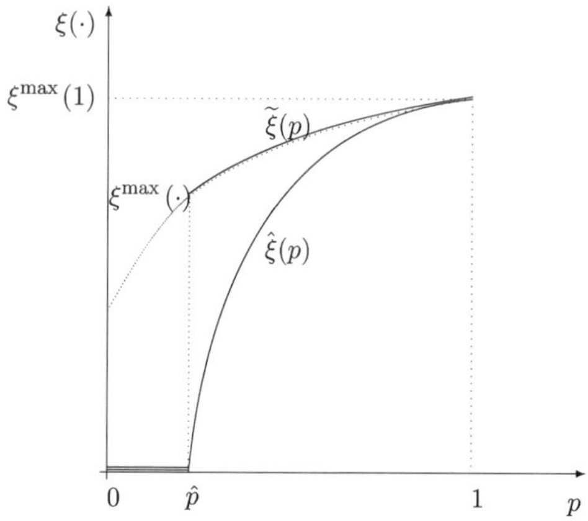

Figure 2. The optimal legally-constrained fine schedule $\hat{\xi}$ (solid curve), the stepwise fine schedule $\tilde{\xi}$ (solid curve), and the legal upper bound $\xi^{\max}$ (dotted curve).

the stepwise fine schedule will induce the second-best outcome, $\hat{p}$, but as discussed, it satisfies only three of the four legal principles and fails the principle of proportionality. To be more specific, any fine schedule $\xi(p)$ between $\hat{\xi}(p)$ and $\xi^{\max}(p)$ for $p \in (\hat{p}, 1)$ such that $\xi(1) = \xi^{\max}(1)$ and $\xi(p) = 0$ on $[0, \hat{p}]$ will also induce the cartel to set $\hat{p}$. Since such scheme also achieves $\hat{p}$ with lower fines, $\tilde{\xi}(p) = \xi^{\max}(p)$ on $(\hat{p}, 1)$ fails the principle of proportionality. This completes the analysis of stepwise fines.

Next, we characterize the **optimal legally-constrained fine schedule** that induces the minimal cartel price, $\hat{p}$, and also satisfies all four legal principles (including proportionality).

Proposition 2 *The optimal legally-constrained fine schedule that satisfies all four legal principles and induces the cartel to set* $\hat{p} = 1 - \sqrt{\beta t(1 + nT)}$ *is given by*

$$\hat{\xi}(p) = \begin{cases} 0, & \textit{for } 0 \leq p \leq 1 - \sqrt{\beta t(1 + nT)}, \\ \dfrac{1}{\beta}\left[\dfrac{1}{n}p(2 - p) - (1 - \delta)v^*\right], & \textit{for } 1 - \sqrt{\beta t(1 + nT)} < p \leq 1. \end{cases} \tag{8}$$

Proof. Similar arguments as in the proof of Proposition 1 establishes that (1) holds at $\hat{p}$ and that this price can be sustained as a cartel price under fine schedule in (8). Next, for all $p < \hat{p}$, each cartel member gets $v(p, 0) < v^* = v(\hat{p}, 0)$. For all $p \in (\hat{p}, 1]$, $v(p, \hat{\xi}(p)) = v^*$. In equilibrium, even though cartel is indifferent between any price $p \in [\hat{p}, 1]$, it will choose $\hat{p}$. Because if not and the cartel would choose $\hat{p} + \varepsilon$ for arbitrary $0 < \varepsilon \leq 1 - \hat{p}$ instead, then we can extend the zero fine to $\hat{p} + \frac{1}{2}\varepsilon$ and make $\hat{p} + \frac{1}{2}\varepsilon$ more attractive than $\hat{p} + \varepsilon$, which would break such an equilibrium.

The fine schedule in (8) satisfies all four legal principles:

1. $\hat{\xi}(p) \geq 0$ for all $p \in [0, 1]$ trivially satisfies the legal lower bound.
2. $\hat{\xi}(p) < \xi^{\max}(p)$ for all $p \in [0, 1)$ and $\hat{\xi}(1) = \xi^{\max}(1)$ also trivially satisfies the legal upper bound.
3. The punishments-fit-the-crime principle is satisfied, since $\hat{\xi}(p) = \frac{1}{\beta}\left[\frac{1}{n}p(2 - p) - (1 - \delta)v^*\right]$ is increasing in p on $(\hat{p}, 1]$, while $\hat{\xi}(p) = 0$ is constant on $[0, \hat{p}]$. This implies weakly higher fines for more grave offences.
4. The principle of proportionality is satisfied, since any fine schedule $\xi(p) < \hat{\xi}(p)$ for all p, will induce a price above $\hat{p}$, while any fine schedule $\xi(p) > \hat{\xi}(p)$ for all p cannot induce $p < \hat{p}$. More specifically, we can lower $\xi(p)$ on $(\hat{p}, 1)$ until $v(p, \xi(p))$ becomes equal to v^*. Lowering it further would increase $v(p, \xi(p))$ above v^*, inducing the cartel to set a price above $\hat{p}$.

This completes the proof. □

The fine schedule (8) is also illustrated in Figure 2, from which three legal principles can be easily verified similar to how it has been done above for the stepwise function. Both legal bounds and the punishments-fit-the-crime principle are satisfied. Within the class of fine schedules under considerations, it is the only one that achieves the smallest attainable optimal cartel price $\hat{p}$ and satisfies all four legal principles. The fine schedule (8) induces the cartel to set $\hat{p}$ as its optimal cartel price. This price lies strictly between the Nash equilibrium price and the monopoly price when the legal upper bound is imposed. In standard oligopoly models without antitrust enforcement, a lower cartel price generally implies a higher social welfare, which is also the case in this chapter. So, the minimal cartel price reduces the deadweight loss caused by the cartel.

This result indicates that the optimal fine schedule should consist of two parts. The flat part indicates price overcharges that should be tolerated given the presence of the insufficient legal upper bound and the increasing part is a downward shift of the first-best fine schedule $\frac{1}{\beta}\pi(p)$ in the absence of both sustainability considerations and legal upper bounds. The downward shift is of the size $\frac{1}{\beta}(1-\delta)v^*$ such that each cartel member is punished maximally at $p^* = 1$, which is the monopoly price in case of the Bertrand oligopoly.

If antitrust enforcement is insufficient to deter cartel activity, some cartel prices can be sustained by the cartel and society incurs a deadweight loss. The important question is how to keep the deadweight loss minimal given the legal upper bound. According to Proposition 2, the effectiveness of the fine schedule in reducing the optimal cartel price can be maximally improved by adopting fine schedule (8). This improvement is achieved by making collusion on lower prices more attractive than collusion on higher prices instead of imposing the maximum fine for all types of offences.[25] Under fine structure (8), the value of collusion on any price above $\hat{p}$ does not exceed the value of collusion on price $\hat{p}$. Hence, this fine structure blocks collusion on any price above $\hat{p}$ (including monopoly price). As a result, the deterrence power can be improved without increasing the level of the fine.

The maximal reduction of the optimal cartel price is achieved by making all prices in the range between $\hat{p}$ and monopoly price as attractive as monopoly price by reducing the fine below the legal upper bound. Moreover, the fine schedule (8) does not punish mild offences of collusion on cartel prices below $\hat{p}$. This result supports the procedure of determination of the base fine in the current U.S. sentencing guidelines, see DOJ (2010), where offences of mild gravity would be assigned a base fine of zero.

Applying the above algorithm, for the range of policy-relevant parameter values, we can identify the corresponding maximal cartel profit (v^*), the minimal cartel price ($\hat{p}$), and the optimal legally-constrained fine schedule ($\hat{\xi}(p)$) that induces the minimal cartel price. We will interpret the minimal cartel price as the **tolerated cartel overcharge**, since this is the lowest

[25] Recall that our results are related to the literature on marginal deterrence by Stigler (1971), Shavell (1992), Wilde (1992), and Mookherjee and Png (1994), where similar intuition is obtained.

Table 1. The Tolerated Cartel Overcharge in % of the Monopoly Price for Parameter Values $t = 0.5$, $T = 1.5$, and $\xi^{\min} = 0$

β	$n = 2$	$n = 3$	$n = 4$	$n = 5$	$n = 6$
0.10	55.3	47.6	40.8	34.8	29.3
0.15	45.2	35.8	27.5	20.1	13.4
0.20	36.7	25.8	16.3	7.8	0.0

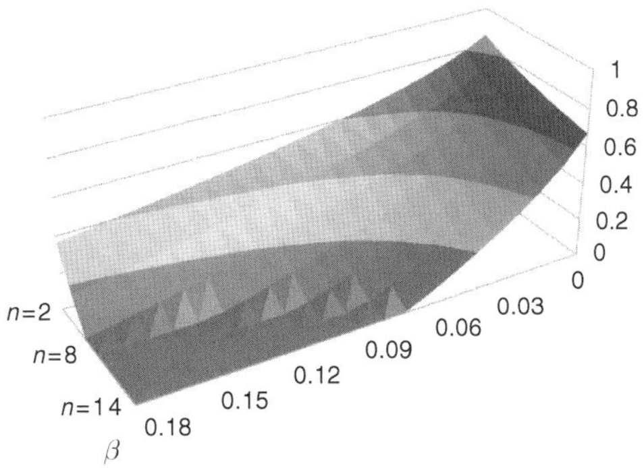

Figure 3. The tolerated cartel overcharge $\hat{p} = 1 - \sqrt{\beta t(1 + nT)}$ for parameter values $t = 0.5$, $T = 1.5$, and $\xi^{\min} = 0$.

cartel price that can be enforced given the presence of an insufficient legal upper bound on fines.

According to Bryant and Eckard (1991), the detection rate (β) in the U.S. has been estimated at the level between 0.13 and 0.17.[26] In Table 1 and Figure 3, we analyze detection probabilities around this range of values. Discount factor calibration is adopted from Buccirossi and Spagnolo (2007) and set at $\delta = 0.9$. Following the current guidelines, we set the minimum fine at 0. Finally, the legal ceiling on the fine is parametrized by the EU system with $0.5(\pi(p) + 1.5)$, which is also comparable with the limited liability restrictions (or no-bankruptcy considerations) as per period illegal

[26]Per-period detection probabilities close to 0.15 have also been employed in the Buccirossi and Spagnolo (2007), Bageri *et al.* (2013), and Katsoulacos and Ulph (2013).

gains (relevant turnover) in our setting with linear demand specified above cannot exceed the value of monopoly gains, which is 1.

In order to give the exact magnitude of changes in cartel overcharges when the detection probability and market conditions change, we also present Table 1. Both this table and Figure 3 show that the tolerated cartel overcharge can vary substantially with the size of the detection probability and the number of firms in the cartel.[27] Under stronger antitrust enforcement, when detection probability reaches 0.2, the full deterrence outcome, where the cartel does not find it attractive to set prices above competitive level of 0, can be achieved for oligopolies with at least six firms. While with a smaller detection rate, e.g., $\beta = 0.1$, the cartel overcharge still can reach up to 55.3% of the monopoly price.

Generally, analyzing the structure of the tolerated cartel overcharge implied by (6), which is given by $\hat{p} = 1 - \sqrt{\beta t(1 + nT)}$, we can state the following result.

Proposition 3 *The tolerated cartel overcharge decreases when the toughness of the enforcement regime increases (i.e., when either the detection probability or the fine multiplier applied to the relevant turnover). Moreover, the tolerated cartel overcharge decreases when either the number of firms in the market or turnover on other relevant markets is larger.*

Proof. Partial differentiation of expression $\hat{p} = 1 - \sqrt{\beta t(1 + nT)}$ with respect to β (detection probability) and t (slope of the legal ceiling) implies $\frac{\partial \hat{p}}{\partial \beta} < 0$ and $\frac{\partial \hat{p}}{\partial t} < 0$ for the policy instruments. Similarly, partial differentiation with respect to n (market conditions) and T (the size of turnover outside the market) implies $\frac{\partial \hat{p}}{\partial n} < 0$ and $\frac{\partial \hat{p}}{\partial T} < 0$. This completes the proof of this proposition. □

Note that the term $1 + nT$ can be rewritten as $n\left(\frac{1}{n} + T\right)$. The term between brackets consists of a cartel member's per-period profit of sustaining the monopoly price and the relevant turnover on other markets. Relatively speaking, the ratio of the profit $\frac{1}{n}$ and T, $\frac{1}{nT}$, shows that the smaller $\frac{1}{n}$ is compared to T, the less incentives the cartel has to collude because the firm's legal ceiling increases in T. Therefore, firms for which the market under consideration is relatively small in terms of their overall

[27] This also confirms similar findings in Katsoulacos and Ulph (2013).

activities will have smaller values of v^* and, consequently, will have a lower minimal cartel price.

4.2. *The impact of legal ceilings*

In this section, we discuss the impact of legal ceilings specified in the sentencing guidelines. The reason to concentrate on legal ceilings is that the antitrust authorities can influence the level of the legal ceiling, when designing or modifying sentencing guidelines, while bankruptcy considerations are not adjustable as these can only be either respected or abolished. We show that the presence of legal ceilings will upset the positive effect of the fines, which could otherwise achieve full deterrence, and analyze numerically the welfare distortions caused by the presence of insufficient legal ceilings.

Current cartel fines in both the EU and U.S. are often proportional to the individual firm's illegal gains $\pi(p)$ (see e.g., Bageri *et al.* (2013) or Katsoulacos and Ulph (2013)). These fines may achieve full deterrence if (1) does not hold for all cartel prices on $(0, 1]$, i.e., $\xi(p) > \frac{\pi(p)(1-(1-\delta)n)}{\beta}$ for all $p \in (0, 1]$. However, by condition (3), these fines are capped by the legal ceiling. Imposing such a full deterrence schedule capped by the legal ceiling, $\min\{\frac{\pi(p)(1-(1-\delta)n)}{\beta}, \xi_1^{\max}(p)\}$ for all $p \in (0, 1]$, lets the monopoly price prevail, as we have shown in Section 4.1. This is also what has been argued by e.g., Bos and Schinkel (2007), Buccirossi and Spagnolo (2007), or Wils (2007).[28] We raise the additional question whether such negative result is always inevitable in the presence of legal ceilings on fines? The answer is No, as with the optimal legally-constrained fine schedule in (8), we achieve a lower cartel price, higher consumer welfare, and lower relative welfare loss compared to capped full-deterrence fine schedules, as our numerical results in Tables 2a and 2b illustrate. The main policy implication is that in the presence of the insufficient legal ceilings, the antitrust agencies should avoid standard proportional fine schedules, even if they could potentially achieve the full deterrence outcome, and rather

[28]They argue that the ceilings on antitrust fines in both the U.S. and the EU are insufficient to deter cartels. They imply that these ceilings make antitrust policies either completely ineffective, such that cartels can sustain all prices including the monopoly price, or at best partially effective in the sense that high prices are still sustainable by the cartel.

Table 2a. The Optimal Legally-Constrained Fine Structure

$\xi_1^{\max}(p)$	v^*	$\hat{p}$	$SW(\hat{p})$	$CS(\hat{p})$	$DWL(\hat{p})$	DWL/TW
$t = 0.50$	3.50	0.452	18.98	11.98	1.023	0.051
$t = 0.25$	4.25	0.613	18.15	9.66	1.861	0.093

Table 2b. The Capped Full-Deterrence Fine Structure

$\xi_1^{\max}(p)$	v^*	p^M	$SW(p^M)$	$CS(p^M)$	$DWL(p^M)$	DWL/TW
$t = 0.50$	n/a	1	15	5	5	0.25
$t = 0.25$	n/a	1	15	5	5	0.25

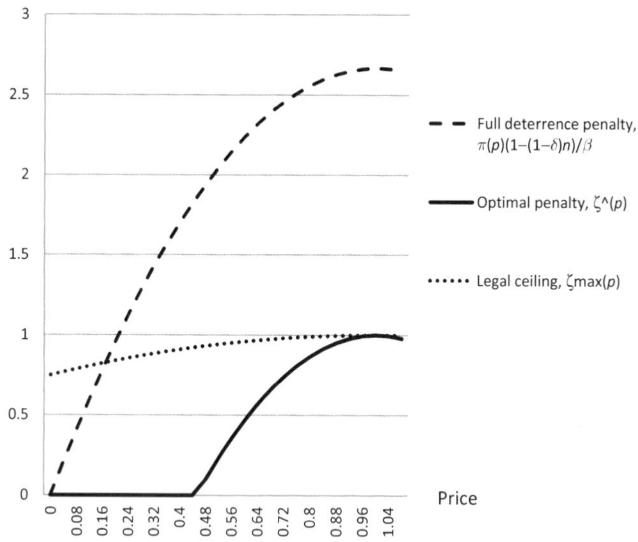

Figure 4. The optimal legally-constrained fine schedule (solid line), the full-deterrence fine structure (dashed line), and the legal ceiling (dotted curve) for parameter values $\beta = 0.15$, $t = 0.5$, $T = 1.5$, $n = 2$, $\delta = 0.9$, and $\xi^{\min} = 0$.

implement an optimal legally-constrained fine schedule that induces a better outcome with a lower fine schedule (see Figure 4, where the optimal legally-constrained fine schedule is given by the solid line, while the lower bound on full-deterrence fine schedules $\frac{\pi(p)(1-(1-\delta)n)}{\beta}$ is given by the dashed line). This discussion is summarized in the following proposition.

Proposition 4 *(i) Antitrust enforcement characterized by capped full-deterrence fine schedules approximated by* $\min\{\frac{\pi(p)(1-(1-\delta)n)}{\beta}, \xi_1^{\max}(p)\}$ *for all* $p \in (0, 1]$ *is ineffective in reducing the cartel price below the monopoly price.*

(ii) Antitrust enforcement characterized by the optimal legally-constrained fine schedule $\hat{\xi}(p)$ *in (8) is effective in reducing the cartel price below the monopoly price.*

(iii) The optimal legally-constrained fine schedule $\hat{\xi}(p)$ *in (8) is always lower than the capped full-deterrence fine schedule on* $(0, 1)$.

Proof. (i) For given β, the full-deterrence fine (or first-best) structure should satisfy $\xi(p) > \frac{\pi(p)(1-(1-\delta)n)}{\beta}$ for all $p \in (0, 1]$. This fine structure destabilizes all cartel activity, since (1) fails for all $p \in (0, 1]$. However, by (3) such fine schedule is infeasible, because it would lie above $\xi_1^{\max}(p)$ at $p = 1$, i.e., $\xi_1^{\max}(1) < \frac{\pi(1)(1-(1-\delta)n)}{\beta}$. Hence, the cartel sets $p = 1$ because this price maximizes $v(p, \xi_1^{\max}(p))$, which upsets full deterrence.

(ii) This follows from the discussion in Section 4.1. The optimal legally-constrained fine schedule $\hat{\xi}(p)$ in (8), which incorporates the legal ceiling $\xi_1^{\max}(p) \leq \frac{\pi(p)(1-(1-\delta)n)}{\beta}$ at $p = 1$, induces $\hat{p}$ specified in (6). Clearly, $\hat{p} = 1 - \sqrt{\beta t(1 + nT)} < 1$ for all $\beta > 0$, $t > 0$, and $T \geq 0$.

(iii) Finally, for the flat part, the inequality trivially holds. Therefore, consider $p \in (\hat{p}, 1]$. Then, $\hat{\xi}(p) < \xi_1^{\max}(p)$ also trivially holds. Next, the following equivalence can be shown:

$$\frac{1}{\beta}[\pi(p) - (1-\delta)\, v^*] < \frac{\pi(p)(1-(1-\delta)n)}{\beta} \iff v^* > n\pi(p).$$

The latter inequality holds for all $p \in (\hat{p}, 1]$. To see this, first note that the monopoly price $p = 1$ is sustainable and the profit function is increasing in p. Therefore, $n\pi(p) < n\pi(1) < v(1, \xi_1^{\max}(1)) = v^*$. This completes the proof. □

Figure 4 clarifies this result. It illustrates the relevant fine schedules mentioned in Proposition 4 for parameter values $\beta = 0.15$, $\delta = 0.9$, $n = 2$, $t = 0.5$, $T = 1.5$, and $\xi^{\min} = 0$.[29] These schedules are the optimal

[29]To simplify the analysis and to concentrate on the pure effects of changing legal ceilings in this section, we assume that $\xi^{\min} = 0$. Obviously, the conclusions of this section will not change if $\xi^{\min} > 0$.

legally-constrained fine schedule (solid curve), $\hat{\xi}(p)$, the (lower bound on the) full-deterrence fine schedule (dashed curve), $\frac{\pi(p)(1-(1-\delta)n)}{\beta}$, that intersects the legal ceiling (dotted curve), $t(\pi(p)+T)$, once at $p = 0.16$. The capped full-deterrence fine schedule consists of the lower envelope of the dashed and dotted curves. As we have shown, even under the fine structure that could potentially achieve full deterrence, the presence of the legal ceiling enables the firms to collude at $p = 1$. On the other hand, the optimal legally-constrained fine schedule implements a tolerated cartel overcharge of 45.2% and, due to the restrictive legal ceiling, antitrust enforcement cannot reduce the cartel price any lower.

In Table 2, we provide numerical values that confirm the ineffectiveness of the standard fine structure in the presence of insufficient legal ceilings of the form $t(\pi(p)+T)$ for two values of t, 0.5 and 0.25, and all other parameter values as in Figure 4.[30] This table essentially considers two variations of Figure 4 and is meant to illustrate the magnitude of cartel pricing and welfare implications of various caps on legal ceilings for both the optimal legally-constrained fine schedule proposed in this chapter and the capped full-deterrence fine structure. Table 2a shows that consumer surplus loss due to the distortion caused by the presence of insufficient legal ceilings could be quite sizable. For the case when the legal ceiling increases due to an increase in t from 0.25 to 0.5, the effectiveness of the deterrence is increased considerably. Note that the minimal cartel price decreases from $\hat{p} = 0.613$ to $\hat{p} = 0.452$, which translates into a reduction of the tolerated cartel overcharge from 61.3 to 45.2%. Also the relative welfare loss due to price distortions is reduced from 9.3 to 5.1%. Both the cartel price and this loss decrease with the level of the legal ceiling suggesting that increasing the legal ceilings would be a good development.

4.3. *The impact of minimum fines*

When positive minimum fines $\xi^{\min} > 0$ are present, we obtain the minimal cartel price by straightforward application of (5). Formally, the **minimal**

[30] In our linear Bertrand model, the discounted social welfare function becomes $SW(p;\delta) = \frac{4-p^2}{2(1-\delta)}$, the deadweight loss is given by $DWL(p;\delta) = \frac{p^2}{2(1-\delta)}$. The maximum total welfare that could be realized in the absence of price distortions is achieved when $p = 0$ and is given by $TW^{\text{comp}}(p;\delta) = \frac{2}{1-\delta}$.

cartel price, denoted as $\hat{p}^{\min}$, will be given by the solution of the following equation

$$\frac{\frac{1}{n}(2-p)p - \beta\xi^{\min}}{1-\delta} = v^* \Leftrightarrow p^2 - 2p + n(1-\delta)v^* + n\beta\xi^{\min} = 0,$$
$$\Rightarrow \hat{p}^{\min} = 1 - \sqrt{1 - n(1-\delta)v^* - n\beta\xi^{\min}}.$$

The intuition behind this method is again based on the minmax principle, where we search for the lowest cartel price attainable under minimum fine that would allow cartel to secure the maximal profits attained under the legal upper bound.

Substituting for v^* from expression (4), we get $\hat{p}^{\min} = 1 - \sqrt{\beta t(1+nT) - n\beta\xi^{\min}}$. This proves the following result.

Proposition 5 *The tolerated cartel overcharge increases when the minimum fine increases.*

Proof.
Partial differentiation of expression $\hat{p}^{\min} = 1 - \sqrt{\beta t(1+nT) - n\beta\xi^{\min}}$ with respect to $\xi^{\min}$ implies $\frac{\partial\hat{p}^{\min}}{\partial\xi^{\min}} > 0$. This proves the result. □

The result of Proposition 5 is illustrated in Figure 5. It shows that the imposition of any positive minimum fine $\xi^{\min} > 0$ results in the downward

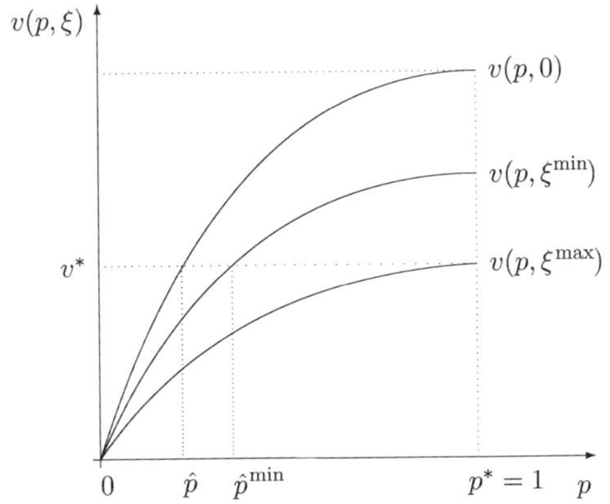

Figure 5. The impact of a positive minimum fine $\xi^{\min}$.

Table 3. The Impact of Minimum Fines under Different Legal Ceilings

$\xi^{\min}$	v^*	$\hat{p}^{\min}$	$SW(\hat{p})$	$CS(\hat{p})$	$DWL(\hat{p})$	DWL/TW
High legal ceiling						
0.0	3.50	0.452	18.98	11.98	1.023	0.051
0.1	3.50	0.480	18.85	11.55	1.154	0.058
0.2	3.50	0.510	18.70	11.10	1.301	0.065
0.3	3.50	0.542	18.53	10.63	1.467	0.073
Low legal ceiling						
0.0	4.25	0.613	18.15	9.66	1.861	0.093
0.1	4.25	0.654	17.89	9.11	2.111	0.106
0.2	4.25	0.700	17.55	8.45	2.450	0.123
0.3	4.25	0.755	17.19	7.81	2.813	0.140

shift of the cartel value function from $v(p, 0)$ to $v(p, \xi^{\min})$ and, hence, the minimal cartel price increases from $\hat{p}$ to $\hat{p}^{\min}$.[31]

Table 3 illustrates the exact magnitude of pricing and welfare implications of imposing minimum fines numerically, where most parameter values are as in Figure 4.

In Table 3, we normalize ceilings under the EU system and the U.S. system such that the fines at the monopoly price are equal and compare the impact of the minimum fine for both low and high ceilings in both the U.S. and EU system. So, we compare the pair consisting of the EU system ceiling $0.5(\pi(p) + 1.5)$ and the U.S. system ceiling $2\pi(p)$ with the pair consisting of the EU system ceiling $0.25(\pi(p)+1.5)$ and the U.S. system ceiling $\pi(p)$. We identify them in the table as high and low legal ceilings, respectively.

For the case with high legal ceilings, once the minimum fine of 0.3 is imposed, the effectiveness of the deterrence is reduced and the tolerated cartel overcharge increases from 45.2 to 54.2%. Also the relative welfare loss due to price distortions increases from 5.1 to 7.3%. For low ceilings, the effects of positive minimum fines are even more pronounced.

[31]Note that the structure of Figure 5 corresponds to the U.S. system with $\xi_1^{\max}(p) = t\pi(p)$ and $\xi_2^{\max}(p) > \xi_1^{\max}(p)$ for all p. Under the EU system, where $\xi_1^{\max}(p) = t(\pi(p) + T)$, with $T > 0$, we will observe a somewhat different shape of the value functions. However, the qualitative conclusions about the impact of minimum fines on the minimal cartel price remain the same.

4.4. *Comparative analysis: three relevant fine structures*

As discussed in Section 4.1, the equilibrium cartel price induced by the optimal legally-constrained fine structure introduced in this chapter, is given by $\hat{p} = 1 - \sqrt{\beta t(1 + nT)}$. This price is clearly below the monopoly price, 1, for all $\beta > 0$, $T \geq 0$, and $t > 0$. We now consider the cartel prices under three alternative fine structures which were proposed in the literature and show that these fine structures lead to higher cartel prices. The alternative fine structures which we consider include fines based on revenues (see e.g., Bageri *et al.* (2013), Katsoulacos and Ulph (2013), or Souam (2001)), fines based on illegal gains (see e.g., Harrington (2004, 2005) or Houba *et al.* (2010, 2012)), and fixed fines (see e.g., Rey (2003) or Motta and Polo (2003)).

A **fine based on revenues (or illegal profits)** is given by $\xi(p) = \alpha\pi(p) = \frac{\alpha(2-p)p}{n}$, where α is the multiplier of the proportional fine. The value of collusion for each individual cartel member, when the fines are based on revenues/illegal profits, is given by[32]

$$V(p, \alpha) = \frac{\pi(p) - \beta\alpha\pi(p)}{1 - \delta} = \frac{1}{n}\frac{(2 - p)p(1 - \beta\alpha)}{1 - \delta}. \tag{9}$$

A **fixed fine** is given by $\xi(p) = F$, where F is a fixed number. The value of collusion under the fixed fines is given by

$$V(p, F) = \frac{\pi(p) - \beta F}{1 - \delta} = \frac{\frac{1}{n}(2 - p)p - \beta F}{1 - \delta}. \tag{10}$$

Analyzing the above value functions, we can state the following result.

Proposition 6 *The optimal legally-constrained fine schedule (8) outperforms fines based on revenues, fines based on illegal gains, and fixed fines that are ineffective in reducing cartel price below the monopoly price.*

[32]Note that in the setting of linear Bertrand model with zero marginal costs analyzed in this chapter, cartel illegal gains and cartel revenues coincide. However, introduction of positive marginal costs will not change the qualitative results of the comparison provided in this section. As shown in Houba *et al.* (2010), proportional fines based on illegal gains cannot reduce the cartel price below the monopoly level, provided that β is fixed. Bageri *et al.* (2013) show that proportional fines based on revenues can only further increase the optimal cartel price, which also applies to the linear Bertrand model with positive marginal costs.

Proof. If $\beta\alpha < 1$, then $V(p, \alpha)$ in (9) is maximized at $p = 1$. This price also satisfies sustainability condition (1), which can be rewritten as $\delta \geq \frac{n-1+\alpha\beta}{n} > \frac{n-1}{n}$. Hence, fines based on illegal profits cannot reduce the cartel price below the monopoly price. Recall that in the setting of the linear Bertrand model with zero marginal costs analyzed in this chapter, cartel illegal gains and cartel revenues coincide. Hence, exactly the same arguments will apply for the case when fines are based on revenues.

If $\beta F < \pi(p)$ for some $p \in (0, 1]$, then $V(p, F)$ in (10) is maximized at $p = 1$. This price also satisfies sustainability condition (1), if $\beta F \leq \frac{1-(1-\delta)n}{n}$. Hence, relatively low fixed fines also cannot reduce the cartel price below the monopoly price.

Finally, recall our analysis in Section 4.1, which shows that the optimal legally-constrained fine schedule (8) induces $\hat{p} = 1 - \sqrt{\beta t(1 + nT)} < 1$, for all $\beta > 0$, $t > 0$, and $T \geq 0$. Hence, the fine schedule in (8) outperforms both fixed and proportional fine schedules as it induces $\hat{p} < 1$. □

This proposition implies that the optimal legally-constrained fine schedule outperforms fines based on revenues, fines based on illegal gains, and fixed fines. We will illustrate this conclusion graphically in Figure 6. In order to make all four schemes comparable, we parameterize the multipliers in the following way: $\alpha/n = F = \xi^{\max}(1) = 1$ in the duopoly case.

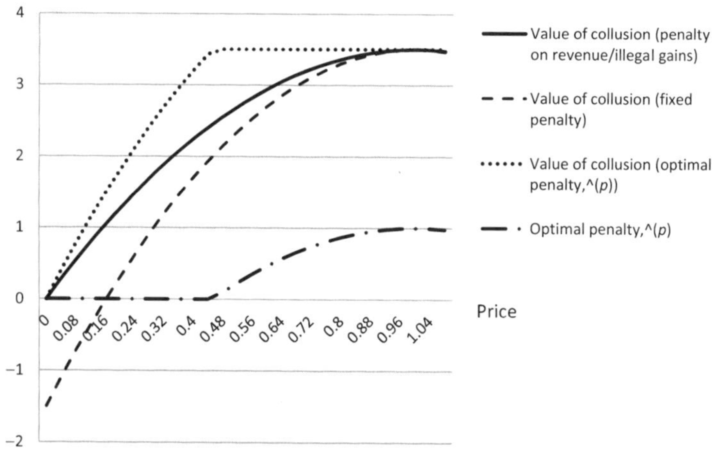

Figure 6. The value of collusion under three alternative fine structures identified in (8), (9), and (10) for parameter values $\beta = 0.15$, $\delta = 0.9$, $\xi^{\max}(1) = F = 1$, $\xi^{\min} = 0$, $\alpha = 2$, $n = 2$.

Furthermore, as before, we take $\beta = 0.15$ and $\delta = 0.9$ for the additional parameter values.

Figurc 6 illustrates the value functions of collusion under three alternative fine structures identified in (9) and (10) and the optimal legally-constrained fine schedule (8). Figure 6 shows that, for the fines of similar magnitude, the optimal legally-constrained fine proposed in this chapter (dotted value function) outperforms both fixed fines (dashed value function) and fines based on revenues/illegal gains (solid value function) in terms of achieving the lowest cartel price where the top is reached. The optimal legally-constrained fine structure induces the minimal optimal cartel price $\hat{p} = 0.425$ and, hence, implies higher social welfare (and a lower deadweight loss). While fixed fines and fines based on revenues or illegal gains cannot reduce cartel price below the monopoly level. This again confirms that the effectiveness of the fine schedule in reducing the optimal cartel price can be maximally improved by adapting the optimal legally-constrained fine schedule (8).

5. Concluding Remarks

We analyze the economic consequences of legal principles in crime enforcement in the framework of classic Bertrand oligopoly model with linear demand. Our analysis establishes the optimal legally-constrained fine schedule that maximizes social welfare given existing legal constraints. This schedule remains below the legal ceiling and there is a range of low cartel prices for which the fine is set to zero according to the legal lower bound. Hence, the main policy recommendation is that if the AA cannot set a high enough fine to deter cartel activity, then it should avoid setting the highest fine schedule that is legally available and instead the AA should set a lower fine schedule that induces collusion at a lower price. In other words, the AA can and should set fines in a smarter manner such that mild offenses are not fined at all. Hence, our results call for a reconsideration of the common wisdom in the economics of crime that setting the fine equal to the available legal upper bound always increases the effectiveness of deterrence.

In the proposed framework, one can easily assess the impact of legal principles on the enforced cartel price. Our approach allows to quantify the economic costs of adapting society's legal principles through the differences in society's deadweight losses. This is illustrated by our numerical analyses of considering alternative ceilings and positive minimum fines. We obtain that increasing maximum penalties by shifting the legal ceiling upwards decreases the cartel's profits, and consequently, reduces the cartel price and increases social welfare. On the other hand, imposing minimum fines will enable the cartel to set a higher price. Therefore, positive minimum fines reduce social welfare and should never be imposed or, if they are currently implemented, they should be abolished. Our analysis provides a technique to adequately deal with such modifications of legal rules.

Furthermore, in the literature on antitrust enforcement, see Harrington (2010), Buccirossi and Spagnolo (2007), Bos and Schinkel (2007), or Bageri *et al.* (2013), it is often argued that corporate antitrust fines are insufficient to successfully deter cartel formation and that the legal upper bounds should be increased. We confirm that increasing the legal upper bound is a right trend in general. But we also show that even in the presence of insufficient legal upper bounds, the effectiveness of deterrence can still be improved by reducing fines for mild offences as our optimal legally-constrained fine schedule prescribes.

We also compare the deterrent effect of the optimal legally-constrained fine structure and the deterrent effects of the other types of fine structures currently looked at in the literature. For comparison, we consider three alternative types of fine structure analyzed in the recent antitrust literature (including fines based on revenue (see e.g., Bageri *et al.* (2013), Katsoulacos and Ulph (2013), or Souam (2001)), fines based on illegal gains (see e.g., Harrington (2004, 2005) or Houba *et al.* (2010, 2012)) or fixed fines (see e.g., Rey (2003) or Motta and Polo (2003)). We conclude that optimal legally-constrained fine structure proposed in this chapter outperforms all three above-mentioned systems.

Finally, implementation of the proposed legally-constrained fine structure is, probably, more problematic than implementation of the standard proportional fine structures based on illegal gains or revenues, since it requires not only the estimation of the gravity of the offence, but also information about market conditions, legal rules, and the detection rate. On the other hand, it can be viewed as a price cap implementation problem, where price cap is implemented through antitrust enforcement and not through sectorial regulation.

References

Bageri, V., Y. Katsoulacos and G. Spagnolo (2013). "The Distortive Effects of Antitrust Fines Based on Revenue," *The Economic Journal*, 123(572), pp. 545–557.

Becker, G. S. (1968). "Crime and Punishment: An Economic Approach," *Journal of Political Economy*, 76, pp. 169–217.

Bos, I. and M. P. Schinkel (2007). "On the Scope for the European Commission's 2006 Fining Guidelines under the Legal Maximum Fine," *Journal of Competition Law and Economics*, 2, pp. 673–682.

Bryant, P. G. and E. W. Eckard (1991). "Price Fixing: The Probability of Getting Caught," *The Review of Economics and Statistics*, 73, pp. 531–536.

Buccirossi, P. and G. Spagnolo (2007). Optimal Fines in the Era of Whistleblowers — Should Price Fixers Still Go to Prison? in V. Goshal and J. Stennek (Eds.), *The Political Economy of Antitrust*, Elsevier, Amsterdam.

Burca, de, G. (1993). "The Principle of Proportionality and its Application in EC Law," *Yearbook of European Law*, 13(1), pp. 105–150.

Connor, J. M. and R. H. Lande (2005). "How High Do Cartels Raise Prices: Implications for Optimal Cartel Fine," *Tulane Law Review*, 80, pp. 513–570.

Connor, J. M. and R. H. Lande (2006). "The Size of Cartel Overcharges: Implications for U.S. and EU fining Policies," *Antitrust Bulletin*, 51, pp. 983–1022.

Connor, J. M. and R. H. Lande (2008). Cartel Overcharges and Optimal Cartel Fines, in S. Waller (Ed), *Issues in Competition Law and Policy*, Vol. 3, AMA Section of Antitrust Law, Chapter 88, pp. 2203–2218.

Connor, J. M. and R. H. Lande (2012). "Cartels As Rational Business Strategy: New Data Demonstrates that Crime Pays," Mimeo. Available at http://www.luc.edu/media/lucedu/law/centers/antitrust/pdfs/events/connor_lande.pdf.

Cooter, R. and T. Ulen (2007). *Law and Economics*, Addison Wesley Longman, California.

Craycraft, C., J. L. Craycraft and J. Gallo (1997). "Antitrust Sanctions and Firm Ability to Pay," *Review of Industrial Organization*, 12, pp. 171–183.

DOJ (2010). "US Sentencing Guidelines (Chapter 8: Sentencing of organizations)". Available at http://www.ussc.gov/2009guid/CHAP8.htm.

EC (2006). "Guidelines on the Method of Setting Fines Imposed Pursuant to Article 23(2)(a) of Regulation no 1/2003," *Official Journal of the European Union* (2006/C 210/02), Brussels.

Fish, M. (2008). "An Eye for an Eye: Proportionality as a Moral Principle of Punishment," *Oxford Journal of Legal Studies*, 28, pp. 57–71.

Fudenberg, D. and J. Tirole (1991). *Game Theory*, MIT Press, Cambridge.

Gallo, J. C., K. G. Dau Schmidt, J. L. Craycraft and C. J. Parker (1994). "Criminal Penalties Under the Sherman Act: A Study of Law and Economics," *Research in Law and Economics*, 16, pp. 25–71.

Harrington, J. (2004). "Cartel Pricing Dynamics in the Presence of an Antitrust Authority," *RAND Journal of Economics*, 35, pp. 651–673.

Harrington, J. (2005). "Optimal Cartel Pricing in the Presence of an Antitrust Authority," *International Economic Review*, 46, pp. 145–170.

Harrington, J. (2010). "Comment on Antitrust Sanctions," *Competition Policy International*, 6, pp. 41–51.

Harrington, J. and Chen (2007). The Impact of the Corporate Leniency Program on Cartel Formation and the Cartel Price Path, in V. Ghosal and J. Stennek (Eds.), *The Political Economy of Antitrust*. Elsevier.

Houba, H., E. Motchenkova and Q. Wen (2010). "Antitrust Enforcement with Price-Dependent Fines and Detection Probabilities," *Economics Bulletin*, 30(3), pp. 2017–2027.

Houba, H., E. Motchenkova and Q. Wen (2011). "Antitrust Enforcement and Marginal Deterrence," *(2011) Tinbergen Institute Discussion Papers* 11-166/1, revised 2013.

Houba, H., E. Motchenkova and Q. Wen (2012). "Competitive Prices as Optimal Cartel Prices," *Economics Letters*, 114, pp. 39–42.

Immordino, G. and M. Polo (2013). "Antitrust, Legal Standards and Investment," *IEFE Working Paper* No. 54.

Katsoulacos, Y. and D. Ulph (2013). "Antitrust Penalties and the Implications of Empirical Evidence on Cartel Overcharges," *The Economic Journal*, 123(572), pp. 558–581.

Jacobs, F. G. (1999). Recent Developments in the Principle of Proportionality in EC Law, in E. Ellis (Ed.), *The Principle of Proportionality in the Laws in Europe*, Hart Publishing, United Kingdom.

Mookherjee, D. and I. P. L. Png (1994). "Marginal Deterrence in Enforcement of Law," *Journal of Political Economy*, 102, pp. 1039–1066.

Motta, M. and M. Polo (2003). "Leniency Programs and Cartel Prosecution," *International Journal of Industrial Organization*, 21, pp. 347–379.

Posner, R. A. (1976 & 2001 second edition). *Antitrust Law: An Economic Perspective*, University of Chicago Press, Chicago.

Rey, P. (2003). Towards a Theory of Competition Policy, in M. Dewatripont, L. Hansen and S. Turnovsky (Eds.), *Advances in Economics and Econometrics: Theory and Applications*, Cambridge University Press, Cambridge.

Sauter, W. (2013). "Proportionality in EU Law: A Balancing Act?," *TILEC Discussion Paper* No. 2013-003.

Shavell, S. (1992). "A Note on Marginal Deterrence," *International Review of Law and Economics*, 12, pp. 345–355.

Stigler, G. (1970). "The Optimum Enforcement of Laws," *Journal of Political Economy*, 78, pp. 526–536.

Souam, S. (2001). "Optimal Antitrust Policy under Different Regimes of Fines," *International Journal of Industrial Organization*, 19, pp. 1–26.

Sullivan, E. and R. S. Frase (2008). *Proportionality Principles in American Law: Controlling Excessive Government Actions*, Oxford University Press, Oxford, USA.

Tridimas, T. (2006). *The General Principles of EC Law*, Oxford EC Law Library, Oxford University Press, Oxford, USA.

Usher, J. A. (1998). *General Principles of EC Law*, European Law Series, Longman, Edinburgh.

Wehmhorner, N. (2005). "Optimal Fining Policies," Paper Presented at the Remedies and Sanctions in Competition Policy Conference, Amsterdam Center for Law and Economics.

Werden, G. and M. Simon (1987). "Why Price Fixers Should Go to Prison," *The Antitrust Bulletin*, 32, pp. 917–937.

Wilde, L. (1992). "Criminal Choice, Nonmonetary Sanctions, and Marginal Deterrence: A Normative Analysis," *International Review of Law and Economics*, 12, pp. 333–44.

Wils, W. (2007). "The European Commission's 2006 Guidelines on Antitrust Fines: A Legal and Economic Analysis," *World Competition*, 30, pp. 197–230.

Chapter 15

Deterrence in Competition Law*

Paolo Buccirossi

Laboratorio di economia, antitrust e regolamentazione
paolo.buccirossi@learlab.com

Lorenzo Ciari

European Bank for Reconstruction and Development
ciaril@ebrd.com
lorenzociari@hotmail.com

Tomaso Duso

DIW and DICE
TDuso@diw.de

Giancarlo Spagnolo

University of Rome Tor Vergata, SITE-Stockholm, and CEPR
Giancarlo.Spagnolo@uniroma2.it
Giancarlo.Spagnolo@hhs.se

Cristiana Vitale

Organisation for Economic Cooperation and Development (Paris)
Cristiana.VITALE@oecd.org

*This chapter is based on a research project we undertook for the Directorate General for Economic and Financial Affairs of the European Commission, with the support of the Directorate General for Competition. We thank Fabienne Ilzkovitz, Roderick Meiklejohn, Adriaan Dierx, Adam Lederer, Francesco Montaruli, and Martin Peitz for their comments on previous drafts of this chapter and Gianmarco Calanchi and Paolo Colonna for their excellent research assistance. Tomaso Duso gratefully acknowledges financial support from the Deutsche Forschungsgemeinschaft through SFB/TR 15.

Abstract

This chapter provides a comprehensive discussion of the deterrence properties of a competition policy regime. On the basis of the economic theory of law enforcement, we identify several factors that are likely to affect its degree of deterrence: (1) sanctions and damages; (2) financial and human resources; (3) powers during the investigation; (4) quality of the law; (5) independence; and (6) separation of powers. We then discuss how to measure deterrence. We review the literature that uses surveys to solicit direct information on changes in the behavior of firms due to the threats posed by the enforcement of antitrust rules, and the literature based on the analysis of hard data. Finally, we argue that the most challenging task both theoretically and empirically is how to distinguish between "good" and "bad" deterrence.

Keywords: Competition policy, law enforcement, deterrence.

JEL Classification Codes: K21, K42, L4.

1. Introduction

Deterrence is a central theme in the theory and the practice of law enforcement; the enforcement of competition law is no exception. Laws are enacted in order to influence behavior such that socially undesirable conduct is not undertaken. A law enforcement system that "taxes" agents for undertaking unlawful behaviors, but is not able to prevent them, represents a waste of resources from an economic point of view as law enforcement is costly. It requires resources to monitor agents' behaviors, to detect infringements, to prove violations, and to inflict punishments. These resources might be devoted to other aims. Moreover, the sanction imposed on apprehended wrongdoers is, at best, a mere transfer that does not improve social welfare. If these costly activities and transfers do not modify the rate at which agents undertake harmful actions — i.e., do not deter other infringements — society does not directly benefit from them.[1]

[1]There are indirect social benefits of law enforcement that may accrue even without deterrence, including restitution to victims (where possible) and re-establishment of justice (important because citizens have preferences for justice), but these are unlikely to justify the large economic costs involved in the public enforcement of the law. Moreover, Bageri *et al.* (2013) show that non-deterring antitrust sanctions can distort economic activity and increase the deadweight loss from anticompetitive behaviors, even in the absence of mistakes in the relevant decisions.

These statements are not new. They date back to the insights of 18th century thinkers like Montesquieu, Beccaria, and Bentham. A large literature, developed from these first contributions, analyses how to obtain optimal deterrence in the enforcement of the law, as well as deterrence in the implementation of competition law. This literature deals with the use of criminal sanctions,[2] the optimal level of fines,[3] the contribution of private litigation and damage suits to the achievement of the public goals pursued by competition law,[4] the implications for deterrence of leniency policies,[5] and the optimal design of merger policy.[6]

This chapter provides an overview of the key determinants of deterrence in the realm of competition law and its enforcement. The aim is to systematize the existing contributions on the deterrence properties of a competition policy regime in order to provide a general overview of the literature highlighting its key results and the areas that could benefit from further research and analysis. Section 2 briefly discusses the economic theory of optimal deterrence and of its determinants, distinguishing between general deterrence and specific deterrence, as well as identifying the cases in which the enforcement activity generates over-deterrence. Section 3 examines how these general findings apply to competition law and policy. It argues that deterrence is affected by three main factors: (a) the level of the loss incurred by those that infringe the law and are detected and convicted; (b) the (perceived) probability of being detected and convicted; and (c) the (perceived) probability of being wrongly convicted or acquitted. The same section analyses which institutional and enforcement features of a competition policy regime affect these three factors. Section 4 deals with the problem of how to measure deterrence. Section 5 presents our main conclusions.

---

[2]See Landes (1983), Werden and Simon (1987), Gallo *et al.* (1994), Kobayashi (1994), Wils (2006a), and Spagnolo (2006).

[3]See Buccirossi and Spagnolo (2007), Connor (2005), Craycraft *et al.* (1997), Geradin and Henry (2006), and Wils (2006b).

[4]Wils (2003).

[5]See Motta and Polo (2003), Aubert *et al.* (2006), Spagnolo (2004), Spagnolo (2008), and Harrington (2008).

[6]See Sørgard (2009), Seldeslachts *et al.* (2009), and Duso *et al.* (2013). Although Nocke and Whinston (2010, 2013) do not directly talk about deterrence, their framework explicitly takes into account that current merger policy decisions affect the profitability and type of potential future mergers in a dynamic setting.

2. The Notion of Deterrence

2.1. *General and specific deterrence*

Deterrence of unlawful behaviors may take different forms.[7] The most relevant ones are: *general deterrence* and *specific deterrence.*

General deterrence, also referred to as *ex-ante* deterrence, consists in preventing agents from undertaking illegal behavior by threatening violators with sufficiently heavy sanctions. The optimal level of general deterrence, from an economic point of view, is achieved when only those conducts that cause a harm to society that is larger than the net gain that accrues to the wrongdoers, are prevented. If the enforcement costs are zero and there is perfect and symmetric information, this level of deterrence can be obtained by setting the actual sanction, S, and the perceived probability of being detected and convicted, a, at a level such that the expected sanction, S^*a, equals social harm, H:

$$S^*a = H. \tag{1}$$

This simple rule, also known as Becker's rule,[8] implies that for all those conducts that are socially inefficient — in that the wrongdoer's gain (G) is lower than the social harm — the expected sanction is greater than the gain (i.e., $S^*a > G$). Therefore, the level of the expected sanction is such that potential wrongdoers are discouraged from undertaking these conducts, as their expected payoff would be negative. On the contrary, all the socially efficient conducts, for which the wrongdoer's gain is larger than the social harm, will be undertaken, as the expected sanction is lower than the gain (i.e., $S^*a \leq G$). In a nutshell, Becker's rule sets the sanction so that it induces the offenders to internalize the social costs of their actions, and in a world with no enforcement costs and perfect information it ensures *ex-ante* deterrence of *all* socially inefficient acts.

Another important form of deterrence is *specific* deterrence, sometimes called *desistance*. This form of deterrence takes place *ex-post*, i.e., after an

[7] For an in-depth criminological discussion of the different forms of deterrence for various types of unlawful behaviors, see Bernard *et al.* (2001). For a review of the basic theory of deterrence, see Shavell (2003). For an extensive discussion of deterrence in the context of competition policy, see Buccirossi and Spagnolo (2007) and Davies and Osmosi (2012).

[8] The design of the optimal sanction is one of the key results of Becker (1968) seminal paper.

unlawful behavior has taken place and has been discovered by the law enforcement agency. This form of deterrence works through a change in the information held by the agents. For example, if agents do not have perfect knowledge of the probability of being detected and convicted, i.e., a in (1), being caught and punished provides them with new information to update their expectations.[9] The very experience of being sanctioned may also have the effect of deterring further wrongdoing through the so-called *punishment-induced deterrence*, which represents a behavioral increase in the salience of the expected sanction.[10]

General deterrence is typically the primary objective of law enforcement, as it can be achieved for a very large number of potential infringements without the need for these to be detected by law enforcers. This allows saving on a number of costs: the costs of the budgets of the courts and agencies involved in the investigation and prosecution of the alleged illegal behaviors, the cost of the distortionary taxation required to finance these budgets, the private costs of litigation, and the social and private costs of imposing sanctions on the convicted parties. In addition, general deterrence avoids the damages that each illegal action would have caused, had it not been prevented. Hence, the most important part of the activity of a law enforcement agency, whose aim is to maximize social welfare, should consist in deterring violations, rather than in identifying and punishing wrongdoers. In an ideal world, this activity should be sufficient to control all misconducts, making desistance unnecessary.

2.2. *Over-deterrence*

The optimal level of *ex-ante* deterrence should not only ensure the prevention of all illegal and socially inefficient actions, but it should also avoid stopping agents from undertaking actions that improve social

[9]Specific deterrence can also operate through a change in the costs and/or benefits of committing an additional crime, when the legal system contemplates increased sanctions for repeat offenders, incapacitation (by imprisonment or disqualification), and special monitoring of convicted wrongdoers; see Stigler (1970), Rubinstein (1979), Polinsky and Rubinfeld (1991), Chu *et al.* (2000), and Emons (2007).

[10]This punishment-induced deterrence effect has been quantified recently in a field experiment on videotape rental by Fishman and Pope (2006).

welfare. In other words, *ex-ante* deterrence, to be at its optimal level, should never become *over-deterrence*. Over-deterrence takes place when the expected sanction is too high, thus stopping agents from choosing courses of action whose gain is actually higher than the harm they cause to society (i.e., $a^*S > H$). Over-deterrence can occur either when the sanction has been set at too high a level,[11] or when the enforcement effort, which determines the level of the probability of being caught and convicted, is excessive.[12]

2.3. *Deterrence in a more complex world*

Becker's rule guarantees the optimal level of *ex-ante* deterrence, but only in a world of perfect information and with no enforcement costs. Over the years, this rule has been refined by a series of contributions that have considered what happens if one relaxes these conditions. In their encompassing survey of the economic literature on the enforcement of law, Polinsky and Shavell (2000) suggest that sanctions should be set so as not to deter all inefficient conducts since the investigation of alleged crimes and the imposition of sanctions has a cost. Sanctions should be set only up to the point at which the harm caused to society by these conducts is larger than the gain that accrues to the wrongdoer plus the value of the resources saved by not enforcing the law.

If one considers that information is difficult and costly to obtain and, thus, that law enforcement agencies may make mistakes when investigating potential crimes, the probability of these errors should be considered when setting the optimal level of the sanction. Indeed, the enforcement agency's errors increase the incidence of unlawful behaviors for two reasons.[13] First, and most obviously, if agents are aware that the agency may acquit wrongdoers (i.e., it commits a type I error), the perceived and

[11]In the case of anticompetitive behaviors, this can happen as the loss an agent incurs is actually given by the sum of "sanctions" imposed by different bodies, which do not coordinate their decisions (e.g., the fines imposed by the competition authority and the private damages awarded by the court).

[12]With regard to the EU, over-deterrence does not seem to be a problem since legal actions for private damages are still rare and the fines imposed on misbehaving firms appear to be too low, see Waelbroeck *et al.* (2004), Veljanovski (2007) and Schinkel (2007).

[13]*See* Shavell (2003); Polinsky and Shavell (2000); Buccirossi *et al.* (2006b).

actual probability of being punished when behaving unlawfully diminishes, leading to lower expected sanctions. Second, if agents are aware that they risk to be unjustly sanctioned despite having complied with the law (i.e., if type II errors happen), the gain from illegal actions increases relative to legal ones, reducing the deterrence effects of sanctions. Hence, if the enforcement agencies make mistakes, optimal sanctions should be higher than the Beckerian level.

If ε_{I} and $\varepsilon_{\mathrm{II}}$ respectively indicate the probability that the enforcement agency incurs in type I and type II errors, the optimal sanction should then satisfy the following adjusted Becker's rule:

$$S^* a(1 - \varepsilon_{\mathrm{I}} - \varepsilon_{\mathrm{II}}) = H.$$

Clearly, if the enforcement agency makes too many mistakes, it is instead optimal to not enforce the law at all (when $1 - \varepsilon_{\mathrm{I}} - \varepsilon_{\mathrm{II}} < 0$). Since information is costly and difficult to obtain, agents may also commit errors in assessing the level of the sanction they could incur when undertaking a specific behavior.

Errors can also be committed by the agents when trying to forecast the effects of their actions and, thus, the reaction of the enforcement agency. This is especially true when behaviors have complex economic effects, as assessing whether they are actually illegal may be difficult both for the enforcement agency and for the agents undertaking them. The complexity of the evaluation of the effects imply that a firm may be deterred from undertaking a perfectly competitive behavior under the mistaken assumption that it is illegal or because it could be perceived as illegal, in which case general deterrence generates a reduction in social welfare. Similarly, a firm may undertake an anticompetitive behavior because it believes that it is not in breach of the law. If such errors are possible, general deterrence becomes less effective and *ex-post* intervention becomes necessary.

This line of reasoning suggests a competition policy regime needs to rely on a mixture of *ex-ante* and *ex-post* deterrence.[14] The relative

[14]See Duso *et al.* (2007) and Buccirossi *et al.* (2006a). However, the recent theoretical analysis by Sørgard (2009) suggests that taking into account the likely deterrence effects of merger control should lead to a rather different interpretation of the results of studies

magnitude of the two should depend on the type of illegal behavior. For example, in the case of cartels, it is hard for companies to make mistakes when evaluating the possible effects of such a practice.

2.4. *Deterrence of anticompetitive behaviors: firms rather than individuals*

Since Becker's contribution, competition law enforcement and optimal deterrence of anticompetitive behaviors have become specific research subjects, which have gone well beyond adapting the results obtained by the economic theory of the public enforcement of law.

One reason behind the development of a specific literature on enforcement of competition law is that the design of the system that ensures optimal deterrence is complicated by the fact that the potential violators are both individuals and firms.[15] Hence, there are a number of additional factors that have to be taken into account in such cases. For example, fines — against firms and individual employees — can be relatively less effective than the imprisonment of managers, because firms are protected by limited liability and they can easily indemnify managers by paying their fines when they acted in the interest of the firm.[16] On the other hand, in setting the optimal sanction against corporations, one should consider that firms can also be sanctioned by the market and may be required to pay private damages (in some cases, treble damages).[17] In addition, anticompetitive behavior may not stem from calculated profit-seeking decisions at firm level, but may result from the presence of a principal–agent problem between shareholders

---

on the *ex-post* evaluation of merger control decisions. If competition policy is effective, it deters *ex-ante* the clearly anticompetitive mergers, leaving those that are more difficult to evaluate and for which errors are more likely to the scrutiny of competition authorities. This is the expected effect for an effective merger control policy, which deters all clearly anticompetitive mergers and focuses its investigations on difficult cases. Recently, analyses of deterrence in merger control have also been attempted. See for instance Seldeslachts *et al.* (2009), Clougherty and Seldeslachts (2013), and Duso *et al.* (2013).

[15]This is actually true for all corporate crimes.

[16]See Beckenstein and Gabel (1982); Kobayashi (2002); Spagnolo (2000; 2005).

[17]For an overview of these principal agent issues for cartel deterrence, see Buccirossi and Spagnolo (2008). And for an illuminating formal treatment of the issue see Aubert *et al.* (2006).

and managers, as well as between managers and their subordinates.[18] Firms try to prevent these occurrences through compliance systems and changes in decision-making practices. Yet, these activities have a cost that should be taken into account when determining the optimal level of deterrence.[19]

It should also be considered that very high fines may jeopardize a firm's financial stability, in which case, they may run against the ultimate goal of competition law: welfare maximization. This consideration is often mentioned in policy debates, as there is a common perception that future competition should increase with the enforcement effort, and that the number of active competitors might be a proxy for the degree of competition. This perception may render very high fines not credible, as agencies and judges may choose not to apply (or to reduce) them when they can seriously jeopardize the existence of a firm. This lack of credibility could in turn reduce their deterrence effect.[20] The argument on bankruptcy further affecting — i.e., on top of the impact of the anticompetitive behavior — the level of competition in the market and the policy it appears to foster have, however, severe limitations. As discussed by Buccirossi and Spagnolo

[18] Buccirossi and Spagnolo (2008) argue that if firms become liable for sufficiently high fines, directors should be induced to choose, within their compliance efforts, those executive contracts that deter management from undertaking illegal actions, even if these increase profit. However, as noted in Harrington (2006), in most cartel cases prosecuted in Europe, the illegal agreement was decided at the top management level and almost no CEO has been fired after their firm was convicted for price fixing. This suggests that in Europe, corporate governance systems are not yet designed to dissuade top management from undertaking anticompetitive behaviors. A likely reason for this is that fines and other sanctions have been too low in Europe, making anticompetitive agreement a profitable undertaking for both agents/managers and principals/shareholders.

[19] Kobayashi (2002) claims that if sanctioning tools were further strengthened in the U.S., where actual fines are high and treble damages can be imposed on misbehaving firms, the result could be higher prices for consumers and a decrease in social welfare. The reason is that, even if large *ex-ante* penalties can increase *ex-ante* deterrence, they also induce corporations to incur higher precaution and avoidance costs up to a point where they become excessive relative to the social gain they bring about, i.e., they can induce over-enforcement.

[20] Craycraft *et al.* (1997) find evidence that courts act according to the idea that bankruptcy should be avoided and reduce fines when a firm's ability to pay appears low. They also find that, in the majority of the U.S. cases they analyzed, firms were imposed fines that were only a fraction of the optimal cartel-deterring Beckerian ones, even though these could have afforded to pay them from their normal cash flow.

(2007), there are a number of qualifications needed when arguing for caps on antitrust fines that ensure the financial survival of firms. For example, if this concern causes fines to be set at too low a level to have a deterrence effect, it may be more costly to society than the risk of driving a few convicted firms bankrupt with higher fines.

Moreover, competition law exists to deter anticompetitive behaviors in all industries. If, for instance, high "optimal" fines lead to the bankruptcy of some convicted firms in an industry, this may temporarily decrease the number of firms in that particular industry but it may also increase competition in other industries through the *ex-ante* general deterrence effect generated by these fines.

In addition, if bankruptcy procedures are efficient, the impact of the financial failure of some convicted firms on competition may be small or even positive. Since the firms driven bankrupt by a fine should be economically sound, they might be sold to new owners who can use the same assets to enter the market and increase again the degree of competition.

Most importantly, linking fines to the firms' ability to pay — so as to always avoid bankruptcy, as is apparently done by U.S. courts, entails a double risk. It can generate distorted incentives for compliance for wrongdoers who only differ in their financial situation. Moreover, it might induce firms to issue more debt to reduce their (apparent) ability to pay and, thereby, the level of the expected fines.[21] Such a policy would add to the social costs of reducing deterrence by limiting the level of the sanctions for competition law violations and by inducing firms to adopt an inefficient financial structure. With the introduction of new competition policy instruments such as leniency programs and rewards for whistleblowers, the issue of firms' limited ability to pay may however lose bite. Buccirossi and Spagnolo (2007) show through a set of simulations that in the presence of well-designed and consistently/parsimoniously administered leniency and whistleblower reward programs, the deterrence effect of fines increases substantially: too generously administered programs of this kind will clearly reduce deterrence and welfare, though they may make the work of a competition authority much easier.

[21]This seems to have already happened in the U.S. with taxi companies trying to limit their liability toward victims of car accidents (e.g., Che and Spier, 2008).

3. The Determinants of Deterrence in Competition Law

Section 2 highlights a key point: both "good" deterrence and "bad" deterrence (i.e., over-deterrence) exist. Good deterrence prevents firms from adopting conducts that, by impairing competition, reduce welfare; while bad deterrence, or over-deterrence, prevents firms from behaviors that, by enhancing competition, improves social welfare. A competition policy regime is more effective the higher its level of good deterrence and the lower its level of bad deterrence.

As shown by the previous analysis, both good and bad deterrence depend on three general features of the competition legislation and its enforcement:[22]

1. the level of the loss that firms and their managers expect to suffer if they are convicted (rightly or wrongfully);
2. the perceived probability of wrongdoers being detected and convicted; and
3. the perceived probability of being wrongly convicted.

It is now important to understand which features of a competition policy regime (i.e., which policy variables) influence the level of deterrence, by affecting these factors. In what follows, we identify and discuss the six sets of policy variables that we believe affect the three key elements of deterrence just listed, which are:

1. The level of the loss incurred as a consequence of the competition law infringements;
2. the human and financial resources employed for detecting violations by the Competition Authority (CA) (or the court);
3. the powers to investigate held by the CA (or the court);
4. the quality of the law;
5. the level of independence of the CA (and of the court); and
6. the degree of separation between the investigator and the prosecutor.

[22]There are other factors that may be relevant, of course, including the degree of uncertainty on the level of the sanctions and, in the case of cartels, the risk of being betrayed by another cartel member rather than discovered by the CA. However, we have chosen to restrict our focus to those we believe to be the main factors, which are the ones outlined above.

3.1. *Features that affect the expected level of the loss: sanction policy, damages, settlements, and market reaction*

The factors that influence the level of the loss that a firm expects to incur if it is found guilty of violating the competition law are: the sanction policy followed by the CA (or the court), the existence and extent of private litigation and, hence, of private damages; and the reactions of the market.

The feature of a competition law regime that has the most evident impact on the level of the loss is the sanction policy. The sanction levied by a CA and/or a court (e.g., fine or imprisonment) for a breach of competition law has a clear and direct impact on the loss suffered by a convicted firm and its executives. Hence, the level and the nature of the sanctions that can be imposed on the firms guilty of breaching competition law and on their managers considerably affect the behaviors these undertake.

In a world with imperfect information, the expectations on the level and nature of the sanctions, and not just what these actually are, play also an important role. These expectations depend on the practice of the CA (or the court) and on the degree of transparency of the sanction policy. The availability of clear and detailed guidelines on how sanctions are set, as well as of previous reasoned decisions can have a strong influence on these expectations.

The loss a firm incurs when it is found guilty of a competition law violation also includes the damage repayments to the affected parties it expects to have to pay. These depend on the extent to which private litigation is possible, on the conditions under which litigation can be started as well as on the limit to the amount and type of damages that can be requested.[23] The possibility to settle the case — both with respect to an investigation of the CA (or the court) and to a private damage action — can also influence the expected loss.[24]

[23]For example, in some countries, no class action from consumers and/or small firms is possible, or an action for damages can only be started when the CA has ascertained the existence of a competition law violation. Similarly, in some countries, treble damages are awarded or the passing on defense is not allowed. All these features of the private litigation regime considerably affect the amount of damages a firm can be expected to pay.

[24]In some countries rather than settle with the CA, the latter can accept commitments and close the investigation.

A final element of this loss is the reduction in equity value or in market share that the firm may expect to suffer. The latter comprises the loss of customers who are unwilling to trade with a firm that has violated the law and the loss of reputation among clients and/or input suppliers, while the former represents the reduction in the stock market value of the firm's shares (when this is quoted in the stock market) that may affect its ability to raise capital.

It is important to note that it is the sum of all these costs, and not just the sanctions imposed by a CA or a court, that is relevant because what determines the behavior of a firm are the overall gains and losses imposed by a given course of action with respect to alternative ones.[25]

It is also important to highlight that the level of the loss depends on two elements: the law on the books and how it is enforced. The sanctions imposed by the CA (or by a court) depend on the criteria set out in the law regarding the type of sanctions and maximum level they can reach, and on how these criteria are actually applied (i.e., enforcement). For instance, if the monetary fine can reach up to 10% of the turnover of a firm, but no fine of this level has ever been imposed, even when a serious breach of the law takes place, firms will not expect to have to pay such a figure, despite what the law says. Similarly, the damages a firm can be expected to pay depend on whether it is legally possible to undertake a private enforcement action, on the legal framework that discipline these actions (e.g., whether class actions are possible or whether there is the treble damage rule) and on how tough courts have been in their decisions.

From this consideration, it emerges that the characteristics of the judicial system matter substantially, both in terms of the expected sanction and of the threat represented by damages. Stock market reactions, instead, only depend on the response of markets to the convictions. Therefore, they do not depend on specific policy variables, but rather on a more diffuse set of norms that may be influenced by many policies.

[25]In some countries, public enforcement and the risk of being imposed a sanction by a CA or a court, represent the major, if not the only loss, that a firm incurs when violating competition law, while in others, private enforcement and damage payments are the bulk of a loss a firm can face. The relative importance of the two varies across legal systems, countries and time (e.g., see the current increase in private damage actions in the European Union).

3.2. *Features that affect the probability of detection and conviction*

The probability agents attribute to the occurrence of being apprehended after breaching the law depends mostly on the policing activity of the CA. This is affected by the amount of resources the CA devotes to this activity and the investigative powers it holds.[26]

3.2.1. Financial and human resources

The enforcement of competition law is a direct result of the quantity and the quality of the financial and human resources that a CA can employ. The greater the amount of the resources and the better their quality, the more likely the competition authority is to identify behaviors impairing competition.

3.2.2. Powers during investigation

Another feature that affects the probability of detection and conviction is the type of investigative powers held by the CA. The stronger these powers, the better the information the CA can gather. These powers can include the ability to inspect the premises of the firm under investigation, the ability to inspect private premises of their employees, the ability to wiretap conversations, the ability to compel the investigated firms to provide information, as well as the ability to compel third parties to cooperate with the investigation.[27]

---

[26]We need to point out that some aspects of the sanction policy may also alter the probability of detection. This occurs through the leniency programs that grant immunity to those firms that reveal the existence of a cartel. One of the deterrence effects of leniency programs works exactly through a modification of the perceived probability that a cartel is uncovered by a CA, as the incentive firms have to cooperate with the enforcer improves the chance that the latter will discover illegal activities that would have remained unknown otherwise. See Buccirossi and Spagnolo (2007).

[27]With respect to the financial and human resources and to the investigative powers, of course, we are not claiming that from a social point of view, it is optimal to set them at their maximum feasible level; we just maintain that there is a monotone positive relation between them and the (perceived) probability of crime detection.

3.3. *Features that affect the probability of errors*

The features discussed in the previous subsection are likely to affect not only the "quantity" of the enforcement activities but also their "quality." If more accurate information is available, the CA is less likely to commit errors of both types (Lagerlöf and Heidhues, 2005). Some characteristics of the sanction policy can also improve the ability of the CA to meet the standard of proof needed to legally prove anticompetitive conduct. For example, leniency programs, when combined with adequate sanctions, can reduce the probability of errors. Full or partial leniency is usually granted if the self-reporting firm provides evidence that contributes to the formation of a legal proof of the agreement or that allows the CA to understand more clearly its functioning and its impact on the market. The evidence provided by the leniency applicant strengthens the case and reduces the probability that firms that are actually guilty are acquitted by the CA or in subsequent judgments.

The probability of errors depends on various features of a competition policy regime. The most important ones are: the quality of the law; the level of independence of the CA (and of the court); and the degree of separation between the investigator and the prosecutor. These are briefly discussed below.

3.3.1. Quality of the law

So far, we have defined deterrence and over-deterrence with reference to the prevention of conducts that reduce or enhance social welfare. However, these may not be the conducts that are declared illegal or legal by the competition legislation. Rules are imperfect and they can draw the boundary between legal and illegal conducts in a way that does not necessary coincide with the boundary between socially-enhancing and socially-damaging behaviors.

The quality of the rules is a matter of judgment, which makes defining this policy variable extremely difficult. However, one can observe whether the competition legislation (and the soft law that disciplines its actual application, e.g., guidelines) has rules that make the division between legal and illegal conducts closer to their effect on social welfare, according to the prevalent economic theory. Key factors, for instance, are whether the competition law allows an efficiency defense, whether the CA can consider non-economic goals in evaluating the effects of potentially abusive behaviors, whether an economic analysis of the effect of the behavior is required, whether the standard of proof is based on a rule of reason or a *per se* prohibition, whether state-controlled firms are exempted even when competition with private firms in the provision of commercial activities, and whether there is a general exemption for one or more industries.

3.3.2. Independence

A further relevant factor affecting the deterrence properties of competition policy regimes is the independence of the CA with respect to political or economic interests. A CA that makes its decisions by taking into account interests that are (potentially) in contrast with those that should guide its activity is more likely to commit both types of errors.[28]

Important elements for determining the level of independence of a CA are its institutional status (i.e., whether it is a court, an independent public sector body, or a branch of a ministry) and whether the government has the power to over-rule a decision made by the CA or to block an investigation.

Ideally, one should consider not only the level of formal independence of a CA, i.e., as guaranteed by the legal framework, but also the level of effective independence, which depends on its actual ability to avoid interference and capture from the government or from the business community.

3.3.3. Separation of powers

A final relevant characteristic of a competition policy regime is the degree of separation between the body performing the investigation on an allegedly anticompetitive behavior and the one making the decision on whether

[28]For discussion of the importance of having a CA that is independent of the government, see Rey (2003), Voigt (2009), Oliveira *et al.* (2005), OECD, (2005a, b) and Høj (2007). Moreover, a CA makes decisions that pursue its true objective if it is not influenced by the "regulated" firms, as argued by the vast literature on the so called "regulatory capture"; see Stigler (1971), Peltzman (1976), Posner (1971, 1974, 1975), Becker (1983), and Laffont and Tirole (1991).

this behavior should be sanctioned. The stronger the separation between prosecutor and adjudicator, the more balanced the decision is likely to be. This, in turn, reduces the probability of an error.[29] Similarly, it matters whether the appeal court is a specialized body with competence only on competition matters or whether it is the appeal body for all judicial decisions, and how long the appeal procedures are (see OECD, 2005c).

3.4. *Conclusions on the determinants of deterrence*

We believe that the six sets of policy variables described in this section — (1) sanction policy and damages; (2) financial and human resources; (3) powers to investigate; (4) quality of the law; (5) independence; and (6) separation of powers — represent the main institutional and enforcement aspects on which the level of deterrence of a competition policy regime depends.

There might be other determinants of deterrence that do not fall within the six categories outlined. However, we believe that these are less important and that the six areas listed are the ones that the CAs and courts, as well as the legislators and governments, should focus on in order to increase the effectiveness of competition policy regimes.

The deterrence properties of a competition policy regime depend also on the quality of the judiciary system and of the institutions in general, as well as on the type of social norms that guide the conducts of the agents. However, these are factors that are more difficult to modify and that are shaped by circumstances. Hence, in this chapter, we focus on those factors more directly linked to the competition policy regime and which are more easily changed.

4. Measuring Deterrence

Measuring deterrence is an extremely difficult task because the deterrent effect implies that firms choose a different behavior from the one they would have adopted without competition legislation and enforcement. To measure this effect, one would have to be able to determine the actions that

[29] See Block *et al.* (2000), Dewatripont and Tirole (1999), Neven and Röller (2005), Duso *et al.* (2007), Posner (1988), and Wils (2004).

firms would have undertaken had they not been constrained by the risk of a sanction, which means measuring the occurrence of certain events in a pure and only hypothetical world (e.g., Davies and Ormosi, 2013).

Any researcher who wants to measure the level of deterrence of the enforcement of a given law or regulation faces this type of problem because it is impossible to directly observe intentions if these do not materialize into actions. In some cases, it is possible to study how the number of breaches has changed over time when there has been a change in the level of the sanction, in the probability of detection or in the enforcement effort. For example, if the length of the maximum imprisonment sentence for a house theft is increased, it is possible to measure its deterrence effect by measuring the change in the rate of break-ins. However, calculating the rate of change is possible only if one has a reliable knowledge of the total number of violations committed in a given period of time. In the case of crimes like bank robberies or homicides, understanding if their total number has changed is relatively easy because most of them are reported to the police. The same does not apply to competition law breaches, a large share of which might go undetected.

Among the different types of anticompetitive practices, cartels are the most problematic because only a fraction of them are likely to be detected. This is especially true when cartels take place in retail markets where it is difficult for asymmetrically informed and often dispersed consumers to determine whether they paid a competitive or a collusive price. Hence, the level of deterrence on cartels cannot be measured by direct observation.

The abuses of a dominant position and anticompetitive agreements other than cartels, instead, tend to be reported more often, because they tend to affect a limited number of large players, who are generally aware of the obligations imposed on dominant firms. However, because of the difficulties faced by firms in judging whether a given behavior is pro or anticompetitive, there is a high risk of over-reporting.

As for anticompetitive mergers, if there is an obligation to notify, there are data on the total number of mergers and on the share that are blocked. In this case, direct observation of the degree of deterrence may be possible. However, the number of blocked mergers may underestimate the number of anticompetitive concentrations because a large share of mergers do not yield the efficiency effects forecasted.

In conclusion, measuring the deterrence effect of competition policy on the behaviors of firms and their managers is a rather complex task. The remainder of this section reviews the literature on the subject. We first examine those papers that tried to assess the deterrent effect of competition policy on cartels and abuses, and then consider the papers on deterrence and merger control policies.

4.1. *Agreements and unilateral conducts*

There are very few studies that try to ascertain the level of compliance with competition law, and hence its deterrence effect, and to understand the factors that influence it. A large part of these are based on surveys of the affected firms or of their legal advisors that attempt to measure the intentions of firms and their managers with regard to anticompetitive practices and how these have been altered by competition policy. These studies obtain mostly qualitative results, but provide some useful insights on the determinants of compliance with competition law.

Beckenstein and Gable (1986) provide the results of a survey of all U.S. antitrust practitioners (external and in-house ones) on changes in the frequency of violations of the Sherman Act and on the causes that led firms to commit them, as well as on the methods adopted by firms to ensure compliance with the act. The responses refer to the period from the late 1950s through the late 1970s. The survey did not report any major change in the frequency of violations over time, even though the degree of enforcement was seen as increasing. Further, the respondents perceived the probability of a cartel being detected as much lower than the probability that an attempt to monopolize was found out. The most powerful deterrence instruments were considered to be the risk of imprisonment and the threat of private suits for damages, followed by fines and the cost of the court cases (which at the time was substantially smaller than today).

Around the same time, Feinberg (1985) explored the effects of the EU competition policy on horizontal agreements and parallel imports in the Member States, relying on an anonymous survey of the opinions of antitrust practitioners based in Brussels. The survey was run in the early 1980s, 10 years after the European Commission introduced financial penalties for breaches of Article 101 (at the time Article 81) and examined the changes it brought about.

The key results reported by Feinberg are that the risk of being investigated and sanctioned by the European Commission was seen having increased since the late 1970s and as having a deterrent value, but there was no agreement on whether antitrust violations were more or less common than 10 years before. He also found that the most common cause of anticompetitive behaviors was considered to be the pursuit of corporate gain. The suggestions put forward by the respondents to promote compliance were higher fines, greater encouragement of private damage suits, and imposition of penalties on the managers of the offending firms.

Nielsen and Parker (2005) followed a slightly different approach in that they surveyed the affected firms, rather than their advisors. The two authors describe the responses obtained from questioning a sample of Australian firms on their level of compliance with the Trade Practice Act (the Australian competition and consumer legislation). Their key findings are that most businesses claim a high degree of actual compliance with the Act and rate the threat of an enforcement action highly.

Nielsen and Parker also find that the level of compliance does not vary much across industries and that larger businesses exhibit a greater level of compliance and greater awareness of the rules than smaller firms do.

Some CAs are directing their attention to the issue of deterrence (see Section 4.2). The UK Office of Fair Trading (OFT) (2007) ran a survey of antitrust lawyers and in-house legal advisors to assess the level of deterrence and over-deterrence that competition law enforcement generates in the UK, as well as the key factors that influence business compliance. The results of this research show that the deterrent effect in the UK is quite high, in particular for cartels and other anticompetitive agreements, but less so for abuses of a dominant position.[30]

---

[30]The study found that companies abandoned, or significantly modified, a large number of possible anticompetitive agreements and conduct because of the risk of being investigated. The survey of antitrust lawyers suggests that over the 2000–2006 period, the following ratios of agreements and initiatives were abandoned, or significantly modified relative to those which resulted in violations: cartels 5:1, commercial agreements 7:1, and abuses 4:1. The company survey produced significantly larger ratios: cartels 16:1, commercial agreements 29:1, and abuses 10:1, showing that external advice is sought only at a late stage in any business planning.

In both surveys, the respondents suggested improving the deterrence aspect of competition law in the UK by spending more on publicity and educational campaigns, encouraging private damages actions, speeding up the decision-making process, increasing the number of criminal prosecutions for cartels, and strengthening the enforcement activity.

Another attempt to quantify the deterrent effect of competition policy through a survey was made by the U.S. Department of Justice (2000). The authors conclude that if the Department stopped enforcing Section 1 of the Sherman Act, there would be an estimated 150% increase in the number of violations over the following five years and an increase (not quantified) in their aggressiveness.

4.1.1. Assessing the deterrence effects of competition policy on cartels using hard data

A few studies try to assess the deterrence effect on cartels using hard data. An OFT commissioned study by Davies and Majumdar (2002) attempts to quantify the deterrent effect of competition policy on cartels by relying on empirical findings made in other studies. The two authors conclude that, on the reasonable assumption that typical demand elasticities are less than 8.5, competition policy has a substantial deterrent effect on cartels, possibly leading to an actual price of about one-seventh of the full monopoly price.

More recently, Brenner (2009)[31] estimates the relationship between leniency applications under the EU 1996 leniency notice, the size of the fines actually imposed, and the duration of the investigations. The study concludes that the EU leniency program had no significant effects on the hazard rate at which cartels break down, nor on their expected duration. Indeed, in 2002, the leniency notice was considerably revised.

Miller (2009) estimates the likely impact on deterrence of the unanticipated introduction of a leniency program by looking at variation in the number of cartels discovered. Miller applies his methodology to all the cartel indictments that took place in the U.S. between 1985 and 2005, and finds that the introduction of the leniency program is likely to have

[31] See also the methodological work of Harrington and Chang (2009).

considerably enhanced the ability of the Department of Justice to detect and deter collusion. He estimates that over that period the cartel detection rate increased by about 62%, and that the rate of cartel formation fell by about 59%. Surprisingly, he also finds that the spike in cartel discovery occurred slightly before the introduction of the leniency program, and that the increased protection from damage suits for leniency applicants (de-trebling of damages) and the strong increase in sanctions for other cartel members, introduced by the Antitrust Criminal Penalty Enhancement and the Reform Act in 2004, did not have any significant effect on the number of cartels uncovered.

Ormosi (2013) adapts capture–recapture methods borrowed from the ecology literature to present a simple and parsimonious tool to estimate time-dependent cartel discovery rates. By allowing for heterogeneity across firms, population dynamics, and time-dependence, the method allows to make inference on cartel detection rates in quite general scenarios. The basic idea of the method is to trap, mark, and release animals several times and then to make inference on population parameters — e.g., size, capture, and survival rates — by observing the proportion of "recaptured" animals. The main result of this study is that cartel detection in the EU during the 1985–2009 period lies between 1/10 and 1/5 of the total number of existing cartels.

4.2. *Mergers*

The deterrence effect of merger control policies is also studied through surveys. Aaronson (1992) describes a survey of the Times top 500 firms, conducted by Coopers and Lybrand in 1991, on their perception of the activity of the UK CAs. From these results, he concludes that competition policy has a low deterrent effect because of a combination of limited knowledge of the rules among top managers and of lack of clarity about the criteria followed by the two CAs in reaching decisions (both around 40%).

In 2005, the Dutch Competition Authority (NMa, 2005) studied the nature and magnitude of the deterrence effect on mergers. Using a survey of 16 competition lawyers, followed by a set of interviews with firms, investment banks and private equity companies, they found that firms try to predict and minimize interventions by the CA. A more recent study by Baarsma *et al.* (2012) completed a similar survey for the Dutch competition authority and finds some evidence that merger policy rarely seems to over-deter, i.e., deter procompetitive merger activity.

The OFT survey previously mentioned also included questions about mergers. The survey of antitrust lawyers suggested that, over the 2004–2006 period, at least five proposed mergers were abandoned or modified for each one merger blocked or remedied by one of the CAs. The survey also suggested that a merger is more likely to be abandoned or modified if there has been a recent inquiry by the Competition Commission in the sector.

4.2.1. Assessing the deterrence effects of merger control using hard data

Very few papers try to assess the deterrence effects of competition policy on mergers using hard data. Stigler (1966) performs an exercise of this type in the mid-1960s. He found that the fraction of horizontal mergers fell relative to that of conglomerate and vertical ones after the U.S. merger control procedure became tougher in the 1950s.

More recently Seldeslachts *et al.* (2009) focus on the impact of different policy tools on the deterrence of mergers using a dataset on merger decisions relative to the 1992–2003 period in 28 OECD countries. The measure deterrence the authors analyze is the change in the number of notified mergers as a function of different merger policy actions. The main explanatory variables are the number of "prohibitions", the number of "authorizations with remedies", and the number of "authorizations with a commitment by the CA to monitor the post-merger behavior". Their findings provide strong support for the hypothesis that prohibitions have a deterrence effect on future merger frequencies, but not for the hypothesis that the imposition of remedies has such effect. However, the authors do not discuss whether the level of deterrence engendered by the prohibitions is the desirable one, i.e., whether it causes over-deterrence.

In a subsequent paper, Clougherty and Seldeslachts (2013) employ deterrence methodology, based on conditional probabilities, to elicit whether different merger policy instruments (investigations, remedies, and prohibitions) impact the composition of proposed merger activity in various U.S. industrial sectors, as in the original study by Stigler (1966). They use data from the annual reports published by the U.S. Department of Justice and the Federal Trade Commission over the 1986–1999 period. They show that the composition of horizontal merger activity is negatively influenced by the application of past antitrust actions more than by past antitrust investigations. In particular, they find both the conditional probability of detection (eliciting an investigation), and even more so the conditional probability of punishment (eliciting an antitrust action) to yield deterrence effects on the relative number of horizontal mergers in subsequent years. However, the conditional probability of eliciting a severe punishment (prohibitions versus remedies) does not indicate significant deterrence. Furthermore, their results for the U.S. suggest that there is no significant difference in the deterrence effect of prohibitions and remedies.

More recently, a study by Duso *et al.* (2013) analyze a sample of 368 mergers scrutinized by the European Commission over the 1990–2007 period, and study the deterrence properties of different merger policy tools. They identify anticompetitive mergers by looking at the share price reaction of non-merging rival firms to a merger announcement and assume that mergers that significantly benefit rivals are anticompetitive, while mergers that significantly hurt rivals are pro-competitive.[32] The remaining mergers are considered to be welfare neutral. Duso, Gugler, and Szücs then analyze, by means of a multinomial probit, the likelihood of a merger being anti- or procompetitive, if compared to welfare neutral, as a function of merger-specific characteristics and the ratio of past decisions to notifications. They find that when the Commission's prohibition ratio increased in the two quarters prior to a newly notified merger, the likelihood of anti-competitive merger is significantly reduced, while the likelihood of clearly pro-competitive mergers is not affected. Hence, prohibitions seem to deter but do not over-deter. They further analyze the effect on deterrence of the major reform of the EU merger regulation accrued in 2004. In the post-reform period, almost no prohibitions are observed yet this lack of prohibitions is partially overcome by an increase in the number of mergers withdrawn, which seem to deter anticompetitive mergers post-reform. Finally, the authors show that an increased use of phase-1 remedies in the past two quarters, significantly reduces the likelihood that a proposed merger is anticompetitive, but only after the 2004 reform.

[32] See Farell and Shapiro (1990) and Duso *et al.* (2007) for a discussion of this methodology.

4.3. *Measuring deterrence by assessing the quality of key institutional features*

A few studies try to measure the effectiveness of competition regimes by assessing how well specific institutional features score against a well-defined best practice and aggregating this information in one or a set of indicators. These features are very close the ones identified in Sections 2 and 3. Since the effectiveness of a competition regime is strongly linked to its ability to deter anticompetitive behaviors, these indicators can be interpreted as measures of deterrence.

An example of this methodology can be found in the studies by Buccirossi *et al.* (2011), Buccirossi *et al.* (2013), Høj (2007), Nicholson (2004), Voigt (2009), and Vitale *et al.* (2013). Each of these studies relies on a slightly different set of institutional features.

4.4. *Conclusions on how to measure deterrence*

Overall, the existing literature on the level of deterrence is quite limited. There seems to be a general agreement on the fact that the pursuit of gain is the main cause behind any competition law violation, which suggests that an appropriate sanctioning policy and an active private enforcement should have a good deterrent effect. Indeed, the answers to those surveys that ask what could increase compliance suggest higher fines, a greater opportunity to bring damage actions, and harsher penalties for the individuals involved. In addition, ambiguity of the law is quoted as another important cause behind abuses of dominant position, which suggests that infringement decisions, to the extent they clarify the scope of the prohibition and determine *ex-post* deterrence, can also play an important role with respect to these infringements. With respect to mergers, which do not lead to sanctions but only to the imposition of remedies or to prohibitions, the latter appear to have the strongest deterrence effect on anticompetitive mergers.

5. Conclusions

To what extent a competition policy regime is able to deter true anticompetitive behaviors is key to its effectiveness. Notwithstanding this obvious proposition, the deterrence properties of the institutional and enforcement features of a competition regime need further research. In this chapter, we try to provide a comprehensive overview of the subject. On the basis of the general economic theory of law enforcement and on its application to the enforcement of competition law, we identify several factors that are likely to affect the degree of deterrence of a competition policy regime. In our opinion, the main institutional and enforcement features on which the deterrence of anticompetitive practices depends are: (1) sanctions and damages; (2) financial and human resources; (3) powers to investigate; (4) quality of the law; (5) independence from political influence; and (6) separation of investigative and adjudicatory power. These influence the level of the loss that agents are expected to bear when breaching the law, the perceived probability of detection and the perceived probability of errors by the competent CA. Deterrence is also influenced by other general features of the context in which the competition legislation is applied such as the quality of the judiciary system and of other institutions and the type of social norms that guide the conducts of economic actors, but these are not characteristics specific to the competition policy regime itself.

A much more complex issue is how to measure deterrence of anticompetitive behaviors. A large number of the attempts to measure deterrence made so far are based on surveys. This is because, especially for non-merger infringements, this method is the only way to obtain direct information on changes in the behavior of firms due to the threats posed by the enforcement of antitrust rules. Surveys have many limitations, including the risk of biased responses and the difficulty of comparing results across countries. Some researchers try to measure deterrence through hard data, but this literature is still very limited and further research is needed to improve our understanding of the phenomenon. A few others have used indicators based on how a competition policy regime scores against an accepted best practice to assess the effectiveness, and hence the deterrence effect, of different regimes.

Finally, the most challenging task, both theoretically and empirically, is how to distinguish between "good" and "bad" deterrence. We identify the features of a competition policy regime that make deterrence stronger. However, this does not mean that any change of these features that increase deterrence is socially desirable. Indeed, more deterrence is needed if and only if the current features of a competition policy regime lead to under-deterrence. If, on the contrary, firms are already over-deterred, then the competition policy regime should be changed so as to make the threat of its enforcement less harsh. Our understanding of this last topic is still unsatisfactory.

References

Aaronson, R. (1992). "Do Companies Take any Notice of Competition Policy?" *Consumer Policy Review*, 2(3), pp. 140–145.

Aubert, C., W. E. Kovacic and P. Rey (2006). "The Impact of Leniency and Whistleblowers Programs on Cartels," *International Journal of Industrial Organization*, 29(6), pp. 1241–1266.

Baarsma, B. (2012). Ron Kemp, Rob van der Noll and Jo Seldeslachts, Let's Not Stick Together: Anticipation of Cartel and Merger Control in The Netherlands, *De Economist*, 160(4), pp. 357–376.

Bageri, V., Y. Katsoulakos and G. Spagnolo (2013). "The Distortionary Effects of Antitrust Fines Based on Revenue," *The Economic Journal*, 123(572), pp. 545–557.

Beckenstein, A. R. and H. L. Gabel (1982). "Antitrust Compliance: Results of a Survey of Legal Opinion," *Antitrust Law Journal*, 51(3), pp. 459–516.

Beckenstein, A. R. and H. L. Gabel (1986). "The Economics of Antitrust Compliance," *Southern Economic Journal*, 52(3), pp. 673–692.

Becker, G. (1968). "Crime and Punishment an Economic Approach," *Journal of Political Economy*, 76(2), pp. 169–217.

Becker, G. (1983). "A Theory of Competition Among Pressure Groups for Political Influence," *The Quarterly Journal of Economics*, 98(3), pp. 371–400.

Bernard, T. J., J. Snipes and G. B. Vold (2001). *Theoretical Criminology*, Oxford University Press, New York.

Block, M., J. Parker, O. Vyborna and L. Dusek (2000). An Experimental Comparison of Adversarial Versus Inquisitorial Procedural Regimes, *American Law and Economics Review*, 2(1), pp. 170–194.

Brenner, S. (2009). An Empirical Study of the European Corporate Leniency Program, *International Journal of Industrial Organization*, 27(6), pp. 639–645.

Buccirossi, P. and G. Spagnolo (2007). Optimal Fines in the Era of Whistleblowers: Should Price Fixers Still Go To Prison? in V. Goshal and J. Stennek (Eds.), *The Political Economy of Antitrust*, Elsevier, North Holland.

Buccirossi, P. and G. Spagnolo (2008). Corporate Governance and Collusive Behavior, in W. D. Collins (Ed.), *Issues in Competition Law and Policy*, American Bar Association, Antitrust Section, Washington, 285, pp. 1–28.

Buccirossi, P., L. Ciari, T. Duso, S. O. Fridolfsson, G. Spagnolo and C. Vitale (2006a). *Ex-post Review of Merger Control Decisions*, DG Competition of the European Commission, 156(4), pp. 453–475.

Buccirossi, P., G. Spagnolo and C. Vitale (2006b). "The Cost of Erroneous Interventions/Non-Interventions Under Art 82," *Office of Fair Trading Economic Discussion Paper*, 864.

Buccirossi, P., L. Ciari, T. Duso, G. Spagnolo and C. Vitale (2011). "Measuring the Deterrence Properties of Competition Policy: The Competition Policy Indexes," *Journal of Competition Law and Economics*, 7(1), pp. 165–204.

Buccirossi, P., L. Ciari, T. Duso, G. Spagnolo and C. Vitale (2013). "Competition Policy and Productivity Growth: An Empirical Assessment," *Review of Economics and Statistics*, 95(4), pp. 1324–1336.

Che, Y. and K. Spier (2008). "Strategic Judgment Proofing," *RAND Journal of Economics*, 39(4), pp. 926–948.

Chu, C. Y. C., S. Hu and T. Huang (2000). "Punishing Repeat Offenders More Severely," *International Review of Law and Economics*, 20(1), pp. 127–140.

Clougherty, J. and J. Seldeslachts (2013). Deterrence of Horizontal Mergers: Empirical Evidence from U.S. Industries, *Journal of Law, Economics and Organization*, 29(5), pp. 1114–1144.

Connor, J. M. (2005). *Optimal Deterrence and Private Antitrust Enforcement* Manuscript, Purdue University, 285, pp. 1–28.

Craycraft, C., J. L. Craycraft and J. Gallo (1997). "Antitrust Sanctions and Firm Ability to Pay," *Review of Industrial Organization*, 12(2), pp. 171–183.

Davies, S. and A. Majumdar (2002). The Development of Targets for Consumer Savings Arising from Competition Policy, *OFT Economic Discussion Paper* 4.

Davies, S. W. and P. L. Ormosi (2012). "A Comparative Assessment of Methodologies Used to Evaluate Competition Policy," *Journal of Competition Law and Economics*, 8(4), pp. 769–803.

Davies, S. W. and P. L. Ormosi (2013). "The Impact of Competition Policy: What Are the Known Unknowns?," *CCP Working Paper*.

Dewatripont, M. and J. Tirole (1999). "Advocates," *Journal of Political Economy*, 107(1), pp. 1–39.

Duso, T., K. Gugler and F. Szücs (2013). "An Empirical Assessment of the 2004 EU Merger Policy Reform," *The Economic Journal*, 123(572), pp. F596–F619.

Duso, T., D. Neven and L. H. Röller (2007). "The Political Economy of European Merger Control: Evidence Using Stock Market Data," *The Journal of Law and Economics*, 50(3), pp. 455–489.

Emons, W. (2007). "Escalating Penalties for Repeat Offenders," *International Review of Law and Economics*, 27(2), pp. 170–178.

Farrell, J. and C. Shapiro (1990). "Horizontal Mergers: An Equilibrium Analysis," *The American Economic Review*, 80(1), pp. 107–126.

Feinberg, R. M. (1985). "The Enforcement and Effects of European Competition Policy: Results of a Survey of Legal Opinion," *Journal of Common Market Studies*, 23(4), pp. 373–384.

Fishman, P. and D. G. Pope (2006). "Punishment-Induced Deterrence: Evidence from the Video Rental Market," *Working Paper*, University of California, Berkeley.

Gallo, J. C., K. G. Dau Schmidt, J. L. Craycraft and C. J. Parker (1994). Criminal Penalties Under the Sherman Act: A Study of Law and Economics, *Research in Law and Economics*, 16, pp. 25–71.

Geradin, D. and D. Henry (2006). The EC Fining Policy for Violations of Competition Law: An Empirical Review of the Commission Decisional Practice and the Community Courts' Judgments, in K. J. Cseres, M. P. Schinkel, F. O. W. Vogelaar (Eds.), *Remedies and Sanctions in Competition Policy: Economic and Legal Implications of the Tendency to Criminalize Antitrust Enforcement in the EU Member States*, Edward Elgar, London, 14, pp. 1–36.

Harrington, J. (2006). "How do Cartels Operate," *Foundations and Trends in Microeconomics*, Now Publishers Inc., 2(1), pp. 1–105.

Harrington, J. (2008). "Optimal Corporate Leniency Programs," *Journal of Industrial Economics*, 56(2), pp. 215–246.

Harrington, J. and M. H. Chang (2009). "Modelling the Birth and Death of Cartels with an Application to Evaluating Antitrust Policy," *Journal of the European Economic Association*, 7(6), pp. 1400–1435.

Høj, J. (2007). Competition Law and Policy Indicators for the OECD Countries, *OECD Economics Department Working Papers*, OECD Publishing, No. 568.

Kobayashi, B. (1994). "Antitrust, Agency and Amnesty: An Economic Analysis of the Criminal Enforcement of the Antitrust Laws Against Corporations," George Mason University School of Law, *Working Paper* No. 02–04.

Kobayashi, B. (2002). "Antitrust, Agency and Amnesty: An Economic Analysis of the Criminal Enforcement of the Antitrust Laws Against Corporations," George Mason Univ. Law and Econ., *Working Paper* No. 02–04.

Laffont, J. J. and J. Tirole (1991). "The Politics of Government Decision Making. A Theory of Regulatory Capture," *Quarterly Journal of Economics*, 106(4), pp. 1089–1127.

Lagerlöf, J. and P. Heidhues, (2005). "On the Desirability of an Efficiency Defense in Merger Control," *International Journal of Industrial Organization*, 23(9), pp. 803–827.

Landes, W. M. (1983). "Optimal Sanctions for Antitrust Violations," *The University of Chicago Law Review*, 50, pp. 652–678.

Miller, N. (2009). "Strategic Leniency and Cartel Enforcement," *American Economic Review*, 99(3), pp. 750–768.

Motta, M. and M. Polo (2003). "Leniency Programs and Cartel Prosecution," *International Journal of Industrial Organization*, 21(3), pp. 347–379.

Neven, D. J. and L. H. Röller (2005). "Consumer Surplus vs. Welfare Standard in a Political Economy Model of Merger Control," *International Journal of Industrial Organization*, 23(9–10), pp. 829–848.

Nicholson, M. W. (2004). "Quantifying Antitrust Regimes," *Federal Trade Commission Paper.*

Nielsen, V. L. and C. Parker (2005). "The ACCC Enforcement and Compliance Survey: Report of Preliminary Findings," *University of Melbourne Legal Studies Research Paper* 150.

NMa (2005). *Research into the Anticipation of Merger Control*, Amersfoort, Twynstra Gudde.

Nocke, V. and M. D. Whinston (2010). "Dynamic Merger Review," *Journal of Political Economy*, 118(6), pp. 1200–1251.

Nocke, V. and M. D. Whinston (2013). "Merger Policy with Merger Choice," *American Economic Review*, 103(2), pp. 1006–1033.

OECD (2005a). *Designing Independent and Accountable Regulatory Authorities for High Quality Regulation.*

OECD (2005b). *European Commission — Peer Review of Competition Law and Policy.*

OECD (2005c). *Relationship between Competition Policy and Economic Performance*, Paris.

Oliveira, G., E. L. Machado, C. B. Guimarães Ferreira and L. M. Novaesm (2005). "Aspects of the Independence of Regulatory Agencies and Competition Advocacy," *ICN–Bonn Working Paper*, III Subgroup.

Ormosi, P. (2013). "A Tip of the Iceberg? The Probability of Catching Cartels," *Journal of Applied Econometrics*, doi: 10.1002/jae.23.

Peltzman, S. (1976). "Toward a More General Theory of Regulation," *The Journal of Law and Economics*, 19(2), pp. 211–240.

Polinsky, A. M. and D. L. Rubinfeld (1991). "A Model of Optimal Fines for Repeat Offenders," *Journal of Public Economics*, 46, pp. 291–306.

Polinsky, A. M. and S. Shavell (2000). "The Economic Theory of Public Enforcement of Law," *Journal of Economic Literature*, 38(1), pp. 45–76.

Posner, R. A. (1971). "Taxation by Regulation," *The Bell Journal of Economics and Management Science*, 2(1), pp. 22–50.

Posner, R. A. (1974). "Theories of Economic Regulation," *The Bell Journal of Economics and Management Science*, 5(2), pp. 335–358.

Posner, R. A. (1975). "The Social Costs of Monopoly and Regulation," *Journal of Political Economy*, 83(4), pp. 807–828.

Posner, R. A. (1988). "Comment: Responding to Gordon Tullock," *Research in Law and Policy Studies*, 2, pp. 29–33.

Rey, R. (2003). Toward a Theory of Competition Policy, in M. Dewatripont, L. P. Hansen and S. J. Turnovsky (Eds.), *Advances in Economics and Econometrics: Theory and Applications* — Eight World Congress, series "Econometric Society Monographs," II(36), Cambridge University Press, p. 82.

Rubinstein, A. (1979). An Optimal Conviction Policy for Offenses that May Have Been Committed by Accident, in S. J. Brams, A. Schotter and G. Schwodiauer (Eds.), *Applied Game Theory*, Physica–Verlag, Wurzburg, pp. 406–413.

Schinkel, M. P. (2007). "Effective Cartel Enforcement in Europe," *World Competition*, 30(4), pp. 539–572.

Seldeslachts, J., J. Clougherty and P. Pita Barros (2009). Settle for Now but Block for Tomorrow: The Deterrence Effects of Merger Policy Tools, *The Journal of Law and Economics*, 52(3), pp. 607–634.

Shavell, S. (2003). "Economic Analysis of Public Law Enforcement and Criminal Law," *Harvard Law and Economics Discussion Paper* No. 405.

Sørgard, L. (2009). "Optimal Merger Policy: Enforcement vs Deterrence," *Journal of Industrial Economics*, 57(3), pp. 438–456.

Spagnolo, G. (2000). "Stock-Related Compensation and Product–Market Competition," *RAND Journal of Economics*, 31(1), pp. 22–42.

Spagnolo, G. (2004). "Divide et Impera: Optimal Leniency Programs," *CEPR Discussion Paper* No. 4840.

Spagnolo, G. (2005). "Managerial Incentives and Collusive Behaviour," *European Economic Review*, 49(6), pp. 1501–1523.

Spagnolo, G. (2006). Cartels Criminalization and their Internal Organization, in K. J. Cseres, M. P. Schinkel and F. O. W. Vogelaar (Eds.), *Remedies and Sanctions in Competition Policy: Economic and Legal Implications of the Tendency to Criminalize Antitrust Enforcement in the EU Member States*, Edward Elgar, London.

Spagnolo, G. (2008). Leniency and Whistleblowers in Antitrust, in P. Buccirossi (Ed.), *Handbook of Antitrust Economics*, MIT Press, Cambridge, MA.

Stigler, G. (1966). "The Economic Effects of the Antitrust Laws," *Journal of Law and Economics*, 9, pp. 225–258.

Stigler, G. J. (1970). "The Optimum Enforcement of Laws," *Journal of Political Economy*, 78, pp. 526–536.

Stigler, G. J. (1971). "The Theory of Economic Regulation," *Bell Journal of Economics*, 2, pp. 3–21.

U.S. Department of Justice (2000). *Antitrust Division Congressional Submission for Fiscal Year 2001*, US Department of Justice, Washington DC.

Veljanovski, V. (2007). "Cartel Fines in Europe — Law, Practice and Deterrence," *World Competition*, 30(1), pp. 65–86.

Vitale, C., C. Klein, I. Koske and A. Alemani (2013). "OECD Indicators on Competition Law and Policy," *OECD Economics Department Working Papers*.

Voigt, S. (2009). "The Effects of Competition Policy on Development–Cross–Country Evidence Using Four New Indicators," *The Journal of Development Studies*, 45(8), pp. 1225–1248.

Waelbroeck, D., D. Slater and G. Even-Shoshan (2004). *Study on the Conditions of Claims for Damages in Case of Infringement of EC Competition Rules*, Ashurst, Brussels.

Werden, G. J. and M. J. Simon (1987). "Why Price Fixers Should Go to Prison," *The Antitrust Bulletin*, 32, pp. 917–937.

Wils, W. (2003). "Should Private Antitrust Enforcement be Encouraged in Europe?" *World Competition*, 26, pp. 473–488.

Wils, W. (2004). "The Combination of the Investigative and Prosecutorial Function and the Adjudicative Function in EC Antitrust Enforcement: A Legal and Economic Analysis," *World Competition*, 27(2), pp. 201–224.

Wils, W. (2006a). Is Criminalization of EU Competition Law the Answer?, in K. J. Cseres, M. P. Schinkel and F. O. W. Vogelaar (Eds.), *Remedies and Sanctions in Competition Policy: Economic and Legal Implications of the Tendency to Criminalize Antitrust Enforcement in the EU Member States*, Edward Elgar, London.

Wils, W. (2006b). "Optimal Antitrust Fines: Theory and Practice," *World Competition*, 29(2), pp. 183–208.

Chapter 16

The Risks and Tricks in Public–Private Partnerships*

Elisabetta Iossa

University of Rome Tor Vergata, CEPR and IEFE-Bocconi
Elisabetta.Iossa@uniroma2.it

Giancarlo Spagnolo

University of Rome Tor Vergata, SITE-Stockholm, and CEPR
Giancarlo.Spagnolo@uniroma2.it
Giancarlo.Spagnolo@hhs.se

Mercedes Vellez

University of Rome Tor Vergata and CEDES
mervellez@yahoo.com.ar

Abstract

Public–Private Partnerships (PPPs) have been implemented broadly around the world in the infrastructure sector — water and sanitation, transports, energy, telecommunications — and, more recently, in the provision of public services — education, health, prisons, water and waste management. Key aspects of the contract design, such as risk allocation and payment mechanisms, significantly affect the PPP outcomes because they affect the incentives of the public and private parties to deliver a public service that satisfies user needs. Nevertheless, contractual provisions used in practice often do not implement the efficient risk allocation. In this chapter, we discuss the crucial role of the public sector in designing and imposing standardized contracts, monitoring their compliance, disclosing contractual information to the general public, and transferring risks to the private sector in order to reduce the likelihood of PPP performance failure.

---

*This chapter is an updated extract of Iossa *et al.* (2007a, b). For very helpful comments, we wish to thank Francesco Totaro, Chris Shugart, and Editor Yossi Spiegel. Elisabetta Iossa thanks financial support from the University of Padua, Grant No. CPDA121089/12.

Keywords: Concession contracts, incentives, public–private partnerships, risk allocation.

JEL Classification Codes: D02, D20, D82, L33, L38.

1. Introduction

Public–Private Partnerships (PPPs) are long-term contractual arrangements between the public and private sectors in which the contractor (typically a consortium of firms) has responsibility for significant aspects of the building and operation of an infrastructure for the delivery of public services. Although there is no unanimous definition of PPPs, most of them include BOT and DBFO contracts.[1] In a BOT contract, for example, the contractor takes responsibility for building (B), operating, and managing (O) assets. Investment in capital assets is also undertaken by the contractor, but it is financed by the public authority, which retains the financial risk. Upon contract expiry, the ownership of the assets is transferred (T) to the public authority under the terms of the original agreement.[2] In a DBFO contract, the contractor is in charge of all the stages of the project: the design (D), building (B), finance (F), and operation (O).

PPPs have been implemented broadly around the world. In the 1980s, the United Kingdom pioneered the development of a particular form of PPPs, creating the Private Finance Initiative (PFI) in 1992 to further promote PPP agreements. As of December 2006, 794 PFI projects had been signed involving around £55 billion of capital value (CBI, 2007; HM Treasury, 2006). Other European countries have also invested in PPPs, especially Ireland, Portugal, Greece, the Netherlands, and Spain (PWC, 2005; EIB, 2004) and large PPP projects have been implemented in the U.S. In a review of PPP activity, PricewaterhouseCoopers (PWC, 2005) reports that 206 PPP

[1] See Hodge and Greve (2007) and EC (2003) for a survey on the definitions of PPPs used in the public management literature.

[2] Variations of the BOT contract can be implemented in practice: Design–Build (DB), Design–Build–Operate (DBO), Build–Own–Operate–Transfer (BOOT), Build–Lease–Operate–Transfer (BLOT), Build–Transfer–Operate (BTO), etc. For instance, in a DB contract, the main benefits arise from making the contractor responsible for designing (D) and building (B) a facility, e.g., a road, while allocating financial, operation, and demand risk to the public authority. In a DBO contract, additional benefits arise from the fact that the contractor operates (O) the facility, and then it has incentives to design and build taking future operation costs into account.

contracts were signed worldwide during 2004–2005 involving $52 billion in investments. Numbers, however, have gone down with the economic crisis: EPEC (2012) reports that in 2012, the value of PPP transactions reaching financial close in the European market amounted to €11.7 billion. This represents a 35% drop compared to 2011 (€17.9 billion) and the lowest market value since 2003.

PPP agreements in developing countries have grown steadily since the 1990s. According to the World Bank's Private Participation in Infrastructure,[3] 2,750 infrastructure projects involving private and public investment for capital value of $786 billion have been implemented during 1990–2003 (in 2002 constant dollars) and about $1,530 billion between 2002 and 2012 (in 2012 constant dollars). Between 1990 and 2003, around 1,000 projects and 47% of the investment took place in Latin American and the Caribbean (LAC) countries (IMF, 2004); similar trend extends to the period 2002–2012.

Since the 1980s, and particularly after the United Kingdom developed the PFI program, PPPs have been introduced in many sectors, mainly water and sanitation, transports, energy, and telecommunications. In recent years, countries with a large experience in this kind of private participation in public services provision, such as the United Kingdom, Australia, Canada, Ireland, and the Netherlands have introduced PPPs in areas such as education, health, and water and waste management (Hammami *et al.*, 2006).

Worldwide experience with PPPs suggests there is no "one-size-fits-all" principle that might simplify the design of a PPP contract for a given objective and sector (Chong *et al.*, 2004). A number of factors influence the likelihood of performance failure in a PPP agreement (though these factors are not specific to PPPs). The first three factors listed below could be considered as "external" to the contract; whilst the fourth factor as "internal":

(1) The characteristics of the targeted sector and the market structure;
(2) The degree of macroeconomic and political instability;
(3) The country's regulatory and institutional framework;
(4) The contract design and management, in particular, the payment mechanism and the risk allocation built-in the contractual terms.

[3]However, this dataset includes contractual arrangements that are not strictly "PPPs" according to our definition, as it includes, for example, service contracts where the contractor takes responsibility only for operations.

Consider these factors briefly. The characteristics of the sector targeted by a PPP contract and the prevailing market structure help in explaining PPP performance. Differences across sectors have for example been observed in the incidence of contract renegotiation for LAC countries. The highest renegotiation incidence corresponds to concessions for essential facilities such as transports and water, where 55% and 74% of the contracts ended up under revision (Guasch, 2004). In the UK, the HM Treasury recommended against the use of PPPs for IT services because fast changing technology make long-term contracts unsuitable.

The degree of macroeconomic and political instability also matters in accounting for PPP outcomes. In an uncertain macroeconomic environment, contract design failures are more likely since it is difficult for the contracting parties to envisage future contingencies and write the contract terms accordingly (thus aggravating problems arising from contract incompleteness). *Ex-ante*, a high aggregate risk level discourages long-term contractual relationships and weakens incentives to undertake investments in infrastructure projects that typically have long maturity. Empirical evidence shows a correlation between macroeconomic instability and renegotiation incidence: the peaks of contract revision occurred when negative shocks hit LAC countries and triggered severe macroeconomic crises. For instance, generalized renegotiations were observed soon after the Argentine hyperinflation in 1990, the Mexican crisis in 1995, the Brazilian devaluation in 1999, the Colombian recession in 2000, and the Argentine crisis in 2001 (Guasch *et al.*, 2003). Moreover, political instability translates into higher risks of government-led renegotiations which may affect the profitability of the project and impact on the insolvency of the private partner.

For similar reasons, the regulatory and institutional framework heavily matter since the quality of contract enforceability and governance are critical factors affecting PPP agreements. In LAC countries, weak governance and the government's lack of commitment not to renegotiate also accounted for the recurrent contract revisions. In many of these countries, the regulatory agencies were rarely given training and instruments to carry on their mandate with competence and even lacked political support from the government. Moreover, in some cases, the government had political control over them, raising concerns on autonomy and accountability issues (Estache, 2006). There were instances in which the private partner considered its main counterparts to be ministers and secretaries rather than the regulatory agency. For example, in the Buenos Aires water concession, the Secretary of Environment and Sustainable Development bypassed the regulators arguing regulation of water provision was too complex to be managed by the regulatory agency.

Aspects of the contract design, such as the risk allocation or the payment mechanism, significantly affect the PPP outcomes. Project-related risks, such as construction risk, cost overrun risk, and demand risk, are allocated through contract design. The sheer complexity of PPP agreements makes contract design a key issue for the success of a PPP project: the contract may transfer an inappropriate type and amount of risk to the contractor. In LAC, most cases of renegotiation or contract termination were due to contract design failing to manage risks (Guasch, 2004). But also in the EU, risk assessment and allocation are problematic issues, leading to contract revisions and unanticipated financial burdens for the public sector (Renda and Schrefler, 2006).

In this chapter, we shall focus on the main risk allocation issues in contract design for PPP agreements, as this is an aspect where PPPs not only have the greatest potential but also the highest risk of failure compared to traditional forms of procurement. Risk allocation issues are key not just because they affect the sustainability and bankability of the PPP project, but also, and especially, because they affect the incentives of the parties involved in the project to deliver a public service that satisfies user needs. Moreover, incentives are a central aspect in PPPs provision, given that the long-term nature of the contract shields the contractor from competition for a long time. We shall argue that the potential for an efficient PPP rests with the way the contract design shapes these incentives. But achieving an efficient contract design and implementation will typically be very difficult because of conflicting interests, unless a system of standardized contracts, regular performance monitoring, and open access to contractual information is in place.

We shall start in Section 2 by discussing the importance of standardized contracts to reduce the risk of contract misspecification and inefficient risk allocation. We shall also discuss governance and transparency issues associated with the public procurement process and the PPPs. In Section 3, we shall discuss the efficient risk allocation and describe the incentive structure and risk transfer between the contracting parties for the main forms of PPPs. We shall then argue in Section 4 that contractual provisions used in practice often do not implement this efficient risk allocation, and we provide some explanations as to why this occurs. In Section 5, we present some policy recommendations and conclude.

2. The Role of Contract Design

2.1. *Contract misspecifications and standardized contracts*

PPP contracts are based on an output specification approach: the public authority defines the basic standards of service whilst the contractor chooses how to meet and possibly improve upon them. This approach incentivizes innovative solutions, allowing for private sector's skills and knowledge to feed into public service provision, and also involves a greater risk of contract misspecifications for the public sector. In particular, problems may arise because output specifications may not be clearly described or defined consistently with the infrastructure needs that the PPP intends to satisfy. Since output specifications form the basis of the contractual obligations, they should be identified by conducting a careful assessment previous to the contract drafting. Mistakes at the contract drafting stage can then be very costly for the public authority because of the long-term nature of most PPP contracts.

A number of factors can lead to contract misspecifications. They can be due to mistakes resulting from an incompetent public authority staff (or the consultants acting on its behalf) in charge of contract drafting. Lack of appropriate incentives for the public authority and thus inadequate effort in information acquisition and processing can also result in contract misspecifications. Corruption and favoritism explain contract misspecifications that lead to the contractor receiving very favorable contract terms. Engel *et al.* (2009) reports that 64 out of 106 PPPs projects audited in China showed signs of corruption.

Making the public authority staff (or its consultant) accountable for its actions so as to provide adequate incentives is not an easy task. Labor market regulations often constrain the use of incentive mechanisms for the public sector and lack of financial stakes make it difficult to provide incentives in the first place. Also, PPP contracts are generally long-term contracts, so when mistakes are discovered, the public sector employee may have moved job already.

In the early stages of PPPs, contract drafting mistakes have often arisen simply because of lack of experience of public administrations on the writing of PPP contracts. In Europe, a challenge for the public sector has been to rapidly build up the capacity and knowledge to devise and implement PPPs, and to manage the PPP contractual relationships over the long-run. The public sector's progress on this front has not kept pace with that of private sector partners. In the UK, recognition of this problem by the National Audit Office has led to a series of programs aimed at training public officials and to an extensive use of external consultants.

External consultants can be a means to acquire competence and knowledge for the benefit of the public authority, but it also has limits. First, the use of consultants does not address the problem of corruption. *A priori*, there is no reason to believe that external consultants are less prone to corruption than public sector bureaucrats, although it could be argued that *large* consultancy firms may have more to lose from being involved in a corruption scandal than single individuals. Second, large consultancy firms that have the specific knowledge to deal with contracts, as complex as PPP contracts, find themselves hired by the public sector in one contract and by the private sector in another. Working for both sides, although at different points in time, may reduce asymmetric information among the parties and be conducive to rogue deals.

To the extent that experience with PPP in a specific sector accumulates, i.e., the PPP market matures, the public authorities should standardize parts of the contracts for that specific sector in order to reduce the likelihood of contract and output misspecification. From ongoing projects in a sector, it is possible to learn what the generic risks are, and then use this information to design a standardized contract (or some parts of it) that allocates these risks properly. The use of standardized contracts also reduces transaction costs resulting from agreeing and drafting the contract, provided that both parties are willing to accept the standardized terms. Standardized contracts are widely used in the UK (HM Treasury, 2007), and are being introduced in Italy.

A question that arises when standardized contracts are designed by the central government is whether local administrations engaging in PPP projects should be required to adopt the standardized contracts (when the national law allows it). On the one hand, compulsory standardized contract terms bring the cost of increased rigidity and, in particular, the cost of loss of valuable local or specific information not reflected in the standardized contract. On the other hand, optional standardized contract terms do not address the possibility that corrupt local administrations purposefully design inefficient contracts to increase the profitability of the project for the firm, neither do they help addressing the cost of incompetent public administrations that choose wrong contract terms. This trade-off could be managed by adopting an "intermediate" approach: the public authority could be given the option to introduce motivated changes into the standardized contract. The benefit of this increased flexibility would then have to be weighed against the cost of a higher risk of corruption and favoritism. This point is further developed in Iossa and Martimort (2013) who analyze the impact of corruption on contract design. They argue that corrupted local authorities may have incentives to keep important contingencies that may realize during the project implementation as unregulated because this contract incompleteness justifies higher risk premium to the private partner. Limited discretion with standardized contract choices may limit this problem.

2.2. *Transparency, confidentiality, and governance in PPP contracting*

Since the "Cadbury report" identified the lack of disclosure in CEOs and directors compensation contracts and the side transactions as crucial determinants of corporate governance failure, most corporate governance codes and regulations incorporate stringent disclosure requirements on the details of crucial contracts (OECD, 2004).[4]

In Public Procurement, stringent disclosure requirements are seen as a potentially powerful remedy to fight corruption (Rose-Ackerman, 1999;

[4]The Cadbury Report, titled *Financial Aspects of Corporate Governance*, is a 1992 report issued by "The Committee on the Financial Aspects of Corporate Governance" chaired by Adrian Cadbury that sets out recommendations on the arrangement of company boards and accounting systems to mitigate corporate governance risks and failures. The report's recommendations have been used to varying degrees to establish other codes such as those of the European Union, the United States, the World Bank, etc.

Kaufmann, 2005). Coppier and Piga (2007) find an inverse cross-country relationship between the level of transparency in public procurement and the perceived level of corruption in a country, as measured by the Corruption Perception Index by Transparency International. According to their estimates, governments' attempts to fight corruption by increasing disclosure and transparency can be effective.

The direct costs of disclosing information on contract terms and performance evaluation appear to be rather small in general (Leuz, 2007), and even more so for repeated procurements and large infrastructure projects like PPPs. Disclosure costs in terms of potential competitive harm for the contractor (and for potential private partners in the phases that precede the signature of the contract) should be rather small when disclosure regards contractual and output-related performance measures. Instead, costs are expected to be much larger when disclosure refers to investment choices and other input-related variables that may convey delicate information about production processes and strategic choices.

However, one cost of disclosure rules that is not often discussed, but that has been identified early in relation to public procurement rules, is that of public knowledge on the price and quality conditions offered by the winning private partners may harm the competitive process by facilitating anticompetitive agreements among competitors. Bid rigging illegally tries to keep procurement prices at a level higher than the competitive one, and prevent competitors from cutting prices by threatening "price wars". And, as George Stigler wrote regarding public procurement auctions: "The system of sealed bids, publicly opened with full identification of each bidder's price and specification, is the ideal instrument for the detection of price cutting" (1964, p. 48).

In comparison with public procurement of standardized products or services, the governance of PPPs is likely to be even more problematic, as for a specific public buyer PPP procurements tend to be infrequent, large, complex, and often asset specific. These features make benchmarking and other standard forms of outside control more complex. At the same time, stakes are higher than in standard procurement, so bad governance can be much more costly.

Early reports on PPP best practices recognized well the particular governance problems of PPP procurement, and therefore suggested (IPPR,

2001) or prescribed (NHS, 2003) great levels of transparency and a widespread and proactive disclosure of contractual terms. *Ex-post* analyses such as Gosling (2004), however, have revealed that even in a country like the UK, with a very good general level of accountability and a lively public debate, non-binding "best practice" recommendations to disclose information were seldom followed by public administrations, even when directly asked for the information. It is clear, therefore, that in countries with weaker general accountability and public debates, non-binding disclosure requirements are likely to have little or no impact.

We mentioned that the standard ground for classifying private information as "confidential" is that, if disclosed, such information could place the contractor in a disadvantageous position relative to competitors.[5] This suggest that there is a trade-off between accountability and willingness of private parties to disclose delicate information on how certain needs could be faced in a PPP. Such information is crucial, for example, in the early stage of assessing the suitability of PPP for an infrastructure project.

The trade-off between accountability and confidentiality should be relevant for information about the production processes and strategic choices of the contractor. The disclosure cost in terms of potential competitive harm for the contractor should therefore be small or absent when disclosure is limited to contractual terms (payment schemes, quality standards, deductions, prices, etc.) and other output-related measures (revenues). As PPP contracts are based on output specifications and the assessment and selection phases are in the past, from a PPP governance perspective, the contractual information that needs to be disclosed once the contract is signed is that about output variables, the business outline, the risk allocation, the payment mechanism and the Public Sector Comparator.[6] Information should be disclosed within a pre-established, short, and binding time limit from the contract signature; a timetable for publishing sensitive

[5]The information sharing literature has shown that disclosure may give a firm either a strategic advantage or disadvantage depending on whether its strategy and the strategy of rivals are strategic substitutes or complements and on whether the information is regarding the firm's own cost, demand, or some industry-wide parameter (see e.g., Vives (1999) for a review).

[6]The Public Sector Comparator regards the PPP suitability assessment, as it estimates the potential gain from a PPP as opposed to in-house provision.

issues could also be determined. The time limit could be established by law information, by the national auditor, and/or by the contract, but in any case it must be short and strictly binding. Notice that such information should imply little or no competitive harm for the contractor.

The arguments for keeping as confidential the contractual and output features that convey no information on inputs are, therefore, extremely weak. In fact, most reports and best practice documents suggest maximal disclosure of PPP documentation, limiting confidentiality to a very strict set of information (HM Treasury, 2007). This notwithstanding, to our knowledge, non-disclosure of PPP contracts remains the norm.

3. Risk Allocation, Incentives, and Types of PPPs

3.1. *The main characteristics of PPPs*

There is no unanimous definition of PPP. We use the term PPP to refer to a contractual arrangement between a public authority and a contractor for the provision of public services with the following four main characteristics:

(1) the bundling of project phases into a single contract;
(2) an output specification approach;
(3) a high level of risk transfer to the contractor; and
(4) a long-term contract duration.

PPPs differ in terms of which stages of a project (such as designing, building, financing, and operating) are *bundled* into the contract. Nevertheless, the term PPP is generally used to indicate a substantial involvement of the private sector in at least the building (or renovation) and operation of the infrastructure for the public-service provision.

PPP contracts are based on *output specifications* in the sense that the public authority defines only basic standards of service, leaving the contractor with the choice as to how to meet and possibly improve upon these basic standards. The idea of the output specification is to provide incentives for innovative approaches, allowing for private sector's skills and knowledge to feed into public service provision. By leaving the private partner's discretion over how to meet the output requirements, scope is created for innovation and flexibility at the project design stage and throughout the contractual period.

PPP contracts are (meant to be) characterized by a relevant level of *risk transfer* to the contractor, although the optimal risk allocation varies with the form of PPP used for the project, as different is the scope of activities delegated to the private sector. For each type of PPP contract, risk is allocated to the contractor through contractual incentives and penalties incorporated within the payment mechanism, and through the activities for which the contractor is responsible.[7]

PPP contracts are generally *long-term contracts* with duration increasing with the level of financial involvement of the private sector in the provision of investments. Upon contract expiry, the public authority regains possession of the assets and can re-tender aspects of the service provision to other providers or take provision in-house.

3.2. *Categories of risks*

In every infrastructure project, there are risks associated with the nature of the project. For example, a project to construct a highway to diminish travel times is subject to the risk of construction delay due to unexpected geological conditions, inefficient construction practices, additional environmental studies to be done before the works begin, unexpected problems raised by their results, or simply construction permits not released on time. Once the construction phase ends, the project faces the risk of not raising sufficient revenues to cover operation costs and recoup invested funds because of traffic volume being lower than expected.

We list below the main types of risk at general level:[8]

(1) *Statutory/Planning risk* alludes to the uncertainty that construction permissions of the infrastructure project may be refused, that unacceptable conditions may be applied to any planning permission granted, and that the planning process may take longer than anticipated and cost more than expected.
(2) *Misspecification of output requirements risk* refers to the possibility that the output characteristics specified in the contract and which form the basis of the contractual obligations are ill or not clearly described.

---

[7] See Grimsey and Lewis (2002) for a discussion of how risk allocation in PPPs differs from that in traditional procurement.

[8] For a further discussion, see Bing *et al.* (2005) and Loosemore (2007).

(3) *Design risk* comprises the possibility of failing to complete the design process in time and within the budgeted cost of failing to deliver a solution that works satisfactorily and meets the requirements set by the public authority, and of changes in technical standards during the design phase.
(4) *Construction and time schedule risk* refer to construction delay and cost overruns that may arise from changes in labor and materials costs, inadequate cost management, inefficient construction practices, adverse site and weather conditions, protester action, delays in obtaining approvals and permits, and the failure of private partners to perform.
(5) *Operation risk* relates to large operation costs and failure to meet availability and performance standards that may arise from shortage of skilled labor, labor disputes, late delivery of equipment, poor maintenance schedule, inadequate cost management, etc.
(6) *Availability risk* covers situations where, during the PPP's operational phase, an underperformance linked to the state of the PPP assets results in services being partially or wholly unavailable, or where these services fail to meet the quality standards specified in the PPP contract.
(7) *Demand risk* alludes to the possibility of making lower-than-expected revenues if the actual demand for service falls short of the demand initially forecasted.
(8) *Risk of changes in public needs* refers to the possibilities that output specifications set up in the initial contract become inadequate because of changes in society's preferences. The relative importance of this risk increases with contract length, as for a longer contract, the chance of changes in public needs is greater.
(9) *Legislative/Regulatory risk* includes the changes in the legislative and regulatory framework, e.g., unexpected modifications in tax legislation, tariff-setting rules, and contractual obligations regarding investment and quality standards.
(10) *Financial risk* comprises operating and capital losses that may result from interest and exchange rate fluctuations, capital controls restricting convertibility and transferability of profits, etc.
(11) *Residual value risk* is the uncertainty of holding a facility (e.g., land, buildings, water plant) whose value at the end of the contract is lower than that anticipated at the start.

3.3. *Efficient risk allocation*

In a contract, the risk allocation between the contractual parties should accomplish two sets of goals: to provide incentives for the parties to undertake efficient non-contractible actions (because they are non-observable), and to provide insurance to a risk-averse party against the project's risks. In a PPP contract, in particular, risk allocation should provide incentives to reduce the long-term cost of a project, to complete the project in time and within budget, to deliver the service at agreed standards, and to insure the risk-averse public and private partners against risk. Risk insurance for the public partner helps to improve its profile of project expenditures by converting variable operation and capital costs into predictable unitary payments. Risk insurance for the private partner contributes to reduce the cost of capital.

In order to accomplish the above goals in the most effective way, two principles should guide the allocation of risk between the public and private partners:

(P1) Given partners with similar risk-aversion, the risk should be allocated to the party that is responsible or has relatively more control over the risk factor, and

(P2) Given partners with similar responsibility or control over the risk factor, the risk should be allocated to the less risk-averse party.

When we put together both the issue of incentives and that of risk premium minimization, we find that *risk is optimally allocated* if the following holds:

(i) When the public authority is more risk averse than the contractor, then risk transfer to the latter helps both to ensure incentives over non-contractible actions and to minimize the total cost of the project. The optimal risk allocation then calls for the contractor to bear all the risk.
(ii) When the public authority is less risk averse than the contractor, then risk transfer to the latter generates a trade-off: it helps to ensure incentives, but it may lead to an excessive risk premium.

Taking into account that in general the public authority is less risk averse than the contractor because of its wider possibilities to diversify risk, the above two principles lead to the following criteria for risk allocation:

(i) The public authority should fully bear risks that the private sector cannot control (or cannot control as well as the public authority) either in terms of likelihood of occurrence or in terms of impact, and that are uninsurable.
(ii) The contractor should bear risks that the private sector can control (or can control better than the public authority) both in terms of likelihood of occurrence or in terms of impact. However, some risk sharing may be appropriate when risk is difficult to forecast and transferring all risk to the contractor may result in an excessive risk premium (i.e., high cost of capital), and unbankable projects.

In light of the above, we discuss below how specific risks should be allocated between the public and private parties in the case of the DBFO model where the contractor is responsible for all the stages of the project.

3.3.1. Statutory/Planning risk

As a general rule, the public authority is best placed to manage the statutory process by virtue of its legislative basis, experience, and resources, and therefore, the contractor cannot control this type of risk as well as the public authority. When the public authority carries out the statutory and planning processes in advance of the tender process, and thus fully bears the associated risk, the benefit is that there is certainty about the conditions to be applied to the project.

In many LAC countries, the public sector faces fiscal constraints and lacks expertise and technical capacity to manage the statutory/planning risk it should bear according to the efficient risk allocation. Hence, the public sector may fail to perform the tasks corresponding to it under such an allocation. It may be argued that, if the public authority cannot effectively perform these tasks, it should transfer them to the private partner. But notice that such a transfer would expose the private sector to the statutory/planning risk it cannot control, i.e., the transfer will be inconsistent with the efficient risk allocation, thus requiring an increase in the risk premium that costs more to the public administration than the risk it has transferred.

Compared to the case where the risk is retained in the public sector, the PPP project becomes more expensive in terms of higher service charges, higher subventions required from the public sector, lower contractor transfers, etc.

3.3.2. Misspecification of output requirements risk

In general, information acquisition and processing by the public authority are always needed at the outset in order to correctly specify the output requirements, and thus reduce the risk of contract misspecification. To provide incentives for public administrations to invest time and effort in information acquisition, it is necessary that the public authority bears the risk of misspecification of output requirements.

However, transferring risk of output misspecification to the public sector may often not suffice to ensure adequate incentives for the public authority, because of the general difficulties in making public sector officials accountable for their actions. Because of these factors, transferring the risk of contract misspecification to the public sector-party may not suffice to ensure minimal contract misspecifications. The problem is particularly severe when PPPs are undertaken by small local administrations who may not have received enough training to deal with complex projects such as PPPs. It is therefore often advisable to design centrally standardized contracts to be used by local administrations, and to set up centralized PPP units to advice local administration (as done for example in the UK and in Italy).

3.3.3. Design, construction, time schedule, and operation risk

Under the DBFO model, the contractor is responsible for designing, building, financing, and operating the facility used to provide public services. The *bundling* of project phases into a single contract is the main characteristic of PPP contracts. If the design, construction, time schedule, and operation risk are transferred to the private sector, the bundling of project phases encourages the contractor to think about the implications of its actions on different stages of the project (from the building to the operation) and thus favors a whole-life cost approach (Bennett and Iossa, 2006; Martimort and Pouyet, 2008; Iossa and Martimort, 2014). Furthermore, bundling may also boost incentives to innovate and gather private information about future costs to adapt service provision to changing circumstances (Hoppe and Schmitz, 2013). This is why design, construction, time schedule, and operational risks should be transferred to the private sector.

Risk sharing may, however, become desirable in situations where the public authority has an informational advantage over the contractor, for example over the value of the assets. This is particularly relevant when the PPP contract involves renovation rather than construction of a facility or infrastructure, as it is often the case for PPPs in transport, water, and energy. It is also relevant for prison services, clinical services, and water services, where the public sector owns assets such as pumps, water pipes, metering systems, etc. In these cases, the authority has better knowledge of the state of the underlying assets and may therefore be in a better position to evaluate (at least some of) the cost and risks associated with service provision, as shown by Martimort and Sand-Zantman (2006).

3.3.4. Demand risk

Payment mechanisms in PPPs can be based on user charges, usage, or availability. In a payment mechanism based on user charges, the contractor gets revenues directly through fees applied to end users of the infrastructure facility. To the extent that users pay the corresponding fees and there are no other payments from the public sector or income guarantees, the demand risk is fully transferred to the private sector. Bearing the demand risk, the contractor has direct incentives to improve performance in order to encourage service usage and thus increase revenues.[9] If the contractor is able to control demand risk, it is efficient to fully transfer this risk to the private sector by implementing a user charge-based payment mechanism.

However, in many sectors, demand is difficult to predict accurately and its associated risks are high. This is often the case in projects involving construction of new infrastructure, like a road, bridge, or tunnel, where the expected revenues are calculated using forecasts of future service demand.

[9]Moreover, it is possible to manage demand by setting a pricing rule that charges users according to usage, e.g., in the transport sector, tolls can vary by vehicle type and time of day.

In these cases, a full transfer of demand risk to the contractor might raise the cost of capital substantially, calling for higher user charges or longer contract duration to reimburse investments. It may then happen that an excessive demand risk wipes out the project's benefits because the resulting cost-covering user charges are so large that users prefer to seek for alternative services, thus making the project unbankable. Under these circumstances, the public authority could lower user fees and pay the contractor a subvention to complement the collected revenue, so the demand risk is partially transferred to the contractor.

A number of subvention schemes may be offered to the contractor when the expected revenues are not sufficient to ensure project bankability. First, capital expenditure contributions (capex) may be offered by the public authority taking the form of: (i) capital grants; (ii) loans; (iii) equity. In order to avoid public sector exposure to construction risk, the construction phase should be funded by the contractor, and capex contributions should be injected only after project completion. Capital grants minimize conflicts of interest, but the public authority should take into account that a capital grant is a sunk cost which is not refunded in the event of contract termination. Moreover, as long as senior debt will be repaid first in case of contractor's default, the use of capex contributions may not be appropriate. Second, revenue support to improve the private partner overall cash flow may be linked to the number of users, thus being equivalent to user charges in terms of incentives and risk transfer. Alternatively, they may decrease over time to provide incentives to encourage usage, or decrease as the usage level increases to avoid windfall earnings under unexpected increase in demand. Revenue support can also take the form of revenue guarantees payable only in years where revenues from user charges fall short of a specified level. It has to be noted that subventions weaken the rationale for PPPs since they reduce incentives for the private contractor, which may make PPPs unsuitable.

A payment mechanism based on usage can be seen as a variant of user charges, in which the public authority pays the contractor, instead of service users. In this scheme, the public authority sets tariffs to be charged on users according to its objectives. After receiving the associated revenues, the public authority makes unitary payments to the private partner depending on the actual usage level.

In most cases, there are bands for usage levels specifying the payment due for each level of usage, and thus setting limits to the demand risk transferred to the private partner.[10] When risk sharing is optimal, bands at low usage levels bound the risk to the contractor that demand is lower than expected. In practice, lower bands provide a certain minimum usage payment to cover debt service, but not to ensure a positive return on equity. On the other hand, using bands at high usage levels caps the number of users for which the public authority should make payments, thus bounding the public authority's financial liability.

In a payment mechanism based on availability, typically used for prisons, schools, and hospitals, the public authority makes unitary payments to the contractor for making the service available regardless of the actual service usage. To encourage good performance, the contract could establish "bonuses" to be awarded if and only if certain target performance levels are reached. In addition, the payment scheme may include deductions if the private partner fails to comply with availability targets. Deductions should depend on whether the contractor can or cannot control the events causing unavailability, the private partner's effort to provide alternative services, the spread and recurrence of unavailability episodes, and the rectification period needed. The weightings of deductions are important: if deductions are too low, it may be convenient for the contractor to under-perform; while if they are too high, risks increase and the contract may require a higher pricing (HM Treasury, 2007). The simplest approach is to categorize various types of performance shortcomings and use a grid of monetary deductions. An alternative two-stage approach is to assign penalty points to the contractor any time a performance failure occurs, eventually attaching more points to a serious and recurrent failure, and to set a rule that translates points into monetary deductions. Generally, deductions are made when a certain number of points have been assigned to the contractor within a defined time period. To provide incentives to perform, there should be an adequate calibration between the seriousness and frequency of a failure, the number of penalty points assigned where applicable, and the financial impact of deductions on the private partner (HM Treasury, 2007).[11]

[10]See Kerf (1998) for an in-depth description.

[11]See also Albano *et al.* (2006) for an in-depth discussion on performance-based payments.

In any case, performance targets should be based on objective measures of service availability and should be established in the contract terms, e.g., lanes ready-to-use in roads and capacity to undertake water treatment works. Therefore, with availability payment and no user charges, there is no demand risk for the contractor. The case of prisons explains their logic: here, the demand (number of prison inmates) cannot be affected by the private sector's action or effort, whilst it does depend on the judicial system, the law and offence rates in specific areas. Transferring demand risk to the private party through a payment contingent on the number of inmates would increase risk premium and the cost of capital without impacting on incentives. Demand risk for prisons should therefore be retained within the public sector. However, to retain incentives, the payment mechanism for prisons should include penalties for poor performance to be deducted from unitary payments (for example, linked to number of suicides or riots in a prison).

3.3.5. Risk of changes in public needs

The public authority is often in a better position than the contractor to acquire information on the likelihood of changes in users' needs. Also, changes in public needs can be indirectly affected by changes in public sector policy (e.g., the demand for underground services is affected by public transportation policies regarding the availability and cost of bus services). For these reasons, the risk of changes in public needs that bring about the need to change output specifications prescribed in the contract should generally be borne by the public authority.

However, the optimal allocation of the risk of changes in public needs should also provide incentives for the contractor to make requested changes in the service provision at a reasonable cost so as to control the impact of risk. Whilst the contractor should be contractually obliged to provide the extra asset/service, changes in public needs can be very costly for the public sector because of the strong bargaining position of the contractor locked into the contract, and because of the lack of accessible alternatives and cost benchmarks. This may make it preferable to introduce some sort of risk-sharing agreement between the private and public partner.

Risk sharing can also help to provide incentives for the contractor to acquire information on the cost of changes and thus inform the decision as to whether those changes are indeed necessary. This is also important since the private partner is often in a better position to identify the best means to satisfy the needs of the public sector.

3.3.6. Legislative/Regulatory risk

Changes in the legislative and regulatory framework affecting operation costs and profits are likely to occur during the concession. When these changes are of a general nature and affect the whole industry, e.g., modifications in tax legislation, the rising costs can be either transferred to the contractor or shared with the public authority. For instance, indexation provisions may allow the concessionaire to pass on the rising costs to consumers through price increases. On the other hand, when changes in law and regulation affect only the concession project, it is often the public authority that bears the risk of rising costs (HM Treasury, 2007). Generally, the risk of changes in law should not lie with the contractor as it cannot control this type of risk. But in many cases, the public authority has little influence over national legislation and the private sector can minimize the impact of the change in law on the service provision. Because of this, there is an argument for risk to be shared between the two parties.

3.3.7. Residual value risk

When the facility is built by the contractor, it is likely that during the design and construction phase, the private partner can undertake non-contractible actions affecting the quality of the assets. For facilities like leisure centers and accommodations that have some value when used for private purposes, incentives are given for the private partner to undertake those actions to the extent that it retains ownership of the assets once the contract expires. However, for most infrastructure facilities like roads, bridges, energy, and water plants that have limited alternative use outside the public sector and service continuation requires the facility to remain in public hands, the public authority should keep ownership of the assets when the contract expires.[12]

---

[12]Bennett and Iossa (2006) show that this is indeed optimal on the incentives of the private partner to undertake non-contractible investments to maintain the infrastructure/facility.

To provide incentives for the contractor to look after the facility during the contract life and specially toward the end of the contract, it is crucial to set out contract clauses providing for a final compensation payable to the private partner conditional on the state of the facility once the contract expires. In this regard, an independent third party can be called to verify the state of the assets in order to compute the compensation to be made. Alternatively, and often most effectively, the entrant could compensate the incumbent contractor the facility residual values (Iossa and Legros, 2004).

4. Limits and Tricks in Risk Transfer

In practice, risk allocation often differs from what the criteria for optimal risk allocation recommend. This may happen for a number of reasons. First, there is the issue of whether governments are able to commit to the risk allocation specified in the contract. The need to ensure service continuation often makes the public authority renege on contractual provisions either by bailing out a contractor in difficulty or by not levying the contractual penalties specified in case of underperformance. If, for instance, an essential facility was found to be massively behind schedule and over budget during the construction stage, the public sector might have to take back full control of the project, as it is the provider of last resort in all PPP projects. Renegotiation is indeed a widespread phenomenon in concession contracts, as reported in Guasch (2004), among others.

Renegotiation practices, however, have serious negative effect in the long run. At tender stage, the possibility of renegotiation may be anticipated by the private sector, creating incentives to act strategically and bid very aggressively to get the contract. Firms who did not anticipate the contract renegotiation (possibly just because they have lower knowledge of the public authority) then lose the tender.[13] Furthermore, the anticipation that the public sector will bail out the firm or not levy the due penalties has a negative impact on the incentives of the private sector to perform during the contract implementation.

[13]See Bajari *et al.* (2014) for an empirical estimate of the impact of *ex-post* renegotiation on the *ex-ante* bidding.

Second, PPP contracts have raised important issues for the public authority regarding accounting practices, which have had an impact on the risk allocation. The need of governments to keep public accounts within limits, at least "apparently", has induced them to use PPPs only because of its accounting treatment. This problem has been particularly severe in Europe because of public debt restrictions due to EU treaty and subsequent agreements. In particular, the accounting treatment of monetary transfers to the private sector for PPP projects of prisons, schools, or hospitals, has allowed the public sector to finance the construction of infrastructure "off the balance sheet". Thus, the undervaluation of the public cost of PPP financed infrastructure has made the fiscal budget look healthier than it actually is. This has led to biased decisions in favor of PPPs as opposed to more traditional procurement arrangements.[14]

The Eurostat, the Statistical Office of the European Commission, has attempted to reduce the incidence of this problem by regulating the accounting treatment of PPPs. In 2004, the EUROSTAT has established that a PPP project can be taken "off balance" only when the contract allocates significant project risks to the private sector, specifically the construction risk, demand, or availability risks. National statistical institutions are supposed to monitor the compliance with the European rule, yet, to our knowledge, legislation enforcement has so far been quite obscure[15]: the data is not accessible to the general public, and public officers have confidentially told us that many PPP projects have been declared "on balance" even if the above risks are not fully transferred.

Third, the budget constraint limits faced by governments have often induced them to resolve to PPPs as if it was "the only game in town", in the sense that it could allow to build infrastructure without having to find the funding to finance them upfront. The private finance aspect of

[14] See IPPR (2001) for a discussion of how off-balance sheet considerations mattered in the early PPP projects in the UK.

[15] EU Member States are obliged to prepare National Accounts to a common format as defined in the European System of Integrated Economic Accounts (ESA 95). These accounts are prepared by national statistical offices and reported to Eurostat. ESA 95 sets out the treatment of PPPs. ESA 95 is available from the Eurostat website at: http://epp.eurostat.ec.europa.eu/portal/page/portal/government_finance_statistics/introduction under "Manuals".

PPPs has been an attractive feature for governments with limited budget. The problem with this approach is that of course the private funding does not come for free, and for prisons, schools, and hospitals, where the public sector typically pays for the service, the private party will recoup its investment via public payments during the operations. Governments with short-term electoral objectives have then a great incentive to build infrastructure through PPPs even when it is not efficient to do so, as they can obtain by the short-term electoral gain whilst committing funding of future[16] governments and future generations. To ensure that the contractor could raise sufficient private finance, these governments have then had an incentive to unduly retain main project risks, even when it was not efficient to do so. In particular, generous revenue or income guarantees have been used to ensure the bankability and attractiveness of the project, leading to an inefficient risk allocation, and hence poor incentives. The following PPP case illustrates when an insufficient risk transfer may arise and how this may lead to a remarkable PPP failure.

4.1. *Case studies*

In this section, we discuss a couple of case studies that emphasize some of the potential benefits, costs, and risks of PPPs. The first case refers to the Transmilenio (TM) Bus Rapid Transit system in Bogota for the provision of urban bus services. The project exhibited bundling of different stages of the service provisions, thus allowing for the internalization of externalities across stages. Contractors were rewarded on a performance-related basis and were in large part residual claimant for demand increase, bearing significant demand and operational risks. Incentives were thus strong, and resulted in an overall successful and efficient PPP project.

The second case study refers to the PPP for London Underground, where the degree of bundling was very limited, because the infrastructure was in part already in place and the core service was kept by the public sector. The political opposition to the project and the negative attention received in the news also contributed to make the private finance particularly expensive. Thus, high costs of capital coupled with inadequate risk transfer and inappropriate revenue guarantees, lead to the project failure.

[16]See Engel *et al.* (2006) for a discussion of these political incentives and their implications.

4.1.1. The TM Bus Rapid Transit System in Bogota (Colombia)[17]

The TM Bus Rapid Transit System was developed in 2000 to upgrade and operate the Bogotá's bus transport system by a partnership between the public sector and a number of private companies. Before the TM project, transport services were provided by bus companies that rented the government-issued routes to small private bus operators serving fixed routes. Since the operators' revenue depended on the number of passengers, there were often "price wars" to attract passengers (Colombians referred to this phenomenon as "war of the cents" because only minimal price reductions were feasible in bus fares). Outcomes from such a system were far from efficient: long delays, oversupply of seat capacity, low quality of service, and high rate of accidents due to fierce competition for passengers. The TM project rationalized bus routes, by building exclusive bus lanes in critical areas of Bogotá and using a system of feeder routes to complement the main lanes, and constructed a modern infrastructure of enclosed bus stops, pedestrian bridges, terminals, and transfer stations.

Contracts and partners: A publicly owned company, TransMilenio SA, was set up to manage and develop the planning and contract drafting stages of the project. It also conducted the tendering to select private partners that would build infrastructure and operate the main routes, the feeder routes, the ticketing system, and the payments system. Following the PPP rationale, there was thus bundling of different stages of the project, with some common services shared across contractors. After launching the TM project, TransMilenio SA was responsible for the management of the new bus transport system, and for conducting monitoring and verification activities in order to ensure quality performance and customer service. In this regard, a system of fines was implemented to penalize the private partners failing to comply with their contractual obligations, responsibilities, and investment requirements.

Financing: Transport construction works, estimated in $240 million for the period 1998–2002 and $480 million for 2002–2005, were funded by the public sector. Most of the infrastructure cost was to be borne by the national

[17]This case study is based on the following sources: Fernholz and Morales Fernholz (2005); TransMilenio SA web page; El Tiempo (several articles).

and local governments. The contribution of the national government was around two-thirds of the infrastructure cost, partly financed with a loan granted by the World Bank. Private partners, on the other hand, provided financing for buses and ticket machines, as in a DBFO scheme. Their invested funds were to be recouped by charging fares to final users, with no subsidies nor guarantees offered by the public sector to the contractors. As the contractors borne demand risk, it had strong incentives to operate the system efficiently.

Activities and risk allocation: To conduct the operation activities, the public authority contracted with different partners and unbundled the operation of buses, the collection of revenues, and the distribution of revenues among the bus operators. The existing bus companies awarded concessions through competitive bidding to operate the bus routes. The award criterion was based in a system of points in which bidders received points according to their experience, bus quality, and emission levels. Thus, TM encouraged the bus operators to provide an efficient, modern, and non-polluting vehicle fleet. The bus operators had to invest in new buses, so financial risk was transferred to them.

The TM project specified in detail the technical requirements for the buses: operators of main routes should have afforded modern buses, and operators of feeder routes could use standard buses. To reduce journey times, both regular and express bus services were to be provided with predetermined schedules and making information available for users through an electronic system.

Payment mechanism: The payment system implemented in the TM project implied that the demand risk was jointly borne by the bus operators since all the revenues collected were distributed among them. However, the revenue distribution was based on the weekly route distance that each bus operator served regardless of the number of passengers transported. Since TransMilenio SA could penalize a bus operator failing to comply with its contractual obligations by reducing its assigned weekly route distance (and so increasing that assigned to the other operators), it turned out that the bus operator's performance affected its share in the revenue distribution (and implicitly the share of demand risk borne individually). In fact, TransMilenio SA was able to reduce up to 10% of the operator's income, thus imposing a significant monetary loss for quality service failure.

In determining the fare level, both the bankability and affordability of the TM projcct were taken into account. In the project planning, a fare level around $0.40 cents had been estimated as consistent with the project's bankability. In fact, one year before the new system was introduced, the fares charged by the existing bus service providers were increased from $0.30 to $0.40 cents. Hence, at the time the new system commenced, there was no price difference between the TM bus services and those provided by the small private bus operators. Since the TM bus services were much faster and of a higher quality, the small private bus operators found it hard to compete for passengers in the parallel routes they were allowed to serve. After the initial fare was set, the contracts envisaged a mechanism to adjust the service charge periodically. Price variation provisions aimed at protecting the bus operators from unexpected changes in operation costs they could not control.

Outcomes and future expansion: By all accounts, the inherited bus transport system exhibited low service quality and high levels of congestion and pollution. But soon after the TM project was launched, significant improvements were achieved in terms of the efficiency, safety, and environmental impact of the system. One year after the TM project was launched, journey times were reduced 32%, implying an equivalent to a one hour/day saving for the average passenger; average speed in the main routes were much higher than before; pollution levels in Bogotá resulting from the bus transport system dropped; and the number of accident fatalities decreased.

In line with the successful TM PPP experience, the government has gradually incorporated the rest of the Collective Public Transportation system (TPC-Transporte Público Colectivo), that serves 69% of public transportation trips, into the Integrated Public Transportation System (SITP). The current TPC presents an oversupply of approximately 7,500 public transportation vehicles that exceeds real passenger demand with the subsequent increase in traffic congestion and pollution. Also TPC's buses are generally old and obsolete, and have been traditionally operated by small-scale bus owners whose remuneration is not linked to service quality. Therefore, the SITP will enhance the quality of the CPT by reducing buses oversupply, renewing the vehicle fleet, designing a route network, formalizing operators' revenues, and integrating travel fares into a unified payment system. Like in the TM, the SITP includes investments in transportation infrastructure, vehicle modernization, and complementary systems. Main infrastructure investments (such as construction of bus stops, passenger transit terminals, and bus storage lots) will be financed by the public sector or through PPP, while investments in vehicles and complementary systems will be financed entirely by the concessionaires over the 24-year life of the concession.

4.1.2. The London Underground (UK)[18]

The London Underground PPP project to rehabilitate and upgrade the London tube was awarded to two private-sector companies (Tube Lines and Metronet Infracos) in 2003 after 19 months of arduous negotiations on the contract terms between the parties. Political challenges, fierce critics, and the uncertainty on contract negotiation led to large costs for the public sector arising from advisory services (£109 million) and delays in the award of contracts: London Underground Ltd. (LUL) paid £134 million to Tube Lines, £116 million to Metronet, and even £25 million to unsuccessful bidders in reimbursements for bidding costs.

The London tube PPP contract was more complex than a typical operation PFI deal involving a continuum of work to improve the tube assets over the 30 years of the contract duration. The Infracos would upgrade and maintain the existing infrastructure while the LUL, a public-sector company subsidiary of Transport for London (TfL), continued to provide transportation services to final users. The Tube Lines consortium was awarded the concession for the Jubilee, Northern, and Piccadilly lines, whereas Metronet signed over the other two PPP contracts, one for the concession of the Bakerloo, Central, and Victoria lines, and another for the District, Circle, Hammersmith & City, and East London lines.

[18]This case study is based on the following sources: NAO (2004a, b); The House of Commons, Committee of Public Accounts (2005) and Transport Committee (2008); Transport for London web site; Public Private Finance (various issues); Public Finance (various issues); *The Economist* (2007a, b); *The Financial Times* (various issues); *The Guardian Unlimited* (various issues).

Risk allocation: The demand risk of the PPP project was borne by LUL since it kept the responsibility for delivering the transportation service and charging user fees. The risk of cost overruns arising during the contract was shared between LUL and the Infracos. The amount of cost overruns to be borne by Tube Line and Metronet were capped to £200 million and £50 million for the first 7.5 years of the contract, respectively, provided they performed in an economic and efficient manner. However, the contracts imposed weak constraints on the Infracos' subcontracting arrangements which led to incentive distortions in the Metronet case: Metronet's shareholders were also suppliers of the consortium, so they were less concerned about cutting costs down because an increase in Metronet's costs would translate into higher revenues for the supplier companies. Hence, Metronet's supply chain arrangement lacked transparency and was vulnerable to outright corporate abuse. In fact, Metronet incurred in large cost overruns estimated four times higher of what initially expected when signing the contract. Arguing that cost overruns were due to LUL's additional works requests, Metronet proposed either to share costs with LUL or to reduce the scale of pledged works. On the contrary, no cost overruns were incurred by the Tube Lines consortium, which had implemented an outsourcing arrangement based on competitive tendering and used to stand up to the additional work requirements of LUL. The debate over the responsibility over Metronet's cost overruns suggests the original PPP contract was poorly designed: the overlapping of interests between Metronet's shareholders and suppliers provided pervasive incentives for cost-reducing efforts.

Moreover, it was expected that private financing involved in the PPP contracts would give incentives for the Infracos to efficiently manage the project's financial risks. However, substantial risk was also borne by the public sector through a debt guarantee granted to the lenders entitling them to recoup 95% of their invested funds in case of early contract termination. According to the House of Commons (2005, 2008), the political opposition and public discontent about handling the maintenance of a prime public asset over the private sector during contract negotiations negatively affected lenders willingness to provide the funds, and led to debt guarantees being provided in order to make the project bankable and ensure that it would go ahead. Moreover, unlike other PFI contracts in the UK, LUL could enact a mandatory sale of the contract to ensure the continuity in service provision in case of early termination, instead of allowing lenders to sell the contract to other providers in order to protect their investment. Despite this public guarantee on private financing, the cost of capital turned out to be £450 million above the cost of capital that would have been observed had the project been financed by the government.

Payment mechanism: The PPP contract specified a payment mechanism consisting of a basic infrastructure service charge (ISC) combined with bonuses and deductions. To the extent the Infracos met performance, availability, and ambience targets, they were entitled to bonuses that increased their revenue, whereas a failure to meet these targets triggered payment deductions. The Infracos' performance in rehabilitating and upgrading the tube was measured by the journey time capability (JTC), i.e., the time needed for a train to complete a journey. Availability was measured by the number of lost customer hours, with penalties varying with the severity of a failure (e.g., breakdowns, signaling, and other failures were penalized more heavily at peak times), and ambience and general conditions of the trains and stations were measured by customer surveys.

Poor performance and penalties: Soon after the contracts began, the Infracos were subject to criticism because of their poor performance. The criticism on safety issues became stronger when two derailments occurred in the tube lines assigned to each of the consortiums. Moreover, the performance targets based on JTC were hardly attained as the rehabilitation works delayed significantly, suggesting the work schedule proposed by the companies were unrealistic. In the first year of the contracts, the companies were fined £32 million by deductions for failing to meet some of the targets, and earned just £12 million in bonuses for achieving other targets.

Despite the large (net) deductions applied to the basic ISC, the consortiums made huge profits. According to the NAO Report (2004a), the Infracos shareholders earned a rate of return around 20%, a third higher than the normal rate of return in private finance deals. Therefore, the impact of payment deductions on profitability must have been small (at least relative to gains from keeping low the quality of supply). Indeed, it has been argued that the deductions were too small considering both the payments made to the Infracos to undertake the pledged work and the inconvenience suffered by final users due to service disruptions. The too low deductions for poor performance appear to have distorted the incentive scheme sufficiently to generate the widespread poor performance of the Infracos together with their high profitability.

By April 2005, Metronet had only started refurbishment work on 13 out of 32 scheduled stations, and was also 12 months behind on the refurbishment of 78 District Line trains. Moreover, it received only £121 million out of the £551 million needed to cover its cost overruns. Thus, poor performance, work delays, and cost overruns resulted in Metronet going into administration between July 2007 and May 2008 after which it was bought by two TfL subsidiaries, LUL Nominee BCV Ltd. and LUL Nominee SSL Ltd., transferring the assets, employees, and contracts to ensure the continued safe operation and renewal of the Tube. According to the National Audit Office, the failure of the Metronet PPP contract was estimated to cost the taxpayers more than £400 million.

The remaining tube lines (Jubilee, Northern, and Piccadilly) remained under the PPP arrangement with Tube Lines until May 2010, when it was fully owned by a subsidiary of TfL. Although Tube Lines did not have Metronet's overspend problems, work delays on the Jubilee Line and funding shortfall problems ended up in its transfer to the public sector hands.

5. Concluding Remarks and Policy Implications

Outsourcing of public infrastructure and services is likely to increase in future years, as part of a general trend that is seeing a reduction of the size of the State in the economy. The recent explosion in public debts will certainly contribute to this trend, even if we are going through a stage where private funds and investments are difficult to raise because of the financial crisis.

With greater outsourcing, the role of the State must change: from direct provider of public services, governments should transform themselves in monitors of the private sector provision. Are governments able to undertake such role? If the monitor have incentives to push for the private provision to pursue its own political agenda, it is unlikely that the monitoring will be effective. As this is a possibility with PPPs, users and citizens must ask for the public sector to be more accountable.

Whether PPPs will then manage to realize the great potential to deliver cost and quality efficient public services, is an issue that will depend on whether the governance problems of PPPs that may prevent an efficient risk allocation will be addressed.

This chapter has emphasized that in this respect, a crucial role will have to be played by the commitment of governments to spread good practices, design and impose standardized contract terms, monitor their compliance, and disclose the relevant contractual information and performance evaluations to the general public, whilst at the same time ensuring that PPPs are used only in those circumstances where risks can indeed by transferred.

References

Albano, G. L., G. Calzolari, F. Dini, E. Iossa and G. Spagnolo (2006). Procurement Contracting Strategies, Ch 4, in N. Dimitri, G. Piga and G. Spagnolo (Eds.), *Handbook of Procurement*, Cambridge University Press, Cambridge, United Kingdom.

Bajari, P., S. Houghton and S. Tadelis (2014). "Bidding for Incomplete Contracts: An Empirical Analysis of Adaptation Costs," forthcoming in the *American Economic Review*.

Bennett, J. and E. Iossa (2006). "Building and Managing Facilities for Public Services," *Journal of Public Economics*, 90, pp. 2143–2160.

Bing, L., A. Akintoye, P. J. Edwards and C. Hardcastle (2005). "The Allocation of Risk in PPP/PFI Construction Projects in the UK," *International Journal of Project Management*, 23, pp. 25–35.

CBI, Confederation of British Industry (2007). *Building on Success: The Way Forward to PFI*, CBI, United Kingdom. Report available at www.cbi.org.uk/bookshop.

Chong, E., F. Huet, S. Saussier and F. Steyner (2004). "Public–Private Partnerships and Prices: Evidence from Water Distribution in France," *Review of Industrial Organization*, 29, pp. 149–169.

Coppier, R. and G. Piga (2007). "Why Do Transparent Public Procurement and Corruption Go Hand in Hand?" in G. Piga and K. V. Thai (Eds.), *The Economics of Public Procurement*, Palgrave, Macmillan, United Kingdom.

EIB, European Investment Bank (2004). *The EIB's Role in Public–Private Partnerships (PPPs)*, Luxembourg. Report available at http://www.eib.org/attachments/thematic/eib_ppp_en.pdf.

El Tiempo. Available at http://www.eltiempo.com.

Engel, E., R. Fischer and A. Galetovic (2006). "Renegotiation Without Holdup: Anticipating Spending and Infrastructure Concessions," *Discussion Paper* No. 937, Economic Growth Center, Yale University.

Engel, E., R. Fischer and A. Galetovic (2009). "Public–Private Partnerships: When and How," *Documentos de Trabajo* 257, Centro de Economía Aplicada, Universidad de Chile.

EPEC (2012). *Market Update: Review of the European PPP Market in 2012*, European Investment Bank, Luxembourg. Report available at http://www.eib.org/epec/resources/epec_market_update_2012_en.pdf.

Estache, A. (2006). *Infrastructure: A Survey of Recent and Upcoming Issues*, Infrastructure Vice-Presidency, and Poverty Reduction and Economic Management Vice-Presidency, The World Bank, Washington DC, USA.

European Commission (2003). *Guidelines for Successful Public–Private Partnerships*, Directorate General Regional Policy, Brussels, Belgium.

Fernholz, F. and R. Morales Fernholz (2005). *Case Study on Mobilization of Private Capital in Bogota, Colombia*, submitted by RTI International to Municipal Finance Task Force.

Gosling, T. (2004). "Openness Survey Paper," Institute for Public Policy Research, United Kingdom.

Grimsey, D. and M. Lewis (2002). "Evaluating the Risks of Public Private Partnerships for Infrastructure Projects," *International Journal of Project Management*, 20, pp. 107–118.

Guasch, J. L. (2004). *Granting and Renegotiating Infrastructure Concessions: Doing it Right*. WBI Development Studies, The World Bank.

Guasch, J. L., J. J. Laffont and S. Straub (2003). "Renegotiation of Concession Contracts in Latin America," *Working Paper* No. 3011, The World Bank.

Hammami, M., J-F. Ruhashyankiko and E. B. Yehoue (2006). "Determinants of Public–Private Partnerships in Infrastructure," *Working Paper* No. 06/99, International Monetary Fund.

HM Treasury (2006). *PFI: Strengthening Long-Term Partnerships*, The Stationery Office, London, United Kingdom.

HM Treasury (2007). *Standardisation of PFI Contracts, Version 4*, The Stationery Office, London, United Kingdom.

Hodge, C. A. and C. Greve (2007). "Public–Private Partnerships: An International Performance," *Public Administration Review*, 67, pp. 545–558.

Hoppe, E. and P. Schmitz (2013). "Public–Private Partnerships versus Traditional Procurement: Innovation Incentives and Information Gathering," *RAND Journal of Economics*, 44, pp. 56–74.

IMF (2004). "Public–Private Partnerships," Paper prepared by the Fiscal Affairs Department, International Monetary Fund.

Iossa, E. and P. Legros (2004). "Auditing and Property Rights," *RAND Journal of Economics,* 35, pp. 356–372.

Iossa, E. and D. Martimort (2013). *Corruption in PPPs, Incentives and Contract Incompleteness*, Paris School of Economics, Paris, France.

Iossa, E. and D. Martimort (2014). "The Simple Micro-economics of Public–Private Partnerships," forthcoming in *Journal of Public Economic Theory.*

Iossa, E., G. Spagnolo and M. Vellez (2007a). *Contract Design in Public Private Partnerships*. Report prepared for the Sustainable Development Network, The World Bank.

Iossa, E., G. Spagnolo and M. Vellez (2007b). *Best Practices in Contract Design in Public Private Partnerships*, Report prepared for the Sustainable Development Network, The World Bank.

IPPR, Institute of Public Policy Research (2001). *Building Better Partnerships*, IPPR, London.

Kaufmann, D. (2005). *Six Questions on the Cost of Corruption with World Bank Institute Global Governance Director Daniel Kaufmann*, in News — The World Bank, Washington, DC.

Kerf, M. (1998). "Concessions for Infrastructure: A Guide to their Design and Award," *Technical Paper* No. 399, The World Bank.

Leuz, C. (2007). "Was the Sarbanes–Oxley Act of 2002 Really this Costly? A Discussion of Evidence from Event Returns and Going-Private Decisions," *Journal of Accounting and Economics*, 44, pp. 146–165.

Loosemore, A. (2007). "Risk Allocation in the Private Provision of Public Infrastructure," *International Journal of Project Management*, 25, pp. 66–76.

Martimort, D. and J. Pouyet (2008). "To Build or Not to Build: Normative and Positive Theories of Public–Private Partnerships," *International Journal of Industrial Organization*, 26(2), pp. 393–411.

Martimort, D. and W. Sand-Zantman (2006). "Signalling and the Design of Delegated Management Contracts for Public Utilities," *RAND Journal of Economics*, 37(4), pp. 763–782.

NAO, National Audit Office (2004a). *London Underground PPP: Were they Good Deals?*, HC 645 Session 2003–2004.

NAO, National Audit Office (2004b). *London Underground: Are the Public Private Partnerships Likely to Work Successfully?* HC 644 Session 2003–2004.

NHS Executive (2003). *PPP in the NHS: the PFI*, Section 1 London, NHS Executive.

OECD (2004). *Principles of Corporate Governance*, OECD, Paris.

PricewaterhouseCoopers (PWC) (2005). *Delivering the PPP Promise: A Review of PPP Issues and Activity*, United Kingdom.

Public Finance. Available at http://www.publicfinance.co.uk.
Public Private Finance. Available at http://www.publicprivatefinance.com.
Renda, A. and L. Schrefler (2006). *Public–Private Partnerships. Models and Trends in the European Union*, Report presented to the European Parliament's Committee on Internal Market and Consumer Protection, Mimeo.
Rose-Ackerman, S. (1999). *Corruption and Government*, Cambridge University Press, Cambridge, United Kingdom.
Stigler, G. J. (1964). "A Theory of Oligopoly," *The Journal of Political Economy*, 72(1), pp. 44–61.
The Economist (2007a). "Britain: Down the Tube; London Underground," London, June 30, 383(8535), p. 42.
The Economist (2007b). "Britain: Underground; overbudget; London transport," London, April 28, 383(8526), p. 36.
The Financial Times. Available at http://www.ft.com.
The Guardian Unlimited. Available at http://www.guardian.co.uk.
The House of Commons, Committee of Public Accounts (2005). *London Underground Public Private Partnerships*, Seventeenth Report of Session 2004–2005.
The House of Commons, Transport Committee (2008). *The London Underground and the Public–Private Partnership Agreements*, Second Report of Session 2007–2008.
Transmilenio SA. Available at http://www.transmilenio.gov.co.
Transport for London. Available at http://www.tfl.gov.uk.
Vives, X. (1999). *Oligopoly Pricing: Old Ideas and New Tools*, MIT Press, Cambridge.

Index

A

abuse of a dominant position, 440, 442, 447
accountable care organizations, 318
accuracy, 369, 370, 381, 383–385, 387
"activity level" model, 368
adverse selection, 193, 218, 293, 315, 317, 328, 332, 334, 335
agency problems, 300, 308, 309
agreements, 195, 219, 236, 237, 274, 305, 370, 395, 440–442, 456–459, 463, 477, 489
airline networks, 31, 33–35, 38, 40, 44, 52
America West, 31, 33, 37, 44–46, 50, 51
anticompetitive, 9, 239, 246, 446, 463
antitrust, 32, 38, 39, 42, 44, 176, 193, 194, 197, 200–202, 204, 206–208, 223, 246, 287, 365, 367–370, 378–380, 385, 389–395, 398, 401, 402, 405, 406, 408, 411, 418, 424, 441, 444, 446, 448
antitrust authorities, 38, 194, 214, 223, 409
antitrust enforcement, 369, 378, 379, 384, 389, 391–394, 396, 398, 401, 402, 405, 406, 408, 411, 412, 418
antitrust fines, 389, 391, 409, 418, 432
antitrust rules, 39, 424, 448
antitrust policy, 32, 38, 379, 384, 390, 394
antitrust law, 194, 246, 365, 391, 395, 442, 445
asymmetric information, 145, 172, 219, 229, 238, 247, 254, 282, 290, 293–295, 301, 305, 317, 321, 330, 461
auction, 141–143, 145, 146, 149, 153, 160, 162, 163, 165, 240, 248, 249, 329, 345, 463
authority, 32, 59, 177, 193, 195, 432, 433, 436, 444, 456, 460, 466, 468–470, 472–477, 480
authorization, 365, 366, 368, 371–373, 377, 386, 445

B

bankruptcy, 118, 389–391, 393–396, 403, 409, 431, 432
bankruptcy considerations, 389, 391, 394–396, 397, 403, 407, 409
bargaining, 142, 146, 234, 240, 245, 251, 253–255, 262, 264, 267, 269, 305, 313, 320, 323–326
Bertrand oligopoly, 389, 391, 392, 396, 401, 402, 417
booms, 116–125, 127–135, 137
business cycle, 115, 116, 126, 129, 130, 134, 136

C

cap-and-trade, 341, 344
capacity, 115, 117, 119–123, 129–131, 136, 137, 246, 342, 343, 348, 349–351, 354, 355, 357, 361, 461, 469, 474, 479
capacity utilization, xvi, 115, 117, 120, 121, 129–131, 136, 137
cartel, 175–179, 185, 188–192, 392, 397, 430, 431, 433, 436, 440–444

cartel agreement, 188, 395–397
cartel detection, 197, 200, 444
cartel fine, 409
cartel overcharge, 390–393, 399, 400, 406–408, 412–414
certificates, 352, 353, 359
classroom experiment, 193, 196–198, 203, 208, 209
CO_2, 339, 340, 344–348, 353, 356
coefficient of variation, 19, 126, 130, 131, 134
coinsurance, 292, 301–304, 306, 307
collusion, 59, 61, 64, 119, 137, 175, 177–179, 189, 191, 193–197, 199–201, 203, 205–208, 239, 248, 313, 320, 391, 398, 399, 403, 406, 416, 417, 444
collusive price, 119, 396, 398, 399, 402, 440
competition, 5, 7, 24, 25, 32, 35, 231–234, 314, 317, 323, 340, 356, 360, 389, 423–426, 428–445, 447–449
competition authority, 32, 195, 428, 432, 433, 436, 444
Competition Commission, 3, 7–11, 445
competition policy, 206, 208, 238, 279, 281–283, 286, 289, 293–295, 298–300, 303, 308, 313, 318, 322, 325, 329, 341, 348, 361, 367, 390, 448
competition law, 424, 430–436, 441, 447, 448
competition policy regime, 425, 429, 433, 437–439, 447–449
competitive interaction, 21, 25
compliance, 176, 178, 179, 185, 189–192, 345, 431, 442, 447, 477, 486
compliance horizon, 177–179, 185, 188–192
concentration, 3–5, 7, 9, 24, 42, 49, 89, 125, 136, 286–289, 295, 304, 320, 323, 440
conduct/unilateral conducts, 424, 426, 428, 433, 437, 439, 441, 442, 448
confidentiality, 462, 464, 465
consumer welfare, 5, 31–36, 50–52, 213, 219, 221, 294, 295, 300, 409
contract design, 455, 457–460, 462
contracting externalities, 216, 218
control group, 46, 47
conviction, 194, 226, 435, 436
cooperation, 242, 262, 298, 317–320
cost shock, 60, 62–66, 68, 72, 74, 80, 89, 90, 180, 185, 186, 188, 189, 191
cost-reducing innovation, 231, 235, 236, 240
counter-cyclical, 115–120, 129, 135–137
court, 214, 239, 251, 268, 369, 394, 427, 431–435, 437–439, 441
crimes, 428, 430, 440
cross-market controls, 228
crude oil, 60, 62–64, 66, 70–78, 80, 81, 89, 90

D

D-i-D approach, 33, 46, 47, 51
damages, 215, 245, 343, 365, 368, 369, 371, 375, 377, 427, 430, 431, 434, 435, 439, 441, 443, 444, 448
decisions, 6, 32, 36, 104, 128, 203, 217, 221, 238, 241, 256, 292, 294, 320, 328, 344, 367, 370, 379, 394, 425, 428, 430, 434, 435, 438, 444–447
demand fluctuations, 115, 117, 119, 120, 136, 137
Department of Justice, 38, 194, 370, 443–445
desistance, 426, 427
detection, 194, 197, 200, 204, 206, 399, 407, 408, 436, 440, 444, 446, 448, 463
deterrence, 115, 117, 124, 128, 136, 369, 373, 375, 377, 382, 383, 385, 390, 391, 406, 408, 411, 412, 414, 417, 423–433, 436–448
diesel, 60, 62, 63, 66, 67, 69–79, 81–84, 88–90
discriminating rule, 378, 379, 381, 382–386
divide and conquer, 148, 153
dominant position, 214, 226, 440, 442, 447
downstream merger, 223

E

eBay, 141–144, 153, 160–165, 170
electricity, 339–344, 347–356, 358–361, 379, 389, 392
emissions trading system, 339, 340
empirical analysis, 31, 32, 52, 61, 63, 69, 90, 236
empirical findings, 141, 144, 443
empirical studies, 81, 286, 298, 306, 314, 320, 399
employees, 256, 290, 296, 297, 299, 303, 304, 317, 320, 325, 430, 436, 485
energy, 62, 339–342, 345–348, 350, 353–357, 359–361, 379, 455, 457, 471, 475
enforcement, 39, 61, 176, 190–192, 194, 251, 286, 365, 367, 369, 373, 378, 381–394, 398, 401, 406, 412, 418, 425, 426, 447, 448
enforcement features, 425, 447, 448
entrant, 37, 115, 117, 120, 121, 132, 136, 213, 216, 218, 220–224, 227, 245, 247, 322, 370, 476
entry, 32, 40, 47, 62, 66, 81, 115, 117, 123–125, 127, 128, 130–134, 136, 137, 243–245, 254, 304, 322, 326, 339, 348, 352, 356
entry deterrence, 115, 117, 128, 136
environmental policy, 339–341, 361
equilibrium multiplicity, 143
error-correction model, 59, 62–66, 68, 80, 89
errors, 48, 281, 291, 339, 369, 380–394, 428–430, 437, 438, 448
European Union, 190, 223, 240, 344, 347, 394, 435, 462
every-day low pricing (EDLP), 5, 8, 10, 15, 19
ex-ante deterrence, 369, 375, 376, 383, 426–431
ex-post analysis, 51
ex-post deterrence, 374, 376, 383, 384, 429, 447
ex-refinery, 62, 63, 66–72, 76–80, 88–90
exclusive dealing, 215, 216, 219, 223, 239, 245, 246, 321, 322, 379
exclusive dealing contracts, 215, 216, 223, 245, 246, 321
exclusive relationships, 226, 319
exit, 40, 47, 116, 137, 340
experiment, 144, 165, 193, 196–198, 201–203, 208–210, 427
exploitable leniency program, 193, 196, 197, 203–206, 208, 209
externality, 222, 245, 249, 312, 344, 346

F

F-test, 68, 71, 72, 75, 76, 83, 88, 89
failing firm, 37
feed-in tariffs (FIT), 348, 353, 357, 359–361
fidelity rebates, 213, 214, 223, 228
financial and human resources, 424, 436, 439, 448
fine reduction, 194–197
fines, 365, 366, 374, 377, 382–385, 389–396, 425, 428, 430–432, 441–443, 447
first mover, 115, 117, 120, 122–124, 127, 131–136, 220
first-stage regression, 62
flight frequency, 36
forcing contracts, 221

G

gaming, 295, 310, 312, 313, 315
general deterrence, 425–427, 429, 432
greenhouse gas (GHG), 340, 341, 345, 361
grocery retailing, 3, 4, 7, 8

H

hard data, 424, 443, 445, 448
HiLo pricing, 5, 8, 9, 19
hold up/hold-up problem, 251, 252, 255, 257, 268, 321

horizontal merger, 32–34, 223, 239, 282, 288, 329, 445, 446
hub-and-spoke (HS) network, 34, 35, 41, 47

I

illegal action, 427, 429, 431
imperfect information, 336, 434
imprisonment, 427, 430, 434, 440, 441
impulse response function, 75–80
incentives, 34, 41, 95, 98, 111, 149, 195, 217, 218, 228, 235, 240, 246, 267, 279, 292, 295, 301, 308, 317, 319, 329, 432, 456, 458–460, 462, 465, 466, 468, 470–476, 478, 480, 483, 485
incomplete contracts, 232, 247, 252, 253, 256
incumbent, 35, 115, 117, 120, 131, 136, 216, 220, 222–224, 236, 249, 289, 370, 379, 385, 476
independence, 340, 424, 433, 437–439, 448
infinitely-repeated Bertrand oligopoly, 396
infinitely-repeated oligopoly, 391
infrastructure, 339, 379, 455–458, 460, 463–466, 471, 475, 477–480, 482, 484, 485
infringements, 424, 427, 433, 447, 448
innovation, 93–95, 98, 196, 231, 232, 234–236, 238, 240, 244, 245, 247–252, 254, 255, 365, 367, 370, 376, 380, 465
institutions/institutional feature, 439, 447, 448
insulating fees, 144, 153, 154, 160
investment, 95, 242, 251, 255, 264, 306, 321, 344, 365, 367, 369, 373, 375, 379, 382–386, 444, 456, 463, 472, 478, 482, 484, 485

J

Judo pricing, 132, 134, 136

L

law, 177, 194, 246, 250, 295, 366, 374, 384, 391, 394, 424, 425, 427–443, 447, 448
law enforcement, 365, 367, 369, 384, 391, 424, 427, 428, 430, 442, 448
leader, 15, 22, 23, 94, 120, 194, 221, 224, 378, 379
leader–follower behavior, 6, 7, 21, 24
legal ceilings, 390, 391, 395, 409, 411, 412, 414
legal principles, 389–393, 396, 398–401, 417
legal standards, 365, 367, 368, 370, 378, 383, 385, 386
legal upper bound, 395–397, 399, 400, 402, 406, 413, 417, 418
leniency policies, 425
leniency program, 193–197, 200, 201, 203–206, 208, 209, 432, 436, 437, 443, 444
liability, 365, 368, 371, 374, 377, 384, 391, 395, 407, 430, 432, 473
licensing, 232, 234–247, 251–254, 256, 326, 370
licensing contracts, 232, 236, 239, 246
limit price, 123, 124, 128
local markets, 10, 59, 60, 69, 81, 82
London Underground, 478, 482
loss, 40, 98, 122, 142, 145, 216, 223, 235, 298, 304, 360, 424, 425, 428, 433–435, 448
low cost carrier, 37, 38, 49

M

managers, 238, 297, 430, 431, 433, 441, 442, 444
market power, 7, 9, 32, 34, 36, 40, 60, 64, 94, 116, 213, 214, 216, 223, 226, 227, 288, 304–306, 325, 329, 330, 378
market share, 5, 9, 24, 38, 99, 106, 109, 119, 134, 144, 160, 163, 176, 213, 216–219, 221, 227, 244, 299, 435

market share rebates, 225
merger, 3–6, 16, 19, 25, 31, 35, 42, 49, 52, 223, 288, 298, 329, 378, 425, 429, 430, 440, 441, 444–447
merger control, 378, 429, 441, 444, 445
merger policy, 288, 425, 445, 446
Michelin II, 213, 214, 217, 224
minimum fines, 389, 390, 392, 393, 395, 402, 403, 412, 414, 418
mistakes, 307, 340, 361, 424, 428–430, 460, 461
monitoring, 175–178, 190–192, 318, 427, 455, 459, 479, 485
moral hazard, 232, 238, 251–253, 257, 292, 301–304, 307
multiplicity of equilibria, 145, 148, 160
multi-brand retailing, 226
multi-market contact, 37, 41, 43

N

national pricing, 10, 11
network effects, 141, 142, 145, 154, 250, 322
network externalities, 142
non-exploitable leniency program, 193, 196, 197, 206, 208, 209
norms, 366, 435, 439, 448
notifications, 446

O

one-stop grocery shops, 7
online auction, 141, 143, 165
opportunism, 216, 361
opportunistic behavior, 216, 234, 268, 269
optimal antitrust fines, 391
optimal cartel price, 397, 398, 399, 405, 406, 415, 417
optimal deterrence, 425, 430
optimal fine schedule, 391, 392, 400, 401, 406
optimal legally-constrained fine schedule, 389–391, 399, 400, 402, 404, 409–412, 415–417
organization, 4, 116, 239, 242, 244, 279, 281, 300, 311, 318–320, 344, 378
output specification, 460, 464, 465, 467, 474
outsourcing, 240, 241, 249, 252, 483, 485
over-deterrence, 367, 383, 425, 427, 428, 433, 437, 442, 445
overt collusion, 193, 197, 205

P

pace of technology transfer, 253, 255–257
participation constraints, 143, 155, 156, 160, 161
pass-through/asymmetric pass-through, xvi, 59, 60–68, 74–77, 78–80, 82–83, 88–90
payment mechanisms, 455, 471
per se rules, 370, 378, 380, 381, 383, 384
petrol, 60, 62–64, 66, 69–83, 86, 88–90
photovoltaic panels, 359
Pigovian tax, 344
platform competition, 143, 145, 146, 153, 155
platform profits, 154, 158
platforms, 141–145, 147, 149, 152, 155, 159, 164, 166, 296
policy, 9, 11, 32, 37, 93, 95, 110, 141, 154, 279, 283, 292, 296, 306, 312, 324, 339, 346, 361, 375, 377, 391, 424–426, 429–439, 441, 443–449
policy variables, 433, 435, 439
Polluter Pays Principle, 344
portfolio competition, 296, 323, 325
post-merger, 4–6, 13, 24, 36, 41, 42, 49, 50, 53, 433, 435, 437, 439, 445
premiums, 287, 357
price comparison, 10, 11
price competition, 3–5, 24, 81, 141, 152, 157, 234, 268, 269, 279, 282, 288, 291, 298, 304–307, 310, 311, 328, 330, 393
price discrimination, 148, 153, 218, 219, 294, 306, 309
price dispersion, 19, 24, 52, 120, 127, 134–136

price effects, 31–34, 36, 37, 43, 51, 52, 286–288
price volatility, 127
price-cost margins, 65, 115–119, 127, 128, 133, 134, 137
pricing strategies, 4, 143, 154, 217, 295
principle of proportionality, 390, 393, 394, 397, 403–405
prisoner's dilemma, 198
private costs, 427
private finance initiative, 456
private suits, 441
pro-competitive, 217, 446
pro-cyclical, 115–117, 120, 124, 125, 127–129, 133–137
product market competition, 231–233
prohibitions, 444–447
proportionality, 389, 390, 393, 394, 397, 400, 402–405
prosecution, 393, 427, 443
provider networks, 282, 290, 294, 297, 314, 326, 327
public policies, 95, 282, 297, 326, 365, 372, 385
public services, 455–457, 465, 470, 485, 486
public–private partnership, 455, 456
punishment, 175, 291, 313, 319, 389, 390, 403, 405, 427, 446

Q

quality discrimination, 220
quality of the law, 424, 433, 437, 439, 448
quantity discounts, 217, 218, 228
quasi-equilibrium, 148, 160, 163

R

R&D, 94, 95, 98, 104, 107, 110, 237, 241, 244, 324, 348, 356, 360, 366, 370, 375
recessions, 116–125, 127–135, 137
reference pricing, 302, 303
regime, 360, 366, 369, 371, 372, 377, 392, 424, 425, 429, 433, 434, 437–439, 447–449
regulation, 282, 297, 322, 326–328, 339, 341, 348, 353, 359, 366, 368, 369, 389–392, 394, 397, 418, 440, 446, 459, 462, 475
remedies, 32, 445–447
renewable energy sources (RES), 340, 341, 348, 350–361
repeated Bertrand model, 397
research joint ventures (RJVs), 195
research-intensive industries, 366
residual demand, 100, 121–123, 132, 227
resources, 95, 107, 110, 224, 233, 359, 371, 385, 424, 433, 436, 448, 469
retail, 4, 7, 10, 60, 62–74, 76, 79–81, 83, 89, 90, 223, 226, 361
risk allocation, 455, 459, 465, 468, 476–478, 483, 486
road fuels, 59–62, 65, 66, 89, 90
"rockets and feathers", 59–61, 63, 64, 72, 81, 82, 88–90
rule of reason, 379, 438

S

sales growth bonuses, 225
sales quotas, 175–177, 179, 191
sales volatility, 175, 186, 189, 191
sanction, 424–437, 439, 440, 444, 447, 448
sanctions and damages, 424, 448
sentencing guidelines, 390, 395, 396, 397, 406, 409
separation of powers, 424, 438, 439
sequential contracting, 214, 220, 226
settlements, 434
signal, 238, 247, 291, 307, 309, 314, 339, 344, 354, 382
social costs, 426, 432
social welfare, 249, 250, 371, 383, 389–391, 393, 398, 405, 412, 417, 418, 424, 427, 429, 431, 433, 437
specific deterrence, 425–427
Stackelberg leader, 120, 213, 221
standardized contracts, 455, 459–462, 470
standardized quantity rebates, 225
state aid, 340, 348, 352, 356, 357, 361

stationarity, 70, 191
subgame perfect equilibrium, 124, 132, 160, 261, 398
subsidies, 303, 304, 306, 346, 353, 356, 360, 361, 480
supermarket, 4, 7, 11, 62, 69, 81, 89, 118, 220
supportable cartel prices, 398,
survey, 34, 45, 53, 69, 234, 236, 281, 285, 286, 303, 320, 365, 424, 428, 441, 442, 444, 447, 456, 484

T

tacit collusion, 59, 61, 193, 196, 197, 199–201, 203, 205, 206, 208, 209
tariffs, 141, 144, 217, 237, 241, 306, 348, 352, 359, 472
technology licensing, 232, 234, 245
technology transfer, 231–236, 238, 241, 242, 244, 247, 248, 251–262, 264–269
time series, 69, 89, 190
timing of technology transfer, 242, 253
traffic density, 34, 35, 41
Transmilenio Bus, 478–480
transparency, 312–314, 434, 459, 462–464, 483
treatment group, 46
truck tires, 224, 225
two-sided markets, 141, 142, 145, 146, 171

U

uncertainty, 152, 235, 237, 239, 243, 282, 290, 294, 313, 360, 367–369, 433, 466, 467, 482
United Kingdom, 59, 60, 62, 288, 297, 311, 456, 457
unlawful behaviors, 424, 426, 428
upstream collusion, 216

V

vertical integration, 231, 233, 234, 256, 257, 259, 267–269, 282, 300
vertical mergers, 223, 323
vertical relations, 213, 214, 217, 242, 245, 317, 320, 321, 323
vertical restraints, 213–217, 227, 228, 300
vertical separation, 233, 234, 256, 258, 261, 265–268
violations, 399, 424, 427, 432, 433, 440–443

W

wholesale, 60, 66, 67, 69, 81, 350, 358, 361
wrongdoers, 424, 426–428, 432, 433

Y

Yahoo, 141–143, 153, 160–163, 165